John Steinbeck

A Literary Reference to His Life and Work

CRITICAL COMPANION TO

John Steinbeck

A Literary Reference to His Life and Work

JEFFREY SCHULTZ

LUCHEN LI

Facts On File, Inc.

Critical Companion to John Steinbeck:
A Literary Reference to His Life and Work

Facts On File, Inc.
132 West 31st Street
New York NY 10001

Library of Congress Cataloging-in-Publication Data

Schultz, Jeffrey D.
Critical companion to John Steinbeck : a literary reference to his life and
work / Jeffrey Schultz, Luchen Li.
p. cm.
Includes bibliographical references and index.
ISBN 0-8160-4300-0 (alk. paper)
1. Steinbeck, John, 1902–1968—Handbooks, manuals, etc. 2. Novelists,
American—20th century—Biography—Handbooks, manuals, etc.
I. Li, Luchen. II. Title.
PS3537.T3234Z86623 2005
813'.52—dc22   2004026100

Facts On File books are available at special discounts when purchased in bulk
quantities for businesses, associations, institutions, or sales promotions. Please
call our Special Sales Department in New York at (212) 967-8800
or (800) 322-8755.

You can find Facts On File on the World Wide Web at
http://www.factsonfile.com

Text design by Erika K. Arroyo
Cover design by Cathy Rincon

Printed in the United States of America

VB Hermitage 10 9 8 7 6 5 4 3 2 1

This book is printed on acid-free paper.

CONTENTS

PREFACE

John Steinbeck is regarded as the quintessential American writer, and his reputation extends worldwide. Yet at home, although Steinbeck has been widely read, he occupies a controversial position; his works have achieved wide popularity but have also received heavy criticism. He is one of the most underrated and misunderstood American writers.

Whatever his faults, Steinbeck was a uniquely authentic writer who, over nearly four decades, produced a body of work—including novels, short stories, screenplays, journals, essays, and newspaper and magazine articles—that evokes life in the 20th century with compassion and lyrical precision. Several generations of young readers in the United States have grown up reading such books as *Of Mice and Men, The Pearl, The Red Pony,* and *The Grapes of Wrath,* and readers from Cairo to Beijing, from Tokyo to Stockholm continue to read Steinbeck's books, which have been translated into dozens of languages. Contrary to many influential critics' predictions that Steinbeck's reputation would decline after his death, an editor from Penguin Putnam in 2002 noted that Steinbeck's books continue to sell more than 2 million copies a year. Fresh adaptations of his works, such as *East of Eden* and *Of Mice and Men,* appear regularly on stage and screen.

In writing, Steinbeck was committed to engaging his readers. By selecting the proper plot, emotion, character, and tempo, he enabled readers to become part of the story. He once wrote, "I want the participation of my reader. I want him to be so involved that it will be *his* story."

When Steinbeck accepted the Nobel Prize in 1962, he declared that the writer's duty was "to declare and to celebrate man's proven capacity for greatness of heart and spirit." He believed that literature could unite people and help them overcome their most enduring fears and troubles. Through the courage and dignity of his characters, his panoramic depictions of his nation, and his reports on the world, John Steinbeck delivered a message of hope for humanity.

Luchen Li
Kettering University

How to Use This Book

The purpose of *Critical Companion to John Steinbeck* is to provide a comprehensive review of Steinbeck's life and an examination of his work. Part I of this book provides Steinbeck's biographical details and explores his development as a writer. Part II provides detailed entries on Steinbeck's works, major and minor, in alphabetical order. Entries on major works contain synopses of the work, information on its critical reception—both past and recent—and subentries on characters in the work. Part III contains entries on related people, places, and topics. Part IV contains appendices, including a chronology; a list of awards; a selected list of major film, television, and theater productions; and bibliographies of Steinbeck's works and important secondary sources.

Any reference to a work by Steinbeck that is the subject of an entry in Part II is printed in SMALL CAPITAL LETTERS the first time it appears in a particular entry. Similarly, any reference to a person, place, or topic that is the subject of an entry in Part III is also printed in SMALL CAPITALS the first time it appears in a particular entry.

PART I

Biography

John Steinbeck

(1902–1968)

On February 27, 1902, John Ernst Steinbeck was born in the bedroom of his parents' house at 132 Central Avenue, SALINAS, CALIFORNIA. He was the third of four children and the only son of JOHN ERNST STEINBECK and OLIVE HAMILTON STEINBECK, both of whom were second-generation Americans and Californians.

Steinbeck's paternal grandfather, JOHN ADOLPH GROSSTEINBECK, immigrated to the United States in the 1860s from his hometown of Düsseldorf, Germany, on a circuitous journey beginning in the Holy Land. He and his brother, both cabinetmakers, had accompanied their sister and brother-in-law, a Lutheran minister, on a religious mission to Jerusalem. There, Steinbeck's grandfather met and married Almira Dickson, whose New England family had traveled to the Middle East to convert Jews to Christianity. Both the Grossteinbecks and the Dicksons endured numerous setbacks and tragedies during their quixotic trek, including shipwrecks, rapes, and the death of Grossteinbeck's brother at the hands of Bedouin tribesmen. Having suffered as well the loss of a farm carved out of the barren desert, the Dicksons returned to New England with their new son-in-law, who changed his last name to Steinbeck. John Adolph then moved to Florida with Almira, but shortly thereafter when the Civil War began, he was conscripted into the Confederate army. Holding no sympathies for the Confederate cause, he deserted and fled to the safety of his wife's family in New England, leaving Almira and their small children, including the writer's father, behind. Eventually, the Confederate government permitted Almira to join her husband in the North. Some 10 years later, John Adolph moved to California, where he purchased a small plot of land near Salinas and established a dairy farm. His wife and six children followed him, and the family later converted the acreage into a fruit farm and set up a successful flour mill.

SAMUEL HAMILTON, Steinbeck's maternal grandfather, began his life near Ballykelly, Ireland. At the age of 17, Samuel sailed for NEW YORK CITY at the height of the Irish potato famine (1845–50), which

John Steinbeck as a child, 1906   *(Center for Steinbeck Studies)*

devastated the primary food crop of Ireland and caused the death of almost 11 percent of the Irish population. In 1849, he married Elizabeth Fagen, a deeply religious daughter of Northern Irish immigrants. Seeking his fortune in the Far West, Samuel sailed around the Horn of South America in 1850 to join his sister in San José, California, and a short time later, Elizabeth made her way to the Golden State via the Isthmus of PANAMA with a small daughter, Lizzie. The Hamiltons lived in or near San José for almost 20 years, while Samuel practiced the blacksmith's trade. In 1871, the family moved to Salinas, and, within two years, began to homestead a ranch near KING CITY, CALIFORNIA about 60 miles south of Salinas. Beginning with an initial 160 acres, the ranch eventually grew to 1,600 acres, as the family accrued land for each family member. Never particularly productive because the soil was so poor, the Hamilton ranch served as a nostalgic backdrop for many of Steinbeck's works, especially THE RED PONY and EAST OF EDEN.

Although Steinbeck had little personal knowledge of his grandfathers because both died when he was still a young child, the family history sparked his imagination and provided themes for many of his novels. Indeed, Samuel Hamilton was a central character in *East of Eden.* Throughout his life, Steinbeck returned to the idea of a human need for a romantic quest to seek one's fortune and to achieve personal goals, inspired often by unrealizable dreams, but always in one to move forward and onward. His grandparents personally represented this vision for the author.

A quiet and reserved man, Steinbeck's father served most of his life as treasurer for Monterey County. Originally employed at flour mills near Salinas as an accountant and manager, the elder Steinbeck lost his position when the Sperry Flour Mill ceased production. He then invested his life savings in a feed and grain store, but the store went into bankruptcy as people gave up animal transportation for the automobile. Still highly respected within the community despite his business failure, the elder Steinbeck filled the office of county treasurer with the help of well-connected friends from 1910 until his death in 1935. Despite his outward appearance of a bookkeeper lost in facts, figures, and ledgers, Steinbeck's father never felt completely at home in an office setting and preferred being outdoors, whether working in his vegetable garden or riding his horse around the county on various official errands. He passed this love for nature and the soil to his son and made certain that the younger John spent at least part of every summer working at the Hamilton ranch.

Far more gregarious and outspoken than Steinbeck, Olive Hamilton yearned throughout her youth for something more than the rural and bucolic existence of the Hamilton ranch. By the age of 17, she had been certified as a teacher, a remarkable educational achievement for a woman at the time, and began a career as an educator in several one-room schoolhouses in the area. When her future husband came courting, his ambition, practicality, and responsibility appealed to her, but more significantly, he had already achieved standing in the town of Salinas as a factory manager. After marriage, she successfully applied her deter-

mination and will to becoming a social and community leader, single-handedly managing numerous clubs and committees for the betterment of Salinas. Despite her tough, no-nonsense exterior, Olive passed to her son a gift for imagination and spirituality. It was she who ensured that the family home always contained diverse and abundant reading material; it was she who first introduced John Steinbeck to the myths and legends of Western literature and who encouraged him to explore the sensuousness and profundities of language.

Throughout his childhood and adolescence, John Steinbeck often appeared to be lazy, mischievous, and spoiled to his neighbors, friends, and family. His three sisters (ELIZABETH STEINBECK AINSWORTH, ESTHER STEINBECK RODGERS, and MARY STEINBECK DEKKER) and his parents gave him special treatment as the only boy in the family. Nevertheless, he was expected to do his share of family chores, and to earn his own spending money. Still, he exhibited a streak of rebelliousness against his parents' demands for self-discipline and responsibility. He began smoking at an early age and routinely failed to deliver the newspapers along his assigned route on time, if at all. Described alternatively as loner by some of his early acquaintances and as a leader of a small clique of neighborhood boys, Steinbeck demonstrated a paradoxical personality, which his later acquaintances affirmed as a lifelong characteristic, alternating between withdrawal and sociability. He did well in his academic studies and was elected class president in his senior year in high school.

In 1919, Steinbeck matriculated at STANFORD UNIVERSITY in PALO ALTO, CALIFORNIA. He had announced an ambition to become a writer at the age of 14 and was insistent on taking only those courses relevant to his stated aspiration. He never adhered to the university's requirements for a degree in English, which was his declared major course of study. Rather, he dismissed certain required courses completely and repeated other courses when he found them interesting and helpful to his writing. In some respects, Steinbeck devised his own independent study program, though not one recognized at the time by Stanford University. During the six years of his enrollment at the school, the author established a pattern of taking a full semester or two of courses and then dropping out or taking a leave of absence in order to earn money for his continuing education with a series of odd jobs ranging from store clerk to cotton picker and ranch hand. From these work experiences, Steinbeck developed a deep appreciation and sympathy for the common laborer, which would prove seminal to his great works of the 1930s.

In 1925, Steinbeck abandoned his intermittent efforts to earn a college degree. After taking a summer job at Lake Tahoe doing maintenance work and driving a mail truck, he earned enough money to ship out on a freighter bound for New York City, where he hoped to make serious headway in his writing career. During the voyage, the ship passed through the Panama Canal and stopped in Panama City, which later formed the setting for Steinbeck's first published novel, CUP OF GOLD. By the time Steinbeck reached New York, he had very little money and immediately contacted his older sister Beth, who lived in Brooklyn with her husband. His brother-in-law found him a job as a day laborer on the construction of Madison Square Garden. Working 10- to 15-hour days left him little time to write. Eventually, his mother's brother, JOE HAMILTON, an advertising executive from Chicago, used his influence to obtain a position for his nephew as a cub reporter with the NEW YORK AMERICAN. Unfortunately, Steinbeck did not do very well with his first serious foray into journalism, often failing to submit his stories in a timely fashion and to complete the assignments given him. The newspaper fired him after several months. Out of work and out of money, the young writer made a last desperate attempt to sell a collection of short stories to Robert M. McBride & Company, a publishing house known for taking chances with unknown authors. His efforts proved fruitless, and acknowledging his defeat, he made the decision to return to California.

Shortly after his return in 1926, Steinbeck found employment as a year-round caretaker for the BRIGHAM FAMILY's summer estate in Lake Tahoe, a job he would keep for more than two years. During the summer months, Steinbeck was kept quite busy, tending to the needs of the family

in residence, even serving as a tutor to the Brigham children. When winter set in after the family's departure, he had far fewer responsibilities. Snowbound and isolated, the solitude proved to be a godsend, because he finally found the time to write without interruption and to establish a routine of writing that he would follow for the rest of his life. He finished the manuscript for *Cup of Gold* and began work on TO A GOD UNKNOWN, his third published work. It was during this time that he met Carol Henning, who would become his first wife (see CAROL HENNING STEINBECK BROWN). Having left his caretaker job, Steinbeck spent the summer of 1928 working at the Tahoe Fish Hatchery with his friend LLOYD SHEBLEY but lost his employment after wrecking his supervisor's truck.

In September 1928, the author moved to San Francisco to be closer to Carol, who worked in the advertising department of the *San Francisco Chronicle*. Relying once again on the help of relatives,

Steinbeck as a teenager, 1919 *(Center for Steinbeck Studies)*

Steinbeck got a job as a warehouseman at the Bemis Bag Company, owned in part by his sister Mary's husband, Bill Dekker. For three months, Steinbeck put in long hours at the factory doing manual labor and continued to maintain a writing schedule, while romancing Carol. Exhausted and mentally drained, he realized he could not maintain this frenetic life. He appealed to his father, who offered the Steinbeck summer home in PACIFIC GROVE, CALIFORNIA, rent free, plus a subsidy of $25 a month to his son, so that he could devote all of his time to his writing. Steinbeck accepted his father's generosity.

In the meantime, Steinbeck's college friend TED MILLER, who lived in New York City, had been searching for a publisher for *Cup of Gold*. In January 1929, Miller wrote his friend with the good news that the Robert M. McBride company, the same firm that had declined Steinbeck's collection of short stories in 1926, had agreed to publish the novel. It was released in August 1929 and sold reasonably well for a first effort, until McBride entered bankruptcy.

The year 1930 proved to be a turning point for Steinbeck. Having achieved the status of a published author, he married Carol in January. He began a lifelong business relationship and personal friendship with the founders of the MCINTOSH & OTIS LITERARY AGENCY, MAVIS MCINTOSH and ELIZABETH OTIS. Perhaps most significantly, considering the influence on his philosophic and literary outlook, he met and developed a deep and abiding friendship with EDWARD RICKETTS, a marine biologist in MONTEREY, CALIFORNIA. Ricketts, who quickly became a fixture on CANNERY ROW within a short time of opening the PACIFIC BIOLOGICAL LABORATORIES in 1923, possessed a curious magnetism for people from all walks of life, from prostitutes and *paisanos* to intellectuals and artists. His workplace eventually became an informal salon for West Coast intelligentsia, including the Jungian psychiatrist Evelyn Ott, the poet Robinson Jeffers, and Joseph Campbell, who later became famous for his work on the power of myth. Ricketts also stimulated Steinbeck's interest in biology and science, leading the author to his PHALANX theory of human organization.

For the next several years, in the midst of the GREAT DEPRESSION, Steinbeck had minor success with his writing. He contributed several short stories to the *North American Review*, including those of *The Red Pony*, and "THE WHITE QUAIL," and "THE MURDER." He also published two additional books, THE PASTURES OF HEAVEN and *To a God Unknown*. Though critically praised, the books did not achieve commercial success, partly because the first publishing firm, Brewer, Warren and Putnam, filed for bankruptcy shortly after publication (ironically, the same difficulty as with *Cup of Gold*), and the second firm, Ballou, did not have the financial wherewithal to publicize the work. During this period, Steinbeck's mother suffered a paralyzing stroke, and Carol and John moved to Salinas to care for her during the year preceding her death in 1934. His father died a year later, shortly before Steinbeck's first popular triumph with TORTILLA FLAT. Although Steinbeck regretted that his parents did not live to see him become a best-selling writer, he took solace in their continuing faith in his talents, and their support of his writing career.

Having established a professional and personal connection with the editor and publisher PASCAL COVICI, later of Viking Press, Steinbeck followed *Tortilla Flat* with a slew of popular and highly regarded works. Over the space of the next four years, Steinbeck wrote and released IN DUBIOUS BATTLE, OF MICE AND MEN, *The Red Pony*, THE LONG VALLEY, and what is commonly regarded as his masterpiece, THE GRAPES OF WRATH. He also wrote a nonfiction account of the migrant worker problem, THEIR BLOOD IS STRONG, a polemical pamphlet deploring the condition of the refugee camps and calling for concerted government action to assist farm laborers. Steinbeck received the first of many awards: the California Commonwealth Club Gold Medal for Best Novel by a Californian in 1935 (*Tortilla Flat*) and 1936 (*In Dubious Battle*); the New York Drama Critics Circle Award for the Broadway version of *Of Mice and Men* in 1938; and the National Book Award and the Pulitzer Prize in 1940 for *The Grapes of Wrath*.

Strangely, Steinbeck resented the effects of his new fame and fortune. A shy and intensely private man, he resisted almost all appeals by his publicist for interviews and biographical material, claiming his work should stand on its own without a personal identification by the audience with the author. For the most part, Steinbeck disliked professional intellectuals. He viewed them as self-promoters whose main concern was the advancement of their own reputation. Steinbeck believed that, for the interests of society, they were more destructive than creative. For him, the role of a writer was to be a true artist. As an artist, he was reluctant to deal with his ideas directly and publicly.

Regardless of his preference for privacy, long-forgotten acquaintances and total strangers began an onslaught of emotional pleas for money. Barraged by letters and phone calls to his home, Steinbeck eventually turned the handling of the bulk of his nonpersonal correspondence over to McIntosh & Otis and applied for an unlisted phone number. One bright aspect of the end of financial problems was the Steinbecks' ability to travel. In 1936, he and Carol took a long-postponed trip to MEXICO, where they stayed for four months, completely charmed by the country and its people. In the summer of 1937, the Steinbecks visited Europe and included in their itinerary the cities of Leningrad and Moscow, the first of several trips Steinbeck would make to the Soviet Union. The couple also renovated the cottage in Pacific Grove and built a new home in LOS GATOS, CALIFORNIA, which they soon sold to build a larger home on a 50-acre ranch nearby.

By 1939, Steinbeck had completely worn himself out. The writing of The Grapes of Wrath had taken a much greater toll on him than any of his previous books; an undiagnosed strep infection gave him chronic and serious pain for almost the entire year; and his marriage to Carol had begun to disintegrate. He and she had always had a volatile relationship, punctuated by fierce fights, but by and large their different personalities had always complemented each other. Now he began to resent what had attracted him to her in the first place— her gregarious sociability, her blunt speech, and the constant flow of her guests in and out of their homes, denying him the peace and quiet he needed to write. She, in turn, resented his taciturnity and

John Steinbeck, as an adult *(Photofest, photo by Breitenbach)*

peevishness and what she perceived as his ingratitude for all the help she had given him during their marriage to the detriment of her own career. Fueled by alcohol, their arguments spilled from the privacy of their home into public battles and led to several lengthy separations. During one such separation, Steinbeck rented an apartment in Hollywood under an alias. His childhood friend MAX WAGNER, who worked as an extra in films, visited Steinbeck and was taken aback by his friend's obvious depression and pain from the lingering strep infection. Max asked a young actress friend of his, GWYNDOLYN CONGER, to bring a bowl of homemade chicken soup over to Steinbeck's apartment to cheer him up. What began as an innocent gesture of kindness eventually led to the affair that ended Steinbeck's marriage to Carol.

In the spring of 1940, determined to find a new direction in his career and to take a break from the hectic activity following the publication of The Grapes of Wrath, Steinbeck funded a six-week marine expedition to the GULF OF CALIFORNIA to investigate invertebrate sea life along the Baja peninsula. Accompanied by his friend Ed Ricketts, four crew members, and Carol, who came along as the designated cook for the voyage, Steinbeck later chronicled the experiences on the trip in a book coauthored with Ricketts, SEA OF CORTEZ. Indicative of the strain in the Steinbecks' marriage, Carol locked herself in her stateroom as soon as the boat set sail from Monterey, and, strangely, the author never mentions his wife's name in the book. From a scientific standpoint, the expedition proved very fruitful but did nothing to mend the rift between the Steinbecks.

During the summer of 1940, along with his wife, Steinbeck returned to Mexico to work on a small film, THE FORGOTTEN VILLAGE, depicting the effects of the arrival of modern medicine on a rural community in Mexico. He had always been fascinated with filmmaking and had worked closely with the famed documentary filmmaker, PARE LORENTZ, on the production of THE FIGHT FOR LIFE to learn the techniques of production and cinematography. Suspicious of the interference of the big movie studios, Steinbeck was determined to make *The Forgotten Village* entirely his own project, although he did seek investments from friends with financial support for the film. In Mexico City, Carol's behavior became even more erratic, and Steinbeck began to fear for her sanity without good reason. He also realized his attachment to Gwyndolyn Conger had grown beyond friendship.

After a debilitating bout with the flu, Carol took an extended trip to Hawaii in early 1941 to recover her health. By this time, Steinbeck had wrapped up the work on *The Forgotten Village* and had begun serious writing on *Sea of Cortez*. Wanting to avoid the distractions of the ranch at Los Gatos, and also desirous of maintaining close contact with his collaborator, Ed Ricketts, Steinbeck rented a small cabin on the outskirts of Monterey. He invited Gwyn to join him for three weeks. Afterward, Steinbeck recognized his marriage had arrived at a crossroads. Torn between his affection for and obligations to Carol and his love for Gwyn, Steinbeck arranged for a curiously inept and insensitive confrontation between the two women when Carol

returned from Hawaii in late April. He brought Gwyn to the house he had rented near Cannery Row, introduced his girlfriend to his wife, and told the two women to work out between them which of the two loved him more. By early May, Carol and John Steinbeck had separated permanently.

Steinbeck threw himself into the completion of *Sea of Cortez,* and by the end of July 1941, he had finished everything except the revision. Pat Covici, and other editors at Viking Press had reservations about the project: first, because it was being written in conjunction with another author, and second, because it was so very different from Steinbeck's previously published works, a nonfiction journal with a wholly scientific section. Steinbeck, who had never cared whether his writing was popular with the public or with literary critics, pressed hard for the book's publication in the form he envisioned, including expensive typefaces and illustrations. At the same time, he began work with the director LEWIS MILESTONE on the screenplay for *The Red Pony.*

Still living in the small rental house in Monterey while the arrangements for his divorce were finalized, Steinbeck received word from Carol that she intended to return to the West Coast permanently from New York, where she had moved shortly after their separation. Dismayed at the thought of living in the same vicinity with his estranged wife, and concerned about Gwyn's reaction, Steinbeck made the momentous decision to relocate to New York. All of his life, except for the disastrous year in New York City during his mid-twenties, had been spent in California, particularly central and northern California. He had been labeled a western writer, since almost everything he wrote took place in California. However, it should not be forgotten that Steinbeck rarely returned to his home state for any length of time after 1941, and thus more than half of his literary career was spent on the East Coast. Biographers and critics alike remark on the shift in Steinbeck's focus after 1941, but whether it was due to a change in geography or a conscious alteration in the author's sense of literary direction begun before the move would be difficult to say.

Steinbeck asked permission of Gwyn's parents to remove their daughter to New York and promised to marry her as soon as the divorce was final. They granted his request, and in September 1941, the couple left hurriedly, the haste made necessary because Steinbeck had been summoned to a conference in Washington, D.C., with President FRANKLIN D. ROOSEVELT and his top intelligence aides. Previously, the author had conferred with the president about the need to counter proliferating Nazi propaganda in Mexico, and Roosevelt wanted to enlist Steinbeck's services for a new agency, the FOREIGN INFORMATION SERVICE (FIS), set up specifically to respond to Axis propaganda with pro-American and pro-Ally information. "Wild" Bill Donovan, later the head of the Office of Strategic Services (OSS), which became the Central Intelligence Agency (CIA), assembled a meeting of prominent playwrights, screenplay writers, filmmakers, and novelists to hear their suggestions about effective counterpropaganda techniques. As a result of this meeting, Steinbeck agreed to participate actively in the FIS.

While living briefly in a small house on the farm of the actor BURGESS MEREDITH, near Suffern, New York, Steinbeck began work on THE MOON IS DOWN, his novel about a small town's resistance to foreign occupation, and also wrote scripts for FIS radio broadcasts. After moving to New York City late in the year, shortly before the United States's entry into WORLD WAR II, he received word that censors had banned release of his documentary, *The Forgotten Village*, for indecency, and that Viking Press wanted changes in the *Sea of Cortez* manuscript to forestall charges that Steinbeck was a socialist. Bewildered by these developments—he was, after all, now working as an unpaid and unofficial government employee out of a sense of patriotism—Steinbeck agreed to minor changes in the book and successfully argued for the distribution of the film, although it never was shown widely in the United States.

On the domestic front, Steinbeck and Gwyn set up housekeeping in New York City and established a pattern in their relationship, even prior to their marriage, which ultimately led to its demise. Because of his increasing involvement in the work for the FIS, Steinbeck was frequently absent, leaving his fiancée to her own devices in a city where

she barely knew anyone. Moreover, with a perhaps overly romanticized view of traditional marriage, he insisted Gwyn give up her singing and acting career and devote herself to maintaining a home. When he was at home, he continued with a long-standing routine of writing most of the day, and he disliked interruptions of his work. Gwyn became more lonely and isolated and retreated into spells of depression and minor hypochondria. On the one hand, Steinbeck found Gwyn's forced dependence on him to be what he wanted in a conjugal relationship; on the other, he found her demands for his attention to be cloying and intrusive.

The spring of 1942 marked the publication of *The Moon Is Down* and the opening of a play based on the PLAY-NOVELETTE. Heavily criticized for its "sympathetic" portrayal of Nazi invaders, Steinbeck was gratified to learn after the war that the work had greatly contributed to the morale of resistance forces in Europe. Meanwhile, Gwyn had moved back to California to be with her family, while the author completed research for a book and movie on ARMY AIR CORPS bombardiers that required visits and inspection of various Army training installations across the country. Steinbeck recognized that the book, BOMBS AWAY, and subsequent movie, served as little more than a recruitment effort, but he was determined to do his part to contribute to American prosecution of the war. However, his frustration with military and government bureaucracy mounted, and he began to seek a more active role. He applied for direct commissioning as an army intelligence officer but was required to obtain a deferment from his local draft board in Monterey County. Despite the recommendation of General Henry "Hap" Arnold, the draft board refused his request because his writings were deemed subversive and suspect. He appealed the decision but was forced to wait for the slow wheels of government machinery to work. By the end of 1942, he agreed to participate in two new projects: the development of a screenplay, A MEDAL FOR BENNY, with his friend JACK WAGNER and another screenplay, LIFEBOAT, for the renowned director Alfred Hitchcock.

Tired of futile attempts to join the military either as a draftee or a commissioned officer, Steinbeck turned to another possible avenue for participation in the war in early 1943. He applied and was accepted as a war correspondent for the *Herald Tribune*. Security clearances and other paperwork needed to be filed and approved before he could travel overseas for the newspaper, but Steinbeck hoped employment in the private sector would be more forthcoming than his futile attempts to serve in the armed forces. Everywhere he turned, he had been stymied by anonymous reports that cast suspicion on his loyalty, despite the fact he enjoyed personal access to the president of the United States and unrestricted entry into heavily classified areas while on assignment for his work with the FIS. While he waited for approval of his bona fides, and issuance of a special passport, his divorce from Carol was granted on March 18, 1943, and he married Gwyn in New Orleans, 11 days later.

By June, the red tape for Steinbeck's assignment with the *Herald Tribune* had been cut, and he left for the European theater of war. He filed reports from London, England; North Africa; and Italy, catalogued later in ONCE THERE WAS A WAR. Though technically prohibited from carrying a weapon as a journalist, Steinbeck participated as an armed combatant in several special operations missions against Nazi forces in Italy, led by an acquaintance from Hollywood, DOUGLAS FAIRBANKS, JR., who had joined British Expeditionary Forces at the beginning of the war. He returned to New York in October, prior to the expiration of his contract with the *Herald Tribune*, a changed man. Though he never complained, he had incurred minor injuries (ruptured eardrums and a twisted ankle) and more lasting psychological distress witnessing the death and destruction of heavy combat. Today, we identify these symptoms as posttraumatic stress disorder, and his emotional instability was further compounded by the lack of communication during his time in Europe from his bride, who strongly protested her husband's voluntary separation from her shortly after their marriage.

Steinbeck immediately began work on *Cannery Row*, a comedic and welcome diversion from his overwhelmingly serious experiences as a war correspondent. He also began to record a basic outline for *THE PEARL*, based on a story first related to him during the 1940 expedition to the Gulf of Califor-

nia. In January 1944, the Steinbecks traveled to Mexico for rest, recuperation, and reconciliation, and with the author's stated intention to do further work on projects pending. Gwyn announced her pregnancy, and the couple returned to New York in March to await the birth of the baby. Their son, THOMAS STEINBECK, arrived on August 2, 1944.

As the war drew to a close, Steinbeck tried to grapple with the trappings of celebrity. He had never come to grips with his "overnight" success, and though he certainly enjoyed the privileges attached to his public recognition—reserved tables at exclusive restaurants, instant acknowledgement by admirers, and acceptance by the highest echelon of literati—he felt his new social status would ultimately corrupt him and turn his attention away from what he believed important. Gwyn relished the attention and inclusion in café society, but Steinbeck redoubled his efforts to avoid publicity and sought projects to reaffirm himself as a serious author rather than a celebrity writer. He made tentative plans to return permanently to California in the hope of regaining a simpler life, surrounded by truer friends and more solid inspiration.

He and Gwyn traveled with the infant Thom to California in October 1944. They purchased a house in Monterey, an old adobe built in the 1830s requiring extensive renovation, and prepared for permanent residency on the West Coast. Wartime rationing delayed repairs to the house, and Steinbeck applied for a license on a business office to continue his work. Aware of the controversy surrounding Steinbeck, the city fathers denied his application, explaining they only wanted professional people. Instead, the author was forced to use an unheated woodshed for his writing. Steinbeck made concerted efforts to renew and reestablish his former connection with his old circle of friends and acquaintances. It became apparent, as time went on, that his previous relationships had altered irrevocably. Steinbeck felt betrayed, used, and abused; his friends believed themselves unappreciated and neglected. Additionally, unsubstantiated rumors circulated about Gwyn's reputation as a gold digger, interested only in Steinbeck's money and influence in the entertainment industry. Only Ed Ricketts welcomed him wholeheartedly.

Steinbeck deferred his decision about traveling back to New York, while he worked on the film version of *The Pearl*. Gwyn had already traveled to Mexico with Thom, because she had been given responsibility for the movie's musical score. In early April 1945, Steinbeck took a train to Los Angeles and then to Cuernavaca, Mexico, where he had rented a villa. During this period, he was also working on the script for the play THE WIZARD OF MAINE, and doing the initial preparation for THE WAYWARD BUS. By September 1945, after delays in the production of the movie, Gwyn departed for New York after a diagnosis of acute food poisoning. With persistent hints from Viking Press that he needed to produce another major work, Steinbeck returned briefly to New York to consult with his agents and editors and discovered his wife was pregnant again. Having at last decided to remain in New York, he purchased two large brownstones, one for investment purposes, and returned to Mexico until December 1945 when the shooting for *The Pearl* ended.

While Gwyn's first pregnancy had been difficult, the second proved excruciating. Afflicted by recurrent dysentery and by other unidentified ailments, Gwyn spent most of the last six months of her pregnancy confined to bed. The brownstone required extensive renovations before being habitable, and Thom, now a toddler, required his father's attention. Steinbeck grew increasingly distracted and found it very difficult to work on the new book, *The Wayward Bus*. He claimed later he had to discard more words than he kept while working on the novel. By April 1946, the new house was ready for occupancy, and Steinbeck, for the first time in his life, had a separate office in which to work. On June 12, 1946, his second son, JOHN STEINBECK IV, was born. Both Gwyn and the baby had postpartum complications, creating more difficulties for Steinbeck's concentration, and he moved his typewriter and other materials to an office at Viking Press. In spite of the chaos around him, including an unexpected monthlong trip to Mexico to resolve postproduction problems with *The*

Steinbeck with his wife Gwyn Conger and son Thom in Cuernavaca, Mexico, during the making of *The Pearl,* 1943 *(Center for Steinbeck Studies)*

Pearl, Steinbeck finished the book in October ahead of his original completion date.

Immediately the Steinbecks took a three-week trip to Scandinavia, which was to be followed by a week in London. Because of the inspiration provided to resistance fighters in Norway by *The Moon Is Down*, King Haakon of Norway bestowed the Liberty Cross on Steinbeck, the first time the medal had been given to a non-Norwegian. All over Scandinavia, people clamored to meet the author, and he was given a hero's welcome at every stop, with the press reporting his every move and word. The couple had invitations to dine virtually every evening and, feeling ill and exhausted, Gwyn asked to return to New York a week early, skipping the visit to London entirely. In hindsight, Steinbeck later claimed his wife had been jealous of the adulation given him.

Upon their return, the Steinbecks threw themselves into a whirl of parties and evenings on the town. No longer homesick for California, Steinbeck began to see New York as the one place where his fame did not prove to be a detriment, partly because many of his friends had just as much celebrity and talent as he. Gwyn enjoyed entertaining and was a superlative hostess. Unfortunately, the strains on the Steinbeck's marriage increased, and in February 1947, the first trial separation for the couple took place when Gwyn traveled for a month to California. During her absence, Steinbeck firmed up plans to make an extended working trip to postwar Europe and then to the Soviet Union with the photojournalist ROBERT CAPA, whom he had met while on assignment in London during World War II. Initially, the plan was to embark immediately, but Steinbeck suffered a serious accident when the brownstone second-floor balcony gave way as he leaned on it. He plummeted to the ground, shattering his kneecap, and required surgery to repair the damage. Capa, Steinbeck, and Gwyn departed for Europe in June, with the first segment of the journey to be spent in France as a kind of renewal for the Steinbecks. The author and photographer then continued to Moscow without having made any advance arrangements with the Soviet government to travel around the country. Despite the lack of preliminary organization, the two were granted unprecedented access to the countryside, visiting Stalingrad, the Ukraine, and Georgia. Steinbeck recorded his impressions of the Soviet Union in *A RUSSIAN JOURNAL*, published the following year.

By the time he returned to the United States in September, Gwyn's resentment of her husband's lengthy absences, and what she perceived as his disregard for her, boiled over. Made increasingly miserable by the atmosphere at home, Steinbeck decided to take another trip, this time to California in January 1948, to do research for a lengthy novel he had been considering a while based on his family history. During the trip, he visited with Ed Ricketts; interviewed family, friends and acquaintances in Salinas; and took extensive notes from back issues of newspapers in Monterey County. He and Ricketts tentatively discussed another scientific expedition to the Northwest, similar to the *Sea of Cortez* voyage, to take place in the summer. When he arrived back in New York at the end of March, he found the tension between him and Gwyn had not abated. Their marital difficulties were exacerbated by health problems for both husband and wife. Then, on May 7, Ed Ricketts's car was struck by a train at a railroad crossing near Cannery Row. Ricketts lingered for four days and died of massive internal injuries. The news devastated Steinbeck, who immediately flew out to California, hoping to see his friend for one last time before he died. He was too late, but he attended the funeral with mourners from every level of society, reflecting Ricketts's impact on the people of Monterey and elsewhere. Steinbeck returned to New York feeling a part of himself had died, and he was immediately informed by Gwyn that she wanted a divorce. The divorce became final by August, with Gwyn awarded custody of the children and Steinbeck left destitute by the property settlement. Gwyn even refused to allow her former husband his reference books, typewriter, personal correspondence, and more—all of which he needed to continue writing.

Steinbeck went on a drinking and womanizing binge, causing concern among his closest friends. Even Pat Covici, with whom he maintained a somewhat formal friendship up to this time, wrote to the author admonishing him about his moral lapses. Though he never fully recovered from what he believed to be Gwyn's betrayal, by immersing himself in manual and mental labor for the next year, Steinbeck eventually began to regain a semblance of equilibrium. In September 1948, he moved into the old family cottage in Pacific Grove, which required extensive repair from tenant damage. The author, always restored by working with the soil, totally refurbished the neglected garden. He painted and plastered the inside of the house and refinished the floors. Doing the work himself was not simply a matter of therapy. He was on the verge of bankruptcy and still owed alimony and child support.

In November 1948, Steinbeck traveled to Mexico with the director ELIA KAZAN to do research for the movie VIVA ZAPATA!, for which he had agreed to do the screenplay. Still floundering and depressed, over the next couple of months Steinbeck returned to Mexico several times, and finally, in February 1949, settled back into his old habit of working at least six hours a day. He made considerable progress on the script for the movie by the end of March and had also begun work on several short stories, plus the initial writing of what later developed into *East of Eden.* He had also fallen in love again.

Her name was Elaine Anderson Scott (see ELAINE ANDERSON STEINBECK), a native Texan, and the wife of the actor Zachary Scott. Steinbeck met her while on a date with Ann Sothern, one of many actresses the author had squired after his divorce. Immediately attracted to Elaine's intelligence and sense of humor, Steinbeck courted her with a vengeance. Elaine's marriage had been moribund for years. She eventually divorced her husband on charges of mental cruelty, apparently well justified because of Scott's frequent violent behavior and addiction to alcohol. Because of her marriage, and the ever-present Hollywood gossip mill, Elaine and Steinbeck were forced to keep their relationship secret. Nevertheless, he began writing to her on a daily basis, often more than one letter, and forwarded them through his friends Max and Jack Wagner. During the summer of 1949, the two spent as much time together as was possible, considering the circumstances, with Elaine and her daughter,

WAVERLY SCOTT, joining Steinbeck and his two sons, who had flown west as part of the divorce custody agreement. Over the summer, Steinbeck began work on BURNING BRIGHT, an allegorical play-novelette, and one of the least successful of all of his works.

After a week holed up with the producer of *Viva Zapata!,* Jules Buck, Steinbeck produced a working script for the movie in November 1949. At the same time, Elaine informed him that she had severed the relationship with her husband and intended to file for divorce immediately. Steinbeck traveled to New York at the end of November and rented two adjacent apartments for Elaine and her daughter and for himself. Having been a Broadway stage manager before moving to Hollywood with Zachary Scott, Elaine introduced Steinbeck to a new group of influential friends, and he became fascinated with the details of drama production. He delighted in being close to his sons once more and in presenting Elaine to his own group of friends. During 1950, Steinbeck was more productive than he had been in years, doing the final revisions on the movie script with Kazan, arranging for the stage production of *Burning Bright,* and writing his memoir of Ed Ricketts for THE LOG FROM THE SEA OF CORTEZ. He also renewed his work on "Salinas Valley," which would be renamed *East of Eden.* In October, *Burning Bright* opened on Broadway to almost completely negative reviews, despite a brilliant cast. Steinbeck uncharacteristically shrugged the criticism off as a valuable lesson. On December 28, 1950, Steinbeck and Elaine were married at the home of HAROLD GUINZBURG, the head of Viking Press.

Moving to a new home only five blocks from the old brownstone in early 1951, Steinbeck plunged himself into the book he regarded as his masterpiece. The quasi-biographical, quasi-fictional, quasi-biblical *East of Eden* presented unanticipated difficulties. He had always agonized over his longer books, but this novel was made doubly difficult because of his personal presence as the unidentified narrator and because he consciously viewed the work as his literary bequest to his sons, Thom and John IV. Hoping to avoid the deep fatigue that followed the completion of his last lengthy novel, *The Grapes of Wrath,* and to establish an unhurried pace to the book, Steinbeck set himself to composing a

John Steinbeck *(Photofest)*

specific number of words each day, no more than 800 to 1,000. Always careful of the sound and rhythm of language, he spent even more care on the literary nuances in *East of Eden*. Steadily, the book progressed, as a result of Steinbeck's taking few hiatuses from the writing process. For this, Steinbeck could thank Elaine. Impeccably well organized, she was a modern-day chatelaine, handling all practical necessities. When Steinbeck's boys were in residence, whether in the house in New York City or on vacation in a summer house, Elaine provided their entertainment and served as their tutor if they were behind in their studies. She provided a buffer for her husband against the noise of the world when he needed solitude and silence for his art.

By November 1951, Steinbeck had completed the novel and began to work on the revisions, which were done by March 1952. Having submitted the manuscript to Viking Press, the author felt almost purged. He and Elaine traveled to Europe, the first of many trips abroad during their marriage. He contracted with *Collier's* magazine to write a series of feature articles about his trip, an arrangement he had relied upon before to subsidize his travels. The couple spent almost six months away

from the United States, visiting France, Switzerland, Spain, Italy, and the British Isles, including the birthplace in Northern Ireland of Steinbeck's maternal grandfather, Samuel Hamilton. Much to his dismay, no one in the village of Ballykelly remembered Samuel, and all traces of the Hamiltons had disappeared.

For his next project, Steinbeck turned again to a stage production, this time a musical comedy based on many of the characters of *Cannery Row*. After numerous false starts, he realized he hadn't the ability to write the book for a musical comedy, and, instead, decided to approach "Bear Flag," the working title for the book, as a straightforward sequel to his earlier novel. He later admitted that SWEET THURSDAY had been only a happy diversion for him, and it could be said, the same is true for most of the writing Steinbeck did during the 1950s. He collaborated on *Pipe Dream* (1954), the RODGERS & HAMMERSTEIN version of *Sweet Thursday*; wrote a satirical fantasy, THE SHORT REIGN OF PIPPIN IV (1957); and edited and revised a collection of his 1943 wartime dispatches for the Hearst syndicate, which was published in 1958 as *Once There Was a War*. During the 1950s, Steinbeck became more involved in politics, agreeing to serve as a speechwriter for ADLAI STEVENSON in his two failed campaigns for the presidency. The first serious concerns about Steinbeck's health arose in the 1950s as well. In 1954, he applied for a life insurance policy and was denied coverage because of an underlying heart condition unearthed during the required physical.

Perhaps, it was the happiness of his third marriage, perhaps the relief from any financial concerns, perhaps his ongoing and frequent connection with his sons (though Gwyn continued to create friction between his sons and him), but the author seemed adrift and unwilling to tackle anything of moment during the decade. Steinbeck established a routine during the 1950s of travel abroad, deriving income from his royalties and journalistic submissions, and relaxing in the comfort of his home in New York City and a summer house purchased in 1955 at SAG HARBOR, NEW YORK. It was not that he had run out of material or of steam. His contributions to the *Saturday Review* and to the British magazine *Punch* demonstrated he maintained a keen wit and remarkable skills in observation. He did keep in mind one important project. It involved a translation into modern vernacular of SIR THOMAS MALORY's *Le Morte d'Arthur,* the book that had charmed him so much as a child, and whose quest theme informed almost all of Steinbeck's body of work. The project was never completed. It was published posthumously in 1976 as *THE ACTS OF KING ARTHUR AND HIS NOBLE KNIGHTS,* but Steinbeck devoted a great deal of energy and research to the work in the late 1950s, much to the dismay of his editor, Covici, and his agents, McIntosh & Otis.

In late October 1959, Steinbeck was treated for a severe kidney infection, and then in early December, he apparently suffered a minor stroke, losing consciousness while smoking a cigarette and setting fire to the bed in which he was resting. He required hospitalization for almost two weeks. Both he and Elaine emerged from the experience severely shaken, and he decided to stop work on the Arthurian legends and begin work on more contemporary subjects. From this came both *TRAVELS WITH CHARLEY* and *THE WINTER OF OUR DISCONTENT.* Both were close and somewhat pessimistic examinations of contemporary America—the first, a chronicle of Steinbeck's journey across the United States in his truck, ROCINANTE, with his poodle, CHARLEY, and the second, the only novel he wrote set in the East. Steinbeck acknowledged freely that he wrote both works in recognition of his own mortality. After he emerged from the hospital, Elaine had begun to treat him as an invalid, and he needed to assert his worth as a competent person and functioning writer.

After submitting the manuscripts to Viking Press, and preoccupied with morbid premonitions of his death, Steinbeck decided to take Thom and John Jr. abroad for almost a year. Along with Elaine, he hired a tutor, Terence McNally, and began the Grand Tour of Europe in August 1961. Steinbeck believed it might be his last chance to ground his sons in the cultural heritage of western Europe and to reestablish an ethical direction he thought his sons had lost during their adolescence. Steinbeck suffered two more "attacks" during their travels, but by the time the family returned in May 1962,

he felt he had done as much as he could to change the course of his sons' lives.

The Nobel Committee awarded Steinbeck the prize for literature in the fall of 1962. Immediately, criticism of the Nobel Committee's choice erupted across the United States from prestigious literary reviews, calling the award a mockery and the recognition of a mediocre talent whose work had been passé for almost two decades. During the press conference held at Viking Press the day after the award was announced, a reporter asked Steinbeck if he believed he deserved the prize. According to Pete Hamill, journalist and essayist, who was present at the question-and-answer period, a look of deep anguish appeared on Steinbeck's face, as he answered, "Frankly, no." Accepting no further questions, the author left the room. For the official awards ceremony, Steinbeck and his wife were greeted warmly in Stockholm. He delivered a speech of remarkable grace, making only a passing comment at the critical carping he had endured. Nevertheless, he did not get over the rejection of his worthiness by the literary elite and never wrote another word of fiction.

In May 1963, Steinbeck once again entered the hospital to repair a detached retina. Unable to see, he stopped writing personal correspondence, which he had continued even during the most severe spells of writer's block. In the fall of 1963, President Kennedy asked Steinbeck to make an extensive tour behind the Iron Curtain as part of a cultural-exchange program. Steinbeck agreed, as long as Elaine would be allowed to accompany him, and they departed in October for an arduous two-month trek through the Soviet Union, Poland, Hungary, Czechoslovakia, and West Berlin. Every hour of every day of their itinerary had been scheduled in advance, and because of Steinbeck's stature as an American icon, he often faced hostile audiences. Toward the end of their trip, the Steinbecks received word of Kennedy's assassination but decided to continue the tour in honor of the late president's memory.

Beset by continuous declining health and personal problems involving his children and ex-wife, Gwyn, who sued him for additional child support in 1964, Steinbeck welcomed a project proposed to him by Viking Press. Viking had commissioned a series of photographs to be taken in every region of the United States depicting ordinary people going about their lives and engaging in ordinary activities. Originally, Steinbeck was asked to provide brief captions for each of the photographs, but as the work progressed, the captions evolved into full-blown essays, and the coffee-table book was published in 1966 as AMERICA AND AMERICANS. Additionally, in 1964, the author began a controversial but personally gratifying friendship with President LYNDON JOHNSON. President Johnson awarded Steinbeck the Medal of Freedom in fall 1964, the highest civilian award bestowed by the United States. Personally loyal to the president, and fundamentally committed to America's efforts to combat the encroachment of communism, Steinbeck found himself embroiled in the budding disagreement regarding the country's involvement in the VIETNAM WAR. His defense of the United States's military commitment in Southeast Asia occupied the author for the rest of his life.

By 1966, both of his sons had joined the military. His son Thom was in basic training in California, and John had already been deployed to Vietnam as a military journalist. Steinbeck arranged to travel to Asia as a war correspondent with Elaine and hoped it would give him an opportunity to see John Jr. while in Vietnam and to witness personally the conditions and parameters of the war. At the age of 65, already weakened by the ailments that would kill him, the author spent six weeks in Vietnam. His assigned military liaison, Major SAM M. GIPSON, JR., later complained he was hard put to keep up with the aged writer, and, indeed, lost track of him on several occasions when Steinbeck chose to accompany troops on missions without informing Gipson. Steinbeck reunited with John Jr. just as his son's unit came under attack by a Vietcong unit. As he did during World War II, Steinbeck acquired a weapon and manned an outpost during a long night of sporadic fire.

Steinbeck and Elaine stopped in Japan on their way back to the United States, and while there, he ruptured a spinal disk helping a delivery man with a load of beer. The circumstances were humorous, but the injury proved deadly. Six months later in October 1967, surgery had to be performed to relieve Steinbeck of immobilizing pain. The operation lasted almost five hours and appeared successful, but it ultimately put a strain on his heart and circulatory system from which he never recovered. His last year was a series of attacks, seizures, and hospitalizations, as the damage from severe arteriosclerosis increased. On December 20, 1968, with Elaine lying beside him on a hospital bed in their apartment in New York, John Steinbeck died. His remains were cremated, then buried in the Hamilton family plot in Salinas, California.

Over his lifetime, John Steinbeck never gave up trying to perfect his craft. From his early childhood, when he would write stories in the margins of his father's work ledgers, until the final stage of his fatal disease, Steinbeck sought ways to expand his repertoire and his skills as a writer. He was not trying to "find his voice." He found it many times and, having used that voice, moved on to another. He compared good literature to musical composition, always seek-

John Steinbeck *(Photofest, photographed by Wm. Ward Beecher)*

ing the perfect sound for a particular genre, the perfect blend of notes and rhythm. In this sense, he is one of the most experimental American writers. On many occasions, he stated his fear of being pigeonholed, identified with one style of writing and one theme, and also his concern that he would become so complacent and reliant on his prodigious facility of expression that he would be unable to break away from previous modes and patterns. His continuous willingness and drive to research and test new ways of literary communication may explain why critics so often lambasted or cavalierly dismissed his work. Over and over, reviewers complained that Steinbeck's latest release, whatever it was, did not stand up to his previous work, or that he had neglected his core values, or he was unequal to the task he set for himself. Which means, of course, the critics missed the point. Steinbeck could not stand still any more than his most memorable characters could.

Steinbeck's work roughly can be divided into three separate periods. The first involves the conflicts inherent in individual consciousness. As we become more self-aware and more active in our environment, we eventually have to come to terms with illusions of self-sufficiency, impractical ideals, and invulnerability. Perhaps the best examples of this perspective can be found in the characters of Henry Morgan from *Cup of Gold,* and Jody from *The Red Pony.*

Steinbeck's next approach sprang from the development and refinement of his nonteleological philosophy based on phalanxes, or human behavior observed in a larger group context, whether of family, community, or nation. He identified human beings as inseparable from a larger organism with its own natural behavior patterns. In other words, the whole is greater than, and different from, the sum of its parts. Representations of this viewpoint can be found in his labor trilogy: *In Dubious Battle, Of Mice and Men,* and *The Grapes of Wrath.*

Finally, in the 1950s and onward, Steinbeck turned to autobiography and away from the stance of an objective observer to a very subjective narrator. His writing became more obviously inward-focused, and the actual process of writing assumed almost a separate character. *East of Eden* and *The Winter of Our Discontent* best demonstrate this approach.

However, to categorize Steinbeck in this fashion ignores the immense complexity of his work and of his intentions. The author frequently described his writing as multileveled and multilayered, appropriate for the most casual and the most discerning reader. Furthermore, it is difficult to label his less known works, such as *To a God Unknown, Sea of Cortez, The Moon Is Down,* and *Burning Bright.* Nonetheless, they are an important part of Steinbeck's literary accomplishments.

In recent years, Steinbeck's reputation among scholars and critics has been redeemed. He has been identified as an early environmentalist, as a proto-feminist, as an advocate for social ethics, and as a proponent of cultural diversity. These labels are insufficient, yet they help outline the many aspects of Steinbeck's literary dimensions.

PART II

Works A–Z

"About Ed Ricketts" (1951)

In 1951, VIKING PRESS republished the narrative portion of the book SEA OF CORTEZ: A LEISURELY JOURNEY OF TRAVEL AND RESEARCH, under the title THE LOG FROM THE SEA OF CORTEZ. In its original format published 10 years previously (1941), the book contained two distinct sections. One offered a scientific documentation of the invertebrate species examined during the expedition, and the other, a travel journal or narrative, detailing the experiences of those aboard the boat, *The Western Flyer*. Unlike the previous edition, which had attributed the authorship of the work to both John Steinbeck and his colleague EDWARD F. RICKETTS, the new edition was credited only to Steinbeck. *The Log from the Sea of Cortez* included a preface titled "About Ed Ricketts," written by Steinbeck to honor and immortalize the man who had been his dearest friend for more than 18 years and who had been killed in a tragic automobile accident a few years earlier. An extremely personal and strikingly intimate portrait of his friend, "About Ed Ricketts" is in many ways a belated eulogy of the man who had the strongest impact on the life and work of Steinbeck.

Among other things, the essay reveals how intimately John Steinbeck based the character Doc in his celebrated novels CANNERY ROW and SWEET THURSDAY on Ed Ricketts; indeed, many of the events and anecdotes related in the novel are derived from actual events in his friend's life. In the essay, Steinbeck recounts nervously showing his friend the typescript of *Cannery Row* and offering to make any changes that he suggested. "Let it go that way," Ricketts replied. "It is written in kindness. Such a thing cannot be bad."

SYNOPSIS

Steinbeck begins "About Ed Ricketts" by writing of the accident that ended his friend's life in April 1948 at the age of 52. Ricketts was fatally injured when his car collided with the Del Monte Express train at a railroad crossing in MONTEREY, CALIFORNIA. Rescuers managed to pull the man, mangled but alive, from the wreck. After lingering for a few days

and slipping in and out of consciousness, he died quickly and quietly. The author writes about the shock occasioned in the Monterey community by the biologist's death and of his own shock, characterizing the essay as an attempt to "lay the ghost."

Steinbeck describes meeting Ed Ricketts at a Monterey dentist's office. The two men became immediate best friends: "After the first moment I knew him, and for the next eighteen years I knew him better than I knew anyone, and perhaps I did not know him at all."

The essay continues, describing Ricketts's business, PACIFIC BIOLOGICAL LABORATORIES, Inc., and the haphazard way that it was operated. Steinbeck writes of Ricketts's love of the truth and his unorthodox use of words in writing and speaking. He describes his friend as having a mind that "had no horizons" and characterizes him as being interested in everything, except the metaphysical or extra-physical, which he refused to think about even as they preoccupied him deeply. The author discusses his friend's close relationship with the people of Cannery Row, and particularly the madam of the nearby cathouse, another character that Steinbeck appropriated for use in his novels.

The essay relates in detail Ed Ricketts's military service during the two world wars, noting that although he was a remarkably unmilitary man he managed to be particularly successful in his unlikely career, first as a company clerk and subsequently in the venereal disease section of the Monterey induction center.

A section of the essay is also devoted to Ricketts's love of alcohol, an affection he shared with the author, as well as his "passionate and profound" interest in music and reading. Indeed, Steinbeck describes his friend's harboring a "deep suspicion" of anyone who did not drink.

Steinbeck discusses his friend's sexuality at some length, stating it "was by far his greatest drive." He defends this encroachment on his friend's privacy on the grounds that Ricketts discussed the subject openly. He goes on to describe a man whose "sexual output and preoccupation was purported to be prodigious," and who felt a "compulsion" to seduce any woman whom he found to be a challenge, including the wives of his friends. But despite Ricketts's

reviewers of *The Acts of King Arthur and His Noble Knights*. Morsberger reveals that John Steinbeck had a lifelong passion for Malory's tales of the Round Table and claimed that the stories of *paisanos* in *Tortilla Flat* was directly related to them. Back in 1956, Steinbeck decided, in the writer's own term, to "translate" the original work of Malory into modern English for readers, so that they could share his enthusiasm with the same understanding as audiences of the 15th century had with Malory's Middle English. According to Morsberger, Steinbeck traveled to England and Italy to prepare for his work, visiting Armando Sapori and Bernard Berenson and becoming good friends with Eugène Vinaver, the world's leading Malory expert, who offered the help that Steinbeck needed to complete his translation work. On these research trips, Steinbeck visited such places as Somerset, Cornwall, Wiltshire, and Wales, while his wife took photographs for his future reference. The arduous research did help him better understand what Malory might have known at his own time, and Steinbeck even learned things Malory did not know about the places where the tales of King Arthur took place. Morsberger reports that, although Steinbeck faithfully translated some of the tales, he greatly expanded others: "Thus long passages are not Malory at all but original Steinbeck in the manner of Malory." According to Morsberger, this is probably why Steinbeck never completed the work. Steinbeck had to put the King Arthur project aside for *The Winter of Our Discontent*. In 1965, he did briefly return to the project, but completed only seven of the tales.

SYNOPSIS

Introduction

The author describes learning to read using a copy of Sir Thomas Malory's *Le Morte d'Arthur* given to him by his aunt. He writes of his fascination with the book and honors it as the source of many of the elements that inspire his own writing: "I think my sense of right and wrong, my feeling of noblesse oblige, and any thought I may have against the oppressor and for the oppressed, came from this secret book." He also tells of his long-held desire to bring to present-day usage the stories of King Arthur and the Knights of the Round Table so that they might be more widely appreciated.

Merlin

This part tells the tale of the English king Uther Pendragon's desire for the Lady Igraine, who is married to the Duke of Cornwall. Merlin the wizard agrees to help Uther conquer the lady. In return, the king promises to place in Merlin's care the male child that the wizard prophesies will be conceived during the affair. Merlin disguises the king as Lady Igraine's husband and Uther consummates his love for the unsuspecting woman. Upon learning that her husband is dead, Lady Igraine agrees to marry Uther Pendragon. Nine months later her child is born and secretly entrusted into the care of Merlin, who places him in the home of Sir Ector, one of the king's most loyal subjects. Uther Pendragon dies, leaving the kingdom without an apparent heir to the throne. England falls into chaos as the various lords struggle for control.

Merlin convinces the archbishop of Canterbury to convene a meeting of the nobles. The archbishop announces that God will give a sign indicating who is to be the new king. A great block of marble is discovered in the churchyard, and upon the block is set a steel anvil in which a sword is driven. Written upon the block is the legend: "Whoever pulls this sword from this stone and anvil is king of all of England by right of birth."

A great competition is convened and each of the noblemen attempts to draw the sword from the stone, but to no avail. Young Arthur, sent to fetch a sword for his foster brother, Sir Kay, finds the lodging house locked. Seeing the mystical sword in the stone, the young boy draws it out and delivers it to his sibling. Sir Ector announces Arthur to be the rightful heir to the throne. England is split into camps that are loyal to the new king and those who feel that his claim is illegitimate. War breaks out.

Meanwhile, foreign invaders attack the lands of the rebellious lords. The war is temporarily halted while the two sides attempt to gain control of their respective kingdoms. Arthur receives a sword with magical properties from the Lady of the Lake, who makes him swear that he will one day grant her a wish. Returning to his castle, Arthur has an affair with the wife of his enemy, King Lot, not realizing that she is his half sister, Morgan Le Fay. Merlin warns Arthur that a child, product of the sinful union, will be born on the first of May, and that that child, who will be named Mordred, will destroy him.

The Knight with the Two Swords

A messenger arrives from the lady Lyle of Avalon bearing a magical sword that may be drawn from its scabbard only by the bravest and most honorable knight. Each of Arthur's men fails the test. Finally Sir Balin of Northumberland succeeds in drawing the sword. The Lady of the Lake arrives at Arthur's court and demands that he honor his promise to fulfill her wish by presenting her with the heads of Sir Balin and the messenger. Sir Balin beheads the Lady of the Lake and Arthur angrily banishes him from his court. Sir Balin vows to regain Arthur's favor by killing Lord Royns, the king's enemy. Merlin predicts that the sword will curse Sir Balin and that everything he does will turn to bitterness and death.

With Merlin's help, Sir Balin and his brother Sir Balan capture Royns and deliver him to Arthur. King Lot attacks the kingdom to avenge himself on Arthur for seducing his wife. Lot is killed and his army defeated. Balin travels to the kingdom of King Pelham, the brother of the invisible knight, Gralon. He beheads the knight during a feast. King Pelham disarms Balin and pursues him through the castle. Balin comes to a chamber where the body of an ancient man lies beside a strangely wrought golden spear. The desperate knight takes up the spear and drives it into Pelham's side. At that moment a great earthquake destroys the castle.

Merlin reveals that the spear he used to kill Pelham is the very same that was used by the Roman soldier Longinus to pierce Christ's side on the cross. By taking up the spear, the wizard explains, Balin has unleashed a terrible plague on Pelham's kingdom. Wishing to escape the death and destruction around him, Balin flees the kingdom. He comes upon a knight, Sir Garnish, who mourns the loss of his lover. Balin convinces him to seek out the woman. They find her in the arms of another man. Sir Garnish kills the couple before killing himself in despair. Balin takes shelter at a castle where he is obliged to joust with a knight. He does not recognize his opponent as his brother, and the two men fight viciously, killing one another and fulfilling Merlin's prophecy.

The Wedding of King Arthur

King Arthur marries Guinevere, the daughter of King Lodegrance of Camylarde. As a wedding gift, King Lodegrance presents Arthur with a round table that was given to him by Uther Pendragon, as well as 100 of his best knights. Arthur determines to establish the Order of the Round Table. On the day of the wedding feast a white stag bounds through the hall and escapes. A beautiful white hound pursues it. One of the knights grabs the hound and leaves the hall. Sometime later a hysterical lady enters the hall and demands that her white hound be returned. At that very moment an unknown knight enters the hall and carries the lady away.

King Arthur charges Sir Gawain to kill the white stag, Sir Torre to recover the white hound, and Sir Pellinore to rescue the lady. Each man sets off on his quest. Gawain tracks the stag to a nearby castle and slays it in the courtyard. He is challenged by the owner of the stag, whom he defeats. The man pleads for mercy, but Gawain ignores his request. Guinevere charges Gawain with the eternal quest of defending all ladies and fighting for their cause. Meanwhile, Sir Torre defeats the knight Arbellus and returns to Arthur's court with the white hound. As Sir Pellinore rides off on his quest he happens across a lady tending to a wounded knight. She pleads for his assistance, and when he ignores her, she curses him that he will not find help in his time of need. Pellinore finds two knights fighting over the lady of the white hound. He kills one of the knights and grants mercy to the second. Merlin tells him that the young lady tending the wounded knight was his own daughter Alyne, born of his love for the Lady of Rule. When Alyne's fiancé dies of his wounds, she kills herself with his sword. The wizard reveals that Pellinore is cursed to have the man he trusts the most allow him to be killed.

The Death of Merlin

Merlin falls in love with the damsel Nyneve. He prophesies that this woman will defeat him, but that he will do anything to have her. The old wizard warns the king that he must carefully guard the sword Excaliber, and also its scabbard, for someone he trusts will steal them. The old wizard rides off with his love. Knowing her power over him, she refuses him, demanding that he teach her the secret arts of necromancy. Beneath a great rock cliff, Merlin creates a wondrous enchanted room for his beloved Nyneve. Nyneve, bored with the old man, casts a powerful spell that traps him inside the rock for all time. Meanwhile, King Arthur receives word that his kingdom has been invaded by an alliance of five kings. The king sends out a call for men and travels to the conquered territories with a small retinue of knights. The little band is set upon by the Five Kings before reinforcements can arrive. Arthur, Sir Gawain, Sir Gryfflet, and Sir Kay ambush the Five Kings and kill them, thus routing the invading army. Sir Bagdemagus, angry that he has not been appointed to the Order of the Round Table, leaves court to go on a quest. During his journeys, he comes to the great rock where Merlin is imprisoned, but he is unable to free the old wizard.

Morgan Le Fay

King Arthur's half sister Morgan Le Fay is cruel and ambitious. She studies magic and becomes proficient in the dark and destructive arts. Poisoned by jealousy, she determines to destroy her half brother, the king. She creates a sword and sheath that look exactly like the famous Excalibur, and secretly swaps them for the originals. Then she seduces Sir Accolon of Gaul to help her in her plot against the king. She arms him with the real Excalibur and sends him to the king.

Arthur, Accolon, and Sir Uryens, Morgan's husband, are pursuing a great stag when they become lost in the forest. Nearby they discover a small ship laden with luxuries and occupied by 12 lovely maidens. The three men stop to rest and take their pleasure, and soon fall into a heavy sleep.

Sir Uryens awakes to find himself in his own bed in Camelot, Morgan by his side. King Arthur, however, comes to his senses in a cold dungeon. He is told that he is a prisoner of Sir Damas, a cruel and cowardly man who is at war with his brother, Sir Outlake. Damas offers Arthur his freedom if he will fight for him against Sir Outlake's champion. The king agrees. Meanwhile, Accolon is escorted to the castle of Sir Outlake, where he agrees to fight for the wounded knight. Arthur and Accolon, failing to recognize one another, engage in vicious combat. Accolon nearly defeats the king with his magic sword, but Nyneve intervenes with magic and Arthur disarms the traitor and discovers his identity. Accolon tells the king of Morgan's plot and begs for his mercy. Morgan steals Excalibur's magic scabbard while Arthur lies in a nearby abbey recovering from his wounds. She casts it into a lake, where it is lost forever.

Gawain, Ewain, and Marhalt

Arthur, angry at Morgan Le Fay's treachery, banishes her son, Sir Ewain, from his court. Ewain determines to win back his uncle's trust. His cousin Sir Gawain joins him. Sir Marhalt, a knight of the Round Table, advises them of a mysterious forest where they might find adventure. The elder knight agrees to join them on their quest and the three ride off into the wood. Soon they happen across three damsels who sit waiting in a clearing for knights-errant who will carry them off on their adventures. Each knight chooses his lady. The women lead the knights to a place where the trail diverges into three paths. Each knight chooses a path and they agree that they will meet again in 12 months.

Sir Gawain rides off with his damsel, who quickly tires of his boasting. She escapes with another knight while her chaperon is occupied in battle. Gawain determines to help Sir Pelleas, a knight who suffers greatly for the unrequited love of a lady named Ettarde; but instead he betrays Sir Pelleas and takes the lady for himself.

Meanwhile, Sir Marhalt and his lady come to a castle where he is challenged to fight a duke and his six sons. They continue on to a tournament where Sir Marhalt wins the grand prize. Finally, they come to an estate that is plagued by a giant. Marhalt defeats the giant, and the two settle down in cozy domesticity for the winter.

Meanwhile, Ewain rides with his lady, Lyne. Lyne explains that she is an expert in the ways of warfare and knighthood. But, since women are prohibited from practicing the masculine arts, she has resigned herself to instructing young knights in the ways of combat. She takes the young knight to her secret mountain estate and engages him in a brutal training regime for 10 months before finally declaring him ready. The two journey to a tournament where Ewain unseats 30 knights and wins the prize. Lyne then leads them to assist a lady who has had her lands taken from her by two dishonorable brothers. Ewain fights the brothers and defeats them, restoring the lady's properties. After 12 months, the three knights return to the clearing in the mysterious woods, and their ladies resume their waiting for the next group of knights-errant.

The Noble Tale of Sir Lancelot of the Lake

Peace is finally restored to England. King Arthur begins to worry that his knights are becoming lazy. He and Sir Lancelot devise a plan to send the knights into the countryside as defenders of the peace. Lancelot leaves on his quest with his young nephew, Sir Lyonel. While Lancelot sleeps under an apple tree, Sir Tarquin rides into the clearing. Lyonel determines to defeat the giant knight, but is instead captured and carried away.

Meanwhile, Morgan Le Fay spots the sleeping Lancelot. She and her three companion witches determine to compete for his favor and they each offer him a gift of their greatest charms. Lancelot professes to love only Queen Guinevere. The four witches angrily banish him to a dungeon to die, but he escapes with the help of a young maiden. He then travels to Sir Tarquin's castle to free his nephew and the other knights imprisoned there.

As Lancelot continues his quest, he is disappointed to discover that his fame precedes him and nobody will challenge him. To make matters worse, damsels demand his services at every opportunity. One day, Sir Lancelot rescues his friend, Sir Kay, the king's seneschal (official in charge of domestic arrangements), from a group of marauders. Kay complains bitterly that his responsibilities for feeding and outfitting the royal court are slowly killing him. The next morning Lancelot swaps his armor with that of Sir Kay. In his new identity he encoun-

ters adventure until finally it becomes known throughout the country that the knight in Sir Kay's armor is really the feared Sir Lancelot.

Finally the errant knight returns to the court of King Arthur where his deeds are celebrated and often exaggerated. He sits with the king and queen in the royal chambers. When Guinevere touches his arm, he feels a jolt of excitement go through him. The queen excuses herself and departs the chamber. When Lancelot leaves, he finds her waiting for him in the dark passageway. Their bodies lock together and they kiss one another passionately. Suddenly ashamed of his betrayal of his king and friend, Lancelot rushes away, weeping bitterly.

Appendix

The Appendix of *The Acts of King Arthur and His Noble Knights* excerpts Steinbeck's letters to his literary agent, Elizabeth Otis, and his editor, Chase Horton, regarding his work on the *King Arthur* project. These letters suggest he wrote at least two drafts of the book, the first of which was primarily a straightforward translation of the Winchester Manuscript, and the second, a looser interpretation in which he transformed the text into a more explicitly novelistic form. The letters also present an interesting insight into Steinbeck's working habits, and his vision of the similarities between Arthur's England and 20th-century America. According to Steinbeck, Arthur belonged to a time when "codes of conduct" from a "recent past had been violated," and the same held true for contemporary America. By examining the Arthurian legend, Americans might regain a sense of purpose and ethical perspective lost in the immediate past.

FURTHER READING

Gardner, John. "The Essential King Arthur, according to John Steinbeck." *New York Times Book Review,* October 24, 1976, 31–32, 34, 36.

Morsberger, Robert E. "The Acts of King Arthur and His Noble Knights." *Western American Literature* 12 (August 1977): 163–165.

Steinbeck, John. *The Acts of King Arthur and His Noble Knights.* New York: Farrar, Straus, and Giroux, 1976.

"Adventures in Arcademy, a Journey into the Ridiculous" (1924)

One of Steinbeck's first published short stories, "Adventures in Arcademy" appeared in the STANFORD SPECTATOR while the author was studying at STANFORD UNIVERSITY in June 1924. The short story is a fiercely satirical attack on the conformity and false morality that Steinbeck found to be a large component of academic life. Written as an allegory, the story traces the adventures of a lone man as he wanders through a fantastic landscape populated by strange creatures. The author's symbolism is mostly indecipherable to the contemporary reader, but some critics have noted that it contains scalding criticism of certain members of the Stanford faculty, as well as a rather contemptuous view of the pretensions of academia. Overall, the short story comes across as somewhat forced and sophomoric. Steinbeck's experiments with satire would be repeated on a number of other occasions, most notably his aborted novel *L'Affaire Lettuceberg*, which became the predecessor to *The Grapes of Wrath*.

America and Americans (1966)

America and Americans was first published in October 1966 by VIKING PRESS. While the project had part of its origin in Viking Press chief HAROLD GUINZBURG's invitation to John Steinbeck to write an introduction and perhaps the captions for a selection of photographs representing a cross-section of American life, it can also be traced back to Steinbeck's own road trip across America, which had already resulted in the popular *TRAVELS WITH CHARLEY*. Steinbeck became absorbed in the project, and this contribution grew into a collection of nine essays, a foreword and afterword, with the photographs interspersed among them. Steinbeck had continued to write and publish throughout the 1950s and early 1960s, although none of the works

of this time matched the reception of his works of the 1930s and 1940s. What became his last novel, *THE WINTER OF OUR DISCONTENT* (1961), and his narrative, *Travels with Charley* (1962), added to the body of work for which Steinbeck received the NOBEL PRIZE IN LITERATURE in 1962 and the United States Medal of Freedom in 1964.

This period when recognition of Steinbeck's work became so tangible also corresponded with his growing friendship and influence with President LYNDON JOHNSON, a relationship that also influenced the tone of *America and Americans*; and with great personal loss, the deaths of his friend and longtime editor, PASCAL COVICI, in October 1964, and of his sister, MARY DEKKER, in February 1965. In the months immediately following Guinzburg's invitation, Steinbeck wrote about the project in several letters, but he seemed not to have worked on it much until after the deaths of his friend and sister, when he became more deeply engaged in the project and began writing regularly again. The letters in which he mentions the project suggest that he is somewhat eager to engage his critics and that he expects that at least some readers will take issue with what he has to say.

Steinbeck begins *America and Americans* with a foreword that indirectly suggests that his work seeks to correct an earlier conversation about America and Americanness that failed to include any "native work of inspection of our whole nation and its citizens by a blowed-in-the-glass American." While he claims he will not attempt to refute anti-American sentiment, he insists that his work will be informed by "a passionate love of America and the Americans." Subsequent chapters take up the questions of who are Americans and how they became Americans, noting that the myth of easy assimilation and welcome has in reality been more difficult and resistant. Steinbeck takes a great interest in representing the contradictoriness of American values and culture, the "dream of home" held high alongside an incipient "restlessness," leading him to suggest that Americans are often more attached to ideas than their realities.

Steinbeck also suggests that the many checks and balances institutionalized in the forms of government both derive from and influence the development of the paradoxical contradictions he describes. In the chapter titled "Genus Americanus," he applauds the proponents of the American Revolution for seeking self-government, but he observes that the purported overthrowing of the class structure that later Americans impute to the Revolution has left space for the development of different kinds of class structures rather than the elimination of class. That space has been filled, he argues, by successive American capitalists whose self-interests, and whose successful selling of the idea of self-interest, have created the Corporation Man and replaced the idea of democracy with the machinations of capitalism. In "The Pursuit of Happiness," Steinbeck criticizes the infantilization of American culture, with its unreflective emphasis on youth and fear of aging that is nevertheless contradicted by its underlying contempt of real childhood and youth.

The last three titled chapters present Steinbeck's perspective on American attitudes and behaviors regarding the land, or, in more contemporary terms, the natural environment, the world, and the future. The chapter on the land reiterates observations that can be found in his work of the 1930s—that Americans use the land and its resources without a thought that they are also using it up. The chapter on the world foregrounds Americans' traditional tendency toward isolationism. Steinbeck explains this tendency as being at least partly environmental in its origin: the American continent was separated from Europe and from Asia by great bodies of water; the land itself was expansive and difficult to traverse. But Steinbeck hopes that the tendency toward isolationism is changing, and he bases that hope partly on his observations that Americans travel more than they once did and reflect more on their position in the world.

The chapter on the world also includes a remarkable analysis of the American tradition in literature, in which Steinbeck traces the development of a national literature that is at the same time derived from its European inheritance and independently developed. He observes here the striking distinctiveness of American literature in its willingness to allow the profession of journalism as a legitimate training ground for the profession of belles

lettres. This unique experience of American writers, that they learned about Americans not simply by observing their fellows but by living and working in the midst of the society, has in Steinbeck's words created a remarkable achievement: It "created a new thing and a grand thing in the world—an American literature about Americans. . . . it has the sweet, strong smell of truth." Even as he applauds this phenomenon, Steinbeck wryly notes that these same writers are never truly honored by Americans without external validation—"only when our literature was accepted abroad was it welcomed home again and its authors claimed as Americans."

Steinbeck's final chapter, "Americans and the Future," and his afterword strike alternately dark and light tones. On the one hand the last chapter calls for a return to an ethical sensibility that Steinbeck feels has gotten horribly lost, in particular because it has lost sight of the value of a less tangible purpose in the overwhelming plethora of material "things" that make up day-to-day American life. On the other hand, and in spite of his dismay at this loss of energy, Steinbeck ends with a statement of his hopes that Americans will choose to be inspired by a small chorus of leaders—he mentions Adlai Stevenson and John Kennedy by name—voices calling them back to act on their ideals. He ends with the observation that America's past experience contains the seeds of its possible future success, if only Americans will commit to moving forward and do not, as he puts it, "slip back."

While it may not be productive to impute the almost bipolar structure of *America and Americans* to the duality of satisfied accomplishment juxtaposed with grievous loss that characterized Steinbeck's personal experiences at this time, it is important to note that *America and Americans* does not share the holistic sensibility of Steinbeck's earlier, lengthy (compared with his wartime journalism) nonfiction works, SEA OF CORTEZ and *Travels with Charley*. *Sea of Cortez* most emphatically represents a dualism unified, in both form and content; the narratives of the crew's experiences alternating with the accounts of collecting and cataloguing zoological specimens are consistently structured to flow almost tidally into one another, nicely reflecting the natural pattern of the biological processes of rest and activity and the waxing and waning of the tides affecting the coastal pools that Steinbeck and his shipmates explore. This alternation works its way explicitly into Steinbeck's narrative as a wholesome and necessary aspect of the work and its role in his text. Similarly, in *Travels with Charley*, an important aspect of this travel narrative is to represent what Steinbeck sees as the intrinsic likeness of Americans, which he argues is their dominant feature, surely outweighing any superficial diversity that separates them. By contrast, *America and Americans* is most strongly characterized by the juxtaposition of paradoxical, irresolvable, and contradictory elements that occupy foundational positions in the America Steinbeck represents here. It is perhaps to Steinbeck's credit that he chose not to reconcile the vision in this book with his earlier tone—that he chose not to make *America and Americans* match the vision of interrelatedness that people seemed to have expected from him.

EARLY CRITICISM

When *America and Americans* was first published in 1966, it was received politely, partly because of the format, which encouraged reviewers to treat it something like a coffee-table book, and partly because Steinbeck, as an established and honored American author, had written it. Some early critics took issue with the harshness of his criticism, but others also criticized his unwillingness to shy away from his admitted and unabashedly "passionate love" for his subject matter. In the first 15 to 20 years after its publication, scholars generally grouped *America and Americans* with Steinbeck's other nonfiction and decreed that it was inferior to the fiction, especially the works of the 1930s and 1940s. Near the end of this "early" period, scholars began reconsidering these earlier estimations. During this process, a number of Steinbeck scholars argued, successfully, that Steinbeck's fiction and nonfiction are stylistically and thematically interdependent, and that reading the nonfiction texts as stories revealed a more deliberate structure and purpose to the works.

CONTEMPORARY PERSPECTIVES

Since the late 1980s, Steinbeck studies in particular have more or less followed a general trend in Ameri-

can literary scholarship, that is, of reconsidering the relationship between what are thought of as the literary and nonliterary works of major writers. Under the rubrics of New Criticism, Steinbeck's fiction was dismissed as "timely" rather than "timeless" because of its connection to topical social issues, only to be reconsidered as New Criticism made space for other critical and theoretical paradigms. Consequently, growing interest in the study of prose nonfiction in general and nonfiction genres, such as travel writing and cultural criticism in particular, have encouraged scholars and other readers to return to Steinbeck's nonfiction for another look. While earlier scholars saw *America and Americans* as a product of Steinbeck's conflicted reaction to the times and the losses of his last years, more recent scholars have seen it as an extension and refinement of work he began deliberately in *Travels with Charley* (see, for example, the editors' introduction to the America and Americans section in the 2002 edition of *America and Americans and Selected Nonfiction*). They have identified a more sophisticated and carefully nuanced examination of the contradictions Steinbeck found but sought to minimize in the earlier work, and they have recognized that the essays did not refer only to the collection of photographs that were their immediate cause. Recent scholars have also suggested that, along with Steinbeck's last work of fiction, *The Winter of Our Discontent* (1961), *Travels with Charley* and *America and Americans* form a sort of thematic "boxed set," illustrating the important relationship between Steinbeck's fiction and nonfiction works, and the complementary relationship that existed between them throughout his career.

SYNOPSIS

Foreword
Steinbeck admits that the text and pictures in *America and Americans* form a body of "unashamed and individual" opinion. The book, he tells his readers, is "informed by America, and inspired by curiosity, impatience, some anger, and a passionate love of America and Americans."

E Pluribus Unum
The author discusses how, in a span of only 400 years, a sense of nationhood was achieved among

the various peoples who settled in America. It was this very process of building the country, he says, that produced the American, "a new breed, rooted in all races." A slow process of cruelty and resentment giving way to acceptance and absorption greeted members of each new ethnic group when they first landed on the American shores. He writes of the completeness of the transformation, marveling that Americans of widely varying description and ethnicity are immediately identified as Americans anywhere else in the world. Only two racial groups do not meet the author's pattern: the American Indian and the Negro. Steinbeck writes of the Indian's persecution and near-extermination, followed by the 20th century's official paternalism.

Paradox and Dream

Steinbeck notes that one of the generalities most often stated about Americans is that they are a "restless, a dissatisfied, a searching people," a nature that results in a state of physical and mental turmoil. He outlines the paradoxes that stem from this condition, each one a generality of behavior opposing another generality of behavior. The greatest example of the American paradox, he writes, is the passionate belief in our own myths. For example, he writes of the American dream of Home, which persists even though the American family rarely stays in the same place for more than five years. The persistence of the American Dream, according to the author, provides a perhaps unachievable ideal, but its existence gives "an indication of its possibility."

Government of the People

Steinbeck writes that the American attitude toward government is a paradox. Americans have a deep fear and hatred of any perpetuation of power—political, religious, or bureaucratic—and this attitude has led to a national conviction that "politics is a dirty, tricky, and dishonest pursuit and that all politicians are crooks." Americans, he argues, are increasingly cynical because of the great publicity given to any instance of official dishonesty despite the number of honest and hardworking politicians in American government. He writes of the presidential elections, during which "the rules of nonsense are suspended . . . as well as memories

of honesty and codes of decency." Americans, he says, demand second-rate candidates and first-rate presidents. As to first-rate presidents, they almost miraculously seem to appear, whether or not Americans appreciate them. As for the power of the American president, Steinbeck regards the executive's power as restrained by a "rebellious Congress," a "half-obedient military," a "suspicious Supreme Court," a "derisive press," and a "sullen electorate."

Created Equal

Steinbeck addresses at length the civil rights problem in America. He discusses the history of slavery, noting that in ancient Greece it was neither a crime nor a sin to own slaves, but rather an accepted institution. However, he says, masters must always live with the fear that their charges will revolt; and thus the paradox of slavery is that, "by its very nature, the slave becomes stronger than his master." He observes that disease, diet, and hard work killed off the weaker slaves in America, resulting in the strong and resistant race that the Southern whites feared. If the North resisted slavery, he says, it is only because it was economically unsuitable for the region. He writes of the Civil War, admiring the bravery and ingenuity of the South against overwhelming northern superiority, and he blames the failures of Reconstruction for the 100 years of social injustice that followed it. Finally, Steinbeck tells the story of his Great-Aunt Carrie's failed attempt to open a school for Negro children in the South.

Genus Americanus

Steinbeck writes about the American concept of the classless society. He describes the American paradox of distrusting position, property, and wealth that are inherited while admiring the same things if they are self-acquired. He describes the great millionaires of the 19th century, vital, boisterous figures; modern millionaires, on the other hand, "live almost like fugitives, secret and shy." The author argues that the corporation has replaced the capitalist as the premier creator of wealth. He describes the corporations' struggle against labor, and the transformation of ownership as shares of stock become more widely distributed in American society. The author criticizes the emergence of "the Corporation Man," a man defined almost completely by his status, contributions, and worth to a faceless corporation. Nevertheless, he admires the efficiency achieved by corporations and the men who work for them, even if corporate efficiency stultifies creativity. He writes of the American tendency to join lodges and secret societies, fulfilling a need "for grandeur against a background of commonness, for aristocracy in the midst of democracy." He condemns the American tendency to denounce, threaten, and punish as "sickness of the soul," and calls certain leaders, men such as Senator Joseph McCarthy, who instigated the 1950s Communist witchhunts, "screwballs."

The Pursuit of Happiness

Steinbeck discusses the problem of youth and age in America. He complains of a "child sickness" that developed during the previous 60 years of material prosperity, during which children were hopelessly spoiled by their parents. The American approach, he argues, has "extended adolescence far into the future so that many Americans have never and can never become adults." At the same time, he worries that longer life expectancies will lead to further problems.

Americans and the Land

Steinbeck writes of the "savagery and thoughtlessness" with which the early settlers conquered and tamed the American continent, and connects it to the abuses of pollution and destruction that plague the cities and the countryside. He describes the land lust of the early pioneers who believed the continent to be limitless in size and bounty. This "land hunger" led to the poisoning of rivers and the leveling of forests, as well as the extinction of species such as the passenger pigeon. The author writes with particular passion of the destruction of the redwood forests native to the region of California where he grew up. Steinbeck worries that when Americans make tools it becomes necessary to use them to prove that they exist, a tendency that led to the bombing of Hiroshima and Nagasaki during WORLD WAR II. He writes that the creation and use of the atomic bomb on these two Japanese cities is an act of which he is horrified and ashamed.

Americans and the World

America's attitude toward foreign nations and foreign people is shaped by its geographical isolation, Steinbeck writes. He complains of the hypocritical snobbery of the few foreign visitors that came to the country before World War I. The American insularity and shyness, he argues, is rapidly coming to an end. He discusses the development of American literature, and the lofty respect awarded journalists in America. An important element of American letters is that the writer is usually not a member of an elite, but rather is forced to work his way up from the bottom practicing a profession that is hardly respected until he is well along in his career. History, remarks Steinbeck, "is what we wish it to have been." He argues that if one wishes to understand a country's history, then a thorough understanding of its literature is necessary. Abroad, however, the sectionalism of American literature has contributed to a distorted understanding of America, a problem that has been helped along by the simplistic fantasy and wanton violence of Hollywood films. Among Americans, the frills and trappings of films and commercials, he concludes, "have created a kind of sullen despair and growing anger and cynicism."

Americans and the Future

Steinbeck concludes by addressing what he feels is the most serious problem facing America and Americans, an issue that he approaches by inspecting mankind as a species. He fears that Americans have become obsessed and laden with tensions, and have lost their sense of purpose. The writer frets that morals, ethics, and charity are disappearing, crime is on the rise, and the desire for survival is on the wane. In America's negation of the symptoms of extinction, however, the writer finds hope and confidence for the future.

FURTHER READING

Cooke, Robert J. "Books." *Social Education* 3 (December 1966): 673–674.

Moon, Eric. "New Books Appraised." *Library Journal* 91 (December 1, 1966): 5,962.

Steinbeck, John. *America and Americans.* New York: Viking, 1966.

———. *America and Americans and Selected Nonfiction.* Edited by Susan Shillinglaw and Jackson Benson. New York: Viking, 2002.

"Atque Vale" (1960)

In "Atque Vale," an essay published in *Saturday Review* July 23, 1960, Steinbeck writes that he is amazed at the qualities that are expected of Negroes. No race, he facetiously claims, has ever offered another such high regard. "We expect Negroes to be wiser than we are, more tolerant than we are, braver, more dignified than we, more self-controlled and self-disciplined," he says. As an illustration of what he means, the author offers a few examples: During the Montgomery bus boycott, everyone assumed that there would be no Negro violence and there was not. In fact, the only violence was done by white people. But our greatest expectation is that Negroes will be honest, honorable, and decent, which explains why there is so much outrage when a Negro commits a burglary or a mugging and why the papers cover it so closely. The author gives as a final example the small handful of Negro children in Little Rock who face insults and spitting and shoving and hatred each morning when they go to school. Perhaps some of the anger against Negroes stems from a profound sense of their superiority, which is rooted in their daily necessity to be composed and courageous.

Ballantine Ale Ad

Steinbeck wrote a few paragraphs for a Ballantine Ale advertisement published on January 26, 1953. They are written in second person, addressing an exhausted, baked farmworker who is tired of water that tastes like dirt and longs for something to quench his thirst. Steinbeck envisions a boss who brings iced bottles of Ballantine Ale to his workers at lunch. He describes in vivid detail the feeling of swallowing the mellow drink. There is a subtle hint

to the boss as well, that sending Ballantine out at lunch is the way to keep happy workers.

"The Black Man's Ironic Burden" (1961)

Originally printed in *Saturday Review* and reprinted in *The Negro History Bulletin* in April 1961, Steinbeck's "The Black Man's Ironic Burden," marvels over how much we must respect and look up to African-Americans. He notes that an African-American must be many times smarter or much more gifted than a white person to be equally recognized. Blacks must be polite as they are spat upon or yelled at. He points out that the only violence that erupted in the Alabama bus boycott was from whites; the same was true in Little Rock. He goes on to say that the little children who went every day to school and got good grades while they were insulted and tormented would go on to be respected and honored by their descendents, while the descendents of the abusers would deny and abhor their legacy. He himself would have trouble not attacking those who attacked his child this way. He decides that African Americans must survive only through knowledge of their own superiority and courage.

Bombs Away: The Story of a Bomber Team (1942)

Bombs Away: The Story of a Bomber Team was written at the request of the U.S. Army Air Force during WORLD WAR II. The project was conceived to publicize the efforts of the armed services in mobilizing to fight the air war in Europe, Africa, and the Pacific. The army granted Steinbeck wide access to its facilities and arranged for the book to be illustrated by the photographer John Swope. Steinbeck and Swope spent more than a month traveling across the United States from airbase to airbase. During this time the two men lived among the cadets. They also had the opportunity to fly in many of the great bombers and fighters in the air force fleet. The book, an unabashed piece of wartime propaganda, follows a group of cadets from recruitment into their respective technical schools, and through the end of their training programs where they come together as a bomber squad. VIKING PRESS published *Bombs Away* in 1942. A Hollywood studio purchased film rights to the book for $250,000, money that Steinbeck subsequently donated to the Air Force Aid Society Trust Fund.

CRITICAL PERSPECTIVES

When *Bombs Away* was first published, reviewers such as Joseph Henry Jackson, Lewis Gannet, Clifton Fadiman, and Harry Hansen immediately responded to Steinbeck's new book. The fact that readers usually read more about the planes than about the pilots made the book even more appealing. As most of the reviewers agree, John Steinbeck's new book is no romance, no fictionalized yarn, but a book of actualities, written specially at the request of the U.S. Air Force. In fact, to write the book, Steinbeck toured for months, visiting training fields all over the country.

In his review of *Bombs Away*, Lewis Gannett compares the nonfiction book to Steinbeck's previous works. According to Gannett, "*Bombs Away* is the meticulously precise life-history of a bomber team: a scientifically precise account of what it is, and how it gets that way, written with passion by a man who deeply regrets that he cannot be part of one" (*New York Herald Tribune*, November 27, 1942). Gannett further notes that *Bombs Away* is not what the reader would expect from the author who had written TORTILLA FLAT, THE GRAPES OF WRATH, and SEA OF CORTEZ. One important thing that Gannett mentions in his review is that the book is more of a textbook or a sermon than a story.

Gannett's view of the book is echoed by reviewer Clifton Fadiman's. As Fadiman warns, it is pointless to say that Steinbeck had written better books than *Bombs Away* because it is not a book in the book reviewers' narrow sense at all; instead, it aims "to set down in simple terms the nature and mission of a bomber crew and the technique and training of it." Steinbeck accomplished this aim

clearly and effectively. Unfortunately, this book, which now is out of print, has received few scholarly responses.

SYNOPSIS

Introduction
The author comments on the American effort to avoid war with Japan and Germany. America during the 1930s, he suggests, was uncertain, and withdrawn into an internal debate over the devastation of the Great Depression. But America's enemies, the author assures us, were mistaken in equating uncertainty with weakness, and German and Japanese attacks restored unity and sense of purpose to the nation. Now firmly committed to the war, it has fallen to the commanders of the military to build the greatest air force in the world. As the development of the air force has been so rapid, it is often misunderstood; therefore, it is the author's intention to explain "the nature and mission of a bomber crew and the technique and training of each member of it."

The Bomber
Steinbeck discusses the history of military air warfare, from observation aircraft to dog fighters of World War I, to the strategic bombers that have recently made their appearance with the onset of World War II. He comments that, unlike the army and navy, which have thousands of years of collective history, the air force is the service branch with the least precedent and the least tradition, enjoying an actual history of less than 30 years. The battles at the Coral Sea and Midway proved that the heavy bomber is the backbone of airpower, and the rise of airpower as a determining factor in modern warfare has placed incredible importance on the development of the bomber crew. The bomber crew is unusual in the ranks of the military because it consists of a team of specialists who share command and responsibility to meet a specific mission. Two types of bombers make up the core of the long-range bombers, the B-17 Flying Fortress and the B-24 Liberator, which in the author's opinion are about equal in performance. The author argues that Americans make superior bomber crews for three reasons: the national tradition of sportsman-

ship and team play; early acquaintance with the workings of machinery and engines; and training in the possession and use of firearms.

The Bombardier

This chapter tells the story of Bill, from Idaho. Bill is selected as a candidate for bombardier school. He follows an intensive 12-week training program that includes training on the ground and in the air before finally graduating and being assigned to a bomber crew. Upon graduation, the bombardier will receive an officer's commission.

The Aerial Gunner

The author lauds the gunners of the air force for their tradition of toughness and courage. The best candidate for aerial gunner is said to be a "slender, short, wiry young man with stringy muscles, a deadly eye, and no nerves." The aerial gunner operates the .30 or .50 caliber guns that defend the ship from attack, as well as 20mm and 37mm guns. Americans are said to make excellent gunners because most males have had experience shooting some type of gun or another. This chapter tells the story of Al, a 21-year-old from the Midwest. Gunnery school lasts for five weeks of intensive training in the maintenance, operation, and repair of weaponry, including training on the ground and in the air before Al finally graduates and is assigned to a bomber crew.

The Navigator

Aerial navigators are selected for being studious and oriented toward perfectionism, for their job is one of mathematics and precision. This chapter tells the story of Allen, a graduate in civil engineering, as he passes through the 15-week program to learn the instruments, maps, and techniques that will make him a navigator. Classes include astronomy, mathematics, and meteorology, and incorporate training on the ground and in the air. Upon graduation, a navigator will receive an officer's commission and will be assigned to a bomber crew.

The Pilot

Although the pilot is considered by the public to have the most glamorous position among the bomber crew, the author emphasizes that the development of the long-range bomber lessens the pilot's individual importance and increases the importance of the bomber crew as a whole. Air force tactics have become group tactics where men and machines work together toward an objective. This chapter tells the story of Joe, a tall boy from a farming family in South Carolina. Joe is followed through an intensive three-part training program as he moves from single-engine training planes to multi-engine bombers. Upon graduation, the pilot receives an officer's commission, and after a week's furlough, he is assigned to a bomber crew.

The Aerial Engineer—Crew Chief

The aerial engineer makes necessary repairs and adjustments during flight, substitutes for the copilot, serves as aerial gunner during combat, and supervises ground maintenance of his ship. This chapter tells the story of Abner, a natural-born mechanic, as he goes through the 18-week training program to learn the care and maintenance of single- and multi-engine planes.

The Radio Engineer

The final facet of the aerial bomber crew is the radio engineer. Modern air tactics make it necessary for bomber crews to maintain radio contact with the command center as well as with other planes. The air force draws radiomen from the reserves of thousands of radio hobbyists around the country. This chapter tells the story of Harris, an amateur ham radio operator. Harris is drafted and put through an 18-week training program from which he will emerge as a technical sergeant and be assigned to a bomber crew.

The Bomber Team

As each of the individual specialists completes his training program he is assigned to a bomber crew, given a ship, and put through vigorous group training exercises. At the end of their training, gunners, radiomen, and crew chiefs receive the rank of sergeant, while pilots, copilots, bombardiers, and navigators become commissioned officers. The men are assigned to a new training base recently carved out of a Florida swamp. Final training simulates combat conditions and the men learn to think in terms of their mission instead of their specialty. While on a practice mission, the crew spots a submarine and successfully sinks it. The crew forms a relationship with their plane, naming it *Baby* and painting the representation of a bathing woman on the side.

Missions

The author discusses the organization of the air force units Wing, Group, and Squadron. The squadron, consisting of 13 bombers, 21 officers and 180 men, is sufficiently small to receive personal supervision and control from an experienced officer. *Baby*'s squadron is sent on its final training exercises. Upon returning, they receive their orders assigning them to their mission.

FURTHER READING

Gannet, Lewis. "Books and Things." *New York Herald Tribune*, November 27, 1942, 19.

Fadiman, Clifton. "Books." *New Yorker*, November 28, 1942, 80–82.

Hansen, Harry. "The First Reader." *New York World Telegram*, November 28, 1942, 11.

Jackson, Joseph Henry. "The Bookman's Notebook." *San Francisco Chronicle*, November 26, 1942, 11y.

Steinbeck, John. *Bombs Away: The Story of a Bomber Team*. New York: Viking, 1942.

"Breakfast" (1936)

Steinbeck's short story "Breakfast" first appeared in print in *The Pacific Weekly,* in 1936. It was subsequently reprinted by VIKING PRESS in *The Portable Steinbeck*, which notes that "Breakfast" is a fragment taken from the working notes that the author made while preparing to write THE GRAPES OF WRATH. Indeed, a similar scene occurs in the novel when the Joad family arrives at the Weedpatch camp in California's Central Valley. "Breakfast" appeared in the collection of short stories THE LONG VALLEY, published by Viking Press in 1938.

No more than four pages long, the story is comparable to ERNEST HEMINGWAY's famous recipe for trout in the *Valiant Swimmers*, in its ability to create a voracious appetite in the reader. On an early morning, with a cold "lavender" mist covering a

country road, a young man approaches a campsite of itinerant farmworkers, where breakfast is being prepared by a girl nursing a baby. Though it is clear the family has very little, the father and son invite the stranger to join them in an expertly prepared meal of bacon, bacon gravy, and biscuits, served with hot coffee. In the morning chill, the five of them, including the still nursing baby, devour their food. The father and son offer the traveler a chance at picking cotton with them. He declines, thanks them for the hospitality, and sets off down the road again. During the interlude, no names are exchanged, but the feeling of peaceful camaraderie, and of happiness in life, are striking.

SYNOPSIS

The narrator describes walking along a country road on a cold early morning when he comes upon a campground. A young woman, a baby in her arms, stands over a small stove. She is preparing breakfast. The narrator describes the pleasant smell of frying bacon and baking bread. A younger man and his father emerge from the tent. They greet the narrator and invite him to eat with them. The men explain proudly that they have been picking cotton and that they have even earned enough money to purchase new clothes. The men generously offer to see if they can get the narrator on their work crew, but he declines and continues on his unknown journey.

"Bricklaying Piece" (1955)

"Bricklaying Piece," which appeared in *Punch* in July 23, 1955, is a short narrative in which Steinbeck describes a drunken old Irish master mason he encountered while constructing a small brick-enclosed flower garden in front of his New York brownstone. The two men begin conversing and Steinbeck comments on his own lack of skill at bricklaying. The mason encourages him to do his best, suggesting that everyone is an expert at something different, and continues on his way. "Bricklaying Piece" is typical of the light prose that Steinbeck wrote in some quantity for popular magazines during the latter part of his career; while it demonstrates the Steinbeck charm, it is a far departure from the work that earned him his fame as a writer.

Burning Bright (1950)

Burning Bright was Steinbeck's 20th book and his third attempt at writing what he called the PLAY-NOVELETTE. OF MICE AND MEN and THE MOON IS DOWN are the other two examples of this style. *Burning Bright* was published in New York in 1950 by VIKING PRESS and at the same time, produced as a play in New York. For the reading public, Steinbeck presented it as a novelette in three acts.

"It is a combination of many old forms," he writes in his prologue, "a play that is easy to read or a short novel that can be played simply by lifting out the dialogue." Steinbeck knew that the average person finds it difficult to read a play; the brief descriptions of scenes and characters intended for the guidance of producer and actor, the hints of changes in the mood or action, require an imaginative awareness that the reader may be incapable of giving, so that in many cases reading a play is like finding a path through a dark field.

After reading *Burning Bright*, it would appear that there is also something unsatisfactory in this play-novelette. The characters are vivid, the scenes sharp, but on the whole the book is a failure because the reader is often bewildered; Steinbeck's four characters appear to be puppets moved by strings, using words put into their mouths by a ventriloquist.

If the author were writing as a novelist and not primarily as a playwright, you might sense the background for the motives of his people; you would certainly know them better, for the novelist is compelled to tell you a great deal more about them, how they live, where they came from, what their families and friends are like, something of their childhood and of their habits and tastes.

The novel was originally titled *Everyman,* and then *Forests of the Night,* before Steinbeck finally renamed it *Burning Bright*, from a line in a poem by William Blake ("Tyger! Tyger! burning bright/ In the forests of the night,/ What immortal hand or eye/ Could frame thy fearful symmetry?"). A dense morality piece in three acts, *Burning Bright* is written in what Steinbeck called "universal language," a curious style that he intended less to sound like realistic dialogue than to operate as a system of rhythm and sound that served to express his ideas. Each act of the novelette features the same characters in a different setting: a circus, a farm, and a small freighter.

It tells the story of Joe Saul, a man who is obsessed with producing an heir to carry on his bloodline. Unknowingly, Joe Saul is sterile. Determined to make Joe Saul happy, his young wife, Mordeen, sleeps with another man to get pregnant. Victor, the father of the child, declares his love to Mordeen and threatens to reveal the truth to Joe Saul, for which he is murdered by Joe Saul's loyal friend, Friend Ed. Joe Saul eventually learns the truth. He also discovers that love transcends blood and that every child belongs to all men, for "it is the race, the species, that must go staggering on."

Since he wrote this work during the cold war, critics have suggested that Steinbeck was influenced by the thought of world annihilation. Steinbeck's position on that possibility is clearly reflected in the lines above. He believed that humankind was basically inextinguishable because it is always looking for ways—despite immense pressures—to continue on.

EARLY CRITICISM

Burning Bright is a play in story form. In one of its first reviews, Harrison Smith calls readers' attention to this new literary form of Steinbeck's. Because of its unique format, Smith finds that there is "a feeling of unreality in *Burning Bright* that may come from his method of handling the story itself." Smith notes that the four characters in the first act are circus people, three men and a woman, who are seen in the dressing room tent of Joe Saul and his beautiful young wife, Mordeen. In the second act the same characters are farmers in a midwestern farmhouse; in the third act they are in the captain's cabin of a cargo ship docked in New York harbor. However, these three incarnations of the same people do not change their way of speaking to suit the scene; they never speak as would sailors, farmers or, doubtless, circus performers. To Smith, the book is just a morality play, and the characters can be labeled as if they were symbols of human virtues and vices. Yet, as Smith regrets, although symbolism in his characters and his plots may be vital to the growth or the decline of Steinbeck as a creative writer, the playwright's rudimentary philosophy, his feverish climaxes, and the story as he has told it, in whole or in part, are "neither credible to the reader nor successful as the elements of a short novel."

Reviewer Norman Cousins provides a unique perspective, reading *Burning Bright* in light of Hemingway's book *Across the River and into the Trees* (1950). Despite the fact that Steinbeck claimed that he had never read Hemingway, in an article titled "Hemingway and Steinbeck" in *Saturday Review,* Cousins writes that *Burning Bright* seems to have been written almost in direct refutation of Hemingway. Just like Hemingway's *Across the River and into the Trees, Burning Bright* is a philosophical summation, but Steinbeck's book is strong where Hemingway's is weak. According to Cousins, Steinbeck reveals moral values where Hemingway reveals monomaniacal meanderings. *Burning Bright* tries to address deep inner conflicts instead of pampering them. The truculent, arrogant, prizefight-conscious, sperm-ridden, perennial soldier-boy of Hemingway's book dies a heroic and glamorous death. The man who meets death in Steinbeck's book is also a pompous and willful brute, but there is nothing heroic about him or his death. To Cousins, he is a pathetic and oafish stud whose twisted ego makes it impossible for him to understand that virility alone does not automatically entitle him to the love of a desirable and understanding woman. However, Joe Saul becomes a real human being. He discovers that love has higher dimensions than he had realized, and that identification with the human family is purpose and fulfillment in life.

After *Burning Bright* was staged in New York, an article appeared in *Theatre Arts* 34 (December 1950), calling it a modern morality play. According to the critic, John Steinbeck not only took the title of his play from "The Tyger," but like Blake, Stein-

beck was also commenting on man's finiteness in a boundless universe and also on the creative richness of love. In this sense *Burning Bright* is an affirmation of faith in the human race, an avowal of belief in the dignity of man stated with unmistakable sincerity.

CONTEMPORARY PERSPECTIVES

Most critics consider the work to be an inferior one by Steinbeck—noting that he had lost much of the subtlety of earlier works dealing with similar themes. Mimi Reisel Gladstein points out that the work suffers because it strains to be profound. She argues that in his earlier works, Steinbeck was able to address complex issues on a series of different planes and from different angles.

In a recent study of the story, which appears in Jackson Benson's *The Short Novels of John Steinbeck,* critics Carroll Britch and Clifford Lewis reveal that the excruciating moral dilemma of the story draws inspiration from emotional crises in Steinbeck's own life. According to the critics, Steinbeck suffered in 1948 when his wife Gwyn divorced him and claimed (falsely) that his second child, John IV, was not his. Although it was a lie, her claim bothered him a great deal, which led to his breakdown. Steinbeck tried to heal his emotional injury in a series of letters to his editor, Pat Covici, who the critics argue may have been a model for Ed in the book. Britch and Lewis state that, regardless of the true source for the story, most scholars today agree that the play has a valuable point: that the family is a private unit, a tribal cell, whose main concern is and always has been its own welfare and survival. The play seems to argue that the evolutionary process has not changed.

SYNOPSIS

Act One: The Circus
Joe Saul, a lithe, middle-aged trapeze artist, sits in his dressing tent putting on his makeup for his upcoming performance. He is obviously unhappy. Joe Saul's longtime friend, Friend Ed, enters the tent in his circus clown costume and asks Joe Saul what is wrong. Joe Saul explains that he does not like working with his new partner, Victor, a

stranger to him, unrelated by blood. Joe Saul explains to his friend the importance of bloodline and admits he is unhappy because he has been unable to have a child. He is afraid that he is sterile and fears that his bloodline will be extinguished. His beautiful young wife, Mordeen, joins the two men in the tent and senses the source of her husband's unhappiness.

Victor, Joe Saul's new assistant, enters the tent. He has sprained his wrist and will not be able to perform for three days. Joe Saul angrily berates the young man, telling him that he does not have it in his blood to be a true acrobat. Victor laughs at him bitterly, telling him that he is a frustrated old man. Joe Saul slaps the petulant youth and walks angrily out of the tent. Victor tells Mordeen that he did not strike back because he is in love with her and did not want to anger her. Mordeen tells Victor that she will do anything to see her husband happy. Victor grabs her and tries to kiss her, but she goes limp in his arms, and avoids his lips. Friend Ed walks into the tent, witnesses the assault, and tells Victor to go away.

Friend Ed tells Mordeen that Joe Saul has gone to town to get drunk. He asks Mordeen if she is able to have a baby. She says that she can, that she was once pregnant. She admits that Joe Saul had rheumatic fever as a child and is probably sterile. Friend Ed says that they must not tell Joe Saul of his sterility, for she would lose him to his self-contempt. She admits to Friend Ed that she is thinking about going to another man to make herself pregnant for Joe Saul. She tells Friend Ed to go find Joe Saul and to protect him in his drunkenness. When Ed is gone, Victor returns to the tent. She tells him she is sorry for what happened. She arranges to meet him in town at a Chinese restaurant. Joe Saul returns to the tent, ashamed in his drunkenness, and quietly goes to sleep.

Act Two: The Farm

Joe Saul, the farmer, sits at the table reviewing the farm's books. He complains to Friend Ed about his assistant Victor, whom he feels that he constantly has to watch since he does not have the blood of a real farmer. He tells Friend Ed about a nightmare that he has in which his land is left fallow and the

wilderness creeps back in upon it. He is worried that he has no heir to continue his bloodline when he dies. Friend Ed asks after his wife, Mordeen. Joe Saul says that she has been sickly during the past weeks. Friend Ed asks if Victor holds a grudge toward Joe Saul for his mistreatment of him. Joe Saul admits that he is ashamed of himself for slapping the young man.

Mordeen enters the kitchen. She announces to her startled husband that she is pregnant. Joe Saul weeps with joy. He insists that they organize a party to celebrate. Victor enters the kitchen for a cup of coffee. Joe Saul proudly tells Victor the good news. Victor conceals his shock. He offers a malicious toast "to the father," knowing full well that the father is he. Seeing the secret hatred on Mordeen's face, he excuses himself from the kitchen. Joe Saul rushes off to town with Friend Ed to buy Mordeen a present. Victor confronts Mordeen about the child. She insists that the child is Joe Saul's. Victor throws himself at Mordeen's feet and declares that he loves her. She rejects his advances, asking him coldly to go away from the farm. Time passes but Victor refuses to relinquish his love for Mordeen and his claim on the child. Victor announces to Joe Saul that he is leaving the farm, that he cannot stand living in a place where he was hit in the face. Joe Saul decides that as a Christmas present for his coming child he will have a complete doctor's examination to prove his health and the purity of the blood that he is passing on.

Act Three, Scene I: The Sea

Victor enters the tiny cabin of a freighter and asks to speak with Mordeen. She tells him that she is having pains, signs that she is about to go into labor. She begs Victor to go look for her husband, Joe Saul. Victor insists to Mordeen that she is his woman and that her child is his. He tells her that she must come away with him or he will tell Joe Saul the truth. She agrees to go with him but while he gathers her suitcase, she slips a short dagger into her coat.

Unbeknownst to Mordeen, Friend Ed has been watching from the door. He asks Victor to speak with him outside on the deck, where he kills the young man and throws him into the sea. Meanwhile,

Joe Saul returns to the ship in a rage. He has had his checkup, which he says revealed that he has a bad heart. Friend Ed accuses him of lying and insists that Joe Saul tell the truth about what the doctor told him. Joe Saul admits that he knows that he is sterile and that Mordeen's baby could not possibly be his; his bloodline will die with him. He angrily decries his wife's treachery. Friend Ed rebukes him for rejecting Mordeen's sacrifice and leaves the ship in disgust. Mordeen cries out and collapses on the floor in pain.

Act Three, Scene II: The Child

Mordeen lies in the delivery room, her child beside her in a bundle. Joe Saul enters the room and approaches his wife. Mordeen, overcome with delirium, tells him that the baby is dead. He reassures his wife that the baby is alive and that he loves it. He has realized "that every man is father to all children and every child must have all men as father."

CHARACTERS

Friend Ed   A character in *Burning Bright,* Friend Ed is Joe Saul's loyal friend. He is a broad, tall man, slow in motion and speech. In the three acts of the novelette, he is a circus clown, a farmer, and a ship's captain. He murders Victor and throws him overboard so that Joe Saul will not learn that Victor is the father of Mordeen's baby. Steinbeck may have modeled Friend Ed on his close friend Ed Ricketts.

Mordeen   A character in *Burning Bright,* Mordeen is Joe Saul's beautiful, golden-haired young wife. In the three acts of the novelette, she is an acrobat, a farmer's wife, and a ship's captain's wife. She sleeps with a man that she does not love to produce an heir for her sterile husband.

Saul, Joe   A character in *Burning Bright,* Joe is a lithe and stringy middle-aged man with large, dark eyes and thick graying hair that he keeps carefully dyed. In the three acts of the novelette, he is a circus acrobat, a farmer, and a ship's captain. Unaware that he is sterile, he is obsessed with preserving his bloodline by producing an heir. Eventually, he

embraces a child that is not his, realizing that "it is the race, the species, that must go staggering on."

Victor   A character in *Burning Bright,* Victor is a strong, athletic young man with dark eyes. In the three acts of the novelette, he is alternately an apprentice acrobat, a farmer's assistant, and a ship's mate. Mordeen sleeps with him in order to produce an heir for her sterile husband Joe Saul. When he discovers that Mordeen is pregnant with his baby, he declares his love for her and insists that she leave with him. Friend Ed, who does not want him to reveal to Joe Saul that he is the real father of Mordeen's baby, murders him.

FURTHER READING

Britch, Carroll, and Clifford Lewis. "*Burning Bright: The Shining of Joe Saul.*" In *The Short Novels of John Steinbeck,* edited by Jackson Benson. Durham, N.C.: Duke University Press, 1990.

"*Burning Bright.*" *Theatre Arts* 34 (December 1950): 16.

Cousins, Norman. "Hemingway and Steinbeck." *Saturday Review,* October 28, 1950, pp. 26–27.

Gladstein, Mimi Reisel. "Straining for Profundity: Steinbeck's *Burning Bright* and *Sweet Thursday.*" In *The Short Novels of John Steinbeck,* edited by Jackson Benson. Durham, N.C.: Duke University Press, 1990.

Smith, Harrison. "A New Form of Literature." *Washington Post,* October 22, 1950, 5B.

Steinbeck, John. *Burning Bright.* New York: Viking, 1950.

"The Cab Driver Doesn't Give a Hoot" (1956)

As part of his Election Notebook coverage for the London *Daily Mail,* John Steinbeck covered the Democratic and Republican Conventions in Chicago and San Francisco, respectively. In this report, published August 14, 1956, he talks about the responses from people on the topic of the election. His cabdriver refused to answer any questions about which candidate he preferred, because he was worried about his tip. Finally he admitted that he thought they were all crooks. A man at the gate affirmed that he was part of the No Opinions and he was going to stay that way until the day he voted—secretly. Steinbeck points out that Americans love the underdog; they might even vote for the underdog when they have been brought to the polls by an apparent shoe-in race. He winds up by talking about the growing impact of television on the election. A friend believed that TV was like an X-ray that turned politicians inside out and showed them up if they were crooks. But Steinbeck also found himself really liking a man whose politics he despised, because television had shown him to be smart and honest.

"Camping Is for the Birds" (1967)

Popular Science ran Steinbeck's editorial "Camping Is for the Birds" in May 1967 next to an opposing view of camping by Erle Stanley Gardner. Steinbeck begins by admitting that he understands the urge to go camping, but he does not really see the romance of it. The desire to camp, he contends, is driven by our flawed memories of being a species that camped out in the open because cities hadn't been built yet. The air was clean and the water was fresh. Being in the everyday grind of the city makes us long for those quiet times, without remembering the discomfort that our ancestors went through.

Steinbeck's view of contemporary camping describes the dream: a large family takes off in a camper, seduced by advertisements that show the camper parked in a beautiful, sunny field. The father in the ad brings the beautiful bass he just caught to his wife so she can cook it up for the waiting children while the dog plays in the meadow. The actuality, he contends, is much different. The kids do not want to be there, the father cannot catch any fish, the mother misses her beautician, and the only place they can park the camper is in a lot crammed with other families in campers.

He argues that the fastest way to end a romance, even with the most accommodating and pleasant woman, is to take her away from her bathroom. He calls it "the Kleenex Curtain." Even friends should not camp together, he says. Too much togetherness leads to resentment. The only good way to go camping is to go alone. Find a good place and stop there. Don't look for a better place. Don't seek out other people. Catch up on your reading. Enjoy the sun, or the rain, whichever comes. When your batteries are recharged, go back to the city. He encourages the reader not to take his word for it, but to find out for himself.

Cannery Row (1945)

Steinbeck's first postwar book and his ninth novel was written while the author lived in his family's cottage in PACIFIC GROVE, CALIFORNIA. Steinbeck spent much of his time wandering and exploring the nearby port of MONTEREY, especially the district of sardine canneries known as CANNERY ROW, where his best friend, EDWARD RICKETTS, ran a biological supply company. The book is influenced heavily by several themes. One theme is the sentimental view of the place itself. Written during WORLD WAR II and after Steinbeck had spent time on the European battlefields, Steinbeck's work ignores the war and instead writes of a simpler time and place. Some critics have suggested that the book was specifically an attempt to escape the harsh realism of the war and infuse some cheerfulness into his reading audience. Steinbeck confirms this approach in several letters to CARLTON A. SHEFFIELD. Another possible motivation suggested by some critics is that *Cannery Row*, which attempts to create a nostalgic scenario, was specifically written in response to Thomas Wolfe's *You Can't Go Home Again*.

Another influence was Steinbeck's fascination with the Arthurian legends. *Cannery Row* tells the story of Mack, the leader of a group of hoboes, and his attempts to stage a party to raise the spirits of their friend Doc. Ed Ricketts served as the inspiration behind the "Doc" character, and in an essay written after his friend's death, Steinbeck recounts nervously showing Ricketts the typescript of *Cannery Row* and offering to make any changes that he suggested.

Ricketts plays another important, influential role in the novel. Many critics such as Michael J. Meyer have suggested that *Cannery Row* is a poetic attempt to communicate the same nonteleological philosophy that Steinbeck and Ricketts developed in THE LOG FROM THE SEA OF CORTEZ. In *The Log* and in *Cannery Row,* Steinbeck tries to explain the philosophy of "is" that was developed while on the expedition with Ricketts. In this philosophical approach, questions of why and how are not important and the user must be careful not to impose any value systems other than what "is" to what is good. In other words, Steinbeck and Ricketts expose a philosophy that states whatever "is" is right.

The novel was published by the VIKING PRESS in 1945. Some initial reviews expressed concern that Steinbeck was abandoning some of his sociopolitical concerns for sentimentality. Others agreed with poet and critic John Crowe Ranson who thought the book was a "funny" work highlighted by "a perfect episode or two." Many of the early reviews were very unfavorable. In fact Steinbeck had upset many in the Monterey area with his celebration of bums and prostitutes. The local reaction against the novel was one of the reasons that led the author to move with his pregnant wife from California to New York City. As time passed, however, *Cannery Row* proved to be immensely popular.

EARLY CRITICISM

Early criticism and reviews of *Cannery Row* often focus on the mischievousness of the jovial characters in the novel and neglect the philosophical depth and social messages conveyed by the author. For example, in his review of the novel in the *New Yorker,* Edmund Wilson notes that *Cannery Row,* like *TORTILLA FLAT,* is amusing and attractive. Wilson's view is based on his comparison of the community-oriented Danny and his friends in *Tortilla Flat* and Mack and the boys in *Cannery Row.* In Wilson's opinion, Steinbeck has created an atmosphere of laziness, naïveté, good nature, satis-

faction in the pleasures of the senses, and indifference to property rights.

In the same vein, when reviewing *Cannery Row,* Norman Cousins focuses on Steinbeck's ability to write about "real people." Cousins applauds Steinbeck's skill in startling readers by portraying "bums" from the street and girls from the brothel as decent, clean, honest, and wholesome human beings. Yet in Cousins's mind, Steinbeck's tribute to the "decent," "honest," and "clean" Mack and his boys and the girls from Dora's Bear Flag is an obsession shared with other modern writers, and often taken to excess. A concern Cousins has with the social and cultural backgrounds of Steinbeck's characters in the novel is that the novelist may be "canonizing the castoff" and "turn[ing] people into something special or freakish." Although he acknowledges Steinbeck's realistic style in the novel, Cousins doubts the literary significance of Steinbeck's obsession with "real people." Cousins further points out that these people, whom he calls the "well-meaning, big-hearted, coarse, ignorant bums, boobs, castoffs, and misfits" of society, flourish in Steinbeck's world. When others "tear themselves to pieces with ambition and nervousness and covetousness," these "bums" are relaxed. As Steinbeck comments directly in the book, "Mack and the boys are healthy and curiously clean."

One of the pioneering Steinbeck scholars, James Gray, author of *John Steinbeck* (1971), views *Cannery Row* from a different perspective. He notices that although the novel appears to be "merely light entertainment" its author intends to challenge the values of an American society "that seeks to make a merit of one of its worst defects." Gray has accurately grasped Steinbeck's views on the moral and ethical contortions of American society. What Gray has pointed out echoes the themes of other novels by Steinbeck, such as THE GRAPES OF WRATH and THE WINTER OF OUR DISCONTENT, and his essays in AMERICA AND AMERICANS. As seen from these works, avarice, unethical business practices, and immoral personal behavior are often described by Steinbeck as the worst of all sins. It may be said that with works like *Cannery Row* Steinbeck has created what Gray calls "anti-heroes" who are concerned more about the well-being of the group than about individuals, in contrast to what the author believed to be the real society. Because of this different view Steinbeck poses in *Cannery Row,* early critics often label the novel as a social protest.

CONTEMPORARY PERSPECTIVES

While early critics like Wilson and Cousins realized the amusement of Steinbeck's realistic style in *Cannery Row,* they failed to point out the in-depth meanings often concealed by the superficial comedy of the novel. Cannery Row, with its biological laboratory and brothel, Lee Chong's general store, and scattering of shacks and old boilers, does indeed pose a picture of carefree life, but the characters in *Cannery Row* represent a mixture of races and a variety of social levels. It may be fair to say that *Cannery Row* is about a lot of things, more than what Wilson and Cousins have noticed. First of all, it is about a place and a community: Doc, Mack and the boys, Dora and her girls, Henri the painter, Blaisdell the poet, Mr. and Mrs. Malloy, the Chinese Lee Chong, Frankie, Richard Frost, an anonymous Chinaman, Tom and Mary Talbot, and Joey. Steinbeck pays particular attention to the makeup of the community on the Row and the communication across social classes and ethnicities. As Charles R. Metzger mentions, in one sense *Cannery Row* is a poetic essay on how to give a good party, particularly when the party is for someone whom the community loves.

Other critical studies on *Cannery Row* further explore Steinbeck's intention in portraying "real people" as healthy and clean. Some scholars argue that the novel reveals Steinbeck's intention to present a picture of the characters escaping into the counterculture. To illuminate the messages in the novel, critics often find Steinbeck's first-person narratives more important than his depiction of "real people." For instance, regarding morals and behavioral ethics, Steinbeck laments in *Cannery Row,* "The things we admire in men, kindness and generosity, openness, honesty, understanding, and feeling are the concomitants of failure in our system. And those traits we detest, sharpness, greed, acquisitiveness, meanness, egotism and self-interest are the traits of success."

Nonetheless, most early critics often miss such satires of modern life. Peter Lisca has noted that *Cannery Row,* reminiscent of *Tortilla Flat,* is a "philosophically based and impassioned celebration of values directly opposed to the capitalist ethic dominant in Western society" (*The Short Novels of John Steinbeck*). He states that Steinbeck believes that those who might be normally called "thieves, rascals . . . bums" may just as truly be described as "saints and angels and martyrs and holy men." Steinbeck makes this clear through the statements of the novel's central character, Doc.

To further illustrate how *Cannery Row* has provided a counterculture theme, Lisca argues that the novel's informing spirit is the *Tao Teh Ching* of Lao-tzu, a Chinese philosopher of the sixth century B.C. According to Lisca, both *Cannery Row* and *Tao Teh Ching* were written in wartime. Reacting to these conditions, both books present a system of human values devoid of all those qualities that had brought on war. For further evidence, Lisca points out some interesting prefatory remarks and other correspondences of statements between the two great works. For instance, Lao-tzu states that "A violent order is disorder," and his corollary statement, "A great disorder is an order" seems to be the theme of the epigraph for *Cannery Row.* In the novel, Steinbeck created a world that is characterized by its rich variety, its benevolent chaos. Such qualities are also seen in all parts of the novel: Lee Chong's grocery store, with its hodgepodge of every conceivable commodity. Yet, Lisca also notes that the world into which *Cannery Row* "escapes" is not a perfect one; not everyone lives according to the Tao. The misfortunes of the "real people" in *Cannery Row* seem to be caused by some unexplainable natural forces.

SYNOPSIS

The novel opens with a description of Cannery Row. During the day, the area is industrious and busy. The sardine fleet brings its catch to the docks while men and women pour in from Monterey to work in the canneries. Then, in the late afternoon, when the last fish is cleaned and canned, the workers depart and the Row is left to the local inhabitants.

Nick Nolte as Doc in the 1982 MGM production of *Cannery Row* *(Photofest)*

(I)

Lee Chong, the owner of Lee Chong's Heavenly Flower Grocery, accepts an old shed in lieu of payment for the large debt accrued in his store by Horace Abbeville, a poor man with a large family. The despondent Abbeville returns to the building that was once his and shoots himself. Mack asks Lee Chong to lend the shed to him and his friends, a group of men with "no families, no money, and no ambitions beyond food, drink and contentment." He offers to keep up the property and ensure that nobody breaks the building's windows or burns it down. Chong recognizes Mack's gentle extortion and grudgingly agrees to rent them the property for $5 a week, realizing that he will never be paid. Mack and the boys move in and the place becomes known as the Palace Flophouse.

(II)

A hard man with a generous heart, Lee Chong digs up his grandfather's bones, tenderly packs them,

and sends them to be buried in China. Meanwhile, Mack and the boys continue their uncomplicated existence.

(III)

The Bear Flag Restaurant is a respectable, orderly whorehouse owned by Dora Flood, a model of generosity and civic responsibility. The Bear Flag's lonely bouncer, William, attempts to join Mack and the boys in the vacant lot. He is heartbroken by their rejection and tells everyone that he is going to kill himself. Feeling obliged to make good on his threats, he reluctantly plunges an ice pick into his heart.

(IV)

A mysterious old Chinaman passes through town every morning and evening. One afternoon Andy, a young boy visiting from nearby Salinas, marches behind the old man shouting insults. The Chinaman turns and stares at his persecutor with deep brown eyes. Andy has a vision of a strange, lonely landscape. When the vision is over, the Chinaman is gone.

(V)

This chapter describes Western Biological Laboratories, a low building filled with a dusty collection of scientific instruments and biological specimens run by Doc, a small bearded man who is greatly loved by the residents of Cannery Row.

(VI)

While Hazel and Doc collect starfish they discuss why Henri the painter is constantly changing and rebuilding the boat that he lives on. Doc speculates that Henri does not wish to finish the boat because he is afraid of the sea. The two men then speculate on the nature of stinkbugs.

(VII)

Mack and the boys fix up the Palace Flophouse and Grill. They decide to celebrate their new home by throwing a party for Doc. Mack suggests that they raise some money collecting frogs, which Doc buys for a nickel each.

(VIII)

Sam Malloy lives with his wife in a large, abandoned boiler in a vacant lot where he rents out lengths of pipe as sleeping quarters for single men. Mrs. Malloy decides to fix up the boiler. She is intent on buying real lace curtains, although there is nowhere to hang them on the windowless metal walls.

(IX)

Doc offers to pay Mack and the boys to hunt frogs while he collects baby octopi in La Jolla. He agrees to advance his friend money to buy gasoline for the trip, but then, doubting his reliability, gives Mack a note authorizing him to draw 10 gallons of gas at the local service station. Mack borrows Lee Chong's broken-down vehicle for the trip.

(X)

Frankie, a young boy with a learning disability, becomes Doc's devoted but incompetent assistant. Hoping to please his patron by serving beer to the guests during one of Doc's parties, Frankie stumbles and spills a tray loaded with glasses on a woman's dress. He hides himself in the basement in shame.

(XI)

Gay, a gifted mechanic, fixes Lee Chong's pickup truck and the boys head off to the Carmel River to hunt frogs. They are almost to the top of a steep hill when the old Model T breaks down. Gay hitches a ride back to town to find a replacement part, but the car that picks him up breaks down. He fixes the car and has a drink with the grateful owner, gets drunk, and is arrested for breaking a window and stealing shoes.

(XII)

Monterey is proud of its brilliant literary tradition: Josh Billings, the great humorist, died and was embalmed in Monterey. The townspeople are horrified when a young boy and his dog are discovered using the dead writer's organs for fishing bait. It is revealed that the mortician disposes of his leftovers in the ditch behind his office. The offending doctor is obliged to gather the organs, wash them, and bury them in a leaden box with the coffin.

(XIII)

Eddie repairs the Model T and the boys drive into the Carmel Valley and set up camp next to the river. An angry landowner appears while they are napping and warns them that they are trespassing. Fast-talking Mack explains that they are gathering frogs for cancer research. He convinces the farmer to let them collect frogs in a shallow pond near his house.

(XIV)

After a wild night at La Ida, Cannery Row's local honky-tonk, two soldiers and their girls sit on the beach and watch the sun rise.

(XV)

Mack doctors the farmer's dog. The grateful farmer tells them that his name is Captain and offers Mack a puppy. Captain unearths a five-gallon keg of corn whiskey that he buried in the cellar during Prohibition. The boys get drunk before remembering that they are there to hunt frogs. Mack organizes them into groups: one group forms to stomp through the shallow pond while another group waits at the end of the pond with flashlights. The hunt is spectacularly successful and the men make a party to celebrate their victory.

(XVI)
A particularly large sardine catch coincides with the arrival of a new regiment in the nearby presidio, resulting in a surge of business for the girls of the Bear Flag Restaurant. Meanwhile, a flu epidemic devastates Monterey. Dora organizes the girls to work in shifts taking care of sick families.

(XVII)
Doc packs up his equipment and drives to La Jolla for the low tide to collect small octopi, stopping periodically for hamburgers and beer. He offers a beer to a hitchhiker that he picks up along the side of the road and receives a lecture about the evil of drinking and driving. He angrily throws the hitchhiker out of the car.

(XVIII)
Doc discovers a young woman's body trapped beneath the surface of a tide pool. He is moved by her beauty and his head fills with strange music. Upset, he reports the body to a fisherman and returns to Monterey.

(XIX)
Homan's Department Store hires a flagpole skater to break his own world's record for skating on a small platform above the store. The event is a big success, but all of Monterey's citizens are left wondering how the skater relieves himself until Richard Frost, a high-strung and brilliant young man, gets drunk and goes to the flagpole to ask the skater.

(XX)
Mack and the boys return with their booty of frogs, which they convince Lee Chong to accept in lieu of cash. They decide to surprise Doc by holding the party in the unlocked offices of Western Biological. The party rages on although the guest of honor fails to appear. The frogs escape during a fight and the laboratory is left badly damaged in the resulting chaos. The ashamed guests depart before Doc returns.

(XXI)
Doc is enraged when he discovers the destruction wrought by the party. He hits Mack, splitting open his lip and loosening his teeth. Mack tells Doc about their plan to throw him a party and offers to pay for the broken equipment. But Doc knows that the boys will never have enough money to pay for the damage and that it will only worry them, so he refuses the offer and cleans the laboratory alone.

(XXII)
Henri the painter decides to mourn the breakup of his latest liaison by getting drunk. While he is stretched out aboard his boat he has a vision of a devilishly handsome young man accompanied by a golden-haired baby. The man removes a straight razor from his pocket and cuts the throat of the laughing baby. Henri screams in terror and the vision disappears. Terrified, he seeks out Doc, who assures him that he doesn't believe in ghosts. A pretty young woman, Doc's date, arrives and is captivated by Henri's story. Much to Doc's chagrin she accompanies the painter back to his boat and ends up living with him.

(XXIII)
Ashamed of the damage they have done to their friend, Mack and the boys become social outcasts on Cannery Row. Doc is unaware of his friends' suffering. A dark cloud envelops the Palace Flophouse and the rest of the Row. The disaster reaches its apex when Mack's puppy gets sick. The puppy recovers and the spell of bad feeling is broken. Mack is unsure of how to make things up to Doc. Dora advises him to have another party and to make sure Doc shows up for it.

(XXIV)
Mary Talbot is a cheerful woman who loves to throw parties to protect her husband, Tom, from the feelings of despondency that come over him periodically. She organizes a party for the neighborhood cats and discovers one of them playing sadistically with a wounded mouse. The sight of such cruelty makes her sad and ruins the party.

(XXV)
Happiness sweeps over the Row and everybody begins making preparations for Doc's party, which the boys have decided to hold on his birthday. Suspicious of his friends' intentions, Doc lies about his birthday, saying it is October 27th.

(XXVI)

Two boys, Joey and Willard, play in the abandoned lots of Cannery Row. Joey admits that his father killed himself by eating rat poison after being unemployed for nearly a year. He tells Willard that the funny thing is that the next day somebody came by to offer his father a job.

(XXVII)

Everybody in Cannery Row prepares a present for Doc's birthday: Dora and the girls make him a colorful patchwork quilt of silken underclothes, Lee Chong wraps a bag of China lily bulbs and a string of firecrackers, Sam Malloy polishes a rod and piston from a rare 1916 Chalmers automobile, and Mack and the boys catch 25 tomcats for Doc to embalm. Doc overhears a drunk talking about the party and he warily begins locking up his breakables.

(XXVIII)

Frankie looks for a present for the upcoming party. He discovers a black onyx clock topped with a statue of St. George slaying the dragon at a jewelry store. That evening he breaks into the store to steal the clock and is arrested. Doc is heartbroken when the police decide to send him away to a mental clinic.

(XXIX)

The big day arrives and everybody prepares for the surprise party. Dora's girls discuss why Doc never comes into the Bear Flag for a trick. Doc sits in the laboratory drinking whiskey and waiting for the party to start.

(XXX)

One by one the guests arrive and present their gifts to Doc. He lays out food and puts music on the phonograph. Liquor flows and the party rages. Some sailors arrive and harass Dora's girls, who are defended valiantly by Mack and the boys. The police arrive to break up the ensuing fight.

(XXXI)

A gopher takes up residence in the vacant lot. The setting is ideal and he builds a fine home. He begins to look for a mate, but no female appears. Finally he is forced to move to a nearby garden where the owner puts out traps every night.

(XXXII)

Doc awakens slowly and surveys the damage left in the wake of the big party. He plays music and sets about cleaning up the mess. He recites "Black Marigolds," a sentimental Sanskrit poem, and is moved by feelings of warmth toward his friends.

CHARACTERS AND PLACES

Abbeville, Horace   A character in *Cannery Row*. A man with two wives and six children, he manages to run a large debt at Lee Chong's grocery. He kills himself after agreeing to give Chong an old shed as payment.

Alfred   A character in *Cannery Row*. The bouncer at the Bear Flag Restaurant, Alfred accidentally breaks the back of a drunk whom he throws out of the brothel.

Bear Flag Restaurant   A Cannery Row whorehouse owned and operated by Dora Flood in *Cannery Row* and then by her sister Fauna Flood in *Sweet Thursday*.

Billings, Josh   A character in *Cannery Row*. A humorist living in Carmel, California, he dies and is embalmed by a local mortician who throws his organs in the ditch, where they are discovered and carried off by a local boy and his dog. When the outraged citizens discover that the body of the respected literary man has been defiled in such a way, they make the mortician gather up the organs, clean them and bury them.

Captain   A character in *Cannery Row*, Captain is a farmer in the Carmel Valley. He allows Mack and the boys to collect frogs from his pond. They have a fantastic party and leave Captain sleeping in his wrecked house.

Chong, Lee   A character in *Cannery Row*, and *Sweet Thursday*, Lee is the owner of Lee Chong's Heavenly Flower Grocery. He is a round-faced and courteous Chinese man who enjoys an important position in Cannery Row owing to the credit that he extends to everyone in the community. Lee rents a shed to Mack and the boys, which becomes known as the Palace Flophouse.

Doc   A character in *Cannery Row,* and SWEET THURSDAY, Doc is the owner and operator of Western Biological Laboratory; he adores science, beer, women, and classical music. Doc is the center of Cannery Row. A deceptively small man, he is loved by all the residents of the Row, but despite his popularity he is lonely and set apart. He has a beard, and his face is said to appear to be half Christ and half satyr. As a competent marine biologist, he established his own lab, where residents on the Row come for parties and conversations on science, art, and philosophy. For his birthday Doc is the recipient of a party thrown by Mack and the boys. His laboratory is destroyed when Mack and the boys decide to throw a surprise party. They make it up to him by throwing him another party for his birthday. At the end of the book Doc reflects on the events of the party, realizing that the "bums" truly loved him.

Eddie   A character in *Cannery Row* and SWEET THURSDAY, Eddie is a resident of the Palace Flophouse. He works periodically at La Ida, a local honky-tonk, where he keeps an empty gallon jug beneath the bar into which he empties the leftovers from all the glasses.

Flood, Dora   A character in *Cannery Row,* Dora is the owner and madame of the Bear Flag Restaurant, a *Cannery Row* whorehouse. She is the model of generosity and civic responsibility. During a flu epidemic she organizes her girls to care for the sick families of the Row.

Frankie   A character in *Cannery Row,* Frankie is a boy with a learning problem who worships Doc and works as his assistant in Western Biological Laboratories. He is sent away to a mental institu-

Left to right: James Keane, Frank McRae, M. Emmet Walsh, John Malloy, and Tom Mahoney as the "gentlemen of leisure" who befriend Doc in the film production of *Cannery Row* *(Photofest)*

tion when he tries to steal a heavy onyx clock for Doc's birthday.

Gay A character in *Cannery Row* and *Sweet Thursday*, Gay is an inspired mechanic who moves in with Mack and the boys of the Palace Flophouse to avoid his abusive wife. He fixes Lee Chong's old pickup truck that the boys take frog hunting. Arrested for breaking into a shoe shop, he is sentenced to six months in jail where he lives the good life by letting the Sheriff beat him at checkers.

Hazel A character in *Cannery Row* and *Sweet Thursday*, Hazel is innocent and kind, if a bit dim-witted. Hazel is a resident of the Palace Flophouse. Hazel's mother named him after a great-aunt in the hope of a possible inheritance.

Henri A character in *Cannery Row* and *Sweet Thursday*, Henri is a French painter who lives on Cannery Row. He is not really French, and his name is not really Henri. Henri lives aboard a boat of his own design that he is constantly building and changing. He does not want to finish the boat because then he would feel obliged to sail it and he is afraid of the sea.

Hughie A character in *Cannery Row*, Hughie is an inhabitant of the Palace Flophouse, who bakes a cake for Doc's surprise party.

Mack A character in *Cannery Row* and *Sweet Thursday*, Mack is the leader of a small group of bums who live at the Palace Flophouse on Cannery Row. Mack throws a party for Doc and destroys his laboratory. Doc smashes Mack's face in anger when he discovers the damage caused by the party. Mack is repentant and decides to make it up to Doc by organizing a surprise birthday party.

Malloy, Sam A character in *Cannery Row*, Sam lives inside an abandoned boiler on a vacant lot in Cannery Row with his wife. He rents lengths of abandoned pipe to homeless workers at the nearby canneries for a nominal fee.

Old Tennis Shoes The local name for Old Tennessee, a cheap blended whiskey guaranteed four

months old and popular among the inhabitants of Cannery Row.

Palace Flophouse and Grill A place in *Cannery Row* and *Sweet Thursday*, this flimsy storage building on a small lot is what Lee Chong receives from Horace Abbeville in payment for his huge grocery debts. Chong rents the building to Mack and his friends for $5 a week. The building is named by Hazel.

Precious A fabulously spoiled bird-dog puppy that is the beloved mascot of the boys from the Palace Flophouse. She is given to Mack by the Captain. The boys are devastated when she is taken ill with canine distemper.

Talbot, Mary A character in *Cannery Row*, Mary is a lovely woman who lives on Cannery Row with her husband Tom Talbot. She loves to throw parties to protect her husband from the feelings of despondency that come over him periodically.

William A character in *Cannery Row*, William is a bouncer at the Bear Flag Restaurant, he is a dark and lonesome man. After threatening to commit suicide he feels obligated to do so and drives an ice pick in his heart.

THE FILM: *CANNERY ROW* (MGM, 1982)

Based on the novel by John Steinbeck

> Screenplay: David Ward
> Director: David Ward
> Producer: Michael Phillips
> Music: Jack Nitzsche
> Photography: Sven Nykvist
> *Doc:* Nick Nolte
> *Suzy:* Debra Winger
> *Mack:* Emmet Walsh
> *Fauna:* Audra Lindley
> *Hazel:* Frank McRae

This 1982 adaptation of Steinbeck's 1945 novel was done by David Ward, the author of the Academy Award–winning screenplay for the movie *The Sting*. The film is really a combination of the stories in Steinbeck's novels *Cannery Row* and *Sweet*

THURSDAY, merging together the hilarity of Mack and his gang of hobos from the former novel with the unifying love story of the latter. Ward invents a mysterious background for the beloved character of Doc, making him into a retired baseball pitcher who lives with remorse after being responsible for a terrible accident. The film received negative critical reaction and was largely ignored by the public.

FURTHER READING

Benson, Jackson J. "John Steinbeck's *Cannery Row*: A Reconsideration." *Western American Literature* 12 (1997): 11–40.

Cousins, Norman. "Real People." *Saturday Review* 28, March 17, 1945, p. 14.

Gray, James. *John Steinbeck*. Minneapolis: University of Minnesota Press, 1971.

Lisca, Peter. "*Cannery Row* and the *Tao Teh Ching*." *San José Studies* 1 (1975): 21–27.

Lisca, Peter. "Cannery Row: Escape into the Counterculture." In *The Short Novels of John Steinbeck*, edited by Jackson J. Benson. Durham, N.C.: Duke University Press, 1990, 111–118.

Metzger, Charles R. "Steinbeck's Version of the Pastoral." In *The Short Novels of John Steinbeck*, edited by Jackson J. Benson. Durham, N.C.: Duke University Press, 1990, 185–195.

Owens, Lewis. "*Cannery Row*: 'An Essay in Loneliness.'" In *John Steinbeck's Re-Vision of America*. Athens: University of Georgia Press, 1985.

Steinbeck, John. *Cannery Row*. New York: Viking, 1945.

Wilson, Edmund. Books. *New Yorker* 20 (January 6, 1945): 62–63.

"The Chrysanthemums" (1937)

Steinbeck's short story "The Chrysanthemums" first appeared in print in *Harper's Monthly Magazine* in October 1937. It was subsequently reprinted in the February 1938 edition of the *Scholastic Journal*. "The Chrysanthemums" later appeared in Steinbeck's collection of short stories, *THE LONG VALLEY*, published by VIKING PRESS in 1938. Pyramid Films eventually made the story into a short film in 1990.

In a letter to his friend GEORGE ALBEE, Steinbeck called the tale "entirely different," and "designed to strike without the reader's knowledge." He wanted the story to be perceived at emotional and instinctive levels, rather than on a purely intellectual level. Perhaps because of the multiple layers, "The Chrysanthemums," along with "FLIGHT" and "THE SNAKE," remains among the most widely read and controversial of Steinbeck's short fiction.

Ultimately, the brief examination of one afternoon in the life of Elisa Allen is about restriction and constriction. Steinbeck immediately sets the mood by describing the Salinas Valley where the Allen ranch is situated as closed off by a blanket of fog. Elisa, too, is closed off by the fence surrounding her flower garden while she works to prepare her prized chrysanthemums for winter, and to transplant some of the shoots for spring. She observes but cannot hear the business discussion her husband, Henry, has outside the fence with two cattle buyers. She has nothing to do with the ranch except for the immediate vicinity of the farmhouse with its "hard-polished windows and a clean mud mat. . . ." Henry leans over the fence and remarks wistfully that he wishes Elisa would devote part of her horticultural gifts to tending the orchard. She dismisses his suggestion, but claims she could do it if she wanted. After asking his wife to accompany him to dinner and a movie in town to celebrate the sale of 30 head of cattle, Henry makes a small joke about perhaps taking in a prizefight as well. Elisa misses the humor entirely, and protests "breathlessly." She has closed herself off from her husband's humor. Within a few short paragraphs, Steinbeck establishes the Allens' estrangement and miscommunication. He also establishes Elisa's strength, almost to the point of masculinity, describing her with such adjectives as powerful, handsome, strong, eager, and lean. Her gardening clothes conceal her femininity with a "man's black hat, . . . clodhopper shoes, . . . a big corduroy apron, . . . and heavy leather gloves."

Shortly after Henry's departure to round up the cattle, an itinerant tinker and his mongrel dog pull up in a dilapidated wagon outside the wire fence enclosing Elisa's garden. The encounter between the attractive traveling repairman and Elisa forms the central tension of the story. In contrast to the humorless conversation with her husband, Elisa immediately makes a joke about the tinker's dog, which retreats under the wagon when confronted by Elisa's ranch shepherds. Asked by the tinker for directions to the Los Angeles highway, Elisa suggests the man's wagon would be bogged down in wet sand over the back road, intimating at her own sense of entrapment. Initially resistant to and suspicious of the traveler's offer to mend any of Elisa's old pots, she succumbs to flattery about her chrysanthemums, and a deceitful request for cuttings to give to one of his valued female customers. She invites him inside her garden sanctuary. Elisa becomes animated and energetic, as she gives the tinker precise directions about the planting process, and prepares a pot of shoots for the tinker to take to his friend. She removes the floppy man's hat, and shakes her long hair free. The dialogue becomes sexually charged as Elisa speaks of the "Hot, and sharp and lovely" appearance of stars; her voice grows husky, and eventually she kneels at the tinker's feet "like a fawning dog," her hand reaching out to touch "his greasy black trousers." Her aggressiveness makes the thinker uncomfortable. Embarrassed by her openness and by the relaxation of the barriers she had so carefully constructed, Elisa hands the pot of cuttings to the tinker, and looks for a couple of battered pans for him to repair. While Elisa watches him work, she asks about his life on the road, and expresses a wish that women could do such things. Additionally, she asserts she could do what he does. He responds bluntly it would be "a lonely life for a woman," accepts the 50-cent payment for the job, clambers back onto the wagon, and leaves with the chrysanthemum cuttings resting next to him on the wagon bench. Elisa watches him leave, whispers "Goodbye," and then softly remarks on the "glowing" appearance of the direction he took as he left.

Coming to her senses after the strangely passionate encounter, Elisa dashes into the house to prepare for her evening out with her husband. She scrubs her body with pumice and harsh soap, in a ritual cleansing, and then dresses in her most feminine attire, taking special care with her hair and makeup. On Henry's arrival, she calls to him to take a bath while she finishes dressing, and then sets out his clothes, carefully and precisely. When Henry emerges from his room, he reacts with surprise to how "nice" his wife looks. Elisa challenges his choice of words, and then further challenges him when he modifies his compliment by saying, "I mean you look different, strong, and happy. . . . [S]trong enough to break a calf over your knee." Bridling, Elisa retorts that she is stronger than Henry knows. Henry, somewhat bewildered, goes out to start the car, and Elisa makes him wait while she puts on her coat and hat. On their way to SALINAS, Elisa sees the chrysanthemum cuttings dumped by the side of the road, discarded by the tinker so that he could keep the flowerpot. She asks Henry about the blood and gore in boxing matches, and he asks if she has changed her mind about going to a prizefight. She tells him, "No," and begins to cry silently. Elisa has been defeated by circumstance and by herself. Her brief glimpse of the possibility of life outside her restricted existence—a life on the road unhampered by the responsibilities of marriage and a farm; a spontaneous sexual encounter with a stranger; a chance to share the artistry of her "planter's hands"—has been shown to be an ephemeral dream.

A host of questions emerge from the story. Why does Elisa react so strongly to the presence of the tinker? Why has she sequestered herself behind her garden fence and inside her home? Why does she hide her femininity under shapeless and masculine clothing? Why does she respond with such irritation to her husband, an apparently decent and kind person? One senses the turmoil, and bitterness of Elisa, but without context, it is difficult to draw any satisfactory conclusion. In this respect, Steinbeck accomplishes precisely what he intended for the story as he described in his letter to George Albee. The reader must create his or her own understanding from personal experience.

play's negative reviews. He questions the emotional nature of the criticism, wondering at the cause of the critics' vehemence.

"Critics—from a Writer's Viewpoint" (1955)

"Critics—from a Writer's Viewpoint," published in *Saturday Review* August 27, 1955, is an editorial written in response to the spectrum of criticism written about SWEET THURSDAY. Steinbeck notes that reading a collection of criticism of his novel depressed him. The writer, he recommends, should never answer his critics, no matter how unfavorable the review. He indicates that this article is not a response to critics, but rather "an attempt to scrutinize and perhaps understand present-day American criticism as it is seen by the writer." He emphasizes that the critic's first interest lies in his own career, and that he is prone to warp a piece of criticism in favor of his own cleverness. Steinbeck also insists that the reader must not forget that critics are people with all the frailties and attitudes of people. A man's writing, he says, reflects himself: "A kind man writes kindly. A mean man writes meanly." Steinbeck also reminds his readers to take into consideration that the critic rarely intends criticism as a career, and that he is probably only doing the job until he can sell a book or a play of his own. Finally, he notes, success in criticism requires building up a large body of readers. To do this critics must attract attention, and destructive attacks attract more attention then praise.

Cup of Gold: A Life of Sir Henry Morgan, Buccaneer, with Occasional Reference to History (1929)

Cup of Gold: A Life of Sir Henry Morgan, Buccaneer, with Occasional Reference to History is John Steinbeck's first novel, as well as the only historical novel that the author wrote. The tale is loosely based on the real life and surrounding myths of the famous 17th century pirate, who sailed the Caribbean in search of Spanish plunder. At the beginning of the story, a young Henry Morgan leaves the family farm in Wales to search out his destiny in the distant Indies. After four years as an indentured servant, Henry uses his intelligence and careful planning to become the most feared pirate in the Caribbean, eventually conquering the greatest prize in the New World, the Spanish citadel PANAMA. But the buccaneer takes no joy in his success, feeling plagued by what he describes as "the disease called mediocrity." He returns to England, where he is knighted by King Charles II and appointed lieutenant governor of Jamaica.

Robert M. McBride & Company, who paid the author an advance of $250, first published *Cup of Gold* in 1930. Steinbeck's friend, Mahlon Blaine, illustrated the cover for the first edition of the novel. The book blends actual history and biography with a theme that intrigued Steinbeck throughout his literary career, the allegorical quest for the Holy Grail, first encountered by the young Steinbeck in THOMAS MALORY's MORTE D'ARTHUR. Many of the characters are overtly drawn from Malory's stories, including the character of the old wizard, Merlin; Morgan's idealized love of Elizabeth, which parallels Lancelot and Guinevere; and, of course, the title, which directly refers to the Grail, itself. The lyricism of the writing reveals Steinbeck's fascination with language, but the overly turgid dialogue, the stylized and highly metaphorical phrasing, and his inability to bring alive the characters caused Steinbeck to express disgust with his work (he referred to the novel as the "Morgan atrocity") even before the book had been accepted for publication. Nevertheless, *Cup of Gold* gave Steinbeck his first taste of success, selling well for a book of its genre. More important, it gave him a valuable lesson about the need to pare down such overwrought diction, what his first wife, Carol, called "Irish blarney," and to shift his attention to the psychology of the individual and the group.

CRITICAL PERSPECTIVES

One of the first reviewers of *Cup of Gold*, Will Cuppy, writing in the *New York Herald Tribune*, found this novel of adventure to be lackadaisical. According to Cuppy, the book "lacks the color and spirit traditional to its genre." However, an anonymous reviewer at STANFORD UNIVERSITY, where Steinbeck went to college, reacted positively to Steinbeck's first novel. The review points out that, rather than the plot or the characters of the novel, "it is the vivid, complete, and truly introspective picture of Henry Morgan's life and character that make the book a thing to be remembered." According to this Stanford review, *Cup of Gold* is a "fanciful, rather weird, and sometimes historical novel" concerning the life of one Henry Morgan. As the review points out, *Cup of Gold* is about dreams and searches for happiness. After all, Henry Morgan is depicted as a youth traveling around the world having women, gold, ships, and even power. But the novel conveys the idea to the reader that Henry Morgan is a lost soul, for he never finds the happiness he dreams of.

However, there has been little contemporary study about Steinbeck's first novel, which the critic Roy Simmonds called "very much an apprentice work."

SYNOPSIS

Part 1

(I)

The Morgan family sits by the fire in their ancestral home, an ancient farmhouse in the Welsh countryside. From an old, respectable lineage, the family consists of Old Robert, a man embittered by his life's failures; his practical, no-nonsense wife, Mother Morgan; his mother, Gwenliana; and his 15-year-old son, Henry. An old man comes to visit, and Robert recognizes the old man as Dafydd, who had worked on the Morgan farm years earlier as a young boy before leaving to seek out his fortune at sea. Henry listens in fascination as Dafydd recounts how he made his fortune as a pirate in the Indies. Despite his riches, the old man expresses his dissatisfaction with his life, and declares that he must return to the jungle, for it has gotten into his blood.

After hearing this exciting tale, Henry tells his father that he want to go to the Indies. Robert asks his son to do two things before he goes: To spend the night thinking about the pain his departure will cause his parents, and to visit the old wizard, Merlin, and listen to his advice.

(II)

The next morning Robert tells his wife that Henry will be leaving soon for the Indies. Ignoring his wife's protests, he insists that Henry must be permitted to go, if only to prevent him from stealing out during the night.

(III)

Henry climbs to the top of a craggy mountain in search of Merlin's round tower. Merlin is an old man with long white hair and beard. He tells Merlin of his plan to journey to the Indies. The old man asks him if he will be seeing Elizabeth before he goes; Henry is startled that Merlin knows that he is secretly in love with the young daughter of one of his tenants. The old wizard warns him to be careful of his childlike aspiration to wish for the moon as "a golden cup." He cautions Henry to keep this vision if he wishes to become a great man, but to recognize the unlikelihood and undesirability of achieving it.

(IV)

Henry decides to visit Elizabeth on his way home. He whistles for her but is then overcome with emotion and runs away.

(V)

Old Robert gives his son five pounds and a letter recommending him to his uncle Sir Edward, the lieutenant governor of Jamaica. After supper, Gwenliana tells the boy's fortune, predicting that he will be a warrior and leader of men. Henry is delighted with the prophecy.

(VI)

Robert and his wife fret over their son's imminent departure.

(VII)

Henry leaves before sunrise to avoid painful good-byes. He begins walking to Cardiff, the closest port. Exhausted by the long walk, he stops in a barn to rest, and dreams of Elizabeth and his parents.

Part 2

The author writes of the rise of England as a sea power, its acquisition of Jamaica and Barbados in the Caribbean, and the practice of sending criminals and indentured servants to work the great agricultural plantations of the New World.

(I)

Henry arrives in Cardiff and is excited by the hustle and bustle of the busy city by the sea. He seeks out breakfast in an inn called "The Three Dogs" where he meets an Irish seaman named Tim. The sailor tells the boy that he works on a ship, *Bristol Girl*, that is soon headed for the Indies, and suggests that Henry might be able to obtain passage on the same boat. Tim strikes a deal with the captain of the *Bristol Girl* to sell the unsuspecting boy into indentured servitude when they arrive in the Indies. The ship sets sail and Henry is put to work in the galley.

(II)

Henry quickly adapts to life on the sea. He eagerly absorbs tales of the infamous buccaneers. He realizes that a man who planned very carefully and who weighed his chances could become a successful pirate. The boat finally arrives at Barbados, where Henry is quickly sold to James Flower, the owner of a plantation, for whom he must work five years to gain his freedom.

(III)

James Flower takes the young slave to his island plantation.

(IV)

The plantation owner, touched by Henry's silent misery, brings him to his house to live with him as his companion and friend. Henry's benefactor teaches him languages and literature, and Henry assumes many of the responsibilities of running the plantation, eventually becoming overseer. He executes his duties coldly and efficiently, improving the plantation's production and stealing the profits a little at a time until he amasses a small fortune.

(V)

After three years on the plantation Henry is 18 years old. He convinces James Flower to purchase a sailing ship to carry their produce to market. He quickly learns to sail the new boat, which he names *Elizabeth*. He purchases a beautiful slave named Paulette, whom he makes his mistress. The slave, afraid of losing Henry, determines to make him marry her. She fails, for Henry loves only the idealized memory of Elizabeth.

(VI)

On the fourth Christmas of Henry's servitude, James Flower gives Henry his freedom. Henry informs him that he "must be off a-buccaneering." He takes leave of his saddened benefactor, promising to return when he has earned the admiration of men.

(VII)

Henry sails to Port Royal to seek an interview with his uncle, the lieutenant governor of Jamaica. Sir Edward, a cold, proper aristocrat, is not happy to see his nephew. He rejects Henry's request that he finance his first expedition as a pirate. Henry meets Grippo, captain of a ship called *Ganymede*, whom he convinces to rent him the command of his ship and crew.

Part 3

The author writes of the Free Brotherhood, the loose band of pirates that, operating from their safe haven on the Island of Tortuga, preyed on Spanish shipping in the Caribbean.

(I)

Henry Morgan begins to stage profitable raids as captain of the *Ganymede*. Mansveldt, the most famous of the Free Brotherhood invites the young man to serve as his vice admiral for a raid on St. Catherine's Isle, where the Dutchman plans to form a republic of buccaneers. After successfully taking the island, Mansveldt is lost in a storm at sea, leaving Henry Morgan the paramount leader of the Spanish Main.

(II)

Time passes. After 10 years of fighting and plundering, Henry Morgan is successful, but he is not happy, for he has grown lonely in his glory. Meanwhile, a rumor sweeps the Main about a woman called La Santa Roja, The Red Saint of Panama. This mysterious woman becomes the object of every pirate's desire, and even Henry begins to covet her. He sends a message to the governor of Panama that he will take the city, the Cup of Gold, within a year.

(III)

Henry Morgan decides he would like to have a friend among his followers. He chooses Coeur de Gris, a young Frenchman with the reputation for being a Don Juan. He discusses La Santa Roja with his new friend.

(IV)

Henry becomes obsessed with the legend of the Red Saint. He tries to forget her in a rash wave of plunder and conquest, but to no avail.

(V)

Sir Edward Morgan is killed leading forces against a renegade island, leaving his daughter Elizabeth an orphan.

(VI)

Old Robert pays a visit to Merlin's mountain citadel. He tells the old wizard of the rumors that he has heard regarding his son's conquests. The old sage suggests Henry still wishes for the moon, and continues to put off adulthood.

Part 4

The author writes of Panama, the Cup of Gold, center of the Spanish domination in the New World. The mythic city, rich beyond comparison, is thought to be impregnable to the bands of buccaneers that roam the Caribbean. Don Juan Perez de Guzman, the governor, hears rumors that Henry Morgan is intent on taking the city but does not believe that it is possible.

(I)

Henry Morgan plans his invasion of Panama. He gathers around him an army of unprecedented size.

(II)

Arriving at the coast, the army of pirates floats up the river to Panama in barges. The plantations along the river are abandoned and the men suffer from hunger as well as the intense heat. Morgan drives his men on tirelessly in pursuit of his goal, la Santa Roja. He thinks that his love for her is purer than the common lusts that drive the other men.

(III)

On the eighth day, the band of nearly starved buccaneers arrives on the outskirts of the city. The Panamanian cavalry is lost in a marsh, and the troops rush about in a disorganized panic, leaving the city nearly undefended. Morgan's army plunders the city. He establishes his headquarters in the palace of the governor and a great pile of booty grows up before him.

(IV)

The next morning, La Santa Roja comes to Morgan. He is disappointed to find that she does not resemble the woman that he has created in his imagination. She is equally disappointed to discover that Henry Morgan is like any other man who wishes only to possess her for the sake of his vanity, and yet lacks the strength of character and the brutality to do so. She laughs at him and he discovers the fragility of his pride. He kills a man to prove his strength, but is unable to win the cold maiden. He falls into despair at "the disease called mediocrity." Merlin's prediction has come true and Henry Morgan finally becomes a man.

(V)

Henry is consumed with the jealous belief that the Red Saint loves Coeur de Gris, and in his rage he kills his young friend. A messenger arrives offering a ransom for the return of La Santa Roja to her husband. Morgan demands 20,000 pieces of eight.

(VI)

The buccaneers riot in drunken celebration while the Red Saint recounts her life to Morgan.

(VII)

The Spanish messenger returns with the ransom of 20,000 pieces of eight. He confides to Henry that the Red Saint's husband is anxious to have her back because she is the heiress of 10 Peruvian silver mines. Fingering his treasure, Henry determines to steal it all rather than divide it among his fellow buccaneers.

(VIII)

The treasure is carried to the coast and loaded in Henry Morgan's galleon so that it might be divided the following day. Morgan presents his men with 40 kegs of rum so that they might celebrate their victory.

The next morning the assemblage of buccaneers awake to discover that their leader has escaped during the night with all the spoils of Panama.

Part 5

(I)
A large crowd waits on the beach of Port Royal for the arrival of the famous Henry Morgan. He is greeted with a roaring cheer and is escorted to the governor's mansion. The governor informs him that they have been summoned to England to answer charges of piracy. He suggests to the pirate that a bribe will buy him the king's pardon. The governor also asks Henry to take charge of his cousin Elizabeth, who has been under his charge since Sir Edward's death. Henry and Elizabeth meet and decide to marry.

(II)
Henry travels to England, where he is knighted by King Charles II, who appoints him to be the new lieutenant governor of Jamaica.

(III)
Sir Henry returns to the Indies to take up his new post, where he must sit in judgment over many of the buccaneers who once worked for him.

(IV)
Sir Henry Morgan dies in his bed of a mysterious illness.

CHARACTERS

Coeur de Gris   A character in *Cup of Gold*, Coeur de Gris is a brave young French buccaneer who is befriended by Henry Morgan, who later kills him out of jealousy when it is suspected that La Santa Roja is in love with him.

Dafydd   A character in *Cup of Gold*, Dafydd is an old man who appears at the Morgan family farm. His stories of adventure and riches incite young Henry Morgan to run away and seek his fortune as a buccaneer in the Indies.

Edward, Sir   A character in *Cup of Gold*, Sir Edward is Henry Morgan's uncle, the lieutenant governor of Jamaica.

Elizabeth   The story *Cup of Gold* has two characters named only Elizabeth. The first one is the young love of Henry Morgan, whom he idealizes into the perfect woman. The second one is Henry Morgan's cousin, whom he marries.

Flower, James   A character in *Cup of Gold*, James is the kindly owner of a Barbados plantation. He purchases the young Henry Morgan as his indentured servant and later frees him from his bondage and adopts him as his son.

Free Brotherhood   In *Cup of Gold*, the Free Brotherhood is the loose band of pirates and buccaneers who prey on Spanish shipping in the Caribbean. They operated from the safe haven of the island of Tortuga. Henry Morgan became the most infamous member of the Free Brotherhood.

La Santa Roja   A character in *Cup of Gold*, La Santa Roja is rumored to be the most beautiful woman in the New World; lust for her inspires Henry Morgan to conquer Panama. When she rejects his love, Morgan ransoms her to her husband for 20,000 pieces of eight.

Merlin   A character in *Cup of Gold*, Merlin is the old wizard with white hair and a long, straight beard who councils the young Henry Morgan.

Morgan, Sir Henry   A character in *Cup of Gold*, Sir Henry Morgan is the most famous buccaneer of the Spanish Main. As a young boy of 15, Henry Morgan sails to the Indies in search of adventure, where he is sold into indentured servitude. After four years, his master adopts him as his son and frees him from his bondage. He sets out to become a buccaneer, eventually known as the most feared pirate in the Caribbean. He captures Panama, "The Cup of Gold," in a quest to gain the love of La Santa Roja, the most beautiful woman in the New World. When she rejects him, he becomes oppressed by the "disease called mediocrity." Morgan ends his pirate career and receives a knighthood from King George II. He marries his cousin, Elizabeth, and accepts the lieutenant governorship of Jamaica.

FURTHER READING

Cuppy, Will. "Books." *New York Herald Tribune*, August 18, 1929, 12.

"The Reviewer." *Stanford Daily*, October 1929, 2.

Steinbeck, John. *Cup of Gold*. New York: Robert M. McBride & Company, 1929.

Simmonds, Roy S. "John Steinbeck." In *Twentieth Century Romantic and Historical Writers*, 2d ed., edited by Lesley Henderson. Chicago and London: St. James Press, 1990, 611–613.

"The Death of a Racket" (1955)

"Death of a Racket," published April 2, 1955 in *The Saturday Review*, is an editorial piece about the Senate testimony of Harvey Matusow which, the author proclaimed would be the end of the McCarthy hearings. Matusow, who was employed by various parts of the government to testify that hundreds of other people were Communists during the era of Senator Joseph McCarthy, had admitted that he lied, and that many other government witnesses had lied as well. The senators who were personally involved, Steinbeck writes, are now claiming that "he [Matusow] was truthful when he testified in your favor, and a liar when against." The author reminds his readers of the story of Titus Oates, the informer who lied about an anti-government plot in 17th-century England, and of another paid government witness who briefly joined the Communist Party and then recanted and offered his services to the government as a paid informer. His testimony was also later revealed to be false. Steinbeck suggests that such people as Matusow are seeking money and fame, "the headiest of all drugs," and that they will do or say anything to maintain themselves in the "dramatic center." He argues that "every bit of the testimony of professional witnesses will have to be inspected in terms of the old-fashioned rules of evidence." The most important result of all this, Steinbeck claims, is the change in the public climate. Steinbeck sensed that the tide had turned against McCarthy and that a more reasoned climate was returning.

"D for Dangerous" (1957)

In just a few paragraphs, Steinbeck puts forth a radical plan for cutting down on the number of careless drivers. Published October 1957 in *McCall's*, he asserts that the laws of the time aren't enough: fines for the first, second, and third offenses; and revocation of the driver's license on the fourth. Instead, he suggests that, after a driver's third accident, a large, red "D" be affixed to his car's license plate. Drivers are always clamoring for low numbers or vanity plates, so why not work it the other way, he asks. The "D" would be removed when the driver goes three years without any accidents, but if the driver has three more accidents, he loses his license permanently. Steinbeck points out that the "D" not only would cause other drivers to be cautious around someone who has already proven himself unreliable, but it would also humiliate the driver into changing his ways.

"Dichos: The Way of Wisdom" (1957)

In the article "Dichos: The Way of Wisdom," published November 9, 1957, in *The Saturday Review*, Steinbeck explains the ancient Spanish tradition of the conversation or contest by *dichos*. Roughly translated, the *dicho* is a "saying," Steinbeck explains, "but in Spanish it is much more than that. It is the reduction of a situation, an idea, a question, or a philosophy to one short pithy sentence." He defines the *dicho* as usually satiric and always true, and lauds the Spanish for being unrivaled masters of the *dicho*. Steinbeck explains the advantage of using the dicho as a courting technique, as is the custom among certain classes in the Spanish-speaking world. There are thousands of *dichos*, some of which are quite ancient. The author explains that he collected a large list of *dichos* while working on the script for the movie *Viva Zapata!* In one scene Steinbeck wanted to write the entire exchange between the Mexican revolutionary general and the well-born girl whom he was courting entirely in *dichos*. Steinbeck excerpts the courtship scene from the movie script to give an example of *dichos* at work. The author finishes by listing a number of well-known *dichos*, such as A thistle is a salad in a burro's mouth and Commend marriage, but keep yourself a bachelor.

Dissonant Symphony (1930)

This is a sequence of linked short stories written early in Steinbeck's career while he lived with his wife Carol Henning Steinbeck Brown in Carmel, California. Although the book was never published, many elements of the book's stories and structure would later resurface in *The Pastures of Heaven*, a collection of short stories published a few years later.

Don Keehan (1958)

An unpublished novel that Steinbeck worked on during the late 1950s. It was said to be a spin-off of Miguel de Cervantes's *Don Quixote* written in the form of an American western. The author considered writing the book in a form readily adaptable into a Hollywood screenplay, reflecting his continued interest in film and the play-novelette form found in some of his earlier works (*Of Mice and Men, The Moon Is Down*). Steinbeck gave up the project after several frustrated attempts.

"Dubious Battle in California" (1936)

In this essay, written three years before *The Grapes of Wrath* was published, Steinbeck urges the large

farmers of California to pay the migratory farmworkers a living wage and treat them well. Published September 12, 1936, in *The Nation*, he begins the essay with a historical account of the way farms themselves have polarized. On one end of the spectrum small farmers with less than 100 acres work the land with their families and a few workers; on the other end large consortiums of investors, banks, and absentee landlords hire managers and farm huge tracts of land.

Then he talks about California's treatment of migratory farmworkers—a repetitive cycle whereby they first import cheap labor from foreign countries, then depress the wages so low that the workers can't make a living. When the labor force begins to organize, race riots and hatred ensue. The cycle begins again with the next group of immigrants that the farmers import. In the 1930s, however, this had changed. The "immigrants" are more like refugees: whole farm families driven out of the Midwest by the terrible droughts. For a brief period, it looked like the cycle would repeat again, but the workers are American, and whole families are there to find good farmland and settle on it, not just men who want to make money and send it back home. The workers are paid an average of 30 cents an hour. A good farmworker can make as much as $400 a year; one with health problems or bad luck will bring in only around $150.

Steinbeck goes on to detail the horrendous conditions of the places these migratory workers must live. If they're lucky the farmer will have a one-room house, with no plumbing or electricity, available for "a nominal" rent of $4–8 a month. One bathroom is provided for up to 300 people. (The farmer who suggested that men and women have separate bathrooms was labeled a communist.) The unlucky workers live in camps by a river, where disease and malnutrition run rampant. The deputy sheriffs visit to memorize faces, so that they can run off any workers who might try to stay on after the harvest.

Attempts by the workers to organize are met with savage protest from the large farmers. When labeling the organizers communists doesn't work, they resort to tear gas or whisper campaigns. Rumors fly that poison gas will be used on the next uprising, or that the water will be tainted with typhoid if the workers cause any trouble. Steinbeck notes that the workers are angry, not afraid, and he urges the large farmers to give their workers the ability to live a respectable life, rather than drive them to action.

"Duel without Pistols" (1952)

Steinbeck wrote "Duel without Pistols" in Italy, where he was traveling as a European correspondent for the August 23, 1952, edition of *Collier's* magazine. The author discovers that his visit to Italy corresponds with a visit from General Ridgway, the commander of the NATO military forces. Indeed, the two men are staying in the same hotel. A few days later Steinbeck's attention is drawn to an article titled "Open Letter to John Steinbeck" in the communist newspaper *L'Unità*. The article's author, Ezio Taddei, uses Steinbeck as a foil to "call General Ridgway a murderer, to bring up moldy propaganda about germ warfare and to describe the degeneracy and brutality of American soldiers." The letter also alleges great atrocities are being committed by the American troops in Korea. Steinbeck is furious and quickly fires back a lengthy response, calling Taddei's charges lies. *L'Unità* contacts Steinbeck and tells him that they would like to publish his letter, but that it is too long. Steinbeck refuses to allow them to cut or edit the letter in any way. The newspaper sends representatives to negotiate with the author. Steinbeck still refuses to accept any cuts or rewrites of his letter. Nevertheless *L'Unità* publishes an edited version that Steinbeck characterizes as "Communistically cut." By which he means that the piece was so mangled that it made no sense, and all of the facts were deleted. Steinbeck responds by having his full letter printed in the Roman daily *Il Tempo*.

"The Easiest Way to Die: Reflections of a Man about to Run for His Life" (1958)

In the article "The Easiest Way to Die," published August 23, 1958, in *The Saturday Review*, Steinbeck

writes that he has recently been approached on the subject of life insurance. In thinking about the article's form and substance, he claims to have discovered an answer that might impact the survival rate of the average American male. He notes the tendency of American businessmen to die quickly after retirement, surmising that it is because most humans are unable to tolerate total and complete idleness. Life insurance, he says, makes the danger much greater. A man who has a family to support is forced to live to fulfill his responsibility. On the other hand, a man who finds himself at 60 with $1 million on his life will find that he is a "sitting duck." Suddenly it becomes "economically unsound" for that man to be alive. A man will do anything that is expected of him, Steinbeck claims, even die. The author reassures his readers that he is uninsured and thus his family is vitally interested in having him live.

East of Eden (1952)

John Steinbeck's 12th novel, *East of Eden* is his longest and most ambitious work. The book, whose working title was *Salinas Valley*, was originally conceived to be a narrative history of Steinbeck's family, written for the benefit of his two young sons, THOM STEINBECK and JOHN STEINBECK IV. *East of Eden*, therefore, is part family history and part fiction. It follows the stories of two families, the Hamiltons, Steinbeck's maternal ancestors, and the Trasks from the 1860s through WORLD WAR II. *East of Eden* borrows heavily from the symbolism of the Bible's story of Cain and Abel. Indeed, the novel's title is a direct reference to the place where Cain exiled himself after murdering his brother ("And Cain went out from the presence of the Lord and dwelt in the land of Nod on the east of Eden"—Genesis 4:16). With the encouragement of his editor and friend, PASCAL COVICI, Steinbeck maintained a daily journal of his thoughts and comments during the writing of the novel, which was published after the author's death as *Journal of a Novel: The East of Eden Letters* (Viking, 1969). *East of Eden* was published by VIKING PRESS in 1952 and became an immediate best seller. In 1955, director ELIA KAZAN released a movie based on a portion of the novel beginning at approximately Chapter 37, part 4. The film, starring James Dean (Cal Trask), Raymond Massey (Adam Trask), Jo Van Fleet (Cathy) and Julie Harris (Abra), is now regarded as a classic.

When Steinbeck first began the research and preparation for *East of Eden* in 1948, he had suffered two devastating losses, the death of his closest friend and mentor, EDWARD RICKETTS, and an acrimonious divorce from his second wife, the former GWYNDOLYN CONGER. Considering the events surrounding its creation, the book was an attempt by the author to regain his equilibrium through the therapeutic task of writing a novel about his origins in the Salinas Valley. Steinbeck claimed his presence was more apparent in this book than any other he had written, and that he brought everything he had ever learned about the craft of writing to fruition in *East of Eden,* saying, "Nothing is held back here." He consciously inserts himself into the text as the narrator, and is himself a minor character in the story, further blurring the line between the historical Hamiltons and the fictional Trasks.

Indeed, one should not lose sight of the intensely personal nature of the book. In *Journal of a Novel* Steinbeck wrote, "I have purged myself of the bitterness that made me suspicious of the self. . . ." Having made his own biography a core part of the work, the author opens himself to speculation about his personal life. The previously private Steinbeck, who had always refused any attempt by the press or the public to delve into his life, unveils a subjective and introspective quality that stands in sharp contrast to his prior objective detachment and the principle of non-teleology. Certainly, he suffered through a dark time just as he began the serious research for the novel. Immediately following the funeral of Ed Ricketts, Gwyn surprised him with her demand for a divorce and also revealed a series of infidelities, causing Steinbeck severe doubts about his worth as a man. Already afflicted by concerns for his artistic value, Steinbeck retreated to California, and the family cottage at PACIFIC GROVE, CALIFORNIA. In a bizarre hermit-like state he confronted his past and

attempted to find a transcendent meaning in life. By the time he completed the work, Steinbeck had found joy in his third marriage to ELAINE ANDERSON STEINBECK. *East of Eden* represents the culmination of his private turmoil, and in his words, "the novel . . . I have been practicing for all my life." The primary theme of the book is the eternal struggle between good and evil, which Steinbeck asserted is the fundamental theme of "all novels, all poetry." It is also a tale of redemption, of the possibility of overcoming one's background, environment, or biologically ordained destiny through self-conscious intervention. Through three generations, the Trask family seems locked helplessly in a tragic reenactment of the poisonous rivalry of Cain and Abel, pitting the "good" sons (Adam and Aaron, or Aron), against the "bad" sons (Charles and Cal). Lurking in the background through most of the book is one of the most radically wicked characters in American literature, Cathy (also Catherine and Kate), who appears bereft of any decency. Lacking the complexity of the other people in the book, Cathy almost becomes a laughable stock villain from a soap opera. Nevertheless, she is needed to present the choices one must make in life: a choice between morality and immorality; between equity and iniquity; between virtue and vice. Like the serpent in the Garden of Eden, she offers temptation to all of the Trasks, and all must eventually confront their own internal moral struggles.

Though the overall mood of the book is pessimistic and dark, the offering of a blessing by a dying Adam to Cal at the conclusion reveals Steinbeck's optimism for a better future. Adam manages to utter the Hebrew word *timshel,* from the Book of Genesis 4:7, to his son, and in doing so, offers Cal forgiveness and the possibility of overcoming the "sins of the fathers." *Timshel,* as interpreted by Steinbeck, is God's gift of free will to humanity, the choice between good and evil.

CRITICAL SUMMARY

In the first chapter Steinbeck introduces two key elements as he describes the Salinas Valley of his youth. Harking back to the sense of mystery felt by Jody in THE RED PONY, the author lyrically portrays the two mountain ranges that formed the valley's boundaries in very different ways. The eastern range, the GABILAN MOUNTAINS, are "full of sun and loveliness" while the Santa Lucias to the west are "dark and brooding." Immediately the reader knows this is a story of contrasts. Additionally, in relating the first European explorers' compulsion to name places and thereby establish their claims to the land, Steinbeck introduces the importance of words and their meanings. He speaks of his fascination with place names as a child "because each name suggests a story that has been forgotten."

The second chapter introduces SAMUEL HAMILTON, Steinbeck's Irish immigrant grandfather, who along with his wife Liza homesteaded a 1,600-acre parcel of barren, arid land in the eastern foothills. It is difficult to determine how much of the biography of Samuel is factual, and Steinbeck notes from the beginning that it is based on "memories which are hazy and mixed with fable." Certainly he would have had little memory of his maternal grandfather, since the man died when John was a toddler. And of course, the later interaction between Samuel and the Trask family is wholly fictional. Nevertheless Steinbeck presents an unforgettable portrait of the patriarch of a large family of nine children, a man whose gifts ranged from the elevated pursuits of poetry and philosophy, to the more mundane talents of blacksmithing, ingenious invention, and even basic medical skills. A man widely admired throughout the Salinas Valley for his humor and wisdom, though not for his business acumen, Samuel developed a well-deserved reputation for kindness and generosity. His wife, Liza, brought a deeply honed "sense of sin" to the marriage, and used her piety and straitlaced strength to protect her family from the temptations of "idleness" and other human weakness.

For the next lengthy section of the novel, Steinbeck brings the reader into the lives of the Trasks whom Steinbeck calls his "symbol family." The Connecticut farmer, Cyrus Trask, returns from the Civil War to his somewhat addled wife and his infant son, Adam. Private Trask has served in only one engagement during his enlistment, but in that one day of combat he lost his leg. While recuperating from the amputation in a remote field hospital,

Cyrus contracts gonorrhea from a camp follower and upon his return home, passes the disease to his religiously fanatic spouse. She, believing it is God's punishment for her imaginary sins, drowns herself in a shallow pond. Needing a housekeeper and caretaker for his infant son, within weeks Cyrus marries Alice, the 17-year-old daughter of a neighbor. With the naïve and pregnant Alice as a captive audience, Cyrus begins to invent a fantastical and heroic military career which "made him the most mobile and ubiquitous private in the history of warfare." Both Adam and his half-brother Charles grow up believing their father to be a bona fide military genius. So convincing are his stories that Cyrus eventually parlays his fictitious martial exploits into a paid position in the Grand Army of the Republic, a private organization representing Union veterans with enormous influence in national politics. He runs his home like a boot camp, subjecting his two boys to harsh discipline and rigorous training, and determines that when they are old enough, each will join the army and follow in his glorious invented past.

As Adam and Charles grow to young manhood, they demonstrate totally dissimilar personalities. Quiet, obedient, and unassertive, Adam nourishes an unspoken filial love for his stepmother, an undemonstrative and almost invisible female presence in the farmhouse. He plants secret gifts for Alice for the sole purpose of bringing an uncharacteristic smile to her face. On the other hand, Charles early on develops an aggressive athleticism and a determination to win no matter the cost. He treats his older brother with affectionate contempt, protecting Adam from the bullying of neighborhood children and also from Cyrus's overbearing punishments. Only once in their mid-teens does Adam accidentally best Charles in a competition, and in retribution for his humiliation Charles beats Adam almost senseless with a baseball bat. From then on Adam knows he must avoid aggravating his dangerous brother, and oddly, Cyrus, who observes his older son's battered body after the drubbing, begins to treat Adam with gentle affection.

Eventually the time nears for Adam to muster in the army, and in an unusual display of compassion and candor, Cyrus speaks with his older son about the hardships and rewards he will face as a soldier. He talks about the lack of individuality and degrading regimentation necessary to build a cohesive fighting force. He speaks of the reward of being part of a larger, more purposeful whole, and gaining enough strength and self-confidence that the instinctual fear of death becomes negligible. Adam begs his father not to force him into the service, and asks him to talk to Charles, who would be far better at soldiering. To Adam's surprise, Cyrus discloses that Charles will remain on the farm, because "Charles must be chained down, not let loose." According to Cyrus, Charles would gain nothing from military training, and worse, it might unleash his vicious propensities. Then Cyrus makes an even more startling admission. After outlining those weaknesses of Adam that Cyrus hopes will be mitigated by military life, Cyrus gruffly confesses that he has always loved Adam better than Charles.

Unfortunately, Charles has observed the unprecedented intimate conversation between his father and brother. Deeply suspicious and resentful, he joins Adam on a walk, and challenges his brother's motives, accusing him of trying to usurp all of Cyrus's affection. He jealously recounts his bitterness over Cyrus's reaction to the previous year's birthday presents from his sons, when Adam had given his father a stray mongrel pup, and Charles had given his father an expensive, pearl-handled knife. Cyrus had cherished the puppy, but had never even used the knife. As Charles's rage builds ominously, Adam attempts unsuccessfully to mollify his brother, recognizing the signs that Charles's anger now overwhelms him. For the second time, Charles brutally and savagely attacks his brother, and with no remorse or compunction, pummels him into unconsciousness. Leaving Adam bleeding on the road, Charles rushes back to the house for a hatchet to finish his murderous act. Adam, coming back to consciousness, instinctively hides in a shallow ditch while his brother searches for him in the dark like a predatory animal. Failing in the hunt, Charles tosses the weapon away, and heads to the neighboring village for a modest celebration at a saloon. Meanwhile, Adam, broken and bloodied, attempts to understand what level of emotional

pain could have precipitated his younger brother's actions.

With this early confrontation, Steinbeck establishes the fundamental premise of *East of Eden*, drawn from the Biblical allegory of Cain and Abel. In Genesis two brothers, sons of Adam and Eve, make separate offerings to God the Father. Cain, the farmer, gives obeisance to the Lord with "the fruit of the ground," while Abel, the shepherd, sacrifices the "firstlings of his flock." God demonstrates appreciation for Abel's offering, but "unto Cain and to his offering he had not respect." In a fit of envy Cain slays Abel, and God curses him for spilling his brother's blood, condemning him to a lifetime of toil and a vagabond existence. But by the same token, God marks Cain with a sign of divine protection, so that none who encounter him will kill him for his fratricide. And it is from Cain's loins that the human race originates. God punishes Cain but also presents him with an opportunity to redeem himself. Steinbeck does not present a perfect analogy between the biblical story and his retelling in a modern setting. Adam, after all, survives his brother's homicidal assault, and becomes a vagabond wanderer during his military career. Cyrus intentionally shackles Charles to the Connecticut farm where he eventually dies in unloved solitude. It is in the relationship between Adam Trask's sons, Aaron and Caleb, where the parallel between the biblical narration and Steinbeck's novel is closer. Still it was never Steinbeck's intent to construct a perfect comparison between the biblical story and *East of Eden*. Rather, he understood the brief but tragically compelling tale of Cain and Abel to be the single most important parable in human literature. In Steinbeck's words in Chapter 34 of *East of Eden*, "Virtue and vice were the warp of our first consciousness. . . ." Steinbeck further suggests that love and hate respectively form the bases of virtue and vice, and notes that human "vices are attempted shortcuts to love. . . ." He concludes by observing "that evil must constantly respawn, while good, while virtue, is immortal."

Adam crawls back to the farmhouse, and is unable to offer an explanation to Cyrus or Alice for Charles's assault except to say to his father, "He doesn't think you love him." Within days, Cyrus arranges for Adam to be enlisted in the cavalry as a private while he lies convalescing in his bedroom. For the next 10 years, Adam fights in the Indian wars, and develops "an increasing revulsion for violence." Rather than becoming inured to death and human misery, as his father had predicted, the notion of "inflict(ing) hurt on anything for any purpose became inimical to him." During Adam's absence from New England, both Alice and Cyrus die, and his only ties to his previous life are the letters that Charles writes out of loneliness and an attempt to assuage the damage he had inflicted on Adam. Charles speaks of being haunted by parental ghosts, and having his life cut short and left "unfinished." Intuitively, he understands that it is he who should be condemned to wander like Cain, but there is no possible redemption for Charles. He has only the rudiments of a soul or conscience, because his capacity for love has been stunted by either congenital defect or parental abuse.

Eventually, Adam leaves the army and continues his soul-searching journey across the United States for an additional three years as a BINDLESTIFF, unwilling to return to New England, and seeking the company of others as rootless as he. By the time he returns to the family farm, his life experiences have brought him to a hard-earned and hard-learned level of compassion, of understanding, and of curiosity and patience. His goodness stems not only from an inherent quality, but from experience. Upon his return home, Adam realizes he is no longer afraid of Charles, though Charles still harbors a pathological resentment of Cyrus's deeper love for Adam. He also learns that Cyrus has left a munificent inheritance to both of his sons, and that the bequest probably derived from extortion and corruption wielded by Cyrus in his elevated position as an official of the Grand Army of the Republic. Charles, too, reveals his discovery that their father had concocted his Civil War biography. For Adam, the revelations provide a sense of quiet joy, confirming that his early disregard for his father was well-founded. For Charles, the knowledge of his father's duplicity brings despair. His rabid devotion to a charlatan has colored his entire life, including the attempted murder of his brother, and his dutiful acquiescence in being the family farm

caretaker. The two brothers agree to live together on the farm, using their father's money for long-deferred improvements, and to try to make amends for the disagreements between them.

Both Adam and Charles have existed far too long independent from each other, and have far too divergent personalities to continue in domestic tranquility. However, Steinbeck guarantees an irrevocable split between the brothers, after suggesting the possibility of reconciliation between them, with the introduction of the character Catherine Amesbury (also Cathy Ames or Kate Albey). It is not an accident that the character of Cathy carries the initials "C" and "A" in her name. She is a catalyst for the choices of the novel's main characters, and she is an elemental force of nature. She does not represent either good or evil, in the sense that these are moral choices available to human beings. Instead, she is like a hurricane or any other natural disaster that may devastate human lives. Cathy has no soul, and lacking a soul, she does not possess free will. She has no capacity for love, affection, or attachment. Her primary motivation is fear, a passion humans share with all sentient creatures, but not one associated positively with human achievement. To put this another way, Cathy does not intentionally do evil. She reacts instinctively, out of a primitive understanding of self-preservation. It is the response of the human beings around her to her capacity to disrupt and destroy that informs Steinbeck's characterization. In short, Cathy is a "monster" with a human form, a monster because she appears in human form without the ethical potential that distinguishes human beings from other creatures. Her skill lies in her chameleon nature. She reflects the aspirations, expectations, and passions of others.

Her biography appalls the reader. Outwardly attractive and morally unassailable as a youngster, Cathy unjustly implicates schoolmates for her "rape" as a 10-year-old child even though she instigated the incident, she impels a teacher's suicide for inappropriate behavior after seducing him, and when confronted by her parents for her suspicious behavior, she sets fire to her family home, killing both her mother and father, then arranges a convenient explanation for her disappearance. Having pilfered her father's company safe before the fire, she makes her way to Boston after the arson, and contrives a love relationship with a whoremaster, Mr. Edwards. Against his better judgment, he becomes besotted by her innocent appearance and genteel manner. When Cathy inadvertently discloses her true intentions and character in a moment of drunkenness, Edwards determines to install her in the most sordid of his whorehouses. Overcome by self-disgust and humiliation en route to her new job, Edwards beats Cathy and leaves her for dead on the outskirts of a rural Connecticut town.

With almost feral strength and determination, Cathy crawls on her belly to the porch of the Trask farmhouse, much as Adam had done years before after his encounter with his brother. A kindred spirit to Cathy in many respects, Charles recognizes the danger she poses. Immediately he protests bringing the young woman into the house and presciently avers, "We'll suffer for it." After sending for the town doctor to treat Cathy's severe injuries, Charles and Adam again argue over treating her in their home, and Adam, already strangely attached to Cathy, threatens to leave if he is not allowed to see her through what will obviously be a lengthy convalescence. Deeply uneasy, Charles nevertheless assents to his brother's insistence on taking care of the girl. Once Cathy recovers sufficiently, the local sheriff interviews her about the assault, and she claims to have amnesia, a ruse she devises based on the doctor's diagnosis of a fractured skull. Later Charles confronts her during the brief absence of his brother, saying he does not trust her or believe that she has lost her memory.

As Cathy rapidly heals, she begins to plan a way to assure protection and money. Taking advantage of Adam's sympathy and growing affection, she manipulates him into offering a marriage proposal. Aware of Charles's suspicions, Adam marries Cathy without preliminaries. Returning to the farmhouse after the civil ceremony, Adam again argues with Charles about his new wife. Charles accuses Cathy of being a "whore," and predicts she will destroy Adam. With these words, Adam accuses his brother of jealousy and announces his determination to move to California. When he informs Cathy of the projected move, she quietly tells Adam she

has no desire to go to California. Gently but adamantly he reminds her of her new responsibility as a wife. Cathy falls silent but then puts her opiate pain medication in Adam's tea, causing him to fall into a deep sleep, and awaits the return of Charles. On her wedding night, having previously claimed to Adam that her injuries prevented her from having intercourse, Cathy joins Charles in his bedroom and has sex with her brother-in-law.

In the beginning of Part II, in the year 1900, Adam and Cathy have relocated to California, after a permanent break between the brothers. Unbeknownst to Adam, Cathy is pregnant, and she attempts an unsuccessful abortion. Finding his wife lying in a pool of blood after spending an afternoon searching for the perfect home for his "perfect" wife, Adam summons Dr. Tilson in a panic. Following an examination in which he senses an inhuman quality in the expectant mother, the doctor threatens to call the police if Cathy tries to get rid of the baby again. Faced with the doctor's serious warning, Cathy's demeanor softens, and she claims her family has a history of epilepsy; thus she does not wish to present her beloved husband with handicapped children. Cathy's pregnancy adds to Adam's joy, and the urgency to find the right property heightens. Concerned about the water table at the old Sanchez ranch that he has decided is the best prospect, Adam seeks advice from Sam Hamilton, "who knows more about water than anybody."

In this way, Steinbeck begins to integrate the lives of the Hamiltons and the Trasks. Never completely successful in bringing together the story of the "actual" Hamiltons, and the fictitious Trasks, the literary device does add an element of familiar reality to what is largely an epic tale of human striving. Steinbeck brings a multidimensional quality to the Hamilton clan, based as they are on members of his own family, which is lacking among the Trasks. The composite strengths and foibles of the Hamiltons add to their believability and likability. Unfortunately, the Trasks never emerge as fully realized, complex human beings, nor are there any surprises about their behavior. Having identified the Trasks as his "symbol" family, it could be argued, Steinbeck never intended to flesh out their characters. The

Trasks are archetypes and therefore may be meant to be both simplistic and predictable.

The Hamiltons also provide an element of humor to what is essentially a dark story. Within minutes of his introduction to Samuel Hamilton by Louis Lippo, Adam Trask is treated to a wonderfully comic story about Tom Hamilton, who has escorted two sisters to a community dance on board an ingenious contrivance of a hay rake and the family sofa. Almost immediately Adam and Samuel form a bond of trusting friendship. Samuel advises Adam to buy the Sanchez place, and agrees to help locate water on the property and sink wells if need be. He also warns Adam that there is a "blackness" and "unhappiness" on the Salinas Valley, that "squeez[es] the light out of it like a sponge." Oddly, on hearing this gloomy observation, Adam insists on returning to his pregnant wife as soon as possible.

In another interlude, Steinbeck lovingly traces the biography of his mother, Olive, as an obvious counterpoint to Cathy. Both women possess an indomitable will, unstoppable in their determination to achieve their self-determined goals. But Olivie's life is marked by service to others, whether as a teacher or later, after marriage to Steinbeck's father, as a mother and community leader. Cathy's concerns revolve only around her immediate needs and private desires. She is incapable of extending herself past the limited boundaries of her own skin.

Having purchased the Sanchez ranch and looking to a boundless future, Adam begins extensive renovations on the old adobe farmhouse, built during the time of the Spanish possession of California. He hires a Chinese cook, Lee, to spare Cathy daily household chores, and lovingly anticipates an idyllic life for his children and his wife. As her pregnancy progresses, Cathy becomes more uncommunicative, and inwardly contemplates a future totally different from that of her husband's dreams. Her hopes are directed toward escape from the dual trap of being a wife and a mother. She senses that Lee has an insight to her private thoughts but dismisses him as an inconsequential servant, unable to affect her life directly.

Eventually, Cathy goes into labor, and gives birth to twin boys, assisted by Samuel Hamilton, who has served as a midwife for all of his nine children. Having met Cathy during an earlier visit to the Trask property, Samuel's unease about the woman is confirmed during the delivery. Cathy bites and snarls, and then after delivery, refuses to see the baby boys. Retreating to the kitchen, Samuel seeks the help of Lee in the treatment of a nasty bite from Cathy, and intones that "a frightened sorrow has closed down" his heart. Cathy presents a force that Samuel has never encountered, one of such "despair" and "dreadfulness" that he fears for the inhabitants of the house. Lee agrees, and both men make an informal pact to help Adam in the coming dark times. Samuel, unwilling to face the inhuman behavior of Cathy again, sends for his imperturbable wife, Liza, to care for the new mother. She assumes complete control of the household, scrubbing it from top to bottom, and develops an unexpected affinity for Lee, whom she approvingly identifies as a Presbyterian rather than a "heathen Chinese." What Liza senses, without articulation, is that Lee has maternal skills equal to her own that will prove vital to the twin boys over the coming years.

Within a week after giving birth, Cathy escapes from the unwelcome constriction of domesticity. She shoots Adam with his service revolver, not with the intent to kill but only to effect an unchallenged flight. The shooting sparks an investigation by the deputy sheriff, Horace Quinn. Adam claims his injury resulted from the careless cleaning of his gun, but Horace understands with the instincts of a policeman that there is more to the story. Investigating the unexplained disappearance of Cathy, he discovers that a new prostitute has joined Faye's SALINAS brothel, which caters to sophisticated tastes in sexual preferences, and that the new "girl" fits the description of Cathy Trask. Horace warns Cathy, now called Kate, to have no further contact with her husband, and the sheriff also chooses to remain silent to protect Adam and his sons.

The stage has been set by Steinbeck for an increasingly intricate pattern of lies. Lies of convenience, lies of benign protection, lies of iniquity and self-serving advancement, and lies of self-delusion all serve to promote a sense of disillusionment and inevitable tragedy. The twins, born to a false mother and a delusional father, cannot come to a good end.

Kate immediately ingratiates herself with Faye. She begins to oversee the day-to-day necessities of the whorehouse, supervising the cleaning, laundry, and cooking, while also becoming a very adept prostitute. In addition to earning Faye's affection, Kate offers a sisterly shoulder to the other whores, gaining their trust and fondness. Eventually, Faye begins to regard Kate as her daughter, and asks her to quit servicing the customers. Kate refuses, claiming she needs the extra income, but secretly she enjoys her new profession because she has developed a special talent for sadism. Faye informs Kate that she has made a new will and left all of her modest fortune to Kate, whereupon Kate makes elaborate plans to poison her benefactor. She steals numerous poisons from Dr. Wilde's medicine cabinet, including a bottle of "nux vomica" (a medicinal form of strychnine) and croton oil (a powerful purgative), and begins to mix increasingly larger doses into Faye's food. To be certain no suspicion will fall on her, she even doses herself with the poisons and falls ill. Dr. Wilde diagnoses botulism from home-canned string beans, and suggests that because of Faye's age, she will not survive the food poisoning. After Faye dies, Kate buries the medicine bottles in the back yard, unaware that she has been observed by Ethel, one of the other whores.

Meanwhile, after the shooting and his wife's desertion, Adam has suspended all the renovations on his property, and withdrawn into silent despondency. Lee has taken over the chores involving the twins, in addition to his housekeeping duties, because Adam views the twins as "symbols of his loss," and perceives them with "thin distaste." Samuel Hamilton encounters Lee in town, and discovers that after 15 months, Adam has yet to name his sons. Infuriated by his neighbor's self-indulgent depression, and armed with Liza's Bible as a source for "good names," Samuel violently confronts Adam, and forces him to awake from his stupor. Startled by the unexpected vehemence from the gentle Samuel, Adam agrees to a ritual naming of the twins. Samuel explains the importance of names, and of giving a child "a high mark" and a "name to live up to."

After a lengthy discussion among the three men, Adam, Lee and Samuel, about the meaning behind the story of Cain and Abel, Lee, the most profoundly philosophical of all the characters in *East of Eden*, offers the core theme of the novel. He speaks of the parable in Genesis as "the symbol story of the human soul," in that God's rejection of Cain's offering led to Cain's belief that God did not love him. Out of the rejection came the murder of his brother, Abel, and subsequent guilt for his crime. According to Lee, the biblical story presents a permanent pattern of rejection, anger, and guilt, and it is this pattern that drives humanity for good and for ill. As darkness falls, the three settle on names for the boys. The smaller, darker boy will be named Caleb after the principal spy sent into Canaan and known for his faithfulness to God. Caleb was one of only two men who reached the promised land after the Exodus of the Israelites from Egypt. The larger, more passive child receives the name Aaron after the brother of Moses and the first high priest of the Hebrews. In a letter to Pat Covici before the publication of the book, Steinbeck referred to Caleb as "Everyman, the battle ground between good and evil, the most human of all. . . ."

The third part of the novel opens in 1911. All of the Hamilton children have left the homestead except for Tom, and have either married or made a success in business. Tom, puzzled by the complexities of modern entrepreneurship, stays with his aged parents. Periodically, he visits his sister Ollie and her family in Salinas, and Steinbeck lovingly relates memories of this favorite uncle who could never adapt either to modernity or to the bucolic existence on the farm. The only one of his children whom Samuel regarded as carrying the seeds of greatness, Tom never achieves his father's expectations, perhaps because Samuel "stood between Tom and the sun. . . ." During a family Thanksgiving gathering at the ranch, after the unexpected death of the oldest sibling, Una, the surviving children determine to remove the elderly Samuel and Liza from the hardships and isolation of the farm to the comforts of town under the pretext of an extended visit with family. Tom is to remain behind, unfulfilled and further isolated.

Samuel, cognizant of his children's artifice, accepts the invitation for a "visit," but nevertheless makes the rounds of all of his neighbors to say good-bye, aware that he will never return. Visiting the Trasks, Samuel counsels Adam to put the past behind him, and to make something of his "fallow" life and "fallow" land. Seizing on the suggestion and eager to convince his friend to stay nearby, Adam proposes to plant the fertile acreage with flowers for seed in partnership with Samuel. Samuel gently refuses, claiming he deserves a rest. He meets the boys, now called Cal and Aron, and notes their differences and how each is already beginning to reenact the roles of Cain and Abel, vying for their father's attention, respect, and love. After supper, Lee relates to Samuel and Adam a lengthy study of the key word in the biblical tale of Cain and Abel. The Hebrew word *timshel,* according to Lee, has been variously translated as "thou shalt" or "do thou" rule over sin, implying in the first translation that Jehovah promised Cain that he and his descendants would conquer sin; or in the second, that mankind had orders from God to rule over sin. After learning Hebrew, Lee engaged the interest of a group of elderly Chinese scholars in his search for the true meaning of the word *timshel.* These Confucian wise men, after several years of discussion and investigation summoned Lee with their findings. The word's exact meaning is "thou mayest," and for Lee the discovery is a moment of infinite importance to mankind. No longer is a man's life-journey one of obedience or predestination. Even after weakness and the great sin of fratricide, Cain still had a choice to change direction and make something beneficial of his life. In Lee's words, "that makes a man great . . . [and] gives a man stature with the gods" because "of the glory of the choice."

As the three men say their farewells outside the barn where Samuel's horse has been stabled, Samuel decides to reveal the whereabouts of Cathy, hoping to stir Adam from his self-pitying lassitude. In blunt and almost callous words, Samuel informs Adam that his wife is now the owner of the "most vicious and depraved" whorehouse in the "whole end of the country," and that Kate takes the "fresh . . . and the beautiful" and "maims them so that they can never be whole again." Shocked, Adam stumbles away into the darkness. Lee ques-

tions Samuel about his decision to expose Kate's secret, and Samuel indicates he drew his inspiration from the discussion about *timshel,* and how choice could free men from the downward spiral of destruction. By disclosing the information, Samuel hoped to remind Adam of his freedom to choose between a vital life and stagnation.

Shortly thereafter, Samuel dies. After attending the funeral in Salinas, Adam stops at a bar to assuage the chill of a rainy day and the chill in his soul. Half-drunk, he asks for directions to Kate's, and the bartender warns him to avoid the place. Undeterred, Adam makes his way to his wife's place of business, and after some hesitancy, Kate agrees to meet with him. Not sure what to expect, Kate hides a loaded pistol on the desk in her bedroom before allowing him entrance. Much to her surprise, Adam displays only curiosity and a sense of relief. Irritated by his critical eye on her fading beauty, Kate does her best to goad him, and alternatively tries to seduce him and insult him. Refusing to rise to the bait, Adam watches calmly as Kate, fueled by potent rum, launches a tirade against men in particular and human beings in general, and speaks of the thriving blackmail business against her more prominent clients. Revolted, but yet unwilling to accept the depth of Kate's corruption, Adam reminds Kate that she is the mother of his sons. Taunting him further, Kate announces that Charles is the father of Caleb and Aaron. Momentarily taken aback, Adam laughs when he realizes it does not matter whether he is the blood father of the boys. Now completely enraged at her inability to damage or dominate Adam, Kate screams for the house pimp, Ralph, and demands that he stomp on Adam with his hard-soled boots. Ralph refuses, and Adam unsteadily makes his way out of the whorehouse, having cleansed his soul and reaffirmed his worth as a human being. In many respects, Samuel Hamilton's final gift to Adam of the truth about Cathy is a form of *timshel.*

Demonstrating his newfound sense of purpose and direction, immediately upon getting off the train from Salinas, Adam approaches Will Hamilton about the purchase of an automobile. The car symbolizes Adam's determination to stop wallowing in the past, and to look to the future. Upon returning to the ranch, Adam discusses his new appreciation for life and the events that precipitated his change in attitude with Lee. Recognizing that his employer and friend has emerged from a private purgatory, Lee asks permission to leave the Trask family in order to open a small Chinese bookstore in San Francisco, a dream Lee has deferred because Cal and Aron needed his surrogate parenthood so desperately due to the emotional absence of their father. Adam agrees reluctantly, now aware of Lee's loving contribution to the household, but asks Lee to stay on until he can become acquainted with his sons and sell or rent the ranch.

Steinbeck then begins to flesh out the characters of Cal and Aron, and introduces Abra Bacon, a young girl who eventually is loved by both brothers. The two boys do not resemble each other either in physical attributes or emotional or intellectual characteristics. Cal is dark and muscular, always scheming with his sharp and observant mind to try to achieve an advantage. Outwardly he resembles his father, but inwardly he carries similarities to his mother and his Uncle Charles. Aron has the blond hair and blue eyes of Cathy, but her youthful innocence was feigned while Aron cannot comprehend deception or duplicity. Indeed his brother's complex and sardonic wit confuses him, because he sees the world only in black and white, while Cal perceives the world in shades of gray with multiple layers of subtlety. For Aron, there is only good and bad, making choices between the two almost instinctive; for Cal, clear distinctions between good and bad can never be possible. What the twins share without any question is love for their father, and for Lee. Ultimately, their love includes Abra as they grow to young manhood.

The reader comes to know the boys as they hunt small game on the Trask ranch. Dressed alike in overalls with turkey feathers taped to their foreheads as they pretend to be Indians, Cal's dominance and manipulation of his brother is immediately apparent. He convinces Aron to share credit for the killing of a rabbit, even though it is clear that Aaron shot the fatal arrow. He then quietly mocks Aron's childish belief that their mother has died and "gone to heaven," having eavesdropped on conversations among men in town that indicated Cathy had run away shortly after giving birth to the twins. For Aaron, this revelation is incomprehensible, because both Adam and Lee had insisted Cathy had died. The idea of lying, even for a beneficial purpose, is beyond Aron's understanding. Deeply upset, Aron attacks Cal, who deflects his brother's antagonism by claiming his story of Cathy's fate was an inappropriate invention. Caught in a sudden rainstorm, the boys return to the ranch house to discover unexpected visitors, the Bacon family, who had sought sanctuary from the downpour. Unaccustomed to the presence of females, let alone children of their own age, the boy's reaction to Abra Bacon further underscores the differences between the two of them. Aron greets the girl with mute and uncertain shyness, and then offers her the gift of the recently killed rabbit. Cal glibly introduces himself, and when Abra responds more positively to Aron than to him, he invents a story about being abused by Lee to garner sympathy, and also suggests that Aron's gift is practical joke as a way to sow distrust between Abra and Aron. Steinbeck describes the boys' differences: "Aron was content to be part of his world, but Cal must change it." After the departure of the Bacon family, Adam announces his intention to move to Salinas so the boys will receive a better education. For Aron, it is a moment of joy, since he knows he will encounter Abra on a daily basis at school. Cal understands the move as an opportunity to investigate the truth about his mother.

Adam determines to make amends with Charles after a decade without any communication with his brother. Much to his dismay, he learns that Charles died six months prior to his letter of conciliation, and that Charles has left his substantial riches to Adam and to Adam's wife, Cathy. Following his decent instincts and the lessons he has derived from life, Adam visits Kate, and gives her the share of Charles's bequest. Deeply suspicious and also certain her husband is a fool, Kate questions Adam's motives. He dismisses her objections because Adam, like Aron, possesses an almost unassailable view of right and wrong, though for Adam, his perceptions stem more from life experience than from a congenital predisposition.

The Trasks move to Salinas, renting the ranch to a family eager to exploit its potential. Lee departs for SAN FRANCISCO, but returns very shortly after acknowledging to himself that the meaning of his life has more to do with his concern for the Trasks than a dream of philosophic discourse in an insular and isolated bookstore. Aron's relationship with Abra deepens to the point that the two promise to marry someday. Cal stands apart, ever observant and cynical, except for his care and concern for his family. Adam, patterning his aspirations after the ingenuity and inventiveness of Samuel Hamilton, stakes almost his entire fortune on a scheme to ship lettuce via refrigerated boxcar to the East Coast. Because of inclement weather and unexpected delays in train schedules, Adam loses every dollar of his investment as the lettuce rots in the railyards. Aron resents the proof of his father's fallibility, but Cal becomes quietly determined to replace the loss, and to make his family financially whole again.

Having suffered the fallout from his father's poor business judgment, and conflicted by the community gossip regarding Adam's foolishness, Aron turns to the solace of religion, and away from Abra. He expresses a determination to be celibate, and begins to study for the Episcopal priesthood. Cal, on the other hand, begins to frequent the less savory neighborhoods in town, including the local gambling dens. He hears rumors about the proprietor of the most infamous whorehouse in town, and realizes the madam must be his mother. After surreptitiously following Kate for eight weeks, Cal confronts her. She cruelly dismisses him, but not before noting the resemblance in their personalities, a similarity that Cal denies. Adam elicits a promise from Cal not to divulge the secret about Kate to Aron. Additionally, Cal decides to encourage his brother to finish his secondary school studies a year early. In this way, Aron can enter college, and move away from Salinas, perhaps never having the opportunity to learn about Kate.

Meanwhile, the United States slowly drifts toward involvement in the war in Europe. After borrowing money from Lee, Cal enters into a speculative business partnership with Will Hamilton, and invests in dried-bean futures. Once the nation declares war on the kaiser, Cal amasses a tidy fortune, and he makes plans to present his entire $15,000 profit to his father at Thanksgiving as a small recoupment for the money lost in the lettuce misadventure. Aron has graduated high school early, made his escape from Salinas and what he believes are unseemly feelings toward Abra, and matriculated at STANFORD UNIVERSITY. Adam has joined the local draft board, and is torn by the life and death decisions he must make about the young men of Salinas whom he sends off to war. The strain takes a toll on his health, and he begins to show signs of arteriosclerosis. Abra, resentful of Aron's idealized vision of her and of his increasing priggishness, grows closer to both Cal and to Lee. By the time Aron returns from Stanford for the Thanksgiving break, Abra no longer harbors romantic feelings for her childhood sweetheart, though she has not admitted her growing attachment to Cal. Aron, unhappy in his college career, has decided to quit the university and make a living farming the family property in the Salinas Valley. Basking in his father's pride in having a son in college and the glow of his homecoming, Aron delays telling Adam of his intentions to withdraw from college. Watching the interaction between Adam and Aron, Cal begins to feel like an intruder between them, and once the Thanksgiving feast is over, he makes a hasty presentation of the money to his father. Much to his surprise and chagrin, Adam rejects the gift, and accuses Cal of war profiteering. Worse for Cal, Adam compares him to his brother, and says he would have been happy if he had followed Aron's path and taken pride "in his progress." Cal burns the money intended for his father, an impassioned "burnt offering" sparked by envy and rejection. Furthermore, stung by his father's rebuff and bitterly resentful of his brother, Cal plots an ugly revenge. Later that evening, Cal invites Aron to accompany him on a surprise excursion. The surprise, of course, is an introduction to Kate and the unwelcome revelation of her kinship to Aron. The next morning Aron lies about his age and hastily enlists in the Army to join United States forces in the trenches overseas.

Kate, crippled by arthritis and beset by threats of blackmail from Ethel, who had observed Kate's disposal of the evidence of Faye's murder years before, has become a virtual recluse in the whorehouse. She has even contracted for a special room without windows or natural light to be built next to her bedroom where she retreats in secret solitude. Unbeknownst to Aron, she observed him during his novitiate studies in the Episcopal Church, and developed a queer attachment to the boy. Now oddly shaken by Cal's brutal introduction of Aron to her, Kate determines to end her life. Before ingesting an overdose of pain medication, she makes out a will, and leaves her considerable wealth to Aron. For Kate, this is not a gesture of kindness or benevolence. Rather, it is recognition not only of the physical similarity between her and Aron, but also of the similarities in their psyches. Neither of them is capable of going beyond the boundaries of their nature. Kate has no concept of anything beyond predation and immediate self-satisfaction. Aron, in his simplistic acceptance of goodness, cannot adapt to morally ambiguous situations. Kate's bequest goes to the son most like her.

As Steinbeck makes clear, the lack of choice due to inherent or learned behavior is also true of Adam. Shortly after Cal's presentation of the money derived from commodity speculation has been rejected by Adam, Lee confronts Cal and implores him not to be bitter or angry about the rejection of Cal's gift. Lee points out that Cal has choices unavailable to his father and that Cal "could control it—if [he] wanted." Referring to Adam's denunciation of Cal's war profiteering, Lee says that Adam "couldn't help it," because "That's his nature." But Lee also observes that Cal has alternatives in his response to his father's rejection. As Lee says, "He couldn't help it, Cal, . . .", but "You have a choice." Of all the Trask family members, only Cal has freedom. Aron hasn't the capacity to surmount the shock of the deception of his father or the sins of his mother; Adam hasn't the ability to go beyond the moral sensibilities he has carefully honed over his lifetime.

As the novel ends, Adam receives word of Aron's death in combat and suffers a stroke. As his father lies dying, Cal berates himself for his role in his brother's death, his responsibility for his father's

illness, and also for Abra's affection, believing he is undeserving of her love and his father's love. Cal, Abra, and Lee gather around the bed where a semi-comatose Adam lies, and Lee demands that Adam forgive and bless his surviving son. Drifting in and out of consciousness, Adam nevertheless, in a final demonstration of love and acknowledgement of Cal's worth, manages to croak the word *timshel*. Cal's fate from that moment is unknowable, but he has been given his father's permission to shed the baggage of childhood and the guilt of his actions, and to make his own way and his own choices. *East of Eden*, like THE GRAPES OF WRATH, allows the reader to draw his or her own conclusions about the fate of the central characters.

Too often *East of Eden* has been interpreted as the story of Cal Trask, the paradigmatic prodigal son. It is not. It is the story of Adam Trask, who continually faces adversity and moral quandaries throughout his life. Always he acts and reacts with human fallibility. His decisions are marked by good and bad consequences, but those decisions stem from good intentions. In this regard Adam Trask represents Steinbeck's alter ego. Steinbeck wrote the book for Thom and John, and he offers his sons the gift of *timshel* in a deeply personal acknowledgement of his own origins and journey through life.

THE CONCEPT OF *TIMSHEL*

In both the novel and its accompanying *Journal of a Novel: The East of Eden Letters*, Steinbeck reveals his investigation into the reinterpretation of the Hebrew word *timshel*, a word presumably mistranslated in various versions of the Bible. The King James Bible gives a crucial passage as "Thou shalt rule over him," (where "him" refers to sin), since it translates the word *timshel* as "thou shalt." The phrase is therefore a prophecy, describing what will happen when people encounter sin. The American Standard Bible, on the other hand, gives the phrase as, "Do thou rule over it," where *timshel* is translated as "Do thou," making the phrase an order. However, the character Lee points out that *timshel* should really be translated as "thou mayest," which implies that the phrase offers people a choice. In the novel, these discussions take place among Adam, Samuel, and Lee, but in life it was Steinbeck and his friend Pat Covici who, through primary research, figured out the true meaning of *timshel.* To them, the discovery that the Hebrew word really means "mayest" implies that man has free will.

In Steinbeck's belief, it is individual responsibility that invents moral conscience. The great asset of any society and human civilization as a whole is the talent and energy of its people. In his mind, neither "thou shalt" nor "thou do" could give human beings the encouragement to explore their souls and their guilts in order to make their own choices for better or for worse. But the translation of *timshel* into "thou mayest" enables the release of the energy in every human being. The freeing of human possibilities is one of Steinbeck's objectives in having the story grounded in the framework of the Cain-Abel story. The departure from God's order or predetermined destiny allows individuals to build their internal Eden in their families and then their community.

EARLY CRITICISM

As Steinbeck's first major novel since the *Grapes of Wrath,* the publication of *East of Eden* generated eager anticipation and perhaps unrealistic expectations among literary critics. Very quickly, it achieved best-seller status with the reading public, but just as quickly reviewers seized upon the book's flaws. Many of Steinbeck's prior admirers expressed disappointment, though couched in cautiously approving critiques. The *New York Times,* a newspaper that had previously applauded almost all of Steinbeck's writing, published a review fairly typical of the book's reception. Orville Prescott praised Steinbeck's effort "to grapple with a major theme" of "good and evil," but suggested the novel was "defaced by excessive melodramatics" and that the character of Cathy would "sicken and . . . bore many" readers. Leo Gurko, writing for the *Nation,* immediately indicated that Steinbeck's "talent has declined," and offered as an explanation for the decline that the author served himself better as indignant social commentator than as a moral judge. The *New Yorker*'s critic, Anthony West, identified Steinbeck's inclusion of himself as narrator as "a genius for dissociation" and, after a lengthy discussion of the plot, concluded there "is

nothing more puerile than a discussion [of good and evil]" where "evil is identified with sexual aberration."

More positively, Harvey Curtis Webster, in his column for the *Saturday Review,* called the book "one of the best novels of the past ten years" and praised Steinbeck for finally addressing "human dignity and what it may achieve." The critic for the *New York Times Book Review,* Mark Schorer, applauded *East of Eden* as a "strange and original work of art" and remarked on the book's "wide-ranging and imaginative freedom." In the *New York Herald Tribune Weekly Book Review,* Joseph Wood Krutch compared the novel to Thomas Mann's *The Magic Mountain* in a risky blend of symbolism and realism, and commended Steinbeck for his mastery of "deft little phrases" and his ability to turn "symbolic figures" into living characters.

CONTEMPORARY PERSPECTIVES

East of Eden never achieved the widespread popularity nor the stature as an American classic of *The Grapes of Wrath* and OF MICE AND MEN. Until Oprah Winfrey featured the book as one of her favorite classics in June 2003, it had largely been ignored by the reading public after its initial publication and the release of the film based on a portion of the book. Scholars and literary analysts of Steinbeck's works, however, have taken Steinbeck's self-professed description of the book as his masterpiece seriously.

Richard Astro, a longtime admirer of Steinbeck, claims the book "does not work" despite the author's "great sensitivity" to his family and to California, because of Steinbeck's "confused narratives." He suggests that Steinbeck allowed "conventional morality to replace science and intuition" as a worldview, and thus abandoned his unique perspective. Other critics have given Steinbeck credit for contributing an early example of "metafiction" in which the author explores the role of the artist as creator and makes the creative process a central theme by deliberately including himself as the narrative voice. Peter Lisca criticizes the book's "scrambled syntax and awkward expression," while praising Steinbeck's warm and loving descriptions of the Hamiltons, noting, however,

Poster from the 1955 film production of *East of Eden*
(Photofest)

that the Hamiltons "are in no way involved in the novel's narrative." Joseph Fontenrose claims that Steinbeck never resolves the novel's central theme of good and evil because of an inconsistency in the author's presentation of the relationship between good and evil. For Fontenrose, *East of Eden* fails because it lacks ethical insight. In response to those who criticize the book for a lack of structural unity and moral certainty, John Timmerman points to the key characters of Cathy Ames, Horace Quinn, Charles Trask, Caleb Trask, Lee, and Samuel Hamilton as paradigms for Steinbeck's vision of moral order and ethical challenges. According to Timmerman, Cathy presents a counterpoint and a choice for each of these men. For Horace Quinn, she represents a challenge to the

social order of the quiet community of Salinas. For Charles and Caleb Trask, Cathy offers tempting psychological seduction and attendant dilemmas. For Lee, Cathy disturbs his philosophical certainty of human progress and free will. Cathy temporarily undermines Samuel Hamilton's connection to his spiritual core. With the exception of Charles, each man overcomes Cathy's enticements, because each has a solid grounding from the love and respect of others.

SYNOPSIS

Part 1

Chapter 1
Steinbeck describes the history of the Salinas Valley from prehistoric times to the settlement of Americans.

Chapter 2
Samuel Hamilton arrives with his wife in the Salinas Valley from Ireland. Finding that all the rich bottomland is taken, they claim a homestead in the marginal land of the barren hills. The land is harsh and dry, unsuitable for farming, and Hamilton must support his family by drilling wells and making tools in his blacksmith shop.

Chapter 3
Turning to the history of the Trask family, the author relates how Cyrus Trask enlists to fight in the Civil War, where he loses his leg. The mother of his first son, Adam, drowns herself, and Cyrus marries a young neighbor, Alice, who gives birth to a second son, Charles. Cyrus convinces everybody, even himself, of his involvement in all the important events of the war. A harsh disciplinarian, he raises his two sons in a heavy-handed military way. Adam Trask retreats into quiet passiveness, while Charles becomes cruel and competitive. Cyrus favors his son Adam. He explains to his son the nature and duties of a soldier and announces that Adam will soon be sent to the army. He decides not to put Charles in the army because of his fears that Charles's aggression will be uncontrollable in the military. Charles is jealous and angry with Adam. He beats his brother savagely and leaves him lying in the grass. Adam, broken and nearly senseless,

hides in a ditch when his brother returns with a hatchet to finish his work.

Chapter 4

Cyrus Trask enlists Adam in the cavalry. Adam's cavalry unit is sent west to eliminate the Indians. Adam is disgusted by the butchery he sees and compensates for it by risking his life to rescue his comrades. During the years of his enlistment he develops a close correspondence with his brother.

Chapter 5

Samuel Hamilton fathers nine children, four boys and five girls. The family lives happily but never prosperously, for Samuel wastes most of his family's money trying to patent his inventions.

Chapter 6

Cyrus Trask receives a commission from the Grand Army of the Republic, and Charles is left alone on the farm. One day, while trying to move a heavy rock, Charles is hit in the head with an iron bar, leaving a long brown scar in the middle of his forehead. After five years Adam is discharged from the cavalry. Unwilling to go home, he reenlists. He receives orders to report to the secretary of war in Washington, where his father has become a powerful man. Cyrus hopes to convince his son to stay with him, offering to secure him an appointment to West Point. Adam refuses, wishing only to return to his regiment.

Chapter 7

Five years later Adam receives his second discharge. With no money and no ambition, he wanders around the country as a hobo until he is arrested for vagrancy and assigned to a road gang for six months. Upon his release he is immediately picked up and assigned another six months. Three days before his second release he escapes and returns to the farm. Meanwhile, Charles receives word that their father has died, leaving his sons a large inheritance. Adam admits to Charles that he hated their father. Charles learns that his father's military exploits were a charade. He wonders if it is possible that their father acquired his unlikely fortune dishonestly, but Adam insists Cyrus never lied and that the inheritance cannot be stolen money.

Chapter 8

Cathy Ames is born to a tanner in a small Massachusetts town. She is a beautiful girl and a natural liar and manipulator. Cathy learns early on that she can use her sexuality to gain power over people. She drives her young Latin teacher to kill himself. After her 16th birthday she announces that she is not going back to school, and the next morning she runs away. Mr. Ames finds his daughter and whips her for leaving. Cathy ingratiates herself to her parents while she prepares for a second escape. She burns down her parent's house while they are inside. Fabricating signs of a struggle, she disappears with the tannery payroll.

Chapter 9

Mr. Edwards, a Boston whoremaster, falls in love with Cathy. He rents her an apartment and showers her with gifts. Tortured by his passion, he determines to get rid of her. He takes her to the countryside and beats her, leaving her for dead. With her last strength, Cathy crawls to a nearby farmhouse and faints.

Chapter 10

Adam and Charles live together in a state of tension, always on the verge of fighting. Adam is restless. He complains that they work too much and should enjoy their money. He leaves the farm and travels to South America. When he finally returns, Charles tells him that it is better he leaves before they fall into fighting again.

Chapter 11

The two brothers discover Cathy's broken body on the steps of the farmhouse. Sensing trouble, Charles wants to take her to town immediately, but Adam insists that they bring her into the house and call for a doctor. She claims to have amnesia. Adam happily cares for the wounded young woman, but Charles is suspicious and encourages his brother to get her out of the house. Adam tells Cathy that he will take care of her and he asks her to marry him. Cathy, realizing that she is helpless and has no money, accepts his offer. They marry the following week while Charles is away from the farm. When Adam tells Charles, he storms angrily out of the house. Later that evening he returns drunk. Cathy drugs her husband's tea and makes love to Charles.

Part 2

Chapter 12
Steinbeck describes the arrival of the 20th century.

Chapter 13
Adam Trask and his new wife move to California, where they look for a ranch in the Salinas Valley. One afternoon, he returns to their King City hotel room to find Cathy nearly dead from blood loss. She has badly botched an abortion attempt. She tells the doctor that Adam does not know that she is pregnant. He warns her that if she does not have the child he will ensure that she is jailed for murder. Adam decides to buy the old Sanchez Ranch, 900 acres of beautiful pastures and rolling hills—some of the best farmland in the Salinas Valley. Adam asks Samuel Hamilton for his opinion of the land. The old Irishman agrees that it is fine land, but that there is ". . . a black violence on this valley . . . as secret as a hidden sorrow."

Chapter 14
The Hamilton children grow up. Olive earns her teaching certificate, becomes a schoolteacher in Salinas, and marries.

Chapter 15
Adam sends his new Chinese cook, Lee, to fetch Samuel Hamilton. Lee and Samuel converse deeply and immediately become friends. Adam hires Samuel to dig wells and build windmills so that he can make "a garden of my land" for his wife. He invites Samuel to stay for dinner. Samuel is overcome by a strange nervousness in Cathy's presence and hurriedly excuses himself. Cathy tells Adam that she does not like the ranch and is going to leave as soon as she can, but her husband dismisses her words for nonsense.

Chapter 16
Samuel wonders why Cathy makes him ill at ease. He realizes that she has the same eyes as a murderer who as a child he saw hanged. He feels guilty for thinking such a terrible thing and resolves to help the Trasks as much as possible.

Chapter 17
Lee announces that Cathy is about to have her baby. Samuel finds the expectant mother crouched silently in the dark with "unforgiving, murderous hatred" in her eyes. While he prepares Cathy for the delivery, she bites his hand savagely, refusing to release him until he grabs her throat and cuts off her wind. Twin boys are born. Cathy will have nothing to do with her new sons. A week later she packs her bags and announces to her husband that she is leaving and that he can throw the babies in a well for all she cares. When Adam tries to prevent her departure she shoots him in the shoulder and leaves him lying on the floor.

Chapter 18
Horace Quinn, the deputy sheriff, comes to the Trask ranch to investigate the shooting. Adam lies despondently in bed. He insists that he shot himself while cleaning his pistol and says that he does not know where his wife has gone. Horace, skeptical of Adam's unlikely story, suspects him of killing his wife. He goes to Salinas to ask the sheriff for advice. His boss informs him that Cathy Trask is now working in a Salinas whorehouse. The two men agree to keep Cathy's whereabouts a secret. Meanwhile, Samuel visits the ranch. He reminds Adam that he has two new sons and advises him to "go through the motions."

Chapter 19
Faye, the matronly owner of the newest whorehouse in Salinas, hires Cathy, who has changed her name to Kate. Kate ingratiates herself with the kindly woman and soon begins to assume many of the responsibilities of running the house. The sheriff tells her that he knows who she is. He tells her to dye her hair a different color and warns her that if she ever tells anybody that she is Adam Trask's wife he will see to it that she is run out of the state.

Chapter 20
Kate and Faye become increasingly intimate, referring to each other as "mother" and "daughter." Faye has a party for Kate and announces that she has made a will, leaving everything she owns to her new "daughter."

Chapter 21

Kate begins to plant the idea among the girls that Faye is sick. True to Kate's word, the madam's health disintegrates during the following months. Kate takes control of the house, winning the confidence of the other girls with presents and pleasant encouragement. She poisons Faye's meals with croton oil, mildly poisoning herself also, to give the appearance of botulism poisoning from bad food. A few weeks later she gives Faye a final, fatal dose and then buries the incriminating bottles behind the whorehouse.

Chapter 22

Adam withdraws completely, leaving Lee to care for the newborn infants. Samuel is outraged to learn that Adam has not named the two boys after more than a year. He insists that Adam name the boys, awkwardly striking him when he refuses. Samuel suggests naming them Cain and Abel, but Adam rejects the idea. The men engage in a long discussion over the true meaning of the Cain-and-Abel story (Genesis 4:1–16). Finally Adam chooses the names Caleb and Aaron from Mrs. Hamilton's worn-out Bible.

Part 3

Chapter 23

Una Hamilton dies and her body is shipped home. The death of his favorite daughter affects Samuel deeply and he begins to show his age. His children meet and decide that Samuel and Liza deserve to have a rest. They agree to trick their parents into retirement by inviting them to come and stay a while with each of them. Samuel realizes what his children are up to and assents to the plan, knowing that he is going away to die.

Chapter 24

Samuel pays a final visit to the Trask ranch. The land has been untouched for many years. He tells Adam that he has become "a fallow man on fallow land" and advises him to find a replacement for Cathy and to try to get on with his life. He tells Adam that he has a medicine that might cure him and also might kill him: Cathy lives in Salinas and runs a whorehouse. Grief-stricken, Adam runs into the night. Samuel explains his decision to

Lee: "I exercised the choice. Maybe I was wrong, but by telling him I also forced him to live or get off the pot."

Chapter 25

Samuel Hamilton dies. After the funeral Adam gets drunk and goes to Kate's place to confront his wife. Kate tells him that the world contains only evil and folly. To prove her point she shows him a collection of photos showing important men from the town engaged in vile and compromising acts. She tells Adam that Charles is the father of the twins. Repelled by what he sees and hears, Adam is finally freed of his wife.

Chapter 26

Adam feels free and happy for the first time in years. Seeing the change, Lee asks to be freed from his service. He explains that he has always dreamed of opening a bookstore in San Francisco and spending his last days arguing ideas and haggling with the customers. Adam asks him to stay a while longer to help him get to know his boys, Cal and Aron, as he prefers to spell his name.

Chapter 27

Cal tells his brother that he overheard some men say that their mother is alive. He says that he is going to run away and find her. Aron insists that his father and Lee would not have lied to them about her.

Chapter 28

Adam proposes to his family that they move to Salinas. Lee suggests that Adam tell them at least some of the truth about their mother. He tells the tragic story of his own mother, who was raped and killed in the Chinese railroad gangs.

Chapter 29

Adam decides to write to his brother after 10 years of silence.

Chapter 30

Adam receives a letter from his brother's attorney advising him that Charles died six months earlier, leaving a considerable fortune to be divided equally between Adam and his wife. Adam and Lee discuss the inheritance and whether or not he should respect his brother's wishes and tell Cathy about the money. Cal, listening at the door while the two men talk, discovers that his mother is alive.

Chapter 31
Adam tells Cathy about her inheritance. Unable to accept that his motive is honesty, she suspects a trap. Adam tells her that she is only part human, unable to see the goodness in people.

Chapter 32
Disappointed by love, Dessie Hamilton decides to sell her dress shop and move back to the ranch to live with her brother Tom.

Chapter 33
When Dessie dies of a sudden illness, Tom blames himself for her death. Unable to cope with his despair, he shoots himself.

Part 4
Chapter 34
Steinbeck develops the central theme of the book, arguing that all existence is built upon a struggle between good and evil, but that evil must constantly be reborn, while good is immortal.

Chapter 35
The Trasks move to Salinas and Lee takes his leave of the family. Six days later the old Chinese servant returns to the Trask family, happy to be home.

Chapter 36
Aron and Abra, a young girl of deep maturity, decide that they will marry when they are old enough. Abra tells Aron that she overheard her parents saying that his mother is alive. Aron will not accept that his father and Lee have been lying to him.

Chapter 37
Adam has the idea of shipping refrigerated cars of vegetables to the East during the winter. He seeks out Will Hamilton for advice. Will tells him that he is a dreamer and should give up the idea. Adam's scheme fails and he loses a spectacular sum of money, nearly bankrupting the family. Aron resents his father for making himself a laughingstock.

Chapter 38
One evening Cal meets Rabbit Holman, a drunken neighbor, who reveals to the boy that his mother is the owner of Kate's whorehouse. Cal accompanies Rabbit to Kate's establishment. What Cal sees there sickens him. Uncertain in his new knowledge, he asks Lee about his mother. Cal views his father with new, compassionate eyes. Meanwhile, Aron decides to be a priest and is confirmed in the Episcopal Church.

Chapter 39
Cal admits to Adam that he knows the truth about his mother. They agree that the truth must be kept from Aron because "he hasn't enough badness in him to stand it." Cal begins to follow his mother and learn her routine. She learns that he is her son and questions him about his father and brother. Cal sees that that she is afraid of him.

Chapter 40
Ethel, an old whore whom Kate has run out of the house, tells Kate that she has evidence that Faye was poisoned. She demands a monthly blackmail payment to keep quiet. Kate has the woman arrested for robbery and thrown out of town.

Chapter 41
Cal seeks Will Hamilton's advice, admitting to him that he wants to make a lot of money to give to his father. He tells the businessman that he is trying to buy his father's love. Will agrees to go into business with the boy.

Chapter 42
As World War I looms, British purchasing agents scour the area to buy needed supplies and Cal's get-rich-quick scheme appears very promising.

Chapter 43
Aron passes his high school examinations a year early and prepares to leave the family and go to college at nearby Stanford University.

Chapter 44
Aron leaves for college. Abra confides to Lee that Aron has always been angry with his father because he did not have a mother. She asks Lee if Mrs. Trask is alive. Cal earns $15,000 speculating on bean prices with Will Hamilton and plans to give it to his father.

Chapter 45

Kate orders Joe Valery, the house bouncer, to find Ethel. Joe discovers that the old woman is dead. He knows that Ethel must have had something on Kate and he decides to blackmail her himself.

Chapter 46

War brings patriotism and xenophobia to Salinas. The town militia burns down the house of Mr. Fenchel, the local tailor, a German who had lived in the town for more than 20 years.

Chapter 47

Aron is extremely homesick at the university. Separated from Abra, he idealizes her in his imagination. His passions express themselves in nightly letters that he writes her from his lonely boardinghouse. The letters make Abra uncomfortable, for she senses that Adam is creating a woman who does not exist.

Chapter 48

Joe continues to put pressure on Kate, who becomes increasingly paranoid.

Chapter 49

Cal realizes that Aron is his father's favorite because he bears a close resemblance to their mother. He gives his father the money at Thanksgiving dinner. Adam accuses his son of profiteering from the war and refuses his gift. Cal is hurt by his father's reaction and overwhelmed with jealousy toward his brother. In anger he takes Aron to the Castroville Street whorehouses and presents him to his mother. The next morning Aron enlists in the army.

Chapter 50

Kate figures out that Joe is trying to blackmail her. She sends a note to the sheriff explaining that Joe is an escaped convict. She wearily considers the events of the night before: Cal and Aron's visit, and Aron's shocked flight. Exhausted and wracked with pain from her arthritic hands, she makes out a will leaving everything to her son Aron and swallows a lethal dose of morphine. Joe is shot and killed while fleeing from the police.

Chapter 51

Cal feels guilty for revealing the truth to his brother. He punishes himself by burning the money,

one bill after the other. Adam suffers a mild stroke after receiving a postcard from Aron informing him that he has joined the army.

Chapter 52

Abra tells Cal that she knows about his mother. She admits that she stopped loving Aaron when she realized that he would never grow up and see the world for what it is: an imperfect place. She tells Cal that she loves him.

Chapter 53

Abra visits Lee. He gives him his mother's old jade button and tells her that he wishes she were his daughter.

Chapter 54

Cal and Abra have a picnic in the countryside. While they are away a telegram arrives at the house indicating that Aaron has been killed in the war. Adam receives the news in disbelief and suffers a stroke that leaves him paralyzed.

Chapter 55

Cal's guilt crushes him: He has killed his brother and injured his father. Everywhere Adam's accusing eyes follow him. He runs to Abra, who insists that they return to the house. Lee brings Cal to the head of Adam's bed. The sick man summons all his strength to raise his hand to his son in blessing.

CHARACTERS AND PLACES

Ames, Cathy "Kate" A character in *East of Eden*, Cathy is born to a tanner in a small Massachusetts town. She is a beautiful girl and a natural liar and manipulator who learns early on that she can use her sexuality to gain power over people. She murders her parents and runs away from home to work as a whore. Adam Trask rescues her and marries her after her pimp beats her and leaves her to die. The beating leaves her with a dark scar on her forehead, "like a huge thumbprint." Cathy runs away from her husband and family to become prostitute in Salinas. She changes her name to Kate and murders her patron who has left her the brothel in her will. Kate's house becomes "the most vicious and depraved in this whole end of the country." Exhausted and wracked with pain from her arthritic hands, Kate swallows a lethal dose of morphine.

Bacon family Characters in *East of Eden*. Mr. Bacon, a county supervisor, and his family are driven into the Trask ranch to seek shelter from the rain. Their daughter Abra, a beautiful, wise girl, becomes Aron Trask's girlfriend. Mr. Bacon is caught stealing money from his business.

Cotton Eye A character in *East of Eden*, Cotton Eye is the piano player at Faye's whorehouse in Salinas. Called Cotton Eye because of his blindness, he is an opium addict. Cathy (Kate) advises him to break his drug habit.

Edwards, Dr. A character in *East of Eden*, Dr. Edwards is a physician who tends Adam Trask after he has a stroke.

Edwards, Mr. A character in *East of Eden*. Mr. Edwards is an orderly and unemotional pimp who runs his girls in a circuit of inns along the East Coast. He falls in love with Cathy Ames, whose restlessness and evil behavior soon make his life miserable. Determined to get rid of her, he takes her to the countryside and beats her savagely before leaving her to die.

Ethel A character in *East of Eden*, Ethel is an old prostitute who is run out of town when she tries to blackmail Kate, as Cathy Ames is known when she owns a local whorehouse.

Faye A character in *East of Eden*, Faye is the owner of a Salinas brothel. She befriends Kate (Cathy Ames's pseudonym) and, adopting her as her daughter, leaves her the whorehouse in her will. Kate later poisons her.

Fenchel, Mr. A character in *East of Eden*, Mr. Fenchel has been a tailor in Salinas for more than 20 years. The local militia burns down his house during the war because he talks with a German accent.

Grew, James A character in *East of Eden*, James is a failed divinity student who teaches Latin in a small Massachusetts town. In the novel James Grew is Cathy Ames's Latin teacher. He is "a pale intense young man" and is mysteriously attracted to Cathy. After Cathy refuses to talk to him, he kills himself, becoming Cathy Ames's first victim.

Hamilton, George The oldest son of Samuel and Liza Hamilton in *East of Eden*. A tall and handsome boy with a courtly manners, he is "a sinless boy that grew into a sinless man." George prospers in the insurance business, but his health starts to be plagued by pernicious anemia after middle age.

Hamilton, Joseph The fourth and youngest son of Samuel and Liza Hamilton in *East of Eden*. As the baby of the family, Joseph is both physically and mentally lazy. He is sent to college because he is not fit for ranch work. Later he moves to New York and becomes an important man in the advertising industry.

Hamilton, Liza John Steinbeck's real grandmother, in *East of Eden* she is the wife of Samuel Hamilton and mother of the Hamilton family. Liza is a hard but humorous woman with a Presbyterian mind and a code of morals. Liza reads only the Bible, which she accepts without question. She comes to the Salinas Valley from Ireland with her husband, and together they raise a family and work a farm that yields modestly.

Hamilton, Lizzie The second daughter of Samuel and Liza Hamilton in *East of Eden*. She has a capacity for hatred and bitterness unique among her family. She marries a young teacher and moves away from the family.

Hamilton, Mollie The fourth daughter of Samuel and Liza Hamilton in *East of Eden*. Mollie has beautiful, blonde hair and violet eyes, the pride of her family. At a young age, she has a speech impediment. Her brother Tom thinks it is caused by a membrane under her tongue and cuts it with a pocketknife. Later in the novel, she marries and lives in an apartment in San Francisco.

Hamilton, Olive John Steinbeck's mother in real life and the youngest daughter of Samuel and

Liza Hamilton in *East of Eden.* Olive becomes a schoolteacher in Salinas at the age of 18.

Hamilton, Samuel The head of the Hamilton family in *East of Eden* and real grandfather of John Steinbeck. Samuel and his wife immigrate to the Salinas Valley in the 1870s where they raise a large family of four girls and five boys. He delivers Cathy Trask's twin sons and attempts to stir life back into their inconsolable father when Cathy packs up and leaves him. Samuel is a good-looking, charming man with a sense of humor, who earns adoration from his friends as a "comical genius." He hides behind a mask of his Irish joviality by telling jokes to people who come to his place. Samuel fails to accept the common standard of wealth and social competition, and he finds pleasure in inventing without profiting. He leaves the ranch and dies in Salinas after his daughter's death makes him realize that he is getting old.

Hamilton, Tom The third son of Samuel and Liza Hamilton in *East of Eden.* Tom is dark-faced, with red skin and dark red hair, beard, and flowing mustache. Yet, lacking the competitiveness that other Hamilton children have, Tom stays on the ranch writing poetry secretly and reading books. He is close to his sister Dessie. Heartbroken by a failed love affair, Dessie returns to the Hamilton ranch, where she joins Tom, who doses her with salt to treat a severe abdominal pain. As a result of maltreatment or lack of proper medical care, Dessie dies. Blaming himself for his sister's death, Tom commits suicide.

Hamilton, Una The oldest daughter of Samuel and Liza Hamilton in *East of Eden.* Una is thoughtful and studious. She marries a chemist named Anderson, an incommunicative man who is determined to discover the secret of color photography. Una moves with her husband near the Oregon border, where she lives in poverty and dies young. Her father is heartbroken when she dies in an accident, or possibly a suicide.

Hamilton, Will Second son of Samuel and Liza Hamilton in *East of Eden.* Will is dumpy and stolid.

More energetic than imaginative, he reacts against his father's individualism and becomes a conservative and a political conformist. A prominent businessman, contracting the cultivation of beans he joins young Cal Trask to make money by during World War I.

Holman, Rabbit A character in *East of Eden,* Rabbit is a farmer from the Salinas Valley. He reveals to Cal that his mother is the owner of Kate's whorehouse.

Lee A character in *East of Eden,* Lee is Adam Trask's dedicated Chinese servant, who serves as Steinbeck's mouthpiece in the novel. The novelist describes him as a philosophical Chinese. Although he was born in the United States, Lee wears a pigtail and speaks pidgin English to strangers. However, he is not only fluent in English but also widely read. He speaks formal and dialect-free English when he chooses to. He speaks pidgin English only to protect his Chineseness. At the Trasks, Lee assumes multiple roles. When their father sinks into despondency, Lee postpones his dream of owning a bookstore to dedicate himself to raising Trask's twin sons. Steinbeck cast Lee in the role of a hero, who is able to view his own life and the lives of others from a detached point of view. Lee views his life with the Trasks as the refuge of the philosopher. The lifestyle in which he finds joy is what Taoism teaches about living: simplicity in desires but wealth in learning. This vision of life parallels EDWARD RICKETTS's understanding of Taoism as "non-acquisition," a way of life in which a man confidently resigns himself to the "sweet brew of life," a philosophy which Steinbeck endorses.

Quinn, Horace A character in *East of Eden,* Horace is KING CITY's deputy sheriff, a fat, intrepid man with a white mustache shaped like the horns of a longhorn sheep. He is elected sheriff of Salinas County. He interviews Adam Trask after the man is shot by his wife. He discovers the incriminating photos that Kate has collected and decides to burn them.

Sanchez Ranch A large ranch in the Salinas Valley that was purchased by Adam Trask in *East of*

Eden. It consists of 900 acres, the remnants of a 10,000-acre property granted by the Spanish king.

Tilson, Dr.   A character in *East of Eden*, Tilson is the King City doctor. When Cathy Trask attempts to abort her pregnancy, he warns her that if she does not have the baby he will ensure that she goes to jail for murder.

Trask, Adam   A character in *East of Eden*, Adam is a tall, handsome man with an unswerving sense of integrity. Deeply in love with his new wife, Cathy Ames, Adam moves to the Salinas Valley where he hopes to found a family dynasty. He becomes heartbroken and withdraws from his family when his wife leaves him and their two sons, Caleb (Cal) Trask and Aron Trask, to work as a whore in Salinas. Ten years later he overcomes his depression after confronting Cathy. He is stricken by a fatal stroke when he learns that Aron, his favorite son, has been killed in the war.

Trask, Aron   A character in *East of Eden*, Aron is Adam Trask's preferred son. Aron is a beautiful boy with fine golden hair and blue eyes, and an expression of angelic innocence. Unable to accept the sin in the world, he joins the army and is killed after he learns that his mother is the owner of a Salinas whorehouse.

Trask, Caleb   A character in *East of Eden*, Caleb is the son of Adam Trask and Cathy Ames. A stern, serious young man, Caleb struggles with the forces of good and evil that he feels within himself. Also called Cal, he discovers that his mother, and his twin brother's, is the owner of a Salinas whorehouse. He gives his father $15,000 in an attempt to please him and earn his love. When his father rejects the gift, Caleb tells his brother, Aron Trask, about their mother's occupation. He feels responsible when his father suffers a stroke after learning that Caleb's brother has been killed in the war.

Trask, Cyrus   A character in *East of Eden*, Cyrus is a Civil War soldier who lost his leg during his first skirmish. Cyrus is a liar and a fake with a natural military mind. He becomes a powerful secretary of the Grand Army of the Republic in Washington by inventing a nonexistent military career. He has two sons, Adam Trask and Charles Trask, whom he raises with an iron discipline. Cyrus sends Adam to the war to learn to be a man and is later heartbroken when his son refuses to join him in Washington. He leaves a large inheritance for his two sons when he dies.

Valery, Joe   A character in *East of Eden*, Joe is an escaped convict who works as a bouncer at Kate's, a Salinas whorehouse. Kate discovers that Valery is trying to blackmail her and she reports him to the police. He is gunned down and killed while running away.

THE FILM: *EAST OF EDEN* (WARNER BROTHERS, 1955)

Based on the novel by John Steinbeck

> Screenplay: Paul Osborn
> Director: Elia Kazan
> Music: Victor Young
> *Cal Trask:* James Dean
> *Abra:* Julie Harris
> *Adam Trask:* Raymond Massey
> *Aron Trask:* Richard Davalos
> *Kate:* Jo Van Fleet
> *Sam:* Burl Ives
> *Will:* Albert Dekker
> *Anne:* Lois Smith

Steinbeck agreed to do the film with Elia Kazan after working with the director previously on the film VIVA ZAPATA! The film adaptation of *East of Eden* was taken from the last part of the lengthy book. The screenplay, written by Paul Osborn, a playwright who had worked on many screenplays and adaptations for film and stage, begins in Book 4 of the novel and concentrates on the relationship of the two Trask boys, Aaron and Cal, and their discovery of the identity of their mother, Kate. It eliminates some characters that are important to the book, including the Trasks' Chinese servant Lee, and leaves out almost all of the important personal details that define the complex character of Adam Trask. The film version also simplifies significantly the character of Abra and portrays Cal as a brooding and destructive youth, very different from the sensitive and confused boy found in the Steinbeck novel. Overall, however, Osborn did an excellent job of turning a meandering, complicated book into a coherent, dramatic film. *East of Eden* was extremely successful, generating large ticket sales as well as four Academy Award nominations, for best director, best screenplay, best actor, and best supporting actress. Jo Van Fleet won the award for her supporting role as Kate.

FURTHER READING

Astro, Richard. "Journal of a Novel by John Steinbeck." *Steinbeck Quarterly* 3 (1970): 107–110.

Barnes, Rebecca. "Steinbeck's *East of Eden*." *Explicator* 55, no. 3 (1997): 159–160.

Curtis, Harvey Webster. "Out of the New-born Sun." *Saturday Review,* September 20, 1952, 11–12.

Ditsky, John. "'I Kind of Like Caleb': Naming in *East of Eden*." *Steinbeck Newsletter* 10, no. 1 (1997): 7–9.

Fontenrose, Joseph. *John Steinbeck: An Introduction and Interpretation.* New York: Holt, Rinehart and Winston, 1963.

Gurko, Leo. "Steinbeck's Later Fiction." *Nation,* September 20, 1952, 235–236.

Krutch, Joseph Wood. "John Steinbeck's Dramatic Tale of Three Generations." *New York Herald Tribune Weekly Book Review,* September 21, 1952, 1.

Lisca, Peter. *The Wide World of John Steinbeck.* New Brunswick, N.J.: Rutgers University Press, 1958.

Prescott, Orville. "Books of the Times." *New York Times,* September 19, 1952, 21.

Schorer, Mark. "A Dark and Violent Steinbeck Novel." *New York Times Book Review,* September 21, 1952, 1, 22.

Steinbeck, John. *East of Eden.* New York: Viking, 1952.

Tagaya, Satoru. "Is *East of Eden* a 'Postmodern Metafiction'?" *Steinbeck Studies* 19 (1996): 14–20.

Timmerman, John H. *John Steinbeck's Fiction: The Aesthetics of the Road Taken.* Norman: University of Oklahoma Press, 1986.

Webster, Harvey Curtis. "Out of the New-born Sun." *Saturday Review,* September 20, 1952, 11–12.

West, Anthony. "California Moonshine." *New Yorker,* September 20, 1952, 121–122, 125.

Wright, Terence R. "*East of Eden* as Western Midrash: Steinbeck's Re-Marking of Cain." *Religion and the Arts* 2 (1998): 488–518.

The Fight for Life (1936)

Steinbeck wrote the narrative portions of this film about the struggle to end the high rate of infant mortality in the United States. The film was commissioned by the FRANKLIN D. ROOSEVELT administration in an attempt to gain public support for health legislation that the president planned to submit to the Congress. *The Fight for Life* was adapted from the book by DR. PAUL DE KRUIF, directed and produced by PARE LORENTZ in 1936. Steinbeck's work on the movie interested him in documentary filmmaking and ultimately resulted in the author's own semi-documentary film, THE FORGOTTEN VILLAGE.

"Fingers of Cloud: A Satire on College Protervity" (1924)

One of Steinbeck's first published short stories, "Fingers of Cloud" appeared in the February 1924 STANFORD SPECTATOR. The story suggests the crude beginnings of the style and subject matter that would later appear in the author's better-known short stories, in his books THE LONG VALLEY and THE PASTURES OF HEAVEN. It tells the story of Gertie, an 18-year-old retarded girl with curly white hair. As innocent and defenseless as the lamb she resembles, she has recently been left an orphan by the death of her mother. Putting her childhood home in order for the last time, Gertie vows that she will sweep and wash dishes no more. She wanders off into the countryside in pursuit of the lovely clouds that hang temptingly in the distance. The clouds turn black and she is caught unprotected in a violent storm. She stumbles into a bunkhouse occupied by migrant Filipino farm laborers. Pedro, the chief of the migrants, takes the frightened girl under his protection and determines that he will marry her for the prestige that will come from the possession of a white wife. The crude man treats her like a child, alternately doting on her with gifts and beating her with a curtain rod. Gertie quickly discovers her husband's "blackness," a metaphor for his cruelty and ignorance, as well as his skin color. When she discovers that the superstitious Filipinos are keeping horses' heads in a large barrel of water to scare off evil spirits, she demands that Pedro forbid the disgusting practice. Pedro refuses and threatens his young wife with another beating. Her innocence turns to disillusionment and she wanders off again in pursuit of the clouds floating wistfully above the distant hills.

"Fishing in Paris" (1954)

In "Fishing in Paris," published in the August 25, 1954, edition of *Punch*, Steinbeck observes that national character traits emerge in different countries' attitudes toward fishing. All Americans, he says, believe that they are born fishermen. The American attitude toward fishing, according to the author, is that it is the fisherman's own personal contest against nature. He describes the American obsession with fancy and expensive fishing equipment and clothing. He also observes that every candidate interested in running for public office invariably expresses publicly an interest in fishing. The British fisherman, according to the author, has a very different approach: he describes the "gentlemanly rules of conduct" set up between the trout and the Englishman, including the use of "improbable tackle" and a bait that the fish are known to find distasteful. Steinbeck then moves on to French fishing techniques. He describes the banks of the Oise River in PARIS, where each fisherman has his particular spot from which he never moves. The typical French fishing equipment, he says, is a bamboo pole, delicate tackle, and a tiny bread pellet for bait. Steinbeck marvels at the simplicity that he suggests is really an understanding between fisherman and fish to let each other alone. He admires the scene because it allows one to be alone with "dignity and peace."

"Flight" (1938)

One of the most successful of the stories in *THE LONG VALLEY*, "Flight" tells the tale of a young boy's initiation into manhood in lyrical and mystical terms. It opens with a brief description of the Torres family farm, a tumbledown place of a few acres perched on a mountain slope above the ocean, where the four members of the poor Mexican-American family struggle to survive. Mama Torres, widowed for 10 years, dotes on her older son Pepé, though she despairs of his indolence. Nineteen years old, Pepé prides himself on being a man, though he spends most of his days playing with his dead father's switchblade, and entertaining his two younger siblings, Emilio and Rosy, with his knife-throwing skills. Mama Torres compares her oldest child to various animals including a "lazy cow," a "lazy coyote," and a "foolish chicken." After sending Pepé off on an errand to MONTEREY, she tells her two younger children that their brother is "nearly a man," despite her previous insults. Pepé returns earlier than expected from town a changed person. His face has grown harder, and his eyes no longer have "laughter" or "bashfulness." He explains to his mother that he killed a man with his father's knife after being insulted, and that he must escape into the hills ahead of the posse pursuing him. Mama Torres outfits her son with his father's coat, his father's hat, his father's rifle along with 10 bullets, and some jerky and water, formally bids him farewell, and warns him to stay away from the "dark watching men." She, Emilio, and Rosy watch Pepé as he rides off toward the mountains, until his figure "had become a grey, indefinite shadow." Pepé is already a ghost, and lost to his family.

From this moment on, the reader understands Pepé will not survive his desperate journey. Indeed, the Torres family holds a mourning ceremony after their loved one departs, and when asked by Emilio whether Pepé is dead, Rosy responds, "Not yet." Pepé has become a man, but in doing so, has lost everything dear to him. All he has left are the mementoes from his father, except for the knife left behind in the body of the man he killed in Monterey. In the first part of his trek into the mountains, Pepé passes through a green and verdant area. He is both relaxed and composed. He increases his vigilance when he observes a fellow traveler on the trail, and realizes he must pay strict attention to his surroundings. The landscape becomes increasingly hot, barren, and dry. Little by little, Pepé begins to resemble the animals around him, and at two points in the story, large wild cats observe him without either fear or aggression. He has become one with the feral creatures of the mountains. The mysterious "dark watchers" also observe him, and are described as unknowable creatures, who "did not bother anyone who stayed on the trail and minded their own business." As his journey progresses, Pepé loses everything connecting him to the valley he left behind. He first loses his father's hat, left carelessly under an oak tree where he spends the first night. The pursuing posse kills his horse, and he suffers a grievous injury to his hand, which becomes infected and gangrenous. He abandons his father's coat when it becomes too uncomfortable on his swollen hand and arm. Finally, reduced to crawling on his belly as his dehydration and the effects of the infection overwhelm him, Pepé loses the rifle. He has also lost his power of speech, because his tongue has become so swollen, all he can do is hiss like a snake when he tries to recite a prayer. As black carrion birds circle overhead, waiting for his death, Pepé reasserts his humanity. Knowing the posse has grown closer by the sounds of the tracking dogs, he manages to climb to the top of an exposed boulder at the top of a ridge. He stands with great effort and deliberately makes himself a target for those who have chased him through the mountains. Shots ring out, and Pepé dies like the man he has become. The earth reclaims him, as he falls into the valley below, and a small avalanche buries his head.

Steinbeck portrays Pepé and the Torres family with extraordinary sympathy. A childish response, accompanied by an obsession with his father's knife, requires Pepé to mature quickly. It also requires his mother to make an ultimate sacrifice, sending her beloved son off to meet the consequences of his action. She knows his attempt to elude justice will be futile, but she wants him to spend his last days in a semblance of freedom. It is a harsh freedom, but Pepé, throughout the few short days left to him, is "stern, relentless, and manly." In the last brief moments of his life, having lost every talismanic inheritance from his father, Pepé emerges fully into manhood, and standing completely on his own, chooses the manner of his death. In this, he surpasses the accidental nature of his father's death, who tripped and "fell full length on a rattlesnake." Pepé's death has meaning, if only to him.

Steinbeck engages in rather obvious symbolism throughout the story. The color black—the color of death—predominates, in Pepé's black hair and clothing; the black trail leading into the mountains; the black, gangrenous flesh of his arm; the black tongue swelling in his mouth; and the black birds circling as they wait for Pepé to die. Even the "dark watchers" silently observing Pepé from afar, carry a sense of morbidity. The environment changes as Pepé travels deeper into the mountain wilderness, and water, the most crucial necessity of life, becomes more and more scarce, underscoring the inevitability of the outcome. Nevertheless, Steinbeck demonstrates his poetic mastery of description. From the beginning, the book is an elegy for Pepé, and a paean to the magnificent, untamed California countryside.

EARLY CRITICISM

As part of a larger anthology, "Flight" received mixed reviews. Harry Hansen, in his column for the *New York World Telegram* spoke of the "highlight" of "the curiously inverted psychology of the Torres family." Ralph Thompson of the *New York Times* described "Flight" as "impressive, but artificial." Stanley Young, for the *New York Times Book Review* praised Steinbeck's "directness of impression" in his ability to convey "one primitive emotion after another." The critic for *Newsweek* suggested that the tale of Pepé was "particularly outstanding," in the collection. LEWIS GANNETT, surprisingly, considering his friendship with the author, bemoaned "the almost climactic monotony" of "dry-country stories, which suddenly break out in a cyclonic last paragraph." He called on Steinbeck to dispense with such tricks.

CONTEMPORARY PERSPECTIVES

Despite the inherent tragedy from the beginning pages, "Flight" still creates an odd sense of optimism for the reader, and remains a favorite assignment for English teachers. It can be approached from many levels, which is clear from contemporary analysis. Peter Lisca, commenting on the dual moral messages in the story, remarks that Pepé's flight demonstrates how humankind, "even stripped of all civilized accoutrements," never fully becomes an animal. On the other hand, Lisca observes that the "theatrical ending [is] disjunctive and perhaps too perfect" in its "symbolism and allegory." The mythical and allegorical quality of the story also receives attention from Dan Vogel, who in commenting on the transition from childhood to adulthood apparent in the story, says that this common experience is both tragic and heroic, and Steinbeck's addition to this myth of initiation has as much power as "Wordsworth or Hemingway." The feminist critic, Mimi Gladstein, applauds the figure of Mama Torres as an invulnerable tower of strength, surviving the death of her husband and oldest child, in order to maintain the younger generation of Rosy and Emilio.

THE FILM: *FLIGHT* (1961)

Based on the short story by John Steinbeck, the film was originally shot as a feature-length film in Monterey County, but was later edited to 30 minutes. The film is now available for limited showing through the Center for Steinbeck Studies.

> Screenplay: Barnaby Conrad
> Director: Louis Bispo
> Producer: Barnaby Conrad
> Music: Laurindo Almeida
> Actor: Efraín Ramírez

FURTHER READING

Gannett, Lewis. "Books and Things." *New York Herald Tribune,* September 19, 1938, 11.

Gladstein, Mimi. " 'The Leader of the People': A Boy Becomes a Mench." In *Steinbeck's "The Red Pony": Essays in Criticism,* edited by Tetsumaro Hayashi and Thomas J. Moore. Steinbeck Monograph Series No. 13. Muncie, Ind.: Ball State University Press, 1988, 27–37.

Hansen, Harry. "The First Reader." *New York World Telegram,* September 19, 1938, 19.

Lisca, Peter. *The Wide World of John Steinbeck.* New Brunswick, N.J.: Rutgers University Press, 1958.

"More from Steinbeck." *Newsweek,* September 26, 1938, 29.

Steinbeck, John. "Flight." In *The Long Valley.* New York: Viking, 1938.

Thompson, Ralph. "Books of the Times." *New York Times,* September 21, 1938, 29.

Vogel, Dan. "Steinbeck's 'Flight': The Myth of Manhood." *College English* 23, (December 1961): 225–226.

Young, Stanley. "The Short Stories of John Steinbeck." *New York Times Book Review,* September 25, 1938, 7.

The Forgotten Village (1941)

Steinbeck wrote the script for the documentary film *The Forgotten Village* in Mexico City during the summer of 1940, together with the director HERBERT KLINE. Steinbeck, realizing that this film would be one of the first film depictions of life in a Mexican village, was enthusiastic about the project, taking an active role in the production and filming, and investing a significant amount of his own money in the project.

Filming in the village of Pátzcuaro, in central MEXICO, Herbert Kline used real Mexican villagers as actors to portray what Steinbeck, in the introduction to the book version, called a simple story: "too many children die—why is that and what is done about it, both by the villagers and by the government? The story actually was a question. What we found was dramatic—the clash of a medicine and magic that was old when the Aztecs invaded the plateau with a modern medicine that is as young as a living man."

The actor Spencer Tracy was chosen to narrate *The Forgotten Village,* but he was blocked from doing so by Metro-Goldwyn-Mayer, the studio that owned his contract. Forced to choose another actor, Steinbeck chose his good friend BURGESS MEREDITH, who had already appeared in the film adaptation of *OF MICE AND MEN.*

The movie was released in the autumn of 1941 together with a book, also bearing the title *The Forgotten Village*, published by Viking Press, which included the narration of the film and 136 photographs from the film.

The release of the film was initially blocked by the State Board of Censors of New York, who believed that it encouraged socialism. Steinbeck appealed to an admirer of his work, Eleanor Roosevelt, whose intervention led to a reversal of the ban.

FILM CREDITS

Story and Script: John Steinbeck
Director and Producer: Herbert Kline

Codirector and Director of Photography:
   Alexander Hackensmid
Music: Hanns Eisler
Narration: Burgess Meredith
Coproducer: Rosa Harvan Kline
Production Manager: Mark Marvin
Assistant Director: Carlos Cabello
Cameraman: Agustín Delgado
Assistant Cameraman: Felipe Quintanar

SYNOPSIS

Juan Diego, a young boy from the village of Santiago, a small pueblo in the mountains of central Mexico, accompanies his mother, Esperanza, on a visit to Trini, the local medicine woman. Esperanza

Scene portraying the use of traditional medicine in Steinbeck's 1941 film *The Forgotten Village* *(Photofest)*

is pregnant and she comes to ask the *curandera* to read the fortune of her unborn child. The old woman assures her that the child will be a boy, born healthy and beautiful. She accepts a chicken as payment for the good fortune that she has read and presents the happy mother with a charm for good luck.

Juan Diego rushes to the fields to share the good news with his father. He and his younger brothers, Paco and Carlos, help their father carry heavy bundles of the harvested corn to the landowner, who takes half of the crop as payment for the land.

Juan Diego goes to school. He is a friend of the schoolteacher, an educated man from another town.

The next morning, young Paco becomes ill. The worried mother calls the *curandera*, who prepares an ancient cure for the sick boy. She attempts to draw the "evil airs" out with an egg. Meanwhile, other children in the village are also becoming ill. Juan Diego discusses the problem with the schoolteacher, who tells him that he believes the sickness is caused by bacteria in the water of the town well. Together they attempt to convince the townspeople that they must seek medical help from the government. But the old *curandera*, fearing for her practice, convinces the people that medicine is bad and that only the traditional cures will work. Paco dies from his illness. A few days later, on the town's feast day, Esperanza gives birth to a baby boy, whom they name Santiago.

People continue to die of the mysterious illness. Juan Diego and the schoolteacher once again attempt to convince the townspeople that they must call a doctor, but the town elders reject the idea. Meanwhile, Juan Diego's little sister Maria also becomes ill. Juan Diego decides that he will walk to the city to deliver a letter to the health authorities requesting help. The young boy, who has never ventured more than 10 miles from his village, sets out for the long walk to Mexico City. On his way he meets a soldier who encourages him on his voyage.

The frightened young peasant reaches the city and makes his way to the hospital. He is told that there are no medical trucks available, but seeing his determination, the hospital officials agree to send a car from the Rural Medical Service.

The *curandera* warns the townspeople against the doctors who arrive with Juan Diego, claiming that they have come to poison them. Juan Diego's parents refuse to let them treat their sick daughter. The doctor's tests show that the water is indeed infected. When Juan Diego and the schoolteacher dump disinfectant powder into the well, Trini accuses them of poisoning the water. The angry peasants drive the doctors from the town. That night, Juan Diego steals his little sister and takes her to the doctors to be injected with serum. When the boy returns home, his father banishes him from the village for defying him.

The sad boy goes to the teacher, who counsels him to go to the government school in the city. He says that when the townspeople see that the medicine has worked they will change their minds and welcome the doctors. "Changes in people are never quick," he says. "But the boys from the villages are being given a chance by a nation that believes in them. From the government schools, the boys and girls from the villages will carry knowledge back to their people, Juan Diego. And the change will come, is coming; the long climb out of darkness. Already the people are learning, changing their lives, learning, working, living in new ways. The change will come, is coming, as surely as there are thousands of Juan Diegos in the villages of Mexico."

CHARACTERS AND SETTING

Juan Diego   Juan Diego is a young Mexican peasant boy from the remote village of Santiago, where he lives with his father, Ventura, and his mother, Esperanza. When his brother Paco gets a mysterious illness, Juan tries to convince the townspeople to request medical assistance from the government. When Paco dies and his young sister Maria also becomes sick, he defies his father and takes her to the doctors to be inoculated. He is expelled from the village and leaves to study in a government school.

Santiago   The fictional setting for Steinbeck's film *The Forgotten Village*, actually the Mexican town of Pátzcuaro. A small village located on the hills of a mountain range, Santiago becomes the scene of a clash between modern medicine and ancient tradition when the townspeople fall prey to a mysterious illness.

Trini Trini is the *curandera* (medicine woman or witch doctor) of the small pueblo of Santiago. When a mysterious illness begins to strike the townspeople, she leads them in resisting the advance of modern medicine, assuring them that only the traditional ways will protect them from the "bitter airs" that are plaguing them.

"A Game of Hospitality" (1957)

"A Game of Hospitality" was written as an editorial for the April 20, 1957, edition of *The Saturday Review*. Steinbeck was preparing to travel to Tokyo to participate in the congress of writers of International PEN, where he had been invited to speak as guest of honor. The author learns that PEN has never been able to hold its conference in the United States because too many of the first-rate authors would be denied visas to enter the country. Steinbeck is astonished by the immigration restrictions applied in his country. He determines to make a list of the people in history who, under contemporary immigration laws, would not be allowed into the United States. His long list includes David (revolution), Martin Luther (troublemaker, inciting to riot), and Adam Smith (advocating overthrow of government). He also lists a few people who, if they had not been Americans, could also not get into the country, including George Washington (insurrection), and Thomas Jefferson (teaching violent revolution). Steinbeck offers up Jesus Christ as his final example, charging him with the crimes of inciting riot, causing civil commotion, disturbing the peace, and being released from jail by the mob.

"The Gifts of Iban" (1927)

"The Gifts of Iban," published March 1927 in *The Smoker's Companion*, was Steinbeck's first commercially published short story, earning the author $7.

The story was submitted under the pseudonym John Stern, which the serious young writer perhaps adopted because he was embarrassed by the story's own lack of seriousness. "The Gifts of Iban" is written in the form of a fairy tale and set in an enchanted forest of fantastic foliage and mythical creatures. It tells the story of a beautiful young fairy named Cantha. Cantha's mother pressures the young woman to marry Glump, the king of the gnomes, who has promised her great riches in exchange for her marrying him. Cantha resists her mother's influence, claiming that she is old enough to have her independence. Cantha is secretly and passionately in love with a poor but handsome fairy named Iban. When Cantha runs away to meet her lover in the forest, Iban promises to make her rich with the gold of the sunbeams and the silver moon reflected on the forest floor. Cantha is swept off her feet by his romantic words and the two are soon married despite the disapproval of Cantha's relatives. Upon examining the treasures that he has promised her, however, she soon determines that they are merely the worthless poetry of a dreamer. Regretting her rash decision, she cruelly accuses Iban of deceiving her and abandons the heartbroken fairy in the forest. Although generally dismissed by both the author and his critics, "The Gifts of Iban" foreshadows the theme of youthful disillusionment that would reappear in Steinbeck's first published novel, CUP OF GOLD.

"The Golden Handcuff: Steinbeck Writes about San Francisco" (1958)

Steinbeck wrote "The Golden Handcuff" for the *Pictorial Living* supplement of the November 23, 1958, edition of the *San Francisco Examiner*. The newspaper had requested that the famous author write about his impressions of the city where he spent much of his childhood and early adulthood. In the sweetly sentimental article, the author reminisces about the four distinct stages in his relationship with the city of SAN FRANCISCO, first hearing mythic descriptions of if from his uncle, JOE HAMILTON, then exploring the city's cultural offerings with his mother. Beginning his studies at STANFORD UNIVERSITY, he entered the third stage. Finally, Steinbeck describes the fourth stage as his "tour of duty as an intellectual Bohemian," during which time he struggled with poverty while trying to write and publish his first book. Indicating how the city has always had an important place in his imagination, he writes that it is "a golden handcuff with the keys thrown away."

"Good Guy—Bad Guy" (1954)

Foreshadowing the sort of cultural criticism that would find its fuller expression in THE WINTER OF OUR DISCONTENT and AMERICA AND AMERICANS, in "Good Guy—Bad Guy," published in the September 22, 1954, edition of *Punch*, Steinbeck writes about the growing influence of television and the nature of its impact for both good and bad. Steinbeck sees television as yet another way for parents to control the activity and noise of children. He describes his eight-year-old son Catbird's obsession with television westerns. Steinbeck does not understand the obsession because the plots of the story never change. His son explains to him that the Good Guy always wears white and that the Bad Guy always wears black. Steinbeck asks his son who the guy in gray is. The boy explains that he is the In-Between Guy—sometimes good and sometimes bad. Later, a friend assures Steinbeck that a whole generation of Americans make their judgments on pretty much the same basis as those outlined by the author's son. After giving his friend's idea a lot of consideration, Steinbeck determines that it is true, illustrating this belief with the example of the McCarthy hearings. Steinbeck portrays McCarthy with all of the classic western characteristics of the bad guy except the black hat and he notes that those who have seen him recognize those characteristics.

The Grapes of Wrath (1939)

Published in 1939 by VIKING PRESS, and considered by many to be John Steinbeck's greatest work, *The Grapes of Wrath* fully established the author's reputation as a "proletarian" writer, a reputation which, in many respects, haunted him both personally and professionally for the rest of his life. Though not a Marxist or socialist, Steinbeck became identified with the radical left after the publication of *The Grapes of Wrath*, and in later years suffered unwarranted criticism from the liberal intelligentsia for his supposed abandonment of communist ideology as his attention shifted away from the plight of the impoverished and oppressed. Additionally, he came under the scrutiny of the FBI, led by the fierce anti-communist, J. Edgar Hoover, who ordered the agency to compile a secret dossier on Steinbeck's leftist activities and associations. Without doubt, governmental suspicions of Steinbeck's ideological sympathies prevented the author from enlisting in the military during WORLD WAR II. Finally, when the Nobel Committee awarded Steinbeck the NOBEL PRIZE IN LITERATURE in 1962, an unprecedented outrage erupted among conservative and liberal critics alike. Conservatives excoriated the Nobel Committee for its selection of a "fellow traveler" and communist supporter. Leftists decried the choice of Steinbeck because of his ostensible co-optation by capitalist society. Steinbeck hated to be labeled or categorized, and most of all, feared to be called a social-political writer. His reaction to the controversy was not only outrage and extended depression, but a growing fear of completing another novel, which he did not attempt for several years afterward. During the late fall of 1939 and the winter of 1939–40, he spent most of his time reading and studying, helped EDWARD RICKETTS with the routine lab work, and worked on the equipment for their field trips.

The Grapes of Wrath is the last of the so-called Labor Trilogy, following IN DUBIOUS BATTLE and OF MICE AND MEN, and represents the literary culmination of Steinbeck's decadelong interest in and identification with the common workingman. Conceived and written during the height of the GREAT DEPRESSION, the book's dedication reads "To

CAROL who willed it. To TOM who lived it," acknowledging the seminal influence on the novel of Steinbeck's first wife, CAROL HENNING STEINBECK BROWN, and TOM COLLINS, the camp manager of the ARVIN SANITARY CAMP, also known as "Weedpatch." Carol had introduced Steinbeck to numerous left-wing political activists during the 1930s, including the author Lincoln Steffens and his wife, ELLA WINTER, and FRANCIS WHITAKER, a leading figure in the American Communist Party. Through these connections, Steinbeck received a commission from George West, an editor at the *San Francisco News,* to write a series of articles detailing the grim conditions encountered by migrant farm laborers. Eventually, these articles were collected and published under the title, "THE HARVEST GYPSIES," and Steinbeck's journalistic assignment gave him the real-life experience that forms the foundation of *The Grapes of Wrath.* During his research for the *San Francisco News,* Steinbeck met Tom Collins, the supervisor of a federally sponsored demonstration camp, intended to relieve the misery of agricultural labor in California. Collins provided Steinbeck with detailed and poignant examples of the "OKIE" refugee phenomenon, and served as an invaluable resource for much of the background in *The Grapes of Wrath.*

The novel was loosely based on a story idea that Steinbeck first developed into a satirical novella titled *L'Affaire Lettuceberg,* which the author completed in 1938 and then promptly burned. Written in a unique style that alternates chapters of narrative with chapters of explanatory and often lyrical prose called interchapters or intercalary chapters, *The Grapes of Wrath* chronicles the adventures and misfortunes of the Joads, a family of "Okie" sharecroppers evicted from their failing cotton farm on the outskirts of Sallisaw, Oklahoma. The first half of the story takes place on the road as the family journeys west from Oklahoma to California, the mythical land of plenty where they hope to begin a new life. The second half of the story centers on the family's struggle to survive in the Golden State as they are exploited by large landowners and persecuted by small-town bourgeoisie. The novel takes its title from the "Battle Hymn of the Republic," which Steinbeck insisted be printed on the endpapers of the original edition. Edited by PASCAL COVICI, *The Grapes of Wrath* became a staggering success, selling almost 500,000 copies before the end of the first year. Steinbeck was awarded the PULITZER PRIZE in 1940 for the novel. To this date, it has never been out of print.

Were the novel merely a propagandistic tract intended to mobilize those dispossessed by the economic disasters of the Great Depression, or appalled by the greedy excesses of uncontrolled capitalism, *The Grapes of Wrath* never would have achieved the status of an American and world classic. Steinbeck patterned the book on far more universal themes, both the biblical story of Exodus, and also humanity's capacity for survival and growth in the face of almost unendurable calamity. Just as important, he populated the pages of his most highly regarded work with unforgettable characters, including a nonhuman character, an indefatigable and indomitable turtle that serves as a metaphor for human determination to carry on and persist without regard to social or physical obstacles. The various family members of the Joad family represent every aspect of the human condition and of human motivation from the most abased to the most exalted. Certainly Steinbeck intended to spark antipathy toward the inequities between the rich and poor of the depression era, and perhaps instigate a rebellion among his readers against the degradations suffered by the victims of the economic upheaval. His polemical message emerges most clearly in the intercalary chapters. Nevertheless, the story was always paramount for Steinbeck, and the saga of the Joads resonates long after the misery of the depression ended. A gentle humor pervades the book. Whether it involves Grampa Joad's inability to button his trousers properly, or the uncontrollable exuberance and curiosity of the two youngest Joads, Ruthie and Winfield, Steinbeck includes a necessary whimsical touch as a counterpoint to the novel's predominantly tragic theme. Most important, unlike the two prior stories that comprise the Labor Trilogy, *The Grapes of Wrath* ends on a note of optimism and hope for the continuation of a boundless human spirit, no matter the setting or circumstance.

CRITICAL SUMMARY

The opening chapter describes in colorful and poetic imagery the origins and effect of an ecological disaster, the DUST BOWL. Part human-made, part natural, a product of poor farming practices and an extended drought, the dust bowl phenomenon swept away the rich but thin topsoil of family farms across the Great Plains. It transformed yeoman farmers into indigents, and indigent farmers into sharecroppers with everyone's life and livelihood mortgaged to the bank. Both the farmers and the landscape in Steinbeck's introductory chapter alter from bright primary colors into gray and white, underscoring the close ties of men to the land they have plowed for generations.

Tom Joad, recently paroled from the Oklahoma penitentiary after a conviction for the manslaughter of an acquaintance who had pulled a knife on Tom during a minor disagreement, cajoles a truck driver into giving him a ride closer to his family homestead despite a sign on the truck forbidding hitchhikers. Tom establishes a bond with the driver based on a mutual dislike of "boss's" orders, and an unwillingness to relinquish the last vestige of freedom from authority. "Sometimes a guy'll be a good guy even if some rich bastard makes him carry a sticker," Tom says as he implores the truck driver for his assistance, and with those words, he establishes an ongoing theme throughout the novel. Working people need a kinship against the abuses and arbitrary dictates of employers. Moreover, Tom's success in convincing the driver to give him a lift demonstrates Tom's natural gift for manipulating people, even to the point of going against their self-interest, as part of a larger collective. Tom Joad, despite his aversion to standing out from the crowd and playing a leadership role after four years of imprisonment, must eventually employ his talents and volatile temperament in the service of a larger whole.

Steinbeck then introduces the symbol of the Okie migration to California in an interchapter. A large box turtle struggles over an embankment onto a concrete road, determined to travel southwest. Described in human terms with "hands" and "fierce, humorous eyes," nothing deters the turtle's slow but steady journey, not even the maliciously deliberate attempt by a truck driver to run over the creature. The turtle stops and withdraws into his shell in protection for a short while, but then continues on his steady way. Eventually, Tom Joad, after being dropped off several miles from the Joad homestead, discovers the turtle on a dust road, and picks up the tenacious reptile as a gift for his younger brother, Al. Placing it inside his rolled-up jacket, Tom could feel it struggling and trying to break free. The turtle, against all odds, in time regains his freedom, and continues his trek southwest, just as the Okies, carrying all of their worldly possessions on the back of dilapidated vehicles, make their way successfully to California.

Under a willow tree closer to his family's home, Tom encounters Jim Casy, a former evangelical preacher, who had baptized Tom years before. Commenting on the turtle, Casy says, "Nobody can't keep a turtle, though," and compares himself to the animal as he describes his escape from the restrictions of traditional religion. In his glory days, during tent revival meetings, he would excite the people and arouse them with the "Holy Sperit" to the point that the women he "saved" would be "so full of the Holy Sperit" that they would offer their bodies to him in sexual communion. Casy began to question the whole notion of sin, and came to the conclusion "There ain't no sin, and there ain't no virtue. There's just stuff people do." Here, Steinbeck introduces another central theme, derived in part from Carl Jung's construct of archetypes and universal unconsciousness. According to Casy, the "Holy Sperit" has nothing to do with Jesus or God. "Why do we got to hang it on God or Jesus?" he asks Tom. "Maybe all men got one big soul," and this universal soul derives its power from love. Made somewhat uncomfortable by the clear heresy, Tom suggests that Casy will be persecuted if he pursues this doctrine. More important, the chance meeting and Casy's unorthodox musings form the beginnings of Tom's future role as a disciple to the former minister.

Tom invites Casy to join him and become reacquainted with the Joad family. As the two men cross a ridge overlooking the Joad farm, they realize the buildings have been partially destroyed and abandoned. Like many tenant farmers during the depression, the Joad family had been evicted by the owner of the property to implement a more efficient and profitable agricultural method than sharecropping. Rather than a system of numerous small tenant farms, owners chose to consolidate their holdings, and pay a daily wage to men on tractors who could cover far more territory and at less cost than a man behind a horse-drawn plow. Resisting their eviction, the Joads ultimately had no choice but to leave when a neighbor and former friend, Willy Feeley, riding one of the monster tractors, plowed through a corner of the house, and filled in the well. The story of the Joads' dispossession comes from another neighbor, Muley Graves, who has also been driven off his farm. Muley, half-crazed by his homelessness, refuses to leave the barren soil of Oklahoma despite the fact his wife and children have departed for California, lured by the promise of high wages from landowners in need of seasonal workers. He calls himself a "graveyard ghos'," haunting the abandoned farms, hiding in caves and fields, and periodically taking potshots at the men on the infernal machines who now control the land. Muley tells Tom that the Joads have moved in with his Uncle John while they pick cotton and prepare for their own migration to California. Muley shares his meager catch of snared rabbits with Casy and Tom, saying "if a fella got somepin to eat and another fella's hungry—why the first fella ain't got no choice." Again Steinbeck emphasizes the importance of selflessness and cooperation even under the most desperate circumstances.

Presaging the upcoming journey of the Joads in an ancient Hudson touring car, Steinbeck takes us into the mind and devious methods of a used-car salesman. In a remarkable interchapter where few of the sentences contain more than 10 words, and most are fragments, Steinbeck replicates the fast-talking spiel of a huckster, selling decrepit jalopies at ridiculously high prices to dispossessed farmers who are frantic to reach the "promised land" of California. Already exploited by the landowners, the gullible sharecroppers become easy victims to yet another group of venal men, who profit from the misery of others.

In the company of Casy, Tom finally reunites with his family at his uncle's farm. Before meeting any of his family members, Tom spots a truck parked in the middle of the yard, surrounded by furniture and other household items. He realizes his family is in the midst of final preparations for the departure to California. The reader is introduced one by one to the Joad family. Each of them comes to life in a few short sentences. Tom's father, Old Tom, at first expresses fear that his hot-headed son has "busted out" of prison, but then conveys his joy that Tom will be able to accompany the family to California. Playing a small joke on his wife, Pa Joad announces there will be two extra mouths for the breakfast Ma Joad is cooking for the three generations of the Joads. Without knowing who has shown up, Ma agrees to share the side meat and bread, and turning to greet the visitors, slowly recognizes her son. So powerful is the bond between the two that Tom bites through his lip in his happiness at being with his mother, and she soundlessly caresses him as if to reassure herself that he is real. Steinbeck describes Ma as the "citadel of strength" for the family.

While Pa goes to the barn to announce Tom's arrival to Granma and Grampa, Ma inquires about Tom's state of mind after years of incarceration. "You ain't poisoned mad? You don't hate nobody?" she asks, and Tom reassures her that he is fine though furious at the destruction of the family farm. Ma tells him not to go off on his own against those who evicted the Joads, and says, "They say there's a hun'erd thousand of us shoved out," and "If we all got mad the same way—they wouldn't hunt nobody down." In this odd statement from such an outwardly gentle woman, Steinbeck reiterates the theme of unity in the face of adversity. Suddenly a scream of joy is heard from the farmyard, as Tom's grandmother hears the news of the return of the prodigal son. "Pu-raise Gawd for victory!" Granma repeats like a litany, and the two cantankerous and seemingly indestructible old folks rush for the farmhouse, followed slowly by Tom's older brother, Noah. Grampa is portrayed as a lecherous and appetitive child, fond of dirty jokes, and matched only in meanness by his wife, who finds comfort in a "shrill ferocious religiosity."

The Joad family packing up their truck for the long ride to California in a scene from the 1940 film production of *The Grapes of Wrath* *(Photofest)*

Noah, unlike any of the rest of the family, has no passion for life, and probably suffered brain damage at birth when his father frantically pulled him from his mother's agonized body. Granma insists on a prayer from Casy before the meal, and although Casy insists he is no longer a preacher, he offers a curious and introspective series of thoughts about finding his way to a new vision of holiness after wandering in the wilderness like Jesus, where all "working together" and "kind of harnessed to the whole shebang" would find holiness and love.

After breakfast Tom inspects the truck purchased for the journey westward, and learns that his younger brother Al had a crucial role in selecting the vehicle, because he had acquired knowl-

edge about engines while driving a truck. Al is a hellion and a skirt chaser who can think of "nothing but girls and engines." Tom also learns that his sister, Rose of Sharon (or Rosasharn) has married a young man named Connie Rivers, and the two will be accompanying them to California. Later that day Tom finds his sister to be completely self-absorbed in her impending motherhood, and her husband to be somewhat immature. Lastly Uncle John appears with the two youngest Joads, Ruthie and Winfield, in tow, after a last trip to town to sell the family's meager belongings. Uncle John, as has previously been explained, bears an extraordinary burden of guilt for the death of his young and pregnant wife many years ago when he refused to call the doctor after his bride developed appendicitis. Since then he has attempted to assuage his culpability by alternating between remarkable acts of kindness and generosity, and drunken licentiousness. The children offer an ongoing comic relief in the novel, and because of their youth, prove the most adaptable to the changes in their lives.

The family must face the heart-wrenching task of sorting through their remaining possessions, and determining what must be left behind or burned. Ma expresses her doubts about the rosy conditions in California described so glowingly in the handbills advertising work for cotton and fruit pickers. Tom admits he has heard stories of far different circumstances, of filthy camps and subsistence wages, but also reminds his mother they have no choice. They must face each day as it comes. Jim Casy asks permission to ride along with the family, and after a raucous family council assembled next to the truck, the Joads accept Casy's request. The truck has become the center of the family's life. Tom reveals he will be violating his parole once he crosses the border out of Oklahoma, but will not be deterred from helping his family in the time of crisis. The entire group pitches in to slaughter and salt down the two pigs for food on the road, and stays up most of the night loading the truck. At dawn with 13 people aboard plus the family dog, and what's left of the family's property crammed into every nook and cranny, the truck creeps slowly on to the road, like the turtle heading southwest. At the last minute Grampa refuses to make the trip, and Ma forcibly drugs him with strong patent medicine, and loads his unconscious body into the back of the vehicle. Despite his prior excitement at the vision of rolling in a tub of California grapes, the irascible old man's ties to the land are too strong, and the prospect of leaving his lifelong home unbearable.

Immediately the family's status shifts from the hardscrabble life of tenant farming, in which the land holds the central concern, to the transitory nature of a road family, and preoccupation with their mechanized home. Al's stature rises since he is the "expert" with the inner workings of a car, and he alternates behind the wheel with Tom, who learned to drive in prison. By the end of the first day the family has driven 200 miles, one-10th of the distance to California, but has also experienced its first tragedies. During a stop for water at a run-down gas station, the dog bolts into the road, and is crushed by a passing motorist. Watching the accident, Rose of Sharon has the first inkling that her pregnancy may not be going well as she experiences a painful twinge at the brutal sight. At sundown the Joads pull off the road next to another migrant couple, Sairy and Ivy Wilson, who have pitched a small tent next to their broken-down Dodge touring car. Almost immediately it becomes clear that Grampa is deathly ill. The Wilsons offer the shelter of their tent to the old man, and after Casy recites the Lord's Prayer at Granma's insistence, Grampa dies of a stroke. Unable to afford the $40 for a pauper's funeral, the men bury the old man in a secluded, unmarked grave, wrapped in Sairy's quilt. In his lifetime Grampa had never left Oklahoma and dies before the Joads even reach the state border. Symbolically the older generation has passed its authority to the younger generation.

The Wilsons and Joads make the decision to travel together, relying on the safety and security of numbers. The Wilsons gain the mechanical expertise of Al and Tom to fix their decrepit automobile, and the Joads lighten the burden of the overloaded truck by shifting some of its passengers to the Wilsons car. A new familial relationship begins to grow, based on joint need, and reciprocal responsibility. After the connection among strangers is formed, Steinbeck addresses the primary theme of *The Grapes of Wrath*. He calls it Manself, the transformation of single individuals, who "hunger for joy and some security" into a vast aggregate of human beings with the same desires and goals. No longer do they identify themselves as "I," but rather as "We," united by common suffering and mutual sharing. This multiplication of single souls into a universal soul is creative, not destructive, and undergirds all of mankind's progress. Toward the end of this interchapter, Steinbeck mentions four revolutionaries—Paine, Marx, Jefferson, and Lenin—and suggests that individual owners may not survive the coming storm of collective outrage.

Now unified, the two families continue the trek westward, at "first in flight" until gradually "the highway became their home and movement their means of expression." The momentum of the road has become their way of life. Only Granma fails to adapt to the rhythm of travel, and has lapsed into delirium. Crossing into New Mexico, with Al driving the Wilsons car, a suspicious rattle becomes a grinding noise as a con-rod bearing goes out. The two cars pull over to the side of the road, and the two brothers confer over the difficult repair job facing them. Tom suggests that everyone but he and Casy continue on to California, while they take the long walk back to the closest town, Santa Rosa, and try to locate spare parts. In Tom's mind, "The nearer our folks get to California, the quicker they's gonna be money rollin' in." Pa agrees to his son's reasoning, but Ma, fiercely agitated, challenges her husband's authority for the first time in her life. Taking up a tire iron, she refuses to go ahead, and threatens to knock him "belly-up." "All we got is the family unbroke," she says, and demonstrates an unshakable determination to keep her kinfolk together. To everyone's surprise, Pa yields to his wife's demand, and a shift in the family dynamic takes place. Ma has now assumed the leadership of the Joads. The old rules and way of life no longer apply.

After some difficulty, Tom acquires the parts to fix the Dodge at a junkyard, where Tom objects rudely to the one-eyed yardkeeper's self-pitying defeatism. No longer content to live one day at a time, and to keep his nose out of others' business, Tom has begun to take Casy's words to heart, and to reach out toward the unfortunate, even if tactlessly. After Tom repairs the Dodge with quiet skill and confidence, he, Al and Casy join the others at a campground where the owner charges 50 cents a night for each carload of people. There they encounter a scrawny, ragged man heading eastward away from California who tells the tale of losing his wife and children to starvation, and of the impoverishment of migrant workers. The ragged man claims the handbills promising work to everyone are part of a devious plot to keep wages low, and the workers from organizing. Ma refuses to believe the story and holds onto the hope for a better future for her family in the green land of California.

Traveling through Arizona, the minicaravan experiences the first discrimination toward "Okies."

Encountering a border guard who warns them to keep moving, they drive all through the night to spend as little time as possible in the state. At the Colorado River, having crossed over into California, the men decide to take a refreshing bath in the cool water, almost as a baptismal ritual. There the men encounter another man who has left California to return to his ancestral home, where "at leas' we can starve to death with folks we know" and not with a "bunch of fellas that hates us." Asked for his opinion, Uncle John points out that the stories of misery and deprivation no longer matter. The Joads will continue on because they no longer have a choice. Crawling into a spot of shade to get some sleep before the nighttime desert crossing, Tom is joined by his brother, Noah. Noah announces he intends to stay by the river, saying "the folks don't really care for me." Noah somehow senses the additional burden his disability will place on the family and walks away, much to his brother's consternation. Tom, however, makes no effort to retrieve his older sibling, accepting the decision as his brother's right.

Back at the camp, Ma and Rosasharn are confronted by an abusive policeman as they tend to Granma. Ordered to vacate the premises immediately, Ma threatens the policeman with an iron skillet, and castigates him for scaring helpless women. He backs away, but not before flinging insults at her. In a panic, Ma sends Ruthie in search of Tom, certain that her ex-convict son will be apprehended by the border patrolman. The family gathers around the campfire where Ma learns that Noah has left. Despite her best efforts, the family is breaking up, and the Wilsons also announce their inability to go on. Sairy's weakness from cancer has overtaken her, and she is too debilitated to travel any further. Leaving most of their cash and the rest of their food for the Wilsons, the Joads decide to cross the desert at night when the oppressive heat will be more bearable. Under the tarpaulin covering the back of the Hudson, Connie and Rose make love quietly while John and Casy discuss the nature of sin, and Ma comforts Granma. In the middle of the desert, the truck is stopped for an agricultural inspection. Ma prevents the officers from examining the vehicle thoroughly, telling them there's "a sick ol' lady" who needs immediate medical attention. Accepting her plea the officers wave the Joads through, and by sunrise they have crossed the desert into the mountains and from there into the central green valley. Everyone except Ma clambers out of the truck to view the wondrous sight, and when Ma finally joins them, they learn that Granma died during the night before the family was stopped at the inspection station. Fearful that her loved ones would be detained permanently, Ma lied to the inspectors, and then spent the rest of the night curled up next to the old woman's corpse. In awe, Casy says of Ma, "there's a woman so great with love—she scares me."

After taking the body to a county coroner's office for a pauper's burial, the Joads press on to their first Hooverville, a squatters' camp of itinerant workers common in the depression. As the men inquire about the possibility of work, the truth of the desperate situation for migrant workers emerges. Men speak of their experiences of constantly being on the road looking for a job, while being hounded by the authorities if they stay too long in one spot. The workers, lured by enticing handbills scattered across the country, show up in droves, and the owners of the farming conglomerates pay the migrants a pittance for difficult long hours. Those who organize or protest have their names put on a blacklist circulated across the state, and the local constabulary arrests the "agitators" on trumped up charges of vagrancy or stealing.

As Tom hears the reality of California, he grows more and more angry. Later, starving and dirty children watch Ma prepare a celebratory stew for her family. In shame, Ma and Uncle John leave their portion for the camp youngsters. After helping a young man named Floyd Knowles fix his car's engine, Al hears of the possibility of work about 200 miles north. Excited, he tells Tom about his plans to head north by himself, but Tom expresses his concern about Ma's reaction if the family continues to break up. Shortly afterward, a labor contractor pulls up in a fancy car accompanied by deputies. The contractor offers the men in the camp work picking fruit in Tulare County, but when Floyd asks to see a contract guaranteeing an hourly wage, he's accused of being an agitator, and arrested on suspicion of breaking into a car dealership. Floyd fights back,

and as he escapes down the line of tents, Tom casually sticks out his foot, and trips the pursuing deputy. Observing the melee from the crowd, Casy steps forward and kicks the downed deputy into unconsciousness. Reminding Tom of his parolee status, Casy urges Tom to hide, and then takes the full blame for the assault. Arrested and driven away in a patrol car, Casy "sits proudly" and "on his face a curious look of conquest."

Alerted by Floyd of the intention of a group of vigilantes to burn out the camp overnight, Tom returns to the Joad family campsite and urges everyone to leave. They pack up the truck, and realize that Connie Rivers has abandoned his wife and unborn child in disappointment at the squalid conditions of California. Hurrying away the Joads encounter a roadblock of armed men, and Tom is forced to play a servile whiner to protect his family from the imminent violence. Following the example of Casy's sacrifice, he quells his temper for the greater good. Ma congratulates her son for his patience, and predicts a "different time's comin'" when "us people will go on livin' when all them people is gone."

Wanting to be treated like human beings again and to achieve some normalcy, the Joads seek out the government camp nicknamed "Weedpatch." Funded by the federal government, similar camps across California allowed the Okies to regain self-respect, have access to a more nutritious diet and to rudimentary health care. Self-governing and autonomous, the camps were off limits to the local authorities, who were intent on bullying the migrants into submission. The camps were not charitable institutions. Those who were allowed a space were expected to work for the rent by cleaning up, or doing other chores to maintain the camp's order. Each family permitted to stay could draw on a $20 allotment at the camp store if they could not find work. For the Joads, Weedpatch was welcome respite from the ordeals of their travel.

Tom finds work almost immediately with the help of the Wallace family, who not only share their breakfast, but also risk having their wages lowered by including an extra man on the work crew laying pipe for a small landowner named Mr. Thomas. Walking to the Thomas farm, Tom learns that the

Wallaces have been in California for 10 months, experiencing mostly famine, and only recently had sold their car in desperation for $10 when it was worth $75. Arriving at the farm, Mr. Thomas informs the group that the Farmer's Association has put pressure on him to lower his hourly wages from 30 cents an hour to 25 cents an hour to keep wages down for the larger landowners. Ashamed by his unwillingness to fight unfairness, Mr. Thomas warns the men that outside troublemakers have been ordered to stage a fight at the weekly Saturday dance in Weedpatch, so that deputies can be brought in to quell the disturbance. Nothing frightens the agricultural conglomerates more than the possibility that the migrant workers will organize, and Weedpatch, by definition, is organized.

For the first time in their lives, the Joads experience modern flush toilets, and hot and cold running water from taps. Ma Joad has a pleasant meeting with Jim Rawley, the camp manager, who inquires kindly about the family's well-being. She and Rosasharn meet the Lady's Committee, which sets schedules for the daily cleaning of the bath facilities. Most of Chapter 22 brings a welcome interlude of humor and happiness. The only dark cloud is a visit to Rose of Sharon from a fundamentalist Christian, Mrs. Sandry, who warns the young woman that her baby is marked by sin. Eventually Ma confronts Mrs. Sandry, and threatens physical violence if she approaches Rose again. Ma turns her back completely on the rigid construction of old-time religion.

Warned by Tom and the Wallaces of the impending raid, the camp security committee makes plans against the threat from outsiders during the Saturday night dance. Immediately the head of the Central Committee stresses the importance of doing no harm to the anticipated invaders. "Don't you hurt them fellas. Don't you use no stick nor no knife or arm, or anything like that." The peaceable kingdom of Weedpatch can only survive if it remains peaceable. Posting extra patrols around the perimeter, and instructing everyone in the camp to maintain a heightened scrutiny of any strangers, the camp committee allows the Saturday night dance to go forward. In eager anticipation of an entertaining evening, the Joads dress in their finest clothing.

Even Rose of Sharon, pining desperately for her derelict husband and ashamed at her abandonment, agrees to accompany Ma to the dance. As expected, the interlopers invade the carefree evening, but are spotted and intercepted by the vigilant security detail before any harm or disturbance takes place. As if on cue, sheriff's deputies arrive in town cars just as the three invaders are quietly escorted from the camp, claiming they have received word of a riot. Disappointed by the quiet atmosphere, the deputies pull away and wait again on the outskirts of Weedpatch for any pretext to destroy the camp.

Chapter 25 amplifies the message of the novel. Throughout the state of California, the modern science of agriculture leads to abundant crops. As the fruit ripens, the market price of fruit decreases. Across the country as the depression deepens, the demand for fruits and vegetables dries up, and the fruit dries up as well, on the branch and the vine. There is no profit to be made from the crop, and, therefore, no reason to hire pickers. Let the crops rot or be dumped into rivers or burned with kerosene, the owners say, rather than incur a monetary loss, as children starve from malnutrition. Steinbeck ends the chapter with the following: "In the souls of the people, the grapes of wrath are filling and growing heavy, growing heavy for the vintage."

After a month at Weedpatch, Ma insists the Joads move on. Only Tom has found work in the area, and that for just five days. She worries that the pleasant atmosphere in the camp has encouraged complacency and stagnation, and the family supplies are perilously low. The next morning, bowing to Ma's authority, the Joads once more drive away in the Hudson. On the way north, a nail punctures one of the tires, and as Tom and Al repair it, a man drives by and offers a job picking peaches at the Hooper Ranch, only 35 miles away. Eagerly, the family follows the directions given, but as they approach, they witness a large police presence blocking the entrance to the Hooper place. Unbeknownst to the Joads, they have been hired as strikebreakers. Paid five cents a box, the entire Joad family, including Ruthie and Winfield, manages only 20 boxes in the first day. Ma takes her dollar credit to the company store, and discovers how little it will buy with markups of 20 to 25 percent. She shames the store manager into giving her 10 cents' worth of sugar, and then returns to the dilapidated shack provided by the Hooper Corporation to prepare supper.

After a skimpy meal, Tom wanders to the front gate to investigate the demonstration he had witnessed earlier that day. Carefully avoiding the armed guards, Tom crawls over the fence, and to his delight encounters Casy in a tent with the strikers. During his imprisonment for the assault on the deputy, Casy translated his philosophy of love and unity into a powerful message, and has become a strike leader. While Tom and Casy share their recent experiences, a sentry alerts them to the approach of the Hooper guards and they attempt to escape. Caught, Casy turns to his persecutors and cries plaintively, "You fellas don't know what you're doin'. You're helpin' to starve kids." A heavyset man crushes Casy's skull with a pick handle. Overcome with rage and revenge, Tom wrenches the pick handle away, and beats Casy's killer to death, but in the process receives a maiming blow to his face.

Marked now as the attacker, Tom creeps carefully back to his family's cabin and waits for the dawn. He relates the story of the dual murders of the previous evening when the family awakes, and predicts accurately the price for a box of peaches will plummet by 50 percent now that the strike is broken. He appeals to Ma to allow him to sneak away, but she is determined to protect her son. Over the course of the day, as Tom hides, Rose of Sharon attacks him for bringing possible harm to her baby; Winfield collapses in the early stages of malnutrition; a host of pickers willing to work for two and a half cents a box storm the Hooper Ranch; and Ma makes plans for the family to make its escape intact. Pa no longer even makes a pretense of having control of his family.

Having made a cavelike nest for Tom in the back of the truck, the Joads leave the Hooper Ranch, and take the backroads north, hoping to avoid the police. After 20 miles, the family spots a sign advertising work for cotton pickers next to a group of abandoned railcars. Tom convinces his mother to allow him to hide in a concealed culvert nearby while his face heals, and the family lives in one of the boxcars and picks cotton. Coming from Oklahoma, the Joad family understands about picking cotton. They enter a period of relative prosperity, and having staked their claim early on half a boxcar, they even have room to spread out and have a modicum of privacy. Unfortunately, Ruthie divulges the family's secret about her older brother and his hiding place during a childish quarrel. Ma makes her way to Tom's sanctuary and bids farewell to him forever. In their last conversation, Ma repeats her blind caresses at the beginning of the book when he returned home from prison. In the darkness of the cave, she memorizes his face with her fingers, and listens to his voice as he announces his intention to follow Casy's example. Tom begins quietly by saying, "I now know a fellow ain't no good alone." And then he builds to one of the most famous passages in American literature. He declares he will be "ever'where" there is injustice, "wherever there's a fight so hungry people can eat," and "wherever there's a cop beating up a guy." Like Paul to Jesus Christ, Tom has become Casy's most fervent apostle and will stand as an evangelical champion to all the little people of the world.

Returning to the boxcar, Ma discovers her family will become further diminished. Al has decided to marry Aggie Wainwright, the daughter of the people who share the abandoned railcar, and take a job as a mechanic in a nearby town. As winter approaches, the migrants know they must accept every job, and Ma agrees to pick a small field of late-planted cotton. Rose of Sharon insists on going along, although the birth of her child is imminent. Returning from the fields, the migrants huddle in the railcars as early winter rains intensify. Beginning with a drought of biblical proportions, the novel ends with a flood resembling Noah's deluge. Rosasharn gives birth to a stillborn baby, while the men of the camp valiantly but futilely attempt to stem the rising water from the nearby river. Uncle John, tasked to bury the baby boy, instead puts him in a box and floats him downriver to remind the town folk of the migrant misery. As the water threatens to inundate the boxcars, Ma leads what remains of her family to an abandoned barn on a hill overlooking the flood. There they encounter a starving man with a young son who has taken shelter from the storm. Wordlessly, Ma communicates with Rose of Sharon, and Rose offers her breast to the starving man. Like Tom following Casy's lead, Rose has accepted her mother's mentorship, and expanded her heart to include the "family of man."

EARLY CRITICISM

Although *The Grapes of Wrath* has been regarded as Steinbeck's major work, debates over the novel's social and artistic values have always been the main concerns of Steinbeck critics. Critical reception of *The Grapes of Wrath* at the time of its publication was largely, but not exclusively, positive. Even reviewers who did not like the book's message of the value of collective behavior and the possibility of revolution nevertheless praised its artistry. A few, however, expressed bewilderment as the novel achieved best-seller status in a very short time.

Though not as common, negative reviews about *The Grapes of Wrath* did emerge. *Time's* critic suggested that the book was a thinly disguised propaganda tract in which "social awareness outruns artistic skill." Burton Rasco, writing for *Newsweek,* indicated the "book has beautiful and even magnificent passages in it," but that it suffered from a lack of organization." From the *Partisan Review,* Philip Rahv called the novel "too didactic and long-winded," and said "its unconscionable length is out of all proportion to its substance." Speaking not as a critic, but as a social commentator, Father Arthur D. Spearman, S.J., in an article for the *San Francisco Examiner,* excoriated the book for its "behaviouristic philosophy of sex-indulgence," its inconsistency, and its promotion of "Communist propaganda." From England, Kate O'Brien, the critic for the *Spectator,* took issue with Steinbeck's style, writing that it "epitomises the intolerable sentimentality of American realism." Another leftist magazine, the *New Republic,* carried a review by Malcolm Cowley, who wrote that *The Grapes of Wrath* shows Steinbeck's pity, not love, to the migrants. However, Cowley did not agree with critics who have said that the novel was the greatest novel of the decade, because "it doesn't rank with the best of Hemingway or Dos Passos." Instead, Cowley ranks *The Grapes of Wrath* with *Uncle Tom's Cabin,*" one of the "great angry books."

Among the early reviews Edmund Wilson's criticism of *The Grapes of Wrath* is probably the most interesting. According to Wilson, "*The Grapes of Wrath* was a propaganda novel, full of preachments and sociological interludes, and developed on an epic scale." Wilson believes that Steinbeck's work was ideologically biased. He points out that the preacher in *The Grapes of Wrath* is disillusioned about human moralities. Wilson further states that the subject of *The Grapes of Wrath,* which deals with human society, is of no more significance than the subject in THE RED PONY, which deals with horses, because, to Wilson, they both are about "loyalty to life itself."

On the positive side, though with some reservations, Charles Poore, in his column for the *New York Times,* praised Steinbeck's "magnificent new novel" and particularly singled out the "characters whose full and complete actuality will withstand any scrutiny." Among other things in the book that Poore liked is Steinbeck's sympathy with the characters; however, Poore disliked the intercalary chapters, suggesting that the author "obscures the story with the moral." Clifton Fadiman, writing for the *New Yorker,* noted the book's faults, especially the ending which he termed "the tawdriest kind of fake symbolism." Still, he suggested that the book "may very possibly be . . . The Great American Novel," and that it "may actually effect something like a revolution." In his review for the *Nation,* Louis Kronenberger called the work "the most moving and disturbing social novel of our time," but went on to say it demonstrated "the work of a writer who is still self-indulgent, still undisciplined." George Stevens, a critic for the *Saturday Review,* called the book "colorful, dramatic, subtle, coarse, comic and tragic," and that it was "worth all the talk" and "anticipation." In his article for the *New York Herald Tribune,* Joseph Henry Jackson identified the novel as "far and away the finest book [Steinbeck] has written," and unlike many of his fellow critics, he thought the intercalary chapters to be one of the book's strengths, contributing to its power and lasting effect.

One of the reasons that critics and readers liked the book in those early years was that thousands upon thousands of people like the Joads had been rolling westward themselves. Steinbeck's story touched the common experience of many such migrants. As Poore pointed out, the book succeeded not because Steinbeck created a world for the reader; instead, the novelist did a superb job helping his readers see, feel, and understand what they themselves had gone through.

Peter Monro Jack speaks of *The Grapes of Wrath* as a novel from the depths of the writer's heart, a sincerity seldom equaled. In his review entitled "John Steinbeck's New Novel Brims with Anger and Pity," he regards Steinbeck as one of a handful of writers, including Hemingway, Caldwell, Faulkner, Dos Passos, and MacLeish, who are looking at America "with revolutionary eyes." Similarly, reviewer Joseph Henry Jackson calls *The Grapes of Wrath* a magnificent book that reflects the work of a mature novelist. Jackson believes that the novel is Steinbeck's best work up to that point.

CONTEMPORARY PERSPECTIVES

Today arguments still persist over the worth of *The Grapes of Wrath*, not only as a literary work, but also as a depiction of the immiseration of impoverished tenant farmers and migrant agricultural laborers. Brad Leithauser, writing for the *New Yorker*, indicated that the "chief wonder of the novel is that it's as good as it is" because the novel shows both Steinbeck's strengths and his weaknesses. According to Leithauser, the writer's strengths include his sympathy for the disenfranchised, moral urgency, and narrative propulsion, whereas his weaknesses are "repetitiveness, simplistic politics, and sentimentality." Keith Windschuttle criticizes the book for mythologizing the "Okies" and perpetuating a portrait of the Great Depression that is "outright false or exaggerated beyond belief." Windschuttle suggests that the theme of the book owes more to Karl Marx's *Das Kapital* than it does to the Old Testament's Exodus.

Within academic circles the novel remains a staple of American literature courses and retains the interest of scholars. Richard Astro notes that the book's overall structure is shaped by Steinbeck's PHALANX theory, "which controls individual men" and "can achieve ends beyond the reach of individual men." According to Astro, the three central characters, Jim Casy, Tom Joad, and Ma Joad, all embrace Steinbeck's "unified view of life." Malcom Bradbury suggests that the work is in the tradition of Ralph Waldo Emerson, whose philosophy of transcendentalism influenced Steinbeck's "naturalism" and "biological and deterministic account of human nature." Bradbury indicates that *The Grapes of Wrath* contains two very American and Emersonian themes: "hopeful American westering" and "heroic evolution." On a more general level, John Timmerman makes note of Steinbeck's claim that the novel has "five layers of meaning," and observes that "readers would easily double the number of layers." The intricacy and multiple levels in *The Grapes of Wrath* help maintain its stature as an American masterpiece.

Among the major studies on *The Grapes of Wrath* is Robert DeMott's *Working Days: The Journals of The Grapes of Wrath, 1938–1941*. DeMott's book examines the journals Steinbeck kept while writing *The Grapes of Wrath*. It reveals the astonishing fact that Steinbeck wrote this dense and complex novel in 100 days, by hand. DeMott provides the journal entries with a biographical introduction, commentary and illuminating notes, which offer an unprecedented insight into the novel.

Other leading critics who have written important works on *The Grapes of Wrath* include Warren French, John Ditsky, David Wyatt, and Barbara A. Heavilin. Situating the novel in the framework of modernism, French argues that the book transcends the ironic detachment of modernism with a new affirmative conception of individual regeneration, claiming that the story of the Joad family in the novel portrays the education of the heart. Ditsky traces the critical reputation of the novel, offering a sizable gathering of reviews and broad selection of scholarship. In emphasizing the significance of *The Grapes of Wrath* in Steinbeck's career, David Wyatt argues that the book offers Steinbeck's view of the California migration as a "result," not a "cause." Wyatt further notes that the work parallels Steinbeck's nonteleological thinking, which holds that the world has no origins or ends.

As for a more recent evaluation of the book, Barbara A. Heavilin suggests that "it is highly possible that the real position of *The Grapes of Wrath* in the American canon," as indicated by how much it is read and how often it is assigned in the curriculum, "may continue to decline in the 21st century." On the other hand, Heavilin also states that the current interest in the self, the individual's identity, may contribute to reversing the neglect of *The Grapes of Wrath* in academia. Another trend that Heavilin has identified is the current educational interest in emotional intelligence, or empathy, which reveals a discovery of the obvious on the part of educators: that human beings are complex creatures whose abilities depend on heart and soul as well as intellect. According to Heavilin, *The Grapes of Wrath* shows that Steinbeck knows all of this most passionately with his own heart, mind, and soul, and the book will probably continue to resonate in the minds and souls of readers for generations to come.

SYNOPSIS

Chapter 1
A drought settles across the midwestern states, followed by savage winds that carry away the arable topsoil, wiping out the meager cotton crops and cutting visibility for hundreds of miles.

Chapter 2
Tom Joad, a lean, brooding man, hitches a ride to the family farm. He is on parole after spending four years in prison for hitting a man with a shovel and killing him in self-defense.

Chapter 3
A land turtle makes its way slowly toward some unseen goal. A truck driver swerves to hit the animal, catching the edge of the shell and spinning it off the highway. The turtle flips itself over and patiently continues its journey.

Chapter 4
Tom encounters Jim Casy, an old family friend, and the two men continue together toward the farm. Casy explains that he gave up preaching because of his deep doubts, leaving him with "the call to lead the people, an' no place to lead 'em." The two men arrive at the farm to find that it has been recently abandoned.

Chapter 5
The landowners foreclose on the farms and force out the sharecroppers. They have discovered that one wage-earning man with a tractor can farm the land of 12 or 14 families. The people leave their land, their houses, and their lives, and the little plots of land are bulldozed into large, profit-earning corporate farms.

Chapter 6
Tom finds the house empty and the family's belongings gone. Muley Graves, a neighboring farmer, finds the bewildered men and explains to Tom that his family has recently moved to the house of his Uncle John, where they are preparing to buy a car and move west. Muley tells how his family moved to California to look for work. But he refuses to leave the place he grew up on, and so he haunts the empty land like a ghost, dodging the farm superintendent and eking out a meager living trapping rabbit and squirrels. The three men settle down to cook dinner. Casy senses that something important is happening to the people. He determines to join the Joad family on their journey west. The three men hide in the fields when the farm superintendent arrives looking for trespassers.

Chapter 7
As the banks foreclose on the farms, a great wave of homeless families prepare to migrate west in search of work. They sweep down on the used-car lots, trading their farm implements and the last of their money for any beat-up old wreck that will carry them and their meager possessions to the promised land.

Chapter 8
Tom and Casy arrive at Uncle John's farm where they find the Joad family preparing to move. All the family's belongings are piled high in the front yard and Tom's father, Old Tom, is busy converting an old Hudson Super Six sedan into a pickup truck. Tom is reunited with his large family: Pa and Ma, Granma and Grampa, Uncle John, and his siblings Noah, Al, Rose of Sharon, Ruthie and Winfield. Ma, "the citadel of the family," is nervous. She worries that Tom is resentful or angry about going to prison. He assures her that he is fine.

Chapter 9

The landless farmers gather together their belongings and take them to town to sell to the brokers and pawn agents who flock to take advantage of their sad circumstances. What that they cannot sell they must leave—or burn. They become restless and the urgency to move sets in.

Chapter 10

Al loads the Hudson with their remaining furniture and farm implements to sell in town. Ma confesses her hopes and fears about what awaits them in California. She has a handbill that advertises the need for fruit pickers there. She dreams of finding work and renting a little white house on the edge of a green orchard. Tom is less optimistic. He tells of meeting a man from California who claimed the fruit pickers live on the edge of starvation in dirty camps. The men return from the town humiliated and defeated: they received only $18 for their belongings. Rose of Sharon, Tom's plump younger sister, presents her new husband, Connie. She tells Tom proudly that she is pregnant. The family decides to leave the following day. In a flurry of activity the men slaughter pigs and salt the meat while the women prepare what remains of their belongings to be packed on the truck. Casy comments to Tom that Ma is looking tired under the strain of the move. While Pa and Al load the truck, Muley Graves appears to say good-bye. He asks the Joads to keep a lookout for his family and to tell them that he is well. He reminds Tom that he will break his parole if he leaves the state. Grandpa, a stubborn, cantankerous old man, refuses to leave the farm. They drug his coffee and load his sleeping figure aboard the truck.

Chapter 11

All across the countryside the land has been abandoned. Empty houses crumble in neglect. Only the great silver tractor sheds are new and alive.

Chapter 12

Highway 66 carries the steady wave of migrants westward toward the rich California valleys. They travel alone or in caravans, individuals, families, entire communities, making their campsites along the roadside, scurrying for spare parts and needed supplies.

Chapter 13

The Joads make their way slowly westward in the ancient Hudson. A gas station attendant tells Tom that 50 or 60 carloads of people pass every day headed for California. Connie and Rosasharn watch a beautiful new Zephyr automobile zoom by, and they dream of someday owning one. They watch helplessly as the family dog is run over in the highway. Rosasharn is afraid that witnessing violence is bad for the baby. The family turns onto Route 66 and they join the stream of migrants on that great western road. Ma worries about Tom crossing the state line and violating his parole. He assures her that he will be all right as long as he stays out of trouble. As night falls, the family pulls into a roadside campground where they introduce themselves to Mr. and Mrs. Wilson, a middle-aged couple from Kansas. The Wilsons are also traveling to California, but their automobile has broken down. Grandpa becomes ill. Mrs. Wilson invites him to rest in her tent, where he dies of a stroke. They have little money and are forced to bury the old man in an unmarked grave next to the highway. Al fixes Mr. Wilson's car and the two families agree to travel together.

Chapter 14

The western states begin to feel the pressure of the great migration, and the landowners grow nervous as the discontented, landless men gather together into groups.

Chapter 15

Al and Mae work at a small roadside diner on Route 66, serving truck drivers and tourists and the occasional beat-up, overloaded wreck carrying a desperate family headed west to find work.

Chapter 16

Rose of Sharon and Connie make plans to live in a town so that Connie can work and study. Mr. Wilson's car throws a rod, forcing the caravan to a stop. The Wilsons offer to stay behind so that the Joads can continue. Tom suggests that the family continue on to California to start earning money while he and Casy stay behind to fix the car. The men agree on the plan, but Ma revolts, threatening her husband with a jack handle. She insists that the family stay together. The others go ahead to make camp while Tom and Al look for a junkyard. Tom tells the one-eyed attendant to clean up and stop pitying himself. He and Al find the needed spare and fix the Wilsons' car by flashlight. At the campground they meet a man dressed in rags who is returning from California. He warns them of the labor contractors exploiting workers for starvation wages. His words make the gathered men nervous and uncertain.

Chapter 17

The traveling families gather together in camps, seeking out one another for support and assurance. And where camps form, solidarity is established and group etiquette develops. Thus they make the transition from farm men to migrant men.

Chapter 18

The family crosses Arizona and arrives at the edge of the great desert. They make camp along the banks of the Colorado River and prepare for the crossing. Tom and his father meet two men who are returning to their homes in the east. They explain that all the land in California is owned and that a man can hardly make enough wages to feed himself and his family. What is worse, they say, is feeling like an outsider, an "Okie," and being looked at with suspicion and hate. Noah leaves the family, telling Tom that he intends to walk down the river and live by fishing. Grandma becomes ill under the stress of the trip. Ma denies that the old woman is dying and refuses to let a group of church ladies pray over her. The sheriff arrives and threatens to run the family in if they do not move along. Mrs. Wilson is too sick to continue. She knows that she is going to die and she asks Casy to say a prayer for her. Meanwhile, Grandma's condition is worsening. The family drives frantically across the blazing desert, trying to escape the heat. Finally they reach the end of the desert, cross the mountains, and descend into the great green central valleys. The family's elation is broken by Ma, who tells them that Grandma died during the night. She did not want to tell anybody before, for fear that it would prevent them from crossing the desert. They take the old woman to the coroner and pay their last few dollars to have her buried in a pauper's grave.

Chapter 19

The western settlers steal the land from the Mexicans and settle down to be farmers. Farming becomes an industry and many of those farmers fail. The lands consolidate into ever larger farms, and the great landowners begin to import labor for planting and harvest. Migrant laborers set up their camps on the edge of every town; they have only two hungers, land and food, and the intensity of their hunger strikes fear in the landowners. A feeling arises: The migrants are invaders and they must be kept down or they will rise up. Police raid the squatters' camps, declaring them a menace to the public health. The migrants move on, looking for another camp farther down the road.

Chapter 20

The Joads stop at a camp outside Bakersville. Floyd Knowles, a young camp resident, explains to Tom that the camps are always called "Hooverville" and that the laborers drift from one to another looking for work or getting pushed along by the sheriffs who do not want them to settle too long in any given area. He explains that there are more workers than there are jobs and that the owners bid down the wages to starvation levels. When Tom suggests that the workers get together and refuse to work, Floyd warns that the authorities bust up any sort of organization and blacklist the leaders. He warns Tom to act simple and say nothing to the cops. While the men talk, Ma prepares supper. The smell of stew brings a group of hungry children to the cooking fire. She does not know what to do as there is hardly enough for her own family. She cannot resist the hungry eyes of the children and gives them each a little taste of stew. After dinner a labor contractor arrives in the camps. When Floyd insists that the man guarantee how much they will be paid, the contractor calls a sheriff and accuses Floyd of agitation. Tom trips the sheriff, allowing his new friend to escape. Casy takes the blame for Tom and is carried away by the police. Uncle John admits that he has been holding out $5. He takes the money and goes off into the trees to get drunk. Meanwhile, Floyd warns Al and Tom to get out of the camp before dark because the sheriff and his buddies will be back to get revenge. The family gathers its belongings while Tom looks for the drunk Uncle John, who refuses to go back to the camp. Tom gives his uncle a measured blow to the chin and carries him to the truck. Connie abandons his wife and the family and heads home. Tom watches from a distance as the sheriff's men burn down the camp.

Chapter 21

The townspeople feel threatened by the hungry migrants who will work for any price, or even just a morsel of food for their children. They form vigilante committees to drive the migrants from their communities. Meanwhile the large farms purchase the canneries and manipulate the prices, driving the small farmers out of business. Anger grows.

Chapter 22

The Joad family moves to Weedpatch, a government camp organized and run by its residents. Tom finds work with Mr. Thomas, a farmer who informs him that the Growers Association is forcing him to lower his wages from 30 cents to 25 cents per hour. He explains bitterly that if he does not cooperate he will be denied a crop loan for the next season. Mr. Thomas warns the men that the Growers Association is planning to cause a riot at the dance hosted every Saturday at the government camp. Meanwhile at the camp, Ma nervously prepares the family for a visit from the Ladies Committee. She is taken with the camp and its amenities.

Chapter 23

The migrant people look humbly for any form of pleasure on the road, making music or even attending religious revival meetings.

Chapter 24

Saturday is the day of the big camp dance. The camp's Central Committee prepares to confront the troublemakers that have been predicted. Guards have been posted around the perimeter of the camp and a group of men mix in the crowd to weed out the troublemakers. Tom spots three men trying to start a fight on the dance floor. The men are surrounded and escorted toward the administration building. They admit that they have been paid by the Grower's Association to start a fight so

that the police could come into the camp and arrest the inhabitants.

Chapter 25

The great California fruit harvest begins. The big farmers destroy the crops to keep the prices up. Mountains of fruit are left to rot and go to waste. The anger deepens.

Chapter 26

After a month without work the Joads are almost out of money. Ma begins urging the men to do something. She worries that winter is coming and Rose of Sharon is nearing term. The men decide that they must leave Weedpatch and head north to the cotton fields. Tom and Al are fixing a flat tire when a man pulls up and tells them that there is work 40 miles away at the Hooper Ranch. As they near the ranch they are stopped by the police who lead them through a group of angry men who surround the ranch. The whole family pitches in picking peaches for a nickel a box and by sunset they have earned a dollar, barely enough to buy supper in the company store. Tom sneaks out of the camp to talk to the men outside. He is surprised to find Casy, who explains that the men are striking. He says that Mr. Hooper will only pay five cents a box until the strike breaks, then he will lower the price to two and a half cents. The strike camp is raided and Casy is clubbed to death. Tom kills Casy's attacker and is wounded by a blow to the head. He makes his way back to the peach camp where he hides in the family's cabin. Rosasharn is hysterical with worry. She fears that the trouble is going to hurt the baby. The family abandons the ranch and finds work picking cotton. They set up camp in an old boxcar that they share with the large Wainright family. Ma makes Tom promise that he will not run away. He hides in the woods while his face heals.

Chapter 27

Winter is on the way. The landowners must bring in the crops before the rain starts. The cotton pickers labor furiously over the fields trying to earn enough money to eat and save a little.

Chapter 28

Ruthie boasts to the camp children that her brother Tom killed a man and is hiding in the woods. Ma warns her son that he must leave. She insists that he take the $7 that she has managed to save. Tom tells her that he has been thinking about the things Casy said and that he has decided to organize the people. Al announces that he and the Wainrights' daughter Aggie are going away so that he can find a job in a garage. The next day, Rose of Sharon takes a chill while working in the field. The family rushes for cover as rain begins to pour down on the countryside.

Chapter 29

Great storms sweep across the region, driving the migrant people under shelter and ruining the remaining crops. Terror comes with the realization that there will be no more work for three months.

Chapter 30

After three days of uninterrupted rain the river is rising dangerously close to the boxcars. The family is unable to leave when Rose of Sharon's fever causes her to go into labor. Pa urges the men to throw up a bank against the rising water. They struggle mightily, but the river carries the dike away and the water continues to rise. Rosasharn's baby is stillborn; Uncle John places the little corpse in a box that he sends floating downstream. The family abandons the boxcar and seeks a dry place. They take cover in a barn where they find a young boy and his dying father. The boy explains that his father has not eaten for six days and that he is dying of starvation. Rose of Sharon lies down next to the old man and offers him her breast.

CHARACTERS AND PLACES

Casy, Jim   A character in *The Grapes of Wrath*, Jim is an ex-preacher who accompanies the Joad family westward from Oklahoma to California. He is middle-aged and stringy, with stiff gray hair and heavy, protruding eyes. After fighting with a sheriff, Casy gives himself up in order to save Tom Joad from prison. While in jail he discovers the power of the group and becomes a labor agitator. He leads the strike of the Hooper Ranch peach pickers before being clubbed to death in a raid.

Feeley, Willy   A character in *The Grapes of Wrath*, Willy is a young man from a sharecropping family. The Joad family consider him a traitor of his own kind because he drives the tractor that plows over the Joads' land.

Graves, Muley   A character in *The Grapes of Wrath*, Muley refuses to leave his land when the bank forecloses on it. A lean, short man, he lives "like a ghost," hiding from the superintendent during the day and hunting at night. When Tom Joad finds the Joad family farm abandoned, Muley tells him of the farm foreclosures and explains that his family is staying at Uncle John's farm.

Hooper Ranch   A location in *The Grapes of Wrath*, the ranch is a large peach orchard where Jim Casy is killed leading a strike, and Tom Joad kills the man who has slain Jim Casy and is forced to go into hiding.

Hudson Super Six   Old-model sedan that Pa Joad converts into a truck for their trip to California in *The Grapes of Wrath*. Despite its dilapidated appearance, and unreliability, the vehicle becomes the Joad family's home during their odyssey to California.

Joad, Al   The third son and Tom's younger brother in *The Grapes of Wrath*. In the novel, Al is 16, a young man who dreams of becoming a mechanic. He is responsible for the old Hudson automobile that carries the Joads on their journey to California, where Al finally leaves his family to marry Aggie Wainright, a beautiful 16-year-old girl. Though he deeply admires his older brother, Tom, Al is interested only in his own fulfillment. Al insists that he has to leave the family and make a life on his own. His adolescent thoughtlessness serves as a contrast to Tom's maturity in the novel.

Joad, Grampa (William James Joad)   A character in *The Grapes of Wrath*, Grampa is a "lean, ragged, quick old man" whose right leg comes out of joint. He and Granma constantly fight and bicker. At the beginning of the novel, Grampa refuses to go to California with the family. Tom has to get him drunk to get him on the truck bound to leave his home. But just beyond Bethany, Oklahoma, on the first night away from his ancestors' homestead, Grampa has a stroke and dies in the tent of Ivy and Sairy Wilson. He is the first casualty of the journey west.

Joad, Granma   She is the wife of Grampa in *The Grapes of Wrath*. She is as cantankerous and mean as her husband. She wears a shapeless Mother Hubbard gown. After her husband dies, she never recovers from sorrow. She dies between Needles, California, and the inspection station at Daggett. To avoid being stopped by the inspectors, Ma Joad sits up with the dead body and tells the inspectors that the old woman is very sick. Granma is buried at Bakersfield.

Joad, Ma   The mother of Noah, Tom, Rose of Sharon, Al, Ruthie, and Winfield in *The Grapes of Wrath*. Ma is "the citadel of the family," and offers an almost mystical source of inspiration for the Joads. She knows all of the strengths and weaknesses of the family, and both encourages and incites her family members to resist the impulse to surrender to their plight. She intuitively understands the necessity of unity for the good of the whole, whether it is the unified endeavors of a family unit, or the far larger organization of migrant farmworkers.

Joad, Noah   A character in *The Grapes of Wrath*, Noah is the oldest son of the Joad family, and apparently suffered congenital brain damage at birth. Though he is not retarded, he is "strange." He speaks little and carries a strange look on his

Jane Darwell as Ma Joad in the 1940 film production of *The Grapes of Wrath* *(Photofest)*

face. He is never angry or upset, nor does he have any sexual urges. When the family gets to the Colorado River, he leaves his family and insists on staying by the river and living a hermit's life.

Joad, Pa (Old Tom)   A character in *The Grapes of Wrath*, Pa, also known as Old Tom, is the father of young Tom, Noah, Al, Rose of Sharon, Ruthie, and Winfield. He is a lean, aging man, whose authority as head of the family is slowly ceded to his wife as he gives in to the helplessness of their situation. He is a good, hardworking man, devoted to the land and to tradition. However, he is unable to expand his vision beyond the immediate concerns of his family, nor is he able to adjust and effectively respond to the series of misfortunes besetting his family. Initially, Pa appears strong and decisive, but by the end of the book, his role as patriarch has completely evaporated, and a new family structure has emerged with Ma as matriarch.

Joad, Ruthie   A character in *The Grapes of Wrath*, Ruthie is the youngest daughter of Ma and Pa Joad. She is 12 years old and is close to her younger brother, Winfield. In a fight with some girls at the boxcar, she inadvertently reveals Tom's role in the killing at the Hooper Ranch, forcing her brother to hide from the police.

Joad, Tom   The second-oldest son of Ma and Pa Joad and the male protagonist in *The Grapes of Wrath*. At the beginning, having recently been paroled from prison after killing a man, he expresses little remorse for his crime, and only the desire to satisfy his own immediate needs. He joins the family in the trek westward, superficially understanding a responsibility to his kin. Eventually, as Tom bears witness to the unrelenting suffering of migrant workers and the injustices levied against them, he chooses to fight for the downtrodden, knowing he may lose his life in the struggle.

Joad, Uncle John   Pa Joad's brother in *The Grapes of Wrath*. Depicted as "the loneliest goddamn man in the world," he blames himself for the untimely death of his wife, and worries that his sins have brought all the troubles down on his family.

He places Rosasharn's dead baby in a fruit box and floats it down the river to remind the people in the towns of the suffering of his people.

Joad, Winfield   The youngest child of Ma and Pa Joad in *The Grapes of Wrath*. He is 10 years old and almost dies from malnutrition and deprivation.

Joad family   The main characters in *The Grapes of Wrath*. This family of poor sharecroppers is evicted from their failing land in Oklahoma and forced to make an arduous migration to California where they are exploited and persecuted. The experiences of the Joad family during the migration from the Dust Bowl to California lie at the center of *The Grapes of Wrath*, and loosely follow the biblical book of Exodus. Like the Israelites, who eventually learned to become one people during the 40 years of wandering in the desert on their way from Egypt to the promised land, the Joads, too, must learn the value of cohesiveness and adaptation to survive.

Knowles, Floyd   A character in *The Grapes of Wrath*, Floyd is a young migrant worker with a wife and a child; he shares his experiences with the Joad family before escaping arrest in a confrontation with a labor contractor.

Rivers, Connie   A character in *The Grapes of Wrath*, Connie is Rose of Sharon's 19-year-old husband. He is a sharp-faced, lean young man of Texas stock, with pale blue eyes. He dreams of learning a trade and living in a town, and finally abandons his wife and disappears.

Rose of Sharon (Rosasharn)   The oldest daughter of Ma and Pa Joad and wife of Connie Rivers in *The Grapes of Wrath*. She is also called "Rosasharn." She has a soft and round face. In the novel she changes from an immature and self-absorbed young woman who is only concerned with outward appearance and romance to a strong and giving adult. As food and shelter become an urgent issue for the Joad family, she complains and worries because she is pregnant. She is a "Jesus lover" at the Weedpatch government camp, where it is predicted that her child will be born dead and damned. Abandoned by her young husband, she gives birth to a dead baby, ending many of her unrealistic dreams for the future. The novel ends with her offering her breast milk to a starving man, which demonstrates her newfound willingness to share her bounty with humanity.

Thomas, Mr.   A character in *The Grapes of Wrath*, Mr. Thomas is the owner of a small ranch. He warns Tom Joad that the valley Growers Association is planning on starting a riot at the Weedpatch Camp.

Wainright family   Characters in *The Grapes of Wrath*, the Wainright family is a large one that shares a boxcar with the Joad family at the cotton camps. Al Joad decides to marry Aggie, the pretty 16-year-old daughter of Mr. and Mrs. Wainright.

Weedpatch Camp   A place in *The Grapes of Wrath*, Weedpatch is a government aid camp set up for migratory workers and their families and administrated by Jim Rawley, a lean, generous man with a thin, brown, lined face and merry eyes. When the Joad family is burned out of Hooverville by angry vigilantes, they seek asylum in Weedpatch Camp. The Weedpatch residents organize Saturday night dances that become famous, attracting people from miles around. The Growers Association plots to start a riot at the camp so that they can send in the police and bust it up.

Wilsons, the   The first couple the Joad family encounters on their trip westward in *The Grapes of Wrath*. Traveling from Kansas to California, Ivy and his wife, Sairy Wilson, lend their tent for Grandpa Joad to die in. Al Joad fixes their car and they agree to travel in caravan with the Joads. Sairy Wilson is slowly dying from breast cancer and can travel no farther than the Colorado River.

THE FILM: *THE GRAPES OF WRATH* (TWENTIETH CENTURY–FOX, 1940)

Based on the novel by John Steinbeck

Screenplay: NUNNALLY JOHNSON
Director: John Ford
Producer: DARRYL F. ZANUCK

Musical Score: Alfred Newman
Photography: Gregg Toland
Tom Joad: HENRY FONDA
Ma Joad: Jane Darwell
Casy: John Carradine
Grampa Joad: Charley Grapewin
Rose of Sharon: Dorris Bowdon
Pa Joad: Russell Simpson
Al Joad: O. Z. Whitehead
Muley: John Qualen
Noah Joad: Frank Sully
Uncle John Joad: Frank Darien
Winfield Joad: Darryl Hickman
Ruth Joad: Shirley Mills

One of the best adaptations of a Steinbeck novel to film, *The Grapes of Wrath* preserved Steinbeck's classic novel in both spirit and letter, making only small concessions for the sake of cinematic necessity. Some critics have claimed that the film softened the novel's criticisms of those Steinbeck judged to be the guilty parties in the oppression of migrant workers. Another criticism is that the film's slight reordering of events gives it a lighter ending than the grim hopelessness offered by the novel. For the most part, however, the film was daringly loyal to the book. Indeed, the film portrayed in such stark realism the horrible conditions of the migrant laborers that *Life* magazine published an article showing scenes from the movie alongside actual photographs of the migratory camps in an attempt to prove to skeptics that the poverty shown in the film was not exaggerated. The film also prompted Woody Guthrie to write his famous ballad "Tom Joad."

FURTHER READING

Astro, Richard. *John Steinbeck and Edward F. Ricketts: The Shaping of a Novelist.* Minneapolis: University of Minnesota Press, 1973.

Bloom, Harold. *John Steinbeck's* The Grapes of Wrath. New York: Chelsea House Publications, 1996.

Bradbury, Malcom. *The Modern American Novel.* New ed. Oxford: Oxford University Press, 1992, 138–142.

Cowley, Malcolm. "American Tragedy." *New Republic,* May 3, 1939, 382–383.

DeMott, Robert, ed. *Working Days: The Journals of* The Grapes of Wrath, *1938–1941.* New York: Viking Press, 1989.

Ditsky, John, ed. *Critical Essays on* The Grapes of Wrath. Boston: G.K. Hall, 1989.

———. *John Steinbeck: Life, Work and Criticism.* Fredericton, Canada: York Press, 1985.

Fadiman, Clifton. Books. *New Yorker,* April 15, 1939, 81–83.

French, Warren, ed. *A Companion to* The Grapes of Wrath. New York: Penguin, 1987.

———. *John Steinbeck's Fiction Revisited.* New York: Twayne, 1994.

Heavilin, Barbara A. *John Steinbeck's* The Grapes of Wrath: *A Reference Guide.* Westport, Conn.: Greenwood Press, 2002.

———. *The Critical Response to John Steinbeck's* The Grapes of Wrath. Westport, Conn.: Greenwood Press, 2000.

Hinton, Rebecca. "Steinbeck's 'The Grapes of Wrath.'" *Explicator* (Winter 1998): 101.

Jack, Peter Monro. "John Steinbeck's New Novel Brims with Anger and Pity." *New York Times Book Review,* April 16, 1939, 88.

Jackson, Joseph Henry. "The Finest Book John Steinbeck Has Written." *New York Herald Tribune,* April 16, 1939, Books section, 3.

Kronenberger, Louis. "Hungry Caravan." *Nation,* April 15, 1939, 440–441.

Leithauser, Brad. "Books." *New Yorker,* August 21, 1989, 90–92.

O'Brien, Kate. "Fiction." *Spectator* (England) 163, September 15, 1939, 386.

"Okies." *Time,* April 17, 1939, 87.

Poore, Charles. "Books of the Times." *New York Times,* April 14, 1939, 27.

Rahv, Philip. "A Variety of Fiction." *Partisan Review* (Spring 1939): 111–112.

Rascoe, Burton. "But . . . Not . . . Ferdinand." *Newsweek,* April 17, 1939, 46.

Spearman, Arthur D., S.J. "Steinbeck's *Grapes of Wrath* Branded as Red Propaganda by Father A. D. Spearman." *San Francisco Examiner,* June 4, 1939, Section 1. 12.

Steinbeck, John. *The Grapes of Wrath.* New York: Viking, 1939.

Stevens, George. "Steinbeck's Uncovered Wagon." *Saturday Review,* April 15, 1939, 3–4.

Timmerman, John. "*The Grapes of Wrath* 50 Years Later." *Christian Century,* April 5, 1989, 341–343.

Weiner, Gary. *Readings on* The Grapes of Wrath. San Diego, Calif.: Greenhaven Press, 1999.

Wilson, Edmund. "The Californians: Storm and Steinbeck." *New Republic,* December 9, 1940, 784–787.

Windschuttle, Keith. "Steinbeck's Myth of the Okies." *New Criterion,* June 2002, 24–32.

Wyatt, David, ed. *New Essays on* "The Grapes of Wrath." Cambridge: Cambridge University Press, 1990.

The Green Lady (1928)

Steinbeck's second attempt at a novel after CUP OF GOLD, *The Green Lady* was based on an unfinished play written by his friend WEBSTER "TOBY" STREET, which, in turn, was derived from a short story written by Street called "Something o' Susie's." In the original story, conflict arises between a rancher, Andy Wane, and his daughter, Susie, when the rancher decides his daughter has lost all respect for the land and for nature after three years of college. In his attempts to develop a three-act drama from the original story, Street expanded the farmer's love for the land into an almost mystical, sexual worship, and tied the land worship to his attachment to his daughter. Because the conflicts seemed to be heading into too many directions, and because the farmer's connection to his daughter hinted at incest, Street asked Steinbeck's help in resolving the difficulties. Both men became distracted by other responsibilities, and eventually Street gave Steinbeck the manuscript with his permission to turn the idea into a novel.

Steinbeck spent more than two years trying to write *The Green Lady* before abandoning the project and then beginning again. The radically rewritten book became TO A GOD UNKNOWN, Steinbeck's third published novel. By the time the novel was published, Steinbeck had retained the lead character's mystical, almost religious attachment to the land and to nature, but had eliminated the conflict between father and daughter. What emerges from Steinbeck's revision of Street's work is a pantheistic amalgam of pagan myths, Greek epics, and the Bible.

"The Harness" (1938)

Originally titled "The Fool," Steinbeck's short story "The Harness" first appeared in print in *Atlantic Monthly* magazine in June 1938. In September of that year, Steinbeck included the story in a collection of many previously published works, THE LONG VALLEY, issued by VIKING PRESS.

Like Pat Humbert from THE PASTURES OF HEAVEN, the central character in "The Harness," Peter Randall, finds himself constrained by social convention, and by his own habits. One of the most admired men in Salinas Valley, Peter appears to his neighbors to be an exemplar of business probity, and sound personal judgment, whose strong character is underscored by his upright and unbending posture. His fellow valley dwellers hang on his every word, to the point where, when Peter announces, "I am going to kill a pig on Saturday," nearly all of his neighbors do precisely the same thing, because it appears to be the "good, safe, conservative thing to do."

Peter lives with his wife, Emma, in a perfectly maintained home, in the middle of a prosperous farm, without the presence of children to disturb the picture of a flawless life. The only imperfection stems from Emma's constant ill health. A scrawny, birdlike woman, Emma rules her house with the same indomitable will as her husband runs the farm. Despite her frequent infirmities, exacerbated by Peter Randall's mysterious once-a-year "business" trips to San Francisco, Emma refuses to hire any domestic help or even accept the help of her concerned neighbors; and yet, her house stays immaculate, "unscarred, uncarved, and unchalked."

Eventually Emma succumbs to her ailment, refusing to the last to consider home nursing care, insisting that Peter was perfectly capable of tending to her needs. A nurse is brought in only when Emma lapses into a coma, and largely to assist an increasingly distraught Peter. On the day Emma dies, Peter collapses into hysteria, alarming and surprising the next-door neighbor, Mrs. Chappell, who had come by earlier. Peter had, until recently, presented a stoic, rigid demeanor, unaffected by ordinary emotion. Mrs. Chappell summons her husband, Ed Chappell, for help, and as Peter's behavior becomes increasingly erratic and maniacal, the doctor, who had driven by to sign the death certificate, injects Peter with a powerful sedative, after Ed and the undertaker wrestle Peter to the ground. Ed feels shame for the inexplicable and uncharacteristic outburst of his friend and neighbor.

Ed stays to monitor the sleeping Peter. When the drugged man finally awakes, he begins to expose a persona to Ed that further disturbs and perplexes him. Peter explains he "snapped . . . like a suspender strap" when Emma died. He wonders whether Emma, watching from the afterlife, will approve of his actions now that she is gone, because "she made a good man of me," and kept him to the straight and narrow. Peter then additionally embarrasses Ed by stripping off his shirt and coat, revealing a shoulder harness and a wide elastic belt, which kept his carriage rigid and his stomach flat, devices that Emma had insisted he wear. He compares Emma's death to the removal of the restrictive harness and belt and then asks Ed if he would join him in a bottle of whiskey hidden in the barn. Ed demurs with some shock at the unseemliness of the invitation. When Peter returns with the bottle, he continues to disclose aspects of his life that mortify Ed by divulging details of the yearly "business" trips to San Francisco. As it turns out, Peter would spend the entire week during these annual visits becoming drunk and carousing with prostitutes, necessary because "I'd've *busted* if I hadn't got away," Peter claims.

Ed chooses to have a drink with Peter, and as he accepts the glass, both men sense a change in the house. Peter becomes more garrulous and speaks of future plans for planting sweet peas down by the river, mostly for their color and smell and also because Emma had never allowed him to consider such a risky and impractical crop. He also plans to keep company with chubby, big-breasted women, because "I am hungry for everything, for a lot of everything." It is as if a dam had burst inside him, spilling out a torrent of repressed feelings held in by the trap of his 21-year marriage, and the physical harness. Outwardly devoted to Emma for two decades, Peter expresses a deep resentment of her control of him and of her insistence on convention and conservative conduct.

In the days after Emma's funeral, Peter goes to work on his farm with single-minded attention, rising long before dawn and turning in shortly after dusk. The farmers in Salinas Valley watch him closely, but none so closely as Ed Chappell, who is concerned that Peter will show signs of his odd behavior on the night of Emma's death. He notices that Peter is slouching and that his stomach seems to bulge, but other than that, Peter seems to be no different except for a strange secrecy about the crop he has been preparing so hard to plant. As the tiny plants emerge from the carefully tilled soil, the shocking rumor circulating in the valley is confirmed. Staid and sober Peter Randall has planted his entire acreage in sweet peas, "the most ticklish crop in the world," requiring almost ideal conditions from the sowing of the seed to harvest. The crop of beautiful, difficult flowers represents Peter's outward manifestation of his desire for freedom from Emma's influence, and of being able to make his own choices and demonstrate his worth without her constant guidance. As it turns out, Peter couldn't have chosen a more propitious time to plant the sweet peas. His bountiful harvest yields to Peter a substantial financial windfall.

Sometime later, Ed Chappell encounters Peter at a hotel in San Francisco, drunk, disheveled and, according to his own admission, only recently returned from a bawdy house. Ed challenges Peter about the desire for change he had expressed when his wife died, including the need to visit San Francisco to purge himself of resentment, and pent-up frustration. Peter tells Ed of a constant imaginary hounding from Emma while the sweet pea crop grew, saying, "She's worried me all year about those peas." His wife is gone, but he still heeds her admonitions. He then announces proudly that he refuses to don the harness again, without realizing he does not need it anymore. He has constructed his own

harness in his mind, as restrictive as the one his dead wife insisted he wear.

Peter, like many of Steinbeck's characters, cannot break free from his personal patterns of behavior, nor the pressures of social conformity, in order to realize his vision of happiness, no matter how flawed the vision might be. In the immediate aftermath of Emma's death, he announced his intention to plant sweet peas and to seek out women wholly unlike his wife. He achieved the first goal, but not the second. The first is in keeping with the image others have of him in the valley—a hardworking farmer, dedicated to his land, even if the crop choice appears bizarre. The second vision of happy and exuberant companionship cannot ever take place in the judgmental environment of Salinas Valley or in his own restrictive parameters. It would betray the image of Emma, and thus undermine his standing in the community.

EARLY CRITICISM

As part of the larger collection *The Long Valley,* and overshadowed by the inclusion of THE RED PONY, "The Harness" received secondary but positive remarks during its second publication. William Soskin, from the *Los Angeles Times* remarked on the "surprising strength, in that borderland story of this world and the mind's world," and the invisible presence ruling an old man. Clifton Fadiman, writing for the *New Yorker,* labeled the story "beautifully written" and the author, Steinbeck, "exceptionally sensitive." The reviewer for the *San Francisco Chronicle,* JOSEPH HENRY JACKSON, referred to "The Harness" as typical of Steinbeck's previous work— "a compound of brutality and tenderness, beauty and ugliness." Finally, Stanley Young, a reviewer for the *New York Times Book Review,* commented that "The Harness" fulfilled "the fine promise of IN DUBIOUS BATTLE, and further added that the story could not be "talked about . . . but must be read."

CONTEMPORARY PERSPECTIVES

As part of Steinbeck's early work, "The Harness" demonstrates an underlying pessimism about the capacity of individuals or larger groups of humankind to overcome the barriers of society in the achievement of ultimate goals. In this, it falls into the nonteleological approach of the author: When we set ourselves to the realization of improbable, and idealistic enterprises, we are often, and perhaps, inevitably disappointed. Maxwell Geismar asks about "the curse which defeats us" in Steinbeck's world. Nevertheless, John H. Timmerman observes that in Steinbeck "hope rises ever renewed." Peter Randall has not lost hope; he has only lost the possibility of ever becoming completely unshackled. He has tasted freedom, and chooses the harness of respectability.

SYNOPSIS

Peter Randall, one of the most highly respected farmers in Monterey County, is married to a stern, sickly woman named Emma. After a long, terrible illness, Emma finally dies. Peter becomes hysterical with grief, sobbing and shouting until the family doctor sedates him. His neighbor, Ed Chappell, agrees to spend the evening with the mourning man. When the morphine finally wears off, Peter wakes up, calm and happy. He explains that he always has done what his wife wanted him to do, ignoring his wicked tendencies, except for one week a year when he went to the whorehouses in San Francisco. Opening his shirt he reveals a web harness that pulls his shoulders back, as well as a wide elastic belt restraining his stomach. The harness is an unambiguous symbol of Peter's enslavement. For 20 years he has been controlled by his wife and now he determines that he will do what he wants. He resolves to his friend that he will slouch and let his belly hang out, that he will hire a big fat housekeeper from San Francisco and plant his 45 acres in sweet peas so that he might enjoy the pleasure of their delicate blossoms. Ed is embarrassed to hear his friend's indiscretions and nervously goes home. The day after the funeral, Peter Randall begins working furiously on his farm. He prepares his land beautifully and refuses to reveal his plans to his neighbors who observe his strange behavior with curiosity. Finally, when the sweet peas begin to bloom, the consensus spreads that Peter is "touched," for although the peas will bring a high price if they are harvested, it is a delicate crop that is prone to failure. Peter sits on his porch every evening, looking over his spectacularly flowered fields and nervously awaiting the harvest. Meanwhile Ed is relieved to discover that his friend has neither hired a fat housekeeper nor significantly departed from his upright habits. Peter has the last laugh when he brings in his entire crop successfully, earning a small fortune for himself. That fall Ed Chappell takes a trip to San Francisco. In his hotel he runs into Peter Randall. Very drunk, Peter invites his friend to his room for a drink. He explains that he has just returned from the San Francisco whorehouses. He admits that he has been under incredible strain waiting for his peas to come to harvest. Ed asks his friend why he never changed things like he said he would when Emma died. Peter's response shows that he is still dominated by his wife's memories even though she is not physically there.

FURTHER READING

Fadiman, Clifton. "Steinbeck Again." *New Yorker,* April 4, 1942, 55.

Geismar, Maxwell. "Decline of the Classic Moderns." *Nation,* May 7, 1955, 402–404.

Jackson, Joseph Henry. "A Bookman's Notebook." *San Francisco Chronicle,* September 28, 1938, 13.

Soskin, William. "Varied Art of John Steinbeck." *New York Herald Tribune,* September 18, 1938, Books section, 7.

Timmerman, John H. *The Dramatic Landscape of Steinbeck's Short Stories.* Norman: University of Oklahoma Press, 1990.

Young, Stanley. "The Short Stories of John Steinbeck." *New York Times Book Review,* September 25, 1938, 7.

"The Harvest Gypsies" (1936)

In 1936, the *San Francisco News* commissioned Steinbeck to write a series of articles about the large number of DUST BOWL refugees who were migrating west to California to work as agricultural laborers. Fascinated by the idea, Steinbeck immediately purchased an old bakery truck to sleep and travel in and headed into the state's agricultural heartland. What he found there shocked and outraged him, and his anger at the situation is tangible in the articles that became the seven-part essay on the plight of the migrant farmworker titled "The Harvest Gypsies" and published between October 5 and 11, 1936. Although based on observations of fact, the vehement articles proved to be incendiary in conservative rural California, and Steinbeck soon found himself the object of a fierce attack by the powerful Growers Associations. The author was accused of being a communist agitator and spent some time fearing for his personal safety. The essays contained in "The Harvest Gypsies" were later collected and reprinted in 1938 in a pamphlet titled "Their Blood Is Strong" by the Simon J. Lubin Society, an organization dedicated to the aid of migrant workers. Steinbeck added his article "Starvation Under the Orange Trees," which had been published earlier that year in the *Monterey Trader*, as an epilogue to the pamphlet. "Their Blood Is Strong" was illustrated with photos by Dorothea Lange, a photographer from the FARM SECURITY ADMINISTRATION. A fine example of the power of Steinbeck's writing, "The Harvest Gypsies" became the inspiration for the author's best-known novel THE GRAPES OF WRATH.

SYNOPSIS

Chapter I: San Francisco News, vol. 34, no. 239 (October 5, 1936)

The first article is an introduction to the problem of the migrant worker. Steinbeck writes that at least 150,000 people are living a nomadic life as starving harvesters. This situation, he explains, is brought about by the unique nature of California agriculture, where an orchard that requires basic maintenance by 20 workers requires 2,000 men during the harvest. This, he says, has resulted in the curious paradox that migrants are needed and hated at the same time. The author gives a brief history of the evolution of migratory labor in California. The migrants of the early period were Chinese, Filipinos, Japanese, and Mexicans. In recent years, he says, these foreign migrants have been replaced by the displaced residents of Oklahoma, Nebraska, Kansas, and Texas. These new arrivals are generally small farmers who have experienced the "curious

and terrible pain" of being driven off their land in the dust bowl. These people, he emphasizes, are not migrants by nature, "they are gypsies by force of circumstance." And the old methods of repression will not work against them. To this end he proposes studying how they live, what is done for them, and what their problems and needs are. He suggests that if California does not address the problem of migrant labor, it may "destroy the present system of agricultural economics."

Chapter II: San Francisco News, vol. 34, no. 240 (October 6, 1936)

In the second article of "The Harvest Gypsies," Steinbeck describes in shocking detail the slow descent into poverty and misery that results from life in the squatters' camps of the California farm belt. He is quick to point out to middle-class readers that camp dwellers were very recently tenant farmers with land and crops and even some savings in the bank. The article attempts to explain how the erosion of the humanity of the camp dwellers is a direct result of the impossibility of their situation. He describes three families. The first family is newly arrived and determined to maintain civility and the integrity of their family under adverse conditions. He insists that the cards are stacked against these new arrivals, and that an inevitable chain of misfortune and sickness will eventually lead to their total demise. The second family has been in the camps for six months. It is a chilling picture that the author paints of the terror of starvation. The camp dwellers lose spirit quickly, Steinbeck writes, as malnutrition takes its inevitable toll on health and spirit. The third family has been in the camp for a year. They are left with "no will, no strength," living little better than animals. The only attention given to the camps by the authorities, the author complains, is when epidemics break out. He closes his description of the camps with a warning that the tendency among the camp inhabitants to steal and to hate is not a reflection of their weakness of character, but rather the result of the intolerable conditions that have been imposed upon them. Such statements led others to accuse of the author of harboring revolutionary sympathies.

Chapter III: San Francisco News, vol. 34, no. 241 (October 7, 1936)

In the third article of "The Harvest Gypsies" series, Steinbeck attributes a large portion of the responsibility for the terrible plight of the agricultural migrants to the existence of large corporate farms, as well as organizations such as the Associated Farmers, Inc., which he cites as controlling not only California agriculture, but also the state's banking, industry, and local government. These large economic interests, Steinbeck writes, hold the smaller farmers hostage to their policies by threatening to cut off their access to vital farm financing. He accuses the large corporate farms of overcharging the migrants for inadequate housing and for failing to provide even the most basic sanitary requirements. The workers are herded like animals, Steinbeck writes, and every possible method is used to make them feel inferior and insecure. As in the squatters' camps, he observes, the dignity of man is attacked. Indeed, it is this appeal to the necessity of dignity that best describes the migrant situation. This attack on basic dignity breeds the conditions of revolt and necessitates increasingly repressive methods, which he characterizes as "a system of terrorism that would be unusual in the Fascist nations of the world," and that "constitutes a criminal endangering of the peace of the state." These are, perhaps, the most incendiary words ever published by John Steinbeck either before or after. Written at the height of the growing wave of radicalism that swept across the country as a result of the GREAT DEPRESSION, this article earned the author the enmity of the holders of economic power, who would henceforth accuse Steinbeck of communist sympathies.

Chapter IV: San Francisco News, vol. 34, no. 242 (October 8, 1936)

In this article Steinbeck continues to develop the theme of human dignity evidenced in the previous articles of "The Harvest Gypsies" series. Dignity, he writes, is a "register of man's responsibility to the community." Conditions in the squatters' camps have robbed the migrants of their dignity and reduced their sense of responsibility, resulting in a breakdown bordering on revolt that is indicated in the first three articles. On the other hand, the author views the establishment of several experimental government camps as a positive example of what can be achieved when dignity and decency are restored to the migrants. The Arvin Camp described in the article provided the model for the Weedpatch Camp in Steinbeck's *The Grapes of Wrath*. The self-government provided the migrants within the Arvin camp, the author argues, revived the social sense of its inhabitants. These camps are, according to Steinbeck, unique experiments in democratic self-government. Steinbeck encourages the Resettlement Administration's plans to expand the number of camps as well as to create small maintenance farms. The Growers Association's opposition to the plan is, according to the author, an admission that "they require a peon class to succeed." Perhaps anticipating the criticism that he will receive for his views, he concludes the article by predicting that any attempt to improve the condition of the migrants will be considered radical by the corporate farmers.

Chapter V: San Francisco News, vol. 34, no. 243 (October 9, 1936)

In this article the author decries the obstacles that prevent migrant families in California from obtaining relief from the various state and federal disbursement agencies. Since the basic requirement to receive most forms of relief is residence, he writes, the very nature of the migrant's work makes him ineligible for relief. Steinbeck traces the history of one Oklahoma family as it tries and fails on a number of occasions to obtain assistance. California communities use three methods for dealing with such problems, according to Steinbeck: The first is to deny that there is a problem. The second is to pass responsibility away from local authorities. The third is to push the problem over county borders. He accuses the counties of creating the problem by refusing to consider anything but the immediate economy and profit of the locality. He indicates that the maximum a worker can make in a season is $400 a year, while the average is around $300, and the minimum is $150 a year. Finally he describes the meager diets of the migrant families, as well as the terrible childbirth problems that result in catastrophic levels of infant mortality.

Chapter VI: San Francisco News, vol. 34, no. 244 (October 10, 1936)

Steinbeck traces the history of migrant labor in California, denouncing it as a "disgraceful picture of greed and cruelty." From the Chinese to the Japanese to the Mexican and Filipino immigrants, he paints a picture of the systematic exploitation of imported labor. In each case, he points out, attempts at organization among migrant workers have been responded to with repression and finally deportation. He condemns the large growers for trampling the migrants' basic right of free speech, assembly, and jury trial. Steinbeck argues that the waves of "foreign peon labor" are leaving the state, "leaving California agriculture to the mercies of our own people," who will not be defeated by "the old methods of intimidation and starvation perfected against the foreign peon." He insists on the need for California agriculture to reorganize its economy so as to provide a higher standard of living for agricultural workers. American pride and self-respect, he feels, is such that the migrants will refuse to accept that role of field peon, "with its attendant terrorism, squalor and starvation."

Chapter VII: San Francisco News, vol. 34, no. 245 (October 11, 1936)

Steinbeck's last installment of "The Harvest Gypsies" series demonstrates his credentials as a "New Deal Democrat," and urges the establishment of a migratory labor board to normalize the relations between the migrant workers and their employers. He proposes regulating migrants' pay by publishing wages and numbers of workers needed in advance of the harvest. Here Steinbeck shows his faith that a governmental solution can abate what he sees as a potential for disaster in California's rural communities. His proposal to organize the farmworkers was seen as a radical, even communistic stance by the farmers and growers' associations of the state. Steinbeck also urges the government to investigate the "terrorist" tactics being visited on the migrants by the large California landowners. Finally, he states that if agriculture requires an underclass, then it is not possible to keep it in a democracy. He complains of the "fascistic" practices being employed in the state, and advocates the formation of a "militant and watchful organization" to maintain the state in a democratic form.

"His Father" (1949)

"His Father," a short story published in *The Reader's Digest* in September 1949, tells of a confused seven-year-old boy whose parents have recently divorced. The boy understands that now the atmosphere in his house is no longer thick with dread, and he's happy about that. That dread, however, has moved out into the street. The other kids know about the divorce; one day they were picking on him, asking him where his father was. Instead of telling them his father was away, the boy told them that his father was inside. When one of the kids announced that the boy's parents were divorced, the boy started charging into his friends, kicking and hitting—but it was as if he was watching it from outside, rather than doing it. His mother had broken up the fight, but since then, the boy can't talk to any of the other kids, because of the bottled-up feelings of shame. Finally, one day, as the boy watches with anxiety one of the other children approaching, his father comes around the corner. Too thrilled to move, he closes his eyes and waits. When his father sits down next to him and says "Hi," the boy shouts to all the other children to come and see his father.

"How Edith Mcgillcuddy Met R. L. Stevenson" (1941)

This uncollected short story was first printed in the August 1941 edition of *Harper's Magazine*. The short story later appeared in *The Portable Steinbeck*, a collection of Steinbeck's works selected by his editor and friend PASCAL "PAT" COVICI and published in 1943. It was reprinted in *Chamber's Journal* in 1950. "How Edith Mcgillcuddy Met R. L. Stevenson" is the author's recounting of a tale told by old family friend Edith Wagner. It is the story of Edith Mcgillcuddy, a young girl from Salinas, California, who, as a childish prank, travels on the train to the nearby port of Monterey, where she has a brief encounter with the famous author of adventure stories, Robert Louis Stevenson, whose works include *Treasure Island, Kidnapped,* and *South Seas Tales*. Stevenson, who resided in the Monterey area during the late 1800s, was a boyhood favorite of John Steinbeck.

SYNOPSIS

In 1879, the small agricultural town of Salinas is humorously characterized as a battleground between the saloons and the churches where a few righteous citizens are constantly trying to hold back a tide of sin and avarice. The McGillcuddys, an upright Methodist family, try to keep their 12-year-old daughter Edith on a straight and narrow path. Young Edith however, often gets into trouble for keeping company with the poor Catholic children of Salinas. One Sunday morning Edith is on her way to Sunday school when she happens upon Susy Nugger, a disheveled little girl from a poor family. Susy invites Edith to join her on a train ride to Monterey to see the "free funeral." She explains that the Alvarez family has hired the local narrow-gauge train to take the family and a large contingent of mourners to Monterey for the funeral of their son 'Tonio Alvarez. Edith easily gives in to Susy's prodding and the two young girls find places on the train's crowded flatcars. Arriving at the funeral, Edith is mistaken for one of 'Tonio Alvarez's many illegitimate children. Susy abandons Edith in favor of a young girl with a large picnic basket. Left to fend for herself in the unfamiliar city, Susy wanders to the shore to see the ocean. On the beach she meets an impoverished ragamuffin named Lizzie, who informs her that there is a woman living in Monterey who smokes cigarettes. Edith cannot believe that such a scandalous thing is possible, but Lizzie offers to show her the woman and her long-haired husband. On the way to see the strange spectacle, Edith and Lizzie stop to gather a pail of huckleberries to sell to the strange long-haired man. The two girls arrive at a white adobe house on the outskirts of Monterey. They

knock shyly on the door and are invited in. Edith is astonished to find the couple stretched out on a white cloth spread on the ground inside the courtyard. The woman is smoking, just as Lizzie claimed she would be. Lizzie accepts a nickel for the huckleberries and runs off with her treasure. Edith stays to drink tea. Suddenly she hears the train's whistle and runs wildly for the station.

"How Mr. Hogan Robbed a Bank" (1956)

The short story "How Mr. Hogan Robbed a Bank" was first published in the March 1956 edition of *Atlantic Monthly* magazine. One of the few short stories to be written by Steinbeck in the latter half of his career, "How Mr. Hogan Robbed a Bank" details a middle-aged shopkeeper's efforts to plan and execute the perfect crime. The story would later be incorporated in Steinbeck's last novel, *The Winter of Our Discontent*.

SYNOPSIS

Part 1

On Labor Day 1955 a 42-year-old clerk at Fettucci's grocery store, Mr. John Hogan, wakes up in his brown shingle house at 215 Maple Street. It is the day he has spent the last year carefully preparing for: He has planned the perfect bank robbery, and this day he will put his plan into action. With his wife and children still in bed, Mr. Hogan leaves early and walks to his job, where he has worked for more than 16 years. He is a man who notices things. During his daily trips to deposit the store's earnings, he has carefully observed the habits and patterns at the bank next door and has determined that the best time to rob a bank is on Saturday morning of a long weekend, when the bank has extra cash for the customers who are leaving on holiday. He has observed where Mr. Cup, the bank teller, keeps the large bills, and he knows the habits and security systems of the bank's employees. Everything has been studied; Mr. Hogan is ready and hardly feels nervous at all.

Part 2

In the course of a year, Mr. Hogan carefully practiced for his crime. Today everything is ready. He arrives at the store, unlocks, and prepares to open as he would any other day.

Part 3

He cuts a Mickey Mouse mask off the back of a box of cereal, flushing the rest of the cardboard container down the store's toilet. At one minute to nine he moves to the front of the store and begins sweeping the porch, greeting each of the bank employees as they pass by. At four minutes after nine he enters the store, puts on the mask, removes a silver-colored pistol from the cash register, and steps out the alley door behind the store. He enters the bank, motions for Mr. Cup to lie on the floor, slips his foot under the floor alarm to prevent it from going off, and quickly removes the large bills from the tray. Upon leaving the bank he turns down the alley, enters his store, tears up the mask and flushes it down the toilet, returns the pistol to the cash register, and hides the pile of bills underneath the top drawer of the tray. The robbery is over by 9:07. That evening he returns home and hides the money in his Knight Templar hatbox.

"How to Recognize a Candidate" (1955)

In "How to Recognize a Candidate," published August 10, 1955, Steinbeck advises the readers of the British humor magazine *Punch* on "some of the more intricate political gambits of the scene" as 1956, an election year, draws near. He describes U.S. national politics as "complicated to the point of mysticism," and proposes limiting his article to a discussion of the candidates. The first step, he writes, is to establish who is a candidate. The author describes the first symptom of candidacy as "Decent Reluctance," when the candidate states clearly, simply, and loudly that he has no desire and little qualification for public office. After this move, Steinbeck writes, the candidate usually swears undying loyalty to another candidate who he knows can't win. The candidate then becomes Family Man, setting aside his mistress until after the election. "If a man takes his wife with him wherever he goes he is running for office," he says. The candidate also becomes open and scrupulously honest, according to the author. "Such is the change in a candidate that it would be no bad thing if everyone were forced periodically to run for office," he humorously concludes.

"I Even Saw Manolete" (1970)

The article "I Even Saw Manolete," written the year before Steinbeck's death in 1968, and published in *A Thousand Afternoons: An Anthology of Bullfighting,* is an interesting if indirect description of the author's changing opinion toward sports and the spectacle of bullfighting and possibly a veiled criticism of his literary rival ERNEST HEMINGWAY. The author describes himself as an interested observer of sports, but without much personal aptitude for them. Team sports, he claims, are a simulation of warfare, while individual sports are mimicry of single combat; both express the age-old struggle for survival. Hunting for sport, however, he does not respect. He has nothing against the killing of animals for food, he writes, but he does not believe that shooting animals proves anything superior about man. As to the other blood sports such as fox hunting and bullfighting, he finds them charming and sometimes beautiful. Although he says that he once found bullfighting to be an expression of the "invincible human spirit and unspeakable, beautiful courage," he now has his doubts about that thesis. The bravery of a bullfighter in the ring, he suggests, cannot stand in comparison to bravery in real life. He give examples of real courage, such as Ed Murrow's defiance of Senator Joseph McCarthy or an African-American going to vote in the Deep South. He concludes the short article with the typical cynicism about human nature that colored his writing late in life.

"I Go Back to Ireland" (1953)

In "I Go Back to Ireland," published January 31, 1953, in *Collier's*, Steinbeck writes of a journey to his ancestral home. The author was half Irish; his maternal grandfather, SAMUEL HAMILTON, and grandmother immigrated to the United States in the late 1800s. Only two people in his family had ever returned to Ireland. He and his wife, ELAINE ANDERSON STEINBECK rent a car and drive from Belfast to Derry, which Steinbeck finds an unfriendly town. He is amazed at the formality and inflexibility of this town where, even with a hefty bribe, he is unable to obtain an after-hours drink. The next morning they ride out to look for Mulkeraugh, the seat of the Hamilton family. Steinbeck discovers that the last Hamilton, Miss Elizabeth, died two years earlier and the Hamilton farm was sold. He is distraught to learn that nobody remembers his grandfather, Samuel, who was apparently forgotten when he immigrated to the United States. Villagers tell Steinbeck the history of the remaining Hamiltons and their deaths as spinsters, leaving no one to inherit the family farm, the contents of which were auctioned off to strangers. He visits the grave of the last Hamilton sisters and the sexton gives him a red rose, which is known as the Hamilton rose and is the only remaining evidence of his family line in Ireland.

In Dubious Battle (1936)

Steinbeck's fifth novel, *In Dubious Battle* was one of the earliest examples of the stark social realism that would make the author famous. *In Dubious Battle* was written in California during the mid-1930s, when political radicalism was reaching its apogee in the United States. Centered on two Communist Party organizers' attempts to stage a small strike in an apple orchard, the novel was Steinbeck's first attempt to address in his literature the grievous injustices that he witnessed against the migrant laborers who flocked to California during the years of the DUST BOWL and the GREAT DEPRESSION. The novel, which takes its title from a line in John Milton's *Paradise Lost* ("In dubious battle on the plains of Heaven"), was published by Covici and Friede in 1936 to mostly positive reviews. Critics on both the Left and the Right praised the book for its lack of propaganda and sentimentality, and for the strength of its characterization, and straightforward style.

Steinbeck struggled with the format for this book. Taking advice from CAROL HENNING STEINBECK BROWN, his first wife, he investigated the attempts to organize migrant workers by radical groups in the fertile fields of central California. Initially, he saw the work as an unadorned and objective journalistic account of the "down and out" itinerant farmworker pitted against massive agricultural conglomerates holding sway throughout California, from their influence with farm owners to the highest reaches of state government. He attended rallies, and secret meetings arranged by the Cannery and Agricultural Workers' Industrial Union, a front for both the American Communist Party, and the Socialist Party of America. He interviewed radical leaders, particularly Cicil McKiddy and Pat Chambers, farm owners, and the workers themselves, in the hopes of producing a series of articles, or perhaps a full-length, nonfiction book about his observations. Eventually, Steinbeck began to view the ongoing labor difficulties as a metaphor for his nascent views of man as part of a PHALANX and chose to incorporate his extensive notes and interviews into this first book of his Labor Trilogy.

What strikes the reader immediately is the preponderance of dialogue. According to Steinbeck himself in a letter to his friend GEORGE ALBEE, almost 80 percent of the book is dialogue. And it is common speech, it is vernacular, it is ungrammatical and profane and sometimes obscene. With *In Dubious Battle*, Steinbeck began to earn his reputation as the most censored author in America. Apart from the dialogue, Steinbeck exhibits his developed gifts for description of natural and artificial settings. From the first chapter when one encounters Jim Nolan, the wide-eyed radical neophyte, living in a miserable single room lit only by a flickering neon light, to his death, struck down and made faceless by an anonymous shotgun blast, Steinbeck brings an evocative power with a bare minimum of narrative to the story.

Also for the first time, Steinbeck includes an eponymous "Doc" character, patterned after his closest friend, EDWARD RICKETTS, who speaks as a Greek chorus, commenting as a neutral observer and critic, inserting the philosophical components into the novel, and acting as its moral fulcrum. "Doc Burton" actually stands in for both Steinbeck and Ed Ricketts in this novel, along with any number of influential acquaintances during this period of Steinbeck's life. Doc appears and disappears at key points of the book, having contributed necessary questions about the motivations of the central players, and a practical concern about the well-being of the minor characters. He is integral as well as the speaker for ordinary human beings, who often find themselves forced into conflicts, manipulated by leaders expressing beliefs and urging action outside the ordinary person's self-interest.

CRITICAL SUMMARY

Jim Nolan and Mac embark on a hastily planned attempt to organize rebellion and stir up ferment among farmworkers in the Torgas Valley. Mac represents the seasoned and hardened veteran of the "people's movement," impelled by ideology and the thrill of organizing the various strike movements; Jim, the eager apprentice, determined to take revenge for his own marginalized life, and for his father's degradation as a "working stiff," his mother's humiliation as the wife of a poor and downtrodden man, and even for the unexplained disappearance of his teenage sister, who may have taken to a life on the streets rather than endure her family's poverty. As the story progresses, Mac becomes less of a dispassionate ideologue, and Jim more of an extremist, blind to anything but the cause. A hint arises even of an unhealthy attachment by Mac to this apprentice to radicalism. As his student becomes more proficient and provocative in incitement of the farmworkers, Mac becomes more careful of Jim's well-being, because he acknowledges the almost monstrous force he has created.

The book is about "monsters" and about victims—monsters on both sides of a "dubious battle," which cannot be won by either the capitalist or communist side, but whose victims lie in the middle of the battlefield, the underpaid, underrepresented underclass of migrant farmworkers who worked in California orchards and fields to keep a can of beans on the table. It is also about the victimized wealthy female contributors to the "Reds," bemused by the seductive words and actions of Dick, the handsome and charming moneyman for the Communists, who bilks lonely women out of cash, livestock and produce. And it is about the terrorized Andersons, father and son, who both lose their livelihoods to vigilantes standing behind the fruit growers, determined to break the will of the strikers through murder, arson, and thuggery. Steinbeck deliberately avoids choosing sides between the central antagonists of his novel. Instead he posits that the force behind the human antagonisms witnessed throughout history comes from self-hatred translated into group hatred. Not driven by ideology, not driven by economics, not driven by religion, but only cloaked in these incentives, humanity finds a reason to do "dubious battle" with others of our own species.

Eventually the "small strike" overwhelms both Mac and Jim. An old man, Dan, falls from an apple tree and suffers grievous injury, providing the immediate cause for a walkout by the fruit pickers. Vigilantes shoot Joy, a brain-damaged supporter of the Reds, furnishing a martyr for the strike, and Mac remarks that Joy has "done the first real, useful thing in his life." Al Anderson's diner is burned to the ground by the same vigilante group, and the arsonists then set fire to Al's father's barn, which contains his entire crop of apples, simply because father and son have shown sympathy to the strikers. Over and over, Mac emphasizes that the end justifies whatever means are necessary, no matter the cost to individuals. He treats the strikers as pawns on a chessboard to further the revolutionary cause among what for him are an ideational collective of farmworkers. In this sense, he is no better than the fruit growers determined to keep the pickers in an assembly line, viewing them as the human cogs in a vast agricultural industry. Mac shows no awareness of the similarities between the opposing forces. His choices emerge from his driving force of ideology, his opponents' perspective from their ledger of assets and debits.

The book comes to a close as Mac mounts a rustic stage in the migrant workers' temporary camp, originally constructed to display the coffin of Joy to all the strikers, and gives a speech to commemorate the death of Jim, with Jim's mutilated body propped up behind him. Initially faltering in his rhetoric as he memorializes the person who has become his close friend, Mac gathers steam and begins to speak of Jim in the abstract, converting him into another symbol for the revolution. The novel ends in mid-sentence as Mac eulogizes his friend. It ends in mid-sentence to demonstrate the inconclusive nature of the labor struggle, and to show that the "dubious battle" will not end. In a letter to MAVIS MCINTOSH, Steinbeck wrote, " . . . where can you end a story of a man-movement that has no end?"

Overall, the tone of the book is very dark, as befits a work whose title comes from John Milton's *Paradise Lost*. Much of the action takes place at nighttime with faces lit by the flickering flames of lanterns or campfires, a parallel to the fires of hell, or in miserable rainy weather, with overcast skies and the strikers huddled together in the mud like consignees to hell. Throughout lies uncertainty: uncertainty about the outcome; uncertainty about the loyalty of various strike participants; uncertainty about the fate of numerous characters, especially Doc Burton, who disappears without explanation toward the end of the book. The reader does not know whether Doc left of his own volition, was taken into custody by sheriffs, or waylaid and murdered by the vigilantes. This uncertainty adds to the sense of foreboding.

Largely, Steinbeck's characterization is excellent, though strangely not of the two primary characters in the novel. Mac's determination to use every event and every person, whether minor or major, becomes repetitive and tiresome. From the time he recommends that Jim take up smoking in order to foster trust among the farmworkers, to the time that he assists in the delivery of London's grandchild, through the bizarre display of Joy's and Jim Nolan's corpses, Mac harps on the utility of these events and people to the movement. Steinbeck had no intention of creating a likable character in Mac, but he also made him somewhat boring and predictable. On the other hand, Jim begins as a fairly sympathetic character, and although his reasons for joining the Communists are largely negative in origin, he initially demonstrates both concern and empathy for the plight of the farm laborers. However, Jim almost instantaneously transforms into a cold-hearted fanatic after being shot during a raid against the "scabs" brought in to replace the striking workers. The alteration is startling, and not fully explored. Even Mac mentions that Jim is "getting beyond" him, and that he is "scared" of his protégé.

Nevertheless, many of the other characters emerge as fully realized human beings, not stock figures or one-dimensional creations. Of particular note is London, a natural leader of men because of his honesty, integrity, bluntness, and sincere commitment to those around him—a stark contrast to the character of Mac. Also Dakin, the only one of the strikers with more than meager possessions, known for his coolness under pressure, who loses his temper, his new truck, and his freedom in a confrontation with the vigilantes and the police. There is also Lisa, London's daughter-in-law who grows from a frightened and naive girl to a compassionate woman, caring for Old Dan as he lies dying from the injury suffered during the fall that brought about the strike.

Taken as a whole, *In Dubious Battle* presents a forceful and realistic account of a historic period in American history. More than that, it offers a timeless portrayal of the dynamics of power, of organization, and of group interaction without ideological overtones or preaching. Steinbeck described the book as "brutal," especially because of his deliberate detachment from "a moral point of view." In this sense, he forces his readers to make their own judgments regarding the worthiness of the two sides—strike organizers and agricultural conglomerates—and even, perhaps, to choose another way, apart from "group man." Doc Burton offers that alternative but also makes it clear that opting for disconnection from a group guarantees loneliness.

EARLY CRITICISM

Critics on both the Left and the Right praised *In Dubious Battle* for its lack of propaganda and sentimentality, and for the strength of its characterization and straightforward style. As expected, Steinbeck's friend, JOSEPH HENRY JACKSON of the *San Francisco Chronicle,* applauded the novel for its "strength, and beauty," and for the fact that it is "splendidly written, excellently conceived and executed. . . ." John Chamberlain of the *New York Times* called the book a "wildly stirring story" while noting the objections of an unnamed Communist to Steinbeck's "complete caricature" of Mac, the strike organizer. *Newsweek's* reviewer spoke of Steinbeck's "brutal directness." Bernard Smith, writing for the *New York Herald Tribune,* said that "Mr. Steinbeck's narrative builds and mounts and at last soars" and further adds that the author is "one of the most gifted writers of our younger generation." Peter Quenell, reporting for the *New Statesman and Nation,* called the book "one of the best novels of social conflict I have yet read." The only prominent negative review was written by Mary McCarthy, penning her "Minority Report" for the *Nation.* She had already expressed a strong dislike for Steinbeck's writing in previous reviews. Among other negative adjectives, McCarthy called the book wooden, inert, childish, and tedious.

CONTEMPORARY PERSPECTIVES

What concerns many of the present-day analysts of *In Dubious Battle* is the historical accuracy of the book. From the beginning, left-leaning readers protested the amoral and dispassionate nature of Mac. Certainly, McKiddy and Chambers, the two Communist organizers interviewed by Steinbeck in his research for the book, demonstrated a deep and concerned relationship with the fruit pickers and other farm laborers. Jackson Benson and Anne Loftis point to Steinbeck's awareness of the misrepresentation, but also demonstrate this was an artistic choice—a way for the author to highlight his primary theme of the mechanistic behavior of men in groups. Led by unemotional machines, men begin to act as unfeeling machines. Others, including Susan Shillinglaw, have noted the lack of Hispanics, Negroes, and Asians among the crop pickers. Steinbeck, having worked among farm laborers from an early age, had a keen awareness of the ethnic and racial diversity of migrant agricultural laborers in California. Again, for the purposes of the novel's theme, the homogeneity of the group becomes cru-

cial. There can be no extraneous or intervening internal conflicts aside from those occurring between groups in confrontation. As to the "reality" of *In Dubious Battle,* the author himself, in a letter to CARL WILHELMSON shortly after the publication of the book, claimed " . . . the Battle with its tricks to make a semblance of reality wasn't very close." Steinbeck consciously chose a fictional format for his first venture into "proletarian" literature, because he had a much grander goal in mind than the depiction of labor strife; he wanted to explore a philosophical viewpoint, which he continued to examine throughout his writing career.

SYNOPSIS

Chapter 1

Jim Nolan checks out of his boardinghouse and crosses the city to the shoddy office of Harry Nilson, a recruiter for the Communist Party. Harry is interested to learn that Jim's father is Roy Nolan, a labor agitator. Jim explains that his father was gunned down three years earlier during an attempt to dynamite the slaughterhouse where he worked, and that his mother died only a month earlier while Jim was in jail on trumped-up charges of vagrancy. Jobless and cut off from his past, Jim feels as if he is dead and he hopes that the party will make him "get alive again." Harry agrees to recommend Jim for party membership and invites him to stay for a few days while they wait for a response from the membership committee.

Chapter 2

Harry leads Jim to a cottage inhabited by three men: Mac, the leader of the group, Dick, a boy, and Joy, a large man with a battered face. Mac explains that Joy has been "screwy" ever since he was left in jail for three days with a broken jaw because the doctor would not treat a "God-damned red." Jim adopts Mac as his mentor, and asks him to use his influence to get him assigned to work in the field as soon as possible.

Chapter 3

Jim is writing letters to party sympathizers when Dick arrives with the news that Joy has been locked up for stabbing a cop. Mac instructs him to contact George Camp, a lawyer and sympathizer, and then to try to collect bail money for their friend. He announces that he and Jim are heading to the Torgas Valley to organize the apple pickers, whose wages have just been cut by the Torgas Valley Growers Association.

Chapter 4

Early the next morning, the two men stow away aboard an empty boxcar. Late that evening, they arrive in the rural town of Torgas. Mac has a list of 50 active party sympathizers in the town, one of whom is Al Anderson, the owner of a diner. Al serves a hot dinner to Jim and Mac. He is excited about the pending strike, but concerned about how it will affect his father, one of the valley's few remaining small apple farmers. Jim and Mac walk to the nearest migrant camp and mix with the residents. London, the leader of the camp, is furious because his daughter-in-law is in labor, and the local hospital refuses to attend her. Mac claims to have experience delivering babies. He organizes the men to heat water and donate clean rags. A tangible change comes over the camp as the men begin working together for a common cause. Later, when Jim asks Mac where he learned birthing, Mac admits that he has never done it before, but that he could not pass up such a good opportunity to gain London's confidence.

Chapter 5

The next morning Jim and Mac begin working in the orchards. Jim meets Dan, a 71-year-old who has been laid off from his job of trimming the tops of apple trees because of his advancing age. The old man tells Jim that things in the camp are coming to a boil; but when Jim suggests that it is time for the men to organize, Old Dan responds cynically, suggesting the laborers will kill each other, and new workers will come to replace them. Mac warns Jim that talking to old people will only convert him to hopelessness. Meanwhile, the two men convince London of the feasibility of a strike. They head off in London's old Model-T to talk to Dakin, the leader of another camp. Dakin looks at the two "radicals" with suspicion. He doesn't like the idea of a strike, but he agrees to participate when Jim suggests that if they accept the low apple wages, the cotton owners will get the same idea.

Chapter 6

The ranch owners sense the growing agitation among the pickers. A foreman offers to pay Jim for information about what is going on. Tension spreads through the ranks. Things finally come to a head, when Old Dan falls and breaks his hip. A faulty ladder becomes a symbol of injustice. Mac instructs London's assistant Sam to convince the workers that they need a leader. The men elect London, who appoints a strike committee. Mac and Jim rush to town to wire for assistance. They receive word that Joy has escaped from jail. Mac pressures Al Anderson, who reluctantly introduces the two men to his father. Mac explains to old Mr. Anderson that the strike will start the following morning, and that he is likely to lose his ranch to the local mortgage company if his apples go unpicked. He offers to see that Anderson's apples are picked for free if he will agree to let the strikers set up their camp in his meadow.

Chapter 7

Dick arrives with Doc Burton, whom Mac places in charge of setting up the strike camp in an orderly and sanitary fashion to prevent the public health officials from closing it down. Dick's job is to solicit local sympathizers for money and supplies. London organizes a meeting with the newly elected strike committee. The meeting is interrupted by the farm superintendent, who arrives with an escort of armed sheriffs. He offers to give London a job if he will call off the strike, and warns that if the problems continue, they will be thrown off the farm and driven out of the valley.

Chapter 8

The strikers move to the Anderson farm, where Doc Burton has laid out an orderly camp. On Mac's suggestion the men elect Dakin to be their chairman. Mac receives news that a train of replacement pickers is to arrive the next morning. The strike committee makes plans to confront the scabs. Later that evening, Mac asks Doc why he helps the strikers if he is not a member of or even a believer in the Communist Party. Doc explains his theory about group men, in which he relates the behavior of men in masses to the behavior of cells in the body. When Jim and Mac attempt to proselytize the police posted outside the camp, they are captured and only barely escape. Mac admits to Jim that he has never seen a valley so well organized and that he is sure the strike will fail.

Chapter 9

The strikers march into town to meet the trainload of scabs. At the rail yard, they are hemmed in on one side by the deputy sheriffs, and on the other side by private security forces. London urges the scabs to join the strike. A group of scabs moves to join the strikers. Suddenly a sniper guns down the leader of the group, Mac's comrade Joy, as he moves across the tracks. The enraged strikers move forward in a silent, menacing mass, forcing the frightened guards to step out of the way. They gather around Joy's fallen body. Mac welcomes the death with excitement, certain that it will steel the striker's determination. Back at the camp, they learn that Al's lunch wagon has been burned to the ground, and that Al has been badly injured.

Chapter 10

The strikers form into groups and depart to picket the fields. Jim joins a group of 50 men led by Sam, who tells of his participation in Bloody Thursday, the famous SAN FRANCISCO longshoremen's strike. The picketers brutally beat a group of scabs. One of the picketers is gunned down, and Jim is shot in the shoulder. The men scatter and flee back to the camp, where they learn that Dakin has been attacked, and his truck destroyed by a mob of vigilantes. London is elected to take his place. Mac admits to Jim that he is afraid that the men will get scared and run. Jim coldly reminds him of how the Greek admiral won the Battle of Salamis by advising his Persian enemies of the Greek escape routes, boxing his men in and forcing them to fight for their survival.

Chapter 11

Jim, Mac, and Doc visit the injured Al, who asks to join the party to fight against the system that beat him and burned his lunch wagon. Doc tells Jim that he has a "religious look in his eyes" and warns him to be careful. Jim admits that he is " . . . happy for the first time . . ." Doc worries that Mr. Anderson will be turned out of the valley for aiding the strik-

ers. Mac assures him that the sacrifice of one man may be necessary for the good of the whole. A heavy rain begins to fall, drenching the camp.

Chapter 12

The next morning Jim visits with Old Dan and then wanders around the camp. He confronts a man who is sowing dissension among the strikers. The strikers hold a funeral for Joy. Mac gives a moving speech telling the men that Joy died for them. Incensed, the strikers prepare to march into town to bury their fallen comrade.

Chapter 13

The strikers carry Joy's body to the town cemetery. Mr. Bolton, the president of the growers association, offers a small raise in wages. He announces that a county ordinance will permit parading on the county roads, and warns that outraged citizens may form vigilante groups. That night the Anderson barn burns to the ground, destroying the entire apple crop. Doc disappears in the confusion. Mac allows Sam to burn down a landowner's house in revenge. Jim warns his friend that he is letting his anger cloud his decision-making. A strange glow comes over Jim's face, and he becomes possessed by a religious-like fervor. He promises to use both himself and Mac to aid the strike with his new intensity.

Chapter 14

Heavily armed police barricade the road and turn back the picketers. Mac flies into a rage at the strikers' cowardice. When Burke, one of the group leaders, accuses London of stockpiling supplies in his tent, London breaks the man's jaw and leaves him unconscious. He leads the angry mob to tear down the police barricade. Exhausted, Jim confesses to Mac that he is afraid that they will be defeated. Mac tries to encourage him.

Chapter 15

The sheriff arrives and announces Mr. Anderson wants the strikers off his land by morning. Mac resolves to stay and fight. He tells Jim to leave and go back to the city, but Jim refuses. A young boy rushes in to tell them that Doc is lying injured in the orchard. Concerned for their friend, the two men plunge into the trees and straight into an ambush. Mac senses the danger and dives to the ground. Jim, however, is killed by a shotgun blast in the face. Mac picks up his friend's body and carries it back to the camp. As the curious men gather around, he climbs up on a platform with the body, and speaks passionately about Jim's selflessness and devotion to the workers.

CHARACTERS AND PLACES

Anderson, Alfred "Al"   A character in *In Dubious Battle,* Alfred is a Communist Party sympathizer in the Torgas Valley and owner of Al's Lunch Wagon, a cozy diner with red stained-glass windows and a sliding door. Alfred's father, Mr. Anderson, lends a five-acre field to strikers as a camp. When vigilantes burn down Al's lunch wagon, he resolves to join the Communist Party and struggle against injustice.

Burke   A character in *In Dubious Battle,* Burke was a strike leader in the Torgas Valley who gets his jaw broken when he accuses London of stockpiling supplies.

Burton, Doc   A character in *In Dubious Battle,* Doc Burton is in charge of health and sanitation at the striker's camp, Doc is a young man with golden hair, large eyes, and a delicate, almost girlish face. When Mack questions his motives for helping the strikers, Doc responds that he does not care about politics, only men. He disappears in the middle of the strike and is not heard from again.

Dakin   A character in *In Dubious Battle,* Dakin is chairman of the strike committee in the Torgas, a coldly controlled man with a thin face and veiled, watchful eyes. Dakin is severely beaten and then jailed when he tries to stop a group of vigilantes from destroying his shiny new Chevrolet truck.

Dan, Old   A character in *In Dubious Battle,* Old Dan is retired top-faller (someone who makes the apples fall from the tops of the trees) who becomes the symbol for the strikers when he falls off of an old ladder and breaks his hip.

Dick   A character in *In Dubious Battle,* Dick is a handsome young man who uses his charm and good looks to solicit donations for the Communist Party. Mack calls him a "bedroom radical." He is in charge of gathering supplies during the Torgas Valley apple picker's strike.

Joy   A character in *In Dubious Battle,* Joy is a Communist Party member who has been beaten and bashed to near senselessness. He becomes a martyr when he is gunned down in the Torgas Valley while leading a group of scabs over to the strikers.

Mac   A character in *In Dubious Battle,* Mac is a large man who is a dedicated member of the Communist Party. He and his protégé, Jim Nolan, organize a strike of the Torgas Valley fruit pickers. Always ready to take advantage of a situation, Mac delivers a baby as a way to enlist the sympathies of the young mother's father-in-law, London, whom he convinces to lead the strike. He sees the murder of his friend Joy as an opportunity to unify the strikers, and sets out to do the same when Jim is murdered in an ambush.

Nilson, Harry   A character in *In Dubious Battle,* Harry is a Communist Party recruiter who lives and works in a small office on the second floor of a dingy three-story building. He befriends Jim Nolan and helps him gain membership in the party.

Nolan, Jim   A character in *In Dubious Battle,* Jim is an intense, lonely man with small gray eyes. He joins the Communist Party in the hope that it will make him feel alive again. He travels to the Torgas Valley to organize a strike among the fruit pickers. He is overcome with religious fervor, becoming a martyr for the strike when he is murdered in an ambush. His father, Roy Nolan, a labor agitator with a famous temper, was shot in the chest and killed when he attempted to dynamite a slaughterhouse where he used to work.

Sam   A character in *In Dubious Battle,* Sam is London's right-hand man during the Torgas Valley apple picker's strike. He proudly recounts his participation in Bloody Thursday, the famous longshoremen strike in San Francisco. When vigilantes burn down the Anderson barn, Sam burns down the house of a large landowner.

Torgas Valley Growers Association   The Torgas Valley Growers Association is a group of bankers and large landowners that control the Torgas Valley in *In Dubious Battle*. Strikes break out throughout the Torgas Valley when the growers association announces a cut in wages. When the strike committee refuses to settle, Mr. Bolter, the association president, promises to drive them from the valley.

Torgas Valley   This small valley of apple orchards in central California is tightly controlled by the bankers and large landowners of the growers association and becomes the scene of terrible violence during an apple picker's strike in *In Dubious Battle*. A fictional geographic location created by Steinbeck, Torgas Valley lies north of SALINAS near Watsonville, California.

FURTHER READING

Benson, Jackson, ed. *The Short Novels of John Steinbeck*. Durham, N.C.: Duke University Press, 1990.

Chamberlain, John. "Books of the Times." *New York Times*, January 28, 1936, 17.

Jackson, Joseph Henry. "*Tortilla Flat* Author Produces Proletarian Novel of Sound Worth." *San Francisco Chronicle*, January 1, 1936, Section D, 4.

"Little Reviews." *Newsweek*, February 1, 1936, 44.

Loftis, Anne. "Literary California: John Steinbeck's 30's Odyssey." *The Californians: The Magazine of California*, January 1, 1989, 48.

———. "The Origins and Impact of *The Grapes of Wrath*." *The Steinbeck Newsletter* (Spring 1988): 4–5.

McCarthy, Mary. "Minority Report." *Nation*, March 11, 1936, 326–327.

Quenell, Peter. "New Novels." *New Statesman and Nation*, May 2, 1936, 670.

Saxton, Alexander. "*In Dubious Battle*: Looking Backward." *Pacific Historical Review* (May 2004): 249–263.

Shillinglaw, Susan. "Steinbeck and Ethnicity." In *After "The Grapes of Wrath": Essays on John Steinbeck in Honor of Tetsumaro Hayashi*, edited by Donald Coers, Robert DeMott, and Paul Ruffin. Athens: Ohio University Press, 1995, 40–57.

Smith, Bernard. "John Steinbeck Comes of Age." *New York Herald Tribune*, February 2, 1936, Books section, 6.

Steinbeck, John. *In Dubious Battle*. New York: Covici and Friede, 1936.

"The Joan in All of Us"
(1956)

In the article "The Joan in All of Us," published January 14, 1956, in *The Saturday Review*, Steinbeck speculates about why it is rare that writers in any language have not thought long and longingly of Joan of Arc (1412–31) as a subject. Having read many of the histories and plays about the famous martyr, Steinbeck concludes that the reason for public fascination with Joan of Arc is obvious: "The story of Joan could not possibly have happened—and did." The improbability of Joan of Arc is so great, he says, that it would not be believed were it not for the evidence and complete historical record that backs it up. Critics, he claims, would find the whole thing impossible. At the time, girls of Joan's social class had no access to political discourse; they were illiterate and considered little more than animals. What is more, military science was a specialized field open only to those born into it. The idea of a girl leading an army is a ludicrous thought given the social context of the time. But Joan took command and she won, and this is why Steinbeck believes writers are drawn to her: "there is not one among us who does not dream that the rules may sometime be set aside—and the dream come true."

"Johnny Bear" (1937)

Steinbeck's short story "Johnny Bear" first appeared in print in *Esquire* magazine in 1937, under the title, "The Ears of Johnny Bear." It was subsequently reprinted in Steinbeck's collection of short stories, THE LONG VALLEY, published by VIKING PRESS in 1938. The central figure in "Johnny Bear" presents a part comic, part tragic idiot savant, whose affliction unwittingly causes deep sorrow. In this he resembles Tularecito from THE PASTURES OF HEAVEN, the character Pirate in TORTILLA FLAT, and Lennie in OF MICE AND MEN. The physically and mentally challenged recur throughout Steinbeck's fiction as catalysts for the unanticipated events of his stories.

Like "THE SNAKE," "Johnny Bear" is a horror story. It falls into the genre of such authors as Mary Shelley and Isaac Bashevis Singer, who created innocent monsters wreaking havoc without any conscious effort or vicious intent. Johnny Bear's preternatural ability to repeat conversations as if he were a living tape recorder leads to disillusion and tragedy. Furthermore, the story raises the questions about a zone of privacy, about appearance and reality, and the extent of human responsibility for those around us.

Along with the short tale, "BREAKFAST," also part of The Long Valley, "Johnny Bear" is unusual in that it has a first person narrator. Never identified by name, the narrator is a stranger to the tiny town of Loma, California, a fictional representation of Castroville, California. The narrator has been hired to drain a swamp to the north of the village. Rather than suffer the misery of living in a temporary bunkhouse next to a noxious marsh plagued by mosquitoes, the narrator rents a room in the town's only boardinghouse. In doing so, he becomes a temporary member of the community, and serves as an objective observer to the events that transpire during the course of the story. Moreover, the narrator's work as a swamp dredger echoes the dredging up of the secret lives of Loma residents.

Like every male inhabitant of Loma, the narrator makes an after-work trip to the Buffalo Bar on a daily basis. The saloon serves as a community "newspaper, theater and club,"—a source of entertainment with nightly poker games and conversation, in addition to being the only convenient place to get a glass of whiskey in the small town during the time of Prohibition. Despite the curmudgeonly demeanor of the owner, Fat Carl, whose bark is worse than his bite, the bar offers the only bright

and convivial spot in Loma for any male "over fifteen years old," because the town itself, as depicted by Steinbeck, is a creepy little place surrounded by a constant malodorous fog. Every night, the narrator dreads returning to his "dismal room" surrounded by the "damp night" and hearing the "far off chattering of the Diesel Engine" dredging the swamp.

Eventually, much to his initial chagrin, the narrator encounters Johnny Bear, a lumbering, deformed, and retarded giant, at the Buffalo Bar. Having struck up an acquaintance with Alex Hartnell, a local farm owner, the narrator is enjoying a quiet conversation about bass fishing when the village curiosity, Johnny Bear, enters the saloon and demands whiskey. The narrator expresses surprise when another patron quietly places a coin on the counter to pay for the "monster's" drink, because "Loma was not a treating town." Hartnell hushes him, and a remarkable demonstration of Johnny Bear's odd gift takes place. He recites word for word, with the precise tone, inflection, and intonation, a conversation that had taken place recently between the narrator and his paramour, Mae Romero. Listening, the narrator becomes increasingly disturbed, and is "cravenly glad Mae Romero has no brothers." At the conclusion of Johnny Bear's recitation, the occupants of the bar silently turn away from the narrator, not in condemnation, but in compassion. Apparently everyone in town has been subjected to Johnny Bear's curiosity, and the only way to prevent being a "victim" is to be accompanied by a dog that can sense the presence of another "animal."

As the evening wears on, the narrator realizes that the inhabitants of Loma will not compensate Johnny Bear with whiskey for any and all of his impersonations of their neighbors. The dialogue must be scandalous and titillating. Johnny returns to the counter, and asks for another drink, after repeating a conversation between a woman and her butcher. No one puts a coin on the bar. However, when the grotesque man offers an argument between two women, one of whom is named Emalin, involving an unrevealed, but clearly devastating dilemma, the whole bar falls silent, and two men step forward to pay for drinks. More astounding, Fat Carl pours a third drink "on the house" for Johnny's performance. Johnny stumbles out into the darkness, and the previous geniality evaporates, as if

"Everyone (had) a problem to settle in his own mind."

The narrator and Harknell leave the Buffalo Bar together, and Harknell explains that the two female voices belong to the most respected, and revered citizens of Loma, Amy and Emalin Hawkins. Daughters of a deceased congressman, the two middle-aged maiden ladies live on a farm tended by Chinese sharecroppers adjoining Harknell's farm. Their lives have always been above reproach, and indeed, as Harknell explains, the two women are symbols of aristocracy and decency for the town, in a place where gentility and decorousness are largely lacking. Johnny Bear's unwitting revelation, even without context or details, has exposed a previously unknown dark secret affecting the two icons of virtue and respectability in the community. Like the dank fog, which obscures the physical features of the town of Loma, the townspeople live in a fog of delusion about the sisters.

Unfortunately, Johnny Bear, having had success in cadging whiskey because of his eavesdropping on the Hawkins sisters, begins to focus all of his efforts on them, even without comprehending a word of their conversations. Shortly after the initial contact with Johnny Bear, en route to the saloon, the narrator and Harknell encounter the town doctor in a rush to the Hawkins's farm. According to the physician, Miss Amy, the younger and gentler sister, has "had a little spell." Several hours later, just as the bar was about to close down, Johnny Bear entered, and began his latest oral imitation, this time speaking in a foreign language, which appears to be Chinese. Curious, the narrator puts a quarter on the bar for Johnny's whiskey, much to his regret. Johnny relates a discussion between the doctor and Miss Emalin, who, deeply distraught, admits she found her sister hanging from a rope, and cut her down before she died. Emalin begs the doctor not to tell anyone, but the secret of the suicide attempt is out, because of Johnny Bear.

Several weeks later, the narrator who had been unable to return to the Buffalo Bar because of a series of ugly accidents with the dredging crew, stops by the saloon for a drink. Shortly thereafter, the news breaks that Miss Amy has successfully committed suicide. Johnny Bear enters the bar, and

demands whiskey. Morbidly curious, Fat Carl pours the misshapen creature a drink, and his narrative begins. Once again, Emalin had found her sibling hanging, and still alive, except this time she chose to leave Amy dangling from a rafter. The doctor asks if Emalin knew her sister was pregnant, and Emalin, revealing a crack in her normally cool façade, softly admits to the knowledge, and requests the doctor not to include the information on the death certificate. Continuing, Johnny Bear speaks in the same foreign language he had mimicked before, and includes a gentle female response in the same language but without the nasal quality. Suddenly Alex Harknell leaps up and demands that Johnny Bear stop. When the idiot continues, Harknell punches him in the face, causing the defective giant to defend himself with a crushing bear hug around Harknell. Fat Carl beats Johnny Bear senseless with a bung starter, and Harknell escapes into the foggy darkness with the narrator. Puzzled by the violence, the narrator asks Harknell why he reacted so vehemently, and Harknell discloses his suspicion that Miss Amy's baby had been fathered by one of the Chinese coolies on the Hawkins's farm.

In this bizarre and affecting story, Steinbeck presents the difficulties of adhering to illusory ideals. Amy and Emalin Hawkins are described variously as the "conscience of the community," "who can't do anything bad," and who "live as though . . . honesty really is the best policy." They demonstrate to the town of Loma an example of behavior that all the residents admire, and strive to achieve without much success. As Alex Harknell says, "It wouldn't be good for any of us if the Hawkins sisters weren't the Hawkins sisters." Johnny Bear is a force of nature, barely human, incapable of comprehending the loftier symbol of Amy and Emalin, and the community cohesion and odd pride offered by the two sisters. As is true in many of Steinbeck's works, nature trumps idealism, whether it is human nature, or the forces of nature. Nevertheless, despite the dire effects of Johnny Bear's "gift," Steinbeck presents the idiot savant in a sympathetic light. Johnny Bear cannot help himself, and his only source of human contact and appreciation comes from satisfying the townspeople's need for malicious gossip.

EARLY CRITICISM

Reaction to "Johnny Bear" as part of the larger collection of *The Long Valley* was mixed. LEWIS GANNETT, in his review for the *New York Herald Tribune*, commented positively about the similarity of Johnny Bear to Lennie in *Of Mice and Men*, and William Faulkner's peculiar characters. Stanley Young, writing for *The New York Times Book Review*, remarked on the "grotesque and haunting character study of "Johnny Bear," and called it "story-telling oblique and effective to the highest degree." Clifton Fadiman, in his column Books for the *New Yorker*, noted that the story was "subtle" and "highly original" but flawed by "the contrivance which some shrewd critics felt . . . marred *Of Mice and Men*." The reviewer for the *Times Literary Supplement* in London called "Johnny Bear" "the cleverest of all, repellent and unforgettable," and J. S., the critic for the London *Times* called the tale "the most original and thoughtful story" in the collection. In his column, Books of the Times for the *New York Times*, Ralph Thompson expressed the hope that in future, "Mr. Steinbeck will avoid cretins, fools, imbeciles, boobies, idiots . . . and particular boneheads," because "(h)e seems to do far better with ordinary people."

CONTEMPORARY PERSPECTIVES

Susan Shillinglaw notes the theme of repressed sexuality recurring throughout *The Long Valley*, of particular interest in "Johnny Bear," "THE WHITE QUAIL," and "THE CHRYSANTHEMUMS." Professor Shillinglaw, borrowing from John Timmerman's insightful analysis, suggests the story also represents another constant Steinbeck subject, that of artistic freedom, and the societal condemnation artists encounter when reporting the truth as they observe it. Peter Lisca suggests the story presents "a conflict of social orders," while Charlotte Byrd notes the similarity between the narrator's storytelling and Johnny Bear's talent.

FURTHER READING

Byrd, Charlotte. "The First Person Narrator in 'Johnny Bear': A Writer's Mind and Conscience." *Steinbeck Quarterly* XXI, 1–2 (Winter/Spring 1988): 6–13.

Fadiman, Clifton. "Books." *New Yorker*, September 24, 1938, 71–73.

Gannett, Lewis. "Books and Things." *New York Herald Tribune*, September 19, 1938, 11.

J. S. "American Tales." *Times* (London), February 17, 1939, 9.

Lisca, Peter. *The Wide World of John Steinbeck*. New Brunswick, N.J.: Rutgers University Press, 1958.

"The Long Valley." *Times Literary Supplement* (London), February 4, 1939, 75.

Shillinglaw, Susan. "Why Is Steinbeck 'Almost Great' and 'Always Read?': Some Reflections." *Steinbeck Newsletter* (Spring 1996): 18–19.

Thompson, Ralph. "Books of the Times." *New York Times*, September 21, 1938, 29.

Young, Stanley. "The Short Stories of John Steinbeck." *New York Times Book Review*, September 25, 1938, 7.

"John Steinbeck's America" (1966)

This seven-part series, published in *Newsday*, November 12–19, 1966, excerpts seven of the nine essays that had been published by VIKING PRESS the month before as AMERICA AND AMERICANS.

"A Lady in Infra-Red" (ca. 1925)

One of Steinbeck's earliest short stories, written while he was a student at STANFORD UNIVERSITY in the 1920s. Set in PANAMA, it tells the story of the pirate HENRY MORGAN. Although never published, "A Lady in Infra-Red" provided the foundation for Steinbeck's first published novel, CUP OF GOLD.

"Let's Go After the Neglected Treasures Beneath the Seas" (1966)

When Ernie Heyn, the editor-in-chief of *Popular Science*, asked John Steinbeck to contribute to the magazine, he submitted an open letter to Heyn about the need for research into the oceans. In "Let's Go After the Neglected Treasures Beneath the Seas," published in September 1966, Steinbeck acknowledges that $21 billion, or even a hundred times that much, is reasonable for space exploration. He believes, however, that at least as much attention should be paid to the undiscovered seas as to space.

Steinbeck contends that, while the space race is motivated primarily by an urge to beat the Russians, discovery of the ocean floor could lead to new places to live as well as new sources of food and valuable minerals. He observed the Mohole Project, which drilled underwater into basalt in the Earth's crust. After that project, geological textbooks were rendered obsolete. Though the discovery was stunning, Congress refused to allot any money to the project.

Steinbeck argues that the hundreds of separate experimental groups that are exploring the ocean should be coordinated, the same way that NASA pulled together all space exploration under one umbrella. He looks forward to the next Mohole expedition with joy.

"A Letter on Criticism" (1955)

In its Summer 1954 volume, *Colorado Quarterly* published an article titled "*The Grapes of Wrath*: A 'Wagon's West Romance'" by Bernard Bowron, a professor of English and American Studies at the University of Minnesota. Bowron found fault with Steinbeck for his condescension toward the OKIES in THE GRAPES OF WRATH. Bowron's article was criticized in a subsequent article written by Warren G. French appearing in the Winter 1955 edition of the same journal, and titled "Another Look at *The Grapes of Wrath.*" "A Letter on Criticism," published in the Autumn 1955 edition of the *Colorado Quarterly,* is Steinbeck's response to the journal's request that he comment on these two articles. The author states that he finds some interest in the two writers' academic skills and terminology, but that neither of them provides much help to either a writer or a

reader. He compares their analysis to a childish parlor game in which no one gets kissed, and further labels the disagreement about *The Grapes of Wrath* as "a bunch of crap," which would only discourage young readers from exploring and enjoying literature. Defending his work from charges of obscurity, Steinbeck suggests that arcane and academic criticism could be likened to examining the "skeletal remains of a pretty young girl," giving no insight or comprehension of the work as a living whole. Finally, Steinbeck reveals that writing books is a lonely and difficult job, and he is having too much trouble just being a writer to worry about criticism.

"Letters to Alicia" (1965–1968)

Between 1965 and 1968 Steinbeck wrote a series of articles in the form of letters addressed to ALICIA GUGGENHEIM, the deceased editor of the Long Island tabloid *Newsday*. The articles, first suggested by Alicia Guggenheim's husband HARRY F. GUGGENHEIM, constitute a strange and controversial body of 87 handwritten letters—of which 77 were eventually published in *Newsday*—that Steinbeck submitted to the paper over the course of four years. These include articles written from the author's home in SAG HARBOR, NEW YORK, as well as from Europe, Israel, and Southeast Asia. Steinbeck addresses such diverse topics as the author's observations on quitting smoking, predictions for the future of the Israeli state, and a vigorous defense of the LYNDON B. JOHNSON administration's policies in Southeast Asia. Steinbeck's "Letters to Alicia" were syndicated to a number of papers, both domestic and international, that subscribed to *Newsday's* Newsday Specials Service.

Lifeboat (1943)

Lifeboat was written by John Steinbeck in 1943 at the request of Twentieth Century–Fox, which was commissioned by the Maritime Commission to do a propaganda film about the merchant marine ships that served as the lifeline of the allied effort during WORLD WAR II. Steinbeck prepared a manuscript about a group of civilians and sailors who are stranded aboard a lifeboat after their ship is sunk somewhere in the Atlantic by a German submarine. After a disagreement with the director, Alfred Hitchcock, over his use of a single set for the film, Steinbeck left the production having only sketched a few scenes and a prose summary. Twentieth Century–Fox then assigned Joe Swerling to prepare the screenplay from Steinbeck's original manuscript. Swerling made various important changes to the story. At the behest of Hitchcock, the final script presented a far more blatant anti-Nazi propaganda vehicle than was the author's original intention. Steinbeck had in mind an antiwar film with the stranded inhabitants of the lifeboat representing a microcosm of a world adrift in a sea of mindless violence with each survivor corresponding to a particular archetype. The black-and-white film was released in January 1944, soon after Steinbeck returned from a six-month stint as a war correspondent in the European war theater. Steinbeck received an Academy Award nomination for the best original story. Especially dissatisfied with Hitchcock's treatment of some of his characters, including the film's portrayal of Joe, the ship's steward, as "a stock comedy Negro," as well as certain derogatory remarks about organized labor and "fellow travelers," the author attempted in vain to have his name removed from the finished film. Steinbeck's unpublished manuscript can be viewed by appointment at several Steinbeck research centers in this country, including the NATIONAL STEINBECK CENTER.

SYNOPSIS

A merchant marine ship is sunk somewhere in the Atlantic by a German U-boat. The U-boat shells the lifeboats filled with survivors before finally being sunk by an Allied aircraft. The damage is total, and the water is filled with bodies and debris. An elegantly dressed woman writer, Constance Porter, sits alone in a battered lifeboat in the fog.

She films the destruction with a small handheld camera. Kovac, the engineer of the sunken ship, swims up to the boat and climbs aboard. Constance tells him that she saw a shell hit the U-boat and sink it. Kovac brings aboard another man: Sparks, the ship's radioman. They search through the wreckage and bring aboard five more survivors: Gus Smith, a seaman; Ms. Mackenzie, a nurse; Joe, the ship's steward; Mr. Rittenhouse, a millionaire industrialist; and a nameless English refugee who suffers from shell shock and carries her dead infant in her arms. The nurse treats Gus, whose leg has been severely wounded in the explosion. Suddenly, a hand rises out of the water. They pull a large man aboard. The man's name is Willie, a German from the sunken U-boat. The survivors argue about what to do with the German. Some of the crew are in favor of throwing him overboard, while others say that they must hold him as a prisoner of war. Finally they agree to keep him on the boat as a prisoner. They hold a ceremony to bury the Englishwoman's baby. Delirious with shock, the woman throws herself overboard during the night and drowns. The next day the crew takes stock of their situation and realizes that they have little food and water and no compass. Constance speaks with the German, Willie, and discovers that he is the captain of the sunken U-boat. Gus's leg turns gangrenous and must be amputated. Willie agrees to do the surgery, explaining that he was a surgeon in civilian life. The amputation is successful and Gus's life is saved. The castaways decide to sail for Bermuda, the closest landmass. Willie directs the boat's course, but Sparks soon realizes that he is leading them in the wrong direction. They discover that the German has a hidden compass and is directing them toward a German supply ship. A severe storm blows in and nearly capsizes the boat, breaking the mast and throwing the remaining food and water overboard. Willie takes command of the boat. He explains that they are far from Bermuda and that the German supply ship is the only hope of salvation. He rows the boat tirelessly as the other survivors slowly succumb to hunger and thirst. Gus discovers that Willie is concealing a bottle of water in his shirt. The German pushes Gus overboard and watches him drown. Discovering what Willie has done, the crew beats him and forces him from the boat to drown. Constance laments that they gave in so easily to their enemy. She urges them to work together, giving up her prized Cartier bracelet in the hope of luring a fish with its shiny diamonds. The bracelet works and they are attempting to land a large fish when the German supply ship appears in the distance. Constance drops the line, losing both the fish and the bracelet. A small launch moves toward them and then turns around and hurries back to the larger ship as shells begin to explode in the water around them. The American fleet sinks the German supply ship. The survivors cheer and discuss what they will do when the approaching ships pick them up. Suddenly a hand appears from the water. They pull aboard a young German sailor and are debating what to do with him when he pulls a gun on them. Sparks disarms the young man, who asks fearfully if they are going to kill him. Sparks indicates all he can think about are the deaths of the mother and her baby, and of Gus. Constance suggests that those who died should make the decision. The film ends leaving the viewer to determine whether the young German sailor lives or dies.

FILM CREDITS
(TWENTIETH CENTURY–FOX, 1944)

Screenplay: Jo Swerling
Director: Alfred Hitchcock
Producer: Kenneth MacGowan
Codirector: Alexander Hackensmid
Director of Photography: Glen MacWilliams
Art Director: James Basevi and Maurice Ransford
Set Designer: Thomas Little
Associate: Frank E. Hughes
Film Editor: Dorothy Spencer
Music: Hugo W. Friedhofer
Musical Direction: Emil Newman
Connie Porter: Tallulah Bankhead
Gus: William Bendix
Willie, the German: Walter Slezak
Alice Mackenzie: Mary Anderson
Mr. Rittenhouse: Henry Hull

Kovac: John Hodiak
Stanley Garrett (Sparks): Hume Cronyn
Joe the steward: Canada Lee

The Log from the Sea of Cortez
(1951)

The name for the log (or journal) portion of Steinbeck's scientific collaboration with his friend EDWARD RICKETTS to study marine life in the Sea of Cortez. There is some debate about whether *The Log* was written entirely by Steinbeck or was a collaborative effort on the part of the two men. While *The Log* does bear many of the distinctive marks of Steinbeck's prose style, the author later insisted that it was based entirely upon notes taken by Ed Ricketts during the six-week journey. For a synopsis of *The Log,* see SEA OF CORTEZ: A LEISURELY JOURNAL OF TRAVEL AND RESEARCH.

"The Lonesome Vigilante"
(1936)

"The Lonesome Vigilante," published in *Esquire,* October 1936, follows a man named Mike in the short time following a lynching. It begins immediately after an African-American man has been hanged in the park. The crowd is beginning to break up and go their separate ways. Some of the men who are left are trying to burn the body. Mike protests this dully, but doesn't try to stop it. He feels empty and slow. He knows that he'll want to remember this later, but he can't seem to focus. As he walks away from the remnants of the mob, he stumbles into a bar to drive off the loneliness that settles on him. A pain in his chest reminds him of being crushed against the jail door and fighting to be one of the men who pulled the rope.

The bartender, a small mouselike man, is the only one in the bar. He had caught the end of the lynching and hurried back to open up because he thought some of the men might be thirsty. He presses Mike for details, and Mike tells him about it. Gradually, a group of men had gathered outside the jail, and finally burst in. The sheriff just yelled at them to make sure they got the right man. The African-American man stood still and closed his eyes while the men in the cell beat him. Mike thinks that the man died when he hit his head on the cement floor, because he didn't struggle when Mike and the others took his clothes off or strung him up. He's disappointed; he wanted to do it right. When he shows the bartender a piece of the African-American's denim jeans, the bartender offers to pay him for it, so he can display it in the bar.

After the bartender closes up, he and Mike walk toward home, and he wonders about the man. He and Mike agree that, although they've known plenty of nice "niggers," this one must have been a fiend, because all the papers said so. The loneliness descends on Mike again.

When he arrives home, his wife accuses him of being with a woman. When he goes into the bathroom, he realizes that that is exactly how he feels.

The Long Valley (1938)

Steinbeck's ninth book, *The Long Valley* is a collection of 12 short stories. Many of the stories included in the volume were written earlier in the author's career and published in magazines such as *Harper's* and the *North American Review*. With the exception of "Saint Katy the Virgin," all of the stories take place in California's Central Valley, and many of them foreshadow themes that Steinbeck would later use in his more famous novels. Some of the stories, such as "THE CHRYSANTHEMUMS," are considered to be among the finest examples of Steinbeck's short fiction, and a few, including "The Chrysanthemums," "FLIGHT," and "THE RAID" were later adapted to film. VIKING PRESS published the book in 1938.

The 12 short stories in the volume are "The Chrysanthemums," "THE WHITE QUAIL," "Flight,"

"THE SNAKE," "BREAKFAST," "The Raid," "THE HARNESS," "THE VIGILANTE," "JOHNNY BEAR," "THE MURDER," "SAINT KATY THE VIRGIN," and "THE RED PONY."

"Madison Avenue and the Election" (1956)

"Madison Avenue and the Election," published in the March 31, 1956, edition of *Saturday Review,* is a humorous article about the virtues and dangers of employing advertising firms to develop political campaigns, a tactic that was first employed in the 1952 presidential campaign between General Dwight D. Eisenhower and Governor ADLAI E. STEVENSON. Relying heavily on the new medium of television, advertising firms produced a series of slick political commercials for both candidates. Chief among the strategies implemented by the professionals, Steinbeck writes, is the trapping of captive television viewers. The trick while the audience is half-hypnotized is to offer a short, sharp message, dangling the candidate before the viewers. The only danger, Steinbeck muses, is that the audience might become confused between advertised products and political candidates: "There is great danger that they will buy a Senator and vote for a cereal." Still more dangerous is the possibility that the candidates will enter into partnerships with the advertising agencies. The author also humorously suggests that a television audience might not be able to resist a chocolate or cream-covered candidate, and might insist on tasting the office seeker before voting.

"The Mail I've Seen" (1956)

In the article "The Mail I've Seen," published August 4, 1956, in *Saturday Review,* Steinbeck writes of the various types of correspondence that he receives as a writer. The correspondence, he says, generally falls within a few categories: fan letters written simply to communicate a reader's admiration; letters that protest the writer's morals or choice of subject; the honest out-and-out denunciations, many of which use profanity to make their point; and the requests from fans seeking autographs or photographs. The writer also receives many thoughtful and intelligent letters discussing some aspect of his work, and indicates that such letters are good and warming to receive. He outlines the many requests for money that come in the mail, particularly in the months after a book is published. Additionally there are always the "bughousers"—those letters from crazy or obsessive fans who make outrageous or obsessive claims. Finally the professional writer often receives invitations from individuals to collaborate on their particular project. Such letters, Steinbeck indicates, claim that the letter writer has an interesting story that would make excellent material for a book; the writer generally refuses to reveal the alleged material without a contractual commitment for fear that the author will steal the idea; and they always end with the business proposition that Steinbeck can write and they can share the profits 50-50. The author recounts the variety of offers that he has received from convicts, old ladies, doctors, and dreamers. Finally the author reproduces in its entirety an offer from a woman of the inside scoop on the world of professional women's wrestling.

A Medal for Benny (1945)

Steinbeck's third WORLD WAR II movie after *THE MOON IS DOWN* and *LIFEBOAT*, *A Medal for Benny* was based on an original story written by Steinbeck and the brother of his childhood friend MAX WAGNER, JACK WAGNER, with whom he had previously collaborated on the film adaptation of his novel *THE PEARL*. *A Medal for Benny* tells the story of a shiftless troublemaker, Benny, who joins the army to escape his hometown and a disordered life. When it is learned that Benny has died a heroic death in battle and posthumously won the Con-

gressional Medal of Honor, his small town decides to remember him as a great man and a hero. The townspeople expect his unwilling girlfriend Lolita to spend the rest of her life honoring the man she never really loved. J. Carrol Naish was nominated for an Academy Award for best supporting actor for his portrayal of Charley, Benny's father, and Steinbeck and Wagner received nominations for the category of best original story.

FILM CREDITS (PARAMOUNT, 1945)

Written for the screen by John Steinbeck and Jack Wagner

> Screenplay: Frank Butler
> Director: Irving Pichel
> Producer: Paul Jones
> *Lolita Sierra*: Dorothy Lamour
> *Joe Morales*: Arturo De Cordova
> *Charley Martini*: J. Carrol Naish
> *Raphael Catalina*: Mikhail Rasummy

"The Miracle of Tepayac" (1948)

In "The Miracle of Tepayac," published December 25, 1948, in *Collier's*, Steinbeck tells the classic legend of Our Lady of Guadalupe, the patron saint of MEXICO. Juan Diego, a humble peasant, lives with his wife Maria Lucia in the little town of Cuautitlan, near Mexico City. Juan Diego is inconsolable when Maria Lucia dies of a fever. He begins to wander in the hills, grieving for his loss. One day he comes to the hill of Tepayac (Tepeyac), where he sees a vision of the Blessed Virgin Mary. She orders him to go before the bishop of Mexico and tell him that a temple must be built on the hill. The poor Indian obeys her. He walks to the capitol and shyly seeks an audience with the bishop. When he tells the bishop about the Virgin's command, the man orders him to go away and reflect on what he has seen. Juan Diego returns to Tepayac to tell the Virgin that he has failed and that she should send somebody more important than he. She commands him to go back and order the bishop to build a temple. Juan Diego returns to the bishop, citing his authority as Mary's messenger. The bishop demands proof and assigns two men to follow Juan Diego to insure that the man does no harm to himself or anybody else. As he walks, the poor peasant is caught up in a cloud that carries him to the Holy Mother. He tells her that the bishop demands a sign. The virgin tells him to go to Tepayac, and there he will find his sign. Upon the hill the man finds a beautiful clump of roses of Castile growing where none could grow before. He gathers the delicate blossoms in his cloak and takes them to the bishop. The roses fall to the floor, revealing an image of the Mother of God on the rough cactus fibers of the cloth. The bishop orders a temple to be built upon the hill of Tepayac, and Juan Diego spends the rest of his days sweeping out the chapel and caring for it until he dies.

The Moon Is Down (1942)

Steinbeck's 14th book, *The Moon Is Down* is the author's second attempt to write a short novel in play form (OF MICE AND MEN was the first). The PLAY-NOVELETTE format attempts to create a literary work in which the original dialogue could be transferred directly to a stage, while at the same time allowing a reader to enjoy the story in book form. The story was written on assignment from the FOREIGN INFORMATION SERVICE, an agency of the Office of Strategic Services charged with combating Nazi propaganda in the United States and abroad. Steinbeck's original version set the story in a small American town invaded by enemy troops. The FIS rejected Steinbeck's submission, feeling it might demoralize the civilian public. Steinbeck revised his manuscript and submitted it to his publisher, VIKING PRESS. The rewrite provided a setting of an unnamed Scandinavian town, invaded by unidentified foreign soldiers. The title is taken from a line in Shakespeare's *Macbeth,* Act 2, Scene 1, in which Macbeth makes his final preparations to betray and kill Duncan in the dead of night while the "moon is down." The novelette was published in 1942. It was

extraordinarily successful, selling millions of copies throughout the world and passing through a remarkable 76 editions. Oscar Serlin purchased the rights for the theater adaptation, which was later nominated for best play by the New York Drama Critics' Circle, where it came in second.

Steinbeck's book was heavily criticized for being too favorable to the occupiers. The enemy troops are portrayed as human beings with their own fears, feelings of tenderness and loneliness, and even compassion for the residents of the town. Much to Steinbeck's surprise after the liberation of Europe, former leaders of resistance forces throughout the continent applauded the book, and revealed its importance in maintaining the will to oppose the Germans. The book had been copied, often by hand, and surreptitiously circulated in many of the occupied countries during WORLD WAR II. It remains a succinct and powerful psychological study of the effects of war on both conquerors and conquered. Steinbeck, himself, was awarded the King Haakon Liberty Cross for the work in 1946.

EARLY CRITICISM

When *The Moon Is Down* was first published, it received mixed reviews. Some lauded its technical craftsmanship; others lamented the author's propaganda in the book. After reading *The Moon Is Down,* the writer Wallace Stegner was disappointed in the book as a whole (*Boston Daily Globe*). He argues that the novel is a story of a "peaceful" people, whose country is invaded and conquered but whose resistance is driven "underground" by an invader. Although Stegner credits the novel for Steinbeck's craftsmanship and realizes that the work was designed for immediate conversion to the stage, he finds the book to be a total failure. Noting the faked setting—the country is not in an actual Nazi-occupied region—Stegner calls the "little people" in *The Moon Is Down* lackadaisical, because "the horrors through which they live have been so constantly before us in the headlines and radio reports that . . . we are calloused to their pain." He believes the literary and social value of the book is nearly nonexistent and that Steinbeck's talent in writing does not come off as well as it does in his previous works, such as *THE*

GRAPES OF WRATH, IN DUBIOUS BATTLE, and *Of Mice and Men*. Stegner's criticism of *The Moon Is Down* extends to his disappointment at Steinbeck's inability to come up with graver and more pressing issues to write about. For instance Stegner views Steinbeck's treatment of Mayor Orden as "a mouthpiece of the democratic way" to be an instance of making literature propaganda.

Like Stegner, Clifton Fadiman feels that both the form and the message in *The Moon Is Down* are unsatisfactory (*New Yorker*). In pointing out the poor qualities of the book, Fadiman regrets that *The Moon Is Down* has a "deceiving" form and an "inadequate" message. Fadiman's criticism of the book gets even harsher when he says that "*The Moon Is Down* is a novel only in a Steinbeckian sense." What Fadiman dislikes most about the book is its play format, a style that Steinbeck had experimented with in *Of Mice and Men*. Fadiman finds the dialogues in the book puzzling because the characters neither "speak" in the conventional style of plays, nor do they "talk" in the realistic fashion of Steinbeck's characters in his previous books.

However, in spite of the somewhat negative reception of the book in the United States, *The Moon Is Down*, both as a book and a play, was well received in Norway, whose experience during World War II was most similar to that of the unnamed country in the story. The play *The Moon Is Down* first opened in Stockholm in March 1943. It was so successful that it was staged in many large Norwegian theaters. The play also won approval from Swedish critics, who praised Steinbeck for his "prophetic insight" (*Time*, April 19, 1943).

Even in the United States, *The Moon Is Down* received many positive reviews. In "John Steinbeck's Story of a Military Invasion Appears on the Stage," Brooks Atkinson, calls Steinbeck "a realist of genuine integrity" (*New York Times*). According to Atkinson, *The Moon Is Down* is not a rhetorical play but one which "cuts deep." Atkinson is impressed by Steinbeck's portrayal of the invaders not as "supermen" but as "human beings, subject to human limitations." Likewise Steinbeck does not portray the people of the occupied town as heroes; these ordinary people are "miners and fishermen with wives and families, subject to the usual needs." According

to Atkinson, though many reviewers and readers have paid special attention to Steinbeck's treatment of the "enemy" characters, Steinbeck's portrait of Colonel Lanser, commanding officer of the invading detachment, is especially notable for transcending the notion that the Nazi invader is a "cold-blooded despot." The character is a "tolerant and forbearing, disillusioned" veteran who understands the military science of conquest and the psychology of the invaded people. Atkinson states that Steinbeck has given the book's most important character to the "enemy." Because of such a changed angle in viewing the characters in the book, Atkinson finds that the theme of Steinbeck's work is not about conflict between the usual heroes and enemies, but one between humanity and inhumanity. Therefore, Atkinson concludes that *The Moon Is Down* is "an impressive and heartening play."

CONTEMPORARY PERSPECTIVES

Since the 1970s, Steinbeck scholars such as Tetsumaro Hayashi, John Ditsky, Donald Coers, and others have done extensive work on *The Moon Is Down*. Many of these critics have tried to make a case for the play-novella as a viable form. Acknowledging that *The Moon Is Down* may have been written and used as propaganda, Coers argues in his introduction to the work that the book may instead be best described "as a work of literature that served as propaganda." In evaluating the dramatic functions of some characters such as Dr. Winter, Hayashi argues that in *The Moon Is Down* Steinbeck does fulfill his mission as a writer, to "declare and celebrate man's proved capacity for greatness of heart and spirit—for gallantry in defeat—for courage, compassion, and love" as Steinbeck states in his Nobel Prize acceptance speech.

In "Steinbeck's 'European' Play-Novella: *The Moon Is Down*" John Ditsky notices the uniqueness of the work. The critic urges the reader and viewer to pay attention to the strangeness of Steinbeck's Europe and his European characters in the work. This strangeness, according to Ditsky, may be observed from "the way in which Steinbeck's characters discover who and what they are through moments of existential crisis, and then react to this discovery by producing language which is sometimes extraordinary." Ditsky further argues that although the play does have generalities, ideals, and speeches that are universally American and European, the play's success in countries that had indeed been occupied during World War II proves a most convincing paradox: Steinbeck, in producing the play and projecting characters "who are not particularly European at all . . . had managed to make a dramatic statement in the delineation of which European audiences could recognize the universal—and themselves." In doing so, as Ditsky argues, Steinbeck helps the reader acknowledge the writer's view of "how and why and when the world becomes a stage."

SYNOPSIS

Chapter 1

Mr. Corell, a popular local storekeeper, organizes a shooting competition in the country for the local garrison of troops. While the soldiers are away, a battalion of enemy parachuters invades the town. The soldiers hurry back, but they are too late. Mr. Corell is revealed to be an agent of the enemy. The leader of the battalion, Colonel Lanser, requests an audience with Mayor Orden in the mayor's palace. The mayor's friend and the town doctor, Doctor Winter, waits in the sitting room when Captain Bentick, one of Lanser's junior officers, arrives to search the mayor's home for weapons. The captain has a list, compiled by Mr. Corell, indicating which houses have firearms. The mayor and Doctor Winter discuss the proper etiquette for receiving the colonel. Lanser arrives, accompanied by George Corell. The mayor asks Lanser to send Corell out of the room. Lanser complies, disregarding the traitor's complaints. He explains to the mayor that they plan to occupy the town and operate the nearby coal mines. He requests that the mayor retain his position and protect the citizens by keeping them orderly and insuring that they continue to work in the mines. He also requests that the mayor allow him and his staff to move into the mayor's palace. Annie, Orden's temperamental cook, is upset by the presence of the enemy troops in the kitchen. In the town's first act of rebellion she throws a pan of boiling water on one, and bites another.

Chapter 2

The colonel and his staff of five officers settle into the mayor's palace. Captain Loft, a young, idealistic soldier, complains that Captain Bentick has been patrolling the town without wearing his combat helmet. Major Hunter, the staff engineer, sits at a table working on a drawing of a railroad siding for his model train set. Lieutenants Prackle and Tonder argue over the merits of a blonde pinup torn from a magazine. Tonder tells Colonel Lanser that he would like to live in the town when the occupation is over. Lanser, weary of the naïveté of the idealistic youth, warns him to wait until the war is over before he starts building his estate. Mr. Corell arrives and is introduced to the staff. He has been injured when a stone fell or was thrown from a cliff as he walked outside of the town, an event which he is sure was only an accident. Lanser tells him that his job is over and that he should return to the capital, but Corell insists on staying. He asks to be appointed mayor in place of Orden. Lanser insists that Corell's life is in great danger and that order and discipline will be easier to maintain if Mayor Orden retains the administration of the town. Captain Loft rushes in to inform Lanser that Captain Bentick has been killed in a dispute with Alexander Morden, a miner who refuses to work in the mines.

Chapter 3

Annie insists to Joseph, the mayor's manservant, that if they shoot Alexander Morden she is going to kill some of them herself. Joseph confides to her that some of the town's men escaped to England during the night. Mayor Orden arrives with his friend Doctor Winter. He is upset at the colonel's insistence on holding a show trial of Alexander Morden in the mayor's palace. He confides his concern about the ambiguity of his position: "The people don't quite trust me and neither does the enemy." Molly Morden, the wife of the condemned man, is shown into the mayor's chamber. She asks the mayor if it is true that he is going to sentence her husband. He assures her that he will not pass judgment on Alexander, whom he has known since he was a boy. The mayor sends his wife to Molly's house to take care of her. He asks Doctor Winter to return and keep him company in the evening. Colonel Lanser explains to the mayor that it is necessary to try Morden publicly since punishment deters other potential criminals. He insists that it will prevent further bloodshed if the sentence emanates from the local authorities. Orden bitterly refuses to be complicit in the trial. He insists that as mayor he does not have the authority to pass a sentence of death. He agrees to be present at the trial so that Alex will not feel lonely.

Chapter 4

It begins to snow heavily. An oppressive mood hangs over the town. Lanser and his staff sit in judgment of Alexander Morden. Captain Loft reads the charges. Alex insists that he hit Captain Bentick, but that he did not kill him. He admits that he was trying to hit Captain Loft when Bentick interfered in the scuffle and was struck by his pick. Alex insists proudly that he is not sorry for his actions, but Lanser insists that the court record reflect that the prisoner was overcome with remorse. After Alex is sentenced to death, Orden makes a speech assuring the condemned man that he, the mayor, is not acting with the occupiers. He tells Alexander to die with the knowledge that the enemy will have no rest until they are gone or dead. A gunshot crashes through the window and wounds Lieutenant Prackle. Lanser orders that the town be searched once again for firearms. He places Mayor Orden in protective custody and issues a warning that for every occupying soldier wounded or killed, "five, ten, even a hundred" townspeople will be executed.

Chapter 5

The occupation drags on for weeks and months. The soldiers begin to feel surrounded and insecure under the cold gazes of the townspeople who never relax in their hatred. The occupiers begin to detest the town and dream of their homes and families. Meanwhile, the townspeople wage a silent campaign of sabotage against the occupiers, destroying the rail lines and interrupting the supply of coal from the mine. The enemy takes control of the food supply, issuing rations to the obedient and withholding them from the disobedient. Their efforts are useless and the officers begin to feel the

strain of their position. Lieutenant Tonder complains bitterly about their situation and dreams of going home. Loft returns from the mines after issuing an order to withhold food from the families of miners who refuse to work. Tonder continues voicing his worries and complaints, becoming hysterical. Loft slaps him across the face, leaving him in stunned silence.

Chapter 6

Violating the curfew, Annie sneaks to Molly Morden's house to tell her that the mayor would like to use her house for a meeting with the Anders brothers, two young men who plan to escape to England that very night. Molly agrees to host the meeting and Annie disappears into the darkness. Lieutenant Tonder appears at her door while she waits nervously for the mayor. He confesses to her that he is lonely and that he has admired her for some time for her beauty. The young widow taunts him, telling him that he must come back with food if he wishes to be with her. Tonder departs, promising to return soon. Annie appears with the two tall, blond Anders brothers, Will and Tom, followed by the mayor and Doctor Winter. The brothers explain that they plan to kidnap Mr. Corell, steal his boat, and escape to England. The mayor asks the brothers to carry a message to the allies requesting explosives for the resistance movement. The meeting adjourns suddenly when Lieutenant Tonder returns. Molly kills Tonder with a pair of scissors.

Chapter 7

Some weeks later under the cover of darkness planes circle over the town dropping small packages. Each package contains a stick of dynamite, instructions for its use, and a piece of fine chocolate. The instructions ask the "unconquered people" to hide the dynamite and to use it for small acts of sabotage in the night, concentrating on transportation routes. The townspeople comb the countryside, gathering the packages and hiding the explosives. The colonel frets that this is only the beginning, that if it is successful grenades or poison will follow it. He issues orders to take the town's leaders hostage and search every house. Lieutenant Prackle confides to the colonel that he is in love

Mayor Orden and Doctor Winter being taken hostage in the 1943 film production of *The Moon Is Down* (Photofest)

with a girl from the town. The colonel wearily assures him that whatever happens in the relationship is of no importance, so long as Prackle can shoot the young woman when it is ordered. He dismisses the young lieutenant and receives Mr. Corell. Corell is a changed man. His arm is bandaged and he wears a bitter look on his face. He accuses Mayor Orden of complicity in the resistance movement. He insists that Lanser arrest the mayor and the doctor and hold them as hostages.

Chapter 8

Doctor Winter is escorted to the mayor's palace. Orden admits to his friend that he is ashamed because he is afraid of dying and has been thinking of escaping or pleading for his life. The doctor reas-

sures him that they are thoughts common to everyone. The mayor recites a passage from the *Apology*, Plato's classic dialogue of the trial of Socrates, which teaches that a good man should not calculate his chances of living or dying, but rather should do what is right. The old friends reminisce about their youth. Lanser enters, followed by Lieutenant Prackle, who announces that they have captured some men with dynamite. Lanser tells the mayor that this must stop and informs him that he is being held hostage for the good behavior of the people. The mayor assures him that he can stop nothing and that the people can do without him. Proudly, he tells the colonel that free men will always prevail over "herd men," those who blindly follow leaders. He barely finished his words when an explosion sounds in the distance. The mayor gives his watch and his chain of office to Dr. Winter and departs, saying "Crito, I owe a cock to Asclepius. Will you remember to pay the debt?" quoting Socrates' dying words. Dr. Winter nods his head sadly and assures his friend that the debt shall be paid.

CHARACTERS

Anders brothers   Characters in *The Moon Is Down*. The two brothers who escape to England carrying Mayor Orden's request for explosives for the resistance movement.

Annie   A character in *The Moon Is Down*. Mayor Orden's ill-tempered cook, Annie gains a reputation as an exponent of liberty when she throws a pot of boiling water on the soldiers who occupy the mayor's palace. Annie becomes an agent for the mayor, helping to coordinate the resistance against the occupying army.

Bentick, Captain   A character in *The Moon Is Down*, Captain Bentick is a member of Colonel Lanser's staff. Bentick is a family man and lover of dogs. He has a strange admiration for the British country gentleman, whose style he affects in his habits and appearance. His is accidentally killed by a swinging pick when he steps into a scuffle between Captain Loft and Alexander Morden.

Corell, Mr.   A character in *The Moon Is Down*, Mr. Corell is a popular storekeeper before the invasion. However, Corell turns out to be an enemy sympathizer who paves the way for the occupation. He arranges to send the local garrison of troops into the countryside for a shooting contest on the day of the invasion. When he demands to be appointed mayor during the occupation, he is rejected by Colonel Lanser, who warns him that his life is in danger. The townspeople revile him as a traitor and attempt to kidnap him and drown him at sea.

Hunter, Major   A character in *The Moon Is Down*, Major Hunter is a member of Colonel Lanser's staff. Hunter is a humorless little engineer in charge of rebuilding the rail lines and town infrastructure damaged by sabotage and bombing.

Lanser, Colonel   A character in *The Moon Is Down*, Colonel Lanser is the commanding officer of the small occupation force. Lanser is an experienced soldier who served in Belgium and France during the previous war. He is haunted by the futility of his efforts and the ignorance of his leaders. Lanser asks Mayor Orden to pass sentence on Alexander Morden to promote public order. He arrests Mayor Orden and holds him hostage for the good behavior of his people.

Loft, Captain   A character in *The Moon Is Down*, Captain Loft is a member of Colonel Lanser's staff. Loft is an energetic and ambitious young man who "thought and believed that a soldier is the highest development of animal life" and who thought of war as "the proper career of a properly brought-up young man".

Orden, Mayor   A character in *The Moon Is Down*, Orden is the longtime mayor of a small town that is occupied by the enemy. He lives in the mayor's palace with his wife, Madame. Orden is sometimes referred to by the honorific "His Excellency." Mayor Orden refuses to pass sentence at Alexander Morden's trial. He assures Alex that his enemies will receive no rest until they are defeated. Actively plotting to resist the occupiers, Orden sends a message to England asking them to send explosives. When the explosives finally arrive, Orden is held hostage to guarantee the good behavior of the people. The mayor assures Colonel Lanser that he will stop nothing and that the people can do without him.

Morden, Alexander   A character in *The Moon Is Down*, Alexander Morden is a wide-shouldered, heavily muscled miner. Alexander accidentally strikes Captain Bentick with a pick and kills him while fighting with Captain Loft, who had ordered him to return to work in the mine. He is sentenced to death by firing squad. His widow, Molly Morden, begs Mayor Orden not to pass sentence on her husband. She is visited by Lieutenant Tonder, who has taken a romantic interest in her. She kills Tonder with a pair of scissors and, with the help of the mayor, escapes into the countryside.

Prackle, Lieutenant   A character in *The Moon Is Down*, Lieutenant Prackle is a member of Colonel Lanser's staff. Prackle is a happy, sentimental young man. He is shot in the shoulder by an unknown sniper.

Tonder, Lieutenant   A character in *The Moon Is Down*, Lieutenant Tonder is a member of Colonel Lanser's staff. Tonder is a bitter poet and dark romantic who longs for death on the battlefield. He suffers a nervous breakdown under the strain of the occupation and utters the phrase "the flies have conquered the flypaper," which is transformed into a song of the resistance. Tonder is murdered by Molly Morden when he seeks her companionship.

Winter, Doctor   A character in *The Moon Is Down*, Doctor Winter is a physician and town historian who is friend and adviser to Mayor Orden. He assists the mayor in planning the resistance against the enemy invaders. He is taken hostage along with Mayor Orden to insure the good behavior of the townspeople.

THE FILM: *THE MOON IS DOWN* (TWENTIETH CENTURY–FOX, 1943)

Based on the novel by John Steinbeck

> Screenplay: Nunnally Johnson
> Director: Irving Pichel
> Producer: Nunnally Johnson
> *Mayor Orden:* Henry Travers
> *Colonel Lanser:* Sir Cedric Hardwicke
> *Doctor Winter:* Lee J. Cobb
> *Molly Morden:* Dorris Bowdon
> *Madam Orden:* Margaret Wycherly
> *Lt. Tonder:* Peter Van Eyck
> *George Corell:* E. J. Ballantine

The film rights were purchased for $300,000 by Twentieth Century–Fox, the largest sum ever paid

for a story by a movie company at that time. Recognizing the novel's shortcomings as a screenplay, Steinbeck recommended to his friend NUNNALLY JOHNSON, the man who had done such a credible adaptation of Steinbeck's *The Grapes of Wrath*, that he "[t]amper with it" in order to make it more suitable for the medium. The final version of the screenplay pays tribute to Steinbeck's talent by preserving the novel's original dialogue almost perfectly. Nunnally, however, took the liberty to embellish certain events to give them more color and dramatic effect. Overall many have suggested that the film version of *The Moon Is Down* is more effective at portraying German brutality than the novel. This, of course, is to misread the author's intention for the work, which was to show that the Nazis were only human and that they could be defeated by their enemy's spirited resistance. Steinbeck himself said that "pictures are a better medium for this story than the stage ever was."

FURTHER READING

Atkinson, Brooks. "John Steinbeck's Story of a Military Invasion Appears on the Stage." *New York Times*, April 12, 1942, Section 8, 12.

Coers, Donald. Introduction to *The Moon Is Down*, by John Steinbeck. New York: Penguin Books, 1995.

Ditsky, John. "Steinbeck's 'European' Play-Novella: *The Moon Is Down*." In *The Short Novels of John Steinbeck*, edited by Jackson J. Benson. Durham, N.C.: Duke University Press, 1990, 101–111.

Fadiman, Clifton. "Two Ways to Win the War." *New Yorker*, March 7, 1942, 52.

Hayashi, Tetsumaro. "Dr. Winter's Dramatic Functions in *The Moon Is Down*." In *The Short Novels of John Steinbeck*, edited by Jackson J. Benson. Durham, N.C.: Duke University Press, 1990, 95–101.

Stegner, Wallace. "Steinbeck's Latest Is an 'Idea Novel.'" *Boston Daily Globe*, March 11, 1942, 19.

Steinbeck, John. "Steinbeck's Nobel Prize Acceptance Speech." In *Nobel Prize Library: William Faulkner, Eugene O'Neill, and John Steinbeck*. New York: Alexis Gregory, 1970, 206.

"Steinbeck in Sweden." *Time*, April 19, 1943, 42.

"More about Aristocracy: Why Not a World Peerage?" (1955)

In "More about Aristocracy," published December 10, 1955, in *Saturday Review*, Steinbeck observes that "it is the nature of men to rise to greatness if greatness is expected of them, and it is equally their nature to be driven to bestiality through the despair of hatred." In modern times the path to the recognition and love that everyone desires is confused, the author argues. He proposes to fix this problem by establishing a world peerage toward which a man may work and through his work contribute to the world. He gives the Congressional Medal of Honor as an example of his idea. He proposes that the general assembly of the United Nations accept on unanimous vote those candidates who are unique among men, making those men citizens of the world, above question, and received with respect everywhere they go. Snob appeal, the author predicts, might have a profound effect on those who strive to keep the world divided and mean. He defends his plan as "not at all a dream-encrusted idealism, but rather a cold and feasible method for utilizing a human frailty, for giving a valuable direction to one of the strongest impulses we have."

"The Murder" (1934)

Steinbeck's short story "The Murder" first appeared in print in the *North American Review* in April 1934. "The Murder" won the O. Henry Award for the best short story of that year. It was subsequently reprinted in the collection of short stories, THE LONG VALLEY, published by VIKING PRESS in 1938. The story depicts the ongoing tension and restrictions of culture, tradition, and gender roles. Like many of the stories in the collection, "The Murder" also portrays almost complete miscommunication between a wife and a husband, leading inevitably to despair or tragedy.

The story opens with the description of a rock formation at the head of a canyon, resembling a medieval crusader's castle. Below it lies an abandoned farmhouse, owned by Jim Moore, who has not lived there for years, but who refuses to raze the building because of his sentimental attachment to the structure as his family's homestead, but more important, because it represents a time in his life when he was the lord of his castle. Jim posts "No Trespassing" signs, and visits the building periodically.

Shortly after his parents' death before his 30th birthday, Jim took a bride, Jelka Sepic, a woman from a culture alien to Jim, but whose beauty and passivity appealed to him. Jelka's sprawling Yugoslavian family repels Jim in many ways, and he is further appalled by the suggestion from his father-in-law on the night of the wedding that Jim beat Jelka hard and often to keep her in line, even without provocation. Nevertheless, Jelka's quiet attractiveness, and obsession in her desire to please him posed a stark contrast to the women Jim had previously known—the whores in the bawdy houses of MONTEREY. Jelka "learned her husband as she learned passages of Scripture" with silent and pious devotion, and soon after their marriage she could anticipate his every whim, mood, or need.

Despite her perfect domestic skills, Jim finds himself unable to hold an ordinary conversation with Jelka. She never speaks unless spoken to, and when he initiates a discussion, her responses are monosyllabic, and barely responsive, as if he were speaking a language completely unknown to his wife. Jelka only shows emotion when Jim strokes her hair and immaculate skin like a pet dog, or makes love to her.

Eventually, Jim begins to miss the companionship and banter of the girls at the Three Star, his favorite whorehouse prior to his marriage, and resumes weekly overnight trips to town in order to have an opportunity to laugh, trade jokes, and chatter. He worries about Jelka being left alone so much, but when asked by others about her whereabouts, he refers to her as another animal in his farm stock. When asked, "Where's your wife?" Jim responds, "Home in the barn." Jelka only leaves the farm to visit her huge family once a month. She has no other friends.

One early summer evening, Jim prepares to make a Saturday night trip to Monterey for his usual visit to the Three Star. Spontaneously, Jim asks Jelka if she would like to go to town and perhaps do some shopping, but she declines politely, much to his relief, pointing out the stores will be closed by the time they arrive. As Jim makes his way on horseback down the canyon, with his rifle in a scabbard on the saddle in case he should come across a deer, he encounters his neighbor, George, who reports finding a rustler's camp with a butchered calf carrying Jim's brand. Thanking George for the information, Jim says, ". . . if there are thieves working, I don't want to lose any more stock," and heads over to the next canyon to investigate the camp. Returning to his farm, Jim discovers a strange horse in his barn, and entering the house quietly, he finds Jelka's overgrown cousin in bed with his wife. Silently going out to the barnyard, Jim has visions of his mother slashing pigs' throats during hog killing. He returns to the house, and with a single shot, blows the cousin's brains out. He then vomits, and rides to town to inform the authorities of the killing.

Returning the next morning with the sheriff and coroner, Jim is informed there is a technical charge of murder, but that it will be dismissed, and that he should go easy on his wife. Jim finds a nine-foot bullwhip, and heads to the barn where he discovers Jelka whimpering in the hayloft. He beats her unmercifully, "as bad as I could without killing" her. Rather than fight back or protest, Jelka struggles to her feet, her bloody dress hanging in tatters from her back, and offers her husband breakfast. Afterward, with a smile, Jelka asks if she will be beaten again "for this"; Jim responds, "Not any more, for this"; and then announces his intention to build a new house.

Did Steinbeck intend by this story to condone domestic violence? Certainly at the time of the writing of this story, there existed unwritten understandings about relationships between husbands and wives, including a double standard about adultery. Jim understood his wife knew of his weekly activities at the Three Star, but he could not accept

her adultery, because her indiscretion threatened his manhood. Jim also got away with the murder of Jelka's buffoonish cousin. Had the roles been reversed Jelka most likely would have hanged, not just because of her sex but because she was a foreigner. In this sense Steinbeck offers a reasonably accurate historical portrayal of small-town America during the time frame of "The Murder."

However, Steinbeck does not make Jim a sympathetic character, no matter how one views the historical setting. Jim views Jelka as a possession, not as a human being, and on the night of the murder, Steinbeck makes it clear that Jim views "rustling" of his property as intolerable. Jim makes no attempt to surmount the cultural miscommunication between him and his wife. Rather he expects her to make all of the effort, and calls her religious rituals peculiar, and her habits odd. He prides himself on a sense of humor, but his humor consists of "pleasant insults," "shame-sharpened vulgarity," and gibes at the expense of his wife. He cannot bear to face the consequences of his brutal action, and asks the coroner and sheriff to clean up the mess in the bedroom, while he makes plans to beat Jelka with a bullwhip.

This is not to suggest that Jelka carries no blame. In her loneliness, Jelka engaged not only in infidelity, but also in incest. Moreover, she sought the brutal punishment inflicted upon her, and immediately forgave Jim for the beating. In her case violent conjugal relationships had been a part of her family tradition since time immemorial. She knew no better but her husband did and actively rejected the Sepic family violence when he first married his bride. Ultimately the couple establishes a new life in a new house, but Jim and Jelka have perpetuated a constrictive and destructive pattern of behavior.

EARLY CRITICISM

"The Murder" received scant attention by critics as part of the longer collection in *The Long Valley.* One reviewer, William Soskin, in a column for the *New York Herald Tribune*, mentions that Steinbeck's treatment of "sophisticated women" like the bizarre woman in "THE SNAKE," and Mary Teller in "THE WHITE QUAIL" showed a "weak point," and Soskin encouraged Steinbeck to examine only "ranch wives, eccentrics and clods like the Jugo-Slavic wife . . . who becomes devoted and faithful after she is beaten." Ralph Thompson, a critic for the *New York Times* noted Steinbeck is "at his best when he doesn't work too hard at it," and further suggested that "the callous Mr. Steinbeck . . . describing a cold-blooded shooting in 'The Murder' . . . is impressive but artificial."

CONTEMPORARY PERSPECTIVES

The story of an abused, underappreciated, and passive wife should resonate with modern readers and critics, and yet this story is largely ignored. Jelka's plight demonstrates the classic version of the now-recognized pathology of the "battered wife syndrome." One of the difficulties lies in the amorphous and nebulous characterization of Jelka, whose actions, or inaction, serve only as a foil and spark for Jim's behavior. Jackson Benson calls "The Murder" "a strange story, a sort of Gothic Western," perhaps influenced by Steinbeck's foray into detective fiction at the time. Robert Davis observes a "psychological renewal in the beating," and Katherine and Robert Morsberger point to the "mysteriously primitive passions" within all of us. John Timmerman, usually an admirer of Steinbeck's work, calls the story "an instance wherein ambiguity . . . degenerates to confusion and obscurantism."

SYNOPSIS

Jim Moore lives in a small house in the Cañon del Castillo, in Monterey County, where he runs a small ranch. He marries Jelka Sepic, a beautiful Yugoslavian girl, the daughter of a farmer in a nearby cañon, or small valley. At their wedding, Jelka's father advises him that Slavic girls are not like American girls; they do not like a man who does not beat them from time to time. Jim soon discovers who his wife is not like other girls. She studies her husband like the Bible, memorizing his every mood and characteristic, and anticipating his every need. But Jim finds his dutiful wife mysterious and impenetrable. Plagued by loneliness, he begins to spend time in the Salinas bars. One evening he announces that he is going to Salinas and asks Jelka if she would like to accompany him. She declines, saying that she would rather stay home and watch the full moon rise.

Riding into town, Jim meets a neighbor who warns him that he discovered the remains of a cow with the Moore brand on it that has been killed by cattle thieves. Jim decides to ride his fields in search of the rustlers. Finding nothing, he returns home, where he discovers a strange horse tied in his barn. He walks silently into his house and discovers Jelka sleeping in the bed in the arms of her cousin. He returns to the house with his rifle and shoots the man in the head. Jelka lies in the bed paralyzed with terror.

Jim rides into town to report what he has done to the sheriff. The next day they remove the body. The sheriff advises him that he will be charged with murder, but that the charge is always dropped in instances of adultery. He warns the distraught husband to go easy on his wife. Jim takes his bullwhip to the barn where his wife is hiding and whips her as severely as he can without killing her. He tells her that they will ride to town and order lumber to build a new house farther down the canyon. She asks him if he will whip her any more for her adultery. He says, "No." She smiles at him warmly, now certain that he loves her because he has beaten her for her indiscretion.

FURTHER READING

Benson, Jackson. "John Steinbeck: The Favorite Author We Love to Hate." In *The Steinbeck Question: New Essays in Criticism*, edited by Donald Noble. Troy, N.Y.: Whitston Publishing Co., 1993, 8–12.

Morsberger, Robert, ed. *Steinbeck/Zapata*. New York: Penguin, 1993.

Soskin, William. "Varied Art of John Steinbeck." *New York Herald Tribune Books*, September 18, 1938. "Books" Section. *p. 7.*

Thompson, Ralph. "Books of the Times." *New York Times*, September 21, 1938, 29.

Timmerman, John H. *John Steinbeck's Fiction: The Aesthetics of the Road Taken.* Norman: University of Oklahoma Press, 1986.

Murder at Full Moon   (1931)

A pulp mystery novel that Steinbeck wrote in a marathon nine days during the early 1930s in the hope of earning some money to ease the tremendous economic pressures that he was under. The novel, a cynical attempt at a standard commercial mystery-thriller, was an embarrassment to the author. Steinbeck submitted the book to his friend and unofficial agent TED MILLER with the instructions that it was to be published under the alias PETER PYM and that no one was to know the identity of the author. Miller circulated the novel to publishers, but it received very little interest. *Murder at Full Moon* remains unpublished to this day.

"The Naked Book" (1951)

Steinbeck muses on the nature of books and our relationship to them in this essay, which first appeared in the November 15, 1951, edition of *Vogue.* He begins by lamenting that books have fallen victim to the need for attractive packaging. This drive to have the most attractive book has driven their cost up so that ordinary people are put off. The high price tag demanded by clothbound books in expensive book jackets also means that publishers are less likely to take a chance on a controversial topic or an unproven author. Book jackets and blurbs pique Steinbeck's ire, as well. To him, books should be valued, shared and passed around for their content, not the packaging. He speculates on the future of books, wondering if any book will be bought by a publisher if it can't easily be turned into a movie. Steinbeck opines that books should be written to be books alone, and that that is the true magic of a book.

"Of Fish and Fishermen" (1954)

In "Of Fish and Fisherman," published October 4, 1954, in *Sports Illustrated,* Steinbeck compares the nature of Americans, the British, and the French by studying the way that they fish. The American, he contends, views fishing as his ultimate conquering of nature. Every American believes he is born to it. He buys tons of equipment, travels hundreds of miles, and worships the strong, intelligent fish that got away. Even politicos get photographed with a fish as par for the course in announcing their candidacy. In Britain, fishing rights are hotly contested, and the British fisherman longs to catch the wily fish, usually named something like Old George, who has escaped all other anglers. He does this with bad equipment and grunting mutters, but when he finally catches Old George, he has a story to bore the local pub for years to come. In France, by contrast, the fishermen all have their local place, and each man keeps to that place. They fish with decorated bamboo poles and use bread as bait. Then they drop the bait into the water and wait. Fishing is a contemplative vacation for the French. Steinbeck regards that as the most admirable of all.

Of Mice and Men (1937)

Steinbeck's sixth novel, *Of Mice and Men* was published by Covici and Friede in 1937. The novel was originally called *Something That Happened* until the author decided to change the name on the advice either of his first wife, CAROL HENNING STEINBECK BROWN, or his best friend, EDWARD RICKETTS. One of them read Robert Burns's poem "To a Mouse" to Steinbeck, and the author was intrigued by the line, "The best laid schemes o' mice and men gang aft agley." *Of Mice and Men* was conceived to be a play in novella form, which resulted in its straightforward, sequential style and extensive use of dialogue. Steinbeck chose this unusual form because he was concerned the audience he truly wanted to reach, the working poor, did not read books, but might attend a play. Originally, Steinbeck had hoped that IN DUBIOUS BATTLE might serve this dual purpose, but because of the complexities of the novel, the numerous settings, and the philosophical intricacy involved in his depiction of a strike of fruit pickers, the author chose to defer his new approach of deliberately writing a book for future conversion to a stage play or movie script. *Of Mice and Men* portrays the same marginalized existence of California farmworkers found in the earlier volume, but on a much smaller scale, and without the obvious theoretical undertones.

The story finds its origins in Steinbeck's own experience working alongside migrant workers during his periodic leaves of absence from STANFORD UNIVERSITY. At the center lie two wandering ranch laborers, common BINDLESTIFFS, or hoboes in the vernacular of the time, George Milton and his retarded charge Lennie Small, whose day-to-day existence consists of eking out a living and avoiding trouble. Overarching their meager reality is a common dream. Both of them have constructed an elaborate scenario in which the two of them will earn enough money for a down payment on a small piece of property where the two of them will "live offa the fatta the lan." Both of them build and rely on the hopes they have for this imaginary "place," and in doing so, set the stage for a tragedy. Much like the characters in *In Dubious Battle* who set their sights on ultimate goals, they will be either disappointed or destroyed by their aspirations. In this, Steinbeck continues his exploration of the nonteleological viewpoint.

From the outset of the book, Steinbeck creates an atmosphere of presentiment, and of foreordained outcomes. He deliberately manipulates the reader, but so obviously that the manipulation is excusable. In the opening chapter, George and Lennie pause on the banks of a protected stream, while George attempts to instruct his companion yet another time about proper behavior. During this interlude, the reader comes to understand Lennie's disability; George's concern and affection for his companion; and most important, Lennie's uncontrolled exuberance for living, and the inadvertently excessive exercise of his great physical strength. Lennie has apparently put himself and George in jeopardy in many circumstances, not simply because of Lennie's disability, but largely because of Lennie's overwhelming need for physical and emotional contact with the soft, weak, and vulnerable, whether animal or human. Lennie does not have the intellectual capacity to erect emotional barriers, or to acquire the niceties of polite intercourse. He operates as a natural force with the most primitive of human inclinations. Because of his mental limitations, Lennie reacts instinctively, not nobly, though his instincts are decent and loving.

George, on the other hand, fully comprehends the ramifications and risks of his unlikely friendship with Lennie. In this sense, he is a far more tragic figure than his friend, because he knowingly chooses to be Lennie's protector, confidant, and surrogate parent. Not much explanation is given about how the incongruous pair began traveling together. The two knew each other as youngsters in the same small town of Auburn, California, where Lennie lived with his Aunt Clara, and was the butt of cruel practical jokes, many of them instigated by George. However, George eventually began to see Lennie as a human being rather than an insensitive target of fun, and when Lennie's aunt died, ". . . Lennie just come along . . . out working." He accepts responsibility for a fellow human being to whom he has no blood connection. His reasons stem from elemental need. As George explains, "Guys like us, that work on ranches, are the loneliest guys in the world." Lennie alleviates George's fundamental loneliness, and stands in for the family he never has had or anticipates having. Lennie adds permanence to George's existence, a sense of purpose, and a goal, even if the goal is unrealizable.

Indeed, almost every major character in the book suffers from loneliness, an ongoing theme in Steinbeck's work. Candy, tasked with cleaning out the bunkhouse, who has lost a hand working on the ranch, and whose presence is barely tolerated on a month-to-month basis, sacrifices his aging and decrepit dog to keep the peace among the other ranch hands, but realizing how empty his sacrifice has been, eagerly offers his nest egg to George and Lennie as a payment on a perhaps nonexistent farm to be part of their dream. Curly, the owner's son, marries a woman of questionable moral character to bolster his own image of himself and to mitigate the male-dominated atmosphere of the ranch. Crooks, the "nigger" stable buck, doubly isolated by his race and consequent segregation from the white ranch hands in his own little shack with books his only comfort, confesses to Lennie, "A guy goes nuts if he ain't got nobody." Even Curly's wife, who remains unnamed throughout the book but who provides the catalyst for the tragic events, constantly seeks the attention of anyone and everyone on the ranch as a way of solace for her shattered dreams to be a movie star, and for the inadequacy of her recent marriage. Only Slim, the teamster, appears to be self-sufficient, but his autonomy may have more to do with Steinbeck's inclusion of another character patterned after Ed Ricketts, the distant and impartial observer of human behavior.

As stated before, Steinbeck unveils the possible tragic consequences in the first chapter. The beginning of the novella, and the end take place in the same setting, suggesting a never-ending circle to human endeavor. Lennie's animalistic nature is underscored by Steinbeck's comparison of Lennie to a bear or a horse, as Lennie lumbers to the stream and drinks his fill. George's rational characteristics and his controlling relationship with Lennie immediately are revealed when he advises Lennie that he should not drink anything but running water. Bits and pieces of the two men's history and relationship immediately surface. George issues orders; Lennie tries to obey. The reader learns certain salient facts. The two are on the run from their previous employer, where Lennie did a "bad thing" involving a young woman with a pretty dress. Lennie carries in his pocket a dead mouse, petted to death by the mentally challenged giant. George is both resigned and dismayed, and admonishes Lennie to return to the very same spot along the banks of the stream, should Lennie get "into trouble," and to "hide in the brush." But he also encourages both himself and Lennie by reciting the clearly oft-told description of their own small piece of land where they are the owners, beholden to no one else, and where Lennie will have rabbits to pet and cosset. It's a set speech, without strong conviction, demonstrating George's understanding of the unlikelihood of the dream, but also of its necessity to both inspire and control his companion. Ultimately, George lose his shaky control over Lennie. Despite his best efforts and admonitions, Lennie kills a newborn puppy and Curly's wife, in back-to-back occurrences. Lennie retreats to the sylvan glade of the original chapter, following George's instructions, where George finds him, reiterates the soothing scenario of a place of their own, and kills his friend with a single bullet to his brain stem.

George cannot control fate, anymore than he could control Lennie. What he can control is the manner of Lennie's death. He saves him from a lynch mob, or lifetime incarceration in a mental institution. In doing so, he affirms his freedom, but also acknowledges the futility of grandiose dreams.

EARLY CRITICISM

With few exceptions, *Of Mice and Men* received rave reviews. Charles A. Wagner of the *New York Mirror* called the book "the closest thing to a little prose masterpiece . . . seen in years." LEWIS GANNETT, writing for the *New York Herald Tribune* praised Steinbeck's compassion and artistry, while Fanny Butcher for the *Chicago Daily Tribune* labeled the work a "remarkable literary feat" without a single "false word." Henry Seidel Canby, as literary reviewer for the *Saturday Review,* said that the small book had "every element of good story-telling," and noted that the "subject matter is deeply felt, richly conceived, and perfectly ordered." Fred T. Marsh in the *New York Times Book Review,* called Steinbeck a "virtuoso" storyteller, and said *Of Mice and Men* was a "thriller" and a "gripping tale," which the reader "would not set down until it is finished." From the *New Republic,* Henry Thornton Moore wrote of Steinbeck's magnificent writing, and said the work was "well-contrived and effectively compressed, driving ahead with a straight and rapid movement. Moore did express concern about Steinbeck's portrayal "of men of goodwill so consistently going down in spiritual defeat." Edward Weeks, in his column for the *Atlantic,* said the book offered proof of "a vital and experienced storyteller." JOSEPH HENRY JACKSON, writing for the *San Francisco Chronicle,* specifically pointed out that the novel is not a "proletarian novel." Jackson distinguished the theme in *Of Mice and Men* from those of proletarian novels, arguing that although the novel does concern workingmen, its central figures are workers who, like any human beings, think, desire, and act on the many and various things that we all think and long for.

The play version of the work also received positive reviews. A critic from *Literary Digest* (December 18, 1937) called the play "the first completely satisfying American play of the season" that "tamed testy critics and tired audiences into stunned reverence." Richard Watts, Jr., writing for *New York Herald Tribune*, labeled *Of Mice and Men* a work of true authenticity. In the meantime, some critics, while acknowledging the quality of the play script, praised the versatile and prodigious George S. Kaufman, for his directing of the play.

On the other hand, four reviews stand out for their negative assessment. The prominent critic Mark Van Doren, of the *Nation*, referred to Steinbeck's writing as "mechanical" and "extreme," and further suggested the author appeared "uninterested in reality of any kind." Similarly, *Time's* reviewer called the book an "oxymoronic combination of the tough and tender," and indicated that a discerning reader would prefer the fairy tales of Hans Christian Anderson. Dorothea Brande Collins of *American Review* stated ". . . surely no more sentimental wallowing ever passed for a novel," and suggested that those who praised Steinbeck's "economy" of style had been overcome by "stag party hysteria." Finally, in reviewing the world premiere of the play in SAN FRANCISCO, Margaret Shedd declared that *Of Mice and Men* is not a great play. She called the adaption "confusing" and stated the "epic material" in the play had been destroyed.

CONTEMPORARY PERSPECTIVES

Of Mice and Men continues to be required reading for many high school advanced placement English literature courses. In this sense, it has become an American classic, still analyzed and debated in American classrooms. Indeed, two of the three reader reviews on the Amazon website were penned by high school students. Moreover, as recently as 1992, the actor Gary Sinise starred in and directed a theatrical release of the movie, which was greeted by great critical acclaim.

The novella has gathered attention from the world of academia. Richard O'Connor, examining the relationship between George and Lennie, avers that Steinbeck could never equal "the tenderness of the relationship between the two men" in his portrayals of the "love of a man for a woman," and suggests that Steinbeck was "baffled by the intricacies of female behavior." Charlotte Cook Hadella calls the book "a human drama for all places and all

times." Finally Antonia Seixas, making note of the original title for the book, *Something That Happened*, suggests that the "hardest task a writer can set himself is to tell the story of 'something that happened' without explaining 'why' . . ." and that Steinbeck demonstrated his mastery by making this difficult task, "convincing and moving."

SYNOPSIS

(1)

Two wandering migrant laborers, George and Lennie, make a crude camp deep in the willow trees next to a shallow river. Lennie is a huge man with large pale eyes, and curiously undefined facial features. He confronts the world with confusion and childlike simplicity, depending totally on his friend and protector, George, a small man with restless eyes and sharp, strong features. The two men have been sent to begin work the next day on a nearby farm. Lennie drinks greedily from the stream until George pulls him back and warns him that he is going to make himself sick. George discovers that Lennie, who has a fascination with small furry objects, is hiding a dead mouse in his pocket. He scolds the large man like a child and throws the mouse into the woods. Lennie goes out to collect firewood to heat their simple meal of canned beans. He returns concealing the dead rodent, which his exasperated protector once again throws into the forest. George instructs Lennie to keep quiet the next day when they present themselves at the ranch. He makes him repeat these simple instructions over and over so that he will not forget them. He reminds Lennie they have just fled a ranch up north near Weed, because Lennie wanted to feel a girl's soft dress, and she accused Lennie of attempted rape. Lennie shrivels under George's reprimand. He begs his friend to tell him about their plans to buy a farm and live off the land. George tells Lennie that they are luckier than most ranch hands who are usually the loneliest people in the world. He assures his friend that they are different because they have each other and he promises that some day they will get some land and have a big vegetable patch and rabbits for Lennie to take care of and pet. He warns Lennie that if there is any trouble he should come back to the river and hide until he arrives.

(2)

Candy, a tall, stoop-shouldered, one-handed old man who is in charge of cleaning the bunkhouse, shows the two men to the bunkhouse. He assigns them beds and begins to tell them about the ranch. George and Lennie are told that they will work with Slim, the ranch's best muleskinner. Curley, the boss's son, enters the bunkhouse looking for his father. He is a small, temperamental young man who boxes semiprofessionally. Spotting big Lennie, he immediately begins bullying the confused giant, who retreats to a dark corner of the bunkhouse. Candy explains that Curley is dangerously jealous of his new wife, whom Candy and the boys brand a troublemaker and a floozy. George warns Lennie to stay away from Curley, reminding him that he should hide by the river if there is any trouble. Meanwhile Curley's beautiful young wife enters the bunkhouse on the pretext of looking for her husband. Lennie looks her over appreciatively and George warns him to stay away from the young woman. Slim enters the bunkhouse and introduces himself to George and Lennie. He is a tall, proud man, "the prince of the ranch," whose demeanor automatically ingratiates him to George. Carlson, another of the bunkhouse residents, suggests that Slim offer one of his new puppies to Candy, so they can shoot Carlson's dog who is so old it cannot chew, and stinks up the bunkhouse. Lennie begs George for a new puppy.

(3)

George and Slim rest in the bunkhouse after a hard day's work. Slim exclaims admiringly that he has never seen such a strong man as Lennie. George thanks the muleskinner for the small brown and white puppy that he has given to Lennie. George explains that he knew Lennie's Aunt Clara and that when she died Lennie joined up with him. He confesses before Slim's "God-like eyes," telling him about the two men's trouble up north. Lennie arrives in the bunkhouse with the small puppy hidden in his shirt. George reprimands him and orders him to return the animal to its mother. Carlson tells old Candy that it is time to get rid of the rheumatic old dog. Candy insists that he has had the old dog for so long that he cannot just shoot him. Carlson

offers to shoot the animal himself, assuring the old man that the execution will be painless. The old man helplessly assents and Carlson leads the dog away on a leather leash. Candy weeps silently on his bunk as they wait tensely for the gunshot that sounds in the distance. Later that evening, Candy listens while George once again describes to Lennie the farm that they are going to buy just as soon as they get some money saved. The old man excitedly offers to pool his money with the two men to buy the farm. He explains that he is afraid that he will be turned off the ranch and left with nowhere to go. George figures that with the old man's money the will have almost enough to buy the land. The three sit considering their plan when Curley and Slim enter the bunkhouse. They are arguing over Curley's wife, who Curley suspects is fooling around with the handsome cowboy. Angry, but afraid of taking on Slim, the young bully attacks Lennie, who smiles innocently from his bunk. Lennie retreats, refusing to respond to Curley's blows. He begs helplessly for George to make Curley stop. "Get 'im," George urges Lennie, who catches Curley's fist in his hand and smashes it to pulp between his powerful fingers. Curley slumps to the floor in agony. Slim warns that he had better tell everyone that he caught his hand in a farm machine, otherwise he will be a laughingstock. Curley agrees to keep quiet.

(4)

George and the men go into town, leaving Lennie alone in the bunkhouse. Lonely, he seeks out Crooks, the negro stable buck, for company. Crooks explains resentfully that he must live alone in the stable because he isn't wanted in the bunkhouse on account of being black. But Lennie's simple mind is untroubled by racism and the Negro finally softens and invites him into the room. Lennie tells his new friend of his and George's plan to buy a farm. The old stable buck maliciously tells Lennie that he would be locked up in a "booby hatch" if George ever left him. Dimly comprehending Crooks's words, Lennie becomes frightened and then mad. He walks threateningly toward Crooks, who senses the danger and placates the large man by him assuring him that he was only talking about himself.

Candy arrives and the men continue discussing their dream farm. They are interrupted by Curley's wife, who claims to be looking for her husband. She asks the men what happened to her husband's hand, studying Lennie's bruised face knowingly. When Crooks demands that she leave his room, she warns him to remember his place, threatening that she can get him "strung up a tree so easy it ain't even funny."

(5)

The next afternoon the ranch hands are absorbed in a horseshoe-throwing competition. Lennie crouches in the barn weeping silently over the dead body of his small puppy, which he has inadvertently crushed with his large, clumsy hands. He is debating what to do when Curley's wife enters the barn. Lennie avoids her eyes, telling her that George does not allow him to talk to her. She explains to him that all the men are outside and that she doesn't have anybody to talk to. Lennie continues to insist that he cannot talk to her because George will be mad. She changes the subject, asking him what he is hiding in his hands. He explains how the puppy died and how George will be mad and not let him have any rabbits. She asks him why he is so nuts about rabbits, and he explains that he likes to pet soft things with his fingers. The vain young woman offers to let him feel how soft her hair is. Lennie becomes excited as he strokes her head harder and harder. When she tries to pull back from his eager hands he closes his fingers on her and hangs on tightly. Frightened, she cries for him to let her go. Lennie panics, closing his fingers over her mouth to prevent her from screaming. He shakes her angrily until her body goes limp, her neck broken. Frightened at what he has done, he disappears from the barn. Candy discovers the dead body and guesses what has happened. Curley and the boys resolve to hunt down Lennie and shoot him. Carlson discovers that his pistol is missing and the men assume that Lennie has stolen the weapon. They resolve to shoot him on sight. George pleads with Slim not to let them hurt Lennie. The mule skinner tells him that it will be worse if they don't shoot him. The posse heads out to find Lennie.

(6)

Lennie flees to the agreed-upon hiding place and waits for his protector to arrive. His head is filled with troubled visions of his Aunt Clara frowning disapprovingly at him for disobeying George and getting into trouble. The vision of his aunt is replaced by the vision of a giant rabbit which tells him that George is going to abandon him. George finds his friend with his hand over his ears, crying out his name. He assures Lennie that he will never leave him. The sound of men shouting to one another can be heard in the distance. George tells Lennie to look across the river and imagine their little farm. Stepping behind his friend he begins to recount the familiar details of the garden and the rabbits. He raises Carlson's stolen pistol in his trembling hand, presses it gently to the base of his friend's skull, and pulls the trigger.

CHARACTERS

Candy   The one-handed old man who cleans the bunkhouse in *Of Mice and Men*. He sadly agrees to let his companions shoot his faithful old sheepdog, which has become rheumatic and must be fed by hand. When he hears George and Lennie's plan to buy their own farm he offers to put in his savings if they will let him live on the farm.

Carlson   A character in *Of Mice and Men*, Carlson is a powerful, big-bellied man. He convinces Candy that it is time to shoot his old rheumatic sheepdog. George steals Carlson's Luger pistol to shoot his friend Lennie.

Crooks   A character in *Of Mice and Men*, Crooks is the negro stable buck who sleeps alone in the stable because the men in the bunkhouse do not want him. His body is bent painfully to the left, the result of being kicked by a horse. A proud but lonely man, he befriends Lennie. Curley's wife threatens to have him lynched when he tries to make her leave Lennie alone.

Curley   A character in *Of Mice and Men*, Curley is the ranch owner's temperamental son, he is a thin young man with brown eyes and a head of tightly curled hair. He wears a leather glove filled with Vaseline on his left hand "to keep it soft for his wife," of whom he is explosively jealous. A semiprofessional prizefighter, he likes to pick fights with men larger than he is. He picks a fight with the unwilling Lennie, who crushes his hand in his powerful fist. He leads the lynch mob when Lennie inadvertently kills Curley's wife.

Milton, George   A character in *Of Mice and Men*, George is a migrant laborer who drifts from ranch to ranch with his friend Lennie Small, whom he protects and keeps out of trouble. He is a small, quick man with restless eyes and sharp, strong features. George and Lennie are contracted to work on a ranch in the Salinas Valley. George comforts Lennie with assurances that some day they will own their own farm where Lennie will have a bunch of rabbits to care for. When Lennie inadvertently kills Curley's wife, George shoots his friend to prevent him from being locked up like an animal.

Slim   Slim is a character in *Of Mice and Men*. He is a tall jerkline skinner (the main driver of a mule team who handles the reins), admired by the other workers who respect his authority on any subject. He befriends George Milton and gives one of his newborn puppies to Lennie Small. When Lennie inadvertently kills Curley's wife, Slim makes George realize that it is better that his friend be shot rather than locked up in a cage.

Small, Lennie   A character in *Of Mice and Men*, Lennie is a migrant laborer who drifts from ranch to ranch with his friend and protector George Milton. He is semiretarded, a child with a giant's body, with a huge, shapeless face, large pale eyes, and wide, sloping shoulders. Lennie likes to pet soft things, particularly small animals. Lennie dreams of the day that he and George will own their own farm, where he will have a bunch of rabbits to pet and care for. Curley tries to pick a fight with him, and he crushes the man's hand in his powerful fist. When he inadvertently kills Curley's wife, George shoots him in the back of the head to prevent him from being locked up like an animal.

THE FILMS: *OF MICE AND MEN*

In 1939 United Artists produced one of the most successful adaptations of a Steinbeck novel to film. This version of *Of Mice and Men* preserved most of the author's dialogue, making only small concessions to the public sensibilities of the time by softening the language. The ending from the book was altered slightly to comply with the movie industry's Hays decency code by suggesting George would be arrested for the murder of Lennie. The movie also expanded the character of Curley's wife, Mae, implying her loneliness was as profound as that of George and Lennie. Nominated as best picture for 1939, the film faced stiff competition from *The Wizard of Oz, Gone with the Wind,* and another film adapted from a Steinbeck work, THE GRAPES OF WRATH, and lost to *Gone With the Wind.* The original score from Aaron Copland, a renowned symphonic composer acclaimed for his American musical themes, added to the film's production quality.

In 1992 Gary Sinise, who played Tom Joad in the successful translation of *The Grapes of Wrath* from the text to stage, produced another film of *Of Mice and Men.* This version owed its inspiration to Sinise's own affection for Steinbeck's work. According to critic Mimi R. Gladstein, this version mainly was changed to meet the sensibilities and expectations of contemporary audiences who have become increasingly "desensitized to violence and brutality." The film significantly altered the portrayal of Lennie's killing of Curley's wife. It lingered on the death scene, amplifying not only the violence, but also the sexual tension of the interaction.

FURTHER READING

Bloom, Harold, ed. *John Steinbeck's* Of Mice and Men *(Bloom's Notes).* New York: Chelsea House, 1999.

Butcher, Fanny. "Books." *Chicago Daily Tribune,* February 27, 1937, 11.

Canby, Henry Seidel. "Casuals of the Road." *Saturday Review,* February 27, 1937, 7.

Collins Dorothea Brande. "Reading at Random." *American Review,* April 1937, 100–113.

Gannett, Lewis. "Books and Things." *New York Herald Tribune,* February 25, 1937, 17.

Hadella, Charlotte Cook. "The Dialogic Tension in Steinbeck's Portrait of Curley's Wife." In *John Steinbeck: The Years of Greatness, 1936–1939*, edited by Tetsumaro Hayashi. Tuscaloosa: University of Alabama Press, 1993, 64–74.

Jackson, Joseph Henry. "Steinbeck's Art Finds Powerful Expression in *Of Mice and Men*." *San Francisco Chronicle*, February 28, 1937, Section D, 7.

Johnson, Claudia D. *Understanding* Of Mice and Men, The Red Pony, *and* The Pearl: *A Student Casebook to Issues, Sources, and Historical Documents.* Westport, Conn.: Greenwood Press, 1997.

Karson, Jill. *Readings on* Of Mice and Men. San Diego, Calif.: Greenhaven Press, 1997.

Marsh, Fred T. "John Steinbeck's Tale of Drifting Men." *New York Times Book Review*, February 28, 1937, 7.

Moore, Henry Thornton. *"Of Mice and Men." New Republic*, March 3, 1937, 118–119.

O'Connor, Richard. *John Steinbeck.* New York: McGraw-Hill, 1970.

Seixas, Tony. "John Steinbeck and the Non-teleological Bus." In *Steinbeck and His Critics*, edited by E. W. Tedlock and C. V. Wicker, 275–280. Albuquerque: University of New Mexico Press, 1957.

Shedd, Margaret. *"Of Mice and Men." Theatre Arts*, October 1937, 774–780.

Steinbeck, John. *Of Mice and Men.* New York: Covici and Friede, 1937.

"Theatre: A Completely Satisfying American Play." *Literary Digest*, December 18, 1937, 34.

Wagner, Charles A. "Books." *New York Mirror*, February 24, 1937, 25.

Van Doren, Mark. "Wrong Number." *Nation*, March 6, 1937, 275.

Weeks, Edward. "The Bookshelf." *Atlantic*, April 1937, 14, 16.

"Young Man's Dream." *Time*, March 1, 1937, 69.

Once There Was a War (1958)

Steinbeck's 24th book, *Once There Was a War* is a collection of the author's articles from WORLD WAR II. In 1943 Steinbeck was granted permission by the U.S. War Department to travel to the European war theater to write a series of articles for the *New York Herald Tribune*. Steinbeck had recently married his second wife, GWYNDOLYN CONGER, and left his young bride to become a war correspondent. He remained in Europe from June to October, traveling first to England, then North Africa, and finally Italy and the Mediterranean. Instead of using the objective style of reporting like the celebrated war correspondents Ernie Pyle and Clark Lee, the author chose a style similar to the storytelling that had made him famous, recounting interesting anecdotes and personal accounts that were both intimate and alive with detail. His columns proved to be immensely popular and were soon syndicated and reproduced throughout the United States and the world. The author indicates that many of his stories were heavily edited both by himself and the official military censors, a common practice to preserve the secrecy of troop movements and the location of strategic facilities. The articles appear as they were originally published, with datelines that indicate only "Somewhere in England" or "Somewhere in Africa," reflecting the restrictions imposed by the censors. Various articles also have sentences or even whole paragraphs cut and marked "removed by censor." Fifteen years after the columns first appeared in *The New York Herald Tribune*, Steinbeck's war correspondence was collected and published in the book *Once There Was a War*, by VIKING PRESS in 1958.

SYNOPSIS

Once There Was a War: An Introduction

Written 15 years after Steinbeck traveled to Europe to write about the allied war effort, the introduction to *Once There Was a War* declares World War II to be "the last of its kind," that is, the last of the long global wars. Writing at the height of the cold war, the author is clearly concerned with the looming threat of nuclear war and annihilation.

Steinbeck notes that upon rereading his war articles after so many years, he finds them to be quite dated, one-sided, and impacted too deeply by the single-mindedness of the Allied war effort, and the romance of war. He writes of the censorship that affects the war correspondent's attempts to document the war, both official censorship and self-censorship. He describes the conventions used by all war correspondents: The infantry private is the bravest and noblest man in the army; there are no cruel or ambitious or ignorant commanders; sex is not a preoccupation of the troops. He justifies such practices as the journalist's attempt to participate in the "war effort." The author remarks that many of his stories are deeply affected by the removal of sentences by the official censors, but he defends the censors as having a difficult and necessary job.

He writes of his admiration for his fellow war correspondents, whom he describes as a crazy yet dedicated group of committed journalists, whose careers took them during their lifetimes to more combat zones than the average military man. He acknowledges feeling like an amateurish trespasser in their company. He confesses to a certain amount of embarrassment for being a witness to the war, and says this shame led him to avoid first-person descriptions in his articles, as if to make his observations the experiences of someone else. He defends the self-censorship of war correspondents as necessary to the war effort, and describes his fellow reporters as highly moral, responsible, and brave men. Finally, he suggests the articles he wrote during the war stand only as nostalgic "period pieces" without much truth or historical value.

England

Troopship—Somewhere in England, June 20, 1943 Describes the loading and departure of a troopship, a complex and highly coordinated process

Somewhere in England, June 21, 1943 The sun sets, and the troopship departs for its secret destination across the Atlantic.

Somewhere in England, June 22, 1943 The men accustom themselves to the boredom and cramped conditions of the voyage.

Somewhere in England, June 23, 1943 Addresses the wild rumors of disease and mutiny that pass through the troopship as it makes its crossing

Somewhere in England, June 24, 1943 A small United Service Organizations (USO) contin-

gent works tirelessly to entertain the troops aboard the ship. The author remarks on the interaction between the performers and the audience, which makes a less than convincing show quite entertaining.

Somewhere in England, June 25, 1943 The troopship nears land. A book distributed to the men describes how to get along with their English allies. The ship docks and the troops are unloaded on the quay. The Red Cross greets them, and serves them coffee and cake.

A Plane's Name—A Bomber Station, June 26, 1943 The author describes a small airbase on the outskirts of LONDON and the crew of a Flying Fortress named the *Mary Ruth*.

News from Home—Bomber Station in England, June 28, 1943 The crew of the *Mary Ruth* go to a pub and discuss their impression of the war news that is published in the American papers. They feel that it is often exaggerated and inaccurate.

Superstition—Bomber Station in England, June 30, 1943 Describes how war breeds superstition and how every soldier has some sort of lucky charm that protects him in combat.

Preparation for a Raid—Bomber Station in England, July 1, 1943 The *Mary Ruth's* crew is briefed for a bombing raid across the English Channel. The men get dressed and make final preparations aboard their bomber.

The Ground Crew—Bomber Station in England, July 2, 1943 The ground crew prepares the plane, inspects the engines and loads the munitions. The plane takes off for its mission.

Waiting—Bomber Station in England, July 4, 1943 The *Mary Ruth's* mascot, a gray Scottie, waits for the bomber's return. The bomber returns safely and the mission is over.

Day of Memories—London, July 4, 1943 The people of London prepare Independence Day celebrations for their American guests and the men are particularly homesick that day.

The People of Dover—Dover, July 6, 1943 The great German guns in Calais, across the channel, bombard Dover daily; meanwhile the citizens of Dover go about their business as if there was no war.

Minesweeper—London, July 7, 1943 The author boards a minesweeper that searches the waterway for enemy explosives.

Coast Battery—Somewhere in England, July 8, 1943 The author writes of the coastal anti-aircraft batteries, one of the rare instances where females participate in actual combat, working as spotters and plotters for the guns and living in barracks alongside the gunners.

Alcoholic Goat—London, July 9, 1943 Wing Commander William Goat, DSO, is the long-time mascot of an RAF wing and an aficionado of beer. The air crews believe that he brings him luck.

Stories of the Blitz—London, July 10, 1943 Anecdotes of the people who have lived through the savage German bombardment of London: "The bombing itself grows vague and dreamlike. The little pictures remain as sharp as they were when they were new."

Lilli Marlene—London, July 12, 1943 The story of a German song named "Lilli Marlene" that tells about a woman sleeping her way through the ranks until she finally meets a brigadier. The song became very popular among the German troops before becoming popular among the British, and finally the American troops.

War Talk—London, July 13, 1943 The author points out that "the nearer one comes to a war zone the less one hears of grand strategy." He writes of the specialized, understated vocabulary used by the combat troops.

The Cottage That Wasn't There—London, July 14, 1943 A sergeant tells the story of having peered through the window of a small cottage at the peaceful domestic scene within during a previous time of the war. The day after telling the story, the sergeant returns to the cottage and discovers only a crater. A German fire bomb had destroyed the cottage.

Growing Vegetables—London, July 15, 1943 The American soldiers often plant gardens on the edges of their airfields and between their barracks. These gardens are carefully tended by volunteers and provide much of the fresh produce that is consumed by the troops. The author writes of the differences between English and American methods for preparing vegetables.

The Shape of the World—London, July 16, 1943 The troops are fighting under clouds of worry that the cost of living is rising and concern that they will return home to find that retooled factories and automatic machinery will mean that there are no jobs for them. They fear a great depression will ensue.

Theater Party—London, July 18, 1943 A German bomber destroys a crowded theater in the middle of London.

Directed Understanding—London, July 19, 1943 Describes the army's attempts to promote understanding between the British and the American troops. Preconceptions and prejudices are often proved wrong by individual encounters.

Big Train—London, July 25, 1943 Private "Big Train" Mulligan is a driver in the motor pool in London who, "after two years in the Army and one year overseas, is probably one of the most relaxed and most successful privates the war has seen."

Bob Hope—London, July 26, 1943 The author writes admiringly of the tireless efforts of Bob Hope, whom he recommends for recognition of service to the nation in wartime. During the war, Hope took his shows all over to entertain the American troops. According to Steinbeck, Hope sometimes did four or five shows a day. He moved from camp to camp, from airfields to billets, and from supply depots to hospitals. According to Steinbeck's exaggeration, soldiers liked and remembered Hope's visits better than the secretary of war's inspections.

A Cozy Castle—London, July 27, 1943 The army takes over an old English castle to be used as a base of operations. The author writes of the contrast between the historic site and its new occupants, claiming there is no point to what he writes except the contrast, or "the change of pageantry."

The Yanks Arrive—London, July 28, 1943 An American troop train arrives at a new training field. The troops are received by two young women from the Red Cross, who prepare doughnuts and coffee for the new arrivals.

A Hand—London, July 29, 1943 A soldier with a wounded hand deals with his painful recovery. He is worried his wife will not want to be with a cripple.

The Career of Big Train Mulligan—Somewhere in England, August 4, 1943 The author writes more about Private Mulligan, whom he describes as having "carried looting, requisitioning, whatever you want to call it, to its highest point."

Chewing Gum—London, August 6, 1943 Describes the little children of the port who have mastered the art of begging sweets and pieces of gum from the arriving soldiers.

Mussolini—London, August 9, 1943 Rumors run rampant aboard a troopship that the Italian dictator Mussolini has resigned or been assassinated and that the war will soon be over.

Craps—London, August 12, 1943 Relates the story of Eddie, a talented craps shooter who is particularly successful on Sundays. He bets a great fortune and then loses it because he does not realize that the ship he is aboard has crossed the international dateline and it is no longer Sunday.

Africa

Plane for Africa—A North African Post (Via London), August 26, 1943 The author is given clearance to travel to Africa. He boards a train and is taken to an airbase to await transport aboard a C-54 cargo plane. Finally, an air combat crew boards and the plane departs.

Algiers—Algiers (via London), August 28, 1943 Describes Algiers, which "has been brought to a nightmarish mess by the influx of British and American troops and their equipment." A polyglot of languages is spoken in the streets, and money is a problem due to the profusion of currencies and exchange rates.

A Watch Chiseler—A North African Post (via London), August 31, 1943 A sergeant of MPs and his lieutenant capture three soldiers who are trafficking in stolen army watches.

Over the Hill—A North African Post (via London), September 1, 1943 Two homesick GIs, "Sligo and the kid," explore Algiers on a 48-hour pass. Sligo, an Italian American, bets his friend 20 bucks that he can get home. He then sneaks into a group of Italian prisoners of war being shipped to the United States and is carried aboard a transport ship even as he protests that he is not supposed to be there.

The Short Snorter War Menace—Somewhere in Africa (via London), September 2, 1943 The author describes the Short Snorter, a tradition that has grown up during the war. The first time a man flies across the Atlantic it is customary that he obtain the signatures of the flight crew on a dollar bill as a gesture of good luck. This tradition has grown until men throughout the armed forces are collecting signatures from their comrades-in-arms.

The Bone Yard—A North African Post (via London), September 5, 1943 Describes a "bone yard" on the edge of a North African city where the remains of broken tanks and artillery pieces are stored so that they may be refurbished or used for spare parts.

Italy

Rehearsal—Somewhere in Mediterranean War Theater, September 29, 1943 Describes the training taking place on the beaches of North Africa in preparation for the coming invasion of Italy. The men train on the beach for the initial landing, and practice entry into enemy towns in Hollywood-style mock-up villages.

Somewhere in Mediterranean War Theater, October 1, 1943 Training for the invasion continues, taking on speed as the departure date draws near. The author discusses the incredible logistical complexity of moving and supplying the modern army. The enemy attempts to bomb the training stations, but is held back by the aerial and ground defenses. The troops board the transports, which form into great convoys and sit ready for the "D" day and the "H" hour.

Invasion—Somewhere in Mediterranean War Theater, October 3, 1943　The untested troops sit aboard their landing craft waiting for action, secretly wondering how they will react when they finally face an actual combat situation. Every man writes a final letter home in the event that he is killed.

Somewhere in Mediterranean War Theater, October 4, 1943　The soldiers land at Red Beach No. 2 near Salerno. A radio operator sits under cover and describes the landing.

Somewhere in Mediterranean War Theater, October 6, 1943　The author describes in intimate detail the combat he experiences during the invasion of Salerno. He reports the minute particulars of war in searing images of never-ending dust, the disemboweled remains of a small girl, and an American soldier crying over a "twitching" body. He writes graphically of his own physical discomfort caused by the lack of hygiene, and inability to change clothes.

Somewhere in Mediterranean War Theater, October 8, 1943　Further description of the taking of the beachhead at Salerno and the enemy's failed attacks on the command ship in the middle of the invasion fleet. There are rumors that the enemy has a new radio-controlled bomb that can be steered remotely to its target. Finally the beach is taken and the invasion moves inland as the hospital ships move inshore to take on their cargoes of wounded.

Palermo—Somewhere in Mediterranean War Theater, October 11, 1943　Describes the action of a PT boat off the coast of Sicily. The captain of the boat describes the strange sensation of landing in a small town to find that it has been completely abandoned by its inhabitants.

Souvenir—Somewhere in Mediterranean War Theater, October 12, 1943　The author claims with mordant humor that Americans primarily wage war to collect useless souvenirs, which either have no value, or are too big to transport back to the United States. He tells the story of Bugs, a soldier who carries an ornate Sicilian mirror through the war on his back only to have it fall off the wall of his barracks and break.

Welcome—Somewhere in Mediterranean War Theater, October 14, 1943　Describes the enthusiastic reception of the invading American troops by the Italian townspeople. Appreciation is shown by applause, embraces, and kisses, and thrown fruits and vegetables. The author claims that it is obvious that the Italian people were never America's enemies, but that each village has a fat, beautifully dressed man who collaborated with the Fascist government.

The Lady Packs—Somewhere in Mediterranean War Theater, October 15, 1943　The celebrated British commandos, whom the author describes as "small, tired-looking men who might have been waiters or porters at a railroad station," are called in to rescue an Italian admiral and his wife held hostage on a little island mined with explosives. The author marvels that the commandos manage to neutralize the enemy troops, rescue the lady and her husband, and return to the island to pick up the lady's luggage.

Capri—Somewhere in Mediterranean War Theater, October 18, 1943　Upon capturing the island of Capri the American troops discover an English expatriate who becomes ecstatic when her rescuers offer her a packet of tea and a pat of butter so that she might bake scones.

Sea Warfare—Somewhere in Mediterranean War Theater, October 19, 1943　An officer of Task Force X tries to convince his comrades that naval warfare is like chamber music: "thirty-caliber machine guns, those are the violins, the fifties are the violas, six-inch guns are perfect cellos." He takes his friends to a local monastery to listen to the evensong.

The Worried Bartender—Somewhere in Mediterranean War Theater, October 20, 1943　Luigi the bartender welcomes the American liberators with enthusiasm. He worries to his new friends that his pregnant daughter is trapped in a nearby town that is being invaded by the Germans. A group of soldiers requisition a captured Italian patrol boat and rescue the bartender's daughter.

The Camera Makes Soldiers—Somewhere in Mediterranean War Theater, October 21, 1943 While preparing a film for the army, the author notices that under the gaze of his camera the troops tend to straighten and strike heroic poses, and that even the severely wounded do their best to look less wounded.

The Story of an Elf—Monday, November 1, 1943 A humorous story about an elf named Charley Lytle that visited the hotel room of a group of tired and thirsty war correspondents and delivered them a case of fine whiskey and another case of cold bottled beer

Magic Pieces—November 3, 1943 The author recounts the many different styles of lucky charms carried by the soldiers into battle. He observes the proliferation of amulets and supernatural talismans during times of great danger and emotional upheaval.

Symptoms—November 4, 1943 The author writes of the reticence of ex-soldiers, even those known to be talkers and boasters, to discuss their experiences in battle. He speculates that this is because battle is so physically and psychologically traumatic that they are unable to remember what happened. He describes the extreme discomfort of warfare and the effects that it has on the body and nervous system.

The Plywood Navy—November 15, 1943 The author joins the crew of torpedo boat 412, part of a force of British MTB and American PT boats whose mission is to interrupt German shipping in the Mediterranean. The gunner on the small boat manages to shoot down an enemy plane.

November 19, 1943 Torpedo boat 412 finds itself in the middle of a large convoy of enemy E-boats and transport ships. The crew manages to sink a large ammunition transport before escaping.

A Destroyer—November 24, 1943 The author describes the destroyer as being the nicest fighting ship in the navy. The destroyer, he explains, is small enough that the captain knows his whole crew personally, and it is continuously at work, the busiest ship in the fleet. He describes the captain and crew of Destroyer X, a recently commissioned ship that has seen action at Casablanca, Gela, and Salerno.

A Ragged Crew—December 1, 1943 Forty American paratroopers are brought aboard the destroyer to capture a German radar station on the Italian island of Ventotene. The crew is ragged from the brutal training that they have received in North Africa. The island is thought to be occupied by a few German troops and a force of two or three hundred carabinieri, as well as a number of political prisoners who are to be released.

Ventotene—December 3, 1943 Upon arriving at the island of Ventotene, a small boat goes toward shore with a loudspeaker and demands the surrender of the island's inhabitants. Flares are sent up indicating the town's surrender. The commodore of the small task force boards a boat to go ashore and accept the surrender.

December 6, 1943 The commodore's boat is lost in the darkness and makes an aborted landing in a false harbor and again on the harbor's breakwater before finally finding the harbor and coming ashore. They take the German guards prisoner and learn that there are 87 enemy troops on the island and that each of their false landings have been mistaken for the landing of a separate force, giving the Germans the impression that they have been surrounded. The five men nervously watch their prisoners while they wait for the 43 paratroopers to land.

December 8, 1943 Reinforcements finally arrive for the five lucky conquerors of the island. The officers meet to discuss what to do about the 87 German troops barricaded on the island. One of the officers volunteers to carry a white flag to speak with the enemy and try to convince them to surrender.

December 10, 1943 The lieutenant walks slowly to the German position carrying a white towel on a stick above his head. He is taken to the three commanding officers. He demands the Germans' surrender, lying that he has a force of 600 men backed by naval cruisers, and assuring them that there is no dishonor in surrendering to a superior force.

December 13, 1943 The entire force of 87 Germans surrenders its weapons and is locked in the town jail cells. The German officers begin to suspect that they have been deceived. They demand to see the commanding colonel. The captain admits that he is the commanding officer and warns them that the building is mined and will be blown up if there is any trouble.

"Open Season on Guests: A Harassed Host Declares Total War on Party Girls and Boys" (1957)

Written as a humorous opinion piece and first published in the September 19, 1957, edition of *Playboy*, "Open Season on Guests" describes the "subtle war" between host and guest in what Steinbeck characterizes as the "battle" of entertaining. Eight guests, the author claims, will invariably show their malice toward the host by requesting eight different drinks or eight complicated variations on the offered menu. The host's only recourse, according to Steinbeck, is the cocktail party, when he has the opportunity to avenge himself on his thankless guests by locking them in an overheated, airtight room with a vile concoction of adulterated liquor. "Open Season on Guests" is typical of the light, trivial humor pieces that the author published during his later years when his articles were greatly in demand due to his literary fame.

"Over There" (1944)

Steinbeck spent six weeks in England, North Africa, and Italy working as a WORLD WAR II correspondent. "Over There," the article he wrote for *Ladies' Home Journal*, published in February of 1944, tried to give Americans the sense of what it was like to be a soldier in those theaters. A series of vignettes, it begins with Steinbeck's coverage of the bombers in England. Very rarely does he call the soldiers by proper names, and frequently, the names he uses are obvious aliases: Lieutenant Blank, for instance. When he describes a planned raid over Germany, he leaves out most details, including times, dates, and the exact location. Although there were most likely security issues that prompted this blurring of the facts, it gives the article a universal quality. The essay is not about one or two specific soldiers; it is about all of them.

Steinbeck's vignettes include the standard war stories. He describes the men suiting up for a raid on Germany. He paints vivid pictures of the roaring engines and the bitter cold flying conditions. For each person who lived through it, the LONDON blitz is summed up in one or two striking images that they can't erase. English girls "man" the turrets on the English coastline, calling in strike coordinates to the men shooting the defensive guns. The American soldiers storm the peaceful beaches of North Africa over and over to prepare for the assault on Italy. Steinbeck reports his own inability to report—or even think—clearly during the actual battle that he joined in.

Sandwiched among these are moments more human than warlike. Consistently the men play cards, tease each other, and look for souvenirs. Steinbeck relates a particularly ironic tale of a guy called "Bugs" who carried a huge carved mirror through battles so he could send it back home. When he tried to hang it up in the house where they were billeted for the night, it fell and shattered. Each crew of gunners kept a dog, and the dog knew its plane was coming before the crew did. Bob Hope winds his way through the countryside, giving the men a laugh and a sense of importance. Nothing, however, could help a soldier more than mail. The man who gets cheery letters from home has a better fighting chance, Steinbeck asserts, than one who gets whining complaints.

Steinbeck gives those waiting back home the smells and heat of Algiers and the desperation of Italy. He talks about small moments of heroism, in which a combined crew of British and Americans rescued an Italian admiral and his wife from a torpedo factory that the Germans were threatening. An officer gives tacit authority to his men to bring a pregnant girl from German-occupied Castellammare to American-occupied Capri, so she could be reunited with her father. He ends his article with a note from NEW YORK detailing the toll that constant battle takes on a person. Those back from the war who don't talk about the battles aren't reticent, he avows. They simply can't remember.

The Pastures of Heaven (1932)

Neither a series of connected short stories, as it has often been described, nor a novel precisely, Steinbeck's second lengthy published work demonstrated a far more mature style than his first book, CUP OF GOLD, published three years earlier in 1929. In the book *The Pastures of Heaven* (Brewer, Warner and Putnam, 1932), Steinbeck found his voice, and began the exploration of themes recurring throughout his career—the elusive nature of unrealized dreams, the sometimes damaging effects of conformity and social convention, and the unforeseen consequences of fate or nature on individuals.

During the process of writing the book, Steinbeck wrote to his close friend TED MILLER and described his approach and intent. Basing the locale of the book on a real valley near Salinas, Corral de Tierra, and the negative impact of a real family on the lives of the people in this valley, Steinbeck wanted to show how ordinary actions could cause extraordinary changes, often tragic or disastrous, without any conscious malice by the initiators. He compared the central family, later dubbed the Munroes, to a "Miltonian Lucifer," described their

behavior and influence as evil, and noted the irony of his proposed title, *The Pastures of Heaven.* As the Munroes become more deeply entrenched in the California valley, Las Pasturas del Cielo (The pastures of heaven), individual and family inhabitants begin to endure experiences more akin to purgatory or hell, and the bucolic, pastoral, and idyllic quality of the valley is altered forever.

In its final form, the book presents the Munroes as not so much evil as catalytic. Some member of the family plays a major or minor role in all of the "chapters" except the first and the last. Their evil, to employ Steinbeck's original term, stems from thoughtlessness and insensitivity, and most oddly, often from a genuine desire to help and contribute to the community. Joined with the Munroes' unwitting effect on the inhabitants of the valley is a nameless curse attached to the Munroe homestead, because of the misfortune of prior occupants. Each chapter can be read separately, but to appreciate the purpose of Steinbeck's writing, they should be read altogether, and in order.

The book begins and ends with the same perspective, of explorers and travelers peering into the valley, and imagining a future of limitless possibilities and a past wiped clean of mistakes. In the first chapter, a Spanish corporal in the late 18th century, having recaptured a group of runaway Indians who had escaped serfdom at a Carmelite mission, pauses at the top of a ridge, and views a completely uninhabited valley verdant with trees and abundant with game. He builds a dream of returning to the valley, and establishing a dynasty, and names the place Las Pasturas del Cielo. The corporal eventually dies of pox, still dreaming of the valley without ever setting foot there. Similarly, in the last chapter (Chapter XII), a bus driver pauses on a ridge overlooking the Pastures of Heaven, and the passengers peer below, see an image of apparent prosperity and happiness, and create a dream based on their individual perception and past. For the corporal and his Indian captives, and the busload of passengers, the valley offers a return to the Garden of Eden.

Chapters II through XI present vignettes, some more powerful than others, about the reality in the Pastures of Heaven. After the corporal's discovery, squatters settle the valley, without grants from the

Spanish Crown. In the early 20th century, when most of the action takes place, an order and complacency has built up among 20 families who reside there. Chapter II not only establishes the geographical setting of the valley in almost lyrical terms but introduces the Munroes, latecomers to the rural utopia, and ultimately the serpents who corrupt the garden. Burt Munroe, patriarch of the family, announces his certainty to a neighbor, T. B. Allen, that he has not only exorcised his own previous failures, but laid to rest the ghosts of the unhappy previous residents of his new home who suffered variously from epilepsy, mental defects, and violent tendencies. Allen astutely remarks that perhaps the Munroes' ill luck, and the sad fate of the previous tenants may have combined forces, gone underground and infected the entire valley.

Early on, therefore, Steinbeck presents a metaphor of Genesis. The Edenic geographical location, uncorrupted and innocent, has a possible Tree of Knowledge at the center, an uninhabited and haunted farmhouse with possibilities for corruption or redemption, waiting only for a quasi-demon or fallen angel. On the other hand, the story of Genesis shows the effect of free will, and teaches that individual choices redound both to the benefit and detriment of each person. Steinbeck demonstrates throughout the book the choices made by his characters in the face of life-altering events.

Jackson J. Benson, in his seminal biography *John Steinbeck, Writer*, recounts Steinbeck's deep interest in the Old Testament during the time he wrote *The Pastures of Heaven*. Part of his exploration came from research on the other novel in progress at the time, TO A GOD UNKNOWN. Part came too from his association with JOSEPH CAMPBELL, later famous for his insightful studies regarding the role of myth in human culture. In *The Pastures of Heaven* Steinbeck examines sin. Each of the central characters in the various chapters violates one or more of the Ten Commandments, or commits one of the seven deadly sins of anger, gluttony, envy, sloth, avarice, lust, and pride. Always in the background lurks a Munroe family member, either as an active or passive participant—the snake awakening awareness and choice. None of the central characters comes

to a good end, though almost all show strength in adversity.

As stated earlier, within this book lies almost every theme, general characterization, or philosophical approach explored by Steinbeck in his later years. One can see the realism, naturalism, and descriptive power of his later works. *The Pastures of Heaven* suffers because of the spotty quality, and varied approaches of the "chapters." Is this real life, or is it fairy tale? In the first category, one encounters the spunky and likeable Molly Morgan, the schoolteacher based on the writer's mother, OLIVE STEINBECK. Lovingly and tenderly portrayed, Molly eventually abandons her teaching position for fear of meeting her long lost father whom she has idealized for years. In the second instance, one reads the strange story of Tularecito, the idiot savant who may have been a foundling born of mythical creatures.

Nevertheless, Steinbeck weaves a magic of his own with this book. He comes very close to combining all of the disparate elements into a coherent whole, and shows a respect for nature, for humanity, and for his readers that would be developed further as his skills sharpened.

EARLY CRITICISM

Because Brewer, Warren, and Putnam filed for bankruptcy almost immediately following the release of *The Pastures of Heaven*, the book did not receive wide circulation. Despite this setback, reviewers who could find a copy were largely positive in their remarks. R. M. Coates of the *New Yorker* called it the "best of the novels" he reviewed during the week it was first published and praised its realism. Margaret Cheney Dawson, writing for the *New York Herald Tribune*, lauded Steinbeck's "charming serenity of style," while Anita Moffett in the *New York Times Book Review* found the book "noteworthy for originality of phrase and image and a strongly poetic feeling."

On the other hand, the critic for the *Saturday Review* called the book "excellent entertainment" but lacking in "creative imagination." Cyrilly Abels, writing for *Bookman*, made note of Steinbeck's "immaturity" and the lack of conclusiveness in *The Pastures of Heaven*, but also said the young author showed great promise. Finally the reviewer for the *Nation*, demonstrating prescience, remarked that if Steinbeck could add "social insight to his present equipment," he would make a "first-rate novelist."

CONTEMPORARY PERSPECTIVES

Not as widely read as Steinbeck's better-known books, *The Pastures of Heaven* still attracts attention from both ordinary readers and Steinbeck scholars, and not just as a historical curiosity. For instance, among the reader reviews at Amazon.com, one finds such praise as "a pleasant, and affecting surprise," ". . . still love it more than anything else Steinbeck wrote," and high regard for its "unique style and structure."

In the early 1980s, Joseph Fontenrose, who had earlier criticized Steinbeck for his mythic and philosophical approaches, revised his opinion with a monograph on *The Pastures of Heaven*, calling it a "surprisingly successful book" with the "stature of his later fiction." Feminist critics have discovered the strong female characters in the book, including Molly Morgan, the Lopez sisters, and Katherine Wicks, with one critic, Mimi Reisel Gladstein, going so far as to say that Steinbeck's women are far more adaptable and indestructible than the men.

SYNOPSIS

Chapter I

In 1776, a Spanish corporal discovers a beautiful fertile valley in central California. The place is so lovely that he names it Las Pasturas del Cielo— The Pastures of Heaven, and he swears to return there to settle. The soldier dies of disease and never returns, but in time small farmers settle the valley.

Chapter II

In 1863 George Battle buys a farm in the Pastures of Heaven and builds a large two-story square house. Mr. Battle marries a wealthy spinster, Miss Myrtle Cameron, who bears him a son, John. Myrtle has epileptic tendencies and is confined to a San José sanitarium after trying to burn down the family's house. George works tirelessly on his farm, paying little attention to his young son. He dies at 65, leaving John as his only survivor. John is a supersti-

tious, passionately religious man who has inherited his mother's epilepsy. He becomes convinced that demons inhabit the farm. One afternoon, while attacking an imagined demonic foe with a heavy stick, he is bitten by a rattlesnake and dies. The townspeople whisper that the farm is cursed, and it lies fallow for 10 years until it is purchased by the Mustrovics, an old couple with tight yellow skin and foreign accents. Their son works tirelessly to restore the farm until they mysteriously disappear without a trace. Finally the ill-fated farm is purchased by Bert Munroe. Bert has decided to return to farming after a series of business failures through mishaps not his fault. He remodels the house and restores the land to an orderly and productive state. His wife and three children, Mae, Jimmie, and Manfred, move into the farm. Returning to farming restores Bert's confidence and his happiness, and he quickly makes friends among the valley residents.

Chapter III

Edward Wicks lives with his wife, Katherine, on a small farm. He is known to be the shrewdest man in the valley and an acute businessman. He pretends that he is laying away money in securities, leading the people of the Pastures of Heaven to believe that he is a rich man. "Shark" Wicks becomes admired for his good judgment and acumen. Katherine gives birth to a daughter, Alice, who grows to be an incredibly beautiful but stupid young woman. Shark is painfully jealous and protective of Alice. Provoked by the rakish airs put on by Jimmie Munroe, he forbids his daughter to talk to the young man. While Shark is out of town at a funeral, Katherine and Alice attend a local dance. Jimmie Munroe invites Alice outside. Her mother discovers the two teenagers kissing beneath a stand of trees. When Shark returns he hears the rumor that his daughter has been with the Munroe boy. In his rage he takes a gun and heads off to kill the young man. On his way to the farm, the sheriff arrests him. The local judge orders him to pay a large bond to guarantee Jimmie's safety. Shark, humiliated, is forced to admit that he has no money and that all of his allusions to his profitable investments are lies.

Chapter IV

Pancho, a Mexican ranch hand, rides home after a night in the local saloon. Hearing a baby crying in the sagebrush beside the road, he stops his horse to investigate. Deep in the brush he finds a tiny child, which says to him in a malicious voice, "Look! I have very sharp teeth." He flings the baby to the ground and rides in terror to the ranch of Franklin Gomez. Mr. Gomez rides back to investigate. On the trail he finds a strangely formed infant. Gomez raises the child, who comes to be called Tularecito, or Little Frog, for its flat face and peculiar body. As the boy grows he becomes uncommonly strong and dexterous, and his strange eyes make people nervous in his presence. When Tularecito turns 11 the state forces him to attend school. The young schoolteacher, Miss Morgan, tells the young boy fairy tales about elves and fairies and gnomes. Fascinated, young Tularecito seeks out the teacher and asks her if she really believes that gnomes exist. She says that they do and encourages him to search for them. He begins spending his nights digging holes in search of the mysterious creatures, his people. He digs a large tunnel in Bert Munroe's orchard. Mr. Munroe, discovering the pit, attributes it to the local boys and begins to fill it in with his shovel. Tularecito attacks him and viciously beats him. Tularecito is committed to an asylum for the criminally insane.

Chapter V

Helen Van Deventer, a woman who "hungered for tragedy and life had lavishly heaped it upon her," becomes a widow when her husband dies in a hunting accident. Six months later she gives birth to her daughter, Hilda. When Hilda turns six the doctor diagnoses her with mental illness and recommends that Helen take her to see a psychiatrist. Assuming the air of a martyr, she determines to endure her child's illness on her own. Young Hilda begins to suffer from terrible hallucinations and dreams. When she is 13 she runs away from home and is found sleeping in a deserted real estate office. The doctor warns Helen that Hilda is getting worse and that she needs to be placed in a hospital for the insane. Helen refuses the suggestion. Mrs. Van Deventer buys a ranch in the Pastures of Heaven, where she builds a luxurious hunting lodge, a memorial to her dead husband, to incarcerate her sick daughter. Bert Munroe walks to the ranch to pay a visit to his new neighbor, but Helen Van Deventer refuses to see him. Hilda calls him from a window and tells him that she has been imprisoned, and if he will help her escape, she will run away with him and marry him. That evening Hilda breaks through the oak bars on her bedroom window and escapes. Helen takes her husband's shotgun and shoots her daughter. The incident is judged a suicide.

Chapter VI

Junius Maltby, a 35-year-old clerk with no aspirations, suffers an attack from a respiratory condition. His doctor recommends that the young man move to a warm, dry climate to recover his health. Junius moves to a boardinghouse in the Pastures of Heaven and marries the owner, a widow named Mamie Quaker. Mrs. Quaker's farm slowly falls into disorder and the couple grows very poor due to Junius's laziness, for he would rather sit by the stream reading novels than work. Their two sons die in an influenza epidemic. Soon thereafter Mrs. Maltby dies in childbirth, leaving Junius with a son named Robert Luis, whom he raises in his idyllic poverty. Junius hires an old German named Jakob Stutz to work the farm, but the two men soon lapse into idleness and philosophical conversations, and the farm continues to decay while the people of the valley watch with scorn and pity. Meanwhile little Robbie grows up under the care of his unlikely guardians, oblivious to his poverty, a serious child, intelligent and thoughtful. When Robbie turns six the school board insists that he must attend school. Robbie quickly overcomes his shyness and becomes a leader of his schoolmates, whom he entertains by inventing a series of elaborate games. That spring Mrs. Munroe convinces the members of the board to give poor Robbie a parcel of shoes and clothing. Robbie, realizing for the first time that he is poor, an object of pity, runs away in embarrassment. Junius feels guilt for his son's shame. He decides to sell the farm and give up his blissful existence to return to San Francisco to look for work.

Chapter VII

Maria and Rosa Lopez inherit a 40-acre farm on a rocky hillside above the Pastures of Heaven. The two sisters open a restaurant, serving enchiladas, tortillas, and tamales to the inhabitants of the valley. Business is slow and the sisters are desperate to increase their sales. Rosa determines to offer herself to her customers to "encourage" their patronage. One evening a customer who is not hungry offers Rosa money for sex. She is insulted at the suggestion that she is a prostitute. The women of the town begin to suspect the true nature of the Lopez business. One afternoon, in a gesture of kindness, Maria Lopez offers a ride in her buggy to Allen Hueneker, the shyest man in the valley. Mr. Munroe sees them together and jokingly tells Mrs. Hueneker, a jealous woman, that her husband has run off with Maria Lopez. She complains to the sheriff, who is forced to shut down the Lopez sisters' restaurant. Maria and Rosa, ashamed, decide to go to San Francisco and become "bad women."

Chapter VIII

Molly Morgan, a pretty young woman of 19, arrives in the Pastures of Heaven to interview for a position as the local schoolteacher. She goes to the house of John Whiteside, the school board clerk. During the interview Molly remembers her childhood of extreme poverty. Her father was a traveling salesman and an alcoholic who came home from his long business trips only rarely and eventually disappeared altogether. Molly's mother died, leaving the little girl an orphan. She worked her way through teacher's college. Mr. Whiteside offers the nervous young woman the job and she boards in the Whiteside house. She is a popular teacher, admired and loved by the inhabitants of the valley, and for the first time in her life she is happy. One afternoon Bert Munroe tells about a drunk that he picked up under a bridge to work on his farm. Hearing his description, Molly becomes terrified that the man is her father. She spends the next weeks in fear of casually meeting him. Unable to stand the possibility that the drunk might be her father, she quits her job and leaves town.

Chapter IX

The Banks farm is the most admired farm in the valley. His neighbors love Raymond Banks, a strong, jolly man. His best friend from high school is the warden of San Quentin prison, and two or three times a year he invites Banks to be a witness at an execution. Banks never fails to accept the invitation. Bert Munroe becomes fascinated by the idea of executions and asks Raymond if it is possible to go with him. Raymond writes his friend and secures an invitation for the two of them to attend the next hanging. But Bert changes his mind at the last minute. He tells of seeing an old crippled man trying to kill a rooster and wounding it brutally when he was a boy. He has nightmares about the rooster and he is afraid that the hanging will also give him nightmares. He tells Banks that he has imagined what it must be like to be hanged and that it is horrifying. That evening Raymond tries to imagine himself being executed. The next day he writes to the warden to tell him that he is ill and cannot attend the execution.

Chapter X

When Pat Humbert turns 16, his feeble parents retire, leaving him to run their small farm and take care of them in their old age. He works tirelessly and is continually bullied by his old father, who spends his days in a rocking chair. When Pat is 30 his parents die. After the funeral, he becomes afraid that their ghosts haunt the sitting room. He locks the doors to the room and throws away the key. Alone and afraid of the spirits locked in his parlor, he spends his days working on his farm and his evenings looking for the company of other men in meetings or at the movies. For 10 years he continues his nightly search for company, hanging on the fringes of any group he can find. One evening during dinner at the Munroe house, Pat overhears Mae Munroe talking about a pretty house that she saw in a postcard. Pat determines to decorate his house and win Mae's affection. He breaks down the locked doors to the sitting room and cleans out all traces of his long-dead parents, even burning the furniture in a great pile in the front yard. Exactingly he goes about constructing a replica of the Vermont sitting room he has heard Mae speak fondly of. After many months of preparation the room is ready. He is planning to invite Mae to his house when he hears that she is to be married to Bill Whiteside.

Chapter XI

Richard Whiteside arrives in the Pastures of Heaven determined to build a seat for the large family he hopes to have. To mark his determination, he builds the largest, finest house in the entire valley, and as a symbol of his permanence, he tops the house with a fine, expensive slate roof imported from the East. He marries his cousin, Alicia, who quickly becomes pregnant. Alicia nearly dies in childbirth but delivers him a son, John. Richard is devastated to learn from the doctor that she will be unable to have more children, thus ending his dreams of a large family. But Alicia becomes pregnant again. The second pregnancy nearly kills her, and the baby dies before birth. Richard places his hope in his son, instilling in him an awe of the great house. John Whiteside grows up and marries, but he, too, fathers only one son, Bill Whiteside. Bill is uninterested in lofty ideas of family and dynasty. A practical, business-minded boy, he marries Mae Munroe and buys a car dealership in the city. John insists that his son will not be able to stay away from the farm for long. That fall, Bert Munroe suggests that John burn back the bushes on a nearby hillside to make way for sheep pasture. The fire burns out of control, and the Whiteside house is burned to the ground.

Chapter XII

A tour bus leaves Monterey and drives through the nearby valleys. Coming upon the crest of a hill the passengers admire the view of the Pastures of Heaven in the distance.

CHARACTERS

Banks, Raymond   A character in *The Pastures of Heaven*. Owner of the most admired farm in the valley of the Pastures of Heaven, he is a strong man who works tirelessly on his farm, his only vacations periodic trips to San Quentin Prison to witness the executions of condemned prisoners. He and his wife give chicken barbecues with homemade beer for the whole valley.

Battle, George   A character in *The Pastures of Heaven*. George moves to the valley of the Pastures of Heaven from upstate New York in 1863 with his wife, Myrtle, and they are the first settlers in the region. He is forced to commit Myrtle to a mental hospital after she suffers an epileptic fit and tries to burn down the family home. George lives on the farm with his only son, John. He is bitten by a rattlesnake while hunting for demons in the bushes around his house. When George Battle dies, John becomes convinced that demons inhabit the farm. The Battle farm is thought to be cursed by the people of the valley and lies abandoned for many years until it is purchased by Bert Munroe.

Humbert, Pat   A character in *The Pastures of Heaven*, Pat is a farmer in the valley of the Pastures of Heaven. When his parents die, he becomes convinced that their ghosts live in the parlor sitting room, which he closes and locks. The lonely man spends his days working on his farm and his evenings looking for the company of other men in meetings or at the movies. One day he decides to win the love of Mae Munroe by making his house the most splendid in the valley. He dedicates himself to remodeling the house, opening the parlor and burning the furniture in a great pile in the front yard. When everything is finally ready, Pat discovers that Mae is engaged to marry Bill Whiteside.

Lopez, Rosa and Maria   Characters in *The Pastures of Heaven*, Rosa and Maria are two poor sisters who live on a ranch on the outskirts of the Pastures of Heaven. The two sisters look almost exactly alike. However, Rosa was a little taller and Maria was a little fatter. Rosa and Maria open a restaurant in their home. To "encourage" their patrons, the two sisters offer themselves to any man who buys two or more plates of food. Their business is very successful until a jealous wife makes the sheriff shut down their restaurant. The two sisters move to San Francisco to continue their work.

Maltby, Junius   A character in *The Pastures of Heaven*, Junius is a lazy dreamer who works as a clerk in San Francisco, then moves to the valley of the Pastures of Heaven and marries the widow Mamie Quaker. The Quaker farm falls into disrepair as Junius whiles the day away dreaming and reading the books of Robert Louis Stevenson.

When his wife dies in childbirth, Junius lives in idyllic poverty with his son, Robbie, unaware that the people of the valley look upon him with scorn and pity. Robbie is obliged by the superintendent to go to school. Robbie becomes aware of his poverty when the people of the town pitch in to buy him new clothes and shoes. Junius, ashamed of neglecting his son, gives up his happy life and returns to San Francisco to look for a job.

Morgan, Molly A character in *The Pastures of Heaven*, Molly is the pretty young schoolteacher adored by the residents of the valley of the Pastures of Heaven. She grew up in extreme poverty, the child of a drunk father who one day disappeared and never returned. The orphan Molly works to put herself through teacher's college before taking a job in the Pastures of Heaven. One day she hears the description of a drunk who is living on the Munroe farm. Afraid that this man might be her father, she quits her job and leaves town.

Munroe, Bert A character in *The Pastures of Heaven*, Bert is a farmer in the valley of the Pastures of Heaven. He determines to return to farming after a series of businesses ventures fail, in his view "acts of a Fate malignant to his success." He prepares the farm and brings his wife, Mrs. Munroe, and his three children, Mae, Jimmie, and Manfred to live there. He quickly becomes a respected member of the community and is elected to the school board. Feeling that his curse has gone away, he does not realize that he has spawned a lot of baby curses that haunt his neighbors.

Tularecito A character in *The Pastures of Heaven*, he is a strange child with fantastic strength, a flat face, and peculiar body that earn him the nickname "Tularecito"—Little Frog. As an infant he is discovered abandoned on a trail in the mountains outside of the valley of the Pastures of Heaven and raised by the ranch owner, Mr. Gomez. He becomes fascinated by the fairy tales of elves and gnomes, and determines that he must be one of them. He begins digging holes in Bert Munroe's orchard in search of the mystical creatures. When Mr. Munroe attempts to fill in one of the holes, Tularecito attacks him

savagely and is committed to an asylum for the criminally insane.

Van Deventer, Helen A character in *The Pastures of Heaven*, Helen is a tall, attractive, but melancholy widow with a handsome face, tragic eyes, and a sharp sense of martyrdom. She gives birth to a daughter, Hilda, after her husband is killed in a hunting accident. Determined to care for Hilda when it is revealed that she is insane, she builds an isolated lodge in the hills surrounding the valley of the Pastures of Heaven. When Hilda escapes from her confinement, Helen finds her and kills her with her husband's shotgun to protect her from the men who would take advantage of her.

Whiteside, John A character in *The Pastures of Heaven*, John is a proud, educated man, who is the most respected resident of the valley of the Pastures of Heaven. John Whiteside is the town's first citizen and the clerk of the local school board. The Whiteside family draws its prestige from their fine white house, the largest and finest house in the valley. Built by his father, Richard Whiteside, the house is intended to be the home of many generations of Whitesides. One day John sets out to burn some bushes cluttering his outlying fields. The fire burns out of control and the flames consume the house.

Wicks, Edward "Shark" A character in *The Pastures of Heaven*, Edward is a farmer in the valley of the Pastures of Heaven. He is a blunt, small, brown-faced man. He is nicknamed "Shark" by the townspeople, whom he deceives into believing that he has earned great wealth through his shrewdness and acumen in investing. His wife, Katherine, gives birth to a remarkably beautiful daughter, Alice. Although beautiful, Alice is also incredibly dull and backward. Her father becomes jealously overprotective of the child, warning her not to even talk to the town's boys. When Wicks hears rumors that his daughter was seen kissing Jimmie Munroe at the town dance, he sets off to kill the boy with a shotgun. The sheriff intercepts him and makes him pay a large bond to guarantee his good behavior. Wicks is humiliated when he is forced to admit that he doesn't have any money to secure the bond.

THE FILM: *MOLLY MORGAN* (PYRAMID FILMS, 1991)

Adapted from *The Pastures of Heaven,* by John Steinbeck

Screenplay: Steven Rosen and Terri Debonno
Director: Steven Rosen and Terri Debonno
Producer: Steven Rosen and Terri Debonno
Molly Morgan: Teressa McKillop
Molly Morgan, child: Eunice Clay
Mr. Morgan: Jeffrey Heyer
Mr. Whiteside: Rollie Dick
Mrs. Whiteside: Louise Nachman
Bill: Norman Stottmeister
Bert Munroe: Dennis McIntyre

Based on the experiences of Steinbeck's mother, this story brings to life the experiences of a daughter with her alcoholic father. Independently produced, the film runs 30 minutes and is available through Mac and Ava Productions.

FURTHER READING

Abels, Cyrilly. "Keeping Up with the Novelists." *Bookman,* December 1932, 877–878.

Benson, Jackson J. *John Steinbeck, Writer.* New York: Penguin, 1990.

Coates, R. M. "Books." *New Yorker,* October 22, 1932, 54–55.

Dawson, Margaret Cheney. "In a Peaceful Valley." *New York Herald Tribune,* October 23, 1932, Books section, 2.

Fontenrose, Joseph. *Steinbeck's Unhappy Valley: A Study of* The Pastures of Heaven. Berkeley, Calif.: Joseph Fontenrose, 1981.

Gladstein, Mimi Reisel. "In Search of Steinbeck: A Continuing Journey." *Nova* (University of Texas at El Paso magazine) (September 1983): 7–9, 12.

Moffett, Anita. "A Sheltered Valley." *New York Times Book Review,* November 20, 1932, 15–16.

"The New Books." *Saturday Review,* November 26, 1932, 275–276.

"Shorter Notices." *Nation,* December 7, 1932, 574.

Steinbeck, John. *The Pastures of Heaven.* New York: Brewer, Warren & Putnam, 1932.

The Pearl (1947)

Originally published in the *Women's Home Companion* as *The Pearl of the World,* Steinbeck's 17th book, *The Pearl,* is a short novel written in the form of a parable. *The Pearl* recounts the tale of a poor fisherman who finds a beautiful, valuable pearl. Instead of bringing him riches, however, the pearl only brings misfortune until the fisherman is finally forced to throw it back into the sea. *The Pearl* is based on a story that John Steinbeck heard while traveling along the peninsula of Baja California with his good friend EDWARD RICKETTS. Indeed, Steinbeck first mentions the story of the pearl in the log of his expedition, SEA OF CORTEZ: A LEISURELY JOURNEY OF TRAVEL AND RESEARCH, which was published in 1941. While in LA PAZ, MEXICO, Steinbeck was told of the story of a young Indian boy who finds a magnificent pearl. The author researched and wrote much of the novel while staying in the city of Cuernavaca, in central Mexico. The novel was completed in 1947, after Steinbeck finished the screenplay for the movie, and was published by VIKING PRESS that same year.

Steinbeck wrote the book after his experiences during WORLD WAR II, and this may explain the darker overtones found in the work. The book also explores the dangerous temptations in the acquisition of unexpected wealth, another subject that found resonance with the author after his unforeseen popular success in the 1930s. Of course the author's deliberate identification of the story as a parable underscores the biblical theme of the sacrifice of a possibility of heaven for material goods. Steinbeck's sympathetic treatment of the Mexican villagers stems from an early connection with Mexicans in California as a laborer working side by side with them on farms in the Salinas Valley.

EARLY CRITICISM

The Pearl received friendly reception upon its publication. Writing for *Library Journal,* Robert E. Kingery praised the novel as a "major artistic triumph." Echoing Kingery's positive comments on the novel, Orville Prescott of the *New York Times* found the theme of the story to have a "universally human quality." These early reviewers were quick to point out Steinbeck's focus on the fundamentals and universal significance of life in the novel. In England, the *Times Literary Supplement* and *New Statesman and Nation* carried articles and reviews praising Steinbeck's skills in storytelling, calling the novel "quasi-biblical" because of the allegorical effect of the narrative. A more detailed review of the novel was provided in "Steinbeck's Mexican Folk-Tale," by Thomas Sugrue, who wrote for the *New York Herald Tribune*. Sugrue looked back at ancient folklore and found that the plot in the novel is similar to that of the passage "Hymn of the Soul" in the Gnostic fragment known as the "Acts of Judas Thomas."

CONTEMPORARY PERSPECTIVES

Later reaction to the work has been mixed. Steinbeck scholar and critic Warren French strongly criticized the book for lacking both insight and worth. French contended that Steinbeck wrote the work for the money and not the value of the story itself. For French and like-minded critics, *The Pearl* marks a decline in Steinbeck's work. While French disliked the work, other critics such as Howard Levant, who wrote *The Novels of John Steinbeck: A Critical Study*, praised the piece for its ability to take an "apparent simple narrative into the darkest areas of human awareness." Levant wrote that "*The Pearl* is a triumph, a successful rendering of human experience in the round, in the most economical and intense of forms." While the reviews of the work have been mixed, *The Pearl* has become one of the most widely read works by Steinbeck, assigned in many high school literature courses.

In his study of *The Pearl*, John H. Timmerman carefully compares the theme or the story in *The Pearl* with the books Steinbeck had read before writing this story. According to Timmerman's examination of Robert DeMott's listing of Steinbeck's readings, there were nine separate works by Jung in his catalog. DeMott revealed earlier that Steinbeck arrived at Jung's works independently of Edward Ricketts although his interest in Jung intensified through conversations with Ricketts. Timmerman argues that "[i]n no work . . . is the

influence [on Steinbeck] more clear and systematic than in *The Pearl*, a work heretofore virtually ignored in psychoanalytic terms". According to Timmerman, Jung's chief influence on Steinbeck was the fundamental premise of Jung's theory that the conscious and the unconscious are necessarily in conflict. Even when one adopts a stylized mask, what Jung calls the "persona," for the conscious part of one's nature—and such a mask is necessary because the conscious is the extroverted part of personality, that by which we meet others—the unconscious part of one's personality will afflict the mask. From this perspective, Timmerman argues that at the most immediate and narrative level *The Pearl* details the explosive conflict of the civilized world, as Steinbeck uses that concept in several other works.

Other critics have interpreted *The Pearl* in a number of ways. Some critics call the work a search for values, or a study of the vanity of human wishes; others call it the struggle of one man against a predatory community, or a lesson showing that man must stay in his own niche and not encroach on others, or, most often, a rejection of materialism. Regardless of all critical perspectives, one must not ignore Steinbeck's advice to the reader. In the prefatory comment, he invites every reader to take his or her own meaning from the story, to read his or her own life into it.

SYNOPSIS

Steinbeck introduces his story by framing it as a morality tale. In this tale, there occur no shades of gray—only black and white, good and evil. It is a parable for all human life, and all draw their own meaning from the story.

Chapter I

Kino awakens at sunrise to find his young wife, Juana, awake and observing him. His baby boy, Coyotito, swings in a cradle-box. Kino cannot remember when things were different. He closes his eyes and listens to his internal music. Juana rises to check on the baby. Then she builds up the fire and begins to prepare the morning cakes of corn. Suddenly Kino notices a scorpion crawling down the rope supporting Coyotito's cradle-box. The Song of

Family is replaced by the Song of Evil in Kino's head as he moves cautiously toward his sleeping son. Before he can grab the scorpion, however, little Coyotito awakens and is stung on the shoulder. Juana sucks the venom from the wound, but she knows that the baby may die if enough poison entered its fragile body. She pleads for a doctor, but no doctor will come to such a poor village, and so she insists that they will go into town to find one. In town, they are refused treatment when the doctor learns that they have nothing to offer in payment except a few misshapen seed pearls.

Chapter II

Juana and Kino return to their village on the seashore. Kino gathers his diving rock and his bas-ket and they paddle out to the oyster bed. Kino hopes to find a pearl with which to hire the doctor to cure little Coyotito. Holding his breath under the water, Kino spies a very large oyster lying under an overhang and brings it to the surface. Inside he discovers an enormous, and magnificent pearl. They return excitedly to their village where Juana finds that Coyotito is recovering from the scorpion sting.

Chapter III

Word of the fabulous pearl spreads quickly through the village and then the nearby town of La Paz. Kino makes plans for his family's future. Everyone is envious of Kino's pearl, and many try to find a way to take advantage of Kino's potential wealth. Later, the doctor arrives at Kino's home insisting

Pedro Armendáriz as Kino and María Elena Marqués as Juana in the 1948 film production of *The Pearl* *(Photofest)*

there is still the danger of relapse. The young father's rage turns to fear and he allows the doctor to examine the baby. The doctor gives the baby a pill filled with a strange white powder and says that the poison should come back within the hour but that the medicine will turn it back. Indeed, the baby sickens and the doctor returns again to treat him. Kino is suspicious that it is the doctor's white powder that worsened the baby's condition, but he cannot be sure. He promises to pay the doctor when he sells the pearl. That night he awakes, sensing that someone is in his house. He leaps at the phantom and is dealt a blow on the head. The attacker flees. Juana cries that the pearl is evil and that they must throw it back into the sea, but her husband refuses.

Chapter IV

The next morning, a curious crowd follows Kino into town to witness the selling of the great pearl. Juan Tomás tells his brother that many years before, the poor pearl fishermen had hired an agent to take the pearls to the capital to receive a better price but the agent disappeared and was never heard from again. Kino remembers that the priest gave a sermon claiming that the loss of the pearls was God's punishment of the fishermen for trying to leave their station in life. The pearl buyers have met and determined a strategy to cheat Kino out of his treasure. The first buyer claims that the pearl is too big, a mere curiosity of nature for which there is no market. He offers Kino 1,000 pesos for the prize. The buyer calls three other pearl brokers to prove that there is no collusion. Kino becomes suspicious and angry. He knows he is being cheated, but he is powerless to do anything about it. Refusing to sell the pearl, he returns to his village. Juan Tomás warns his brother to be careful because he is defying the structure of things. Kino decides that he must journey to the capital to sell the pearl. That night Kino is attacked again, but he has buried the pearl in his hut and it is safe. Juana insists that the pearl is evil and should be returned to the sea, but Kino again refuses to consider it.

Chapter V

Kino awakes in the night and discovers Juana fleeing with the pearl, which she plans to fling into the

sea. He catches his wife, takes back the pearl, and beats her. On his way back to the hut he is ambushed and the pearl is knocked from his hand. He kills the attacker with his knife. Juana finds the pearl in the path, but instead of going through with her plan, she returns it to Kino. Kino discovers that his canoe is destroyed and his house in flames. He and his wife hide in Juan Tomás' house while the villagers scour the ashes for their remains. When night falls they gather their meager belongings and flee to the North.

Chapter VI

Under the cover of darkness the young family escapes north on the road to Loreto. When the sun begins to rise they find a place to hide and rest. In the distance Kino notices two trackers on foot and a horseman armed with a rifle. They head inland toward the nearby mountain range, no longer bothering to conceal their tracks. They continue their flight until they discover a green place with a spring, and hide in a cave above the spring as night falls. Their pursuers arrive and set up camp. Kino slips silently into the camp to ambush the men. As Kino nears the crouching rifleman, Coyotito's muffled cry comes from above. The rifleman stands and fires toward the sound, thinking it is a coyote. Kino kills all three of the trackers, but then hears Juana's hysterical cry. Coyotito is dead, killed by the blind shot of the rifleman. Juana and Kino return to La Paz bearing in a bloody bundle the body of their dead son. They march silently to the water's edge where Kino raises up his arm and flings the pearl into the sea from whence it came.

CHARACTERS

Doctor, The   A character in *The Pearl*, the doctor is a fat and selfish man who dreams of leaving LA PAZ, MEXICO, and returning to "civilized living" in France. He refuses to treat Kino's infant son Coyotito when a scorpion stings him. When Kino discovers a great pearl, the doctor rushes to his home and pretends to treat the already recovering child.

Juan Tomás   A character in *The Pearl*, Juan Tomás is Kino's elder brother and adviser. He lives with his wife, Apolonia. When Kino is ambushed and kills a man, Juan Tomás hides him and advises him to flee to the North.

Kino   A character in *The Pearl,* Kino is a poor, young fisherman with black hair, a thin mustache, and bright eyes. He is married to Juana, a quiet and devoted young woman. Together they have a young son, Coyotito, whom Kino dreams of being able to send to school. While fishing for a pearl to pay for a doctor for his son, Kino discovers the Pearl of the World, the greatest pearl anybody has ever seen. The pearl brings great tragedy to the young family, forcing Kino and his family to flee LA PAZ, MEXICO, and finally resulting in Coyotito's death. Angrily, Kino flings the pearl back into the sea.

Pearl of the World   The beautiful pearl, as large as a seagull's egg, that Kino discovers while diving in *The Pearl.* The pearl brings nothing but evil and misfortune until Kino finally throws it back into the sea.

THE FILM: *THE PEARL* (RKO, 1948)

Based on the novel by John Steinbeck

Screenplay: John Steinbeck, Emilio Fernández, and Jack Wagner
Director: Emilio Fernández
Producer: Oscar Danugers
Kino: Pedro Armendáriz
Juana: María Elena Marqués

Steinbeck collaborated closely on the production of the film in 1945 and 1946. In November 1947 the novella version of the story was published by Viking Press. Although there are differences between the film version and the novella, the theme of story remains the same. For example, certain characters and events were added to or eliminated from the film to give it more dramatic coherence. The film version lacks that strong flavor of parable that gives the novel its unique and powerful style. Unable to find strong interest for the screenplay in Hollywood, Steinbeck doggedly pursued a Mexican production company to make the film in MEXICO with Mexican actors. The writer poured considerable time and effort into the production of the film, often spending weeks and

even months at a time on site to oversee the shooting. The film was released in 1948 and represented one of the first Mexican films to receive wide distribution in the domestic market in the United States.

FURTHER READING

"At Home and Abroad." *Times Literary Supplement* (London), November 6, 1948, 621.

French, Warren. *John Steinbeck.* New York: Twayne, 1961.

Johnson, Claudia D. *Understanding Of Mice and Men, The Red Pony, and The Pearl: A Student Casebook to Issues, Sources, and Historical Documents.* Westport, Conn.: Greenwood Press, 1997.

Karson, Jill, ed. *Readings on The Pearl.* San Diego, Calif.: Greenhaven Press, 1999.

Kingery, Robert E. "The Pearl." *Library Journal* (November 1, 1947): 1540.

Levant, Howard. *The Novels of John Steinbeck: A Critical Study.* Columbia: University of Missouri Press, 1974.

"New Novels." *New Statesman and Nation,* November 6, 1948, 400–401.

Prescott, Orville. "Books of the Times." *New York Times,* November 24, 1947, 21.

Steinbeck, John. *The Pearl.* New York: Viking, 1947.

Sugrue, Thomas. "Steinbeck's Mexican Folk-Tale." *New York Herald Tribune,* December 7, 1947, 4.

Timmerman, John H. "The Shadow and the Pearl: Jungian Patterns in *The Pearl.*" In *The Short Novels of John Steinbeck,* edited by Jackson J. Benson. Durham, N.C.: Duke University Press, 1990, 143–161.

"A Plea for Tourists" (1955)

This essay, first published in *Punch,* January 26, 1955, was written while Steinbeck was living in France with his wife and family. At the time he was writing a series of columns about PARIS for the French magazine *FIGARO LITTÉRAIRE.* As an American traveling abroad, Steinbeck was genuinely concerned about the impression that he made on his foreign hosts; but after spending a significant time traveling, he came to believe that tourists were not really getting a fair shake on the Continent. In reality American tourists had saved their hard-earned money to experience the great American dream of the grand European tour; and yet when they arrive "they find themselves scorned, and they suspect they are being cheated." He complains that the bad behavior of a few tourists is attributed to them all. He asks why such contempt exists for American tourists when what they are really doing is offering the greatest compliment one people can pay another. Steinbeck complains of the dislike that greets many visiting Americans, making them "even more quiet and shy than usual." Tourism, he insists, if the tourist is not too badly treated, is a way to lose some isolation and suspicion of foreigners, for it is difficult to hate people you know.

"A Plea to Teachers" (1955)

"A Plea to Teachers," published in *Saturday Review* on April 30, 1955, is written as a humorous editorial letter to America's teachers, who Steinbeck claims "have with the best and highest intentions released a monster." He complains that for the past few years he has been receiving letters from children requesting his assistance with the term papers that they have been assigned to write about the author. As more and more letters arrive, their tone is slowly changing. He notes that some of the students actually blamed him as the cause of their having to write a term paper. Steinbeck claims that the students are even beginning to hold him responsible for their grades, and he begs the teachers to call their students off because they are creating angry students and because they are making him "seriously consider shooting the postman."

"Positano" (1953)

Essay published in *Harper's Bazaar*, August 1953. "Positano" explores the charm of an ancient but still thriving fishing village that climbs up the side

of a mountain on the southern Italian coastline. Steinbeck and his wife traveled there on the advice of several friends, in a taxi driven by a crazed Italian named Signor Bassano. He describes being huddled in the backseat, weeping with his wife while Signor Bassano hurtled the taxi along skinny roads carved into the sides of cliffs overhanging the ocean. When they finally arrive at Positano, they find it beautiful—so charming, in fact, that he worries briefly about telling anyone else about it, lest it be overrun with tourists and lose its natural attraction. He decides that the steps are too steep, the roads too narrow, and there just isn't enough room for the tourist hordes to descend, so it's safe.

He goes on to describe the town: the mayor is a Communist nobleman; the Emperor Tiberius used to get his flour from there; every year there is a festival to reenact the night when Saracen pirates stole a Byzantine painting of the Virgin Mary but returned it when they received a vision. The town used to be a shipping center, but after steamships began to rule the ocean, about three-quarters of the population immigrated to America in the 1860s. Now it's a small fishing village that competes for fish and salvage with another nearby village, Praiano. Several writers, including John McKnight, who recommended Positano to the Steinbecks, have stayed there to finish books. Steinbeck wraps up the essay with a funny anecdote about a Thanksgiving turkey that McKnight and his wife nearly lost to the ocean, but which was returned by the industrious Positano fishermen. Apparently, the turkey tasted of saltwater, even after it was cooked.

"A Primer on the 30's" (1960)

In 1960, Steinbeck wrote an essay for *Esquire* about the 1930s. Although he talks about the '30s from his point of view, the essay does give a more global look at many of the experiences of the time. Steinbeck reflects that the decade seemed to have been designed—bookended by economic collapse at the beginning and the Great War at the end. He begins in 1929, giving a glimpse of the paper-rich stock market tycoons who were just months from losing it all, including a friend's uncle, who dropped to $2 million (in cash) instead of $7 million. The man shot himself one day because he thought he would starve to death on only $2 million. Steinbeck details the run on the banks, and Herbert Hoover's political gaffes that led to Roosevelt's landslide victory, including sending out Douglas MacArthur to lead the army against a group of former soldiers who were protesting the delay in funds they had been promised. Steinbeck and his friends weren't badly off. They'd never had the money to begin with, so they didn't miss it. They lived off the sea and the land, and made great parties for any excuse out of whatever they could get their hands on. One of the saddest moments for Steinbeck seems to have been the death of his Airedale because he couldn't afford to pay the vet to cure her.

He wrote constantly, even though he couldn't get on one of the Works Progress Administration (WPA) writing projects. His agents paid postage so he could send submissions out. He speaks glowingly of the WPA, listing the many worthwhile projects that they completed, and of the National Theater, ended abruptly by the Senate. Just when the United States was on its way to recovery, a massive drought hit most of the country, and Steinbeck was sent out by the *San Francisco News* to cover a group of migrants from Oklahoma. Although he never states it outright, this must have been the main event that led him to write *THE GRAPES OF WRATH*.

He gives a sense of the extreme emotions of the times: The '30s saw the rise of Hitler, Mussolini, and the KKK, as well as the surge of COMMUNISM in America. Steinbeck dismisses most of the Communists that he met as middle-class dilettantes, more interested in fighting than in taking over. He was threatened by the KKK on occasion.

In the later '30s, he observes, the country must have been on an upswing, because his writing was starting to do well. He sold a book to a movie studio for $3,000, more money than he could imagine. Strikes, race riots, and the Dies Committee began to take over American consciousness. Steinbeck himself was denounced by the Dies Committee for giving money for medical aid to the Spanish loyal-

ists (along with Shirley Temple). He met President Roosevelt, who continued to call on Steinbeck to make him laugh until his last days. Toward the end of the decade the specter of war, the other bookend, was rising in Europe.

He ends the essay by looking in on a brokerage house and watching the audience stare at the stock trading board in a way eerily reminiscent of the attention paid in the late 1920s.

"The Raid" (1934)

A precursor to Steinbeck's 1936 novel, *IN DUBIOUS BATTLE*, "The Raid" was first published in the October 1934 edition of the *North American Review*. The short story received criticism for what many viewed as its glorification of socialism, but it also garnered praise for its strength of characterization and setting. "The Raid" was subsequently reprinted in Steinbeck's collection of short stories, *THE LONG VALLEY*, published by VIKING PRESS in 1938. Pyramid Films made the story into a short film in 1990.

"The Raid" served as the first of Steinbeck's examinations of the plight of the workingman during the GREAT DEPRESSION. Despite the impression of socialist and communist sympathizers during the 1930s that Steinbeck's ideology grew out of Marxism, the author found the communist agitators' political philosophy to be unrealistic and dehumanizing. He did, however, deeply admire those who stood up for principle and were willing to suffer privation or discomfort for their beliefs.

Like Mac and Jim, the lead characters of *In Dubious Battle*, the two central characters of "The Raid," Root and Dick, share the same relationship, a seasoned veteran of the labor conflict and his young, inexperienced protégé. Both display an intense commitment to an unnamed proletarian party, though one can infer from the interchange between Root and Dick that it is affiliated with the Communist Party. Early on, Root speaks bitterly of the negative reaction of his father to Root's embrace of radical politics, and, speaking of the American workingman in general, he complains,

"They hang on to their chains." This is clearly a direct reference to one of the most famous passages in Karl Marx and Friedrich Engels's *Communist Manifesto,* which proclaims, "The proletarians have nothing to lose but their chains. They have a world to win. Working men of all countries unite!" Root has spent time reading the literature of the movement without any practical experience in the field; a point underscored by Dick, who tells the young novice, "The way to learn is to do. You never really learn nothing from books."

From the outset of the story, Steinbeck sets a somber tone. The two men hurry purposefully through a dark and rundown area of a small California town with the smell of "fermented fruit" hanging in the air, and the sound of "mournful" train whistles echoing in the darkness. Almost immediately, the reader understands that Root is fearful of the outcome of the evening meeting the two of them have organized with sympathizers of the party. Though he first denies any apprehension, Root presses Dick for guidance about what he should do if anticommunists raid the meeting and threaten physical violence. Dick bluntly tells the young man that if he runs, he will be evicted from the organization. He says "We got no place for yellow bastards," and besides, "it's good publicity." Root promises to do his best to hold his ground, but points out, "How do I know what I'll do if someone smacks me in the face with a club?"

When the two arrive at the abandoned, and decrepit storefront where the meeting has been scheduled, Root's lack of experience again becomes apparent. He's forgotten to fill the oil lamps, one of two tasks given to him by Dick in preparation for the gathering, and has only brought two matches to light the lamps. Dick excoriates Root for his incompetence, and then the two of them begin to wait for the arrival of the first attendees. As the time for the meeting passes, and no one appears, both men become more skittish, though Dick is better able to hide his fear. The tension builds, and Steinbeck increases the ominous nature of the setting with little details—a squeaky door, a half lit, menacing poster of a party leader, and the distant howling of a dog. After the two wait more than 30 minutes, footsteps are heard outside, and a day laborer bursts into the room, warning Dick and Root of the impending arrival of a raiding party charged with disrupting the meeting. The worker encourages the two party activists to leave the building immediately. Dick refuses, stoically saying, "We got orders to stay," but in a telling moment, relaxes his bravado and shivers slightly. He knows what lies ahead.

Dick begins to do his utmost to bolster Root's courage. He reminds Root that their martyrdom and their willingness to stand "steadfast" will further the cause. He encourages Root not to resist, nor to bear any animosity to the men who will conduct the raid, because they are part of an evil "System," not acting independently. In this respect, Dick is as much a part of a "System" as his ideological opponents, but he cannot comprehend the similarity. He assures Root that whatever injuries they may sustain will not hurt, perhaps reassuring himself, or speaking from experience.

After an interminable wait of 90 minutes, the raiding party surrounds the building, and some members of the vigilante group rush through the door. Dick and Root stand passively while the raiders try to determine their next move. Root glances at Dick, and notices his partner's apparent intention to allow Root the first reaction to the raid. Root steps forward, and begins to speak, "Comrades. You are just men like we are." Immediately, he is clubbed to the ground by a two by four. When he struggles to get to his feet, he is beaten to unconsciousness, but not before seeing a "hard smile" on Dick's face. Dick has produced another soldier for the party.

Root drifts in and out of awareness, and awakes in a jail cell, incarcerated with Dick for "inciting to riot." Root's greatest fears have been realized; he has been "smacked in the face with a club," and his nose has been broken in several places. But he has survived the encounter, and is no longer an untried neophyte. The reader learns just how young Root is. He is underage, somewhere between the ages of 18 and 21. He has earned Dick's respect and, more important, has tested his own limits and discovered strengths he had not imagined he possessed. As Root lapses back into unconsciousness from the pain of his injuries, he compares his encounter with the raiders to that of Christ on the cross, who called out, "forgive them because they don't know what they are doing." Dick admonishes Root to "lay off that religious stuff. . . ."

For Steinbeck, the comparison between the ideology of communism, and the core teachings of Christianity is paramount. Both present an eschatological framework of ultimate or last things. For the Christian, it is Judgment Day, or the beatific vision. For Marxists, it is the dictatorship of the proletariat, and a utopian secular community. Both are either unrealizable, or unknowable, and based on the faith of the participant. However, they also both rely on a "principle," to spur action from individuals and from a group of human beings. "The Raid" provides another early example of Steinbeck's approach to the PHALANX—the notion that individuals' behavior is transformed through their involvement in group interaction.

Despite the difference in context and setting, "The Raid" offers a coming of age story, very much like THE RED PONY. Root perceptibly matures over the brief time span of the narrative, even beyond the limited perspective of his mentor. Aside from the fact he has explored the literature of the party more extensively than Dick, Root eventually realizes his role in the organization is about more than "taking orders." It is about a genuine desire to help his fellow man, and this desire is not confined to a particular philosophy or mindset. What carries weight for Steinbeck is the willingness to contribute to the benefit of other human beings despite hardship and ugly consequences. In a letter to ELIZABETH OTIS in 1935, Steinbeck denigrated the "intellectual" Communists, but praised those of his acquaintance who "don't believe in ideologies and ideal tactics" but "do what they can under the circumstances."

EARLY CRITICISM

Almost uniformly well received as part of *The Long Valley*, "The Raid" was recognized by attentive reviewers as a preliminary examination of labor strife in California preceding *In Dubious Battle*. The *New York Herald Tribune*'s reviewer, William Soskin, praised "the tense portrayal of an attack upon a couple of Communist organizers," and also

made note of the "irony" and "compassion" of the situation. A reviewer from the same newspaper, Lewis Gannett, observed, "John Steinbeck has some strange affinity for violence, but he is never lost in it." Harry Hansen, writing for the *New York World Telegram* gave a simple one-word description of the story—"excellent." Stanley Young, writing for the *New York Times Book Review*, gave the story a mixed review. He found it a "courageous but bitter little story" with "topical political implications," but too "fictional" for his tastes.

CONTEMPORARY PERSPECTIVES

Today, reviewers and academic critics tend to view "The Raid" and *In Dubious Battle* as inseparable, the first being a smaller version of the second. Grant Tracey, affiliated with the *North American Review*, while acknowledging the connection between the two works, says that "The Raid" "crams a lot of dignity into the two men's personalities," and that the story is "perhaps one of the most intriguing stories in *The Long Valley*." It does not mince words, and the labor conflict is secondary to the relationship between Dick and Root. John Timmerman praises the story for its unflinching exploration of "the human condition."

SYNOPSIS

Part I

Two men walk through the back streets of a dark California town. Root is a young man, while Dick, his mentor, is much older. They are headed to a rendezvous where they have organized a Communist Party meeting. Root nervously whistles a tune to himself; it is his first meeting and he is frightened. Dick accuses him of being "scared as hell." The young man asks what they will do if the meeting is broken up. His mentor tells him that they have orders not to run away. Root admits that he is scared, never having faced the possibility of violence before.

Part II

The two men prepare an abandoned warehouse for the meeting. They begin to grow nervous when the other men fail to show up on time. Dick assures Root that they have orders to hold the meeting and they will wait as long as they have to. He tells the young man that if he is scared he should take strength from the image of their leader on the posters that they have tacked up on the warehouse's barren walls. Suddenly a man appears and warns them that a raiding party is on the way and that nobody will attend the meeting. Dick tells him that they are going to stay and take the attack because they have orders to do so. He rejects the man's offer to stay with them.

Part III

The man runs off in the darkness. Root expresses his sense of fear. Dick coldly tells him they are both there to serve as an example to the workingmen who need a model of "steadfastness," and to the public at large who need to be reminded of injustice. He assures his young friend that they will not be killed, only hit and kicked. Those who physically attack them will not be attacking men, but "principle." The two men listen tensely for the expected approach of footsteps. Suddenly, a crowd of men bursts in carrying clubs and sticks in their hands and surrounds the two men. Root looks nervously at his friend and sees the older man looking at him expectantly. As he is clubbed to the ground he looks up to see Dick smiling at him proudly.

Part IV

Root returns to consciousness to discover that his face is heavily bandaged. He and Dick are in jail on charges of inciting a riot. Root proudly tells Dick that the beating didn't hurt.

THE FILM: *THE RAID* (PYRAMID FILMS, 1990)

Based on the short story by John Steinbeck

> Screenplay: Steven Rosen and Terri Debonno
> Director: Steven Rosen and Terri Debonno
> Producer: Steven Rosen and Terri Debonno
> *Root:* Matthew Flint
> *Dick:* John Rousseau

Produced by Mac and Ava Motion Pictures, *The Raid* is a short film lasting 23 minutes. The screenplay comes from one of Steinbeck's earliest short stories, of the same title, depicting two labor organizers during the Great Depression, preparing a storefront for a labor rally. The workers never show up for the rally. Instead, the two men are attacked and brutally beaten for their part in encouraging farmworkers to strike. This film has limited distribution but can be obtained through the producers.

FURTHER READING

Timmerman, John H. *John Steinbeck's Fiction: The Aesthetics of the Road Taken.* Norman: University of Oklahoma Press, 1991.

Tracey, Grant. "Steinbeck Revisited." *North American Review,* September/October 2000, 18.

Young, Stanley. "The Short Stories of John Steinbeck." *New York Times Book Review,* September 25, 1938, 7.

"Random Thoughts on Random Dogs" (1955)

In this rambling article, published October 8, 1955 in *The Saturday Review,* Steinbeck writes of an expert on the emergence and development of the human species who argues that the domestication of the dog was of an importance equal to the use of fire because the dog doubled man's perceptions and gave him security so that he could rest. Steinbeck describes how the uses of dogs have changed over the centuries, mentioning the small white dogs carried by ladies in the Middle Ages to keep fleas away from themselves. In our day, the author claims, most dogs stave off loneliness. According to Steinbeck, the old cliché that owners and dogs resemble one another is true. He writes that in America styles and dogs change, and that there is a tendency to breed nonworking dogs to extremes. He tells the story of a cab driver who takes in unwanted dogs. He writes of an English setter named T-Dog that he once owned who ran away from him. Steinbeck was convinced that the dog was a seer and had run off to be a missionary. Finally, Steinbeck writes of the qualities of a white bull terrier that he has always wanted but never had, and he wonders if he still exists in the world.

"Reality and Illusion" (1954)

First published in the November 17, 1954, edition of *Punch*, "Reality and Illusion" was written while Steinbeck was living in France with his wife and family. At the time he was writing a series of columns of his impressions of PARIS for the French magazine FIGARO LITTÉRAIRE. In a piece that demonstrates the author's fascination with the city, he complains that he is constantly being told, particularly by Parisians, that he does not know the "real" Paris. He describes his experiences walking about the city and sitting in the local cafés—but each experience is not definitive and fails to capture the city's essence. He asks himself what constitutes the real Paris. It seems that no matter what he does, it is either the wrong place at which to experience the real Paris or the wrong time. In the end he decides that no Paris he can see is the "real" Paris except to him. He determines to discover his own definition for the city and to defend it against all others who claim that it is not the correct one.

The Red Pony (1938)

During its early publication history, *The Red Pony* appeared in various venues. After submission by the MCINTOSH & OTIS LITERARY AGENCY, Steinbeck's representatives in New York, the *North American Review*, one of the most prestigious monthly literary magazines during the 1930s, agreed to publish two stories from the sequential collection of four that make up *The Red Pony*, "The Gift" and "The Great Mountains" in November and December 1933. Four years later, Covici and Freide issued a limited and expensive edition of 699 copies, which contained those two stories and "The Promise." Finally, *The Red Pony* reappeared in 1938 as part of THE LONG VALLEY, a collection of short stories. *The Long Valley* included the short story "The Leader of the People," considered to be the fourth part of the *The Red Pony*, and VIKING PRESS republished the novella in 1945.

For Steinbeck, the original *North American Review* publication marked an important turning point in his career. Though he was unimpressed by the cachet of the magazine, and was concerned by its limited circulation, the acceptance of the two "pony" stories, as he called them, and three later stories, "THE RAID," "THE MURDER," and "THE WHITE QUAIL" gave a needed boost to his writer's ego. The journal paid well for the time, and Steinbeck needed the money rather desperately. He and his wife, CAROL HENNING STEINBECK BROWN, had been living on the largesse of his parents, and had actually moved in with them when his mother, OLIVE HAMILTON STEINBECK, suffered the effects of an ultimately fatal stroke.

The Red Pony is a relatively short novel that follows the experiences of a young boy, Jody Tiflin, as he grows up on the family ranch in the Salinas Valley. Written in words of almost poetic imagery, it has become a classic "coming of age" tale about the process of maturing, and developing those attributes necessary to be a fully realized human being. At the beginning of the novelette, Jody is a typical young boy—somewhat selfish, lazy, and irresponsible. He resents his father's stern demeanor, and resists, in surreptitious ways, the strict rules of his home life. The gift of the red pony begins to change his life, as he takes charge of another living creature. He also learns about the fallibility of trusted acquaintances when Billy Buck's expertise fails to save the life of the colt. He gains knowledge about the value of extending himself beyond the narrow parameters of his personal concerns, and, indeed, by the end of the fourth section, Jody's empathy for others has gone beyond that of his father, who doesn't want to be bothered by the reminiscences of his father-in-law, just as he didn't want to be bothered by his son's problems earlier. In this sense, the book is also about the interaction among generations, and the importance of remembering the past while confronting the future. Each story can be read separately, though read as a whole, the reader encounters various recurring themes in Steinbeck's work—the PHALANX theory of group behavior, an early example of nonteleological philosophy, and the "westering" impulse that is so much a part of the American experience. Each story, as well, centers on a different approach to death, as witnessed and experienced by the young

Robert Mitchum as Billy Buck and Peter Miles as Jody in the 1949 film version of *The Red Pony* (Photofest)

boy, Jody. On a personal level for the author, the theme of death allowed Steinbeck to lessen the burden of his helplessness as he watched his mother die. Long after the publication of *The Red Pony*, Steinbeck noted that the story was written during a time of "desolation in my family," and that the writing was an "attempt . . . to set down this loss and acceptance and growth."

EARLY CRITICISM

Because *The Red Pony* first appeared as a limited edition in 1937 costing $10, an exorbitant price at the time, many commentators focused on the decision of the publisher or author to issue the slim volume of three stories to such a small audience and for such a ludicrous cost. For example, *Time* magazine's critic expressed bafflement at the "famine price" of the

small book, and called it particularly "remarkable in view of Steinbeck's proletarian themes." Writing for the *Saturday Review*, Christopher Morley noted the "deluxe limitation," but also recommended the book for its "beauty and pain" and "illuminated simplicity." Ralph Thompson, in a column for the *New York Times*, also advised his readers who could "afford a handsome sum" to make the purchase, and indicated they would be "well rewarded" by the "little masterpiece." Eda Lou Walton, a critic for the *Nation* detested the book. She excoriated Steinbeck's work for its "forced and obvious symbolism," lack of "authenticity," and reliance on "Freudian psychology."

With the addition of "The Leader of the People" a year later in *The Long Valley*, critics uniformly praised *The Red Pony* as the best of the collection of stories. The *New York Herald Tribune*'s reviewer, William Soskin, called the novella "magic," praising Steinbeck for his "thoroughly realistic grasp of life in the child's perspective," and added that "it is hard to recall a work so impressive." LEWIS GANNETT, also writing for the *Herald Tribune*, indicated "the Jody stories are almost miraculously good." From the *New York World Telegram*, Harry Hansen told his readers, "Don't miss 'The Red Pony,'" while Red Thompson of the *New York Times* particularly liked Steinbeck's characterization of Jody, writing that "the combination of toughness and tenderness make [Jody] a memorable figure." One of the *New Yorker*'s critics, Clifton Fadiman, called *The Red Pony* a "masterpiece" and a "heart-breakingly true picture of childhood."

CONTEMPORARY PERSPECTIVES

The Red Pony remains a rich source of literary analysis. Like much of his work, Steinbeck intended the book to be read on many levels. Moreover, since the four stories were written over a five-year period, from 1932 to 1938, they demonstrate Steinbeck's increasing aptitude with his profession. As John Timmerman has noted, *The Red Pony* shows the author's growing skill in translating his own personal and unremarkable experiences into universal fables through the "alchemy of art."

Peter Lisca, noting Steinbeck's childhood familiarity with *The Golden Bough,* a book which included a chapter on puberty rites, suggests that one of the central themes of *The Red Pony* is Jody's passage through a lengthy initiation ceremony that takes him from the innocence of childhood to the mysteries of adulthood. Though Jody's experiences do not involve the elaborate rituals of primitive cultures, nevertheless he must fulfill specific tasks in order to pass to the next level until he is finally rewarded with recognition of his manhood. The deaths of the pony Gabilan and of the mare Nellie represent blood sacrifices that often accompany tribal initiation rites, and introduce Jody to the "existence of death and evil in the world view which is his inheritance as an adult."

Continuing this examination of the spiritual component to the novella, Richard F. Peterson compares the old *paisano*, Gitano, to a priest, and

Jody to a novitiate in an ancient search for meaning beyond the day-to-day routine of life. For the young boy the Great Mountains offer a "sense of wonder and mystery," and Jody seeks answers from Gitano about the deep secrets of the mountains where he had journeyed as a boy. Just as one cannot have a direct knowledge of God, Gitano cannot express a direct knowledge of the mountains. Jody begins to understand that certain mysteries cannot be articulated, only experienced.

Richard Astro finds *The Red Pony* a "valuable tool to probe" the complexities of Steinbeck's non-teleological viewpoint. According to Astro, Steinbeck deliberate avoids characterizing any of the central figures of the book as "bad" or "good." To do so would require a retreat to teleological thinking by which all actions are judged by ultimate goals or rigid principles. Astro states that Steinbeck objectively "lives into" the lives of the Tiflins, and "move(s) beyond causes and reasons to the 'whole picture.'"

SYNOPSIS

"The Gift"

The title refers to an unexpected present from Jody's father, Carl Tiflin, an undemonstrative and rigid disciplinarian whose numerous regulations chafe at Jody's boyish desire for freedom from restraint. Without fanfare, Carl acquires a red colt for his son at a sheriff's auction, with the stipulation that the pony will be sold if Jody fails to care for the animal. In this, Carl wishes to please his son, but also wants to teach self-discipline to the slightly unruly boy, a more lasting and valuable bequest in Carl's mind. Finally, the gift refers to the unswerving patience of Billy Buck, the Tiflin hired hand, who shows Jody how to provide for and train the young horse, often over the objections of Carl Tiflin, who eventually begins to resent Jody's obsession with the colt and the closeness of his son to Billy Buck.

Jody names the pony Gabilan after the mountains edging the Salinas Valley to the east, because they are "the grandest and prettiest thing he knew." Immediately, the boy shows a new maturity, grooming the animal at first light before he goes to school and becoming more conscientious about his routine chores on the Tiflin ranch. He acquires a certain respect among his schoolmates as a horse owner, and although the pony is still too young to ride, Jody excitedly describes to his friends his plans to ride the horse bareback through the brush, and to help his father in tending the Tiflin stock after Gabilan is trained. Billy Buck, "a fine hand with horses," assists Jody in every aspect of his interaction with the young animal, from soothing communication with the frightened colt to training with a halter, saddle, and bridle, and to keeping the pony's coat shiny, and his hooves trimmed. Carl Tiflin pragmatically objects to Gabilan's schooling, suggesting the animal was becoming "a trick pony," without "dignity" or a "character of his own," but Jody revels in his horse's rambunctious nature and aptitude for learning. In this, the pony is Jody's alter ego; both of them are young and spirited, with previously unacknowledged talents.

Jody fervently anticipates his first ride on Gabilan's back, scheduled for Thanksgiving, but at the same time, has nightmares about the ride, worried that he will be thrown and be too afraid to remount his horse, suffering shame; or that he will experience grievous injury if thrown. He also worries about the pony's health as the winter comes early to the Salinas Valley, bringing constant miserable rain and chilly weather. He keeps the pony in the barn, with only short periods in the corral after returning from school, to prevent the young horse from catching cold. Eventually, a bright and sunny day dawns, and Jody, with some hesitation, lets the colt out before he leaves for school, asking Billy Buck to return the animal to the barn if the weather changes. The weather changes; Billy Buck forgets to return Gabilan to the shelter of the barn; and Jody's worst fears come true. The pony develops severe distemper despite Billy's assurances that a "little rain never hurt anything."

Recognizing his mistake, Billy does everything he can to rectify it, spending his every free moment nursing the sick horse. At the same time, Carl mocks Jody's concern, pointing out that a "horse isn't any kind of lap-dog," and telling feeble jokes to cheer his son up, without any success. In increasingly graphic passages, Steinbeck traces the pony's deterioration and the efforts of Billy and Jody to keep the horse alive. Eventually Billy performs a tracheotomy on the colt with Jody's assistance, and Jody sleeps in the barn to monitor Gabilan's illness. Carl does not understand his son's distress, and tries to distract him with the offer of an excursion "over the hill." Billy responds angrily to the insensitivity of the remark and challenges his boss's authority by saying, "It's his pony, ain't it?"

Jody comes to terms with the inevitability of Gabilan's death, but chooses to continue sleeping next to the dying animal. He awakes to find the pony gone, having escaped from the barn during a windstorm that blew the doors open. Tracing the hoof marks through the grass, he finds Gabilan in the final throes of death, being attacked by a flock of buzzards. Rushing down a small hillside, he attacks the lead buzzard and beats it to death with a rock. Carl and Billy find him still pummeling the bird to a pulp. Carl asks Jody if he realizes the buzzard didn't cause the pony's death, and Billy retorts to Carl as he lifts the blood-covered and exhausted boy to return home, "Course he knows it. . . . Can't you see how he'd feel about it?" The disconnection between Carl and his son, and Billy Buck's clear empathy for Jody's mental anguish is abundantly obvious.

Billy has his own cross to bear. He has failed Jody, not only in his assurances to keep the pony out of the wet weather, but also in his inability to save the horse after Jody trusted him to cure the beloved pony. Jody must come to grips with the imperfection of adults. He also begins to recognize the miscommunication between his father and himself. Carl's reaction to the training, illness, and subsequent death of Gabilan exposes a gap of understanding, and a different level of shortcoming. Jody possesses a nascent capacity to extend himself past the practical aspects of life, into the spiritual and empathetic connections among all living creatures—a gift beyond his father's imagination. Though he continues to respect his father and his father's dictates, Jody no longer views Carl as omniscient.

"The Great Mountains"
Having experienced the cruelty of life, Jody has become cruel at the beginning of the next story in

the series. He casually destroys swallows' nests in the barn; he tortures Double Mutt, the family dog, with baited rat traps; and kills a thrush with his slingshot out of boredom, meanness, and perhaps a continuing resentment of the predatory birds that attacked the dying Gabilan. Daydreaming, he imagines the "secret mysteries" of the Great Mountains to the west of the family ranch, and of exploring "the possibility of ancient cities" in their uncharted wilderness.

An old man approaches the entrance to the Tiflin ranch, disrupting Jody's imaginary journey to the west, and solemnly declares to Jody, "I am Gitano, and I have come back." Unsure of what to do, but excited about the visitor and the break in his routine, Jody seeks help from his mother. The old man follows Jody, and repeats his initial declaration to Mrs. Tiflin, adding he has returned to his childhood home and "will stay here . . . until I die." From the outset of this section of *The Red Pony*, Gitano has a mystical quality and presents a link between everyday life and the unknown. There is nothing revealed about his life other than his birth close to the Tiflin ranch, in a now disintegrated adobe farmhouse on the outskirts of the Tiflin property. He stands presciently poised on the edge of death, calmly aware of his imminent mortality, and seeks only a last renewal of his earliest memories.

Carl Tiflin responds with his usual pragmatism. Gitano cannot stay, despite the old man's offer to do odd jobs around the ranch without remuneration, except for room and board. In Carl's estimation, an enfeebled old man is of no use on a working farm. He does permit Gitano to spend the night, and tasks Jody with showing the aged *paisano* to his temporary lodging in the bunkhouse. After a period of shy hesitation, Jody musters the courage to ask Gitano if he has ever gone into the Great Mountains to the west, and Gitano responds in the affirmative, but claims he remembers nothing of his boyhood journey other than a sense of quiet.

Shortly before supper, Jody takes Gitano to the corral to view the horses. An aged horse, spindly and hobbled by rheumatism, makes his way to the watering trough, and Jody explains this horse is named Easter, is 30 years old, and is the last relic of Carl's youth. Gitano observes the horse is "No good

anymore," and seizing on the remark Carl cruelly gibes, "Old things ought to be put out of their misery," even though Carl fondly remembers Easter's youthful strength, grace, and agility, and his pleasure in the horse when the animal was young. At supper Carl continues his insistence that Gitano move on in the morning, despite the half-hearted protests of Billy Buck and Mrs. Tiflin against turning out an old man who has traveled a long distance to return home. Quietly observant, Jody "knew how mean his father felt."

After dinner, Jody unobtrusively returns to the bunkhouse, and discovers the old man with an ancient sword carved intricately on its hilt and glittering in the lamplight. Overcome by curiosity and a sense of awe, Jody asks Gitano about the origin of the rapier. Gitano tells the young man that the sword is a family heirloom passed through generations, its provenance and history lost. He then dismisses Jody, indicating he wants to go to bed.

The next morning, Gitano and Easter have disappeared. A neighbor reports seeing an old man riding an unsaddled old horse along a rugged trail headed directly into the Great Mountains. The old man appeared to be carrying a shiny weapon. When asked by the neighbor if someone should go after the old man, Carl responds, "Hell, no. Just save my burying that old horse." Jody looks to the Great Mountains and believes he can see a small speck climbing over the most distant ridge. He becomes "full of a nameless sorrow," his soaring imagination accompanying Gitano and Easter on their final journey while he sadly rejects his father's dismissal of "useless old things."

"The Promise"

The title of the third of the four stories in *The Red Pony* carries multiple meanings. It refers to the promise Jody makes to his father to take on extra chores in order to acquire a pony of his own to replace the ill-fated Gabilan. It refers to the promise Billy Buck makes to Jody to be certain this new colt will survive. It also refers to the promise of maturity, decency, and responsibility that Jody shows as the story progresses.

At the beginning, Jody plays an ugly prank on his mother, packing his lunch bucket with numerous slimy creatures he captures on his way home from school, knowing she will be startled when she opens the bucket for cleaning. Summoned to the barn by his father, a bargain is struck. Carl offers Jody another chance for a horse of his own, with the proviso that Jody take on extra responsibilities around the ranch and stop behaving like a child. Thrilled by the opportunity and encouraged by Billy Buck's offer to help in any way possible, Jody agrees to the stipulations.

The boy's first difficult challenge is overseeing the mating between the Tiflin mare, Nellie, and the neighbor's stallion. Aware that Nellie is Billy Buck's favorite horse on the Tiflin ranch, Jody fears Nellie will be killed by the violence attendant to the mating between the horses. Never having been exposed to the mysteries of procreation and gestation, Jody soon begins to gain practical experience with assistance from Billy Buck and his mother. He pitches in without complaint about the additional chores assigned him by his father, and furthermore, he takes on the care and feeding of Nellie as her pregnancy advances. He imagines the birth of a coal black foal, named Black Demon, with whom he will perform daring equestrian feats, even to the point of being called by the president to assist the country in a time of national crisis.

Wary of promising too much to Jody after the unhappy demise of the red pony, Billy Buck outlines every possible bad outcome, including killing a foal in *utero* if it presents as a breech birth during the mare's labor. This is a prospect Billy can barely stand contemplating, because of his attachment to the mare. Nevertheless, the pregnancy appears normal until the final stages when Nellie's due date comes and goes.

A month overdue, Nellie at last shows signs of throwing the colt in the wee hours of a February morning. Jody and Billy rush to the barn, and after examining the mare, Billy recognizes the colt is turned completely around in his mother's womb, and cannot be born normally. He orders Jody out of the stall, knowing he must take drastic measures. Jody refuses and watches Billy kill Nelly with a sledge hammer to her forehead, and then remove the foal with a buck knife from the mare's belly. Dumbstruck, Jody stands immobile as a bloody and

distraught Billy Buck presents the black foal to him. Billy has fulfilled the promise he made to the young boy after the death of the red pony, and now challenges Jody to honor his promise of becoming a man. The violence of Nellie's death poses a remarkable contrast to the love inherent in Billy's sacrifice.

"The Leader of the People"
Similar to Gitano in "The Great Mountains," Jody's maternal grandfather plays a central role in the final installment of *The Red Pony* as a man at the end of his life. Unlike Gitano, who seems to have had no regrets about his long life, the grandfather seems interested only in reliving the events of 50 years past when he led a wagon train across the Great Plains to the shores of the Pacific Ocean. Jody's compassion and empathy for his grandfather's experiences completes the saga of the boy's growth from oblivious child to the first stage of maturity.

As the story opens, Jody eagerly anticipates a mouse hunt to exterminate the last vestiges of the rodents that took up residence in the winter haystacks. It is a chore of great responsibility in his mind, and one particularly suited to a young boy accompanied by the family dogs. Billy Buck, always cognizant of Carl's prickly and demanding exterior, suggests that Jody wait for his father's permission.

When Carl arrives on horseback with what appears to be a letter in his hand, Jody excitedly rushes to the house to inform his mother before his father can deliver the missive, in eager anticipation of the letter being read aloud. Inexplicably delayed by the post office, the letter announces the imminent arrival of Mrs. Tiflin's father. Immediately, Carl reacts negatively to the news, complaining that the old man never does anything but reminisce about his experiences leading a wagon train on a westward trek across the Great Plains to California. When Mrs. Tiflin uncharacteristically criticizes her husband's reaction, Carl turns on his "big britches" son, and orders him out of the house so the boy will not witness the challenge to his authority. Jody eavesdrops on the ensuing conversation between his parents, as his mother softly explains to her husband the centrality of the westward migration to her father's life, and pleads with Carl for understanding. Impatient and irritated at his wife's morally superior argument, Carl storms from the house.

After asking permission from his mother, Jody walks enthusiastically up a hilly trail to meet his grandfather. For Jody, the old man's tales of his "westering" hold a fascination with their details of encounters with Indians and buffalo stampedes, and of near starvation and killer droughts. Moreover, the grandfather treats his grandson with dignified respect and gentle humor, without the incipient cruelty of Carl's sarcastic gibes, and authoritarian manner. In Jody's eyes his grandfather is the last representative of a bygone world, populated by "a race of giants." Greeting the old man as he arrives in a horse drawn cart, Jody invites him to participate in the mouse hunt the following day, apologizing for the tameness of the activity, saying it would not "be much like hunting Indians." Instead of mocking Jody, the grandfather remarks on how the army's butchering of Indian tribes "wasn't much different from your mouse hunt."

Jody's parents and Billy Buck welcome the grandfather at the farmhouse. Billy Buck, whose father had accompanied the old man on the wagon train as a mule skinner, "held Grandfather in reverence, and had even shaved a week's worth of beard to show his respect. Over supper that evening Mrs. Tiflin and Billy Buck listen politely to the oft-told stories of the grandfather's leadership of the migration to California. In a demonstration of rude impatience, Carl finally begins to cut further narrations short, commenting snidely that he had heard the story "Lots of times." Only Jody encourages more tales of the westward movement, not only out of boyish interest, but also to assuage any hurt from Carl's discourtesy. As his bedtime nears Jody remembers to request his father's authorization for the next day's mouse hunt. Surprisingly Carl grants permission without a quibble.

The next morning Jody arises early to make preparations for the morning's adventure with his grandfather, carefully selecting appropriate sticks from the scrap pile, and constructing a homemade flail to beat the haystack and drive the rodents into the open. Shortly Mrs. Tiflin calls everyone to

breakfast, and while waiting for the grandfather's arrival from the bunkhouse, Carl once more begins to complain loudly about the repetitive nature of the old man's storytelling. Unfortunately the grandfather quietly enters the kitchen as Carl's angry diatribe continues, and it becomes apparent he has heard the whole petulant discourse. Deeply ashamed, Carl attempts to retract his statement, falsely claiming the words were said in jest. The grandfather, rather than berating his son-in-law, kindly apologizes instead for having bored or annoyed Carl and thanks Carl for identifying his obsession with his past. Dispirited, the grandfather refuses Jody's invitation to join him in the long-awaited mouse hunt, and then announces his intention to avoid story-telling unless someone specifically requests the recollection of his long-ago adventures. Wandering outside, Jody realizes the mouse hunt no longer interests him, and he returns to sit on the front steps next to his grandfather. The old man, in a speech that introduces several recurrent themes in Steinbeck's writing, speaks poignantly of the insignificance of his role in the movement across the United States to the West. What was important was the transformation "of a whole bunch of people made into one great crawling beast," and driven by an instinctive impulse to seek new experiences at an unexplored frontier. This phalanx ultimately came together not for a specific goal or purpose, but for the movement itself. Jody quietly suggests that perhaps he "could lead the people some day," and his grandfather sadly observes that the Pacific Ocean presents a permanent barrier for the "westering" urge, and that Carl is corrects. "Westering isn't a hunger any more." Deeply sad, Jody reaches out to his disconsolate grandfather and offers to make him lemonade. In doing so, he shows a greater insight and compassion that his father's, and also belies his grandfather's denial of any new frontiers. Jody has entered the frontier of manhood.

CHARACTERS

Buck, Billy   A character in *The Red Pony*. The chief cowhand at the Tiflin family ranch, he is the best horse man in the county, but Billy disappoints young Jody when he is unable to save his sick pony Gabilan. Feeling responsible for the death of the pony, he sacrifices a mare to insure that Jody's new colt is born healthy.

Gitano   A character in *The Red Pony*, Gitano is an old, tired *paisano* who appears at the Tiflin ranch. He tells the Tiflin family that he was born on the land that the ranch is built upon and insists that he is going to die there. When Mr. Tiflin turns the old man away, he steals an old mare and rides off toward the great mountain range in the distance.

Tiflin family   A small family that lives on a sprawling ranch in the Salinas Valley in *The Red Pony*. Carl Tiflin, the head of the family, is a harsh disciplinarian. His wife, Ruth Tiflin, is a kindly woman who looks lovingly after her 10-year-old son, Jody. The family shares the ranch with their two dogs, Doubletree Mutt, and Smasher. One day Carl gives Jody a pony and charges him with its care, but the pony catches a cold and dies when the ranch hand Billy Buck fails to put it in the barn out of the rain. The Tiflins drive away old Gaitano when he returns to die on the land where he was born. Jody learns about sacrifice when Billy Buck is forced to kill the family's mare to save the life of Jody's new colt. The family listens to the stories of Grandpa Tiflin, a bearded, dignified old man whose one great adventure in life was leading a wagon train west to the Pacific Ocean.

THE FILM: *THE RED PONY* (REPUBLIC, 1949)

Based on the story by John Steinbeck

Screenplay: John Steinbeck
Director: Lewis Milestone
Producer: Lewis Milestone
Music: Aaron Copland
Jody: Peter Miles
Billy Buck: Robert Mitchum
Alice Tiflin: Myrna Loy
Fred Tiflin: Shepperd Strudwick
The teacher: Margaret Hamilton
Beau: Beau Bridges

Steinbeck worked together with Lewis Milestone in the early 1940s to write the screenplay for the adaptation of his classic short story. Because of preproduction difficulties and the onset of WORLD WAR II, the film did not appear in theaters until 1949. In preparing the screenplay, the two men were confronted with many difficulties that demanded important changes in the structure of the story. The most important difficulty was that the novel *The Red Pony* is really a loosely related collection of four short stories lacking a central unifying story. The author chose to fuse the stories from "The Gift," "The Promise" and "The Leader of the People" into a continuous narrative with a new ending, leaving out altogether the second chapter "The Great Mountains." The famous symphonic composer Aaron Copland, whose orchestral works are among the most acclaimed in the 20th century, wrote an original score for the film. The film did not manage to capture the drama and intense understanding of the pain of growing up that Steinbeck expresses in the famous short stories, however, and it received a lackluster reception from the public.

FURTHER READING

Astro, Richard. *John Steinbeck and Edward F. Ricketts: The Shaping of a Novelist.* Minneapolis: University of Minnesota Press, 1973.

Benson, Jackson, ed. *The Short Novels of John Steinbeck.* Durham, N.C.: Duke University Press, 1990.

Fadiman, Clifton. "Books." *New Yorker,* September 24, 1938, 71–73.

Gannett, Lewis. "Books and Things." *New York Herald Tribune,* September 19, 1938, 11.

Hansen, Harry. "The First Reader." *New York World Telegram,* September 19, 1938, 19.

Johnson, Claudia D. *Understanding* Of Mice and Men, The Red Pony, *and* The Pearl: *A Student Casebook to Issues, Sources, and Historical Documents.* Westport, Conn.: Greenwood Press, 1997.

Lisca, Peter. *John Steinbeck: Nature and Myth.* New York: Crowell, 1978.

Morley, Christopher. "Boy against Death." *Saturday Review,* September 25, 1937, 18.

Peterson, Richard F. "Home Was Blind: John Steinbeck on the Character of William Faulkner." In *Steinbeck's Literary Dimension: A Guide to Comparative Studies. Series II,* edited by Tetsumaro Hayashi. Metuchen, N.J.: Scarecrow Press, 1991, 9–14.

Soskin, William. "Varied Art of John Steinbeck." *New York Herald Tribune*, September 18, 1938, Books section, 7.

"Steinbeck Inflation." *Time*, October 11, 1937, 39.

Steinbeck, John. *The Red Pony*. New York: Covici and Friede, 1937.

Thompson, Ralph. "Death and Jody." *New York Times*, September 29, 1937, 21.

Timmerman, John H. *John Steinbeck's Fiction: The Aesthetics of the Road Taken*. Norman: University of Oklahoma Press, 1986.

Walton, Eda Lou. "The Simple Life." *Nation*, October 1, 1937, 331–332.

"Report on America" (1955)

"Report on America," published June 22, 1955, in *Punch*, is a rambling article that proposes to explain life in America to the readers of the British humor magazine, *Punch*. He reports the conviction of Mickey Jelke on charges of operating a prostitution ring and reminisces about the "houses which catered to the base but gay impulses of men" in his own hometown of SALINAS, CALIFORNIA. He describes how the righteous ladies of the Salinas women's club sought to shut the houses down until the troubled District Attorney explained to them that their own husbands collected exorbitant rent on the properties. In a separate section, Steinbeck describes President Dwight Eisenhower's habit of practicing his putting on a small stretch of level turf just outside the executive offices of the White House. He notes that golf has taken the place of fishing as national political training, and that it is viewed as a character building exercise. He observes facetiously that Eisenhower's golf game is not good enough to create political jealousy, but that if it improves, there may be trouble. Steinbeck describes the national furor that arose when the president ordered two squirrels trapped and removed from the White House putting green. After vehement protest from "squirrel societies," the president, Steinbeck writes, was forced to hold a press conference to claim that the matter had not been brought to his attention.

A *Russian Journal* (1948)

A lengthy travel essay, *A Russian Journal* was John Steinbeck's 18th book. He conceived of the idea while drinking in a bar with his friend, ROBERT CAPA, a war photographer. The two men were convinced that the whole truth about Russia was not being portrayed in the press. They decided that Steinbeck would write a simple essay in journal form that would be complemented by Capa's photography. Their objective was to avoid the loaded political issues of the day, and instead, address the issue of the Russian people themselves, how they live and what they think. Steinbeck had made a brief visit to the Soviet Union once before while on a tour with his first wife, CAROL HENNING STEINBECK BROWN, in 1937. Steinbeck used his not insignificant influence to obtain the necessary visas and permits for himself and Capa. Shortly before their departure, however, Steinbeck fell and broke his kneecap, requiring him to remain bedridden for two months. The two men finally departed on July 21, 1947, arriving in Moscow via Stockholm. During their two-month stay the men traveled to Moscow, Stalingrad, the Ukraine, and Georgia. Returning home, Steinbeck wrote a series of articles for the *New York Herald Tribune*, followed by the book, *A Russian Journal*, which was illustrated with Capa's photographs. The resulting journal, although politically naïve, provides an interesting and entertaining look at the postwar Soviet Union. VIKING PRESS published *A Russian Journal* in 1948.

EARLY CRITICISM

Most reviewers credited the contribution Steinbeck made for American readers to see the Russians as blood-and-flesh human beings, a perspective that readers rarely had during the early cold war era. One of the first reviews of the journal, an article titled "Russian Journal," was published in *Time* on January 26, 1948. The article comments that although Steinbeck and Robert Capa did not bring back any exciting news about their trip or about the Russian people, their journal did prove that "the Russians are people after all." Oriana Atkinson, who reviewed *A Russian Journal* for the *New York*

Times Book Review, called the journal "an illuminating and interesting report about the Russian people," and praised John Steinbeck and Robert Capa's superb reporting job. Atkinson pointed out the simplicity and honesty Steinbeck applied in reporting on a people toward whom Americans were hostile at the time. Richard Watts, Jr., who reviewed *A Russian Journal* for *The New Republic,* observed that Steinbeck and Capa's work is an "ugly symptom of the sensitive state of Russian-American relations." As Watts points out, the journal simply shows an American writer's comparison between the "unregulated confusion of American life" and the "moralistic Russian planning." But Watts acknowledges that Steinbeck filled the book with genuine and uncritical affection for the Russian people, and that the book indicates Steinbeck's belief in peace. Of course, neither Watts nor Steinbeck predicted the disintegration of the Soviet Union at the time *A Russian Journal* was published. But, nonetheless, Steinbeck's writing did help his American readers to understand the Russians emotionally.

CONTEMPORARY PERSPECTIVES

Susan Shillinglaw is one of the few Steinbeck scholars who have done serious research about *A Russian Journal.* According to Shillinglaw, *A Russian Journal* is an important book in the Steinbeck canon, much more so than has been acknowledged. The trip to Russia, as the critic observes, marks a crucial stage in Steinbeck's gradual shift from his 1930s commitment to the collective good to his subsequent concerns with individual consciousness. According to Shillinglaw, Steinbeck and Capa captured a few of those individual Russian souls who endured in a system ready to smother all creativity.

SYNOPSIS

Chapter 1

In New York City in March, 1947, John Steinbeck and the photographer Robert Capa decide that the news available to the public regarding the nonmilitary aspects of life in the Soviet Union is wholly inadequate, thus promoting the lack of understanding that has resulted in growing tensions between the two countries. They determine to make a trip together to Russia to do a "simple reporting job, backed up by photographs." Before leaving, the two men are offered much advice and many warnings about Russia, primarily by people who have never been there and know nothing about it. They are cautioned repeatedly that they will arrive in the Soviet Union and promptly disappear—it seems that everybody has heard the stories of disappearances, but nobody knows anybody who has disappeared. Steinbeck jokes that the well-intentioned advice only loaded him down with "rumors."

Chapter 2

Steinbeck cables a colleague from the *Herald Tribune* to arrange for their reception in Moscow. The two men arrive aboard an old American C-47 military transport plane that has been converted for civilian use. At the Moscow airport they discover that no one has come to meet them. As neither man speaks Russian nor carries rubles, they are unsure of what to do. A French courier escorts them to their hotel where they learn that no reservations have been made for them. During the next few days they sleep in rooms belonging to numerous American correspondents while they try to arrange for their own accommodations.

Chapter 3

The more experienced American correspondents in Moscow help the two men arrange their stay and coach them in how to properly conduct themselves in the Soviet Union. Steinbeck describes the incredible system of bureaucracy and bookkeeping that burden every process in the Soviet Union, included getting served at a restaurant. They note that the buildings and public places of Moscow are being restored and decorated in preparation for the celebration of the city's 800th anniversary, as well as the 30th anniversary of the November Revolution. VOKS, the official writer's union, takes charge of the two men and arranges for them to have an interpreter and guide. They learn that accredited correspondents are not allowed to leave the city. The two men apply for permission to travel outside Moscow to the republics. They must also apply for permission to take photographs, as it is illegal to do so without proper documentation. The

VOKS official is suspicious of their intentions. He complains that many man have arrived and spoken highly of his country, only to return to the United States to write negative propagandistic stories about the Soviet Union. Steinbeck assures the man that he wishes only to write the truth as he sees it. Steinbeck complains that foreign correspondents are subject to government censorship and that a new law bars the divulgence of agricultural, industrial, and population figures. The two men are assigned a young female interpreter, Svetlana, whom they dub "Sweet Lana." An attractive woman, Sweet Lana does not approve of drinking or makeup or dancing. Steinbeck remarks on the seriousness and competitiveness of Russian youth. The men and their guide tour Moscow, visiting the Lenin Hills, the Lenin Museum, and an air show that is attended by Stalin. Capa finally receives permission to take photographs, but the camera arouses suspicion everywhere they go. Steinbeck describes the large Moscow department stores and markets. Permission arrives for the two men to leave Moscow and they prepare to travel to Kiev.

Chapter 4

The two Americans are assigned a new interpreter, Mr. Chmarsky. Steinbeck discusses the ubiquity of images of Stalin throughout Russia, noting that this would be a frightening phenomenon to American who fear and hate power invested in one man. Arriving in the Ukraine, Steinbeck comments on the terrible destruction visited upon Kiev by the Germans, noting that 15 percent of the population was killed, not including soldiers. He sees large gangs of German prisoners of war working to remove the rubble. Their guide in Kiev is the Ukrainian writer Alexis Poltarazki, with whom he describes having a fine feeling of friendship. Steinbeck describes seeing a Ukrainian woman furiously attack a man who pushes to the front of a queue. The Ukrainians ask the men many curious questions, particularly why the American newspapers constantly speak of attacking Russia. The people are tired of war and covetous of peace. The two men visit the ruins of the irreplaceable architectural treasures that were destroyed by the Nazis. They attend a performance of the Ukrainian

morality play, *Storm*, as well as a performance of the circus. They visit a nightclub where they meet the Ukrainian playwright Alexander Korneichuk.

Chapter 5

The men arrange to visit a Ukrainian farm village. Of 362 houses, only eight are left standing after the war. Steinbeck notes that the Germans killed all the farm animals and destroyed the tractors and equipment. Even the fruit trees were destroyed. The peasants work tirelessly to rebuild their village and harvest their crop of cucumbers, potatoes and tomatoes. He remarks that despite the destruction, the people are not sad. The harvesting is done by hand and there is a noticeable shortage of men. The villagers prepare a splendid lunch for their guests from their meager resources. Steinbeck comments on the great admiration that the Russians hold for FRANKLIN D. ROOSEVELT, noting, "in the minds of little people all over the world he has ceased to be a man and has become a principle." The farmers ask many questions about farming techniques and machinery in the United States. They question the two Americans about politics, asking how the United States can support reactionary governments like the fascist Francisco Franco in Spain, the oppressive dictatorship of Rafael Trujillo in the Dominican Republic, and the military dictatorship of Turkey. Later they travel to another more prosperous farm that was not so badly destroyed by the Germans. They learn that the Germans have killed all of the animals and many of the men of the village. Steinbeck notes the number of crippled men and wonders why there are so few artificial limbs in the Soviet Union. The farm machinery was destroyed and the people are forced to harvest by hand. The villagers prepare a great feast for the two visitors, as well as a dance and the performance of a propaganda play. Later a literary magazine interviews Steinbeck.

Chapter 6

Steinbeck and Capa return to Moscow. They visit the display of war trophies in Gorki Park and then watch the boat races on the Moscow River. They join the thousands of people who wait in line in Red Square to stare at Lenin in his glass casket. They travel on another C-45 to Stalingrad. Steinbeck describes the terrible devastation around the city. At last they come to the city, which was almost totally destroyed by the German siege. Steinbeck describes the ruined expanse as "fascinating," and he looks with wonder on the people who go about their lives in the rubble, living in cellars and holes in the ground, like cave dwellers in the 20th century. They visit a famous Stalingrad tractor factory where the workers continued to build tanks even as German shells destroyed the factory bit by bit. Capa does not receive permission to take photographs of the factory, and Steinbeck notes that most of the machinery in the plant is made in America. The two men hire a boat to cruise the Volga River, and later, they visit the office of the architect who is responsible for planning the reconstruction of Stalingrad. They inspect the blueprint plans of grandiose buildings and Steinbeck observes the Soviet fascination with American skyscrapers, and industrial facilities. Steinbeck asks to see the gifts to the city of Stalingrad from the people of the rest of the world and is surprised when a long line of men appear, each bearing one of the treasures, for the city's museum has also been destroyed. Steinbeck looks upon the gifts of ceremonial swords and lofty words with dismay. He makes note of the Soviet need for bulldozers, not for ostentatious ornaments, and lavish praise. They watch the sturgeon fisherman in the Volga as they remove and ice the famous Russian caviar.

A Legitimate Complaint by Robert Capa
Robert Capa writes a brief interlude describing living and traveling with John Steinbeck.

Chapter 7
Steinbeck and Capa prepare to travel to the republic of Georgia. The Russians told the two men that Georgia is a veritable Soviet paradise. Their plane lands in Sukhum, on the Black Sea, before continuing on to the Georgian capitol of Tbilisi, formerly Tiflis. Steinbeck describes the Georgians as dark, strong gypsies. Landing in Tbilisi, close to the Turkish border, they are met by a delegation from VOKS, which escorts them into the 1,500-year-old city. Filled with many ancient castles and churches, Tbilisi is an ancient city of tourism. It was spared during the war, and Steinbeck describes it as being incredibly

clean, and the people less touched by the war than in any other part of Russia. They are assigned a jeep to tour the churches and archeological treasures of the monumental valley. Later they attend a game of soccer, the most popular sport in the Soviet Union.

Chapter 8
The two men meet with the Tiflis Writer's Union. Steinbeck compares Russian and American attitudes toward writers, and notes that the Soviets have more respect for the profession. They visit the ancient Georgian capital of Mtskheta, where they visit many ancient churches and monasteries. They travel to Gori, Stalin's birthplace and a national shrine. The author comments on the veneration and hero worship afforded to Stalin, calling it unequaled in history. They travel by train to Batumi (Batum), a vacation resort on the Black Sea. Their continuous traveling exhausts the two men. They visit a large state-run tea plantation, which Steinbeck describes as being run like an American corporation. They are feted with a large feast before returning to Tbilisi by way of Batumi. A large party with all of Georgia's composers and poets and novelists is arranged for the two men.

Chapter 9
Steinbeck and Capa return to an extremely crowded Moscow for the anniversary celebrations. Capa anxiously tries to get the necessary clearance to leave the country with the thousands of photo negatives that he has accumulated. The two men travel to Klin, the home of Tchaikovsky, to the University of Moscow, and attend several performances of the Russian ballet. On a tour of the Kremlin, Steinbeck speculates on the lives of royalty, and remarks on how removed the Russian monarchy must have been. Finally, a farewell party is organized for the two men by the Moscow Writer's Union. Capa is given permission to leave the country with his photos, and the two men fly home. The author concludes that readers of the book, whether on the Left or the Right of the political spectrum, will misinterpret the book's intention. He asserts there are no conclusions to be drawn from the trip except that the Russians are like everyone else, both bad and good, but with the good outnumbering the bad.

FURTHER READING

Atkinson, Oriana. "John Steinbeck and Robert Capa Record a Russian Journey." *New York Times Book Review,* May 9, 1948, 3.

"Russian Journal." *Time,* January 26, 1948, 58–59.

Shillinglaw, Susan. Introduction to *A Russian Journal,* by John Steinbeck. New York: Penguin, 1999.

Steinbeck, John. *A Russian Journal.* New York: Viking, 1948.

Watts, Richard, Jr. "The Eye of the Observer." *New Republic,* April 19, 1948, 22–23.

"Saint Katy the Virgin" (1936)

The only short story in THE LONG VALLEY that is not set in California's Central Valley, "Saint Katy the Virgin" is a comic allegory that takes place in an unidentified European country during the Middle Ages. Originally written by Steinbeck while a student at STANFORD, the style is reminiscent of Mark Twain's satires. The author was so attached to the parody that he prevailed upon PASCAL COVICI to issue a limited, special printing of the story as a Christmas gift book in 1936. It did not receive widespread publication until it was included in *The Long Valley* in 1938, and was so dissimilar from the rest of the collection that critics and readers barely knew what to make of the fabulous story. Many Catholic believers condemned the chronicle as blasphemy, tracing as it does the canonization of a vicious sow, Katy, who is redeemed by faith. Other readers recognized and appreciated Steinbeck's quirky and coarse sense of humor. More seriously, the work traces the origin of legend, and demonstrates Steinbeck's early willingness to explore various literary venues.

SYNOPSIS

In the village of P—— in the year 13—— lived an evil man named Roark. One day, Roark's pig gives birth to a healthy litter of piglets. One of the piglets, Katy, demonstrates as many evil inclinations as Roark. She eats her siblings, other farm animals, and even her own litter of piglets. Because Roark hoped to sell the piglets, he prepares to slaughter Katy. Brother Colin and Brother Paul arrive from the monastery at Roark's doorstep to ask for tithes. In a moment of inspired wickedness, Roark donates Katy to the two delighted friars. The brothers lead the pig out of its sty by a rope. Katy attacks both friars, and chases them up a tree. In desperation, Brother Paul dangles a crucifix from a bit of string, and chants an exorcism. The brother's ritual transforms both Katy and Roark into good creatures. The abbot is infuriated that the pig cannot be slaughtered because she has become a Christian. Katy travels the country curing the sick, and eventually becomes a saint, and a "virgin by intent." To this day, in the chapel of M——, there is a gold reliquary with the bones of Saint Katy the Virgin, which are said to cure feminine troubles and ringworm.

"Sea-Cow" (1951)

This section was excerpted from the THE LOG FROM THE SEA OF CORTEZ and published in the December 1951 edition of *Argosy.* The "Sea-Cow" of the title is not an animal in the traditional sense of the word. It is an outboard motor, which, Steinbeck insists, has developed life and intelligence. Even Tex, the savant-like engineer, could not get the Sea-Cow to work with any reliability. Over time, they observed a set of rules of behavior that seem to govern the apparently animate engine, including an ability to read minds. On one occasion when the men are about to destroy it, the engine roars to life and saves itself. It will not run unless conditions are absolutely perfect for rowing, but when rowing would be a chore, it stubbornly refuses to even try. Though the narrator and his compatriots suspect that if the Sea-Cow ever figures out how to reproduce itself, the human race is in jeopardy, they do not destroy it. Instead, they shine it up and touch up the paint and sell it to another unsuspecting crew.

Sea of Cortez: A Leisurely Journal of Travel and Research (1941)

Sea of Cortez: A Leisurely Journal of Travel and Research is among the most important, yet least understood, works by Steinbeck. The book resulted from a record of the scientific expedition by Steinbeck and marine biologist EDWARD F. RICKETTS to the GULF OF CALIFORNIA in the spring of 1940. It includes detailed cataloguing of life in the gulf preceded by a philosophic-scientific narrative, which was published separately in 1951 by VIKING PRESS as THE LOG FROM THE SEA OF CORTEZ. While John Steinbeck's name was listed as the sole author, the title page also included the explanation that the current text was "the narrative portion of the book, *Sea of Cortez* (1941) by John Steinbeck and E. F. Ricketts." *The Log* is true to its subtitle; it faithfully replicates the 29 chapters of the original narrative without revision. (It even duplicates a seeming error in documentation from the original account: both the 1941 and the 1951 publications label Chapter 25 as the entry for April 22. Logically this chapter should be the journal entry for April 4, since it falls between the chapters that record the events of April 3 and April 5. Apparently, neither Steinbeck nor his editors chose to correct the mislabeling, and later editors have also left it uncorrected and without comment.) *Sea of Cortez* is the product of a 32-day collecting trip that Ricketts, Steinbeck, and Steinbeck's first wife, Carol, made in March and April 1940, renting a purse-seiner, *Western Flyer,* to sail around Baja California and collect zoological specimens along the shores of the Gulf of California. Steinbeck's narrative relates the story of his and Ricketts's decision to make the trip, their initial attempts and final success at procuring a boat and persuading a small crew to accompany them and assist in their project, and the experience of sailing in and out of little ports, bays, and harbors, negotiating with local governments, as well as bands of eagerly industrious young boys for permission and assistance, respectively, in collecting and storing specimens.

The Log was initially published with a prefatory biographical remembrance Steinbeck had written to honor his late friend and collaborator, Ed Ricketts; later editions of *The Log* placed the remembrance, "ABOUT ED RICKETTS," as an appendix. In this position, "About Ed Ricketts" more appropriately replaces the "Note on Preparing Specimens" that ended Steinbeck's narrative contribution to

Sea of Cortez, as well as the lengthy annotated Phyletic Catalogue that Ricketts had prepared after the trip and the 42 pages of plates and charts that Viking generously included to illustrate the earlier work.

Between the sometimes mundane, sometimes almost studiously comical accounts of the activities and occasional adventures of the crew, Steinbeck regularly waxes philosophical about the abundance and variety of life to be found in the tide pools, shallows, and deeps of the Gulf of California and its coastal environs. He compares the richness and variety of life in the gulf to the human condition, although the comparisons do not always make the point he seems to intend. Most of the descriptions of the interconnectedness of the animals in their natural environment attain a lyricism and cadence that emphasize their beauty. The poetry of the natural history of the zoological specimens is more often contrasted with rather than complementary to the comedies of human activity that Steinbeck also recounts.

Sea of Cortez was Steinbeck's second lengthy work of nonfiction, something he began work on almost two years after he published THEIR BLOOD IS STRONG, a nonfiction account of the migrant labor problem in California. It was also the second work planned in collaboration with his longtime friend, biologist Ed Ricketts; however, they ended up never actually getting beyond the planning stage of the earlier project. While Steinbeck had clearly been interested in marine biology for some time before the trip, the work he would do to write the narrative would mark a pronounced departure from the subject matter that had occupied him for most of the decade prior to the publication of *Sea of Cortez.* In particular, IN DUBIOUS BATTLE (1936) and THE GRAPES OF WRATH (1939) had linked Steinbeck's name with the plight of migrant workers. Some of Steinbeck's biographers have suggested that the collecting trip with Ricketts afforded Steinbeck an opportunity to separate himself from the negative publicity generated by criticism of *The Grapes of Wrath* as a "vulgar" work with a socialist bent. *Sea of Cortez* itself lends plausibility to this argument: on several occasions in the narrative, Steinbeck comments appreciatively on the seemingly self-sufficient focus of the communities of creatures in the tidal pools the collectors visit, on the ability he imagines they have to exclude the outside world from consideration. About the collectors themselves he notes that "the world and the war had become remote to us; all the immediacies of our usual lives had slowed up. Far from welcoming a return, we rather resented going back to newspapers and telegrams and business." While the trip may have brought Steinbeck some relief from the debate about the value of his work, it must also have been gratifying to receive both the National Book Award and the PULITZER PRIZE shortly after his return.

When Steinbeck returned to the narrative, this most tangible result of the collecting trip, a decade later, at least some of the gratification of his professional accomplishments may have attached to the work, along with the pleasant memories of the time of its preparation. It is surely no coincidence that the republication of the narrative as *The Log* came relatively soon (about two years) after Ed Ricketts's gruesome accidental death after his car was hit by a train. The appendix eulogizing him is Steinbeck's well-intentioned but ultimately unfocused attempt to bring the image of his late friend closer to the comprehension of his readers. The remembrance recounts the events leading up to Ricketts's death and the stunned, grief-filled reactions of his friends, along with a string of anecdotes about Ricketts's education, professional practices, sociability, and sexual legerdemain, punctuated by Steinbeck's several addresses to the reader in which he self-consciously acknowledges that the account has not done justice to the man.

The Log begins with the straightforward claim that "the design of a book is the pattern of a reality controlled and shaped by the mind of a writer." Steinbeck goes on to explain that the process by which they collected the knowledge accumulated during the trip and related in the narrative is less important to him than making the point that the knowledge is not reported but constructed. He claims for the text in its entirety a kind of subjective accuracy. In a manner that seems to anticipate the process of thick description employed by cultural anthropologist Clifford Geertz, Steinbeck tacks back and forth between the heavily layered descrip-

tions of the activities of the collectors and their shipmates, the boat's owner and the three fishermen hired to accompany Ricketts and the Steinbecks; and the lyrically beautiful descriptions of the landscape and the sea creatures, both before and after they have been collected. The opening chapters justify the trip through a scientifically organized review of the literature, which finds all previous accounts deficient in some respect; they recount the subtly comical process of finding and provisioning the boat and collecting the crew; and they launch the expedition. Most of the following chapters are numbered and dated; early and middle chapters usually follow the pattern of describing the *Flyer's* entry to a port of call, the conditions for collecting, the actual process of collecting and storing specimens, the crew's interaction with the local community, and the process of departure. In these early chapters, the narrative conveys a sense of wonder in the richness and variety of samples to be collected, remarking often on the beauty, the abundance, and the interconnectedness of the various specimens being collected. Of particular emphasis is the observation that there is so much life in the gulf. At one point, Steinbeck reports that the collectors wonder if earlier expeditions actually did the work they claimed, since they seem to have collected so much less than the current group is finding, even though those other trips were better provisioned and better equipped than *Western Flyer* and her crew. Steinbeck also notes repeatedly in these earlier chapters how interrelated are the activities and abundance of the varied species, at some times referring to the "complexity of the life-patterns" and at others to the balance between species. He comments several times that their decision to collect the commonplace and to observe quantities of typical specimens rather than distinctive samples enables them to represent better a holistic view of the natural environment. In almost every chapter, the details of collecting and cataloguing are presented in tandem with the adventures of the crew: Their periods of storytelling, of eating and drinking, of getting into and out of various scrapes while in port provide what Steinbeck calls a beneficial alternation in pattern and design—not only in the book and in the trip it records, but in life as well.

Literally at the center of the trip and the book comes the religious holiday of Easter Sunday; neither the scientists nor the fishermen on board care for the event as more than a calendar day, but Steinbeck uses the coincidence of the date to break the pattern of the narrative and present a lengthy meditation on "teleological and nonteleological thinking" as a prelude to an initial summary conclusion of sorts, on the connectedness within "the whole world of fact and fancy," the holistic nature of being. It is a thesis that clearly reflects Ed Ricketts's thought and work; its insertion at the very center of *The Log* represents Steinbeck's deep respect and sympathy for Ricketts's worldview.

While the pattern of collecting and cataloging probably remained uniform throughout the actual expedition, a probability indicated by the similarity of the activities reported in the earlier and later parts of the narrative, the pattern of their presentation shifts noticeably. The adventure narratives still alternate with the collection accounts and the descriptions of the specimens, but they are more condensed and less discursive that some of the earlier adventures, although they are often among the most memorable stories of the narrative, such as crewman Tiny's encounter with the giant manta that transforms him temporarily into an Ahab-like figure seeking vengeance against this substitute Moby-Dick, or Tex's revolt against the "pre-marriage diet" on which he is temporarily placed. For almost the last quarter of the narrative, Steinbeck chooses to talk about the evening bouts of storytelling among the crew rather than to show and tell those stories in *The Log*. While he seems almost hurried in making an end to the narrative, he suggests that the crew are reluctant to end their trip: "At last we picked up the collecting buckets and the little crowbars and all the tubes, and we rowed slowly back to the *Western Flyer*. Even then, we had difficulty in starting. Someone was overboard swimming in the beautiful water all the time." In spite of the almost rushed pace of the narrative, Steinbeck deliberately returns to the more lyrical prose of the earlier chapters as he makes his ending: "This trip had dimension and tone. It was a thing whose boundaries seeped through itself and beyond into some time and space that was more than all the Gulf and more than all our lives. . . . The *Western Flyer* hunched into the great waves toward Cedros Island, the wind blew off the tops of the whitecaps, and the big guy wire, from bow to mast, took up its vibration like the low pipe on a tremendous organ. It sang its deep note into the wind."

EARLY CRITICISM

Published early in December of 1941, just days before the attack on Pearl Harbor, *Sea of Cortez* went virtually unnoticed, given both the controversy stirred by and the acclaim accorded to *The Grapes of Wrath* not long before the gulf trip. More than one of Steinbeck's literary biographers has suggested that *Sea of Cortez* was published by Viking as a sort of indulgent favor to one of their successful authors, further, they suggest, it would never have been published after December because of the paper shortage during the war. But it is also useful to parallel Steinbeck's experience with that of Rachel Carson, whose 1941 book, *Under the Sea Wind,* was published to very favorable reviews but also went largely unnoticed because it was so unrelated to the events of America's entry into the war. Ten years later, when *The Log* was brought out, Steinbeck's status as an important American writer was secure, but his sales were sagging, and the reissue of the narrative in this less expensive version, minus the beautiful but expensive plates and the Phyletic catalogue, was intended to get his name and his work back in the public eye. The reissue saw only modest sales, however, and reviewers were attentive but not effusive in their comments on the book.

Among the few early reviewers of *Sea of Cortez* was Scott Newhall of the *San Francisco Chronicle,* who acknowledges that it took some courage for Steinbeck, an established author, to write something as prosaic as a description of a voyage to the Gulf of California. But Newhall laments Steinbeck's hasty desire to deviate from the writer's duty and be a philosopher instead. Regarding the literary values of the book, Newhall called *Sea of Cortez* a combination of travel log, biology, and philosophy rather than a work of fiction. Therefore, *Sea of Cortez* could not be considered among Steinbeck's best literary work.

However, in contrast to Newhall's perspective, Joel W. Hedgpeth, writing in the same issue of the *San Francisco Chronicle,* calls the book the first large-scale attempt to include both the results of a scientific expedition and human activities. Hedgpeth regards the insertion of human activities, many of which are Steinbeck's philosophical notes about the expedition, as essential to the purpose of any scientific research. According to Hedgpeth, the book appeals to different tastes of a variety of readers. While the general reader may see the contents of the book as a "wilderness of uncouth nomenclature and meticulous minutiae," a marine biologist may find it an excellent text about the marine invertebrates of the Gulf of California.

Hedgpeth's view seems to best illustrate the original inspiration the authors of the book had. Neither John Steinbeck nor Edward Ricketts believes that the study of biology, especially the amazingly varied and complex life of the tidal regions, should be the exclusive fare of professional scientists.

CONTEMPORARY PERSPECTIVES

This book, like much of Steinbeck's nonfiction, has often been dismissed as less important than his fictional works. Early scholarly attention to *Sea of Cortez* did not begin until the 1960s. The book was seen by some critics from this period as something of a diversion because it departs so markedly from the subject matter of Steinbeck's other writings. Most scholars assumed that the scientific parts of the account are entirely the work of Ed Ricketts and that the narrative and philosophical commentary were mostly Steinbeck's. However, Tetsumaro Hayashi's careful research on the composition of the original narrative and the appendix first published with *The Log from the Sea of Cortez* shows that the relationship between the two writers and their collaboration is more complicated.

Not until the 1990s did a wide variety of scholars and critics pay serious attention to Steinbeck's nonfiction and in particular to *Sea of Cortez* and *The Log.* Steinbeck scholars have reviewed and revised their sense that the nonfiction is altogether less important to a general understanding of Steinbeck's work. In particular, Warren French and

Richard Astro have paid considerable attention to material of the gulf expedition and recognized its greater value within Steinbeck's career. In addition, a general reevaluation of nonfiction works on the natural environment have sent a different audience of scholars back to Steinbeck's works, as well. They often note the importance of Steinbeck's holistic perspective regarding the interrelatedness of species, the balance between the abundant varieties and numbers of creatures as they are described in *The Log,* and the patterns of alternation and rotation that derive from Steinbeck's observations of the natural environment and form the bases of his narrative.

Recent scholarship has paid particular attention to the philosophical, environmental, and ecological significance of *Sea of Cortez.* In the 1997 *Steinbeck and the Environment: Interdisciplinary Approaches,* edited by Susan F. Beegel, Susan Shillinglaw, and Wesley N. Tiffney, Jr., several scholarly essays are included to discuss the *Sea of Cortez* from contemporary perspectives. James Kelley draws on a wide range of philosophies to show how Steinbeck and Ricketts may well have anticipated the study of "deep ecology." Kelley also argues that the authors of the book viewed science based on ecological principles as a "noble human undertaking" and a rational means of achieving global understanding. Therefore, the philosophy of *Sea of Cortez* is increasingly relevant to today's concept of green revolution. Mimi Gladstein, Roy Simmonds, and Warren French are among the contributors who have placed *Sea of Cortez* in the context of 19th- and 20th-century philosophical streams of American environmental thought; they compare Steinbeck's ecological reasoning to that of 1990s "ecowarriors." According to these critics, *Sea of Cortez* proves to be a work ahead of its time, with a holistic view of nature.

One of the most significant scholarly studies of *The Log* in recent years may be Michael J. Meyer's "Living In(tension)ally: Steinbeck's *The Log from the Sea of Cortez* as a Reflection of the Balance Advocated in Lao Tzu's *Tao Teh Ching,*" published in *Beyond Boundaries: Rereading John Steinbeck.* Meyer argues, from a comparative study of *The Log* and *Tao Teh Ching,* that although Steinbeck did not own a copy of Lao-tzu's *Tao Teh Ching*, the text was available to him at Ed Ricketts's lab. According to Meyer, there is evidence in *The Log* that Steinbeck was undoubtedly influenced by Taoism, which can be seen in other Steinbeck works. Focusing on *The Log*, Meyer reveals that Steinbeck's connection to Eastern thought, particularly Taoism, may account for the author's popularity in Asia.

SYNOPSIS

During the months of March and April 1940, John Steinbeck and his close friend, marine biologist Edward F. Ricketts, chartered a fishing boat and set out on a six-week expedition to collect biological samples in the Gulf of California. Also known as the Sea of Cortez, the Gulf of California is a long, narrow body of water that separates the Baja California peninsula from mainland MEXICO. The authors write with charm and affect about the nature and purpose of their expedition. Steinbeck makes clear

in his prefatory remarks that, although he and his partner referred to the trip as an expedition, the word both amplified and diminished the purpose of the voyage. Not a purely scientific gathering of marine specimens; not simply a way to gather experiences for a literary work; not just a way for two good friends to have fun—the trip was all of these and more. Most of all it was a way for both of them to satisfy their curiosity.

Early March

The narrative portion of *Sea of Cortez* begins with a lengthy description of the complicated preparations implicit in the organization of the expedition. The authors write about the inadequacy of existing charts and maps of the region to which they are headed—in the 1940s most of the Baja peninsula was isolated and unpopulated. The first problem encountered is the hiring of a boat, which proves to be difficult due to the unusual purpose of the trip. They finally succeed in chartering a 76-foot

The *Western Flyer*, the 76-foot vessel captained by Tony Berry during the expedition that inspired *Sea of Cortez* (*Mr. Pat Hathaway photo collection, Monterey*)

purse-seiner named *Western Flyer,* captained by a fisherman named Anthony "Tony" Berry. A crew is contracted, consisting of Tex Travis, engineer, and seamen Sparky Enea and Tiny Colletto. Once the charter is signed, the men begin to move the equipment on board, including food, equipment for collecting, preserving, and storing specimens, books and reference materials, and photographic supplies. The authors discuss the boat and the sailor as representative of an archetype. They believe the strong identification of man with boats suggests the ocean is buried very deeply in the human subconscious. The authors discuss the members of the crew and their dissatisfaction with the Hansen Seacow, a constantly failing outboard motor purchased for the expedition. The boat is loaded and prepared for departure, a process characterized by the authors as "makeshift," since neither of them is experienced in provisioning for an extended sea voyage. On the afternoon of March 11, 1940, the *Western Flyer* sets sail from Monterey Bay. The first destination is San Diego. The authors speak admiringly of Tony's familiarity with the boat and his navigational skills.

March 12

The *Western Flyer* arrives at San Diego Harbor to fuel up and bring aboard the last supplies. It is to be the final stop before beginning the long trip to the Baja peninsula. The men note the harbor is bustling with activity as the country prepares for war. After they depart from San Diego, several days of sailing bring the ship to the southern tip of Baja California.

March 16

In Magdalena Bay, Tiny harpoons a sea turtle, which is dissected and cooked unsuccessfully. The collection of specimens begins while the boat is still in transit. Trawling and netting for food, as well as for scientific purposes, will continue throughout the trip.

March 17

The boat arrives in Cabo San Lucas, a small town on the tip of the Baja peninsula, and the men go ashore where an official entourage greets them and clears them through customs. Afterward, the men

set out to begin their first day of shore collecting. The authors explain their scientific method for the trip, which is to look for group patterns rather than individual behavior. That evening, the crew returns to the small town, which has recently been devastated by a severe winter storm. In a bar they purchase a local liquor, *damiana,* famed for its properties as an aphrodisiac. The authors comment on the propensity of some biologists to use vulgar references in Latin for various species they name.

March 18

The crew rounds the tip of the Baja peninsula and begins collecting at the Pulmo Reef, the only coral reef from which collections will be made during the trip. At the reef they meet a few of the local Indians who silently observe them, and sell them a matchbox of worthless, misshapen pearls. The authors talk of the poisonous and spiny animals that populate the coast, from which they will receive many painful stings during the course of the expedition. After collecting, they head north toward Point Lobos on Espíritu Santo Island. The authors begin to expound on a topic that, aside from the geographical distribution of marine invertebrates, is the central theme of the book: the impact of teleologies on man's perception of the world, and the need to escape the conditioned systems of teleological thought.

March 20

The crew collects specimens on the southern end of Espíritu Santo Island. The authors trace an elaborate analogy between the rise and extinction of species and the flowering and decay of individuals and families in human society. They discuss the "ethical paradox" that the "good qualities" such as wisdom, tolerance, and kindliness often lead to failure, while the "undesirable qualities" such as cruelty, greed, and self-interest are the cornerstones of success. The *Western Flyer* sails to LA PAZ, the peninsula's largest town. The authors recount a story of a poor fisherman who finds a great pearl that, rather than bringing him wealth and fame, instead brings only misfortune until he finally flings it back into the sea. This story becomes the inspiration for Steinbeck's novel and movie, THE PEARL.

March 22
The crew attends Good Friday mass at a small church in La Paz. That afternoon they collect specimens at El Migote, a sandy peninsula near La Paz.

March 23
The *Western Flyer* departs La Paz and continues north to Amortajada Bay on the southwestern tip of San José Island, where they will engage in further collection on the Cayo Islet.

March 24
This chapter forms the philosophical cornerstone for the book, underscoring in some detail the authors' worldview. The authors continue their discussion of nonteleological thinking. From their perspective, the appropriate way to examine the world is to dispense with an idealist framework based on what could be, or should be, or might be. Rather, nonteleology examines what "is"—the "what" and the "how," and not the teleological "why" of existence. The authors fundamentally challenge many of the accepted methods and results of rationalism. They present a series of examples of teleological thinking versus nonteleological thinking. The crew continues up the coast and collects on the Marcial Reef.

March 25
The *Western Flyer* arrives in Puerto Escondido, where a ranch owner invites them to hunt bighorn sheep. Indeed, the Indian porters do the tracking and hunting while the other men converse and enjoy the rugged mountains. Though the hunting excursion is unsuccessful, the men enjoy the brief respite on land. Returning to the boat, the authors review the progress of the expedition and are pleased with the results thus far, noting that in only nine days of collecting in the gulf they have gathered many more samples than other, better-funded expeditions.

March 27
The voyage continues to the port of Loreto, home to the oldest mission on the peninsula, where they visit the shrine to Our Lady of Loreto and bring aboard supplies. The authors discuss the Spanish colonization and the role of the icon. They sail north to Coronado Island and continue collecting.

They comment on the geographical distribution of animals in the gulf and speculate as to theories of the formation of the peninsula.

March 28
Exhausted, the crew takes the morning off before continuing their collection at the large Concepción Bay. The authors listen to the sounds of doves in the brush and hypothesize about the deep subconscious responses to certain scents and sounds.

March 29
Fearing malaria, the crew avoids the small town of Mullege, and heads for San Lucas Cove. The authors discuss the virtues of alcoholic beverages, of which they are consuming an incredible quantity during the voyage.

March 30
Skipping the large mining town of Santa Rosalia, the *Western Flyer* sails north to San Carlos Bay.

March 31
The authors describe the desolation of the northern extremes of the peninsula, as well as the psychological changes they have experienced. They have put aside the concerns of the approaching war, and economic uncertainty. That evening, they drop anchor in San Francisquito Bay. The authors note that they have taken more than 50 unknown species thus far. The authors describe their understanding of ecology as an increasingly complex organization of individuals into larger and larger organisms. This idea becomes central to many of the works of John Steinbeck, and is sometimes identified as the PHALANX.

April 1
The crew heads toward Angeles Bay, their last stop on the peninsula. In the bay, they receive a cold welcome from an encampment of Mexicans and Americans whom they believe to be gun smugglers.

April 2
They continue to Porto Refugio, at the upper end of Guardian Angel Island, a large uninhabited island that is said to be inhabited by rattlesnakes and other venomous reptiles.

April 3

Leaving Guardian Angel Island, the *Western Flyer* sails through a school of whales and then on to the island of Tiburón, home of the Seri Indians, a fierce tribe famous for cannibalism.

April 22

(This date seems to be an inconsistency or an error.) The boat heads for Guaymas, on the Pacific Coast of mainland Mexico. Again touching on the theme of ecology, the authors speculate on the behavior of large schools of fish, observing that they act more as a single organism than a group of individual organisms, and further postulate the existence of larger organisms consisting of the interrelationship among species.

April 5

The *Western Flyer* arrives in Guaymas. The authors observe the encroaching modernity of roads and high-tension power lines. They speak about the different perceptions of time and material value that separates Indian cultures from those of the white man.

April 8

The crew is outraged by the destruction wrought by a large Japanese fishing fleet that is dredging the bottom of the gulf outside Guaymas for shrimp. The authors write of the perverting effects that governments and organizations have on otherwise good men. The men attempt to hunt giant manta rays in the gulf, without success, before continuing to Estero de la Luna for further collecting.

April 11

The crew makes its penultimate collecting stop at the Agiabampo estuary. Returning to the discussion of ecology, the authors discuss the efficiency of nature as a complete system, with each living thing having a place and making a contribution to a larger whole. They theorize that this principle also applies to man, and that, out of the chaos of history, a pattern emerges for human conduct. The men make a final collecting stop at San Gabriel Bay, and then begin carefully stowing equipment and collections for the voyage home.

April 13

The *Western Flyer* rounds the tip of the peninsula and begins the journey northward toward Monterey, California. The authors remark that despite the numerous quantities of sea animals collected on the trip, the most important collection was of the images and memories of an unusual and enjoyable voyage.

FURTHER READING

Beegel, Susan F., Susan Shillinglaw, and Wesley N. Tiffney, Jr., eds. *Steinbeck and the Environment: Interdisciplinary Approaches.* Tuscaloosa: University of Alabama Press, 1997.

Hedgpeth, Joel W. "The Scientific Second Half of the *Sea of Cortez.*" *San Francisco Chronicle,* December 14, 1941, 26.

Kelley, James. "The Geoecology of Steinbeck Country." *Steinbeck Newsletter* (Spring 1997): 1–6.

Newhall, Scott. "John Steinbeck's Chioppino of Biology and Philosophy." *San Francisco Chronicle,* December 14, 1941, 26.

Shillinglaw, Susan and Kevin Hearle, eds. *Beyond Boundaries: Rereading John Steinbeck.* Tuscaloosa: University of Alabama Press, 2002.

Steinbeck, John. *Sea of Cortez: A Leisurely Journal of Travel and Research.* New York: Viking Press, 1941.

"The Secret Weapon We Were Afraid to Use" (1953)

The article "The Secret Weapon We Were Afraid to Use," first published in *Collier's* on January 10, 1953, recounts an event from the early days of WORLD WAR II. Steinbeck and a friend, Dr. M. H. Knisely, discuss ways to defeat a regime such as Hitler's Nazis or Mussolini's Fascists. They determine that such a weapon must have the following characteristics: it must increase the pressure of the state on the people beyond the breaking point; it must work from within, not from without; and it must not be effective against us. Steinbeck and his friend devise such a weapon and arrange to meet President FRANKLIN D. ROOSEVELT to propose their solution. The president likes the idea and sends the two men to the secretary of the treasury, Henry Morgenthau. Morgenthau is outraged by the plan. Their plan, he explains, is to have the government turn out billions of dollars' worth of counterfeit enemy currency in common denominations. The bills would be dropped upon the countries by air, thus undermining their economic system. Convinced of the viability of their idea, Steinbeck argues that it is a tool that still might be used in case the United States goes to war with Soviet Russia. He concludes the article with a fictional account of how the plan might work and the chaos that would result within the enemy's borders.

The Short Reign of Pippin IV: A Fabrication (1957)

Steinbeck's 10th novel, *The Short Reign of Pippin IV: A Fabrication* is one of his most unusual works. The inspiration for the book occurred to the author in PARIS, where he lived for some months writing articles for the French weekly FIGARO LITTÉRAIRE. The book takes place, in part, at a rented house at Number One Avenue de Marigny, the house John and his third wife, ELAINE ANDERSON STEINBECK rented during their months in Paris. *The Short Reign of Pippin IV: A Fabrication* is a satirical fantasy about the restoration of the monarchy to France, and in many ways a tale of the moral disintegration that Steinbeck saw in Europe and the United States. Pippin, a distant relative of the Emperor Charlemagne, is crowned king of France in the hope that he will unify the multitude of squabbling parties that plague the government. The unlikely king soon discovers that he has been made a fall guy for politicians who have no intention of sacrificing their own interests for the good of the country. Viking published the book, illustrated with drawings by WILLIAM PÉNE DU BOIS, in New York in 1957. It sold well and became a Main Selection for the Book-of-the-Month Club.

Steinbeck had to fight for the publication of the book. The two people in the publishing business closest to him throughout his career, ELIZABETH OTIS, his agent, and PASCAL COVICI, his editor, disliked the book enormously. They pleaded with the author to drop the project while he was still struggling with preliminary drafts, but Steinbeck stubbornly insisted on having the book printed, if only in a limited edition. Once the Book-of-the-Month Club featured the novel, it achieved a modest popularity, though critics labeled the work superficial and bland. The book, according to most critics, suffers largely because Steinbeck seemed to have no clear plan for it. According to critic Howard Levant, the book fails especially when it tries to move from a silly little diversion to a more serious work. Levant writes that "Pippin's will to institute the good life is a more serious matter than the bulk of the novel's comic dance . . . can sustain." The work has remained a minor one

SYNOPSIS

M. Pippin Arnulf Héristal lives with his wife, Marie, and his daughter, Clotilde, in a narrow building that was once the coach house behind a venerable mansion at Number One Avenue de Marigny, in Paris. The Héristal household is comfortable without being extravagant, and the family derives its income from rents on certain vineyards in the Loire Valley, the remainder of what was once a great family estate. An amateur astronomer, Pippin's proudest accomplishment is the codiscovery of the Elysée comet, which he made in 1951.

Pippin is on the roof peering through his telescope when he discovers an unpredicted meteor shower. Unfortunately his camera is inadequate to take pictures of his discovery. His wife, responsible for the outgo of money in the household, denies him the money to purchase a new camera. She reminds him that they must build a new cooperage on their estate and tells him they do not have the money for his expensive hobby. Pippin storms angrily out of the house, intent on sharing his bitterness with his friend and uncle, Charles Martel (Uncle Charlie), the owner of a small art gallery and antique store.

Pippin explains his problem to his worldly uncle, who offers to lend him the money to buy the camera secretly. He assures him that this will make

Marie guilty of having denied her husband such a small luxury. Meanwhile, Marie visits her friend Sister Hyacinthe, an ex-cabaret dancer who, wanting to rest her feet, has joined a religious order. Sister Hyacinthe advises her friend that men are like children and that she should consent to the purchase of the camera so that he will have to confront the impracticality of the expenditure.

Marie returns home and implores her husband to purchase the camera, which he, having already purchased a camera with his uncle's loan, refuses to do. Clotilde clumsily stumbles into the room. After becoming famous for her novel *Adieu Ma Vie,* Clotilde has decided to pursue a film career and is on her way to a screen test for *The Ragamuffin Princess.*

The French government has fallen for lack of a vote of confidence, and the fractured parties of the National Assembly are unable to form a coalition government. The political system falls into disorder until a member of the Royalist Party makes the unlikely suggestion that the monarchy should be restored to France. All parties agree to the idea, each thinking that the change will in some way benefit their own party's agenda. After days of squabbling over which royal lineage should take the throne, they agree to restore the last living ancestor of the great French emperor Charlemagne, Pippin Arnulf Héristal.

Pippin, meanwhile, is tirelessly monitoring the meteor shower that he has discovered. Working at night and sleeping during the day, he is unaware that the National Assembly has just named him Pippin IV, king of France. When he hears the unbelievable news, he rushes to the gallery of his Uncle Charlie. Uncle Charlie suggests that perhaps the politicians are looking for a patsy. Unfortunately, he tells his nephew that he has no choice but to accept the crown.

The country excitedly prepares for the coronation of their new king. The nobility, having greatly increased in number during the years of the republic, occupy Versailles and clamor for their hereditary rights. The country insists that the king take a royal mistress. Unable to find time for his hobby, Pippin becomes desperate. His uncle recommends that he hire an American publicity firm to handle

the details of the monarchy. Pippin studies the kings of history to look for answers and examples of how to rule the country.

Pippin's daughter Clotilde, now the princesse royale, falls in love with Tod Johnson, the son of the American millionaire H. W. Johnson, the Egg King of Petaluma. Meanwhile, Pippin IV is crowned at Reims. During the triumphant procession down the Champs Elyées, the king escapes from his coach unnoticed and returns to the quiet of his telescope. He visits Uncle Charlie, who is being driven to despair by the long lines of courtiers and cronies who gather in front of his shop hoping to take advantage of his relation to the king. Pippin complains that Versailles has been overrun by aristocrats and that the privy council is as fractious as the recent Republican government.

Marie arranges for Sister Hyacinthe to be uncloistered and moved to a cell in Versailles where she will serve as the lonely queen's companion and adviser. Meanwhile, the king begins to realize his dilemma. He doesn't have the power to effect change, and is certain that the men who have given him the crown have no real intention of giving him any power. Uncle Charlie warns him that if he takes power the people who made him king will turn against him.

Marie senses that her husband is listless and uneasy. She asks Sister Hyacinthe to talk to him and discover what is wrong. Pippin admits that he is worried about being king. Desperate to escape from the sycophants surrounding him, he discovers that by putting on normal clothes he can wander through the city, and even the palace, without being recognized. In his new disguise, he goes to visit Tod Johnson, who advises him that he cannot rule without money and organization. Tod offers to help him sell patents of nobility to American millionaires in order to raise money for the crown.

Meanwhile, the new era of prosperity in France has come to be known as the Platinum Age. The parties begin debating their contributions to the Code Pippin, the new constitution that will determine the laws of the land. Amid the prosperity, however, a feeling of nervousness and restlessness begins to grow among all the classes, inspired by the odd behavior of the king. Uncle Charlie confronts Pippin about his new habit of dressing as a commoner and making inquiries among the people. The king explains that he is trying to understand his people. He expresses his outrage and the conditions of injustice in his kingdom, declaring that he is determined to do something about it. Uncle Charlie warns him of the possibility of failure and that the guillotine can be resurrected.

Pippin tells Uncle Charlie that he is planning on making some suggestions to the constitutional assembly based on his observations of the conditions of injustice in the country. Charlie tells him that he is a fool and says that he is leaving the country until the trouble blows over. The king asks his uncle to take Marie and Clotilde to the countryside the next day when he is scheduled to address the assembly.

The following afternoon King Pippin IV appears to address the opening of the assembly that will create the Code Pippin. At the request of the nobility, he is dressed in a grand marshall's uniform and a long purple velvet cape trimmed in ermine. The uniform, which is borrowed from a museum and far too big for the diminutive king, is held together with safety pins. Pippin proceeds with his speech, chastising the government for its failure and giving it a long list of royal decrees, including demands for fair wages and reorganization of the government. The king's speech is followed by a shocked silence from the politicians in the audience. When Pippin turns to leave, his cape falls from his shoulders, revealing to the crowd the row of safety pins that hold up his uniform and the baggy crotch of his trousers. The crowd begins to laugh hysterically at his retreating figure.

France falls into a chaos of rioting and pillage. Sister Hyacinthe discovers the king quietly playing the harmonica in the royal chamber. She gives him her nun's habit to use as a disguise so that he may escape from the palace, but he refuses to leave with her. He is alone at the gates of Versailles when Tod and Clotilde arrive to rescue their father and take him to asylum across the English Channel. But Marie is not with them and he refuses to leave without her. The Assembly meets and declares France a republic, deposing and outlawing

the king. Pippin returns to Paris on his motor scooter and enters his house at Number One Avenue de Marigny only to discover that Marie is there and that she has cleaned it in preparation for his homecoming.

CHARACTERS

Johnson, Tod   A character in *The Short Reign of Pippin IV: A Fabrication,* Tod is portrayed as the ideal American in looks and manners. He is tall, blue-eyed, reasonably educated and soft spoken. Tod is the son of millionaire chicken tycoon H. W. Johnson, the Egg King of Petaluma, California, who was reputed to have 230 million white leghorn chickens in his vast empire. He is the boyfriend of Clotilde, the princesse royale and daughter of Pippin Arnulf Héristal, the king of France, to whom he becomes an adviser on matters of government.

Martel, Charles   A character in *The Short Reign of Pippin IV: A Fabrication,* Charles Martel is also called Uncle Charlie, the uncle and adviser of Pippin Arnulf Héristal, the king of France The proprietor of a small but prosperous art gallery and antique store in the Rue de Seine in Paris, where he peddles forgeries to unsuspecting buyers.

Pippin Arnulf Héristal   A character in *The Short Reign of Pippin IV: A Fabrication,* Pippin is 54, lean, handsome and healthy. He is an amateur astronomer who lives in Paris with his wife, Marie, and his daughter, Clotilde, on the rents of a small piece of ancestral land in the Loire Valley. His proudest accomplishment is his codiscovery of the Elysée comet.

When the scheming members of the National Assembly decide to restore the monarchy to France, it is discovered that Pippin is the distant descendent of Emperor Charlemagne. He is crowned Pippin IV, king of France, to great domestic and international fanfare. Pippin slowly realizes that "a king without power is a contradiction in terms, and a king with power is an abomination." Unwilling to play patsy for the fractured and inefficient government, he sets out to be the best king possible under the circumstances. When he attempts to interfere during the deliberations on the Code Pippin, he is promptly deposed from the throne and the republic is restored to France.

His wife, Marie, is a buxom, pleasant woman and a good manager who knew her province and stayed in it. His daughter, Clotilde, 20 years old, is intense, violent, pretty, and overweight. She became famous at age 15 for her novel, *Adieu Ma Vie*, which was later made into a movie. Shortly after receiving the title princesse royale, she falls in love with Tod Johnson, the son of an American millionaire.

Sister Hyacinthe   A character in *The Short Reign of Pippin IV: A Fabrication*, Sister Hyacinthe (née Suzanne Lescault) is the childhood friend of Marie Héristal. She worked as a cabaret dancer in the Folies Bergère before, wanting to rest her feet, she took the veil in an order of contemplation. As a nun she radiated such peace and piety that she became an ornament to her order. She becomes the personal adviser to Marie's husband, Pippin IV (Pippin Arnulf Héristal), king of France.

"The Short Short Story of Mankind, a Fable" (1966)

An essay first published in *Adam*, August 1966. A very short history of time illustrates the still-unchanged nature of man: survival. It begins with a couple of cavemen talking about the upstart tribe down the way. They still live in trees, but they've got nets for catching animals. One of the cavemen wants to go live with the tribe to take advantage of their advanced technology. The older cavemen scorn the tribe as foreigners just looking to take over. Then we hear about a series of inventors and freethinkers who pop up just when things are going okay, and shake everything up. They first get vilified as dangerous, but gradually, everyone goes along because those who don't go along die out.

Eventually, for survival, tribes merged into a state, then a league, and then a nation. Nations could defend themselves with natural boundaries okay until the jokers went and invented long-range

weapons like missiles and the atom bomb. In the end, Steinbeck asserts that man has always done what he had to do to survive. If man—faced with missiles and atom bombs and the UN—doesn't knuckle down and do what he has to do to survive, he'll be dumber than the cave people were. Steinbeck believes we're exactly as dumb—and bright—as the cave people.

"The Snake" (1935)

Steinbeck's short story "The Snake" first appeared in print in *The Monterey Beacon* in 1935. It was subsequently reprinted in the collection of short stories, THE LONG VALLEY, published by VIKING PRESS in 1938. In the essay "ABOUT ED RICKETTS," Steinbeck's tribute to his best friend, the author says that "The Snake" is based on a real event that occurred in ED RICKETTS's laboratory, PACIFIC BIOLOGICAL, in MONTEREY, CALIFORNIA. Recorded clinically and objectively in the essay, the incident receives a much more subjective treatment in the short story, and Steinbeck involves the reader far more in the two personalities at its core, Doc Phillips, and his unnamed female customer.

The story presents a series of contrasts—the coolly detached scientist, and the almost feral woman; the sterile setting of the laboratory as a backdrop for primitive biological urges and processes; the equal mixture of attraction and revulsion—creating an overall impression of sexual tension repressed by a thin veneer of civilization. Moreover, the short tale presents chilling and macabre overtones of horror, and also a hint of the supernatural. Finally, it presents an unsubtle aversion to overt female sexual overtures.

EARLY CRITICISM

With its psychosexual underpinnings, "The Snake" attracted attention as part of the larger collection in *The Long Valley*. Most of the reviews were positive, though JOSEPH HENRY JACKSON of the *San Francisco Chronicle* said he liked "The Snake" the least of all of the anthology; and Harry Hansen, writing for the *New York World Telegram* called

"The Snake" "a synthetic attempt to identify a mental state with an episode." Nevertheless, most praised Steinbeck's gift for clinical observation in the story. Wilbur Needham, from the *Los Angeles Times* remarked on the strength of Steinbeck's descriptive powers "in the story of a scientist interrupted . . . by a woman whose aura has a Freudian gleam about it." William Soskin, from the *New York Herald Tribune* referred to "The Snake" as "a gripping little horror playlet . . ." which demonstrated the author's "gift for concrete realism." And from London, the critic for the *Times Literary Supplement* applauded Steinbeck's "refus(al) to blink an eyelid at whatever climax of horror . . ." especially the "pathological" woman in "The Snake."

CONTEMPORARY PERSPECTIVES

"The Snake" continues to attract readers. One recent anonymous online reviewer calls the story "a revelation, and almost Hitchcockian in its perversity." Another anonymous reviewer points to the "slightly veiled panic regarding female sexual desire." The critic John Timmerman has called "The Snake" an example of Steinbeck's ability to translate actual events into a powerful storytelling experience.

SYNOPSIS

"The Snake" opens with Doc Phillips returning to his laboratory, which also serves as his home, after an expedition gathering starfish along the Monterey shoreline. Clearly he has established a routine wherein his private life merges with his business. While he waits for water to boil for his supper, with clinical impassiveness he prepares the most recent tidal pool collections for examination, then euthanizes a cat, and feeds and pets the remaining caged felines. He uses the available lab equipment to prepare various slides, and also to prepare his dinner. After "bolting" a meager meal of canned beans, he sets up the equipment for a time-phased, observational experiment with the starfish, and draws sperm from between their rays. One immediately recognizes that Phillips is single-minded and immersed in his work, and that he is unaffected by the less pleasant aspects of his experiments. What would make most human beings either uncomfort-

able, queasy, or nauseated, has no apparent impact on Phillips. He is a pure, unsentimental scientist, unhampered in his search for knowledge by a standard of normal human sensibilities. Nevertheless, the untidiness of his laboratory spilling over into his living arrangements suggests an unresolved internal untidiness. His physical organization and mental organization may not be wholly detached and objective.

There is a knock on the door, and Phillips greets a strange female visitor, arriving after business hours. The woman is described as dressed in black, with black, dead eyes and black hair, almost sepulchral. There is no indication by Steinbeck that the two know each other, nor that they meet for the first time. Their prior history is unknown. Phillips admits her to his workplace, and asks for time to complete the timed experiment he has begun. She agrees to the delay, but also indicates she has no interest in his present activities. He, offended by the lack of interest in his work and her coldness, describes to her in great detail the complicated process of drawing sperm from starfish, and maintaining the records of the starfish mating from beginning to end. Phillips is the first to introduce a sexual aspect to the interaction, although indirectly. His visitor responds not at all.

Phillips, now determined to elicit some reaction from his visitor, ups the ante, and begins to prepare the previously euthanized cat for shipment to a high school science class, or another venue needing embalmed animals. He puts catheters in place to drain the blood from the cat and inject formaldehyde, and then quickly peers at his visitor. She appears unconscious. His previous nervousness increases when she awakes from her unaware state, and asks if he has rattlesnakes, particularly male rattlesnakes, for sale.

As the story progresses, Phillips's tidy routine and mind, and his own sense of masculine superiority are challenged. In the short space of her visit, the female visitor disrupts the proper completion of his experiment with starfish reproductive cycles; she gives him doubts about the natural pattern of life and death; and most important, she ties life and death to a sexual need. His initial attraction to his bizarre visitor turns to revulsion, as she exhibits inordinate attention to the feeding of her snake, including mimicking the snake's movements as it kills and swallows a laboratory rat. She shows much more interest in the phallic symbol of the snake than in the human male in her presence. After she leaves, Doc Phillips considers destroying the rattlesnake, now defiled and removed from its natural order. He even thinks about uttering a prayer, having been exposed to a possible denizen of the netherworld, but realizes he has no faith in a deity. He senses his exposure to evil, but without a belief in evil's antithesis, he is left without an ameliorative ritual. The woman never returns to the laboratory, though Phillips looks for her with a combination of eagerness and apprehension over a period of months, and even pursues women down the street who resemble his mysterious visitor.

As is true of most of his work, Steinbeck does not provide easy answers to the inevitable questions arising from the story. Does this bizarre and sinister woman represent all women in her apparently emasculatory powers? Doc Phillips, at the beginning, wants to "conquer" her, and perhaps, lure her to bed, but her lack of interest in him combined with her apparent obsession with the more powerful rattlesnake serve to turn him away from her in active repulsion. Does she represent an elemental force of nature in counterpoint to Phillips's scientific pursuits? Most likely, Steinbeck wanted his readers to draw their own conclusions.

FURTHER READING

Fadiman, Clifton. "Books." *New Yorker,* September 24, 1938, 71–73.

Gannett, Lewis. "Books and Things." *New York Herald Tribune,* September 19, 1938, 11.

Girard, Maureen. "Steinbeck's 'Frightful Story': The Conception and Evolution of 'The Snake.'" *San José Studies* 8 (Spring 1982): 32–40.

Hansen, Harry. "The First Reader." *New York World Telegram,* September 19, 1938, 19.

Jackson, Joseph Henry. "A Bookman's Notebook." *San Francisco Chronicle,* September 28, 1938, 13.

Lisca, Peter. *The Wide World of John Steinbeck.* New Brunswick, N.J.: Rutgers University Press, 1958.

"The Long Valley." *Times Literary Supplement* (London), February 4, 1939, 75.

Needham, Wilbur. "New Steinbeck Book: Event of Autumn." *Los Angeles Times,* September 18, 1938, part 3, 6.

Soskin, William. "Varied Art of John Steinbeck." *New York Herald Tribune,* September 18, 1938, Books section, 7.

Timmerman, John H. *The Dramatic Landscape of Steinbeck's Short Stories.* Norman: University of Oklahoma Press, 1990.

Young, Stanley. "The Short Stories of John Steinbeck." *New York Times Book Review,* September 25, 1938, 7.

"Some Thoughts on Juvenile Delinquency" (1955)

First published May 28, 1955 in *Saturday Review,* "Some Thoughts on Juvenile Delinquency" is an editorial about the social roots of juvenile delinquency. Juvenile delinquency, Steinbeck claims, is a comparatively recent manifestation, which Steinbeck blames on parents. While people are responsible for the behavior of their pets, parents do not seem to be responsible for their children, and likewise the children feel no responsibility toward their parents. One of the virtues of the Middle Ages, the author claims, is that every member of the family was responsible for every other member under feudal law. While this meant that if a person committed a crime his whole family was affected and even punished, it also meant that the group took honor from the honorable deeds of one of its members. Not finding mutual responsibility at home, Steinbeck suggests, kids look for it in gangs because children want a larger societal connection. He argues that the very traits demonstrated by kids in a gang are courage and dedication, things that would be considered virtues in another context. Man is a double thing, he concludes, both a group animal and an individual, and he cannot be the second without being the first.

"The Soul and Guts of France" (1952)

"The Soul and Guts of France" was an article written by Steinbeck in France while on a European tour as a correspondent for *Collier's* magazine and first published August 30, 1952. According to Steinbeck, Parisian papers are even further from the people than are American papers. He proposes that one should talk to the farmers if he really wants to know the mood in a country. Thus Steinbeck determines to visit the people of the small village of Poligny, "the soul and guts of France," to find out what the French people are thinking and talking about. In the village he stays in the house of an old schoolteacher who raises grapes. Steinbeck discusses wine, the village industry. After enjoying the wine the men turn to politics. Many of the villagers fought in the resistance or were made prisoners in the German concentration camps during WORLD WAR II. The men discuss allegations that the United States is using germ warfare in Korea, which Steinbeck hotly denies. Then they discuss the charge that most American aid money goes only to the large businesses, driving the smaller ones out of business. The author is given a tour of the village wine cave, a ruined 12th-century church. The villagers tell how they fought for the Communist resistance but left the party when the party leaders demanded that they swear never to fight the Red Army, for they are Frenchmen.

"Starvation Under the Orange Trees" (1937)

"Starvation Under the Orange Trees," published in *The Monterey Trader* in 1937, was written by Steinbeck in response to the increasingly desperate situation of the migrant agricultural workers that he first uncovered in his October 1936 exposé "THE HARVEST GYPSIES" for the *San Francisco News*. The author's anger at the situation is tangible, as he writes that despite the year's rich harvest, the inci-

dence of malnutrition and starvation in the labor camps is increasingly grave. He denounces the California growers' associations, which he compares to other large financial cartels, for holding public meetings and making declarations against "reds" and "foreign agitators." The author's bitter words probably reflect his anger and frustration in the face of like charges that had been constantly raised against him since the publication of the original "Harvest Gypsies" articles. Ending his article with a warning, almost an ultimatum, Steinbeck notes that the harvest season will soon draw to a close, and that the conditions in the migrant's camps will become steadily worse until the state is faced with the possibility of mass starvation among the thousands of workers. He warns that hunger will become anger and this anger, fury, if something is not done soon. The article was later added as an epilogue to "THEIR BLOOD IS STRONG," a pamphlet compiling the original "Harvest Gypsies" articles, published by the Simon J. Lubin Society. The society was an organization that promoted cooperation between family farmers and migrant laborers, and worked to diminish the power and influence of California's agricultural conglomerates. Proceeds from the pamphlet were used to assist migrant workers.

"The Summer Before" (1955)

In "The Summer Before," published May 25, 1955, in *Punch,* Steinbeck describes an event that happened during the spring when he was six years old in the small town of SALINAS, CALIFORNIA. He describes the arrival of spring when he was six years old. One of his friends, Willie Morton, had arrived in Salinas the previous year. Steinbeck writes that when he and his friends went periodically to the Salinas River to pass the afternoons swimming, all the children in the town were allowed to go, except Willie Morton. Mrs. Morton, Willie's mother, seems strangely attached to her son, and is driven into a rage when the children invite Willie to go to the river to swim with his peers. Finally, near the end of the summer, Willie tires of missing all the fun and determines to join his friends at the river. The rowdy group of children march to the water, undress, and dive in happily. Willie, however, remains on the shore, refusing to shed his clothes and enter the water. Late in the afternoon, the group is walking home when they notice that Willie is missing. They return to the river and find him drowned under the water, the strap of his suspenders caught on a submerged branch. When they remove his body, his overall strap breaks and his pants come off. The startled children discover that Willie is a girl.

This article reveals Steinbeck's skill with the short, journalistic feature article. In four short pages, the author reveals biographical details of an influential incident in his youth with two shocking revelations at the conclusion.

Sweet Thursday (1954)

The sequel to CANNERY ROW, *Sweet Thursday* has seldom received the praise lavished upon its predecessor, published nine years earlier in 1945. All the same, for those who respond to its whimsical charm, *Sweet Thursday* is one of the most purely pleasurable works in John Steinbeck's canon.

Legend has it that Queen Elizabeth, admiring Shakespeare's prodigal character Falstaff in the *Henry IV* plays, asked the Bard to write a comedy of "Sir John in Love"—hence *The Merry Wives of Windsor*, a play that has delighted audiences more than critics. By the same token, *Sweet Thursday* is "Doc in Love"—and if much of the richness, subtlety, and tragicomic sense of *Cannery Row* is lost, a good deal of comic energy remains, accompanied by a fair amount of sentiment. It is a telling fact that the 1982 Hollywood adaptation called *Cannery Row* is more than 80 percent based on *Sweet Thursday*.

The sequel started life as a scheme for a musical adaptation of *Cannery Row*, originally for Frank Loesser (whose colorful lowlife characters in his 1950 *Guys and Dolls* must have seemed the natural kinfolk of Steinbeck's bums and harlots), but ulti-mately for RODGERS & HAMMERSTEIN. At some point Steinbeck realized that a new tale rather than a reworking of *Cannery Row* would be required for a musical; and that rather than coauthoring a script he would be better off writing a novel that could then be adapted as the Broadway artists desired. Thus *Sweet Thursday* was published in June 1954, a year and a half before the New York opening of the newly named *Pipe Dream*.

In the earlier novel Steinbeck immortalized a rundown district of MONTEREY, CALIFORNIA, he named CANNERY ROW (a name that the real Monterey would officially adopt for one of its streets in 1958). In the sequel, which looks back to the immediate postwar days as the original had looked back to the 1930s, much has changed: a number of people have died or moved out of town, the canneries themselves have closed, and a new mood of uncertainty is in the air. And yet, little has changed, for some of the gaps left by the departure of old characters have been filled rather neatly, and the easygoing lifestyle of the derelicts and prostitutes continues as before.

Like *Cannery Row*, *Sweet Thursday* centers upon four neighboring locations. The bums, headed by Mack, with the slow-witted Hazel as one of his devoted followers, continue to live rent-free in the Palace Flophouse. That jolly brothel the Bear Flag Restaurant is helmed by Fauna (née Flora, sister of the late Dora), who says of its name, "if you were hustling a state you should do honor to that state." (*Bear State* was Steinbeck's working title for the book.) Lee Chong's grocery/general store is now owned and operated by the much less genial though amusingly mercenary Joseph and Mary (nicknamed J&M by the locals), a Mexican American who houses illegal immigrants on the side. Finally, the Western Biological Laboratory is manned by Doc, the soulful, kind-hearted, tough-minded, heavy-drinking intellectual/scientist of the group, who makes a modest living for himself by collecting marine specimens and preparing them to sell to labs. The canneries may be gone, but Cannery Row is still a neighborhood where everybody socializes with, spies on and gossips about everybody else, mostly in a good-natured way.

Cannery Row was strikingly plotless—a novel held together not by a chain of events but by its setting (tidal pools as well as the Row), its view of life in biological terms and a brilliant overarching style. Doc drives south to collect specimens, Mack and the boys plan a surprise party that turns into a disaster, people get drunk, and that's about it— hardly a novel of suspense. *Sweet Thursday*, befittingly for a book that wanted to be a musical comedy, is much more plot-driven, simply by its introducing a love interest for Doc in the form of Suzy, a young drifter who checks out the Bear State soon after hitting town. Fauna, a matchmaking madam if there ever was one, hires her despite intuiting that the girl is suited more for marriage than for professional life. Indeed, it is not long before the entire cast of characters has decided that Doc and Suzy need one another. They try to engineer casual meetings between the two, then a dinner date, and ultimately marriage, despite the fact that Doc and Suzy have frequent and heated quarrels. This storyline worked for Shakespeare in *Much Ado About Nothing* (where friends connive to make Beatrice and Benedict fall into one another's arms), and it works here.

All this is not to say that *Sweet Thursday* is tightly plotted like some French farce. It has plenty of digressions, but it calls more attention to its own looseness than *Cannery Row* does. In a *Huck Finn*–like prologue, Mack complains to the boys that he "ain't never been satisfied with that book *Cannery Row*. I would of went about it different." Besides having proper chapter divisions with titles, a good book should occasionally "break loose with a bunch of HOOPTEDOODLE," but in separate chapters so it doesn't "get mixed up with the story." Steinbeck kindly supplies, for the new book, not only chapters with whimsical titles but two entitled "Hooptedoodle," featuring appropriately digressive material. Other chapters have moments of playful excess as well, and at least one new character, the exasperating and completely cartoonish Jingleballicks, has little connection to the romance plot.

Indeed, a spirit of playfulness runs through the entire novel. To be sure, some readers may find Steinbeck's tongue-in-cheek narration arch at times rather than genuinely funny, or the whimsy a little strained, as in the story of Lee Chong going off to the South Seas. Worse, perhaps, the book may seem to come dangerously close to the border separating humor from cuteness. Certainly there is nothing remotely like *Cannery Row*'s scene of the discovery of the drowned girl, or its thought-provoking parallels between human life and tidal pools. When *Sweet Thursday* approaches seriousness, it leans toward sentimentality, with its prostitutes with hearts of gold and a lengthy speech Fauna delivers to Suzy on self-confidence and liking oneself. But Steinbeck's jaunty pace and winks at the reader keep the book from drifting too far into sobriety; even Fauna approves of marriage partly because "it sent her some of her best customers." The comic-romantic dinner scene between Doc and Suzy is deftly staged, and the lengthy description of a Sweet Thursday (a joy-filled day after a Lousy Wednesday) is brilliantly written. There is even a quirky charm in Suzy's decision to fix up a nice home for herself in an abandoned boiler cylinder (the source of the musical's title).

As in *Cannery Row*, Doc occupies the center of the book. In the opening pages, when we read of his army life, he certainly seems like the old Doc: "He whiled away his free hours with an unlimited supply of government alcohol, made many friends, and resisted promotion." And back home, "People made pilgrimages to the laboratory to bask in Doc's designed and lovely purposelessness," as before. But now he feels at times a terrible dissatisfaction with his old life, or more precisely, he hears three voices inside himself: the "top" voice is that of the happy marine biologist, but the middle one is constantly mocking his accomplishments and claims of scientific objectivity, and the lowest one is a pure sensation of loneliness. Seeking purpose after all—or "some sort of obscure self-justification," as he puts it—he struggles against writer's block to compose an article on apoplexy in octopi, essentially to prove that they have emotions like humans. (Critics have suggested that Steinbeck here models Doc upon himself rather than his friend ED RICKETTS, the inspiration for the Doc of *Cannery Row*.) Of course, what he really needs is love. Readers can debate whether the Doc of *Sweet Thursday* is a disappointing reduction of the detached scientist of *Cannery Row* or the embodiment of an older writer's belief that no man is, or need be, an island.

EARLY CRITICISM

Upon its publication in June 1954, *Sweet Thursday* received a good deal of attention and sold very briskly. But the reviews were mixed: most offered either mild praise or sweeping condemnation, with very few finding it a major Steinbeck novel or bothering to distinguish its virtues from its flaws. The *New York Times* did extravagantly call it "Steinbeck at his best and magnificently entertaining"—yet the rest of the review found it simply good "hammock" reading. The "summer" theme was carried on by *The Nation*, which deemed the book "a minor pleasantry from a major novelist . . . designed to go nicely with the cool highball and a warm sun." (The magazine's report on the real Cannery Row three months later more harshly condemned the novel as an irresponsible pipe dream, in the face of continued unemployment since the depletion of the sardine population.) Only a few reviews castigated the novel as did *Time* ("reads like stuff that has been salvaged from the wastebasket") and *The New Yorker* ("labored, self-conscious, and drenched with artificial sunlight and good feeling"). Abroad, the book received a similar balance of reviews: "a genuine harebrained charm" (*Times Literary Supplement*) vs. "Hollywooden" (*New Statesman*). *Dublin Magazine* noted astutely enough that the plot hinged upon Doc achieving "Fulfillment" when he "rediscovers . . . the great truth that bad hustlers make the good wives." What might astonish the 21st-century Steinbeck reader is how many reviews simply saw *Sweet Thursday* as "more of the same" from the author of *Cannery Row,* as if the earlier deeply complex book were only a lazy summer treat.

CONTEMPORARY PERSPECTIVES

Dismissed as a very minor work by most Steinbeck scholars from the 1960s onward, *Sweet Thursday* was still receiving limited appreciation in the 1990s. Typically, it was not one of the 10 books singled out in *A New Study Guide to Steinbeck's Major Works, with Critical Explications* (1993); and in Warren French's

John Steinbeck's Fiction Revisited (1994), he still considered it a failure "as an attempt to update a vanished world" and worse, "a superficial and often vulgar attempt to exploit the engaging characters of his earlier work." But the book has received more favorable studies. Three such essays are collected in *The Short Novels of John Steinbeck,* though one is from 1960 and a second from 1971. The latter essay, by Louis Owens, argues that the book is only superficially a romantic comedy: on a deeper level it is deliberate self-parody as a means of "cutting away from the past," that is, the author's past writings and California life, and a book about writing itself. (In the same volume, Mimi Reisel Gladstein faults the novel for its "straining for profundity" and for Suzy as a "contrived" character.)

The most extended defense of *Sweet Thursday* as a major work of art is to be found in *After The Grapes of Wrath: Essays on John Steinbeck* (1995). Robert DeMott argues, like Owens, that the book is about writing itself, but more than that, an early example of postmodernist "experimental meta-fiction" about Steinbeck's "own emotional and creative processes." DeMott also draws attention to the strong influence of the comic strip *Li'l Abner* by Al Capp—a great artist in his own right to DeMott and to Steinbeck himself—on *Sweet Thursday.* One other noteworthy commentary on the novel is Jay Parini's in his important 1995 biography of Steinbeck. Though he sums up the book as "charming, if somewhat fluffy and cartoonlike," he devotes most of three paragraphs to an appreciation of the author's handling of the love theme, with the older Doc realizing that his customary detachment does him little good in the face of a need for a love relationship.

Since the mid-1990s *Sweet Thursday* has been gaining recognition from the perspectives of cultural studies, in part because of the book's use of stereotypes of the larcenous Chicano.

SYNOPSIS

(1)

Doc, the owner of Western Biological Laboratories, returns from the war to find his lab abandoned and in disarray. He drinks beer with his old friend Mack, who fills him in on the changes that have come to Cannery Row during his absence.

(2)

Joseph and Mary Rivas ("Joseph and Mary" is the individual's first name), a career criminal, purchases Lee Chong's Heavenly Flower Grocery to serve as a cover for his real business, the smuggling of illegal immigrants from MEXICO.

(3)

Doc returns to his work listlessly, unable to fully resume his old life. Mack is concerned for his friend. He talks to Fauna, the owner of the local brothel, The Bear Flag Restaurant, who decides that Doc needs a woman. Meanwhile, Doc captures 28 baby octopi and decides to write a scientific paper on their emotional responses.

(4)

Joseph and Mary is confounded when Doc explains to him that there is no way to cheat at chess.

(5)

Suzy arrives in Monterey and is questioned by Joe Blaikey, the town constable, who warns her to stay out of trouble. She asks for work at the Bear Flag Restaurant. Fauna hires Suzy although she realizes that she is not really cut out to be a hustler.

(6)

Doc sits in his laboratory unable to write his paper.

(7)

Joseph and Mary advises Fauna that she made a mistake hiring Suzy.

(8)

Mr. Deems, a local philanthropist, donates a roque court for the amusement of the elderly residents of Pacific Grove. Roque is a difficult form of croquet played on a hard court. Within two years a savage competition has grown between the two local teams, the Blues and the Greens. As the roque tournament draws near, violence ensues between the opposing teams and the town becomes bitterly divided. Mr. Deems is horrified when he sees the trouble that his roque court has created, and on the night before the tournament he sends bulldozers to destroy the courts. The town is reunified in its collective rage toward Mr. Deems, who is driven out of town.

(9)

Doc's friends meet to find a solution for their friend's depression. Fauna reads Hazel's horoscope, which predicts that he will become president of the United States. They decide that Fauna should do Doc's horoscope and Mack is appointed to discover his birth date. Mack speculates that Doc is using the paper as an excuse for something more important.

(10)

Doc meets a large, bearded stranger who claims to be a seer. He invites Doc to have dinner with him at his camp among the dunes. The Seer explains to Doc that he takes all his food from the sea and that he would be self-sufficient except for his craving of sweets, which drives him to steal candy bars from the local Safeway. Doc tells the Seer that he wants to do something meaningful in his life, but that he cannot seem to do it. The Seer tells Doc that sometimes a man cannot do everything alone. Sometimes he needs love.

(11)

The boys of the Palace Flophouse hold a meeting and decide to find Doc a "dame."

(12)

Joe Elegant, the Bear Flag's cook, discusses with Suzy the novel he is writing.

(13)

Wide Ida, the owner of *La Ida,* a local honky-tonk, tells Doc that she has heard he is having some trouble with his paper. His frustrations are confirmed by Ida's pity and he vows to buy a new microscope and return to La Jolla for the spring tides to collect more octopi.

(14)

Mack realizes that Joseph and Mary must have acquired ownership of the Palace Flophouse when he bought the grocery from Lee Chong. He sets out to find a way to transfer the ownership of the property and save the flophouse residents' home.

(15)

Fauna gives etiquette lessons to the girls of the Bear Flag. She shows Suzy the gold stars on the wall commemorating the girls from the Bear Flag who have married well. She sends Suzy to deliver a cake and cold beer to Doc. Fauna wishes that she could find a husband to take Suzy out of the Bear Flag.

(16)
Mack explains to Doc the difference between his dishonesty and the dishonesty of Joseph and Mary. Mack claims he doesn't fool anyone with his dishonesty, nor does he fool himself.

(17)
Doc tells Suzy that going to a whorehouse is a sad substitute for love, to which Suzy responds sharply, asking him what his interest in sea animals is a substitute for. She tells him that everybody is laughing at him because he cannot finish his paper. Doc sees the truth in her words and is hurt by it. He observes that Suzy is the only completely honest woman that he has ever met.

(18)
Fauna admits that she is looking for a wife for Doc and she offers to help Suzy get him. Suzy pleads that she is not good enough for him. Fauna reads Suzy's horoscope, which predicts that she is going to marry a Cancer. She says that the best marriages are those that are arranged by a disinterested party. Suzy goes to Doc and tells him that she wants him to write his paper.

(19)
Mack asks Joseph and Mary to help him organize a raffle to buy Doc a new microscope. He offers the Palace Flophouse as the prize, and schemes to fix the raffle to make sure that Doc wins. Joseph and Mary admires the plan and agrees to help. Mack's hope is to have the raffle before Joseph and Mary realizes that he is the owner of the property.

(20)
Fauna tells Doc that she would like to find a way to get Suzy out of the Bear Flag. She asks Doc to make a play for Suzy, telling him that if somebody treats her like a lady, then she will no longer want to work in the whorehouse. Doc hesitantly agrees to her plan.

(21)
Mack and the boys begin peddling their raffle tickets. The tickets sell quickly to the townspeople, who relish the idea that Mack is playing Joseph and

Mary for a sucker. The boys plan to hold the raffle the following Saturday. Doc lies to Mack, telling him that he was born on the Fourth of July. Fauna is delighted by the news that Doc is a Cancer, just as Suzy's horoscope predicted. She recommends that they make the raffle an engagement party. Meanwhile, Suzy is excited and nervous because Doc has invited her out to dinner.

(22)
Fauna advises Suzy how to behave for her upcoming dinner. Suzy admires her mentor's expertise and is so stunned by her generosity that she tells Fauna that she loves her. That evening Doc arrives for the date in a leather jacket and army pants. When he sees how beautifully dressed Suzy is, he excuses himself to make a phone call and returns in a jacket and tie.

(23)
Doc escorts Suzy for dinner at Sonny Boy's restaurant on the wharf in Monterey. Fauna has called ahead and made all of the arrangements for a secluded table with flowers, wine, and even a piano player. Suzy's shyness is overcome by a warm wave of feminine intuition. She is overwhelmed by a sense of fate when they are served their horoscope, fish and crab, Pisces and Cancer.

(24)
Suzy is concerned that Doc will be bothered because she works at the Bear Flag. Fauna advises her to never try to escape from anything because a fugitive never gets away. Fauna gives Suzy money to buy a dress and sends her on an errand to San Francisco, telling her to return in the morning.

(25)
Doc returns from collecting specimens to discover that Suzy has cleaned the laboratory and left a stew simmering on the stove. His friend Old Jingleballicks arrives unexpectedly and promptly sits down to eat the undercooked stew. Doc leaves to buy beer and returns with Joseph and Mary, whom Old Jay cheats out of $25 by inventing new chess rules.

(26)
Mack confides to Fauna that neither he nor the boys have appropriate clothes for the party. Fauna

solves the problem by suggesting that they organize a costume party with "Snow White and the Seven Dwarfs" as the theme.

(27)

Everyone in Cannery Row begins preparing their costumes for the big party. Mack and the boys decide to dress as trees, all except Hazel, who decides to go as Prince Charming. He asks Joe Elegant to help him make a costume. Meanwhile, Doc and Old Jingleballicks go on a drinking binge. Doc denies that he is in love with Suzy, who he says is an "illiterate little tramp." Old Jay reminds him that he is "putting a lot of energy into denying something which, if it is not true, deserves no denial."

(28)

Doc and Old Jay arrive at the party in a drunken and disorderly state. Joe Elegant plays a horrible trick on his friends by making Hazel an unusual Prince Charming costume, with a drop-down seat, and Hazel's buttocks painted with a bull's eye. Mack tells Whitey No. 2 to "kick the bejeezus" out of Joe Elegant, who has already left town. Doc wins the drawing and admits to Mack that, before leaving Cannery Row, Lee Chong deeded the Palace Flophouse to its inhabitants so that they would always have a place to live. Mack asks Doc not to tell the boys that their great scheme was unnecessary. He requests that Doc retain ownership of the Palace so that they will never be tempted to sell it. Fauna and the girls arrive with Suzy who is resplendent in a white wedding dress: Snow White, the bride. Suzy reads the look of shock and doubt on Doc's drunken face and rushes out of the party. Fauna catches her and tells her she is a "goddam grandstanding bitch," to which Suzy replies tearfully that she loves Doc.

(29)

Suzy leaves the Bear Flag and takes a job as a waitress in the Golden Poppy. She borrows $25 from Joe Blaikey and moves into the boiler in the vacant lot. Fauna visits the boiler to see if she is all right. Suzy tells her mentor to forget about Doc, that she wasn't good enough for him, but that she is going to be good enough if another guy comes along.

(30)

Hazel begins to prepare himself for his presidential destiny. He attempts to understand what happened at the masquerade, but his efforts are fruitless. When Mack refuses to get involved further, Hazel decides that he must fix things himself.

(31)

Hazel decides that he must start listening and remembering what people say regarding Doc's problem.

(32)

He visits all of his friends on the Row, asking them their opinions about Doc. Suzy tells Hazel that she doesn't want to have anything to do with Doc unless he's sick or breaks a leg. Doc admits to Hazel that he likes Suzy. Hazel warns Doc that Joseph and Mary is hanging around the boiler.

(33)

Doc is wrestling with himself over what to do about Suzy when he hears the sound of the boiler door clang shut. Joseph and Mary is puzzling over why Suzy has slammed the boiler door shut on his hand when Doc grabs him from behind and locks his fingers around his throat. He warns Joseph and Mary to stay away from her.

(34)

Suzy steps out of the boiler to find that Doc has left her a giant floral tribute. She visits Fauna to bathe and borrow perfume and then returns to her boiler to wait for Doc's visit.

(35)

Doc dresses in his best clothes and visits Suzy in the boiler. Suzy refuses to listen to his apologies. She tells Doc that she is looking for "the kind of guy that if he ain't got me he ain't got nothing." Doc tells her that the guy she describes is him, but she doesn't believe him. Doc is heartbroken. He arrives back at the lab to find a telegraph from Old Jay congratulating him on the new octopus research section that has been created for him at the California Institute of Technology.

(36)

Hazel visits the Seer, who is in jail for stealing candy bars. He asks him if it is okay to hurt a friend if it is the only thing that will get him out of trouble. The Seer agrees that sometimes it is necessary. Late that night Hazel sneaks into Doc's laboratory and breaks Doc's arm with an indoor ball bat.

(37)
Anguished and in pain, Doc calls the local doctor, who puts his arm in a cast. He is embarrassed because he cannot explain how the injury occurred and is in a state of panic because now he will not be able to drive to La Jolla the next day to collect octopi.

(38)
In 1924 the monarch butterflies failed to appear in Pacific Grove, ruining the annual butterfly festival. They have failed to appear again and the townspeople are in a panic.

(39)
The missing monarchs arrive in Pacific Grove. Word spreads through the town of Doc's broken arm but nobody offers to drive him to La Jolla. Mack realizes that it was Hazel that broke Doc's arm. Hazel tells Mack that he has tried and that he cannot live up to being president of the United States. Fauna relieves Hazel of his burden by telling him that she made a miscalculation with the horoscope and that he will not become president after all. Meanwhile, Hazel's plan pays off when Suzy offers to drive Doc to La Jolla and Doc tells Suzy that he loves her.

(40)
The boys of the Palace Flophouse give Suzy a crash course in driving and Suzy and Doc drive away to the La Jolla tides. Mack tells Hazel that he would have made "a hell of a president."

CHARACTERS AND PLACES

Bear Flag Restaurant   A Cannery Row whorehouse owned and operated by Dora Flood in CANNERY ROW and then by her sister Fauna Flood in *Sweet Thursday.*

Blaikey, Joe   A character in *Sweet Thursday.* The well-liked Monterey town constable. When Suzy arrives in town he warns her to stay out of trouble, gives her a recommendation for the Bear Flag

Restaurant, and lends her money when she decides to quit the Bear Flag and live on her own.

Chong, Lee   A character in CANNERY ROW who is remembered in *Sweet Thursday,* Lee was the owner of Lee Chong's Heavenly Flower Grocery. A round-faced and courteous Chinese man, he enjoyed an important position in Cannery Row owing to the credit that he extended to everyone in the community. Chong rented a shed to Mack and the boys, which became known as the Palace Flophouse. During the war Lee Chong sold his store to Joseph and Mary Rivas so he could buy a schooner to go trading in the South Seas, and was never heard from again. Before he left, he deeded the Palace Flophouse to Mack and the boys, and paid 10 years' worth of property taxes on it.

Deems, Mr.   A character in *Sweet Thursday,* Mr. Deems is a philanthropist who donates a roque court for the amusement of the elderly residents of PACIFIC GROVE. He later decides to bulldoze the courts to put an end to the violence they are causing and is driven from the town.

Doc   A character in *Sweet Thursday* and CANNERY ROW. Doc is the owner and operator of Western Biological Laboratory, he adores science, beer, women, and classical music. Doc is the center of Cannery Row. A deceptively small man, he is loved by all the residents of Cannery Row, but despite his popularity he is a lonely, set-apart man. He wears a beard, and his face is half Christ and half satyr. As a competent marine biologist, he established his own lab, where residents on the Row would come for parties and conversations on science, art, and philosophy. After a problem-wrought courtship he falls in love with a whore named Suzy. The character of Doc is modeled after EDWARD F. RICKETTS, the marine biologist who was Steinbeck's closest friend.

Eddie   A character in *Sweet Thursday* and CANNERY ROW, Eddie is a resident of the Palace Flophouse. He works periodically at La Ida, a local honky-tonk, where he keeps an empty gallon jug

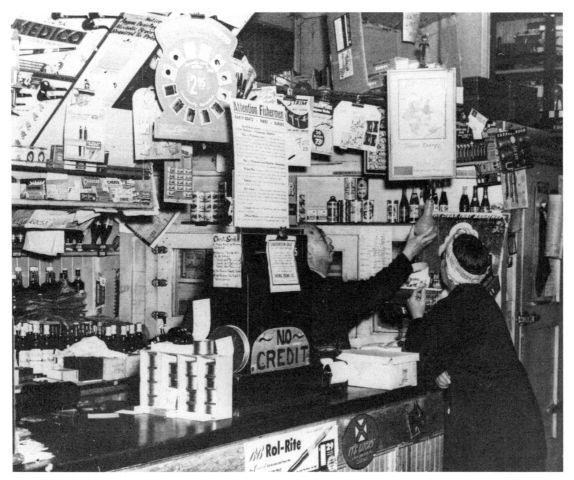

The real-life Lee Chong's grocery, which inspired Steinbeck's *Cannery Row* and *Sweet Thursday* *(Center for Steinbeck Studies)*

beneath the bar into which he empties the leftovers from all the glasses.

Elegant, Joe A character in *Sweet Thursday*, Joe is the cook at the Bear Flag Restaurant. Joe is a pale young man who sneers most of the time and smokes foreign cigarettes in a long ebony holder. Joe spends years writing a novel, *The Pi Root of Oedipus*. Feeling outcast, he takes his revenge on the people of Cannery Row by designing Hazel's Prince Charming costume for the big costume party.

Flood, Flora "Fauna" A character in *Sweet Thursday*, Fauna is Dora Flood's sister. Her real name is Flora, but she changed it when somebody said to her that she seemed "more like the fauna type." When her sister Dora dies in her sleep she takes over the operation of the Bear Flag Restaurant and sets out to turn it into a sort of finishing school for girls. A heavy but graceful woman, she has orange hair and carries herself with elegance. Fauna is a successful businesswoman, benevolent but solvent, public-spirited but privately an individualist. She is concerned with the improvement of her girls and her highest accomplishment is to see them well married. She sets out to make a match of Suzy and Doc, but her plan almost comes to an unhappy end.

Gay A character in *Sweet Thursday* and CANNERY ROW, Gay was an inspired mechanic who moved in with Mack and the boys of the Palace Flophouse to avoid his abusive wife. Gay is killed in WORLD WAR II, by a piece of antiaircraft fallback in LONDON. The boys of the Palace Flophouse preserve his bed untouched as a sort of shrine.

The Golden Poppy Restaurant The Golden Poppy Restaurant is a local Monterey diner run by Ella, a harried and irritable woman in *Sweet Thursday*. Suzy takes a job there as a waitress after the disastrous results of the Palace Flophouse masquerade party.

Hazel A character in *Sweet Thursday* and CANNERY ROW, Hazel is innocent and kind, if a bit dim-witted. Hazel is a resident of the Palace Flophouse. Hazel's mother named him after a great aunt in the hope of a possible inheritance. Hazel becomes overburdened with responsibility when his horoscope reveals that he will become president of the United States. He determines to solve Doc's problem with Suzy, finally deciding to break his arm so that she will be forced to take him to La Jolla for the spring tide.

Henri A character in *Sweet Thursday* and CANNERY ROW, Henri is a painter who lives on Cannery Row, though he is not really French and his name is not really Henri. Henri lives aboard a boat of his own design that he is constantly building and changing. He does not want to finish the boat because then he would feel obliged to sail it and he is afraid of the sea. One night Mac and the boys glue a bunch of barnacles and seaweed to the bottom of his boat. Unable to shake the horrifying notion that his boat was going out to sea while he was asleep, Henri sells his boat and leaves town.

Jingleballicks, Old (Old Jay) A character in *Sweet Thursday*, Old Jay was a stubby man with yellow hair and bright eyes. He was born very rich and spends his life contributing millions to charitable institutions, even while he sponges off of his friends. During the war Doc left Old Jingleballicks in charge of Western Biological Laboratories, only to return to find that it had been abandoned for

years. Old Jay endows an octopus research center in Doc's name to force him to write the scientific paper that has been plaguing him.

Las Espaldas Mojadas The band of Mexican illegal immigrants organized and exploited by Joseph and Mary Rivas from his headquarters at Lee Chong's Grocery on Cannery Row in *Sweet Thursday*. The phrase is Spanish for "wetbacks."

Mack A character in *Sweet Thursday* and CANNERY ROW, Mack is the leader of a small group of bums who live at the Palace Flophouse on Cannery Row. He organizes the residents of Cannery Row to search for a solution to Doc's loneliness. He invents an elaborate scheme to steal the Palace Flophouse from Joseph and Mary Rivas, only to discover that it was deeded to him by the previous owner, Lee Chong.

Palace Flophouse and Grill A place in *Sweet Thursday* and CANNERY ROW, this flimsy storage building on a small lot is what Lee Chong received from Horace Abbeville in payment for his huge grocery debts in *Cannery Row*. Chong rented the building to Mack and his friends for five dollars a week. When Lee Chong sells his grocery and sails for the South Seas, Mack and the boys become afraid that the new owner, Joseph and Mary Rivas, will sell their home. They scheme to raffle the Palace, fixing the contest to ensure that Doc wins the drawing. Later they learn that Lee Chong had deeded the Palace to them when he sold his grocery and left Cannery Row.

The Ready Room A place in *Sweet Thursday*, the recreation room that Fauna Flood built for the girls of the Bear Flag Restaurant. A large and pleasant apartment with three windows overlooking Cannery Row, it was a place to relax, to read, to gossip and to study, and some of these things were actually done by the girls of the Bear Flag.

Rivas, Joseph and Mary A character in *Sweet Thursday*, Joseph and Mary Rives ("Joseph and Mary" is the character's first name) purchases Lee Chong's Heavenly Flower Grocery, from which he manages crews of illegal workers from Mexico. As a smuggler of illegal immigrants, he is said to be in the "wetback business," *wetback* being an offensive word used to describe illegal Mexican immigrants. Joseph is a smart, snappy dresser, also known as the *patrón.* Everything he does naturally turns against the law. Joseph's nephew, Cacahuete, works in the grocery and plays trumpet in the band Las Espaldas Mojadas (The Wet Backs).

Seer, the   A character in *Sweet Thursday,* the Seer is a big, bearded stranger with the lively eyes of a healthy baby and the rugged, chiseled face of a prophet. He lives beneath the pine trees in the dunes beyond the lighthouse near Cannery Row. The Seer has a passion for candy bars, which he must steal from the local Safeway supermarket. He meets Doc on the beach and invites him to dinner. The Seer is arrested when his sweet tooth gets the best of him and he steals three candy bars.

Sonny Boy   A character in *Sweet Thursday,* Sonny Boy is the Greek owner of the restaurant on the wharf in Monterey where Doc takes Suzy on their first date.

Suzy   A character in *Sweet Thursday,* Suzy is a pretty, outspoken young prostitute who works in the Bear Flag Restaurant. The Bear Flag's owner, Fauna Flood, decides that Suzy isn't cut out to be a hustler and tries to find her a husband. Suzy falls in love with Doc, who rejects her, only to finally fall in love with her.

FURTHER READING

"Back to the Riffraff." *Time,* June 14, 1954, 120, 122.

"Book Reviews." *Dublin Magazine,* January–March 1955, 66.

DeMott, Robert. "*Sweet Thursday* Revisited: An Excursion in Suggestiveness." In *After The Grapes of Wrath: Essays on John Steinbeck,* edited by Donald V. Coers, Paul D. Ruffin, and Robert J. DeMott. Athens: Ohio University Press, 1995, 172–196.

"Fiction." *Times Literary Supplement* (London), November 26, 1954, 753.

French, Warren. *John Steinbeck's Fiction Revisited.* New York: Twayne, 1994.

Gill, Brendan. Books. *New Yorker,* July 10, 1954, 70–72.

Gladstein, Mimi Reisel. "Straining for Profundity: Steinbeck's *Burning Bright* and *Sweet Thursday.*" In *The Short Novels of John Steinbeck: Critical Essays with a Checklist to Steinbeck Criticism,* edited by Jackson J. Benson. Durham, N.C.: Duke University Press, 1990, 234–248.

"A Minor Pleasantry." *Nation,* July 10, 1954, 37.

Moore, Ward. "Cannery Row Revisited." *Nation,* October 16, 1954.

"New Novels." *New Statesman and Nation,* November 6, 1954, 589–590.

Owens, Louis. "Critics and Common Denominators: Steinbeck's *Sweet Thursday.*" In *The Short Novels of John Steinbeck: Critical Essays with a Checklist to Steinbeck Criticism,* edited by Jackson J. Benson. Durham, N.C.: Duke University Press, 1990, 195–203.

Parini, Jay. *John Steinbeck: A Biography.* New York: Henry Holt, 1995.

Poore, Charles. "Books of the Times." *New York Times,* June 10, 1954, 29.

Steinbeck, John. *Sweet Thursday.* New York: Viking, 1954.

"Television and Radio" (1957)

A letter first published in the *New York Herald Tribune* on August 23, 1957. As part of a selection of guest writers who filled in for John Crosby, television writer, John Steinbeck contributed a letter to Crosby. Steinbeck admits to being flattered at being asked to fill in, but submits a letter of complaint instead. Rather than a standard complaint against television, he complains instead about his lack of ability to watch television. He laments that he invariably misses all the good shows; he's just too busy reading, or talking, or listening to music. The days that he does watch television are invariably the days when there is nothing good on. He goes on to list the few great shows that he has seen, and to bemoan the mediocre ones. He worries that he is too old to learn how to take pleasure in being told what brand of cigarettes to smoke or the answers to the $64,000 questions. Although Steinbeck respects Crosby's job, he wonders what Crosby could be up to on his vacation; is he relearning the art of conversation or is he nervously waiting to get back to the ceaseless chatter of the TV? Steinbeck finally posits that the children will be all right. They have grown up with television, so it is a way of life. But he is not quite sure he wants to share in that way of life.

"Their Blood Is Strong" (1938)

See "THE HARVEST GYPSIES."

"Then My Arm Glassed Up" (1965)

"Then My Arm Glassed Up" is a one-page, nearly stream-of-consciousness essay on sports that first appeared in *Sports Illustrated* on December 20, 1965. Steinbeck veers between lists of sports that he likes and dislikes, and a more philosophical look at the history of sport and its contemporary meanings. Steinbeck begins by declaring that he is an observer, rather than a participant. The title of the essay refers to the end of his javelin-throwing days, when his arm glassed up. He looks briefly at the derivation of sport: both the word and the activity. Team sports represent battles and individual sports provide an outlet for single combat. He does not admire sport hunters, although he thinks fox hunting serves the purpose of keeping the population of the English aristocracy in check and provides fine horses. (The fox population isn't affected, he observes dryly.) He loves fishing, but not big-game fishing. He wonders if senior citizens should have their own sports, like vine racing, in which two combatants plant a vine, and wait to see which grows faster. (The same can be done with oak trees.) Then he goes on to deplore bullfighting, which he has researched and seen in person. He sneaks in a poke at ERNEST HEMINGWAY here, imply-

ing that he has more experience watching bullfighting than Hemingway does. Although he recognizes that bullfighters are brave in the ring against crippled bulls, he notes that their courage does not extend outside the ring. In the end, he declares that the kind of courage that is important to the world—the kind shared by Edward R. Murrow, an African-American voting for the first time in Alabama, and Dag Hammarskjold—is the only kind of courage that is necessary.

To a God Unknown (1933)

The inspiration for Steinbeck's third novel, *To a God Unknown,* came from the play *A Green Lady,* written by his Stanford friend WEBSTER "TOBY" STREET in the late 1920s. Steinbeck began the original draft of the novel, which he called THE GREEN LADY, early in his career—it represented only his second attempt at producing a full-length novel. Unsatisfied with the first draft, he abandoned it and started over with a new story, changing its title to *To an Unknown God.* Every publishing house that Steinbeck contacted rejected this second draft of the novel. Frustrated and nearly broke, he set the manuscript aside to write what would become his second published novel, THE PASTURES OF HEAVEN. Upon completing *The Pastures of Heaven,* Steinbeck rewrote *To a God Unknown* for a third and final time. In 1933, ROBERT O. BALLOU published the novel.

This book shows the clear influence of a young scholar whom Steinbeck had met in MONTEREY, CALIFORNIA, during the time the book was in progress. JOSEPH CAMPBELL, who later became famous for his comparative studies of human mythology, met the author through EDWARD RICKETTS, and the three spent many long hours discussing literature, psychology, and religion. *To a God Unknown* displays Steinbeck's early exploration of man's role in nature, of nonteleological thinking, and of the ultimate flaws in the American dream.

Unfortunately the novel fails on many levels, perhaps reflecting its origin, and the massive revisions required by Steinbeck to fit his evolving view of its themes and characters. Toby Street originally conceived a three-act play, dealing with a father, Andy Wane, his adoring relationship with his college daughter, Susie, and an intermingled, obsessive love for his ranch land. Upset by his daughter's growing indifference to his own mystical connection to his property, and blaming it on her newfound interest in books, Andy forbids Susie to return for her senior year. He sets a further barrier by refusing to sell forest acreage to a lumber company to pay for the tuition. By the time Street asked Steinbeck for help with the play, it had already taken a direction that disturbed him: hints of incest, and sexual attachments to an earth goddess. The title, *The Green Lady,* referred to this spiritually perverse connection, a Mother Earth who should be worshipped and subdued at the same time, whether literally in the normal process of agriculture, or figuratively, in the symbolic person of Susie.

The subject matter intrigued Steinbeck. Never one to be put off by middle-class moral sensibilities, and already deeply involved in the study of myth, pantheism, animism, and the origins of religion, he threw himself into the project off and on for almost six years, often to the neglect of his other writing. Throughout his career, Steinbeck labored over his writing, trying to find the perfect diction and rhythm for all of his works, and to make the language flow easily and apparently effortlessly. With *To a God Unknown,* the labor shows in forced allusions and allegories; in turgid monologues, and unsympathetic characters; in a mishmash of obvious and obscure religious symbolism ranging from traditional Catholicism to sun worship. Perhaps writing the book in fits and starts, and with so many revisions and changes of direction affected its coherence.

CRITICAL SUMMARY

In its final version, *To a God Unknown* provided another example of the "westering" impulse so identified with Steinbeck in later years, a primordial need for people across the globe, but especially in America, to pick up and move on to another frontier, ever westward to the edge of the Pacific Ocean. The protagonist, Joseph Wayne, leaves Vermont for California after receiving his dying father's blessing, even though he is the third son of four. He travels westward in search of land, because he recognizes there is not enough family land available in Vermont to be divided among all of the brothers. Spending his first night alone on his newly claimed homestead in the valley of Nuestra Señora, Joseph is overcome by his ecstasy, and copulates with the earth, spilling his seed in the ground in the first of many fertility rituals. Shortly thereafter, Joseph feels the spirit of his dead father enter a magnificent tree on the property, and begins to hold conversations with, and even to make sacrifices to the tree in an informal rite of ancestor worship.

Eventually his brothers and their wives join Joseph in California, without explaining the abandonment of the family farm in Vermont. But each represents a different aspect of spiritualism. The oldest brother, Thomas, almost animistic, with a mystical connection to animals but not colored by sentimentality, arrives with his wife, Rama, who becomes a physical embodiment of the Earth Mother. Burton, the second brother, a pious and Puritan fundamentalist, who disapproves of anything deviating from The Word, brings his wife, Harriet, and lives an almost monastic life, having kept the Lord's admonition to be fruitful and multiply four times. The youngest of the brothers, Benjy, accompanied by his wife, Jenny, is a human Pan, compelled only by enticements of wine, women, and song, and in constant search for Dionysian revelry. Shortly after the brothers' reunion, Joseph finds another talisman in a remote corner of the property in a mystical glade, a huge rock that had been the site for prehistoric Native American religious ceremonies. The fifth chapter sets the conflict, and additionally, in a heavy-handed bit of foreshadowing, a meteorological anomaly of severe cyclical drought has been introduced as a future possibility for the Wayne homestead.

Joseph begins a single-minded pursuit of the village schoolteacher, Elizabeth, who initially is both repelled and drawn to this strange man, whom she views in almost biblically patriarchal terms. He makes it clear from the outset that he intends to marry her, and make her the mother of his children, and that his choice of her is more one of practicality than attraction. She also is torn by an inexplicable lust for Benjy, the drunken balladeer, who sings beneath her window at night. Elizabeth eventually bows to practicality and to Joseph's insistence.

Benjy dies early, killed while seducing the fiancée of one of the ranch employees on his brother's wedding night, suggesting, perhaps, that bacchanalian excesses must serve a larger purpose than the pleasure of the individual. Joseph protects his brother's killer, Juanito, and assists him in escaping from the authorities, offering the first blood sacrifice to the land. Benjy's escapades threatened the property and the security of the Wayne homestead. Meanwhile, the homestead grows ever more prosperous and fecund, the livestock ceaselessly multiplying, seemingly without much effort on the part of Joseph. To underscore the notion of Joseph being the phallic symbol for the Wayne homestead, Steinbeck introduces an element of bestiality. In a comment to Burton, Joseph says that if the lead bull were not capable of fertilizing the cows, he would step into the bull's place. Burton rightfully objects to the remark, and as the book progresses becomes more disturbed by his brother's descent into paganism.

Ultimately Burton's disgust and fear for his brother's soul bring disaster to the Wayne ranch. After a series of what Burton understands as sacrilegious events, including a winter fiesta on the property that culminates in a drunken orgy, a Catholic mass, and Joseph offering wine and his newborn son to the Tree/Father, Burton leaves. Before he leaves, he girdles the tree in which Joseph believes the spirit of their father resides, causing it to die a slow death. Almost immediately, drought and famine descend on the region. Elizabeth dies in a queer accident at the rock altar, and a brief period of rain dampens the parched soil. Wayne livestock collapse and die for lack of food and water. Joseph decides to send his brother Thomas and his family, and his own infant son to the San Joaquin Valley with the remaining livestock, but not without another odd interlude. Thomas and Joseph travel to the Pacific Coast, and meet an old man, a sun worshiper, who sacrifices small animals to guarantee sunrise.

After the departure of his family, Joseph moves to the clearing where the talismanic boulder lies, and begins an ascetic cleansing while tending to dying plant life surrounding the rock. He replicates the 40 days and 40 nights of Christ in the New Testament, and also of numerous other martyrs who suffer for their beliefs. He is joined by Juanito, who participates in the ritual, but who convinces Joseph to seek counsel from the village priest, Father Angelo. The padre is unable to offer Joseph any solace. Joseph returns to the rock, opens his veins, and as he lies dying, the skies open up and the rain falls.

One searches very hard for any positive attributes to this book. On the surface, *To a God Unknown,* presents a fictionalized account of mankind's search for a deity or deities. Its pantheism is glaringly obvious, and yet, there seems to be no recognition of the underlying importance of belief. Steinbeck's agnosticism has been well documented. Perhaps his lack of commitment affected the outcome. One never knows whether Joseph is a priest or shaman, a minor deity, or simply a delusional individual. Was there a cause and effect in the ultimate sacrifice at the end of the book, or was the rainfall ending the drought a coincidence as Joseph ended his life? Or did Steinbeck intend to say that all spiritual and mythical constructs are in the end meaningless? None of these questions can be answered through Steinbeck's prose. On at least two occasions, Joseph rises from his body, and becomes the mountains, the rocks, the trees, and every part of the Earth, suggesting a metaphysical and creative component to the central character. Yet, on the other hand, Joseph sacrifices everything he holds dear, including his child, and achieves nothing.

The best parts of the novel can be found in the lyrical descriptions of the land, and the graphic portrayals of rural farm life at the turn of the 20th century. One can almost smell and see the Wayne homestead in Joseph's first exploration; taste the food at the New Year's Eve fiesta; and feel the despair of a farmer in finding the bloated carcasses of dying livestock. When the characters are not making speeches to further the story, Steinbeck shows a wonderful ear for ordinary dialogue. But he never makes it clear why Joseph, patterned after great spiritual leaders, could inspire anyone. Referencing his ongoing work with *To a God Unknown*, Steinbeck expressed his belief "that only gods, kings, and heroes are worth writing about." Joseph Wayne may have been intended to be all of those archetypes, but by stretching the metaphor, Steinbeck created a protagonist who was none of them.

EARLY CRITICISM

Coming as it did on the heels of *The Pastures of Heaven*, which garnered positive critical response, *To a God Unknown* puzzled reviewers who read the book. As was true for Steinbeck's two prior lengthy published works, the company holding his contract shortly went out of business. For those reviewers who had an opportunity to read the work before it went out of print, the book was a critical disaster. Although she liked the book overall, Margaret Cheney Dawson of the *New York Herald Tribune* remarked that readers of Steinbeck "may be dismayed to find Mr. Steinbeck on so different a tack." Others called it ". . . a curious hodgepodge of vague moods and irrelevant meanings," (Virginia Barney, *New York Times Book Review*); and "half-baked mysticism" (V. S. Pritchett, *Spectator*). Notably the book received many short and quick responses on its publication. They constitute a mixed feeling about the changed style in Steinbeck's new book. In the *Nation*'s column "Shorter Notices", a reviewer called *To a God Unknown* "pitifully thin and shadowy."

The reviewer in *New Republic* commented that *To a God Unknown* indicates Steinbeck's departure from the sharp characterization of his first book to mystic symbols of nature worship. Citing the Christ figure in the novel, the reviewer noted that Steinbeck writes of his principal character with the fervor of a faithful apostle. Yet, unlike Christ, Joseph had no creed, no desire to be remembered, no human emotional indulgences such as pain and sorrow.

Harold Brighouse in the *Manchester Guardian* wrote that the novel is built to a climax dealing with drought, at which Joseph Wayne sacrifices his own blood to the rain god, and we are unconscious of the absurdity. It is an action for which Steinbeck has prepared us; it is also a poet-novelist's victory over common sense.

CONTEMPORARY PERSPECTIVES

Like *Cup of Gold*, neither casual readers nor scholars find much worth in *To a God Unknown*, except as an example of the development of a renowned author. Many believe that the book says more about Joseph Campbell and his influence than about Steinbeck himself. In the work one can see elements of nonteleological philosophy and the unity between mankind and environment that emerged in later writings. However, careful critics like Robert DeMott and Peter Lisca have done some excellent scholarship on the theme and style of the book. Lisca believes that *To a God Unknown* considers not only the problem, "Who is He to whom we shall offer our sacrifice?" but also the nature of man's proper relationship to God. Building on other scholars' views of the book, DeMott further notices that a good understanding of the image of the main character, Joseph Wayne, helps readers to extricate the author's intentions with the book. According to DeMott, Joseph Wayne is a hero and a god-like man. Different from the historical Jesus Christ, Joseph is the symbolic type of a Christ-like individual who signifies psychologically the human self. He represents the projection of an important and central archetype. Thus for DeMott, Joseph's process of individuation, his transformational journey, is the subject of the novel. This is a journey in which the man must encompass his darker half before he comes to symbolize the mythic ideas. Therefore, *To a God Unknown* is not a mystical novel corresponding to Campbell ideas of mythology, instead, it is a visionary one. Much like the dance Joseph witnesses at the fiesta, the book attempts to be "breaking through" to a different vision.

SYNOPSIS

(1)

Joseph Wayne, a brooding, serious man, asks his elderly father's permission to move west and homestead in California. He is worried that their Vermont farm is too small to be divided among him and his brothers, Thomas, Burton, and Benjy. The elder Wayne asks him to wait until he dies so that his spirit can accompany him to the new land. Joseph insists that he must leave soon before all the good land is taken. His father reluctantly agrees to let him go. The old man tells his son that he intends to give him the special blessing that has been passed from father to son throughout the generations: "There's something more strong in you than in your brothers, Joseph; more sure and inward."

(2)

Joseph registers a 160-acre homestead in the Valley of Nuestra Señora in central California. He meets Old Juan, a resident from the nearby town of Nuestra Señora. He promises Old Juan that he will make a party for his neighbors when his house is built. As Joseph rides through the thick pine forest that borders his land, he is suddenly aware that his father is dead and that his spirit has come to California to watch over him. Joseph determines to become the guardian of the land.

(3)

Romas, an old Mexican teamster, delivers a load of lumber to the Wayne ranch with his son Willie and the skinner, Juanito. Joseph asks Romas why nobody has homesteaded the land in the valley. The old man tells him that 10 years of drought killed the livestock and drove many of the valley's inhabitants away. The drought, he warns, has occurred at least twice in memory.

(4)

Juanito returns to the ranch to become Joseph's cowhand and loyal friend. He brings a letter from Joseph's brother, Burton, who writes of their father's death and says that his brothers would like to move west to join him. Joseph suddenly senses that his father's spirit inhabits a great oak tree standing next to the house that he is building. He kisses the bark of the tree, welcoming his father.

(5)

Joseph's three brothers arrive with their families, each filing a homestead on the adjoining land.

(6)

Having received his father's blessing, Joseph becomes the patriarch of the clan. He is obsessed with the land and believes himself to be both its guardian and source of its fertility. Seeing himself as the only unproductive thing on the land, he decides to find a wife.

Joseph, Thomas, and Juanito ride out to inspect the land. Thomas asks Joseph why he hangs dead animals on the great oak tree. Joseph admits he believes that their dead father lives in the tree. The three men are drawn to a large circular clearing in the center of a thick stand of pines. In the middle of the glade is a rock. A small stream runs from beneath the rock and across the clearing. Juanito explains that the old Indians consider the place holy.

(7)

Joseph awkwardly begins courting Elizabeth McGreggor, the pretty young schoolteacher in the town of Nuestra Señora, finally asking her to marry him.

(8)

Joseph tells Juanito that he might soon be married. Juanito confides that he too will soon be married to Alice Garcia, a young woman from the town. Elizabeth agrees to marry Joseph.

(9)

Joseph takes his fiancée on a tour of the Wayne ranch. He is surprised when she asks him if she may climb the great oak tree. He helps her into the tree.

(10)

Joseph and Elizabeth are married in Monterey. Traveling back to the ranch they cross over a pass into the Valley of Nuestra Señora. Elizabeth is afraid to go through the pass, for it is symbolic of the life that she is leaving behind. She imagines an image of herself as a little girl sadly turning around and walking away, leaving her alone to face her new life.

(11)

The newlyweds pass through the town of Nuestra Señora, where the residents shower them with gifts. As they near the ranch they meet Juanito, who asks Joseph to meet him at the rock in the clearing. Returning to the ranch, Joseph discovers that Juanito has murdered Benjy after discovering him in bed with Alice, Juanito's fiancée. Joseph instructs his brother to report Benjy's death as accidental. Reporting Benjy's death to the oak tree, he suddenly understands the implication of the blessing he received from his father. In him are both good and evil, and he cannot judge either one.

(12)
Rama, Thomas's wife, takes charge of Elizabeth, explaining that Benjy has been killed. In a moment of intimacy, she tells her that Joseph is special, a symbol of the "earth's soul." When Elizabeth accuses her of being in love with Joseph, she insists that she does not love him, but that she worships him.

(13)
Joseph rides out to the rock to find Juanito. The young cowhand gives him his pocket knife so that he may kill him and avenge his brother's murder. Joseph refuses, telling him that what happened was expected. Juanito says that he cannot live near the grave of an unavenged man. He decides to leave the ranch until the body has decomposed and the memory of the knife is gone.

(14)
Benjy's widow, Jennie, returns to the East. Alice, pregnant and in deep mourning because of her lover's absence, moves in with Joseph and Elizabeth.

(15)
Joseph waits anxiously for the rains. He and his brother kill a pig by the oak tree, as though making a sacrifice to their father. Prodigious rains come to the valley, promising a prosperous year. Joseph, remembering his promise to make a large feast, decides to hold the event on New Year's Day.

(16)
Old Juan returns after Christmas to help the family prepare for the fiesta. Father Angelo, the town priest, agrees to give a mass before the party. After the mass, Joseph consecrates the party by filling a cup with wine and pouring it out on the ground and then refilling the cup and drinking its contents in one thirsty gulp. Later, the priest observes him offering wine to the oak tree, and warns him of blasphemy. Wine and whiskey are consumed in great quantity, and the partygoers dance crazily in an increasingly bacchanalian celebration. His brother Burton refuses to take part in the fiesta, complaining that it is devil worship. As the party reaches its orgiastic culmination, a heavy rain sud-

denly washes down upon the valley. Elizabeth announces that she is pregnant. Late that night Joseph goes out to the tree to announce that a baby will be born. Burton observes him from the shadows as he lays an offering of meat in the crotch of the tree. Worried for his brother's soul, he begs him to repent and cut down the tree.

(17)
Heavy rains bring abundance to the valley. Elizabeth prepares for the birth of her child. One afternoon, while Joseph is away, she drives her buggy to the distant pines and discovers the grove with the mysterious rock. A sensation of evil comes over her and she flees the glade.

(18)
Joseph delivers his son with Rama's help. Elizabeth learns of Joseph's relationship with the oak tree.

(19)
Joseph names the new baby boy John, after his father. He takes his son to the tree to put him in its branches. Burton, understanding his intention, forbids him to do it, but Joseph refuses to heed his brother's warnings. Indignant, Burton decides to leave the ranch and move to Pacific Grove with his family.

(20)
The next week Burton moves away from the ranch. Joseph senses that something is wrong. The leaves of the oak begin to lose their luster and he fears that it is dying. Digging down along the trunk, Thomas and Joseph, discover that Burton has removed a band of bark under ground level, and has, therefore, killed it.

(21)
Fall and then winter arrive and no rain falls in the valley. The dryness begins to worry Joseph. Elizabeth asks him to take her to the rock so that she can dispel her fear of it. The next morning they ride to the glade. Elizabeth climbs upon the rock. Suddenly she loses her grip and falls, breaking her neck. A gentle rain begins to fall on the glade. Joseph carries his wife's body to the ranch, where Thomas takes charge of it. That night Rama enters Joseph's bedroom and makes love to him.

(22)

The drought worsens and the land becomes gray and lifeless. Joseph feels that he has failed to protect the land. He and his brother Thomas decide that they must drive the cattle as soon as the remaining hay is gone. The two brothers decide to ride over the western mountains to get a glimpse of the ocean while the cattle eat the remaining feed. They meet an old man who lives on a cliff above the ocean. He explains that every evening he watches the sun go down from his cliff, and that he is the last man in the western world to see the sun each evening. The old man shows Joseph to a stone altar on the edge of a cliff, where he sacrifices an animal as the last rays of the sun disappear.

(23)

The following morning the two men head back to the ranch. They find the land littered with the remains of dead cattle. Joseph gives his son to Rama, explaining that such a sacrifice might help the land. He closes up the house and goes to the glade, where he finds that there is still a trickle of water in the stream. He begins to carry water to the rock. Joseph resolves to live in the glade and care for the rock until the rains come.

(24)

Joseph dedicates himself to the rock, leaving it only to purchase supplies. Juanito returns with a letter from Thomas indicating that they arrived in green pastures with only 100 cattle. Joseph observes that the little stream is shrinking. Juanito, concerned for his friend's sanity, convinces Joseph to go to town and talk to Father Angelo. The priest assures him that the land will not die and warns him that he should be more concerned about his own soul.

(25)

Juanito presents his young son to Joseph, and shyly explains that he bears Joseph's name. He asks Joseph to bestow his blessing upon the child. On his way back to the glade, Joseph rescues a small calf whose mother has died. When he arrives back at the rock, he discovers that the steam has dried up. Remembering the old man of the sunsets, he kills the calf and pours its meager trickle of blood upon the dry streambed. Feeling that he must make a larger sacrifice, Joseph climbs upon the rock and cuts his wrists. As his life slowly trickles away, he feels his body become light and rise into the sky, from which a heavy rain begins to beat down. "I should have known," he whispers. "I am the rain."

(26)

The people of Nuestra Señora gather to practice their ancient rituals to thank the gods for the return of the rain.

CHARACTERS AND PLACES

Angelo, Father A character in *To a God Unknown*, Father Angelo is the priest of Nuestra Señora. He gives a New Year's Day mass at the Wayne ranch. When Joseph Wayne comes to him and begs him to pray for rain, he assures him that he would be better off praying for his soul.

Juan, Old A character in *To a God Unknown*, Old Juan is a peddler who welcomes Joseph Wayne to the Valley of Nuestra Señora. Joseph promises the old man that he will host a large fiesta to celebrate his new ranch. The old man returns with his son-in-law Manuel and helps organize the party.

Juanito A character in *To a God Unknown*, Juanito is Joseph Wayne's ranch hand. He has dark, Indian skin and blue eyes, which he claims to be a result of his Castilian ancestry. His wife, Alice, is a young woman from the small town of Nuestra Señora. Juanito stabs Benjy Wayne in the back when he discovers him with his wife, killing him. He tells Joseph Wayne that it is his right to kill him since he has murdered his brother, but Joseph refuses to take revenge on his friend. Juanito leaves the Wayne ranch rather than live beside the grave of an unrevenged man. He names his son Joseph after his benefactor and asks him to give his blessing to the child. Later, Juanito's wife became a helper at the Waynes house.

Nuestra Señora A place in *To a God Unknown*, Nuestra Señora (Spanish for "Our Lady") is a small town populated mostly by Indians and Mexicans. It lies at the southern end of the Valley of Nuestra Señora and is the closest town to the Wayne ranch.

Romas A character in *To a God Unknown*, Romas is a teamster from Our Lady. He helps Thomas drive the remaining Wayne cattle to greener pastures.

Valley of Nuestra Señora Also known by the English name "The Valley of Our Lady," this long, fertile valley in *To a God Unknown* was carved out by the San Francisquito River in central California. Joseph Wayne moved here and claimed a 160-acre homestead.

Wayne, Benjy A character in *To a God Unknown*, Benjy is the youngest of four brothers. He is a drunkard and a seducer of women. He is married to Jennie, a young woman from the East Coast. Juanito stabs him in the back and kills him when he discovers that Benjy has been in bed with his new wife.

Wayne, Burton A character in *To a God Unknown*, Burton is the second of four brothers, a stern, religious man. His wife, Harriet, is a soft, sickly woman. When his brother Joseph Wayne refuses to renounce his pagan adoration of a great oak tree, Burton leaves the ranch and moves his family to PACIFIC GROVE, but before he goes he secretly kills the tree by girdling the bark just below the dirt's surface.

Wayne, Elizabeth A character in *To a God Unknown*, Elizabeth Wayne is the wife of Joseph Wayne and daughter of Mr. McGreggor from Monterey, California. She is pretty and intelligent, and at the age of 17 she becomes a schoolteacher. At her wedding, she feels that her husband's face resembles that of Christ. On the same day she arrives at the Wayne ranch, Benjy Wayne, her husband's younger brother, is killed by a man whose wife he had stolen. In the story Elizabeth is drawn mysteriously to a rock in the woods. On a return trip to the rock she climbs it, but slips off and dies of a broken neck.

Wayne, Joseph A character in *To a God Unknown*, Joseph is the third of four brothers. He receives an ancient blessing from his dying father and becomes the patriarch of the Wayne family. He wears a dark beard and has blue eyes, a large nose and high, hard cheekbones. Joseph leads his brothers from their small farm in Vermont to the Valley of Nuestra Señora in central California, where they homestead a large ranch. He marries Elizabeth McGreggor, the schoolteacher in the small town of Our Lady, a determined, pretty woman, tall and lean with a small nose and eyes set wide apart. After giving birth to Joseph's first son, John, Elizabeth falls and breaks her neck. Determined to save the land from a terrible drought, Joseph sacrifices himself to bring rain.

Wayne, Rama A character in *To a God Unknown*, Rama Wayne is Thomas Wayne's wife and the mother of three daughters. Rama is a strong woman respected by all the children of the Wayne family. She is also an authority on the Wayne farm. When Elizabeth arrives at the ranch, Rama tells her that her husband, Joseph, is not an ordinary human being and that she should worship him. After Elizabeth's death, she takes care of the infant and gives herself to Joseph sexually when he is drunk due to his sorrow for his wife's death.

Wayne, Thomas A character in *To a God Unknown*, the eldest of four brothers, a quiet, strong man with golden hair and a long mustache, Thomas has a strong kinship with animals of all kinds. He supports his younger brother, Joseph Wayne, far more than the other two brothers, Benjy and Burton, because Thomas has his own mystical connection with nature. Benjy is a womanizing drunkard, and Burton a devout Christian offended by Joseph's animism. Only Thomas appreciates the fundamental beliefs behind Joseph's actions. Thomas's wife, Rama, is a strong, full-breasted woman, "nearly always contemptuous of everything men thought or did."

FURTHER READING

Barney, Virginia. "Symbols of Earth." *New York Times Book Review,* October 1, 1933, 18.

Brighouse, Harold. "Pan in California." *Manchester Guardian,* March 27, 1935, 7.

Dawson, Margaret Cheney. "Some Autumn Fiction." *New York Herald Tribune*, September 24, 1933, 17, 19.

DeMott, Robert. Introduction to *To a God Unknown*, by John Steinbeck New York: Penguin, 1995, vii–xxxix.

Hayashi, Tetsumaro. "John Steinbeck: The Art and Craft of Writing." In *A New Study Guide to Steinbeck's Major Works, with Critical Explications*, edited by Tetsumaro Hayashi. Metuchen, N.J.: Scarecrow Press, 1993.

Lisca, Peter. *The Wide World of John Steinbeck*. New Brunswick, N.J.: Rutgers University Press, 1958.

Pritchett, V. S. "Fiction." *Spectator*, April 5, 1935, 580.

"Shorter Notices." *Nation*, October 18, 1933, 456.

Steinbeck, John. *To a God Unknown*. New York: Robert T. Ballou, 1933.

"To a God Unknown." *New Republic*, December 20, 1933, 178.

Tortilla Flat (1935)

Steinbeck's fourth novel, *Tortilla Flat* tells the story of a group of rough-and-tumble hoboes and *paisanos*—people of mixed Spanish, Mexican, and Caucasian heritage living in the poor shantytown area around MONTEREY, CALIFORNIA. During the early 1930s, Steinbeck had lived close to the area that was known as TORTILLA FLAT with his first wife, CAROL HENNING STEINBECK BROWN. At that time, Steinbeck and his friend EDWARD RICKETTS explored the area thoroughly, often drinking and carousing with the inhabitants. Steinbeck also made the acquaintance of a schoolteacher and aspiring poet from the area named SUE GREGORY, who related to the author many of the comically romantic stories of *paisano* life that would provide the backbone of the novel *Tortilla Flat*. After being rejected by numerous publishing houses, the book was finally accepted by the firm Covici and Freide, whose part-owner PASCAL COVICI had recently recognized the author's potential. Released in 1932, the book was an instant sensation, becoming the writer's first commercial success, and finally freeing him from the economic problems that plagued him during his early years as an author. That same year, Paramount purchased the film rights to *Tortilla Flat*, setting the stage for Steinbeck's introduction to Hollywood.

In the preface, Steinbeck draws a deliberate parallel between Danny's story and the basic composition of the Arthurian legends, a point underscored by Steinbeck when he constructed the chapter headings in the same format as SIR THOMAS MALORY's *MORTE D'ARTHUR*, and presented a stylized speech pattern, akin to archaic English. Danny takes on the role of King Arthur, even if unwillingly. He serves as the head and rallying point of the band of friends, with his inheritance of two homes from his grandfather representing a modern Camelot. Though his friends and he are certainly not knights in the classical sense, they do seek adventures to prove themselves, and observe a code of conduct as binding as that of the Round Table. When Danny dies, the group disbands, just as Arthur's death shatters the unity of his knights. But also with Danny's death, the tales of his life take on epic and mythical proportions. In a sense, Danny becomes the "once and future king" of Tortilla Flat.

One must be careful in ascribing too much similarity between the Arthurian canon and *Tortilla Flat*, however. For example, Chapter VIII, "How Danny's friends sought mystic treasure on St. Andrew's Eve. How Pilon found it and later how a pair of serge pants changed ownership twice," was described by Steinbeck in a letter to MAVIS MCINTOSH as the *paisano* version of the Quest for the Holy Grail, but he also notes "that the search of the forest is not clear enough. . . ." The search in *Tortilla Flat* has a much more secular and far-ranging foundation, which Steinbeck found in the legends of King Arthur. It is the search for friendship and camaraderie; of an individual's transformation and enhanced potential in a group situation; and of the successes and failures of people interacting with and inseparable from their environment. A reader familiar with Malory looks in vain for precise congruence between the central figures of the story of King Arthur, and the characters in *Tortilla Flat*. Danny clearly is King Arthur. But where is Guinevere, or Lancelot, or Galahad? Or Mordred, and Morgan LeFay, the most notable villains of the

Round Table legends? No nobility of purpose, or higher end is intimated except for the loyalty, devotion, and joy discovered by Danny's cohort of disparate *amigos* during their brief collaboration and collusion in the pursuit of temporal pleasure. Steinbeck makes them heroes of a different sort. Despite their amoral, and immoral behavior, most of the major and minor characters in the book demonstrate a remarkable ability to survive poverty, congenital deformity, and social disapproval, sometimes with ingenuity, sometimes with self-delusion, but most of the time through the bonds of friendship. Steinbeck creates a fully realized and likable cast of characters whose adventures do begin to resemble the often fruitless exploits of King Arthur's knights.

In spite of the comic overtones, *Tortilla Flat* is not a comedy. From a classical perspective, the distinction between a comedy and tragedy is that in a tragedy, the hero dies. Danny tumbles to his death into a drainage ditch toward the end of the book, and before then, does everything he can in a fit of apparent madness, to sever the fraternal ties among his close circle of friends. What Steinbeck attempts, with much success, is a wholly modern form—a blend of tragedy and comedy—the so-called "black" comedy. A casual reader cannot help but be amused by the thought process of Pilon, as he contemplates a new bit of thievery, or connivance to insure a roof over his head, a solid meal, or jug of wine. Or the story of Teresina Cortez, who conceived her first child at the age of 14, and continued

Spencer Tracy (second from right) as Pilon and John Garfield (with guitar) as Danny in the 1942 film production of *Tortilla Flat* (Photofest)

to produce babies regularly until they numbered nine; and then jeopardized her family's health through the largesse of Danny's "Round Table" with a diet that varied from the accustomed regimen of tortillas and beans. And the mentally challenged Pirate—never given a real name, though most of his five dogs have both a given and surname—who comes to live with Danny, in a chalked-out circle on the living area floor, dreaming of making religious obeisance to St. Francis of Assisi through the gift of a gold candlestick to the church in memory of one of his deceased dogs.

In a noteworthy chapter of self-revelation, Steinbeck demonstrates one of his purposes with this book, to distinguish between wholesome and unwholesome laughter. In Chapter XIV, "Of the good life at Danny's House; of a gift pig, of the pain of Tall Bob, and of the thwarted love of the Viejo Ravanno." The inhabitants of Danny's house begin to exchange stories in what amounts to verbal jousting, each "knight" attempting to overcome the other with his prowess in relating a tale, or remembrance of Tortilla Flat inhabitants. The first stories amount to gossip, centering on a particular woman, Cornelia, whose favors and temperament achieve renown with the *compadres.* As the night wears on, the stories become more profound, more complicated, and indicative of a central theme. Jesus Maria speaks as the resident philosopher, and "great-hearted man." There are stories that make people laugh, but with a bad kind of laughter, he says, and these stories never serve any purpose except to harm. He gives the example of Tall Bob, who shoots off his nose to give himself stature and respect in the community as the animal control officer. Jesus Maria then speaks of a different kind of story, ". . . when you open your mouth to laugh, something like a hand squeezes your heart." These are the stories at the heart of *Tortilla Flat*—funny, but instructive and poignant at the same time. Not of mockery or deprecation of the simple *paisanos* outside the respectable people of Monterey, but a realistic portrayal of human beings whom John Steinbeck knew and liked. Human events that make us laugh, and at the same time, make us cry.

In *Tortilla Flat*, Steinbeck demonstrates a shift from the historical, episodic, and metaphysical approaches of his three previous novels. None of them was grounded in an experiential reality, but found their inspiration only in the mind of the author. His descriptions of the denizens of Tortilla Flat came from day-to-day and side-by-side connections with the *paisanos*—his neighbors, friends, and fellow-sufferers in the early years of the GREAT DEPRESSION. After years of living from hand to mouth, Steinbeck understood very well the importance of good friends, no matter their background, and of the value of community. Five years after the publication of *Tortilla Flat,* in a subsequent reprinting, Steinbeck wrote a foreword in response to those who criticized his "paternalistic" denigration of the brown-skinned, non-Anglo citizens of Monterey, and to those of his readers who found the unstructured portrayal of *paisanos* good reason for discriminatory action, and possible expulsion from the United States—two sides of the critical coin he often faced from the liberal and conservative communities. He subtly criticizes those who find the *paisanos* "quaint" and "vulgar," and apologizes for his role in creating or reinforcing the negative image. He then vows never again to subject a vulnerable class to the inspection of "decent" folk. Happily, he broke his vow.

Tortilla Flat offers an introduction to what later became known as "The Labor Trilogy," or "The Great Proletarian Novels" (*IN DUBIOUS BATTLE, OF MICE AND MEN,* and *THE GRAPES OF WRATH*). Steinbeck wrote the book during the period between the death of his mother and of his father, and described it as lightweight, a way to relieve the stress from deaths of loved ones, and an easy literary diversion from more reflective topics. Much to his surprise *Tortilla Flat* sold more copies than any of his prior works and even brought the attention of Hollywood studios. Never again did Steinbeck create characters, plots, or themes out of whole cloth, solely the product of his own active imagination. He found inspiration in real people and real events.

EARLY CRITICISM

Tortilla Flat achieved both national and international acclaim without gaining Steinbeck a reputation as an author to be considered seriously. What perplexed and delighted many reviewers was how such reprobates could be presented in such a positive light, and with such affection. LEWIS GANNETT, of the *New York Herald Tribune,* called it "a book to cherish," and denied that his wife's role as illustrator had anything to do with his opinion. William Rose Benét, from the *Saturday Review,* marveled at Steinbeck's ability to portray unscrupulous scoundrels with hysterical humor. Fred T. Marsh, in the *New York Times Book Review,* remarked on Steinbeck's "gift for drollery," but doubted that life in the real Tortilla Flat was as amusing or satisfying as the author portrayed. Reviewer Ella Winter of the *San Francisco Chronicle,* granted a rare personal access to Steinbeck, gushed about the author's large, bony frame and piercing blue eyes, and then spoke of his "wise, light, and wistful touch" of humor. One of the few negative evaluations came from Helen Neville, writing for the *Nation.* She accused Steinbeck of writing with "indifference" of the desperate plight of the underclass, and of imposing an "urbane and charming gaiety" upon a subject matter "rife with possibilities" for social upheaval. Steinbeck's long-term friend, JOSEPH HENRY JACKSON (*San Francisco Chronicle*), set Miss Neville straight, perhaps with the benefit of inside information. In Jackson's evaluation, the author never intended to write "a fine sermon," but only "a funny story." Regarding Steinbeck's portrayal of life on Tortilla Flat in Monterey, Harry Hansen wrote in the *New York World Telegram* that "the characters of Tortilla Flat belong to the immortal bank of vagabonds who romp through the books of all nations.

CONTEMPORARY PERSPECTIVES

Steinbeck's critics, particularly Warren French and Peter Lisca, find that a complete understanding of *Tortilla Flat* has often been hindered by some common misinterpretations of the novel. Typical comments on the book affirmed that it celebrated the virtue of being unmoral without apology, that the characters are not quite human beings, and that the book glorifies man as animal. Another misinterpretation of *Tortilla Flat,* as French pointed out, began with Lewis Gannett's introduction to the *Portable Steinbeck.* To better understand the book, French suggests that it be read as a work which uses

novelistic techniques—such as character development, incident, setting, and symbols—to make a dramatic presentation of a flawed society. In the past few decades, Steinbeck scholars have compared Danny and his friends to the knights at King Arthur's Round Table. Recently Susan Shillinglaw has pointed out that *Tortilla Flat* could be rich text for ethnic and cultural studies. The conventional "shiftless and lazy" stereotypes of a non-Anglo population found in *Tortilla Flat* appear to be a ridiculous mistake considering the mixed ethnic origins of most of the characters, whose names reflect national backgrounds from the Spanish, the Irish, the Italian, and Asian—in short, a microcosm of American and Californian immigrants. Instead, Steinbeck describes a community with a natural ebb and flow, defined by old and new patterns of behavior, infinitely adaptable, and resilient. Feminist critics examine the whore/Madonna characteristics of the central female characters, and their role as "victims" of Danny and friends who make it a vocation to pursue the "ladies" of Tortilla Flat, but overall, the women have better survival skills, and inherent knowledge than the men, and more traditional scruples than their male counterparts.

Ultimately, *Tortilla Flat* provided a staging area for Steinbeck, and gave him the impetus to direct his literary sensibilities from inward motivation, to outward examination of people, places, and events with which he had familiarity and insight.

SYNOPSIS

Preface
Danny, 25 years old, is a homeless, jobless resident of Tortilla Flat, an uphill district above the town of Monterey, California. Tortilla Flat is inhabited primarily by poor *paisanos.* War is declared with Germany, and Danny along with his friends Pilon and Big Joe enlist in the army during a fit of drunken patriotism.

Chapter I—How Danny, home from the wars, found himself an heir, and how he swore to protect the helpless
Returning home from World War I, Danny discovers that his grandfather has died and left him an inheritance of two small houses. Carefree Danny is

burdened by the weight of this new responsibility. He is jailed for drunken and disorderly conduct and promptly escapes. While hiding from the law, Danny is reunited with his friend Pilon. Pilon predicts that Danny's new position as a property owner will cause him to forget his friends. Danny swears to share his new house with Pilon.

Chapter II—How Pilon was lured by greed of position to forsake Danny's hospitality

Danny and Pilon move into the larger of the two houses, a simple construction of three rooms, a bed, and a stove. The responsibility of ownership begins to weigh on Danny. He wishes that the house were Pilon's so that he could come and live with him as a guest, rather than a host. Pilon decides that he wants his own house. He suggests that Danny rent him the second house. Danny agrees to rent the house for $15 a month.

Chapter III—How the poison of possessions wrought with Pilon, and how evil temporarily triumphed in him

Pilon moves into Danny's other house, a house exactly like Danny's, only smaller. Pilon feels oppressed by his unpaid rent and decides to work, earning $2 cleaning squids for Chin Kee. He decides that a gift of two gallons of wine would be a better expression of friendship than cash. Armed with the wine, he begins the ascent to Danny's house. Pilon is raised to a state of spiritual elation by a beautiful view of the gulls soaring over the harbor. He is wrestling with the temptation to keep the wine for himself, when he stumbles upon his friend Pablo Sanchez. Pablo has just been paroled from jail. Pilon, saved from selfishness, promptly invites Pablo to the house to share the wine. He convinces his friend that it is a fine thing to live in a house and agrees to rent him a room for $15 a month, freeing himself of his debt to Danny.

Chapter IV—How Jesus Maria Corcoran, a good man, became an unwilling vehicle of evil

Pilon worries that Danny will decide to marry and begin asking for the rent. He and Pablo visit Danny, who expresses amorous interest in his neighbor, Mrs. Morales, a widow with more than

$200 in the bank. Danny asks his friends for rent money to buy her a box of chocolates. Pilon and Pablo react angrily. They accuse Danny of being a miser and making inhuman demands on them. On the road home, they find Jesus Maria Corcoran lying drunk in a ditch. He tells of finding a rowboat washed up on the beach and selling it in Monterey for $7, with which he bought two gallons of wine and a pair of silk drawers for Arabella Gross, a local whore, before being thrown in jail. He has $3 left, and his friends quickly set out to relieve him of it. They agree to rent a room to Jesus Maria for $15 a month, of which he must pay $2 in advance. Rather than give the money to Danny, however, they agree that a gift of wine would be more appropriate.

Chapter V—How Saint Francis turned the tide and put a gentle punishment on Pilon and Pablo and Jesus Maria

Pablo and Pilon decide that it would be unwise to give Danny two gallons of wine. Pablo seduces the wife of Mr. Torelli, the owner of the local trading post, relieving her of a little dinner and then some firewood. Jesus Maria returns to the house, his face bloody and his clothing torn after fighting with some sailors. A candle topples while the drunken men sleep, setting the small house aflame. Jesus Maria, awakened by a falling shingle, rescues his friends. The house burns to the ground. Danny receives the news of the disaster indifferently.

Chapter VI—How three sinful men, through contrition, attained peace. How Danny's Friends swore comradeship

Danny examines his ruined house and his newly lost social status as a man with a house to rent. His anger quickly diminishes, however, replaced with relief that he no longer has to bear so much responsibility. Pablo, Pilon, and Jesus Maria decide that it is best to admit their guilt and accept their friend's punishment. The three penitents arrive at Danny's house armed with a stolen picnic lunch and a silk brassiere for him to give to Mrs. Morales as a gift. Danny accepts his friends' contrition, and they all enjoy the stolen feast. The three men move in with Danny.

Chapter VII—*How Danny's Friends became a force for good. How they succored the poor Pirate*

Pilon devises a plan to uncover the hidden treasure of Pirate, a halfwit who lives with his five dogs in an abandoned chicken house. Unable to convince Pirate to reveal the whereabouts of his stash, he tells him that his friends are worried about him living all alone, and invites him to live in Danny's house. The astounded Pirate moves in the next day. Still unable to discover the location of the treasure, Pilon and friends decide to scare him. They tell him stories of fortunes that were hidden by their selfish owners only to be discovered and stolen. The next morning the worried Pirate decides to entrust his friends with his treasure, which he is saving to buy a golden candlestick for Saint Francis. Pilon and his friends realize they have been defeated, for honor forbids that they steal money that has been entrusted to their protection.

Chapter VIII—*How Danny's Friends sought mystic treasure on Saint Andrew's Eve. How Pilon found it and later how a pair of serge trousers changed ownership twice*

Big Joe Portagee returns from the army. It is Saint Andrew's Eve, a day when it is believed that buried treasure reveals itself by throwing up a faint phosphorescent light. Pilon and Big Joe wander through the dark forest, where Pilon spots the telltale sign of buried treasure. He carefully marks the spot, and makes plans to return the following evening. Big Joe moves in with Danny and his friends. Big Joe steals one of Danny's blankets, which he trades in Torrelli's store for a gallon of wine. Pilon rebukes him for stealing from their friend and decides that he must pay for his perfidy by doing all the digging. That evening they return to claim their treasure. After many hours of hard excavation, Big Joe's shovel unearths a geological survey marker. The men drown their disappointment with the remaining wine. Pilon awakens with a powerful thirst and decides to take Big Joe's blue serge trousers as punishment for stealing Danny's blanket. He trades the pants in Torrelli's store for a liter of wine and then steals them and the blanket back. He returns to the beach and returns the pants to his grateful friend.

Chapter IX—*How Danny was ensnared by a vacuum cleaner and how Danny's Friends rescued him*

Danny determines to win the affection of Sweets Ramirez with a jug of wine and a gift. He buys her a vacuum cleaner. The gift elevates Sweets to the top of Tortilla Flat society. She proudly pushes the vacuum through her house, even though there is no electricity in Tortilla Flat. Danny begins spending all his evenings with the grateful Sweets, much to the chagrin of his friends, who decide that it is time for the relationship to end. They convince Danny that Sweets intends to demand that he install electricity for the vacuum. Danny is outraged. Pilon steals the vacuum and trades it to Torrelli for two jugs of wine. Torrelli discovers that the vacuum has no motor.

Chapter X—*How the Friends solaced a Corporal and in return received a lesson in paternal ethics*

Kind-hearted Jesus Maria Corcoran rescues a young Mexican corporal with a sick baby boy. The child dies, and the corporal tells the sad story of how his wife was stolen by his captain, and how his only desire was that his child grow up to be a general so that he might have more good things than his father.

Chapter XI—*How under the most adverse circumstances, love came to Big Joe Portagee*

Big Joe seeks shelter from the rain in the house of Tia Ignacia, a middle-aged widow. Ignacia offers Joe a glass of wine and makes a sexual advance. Joe resists and falls asleep. Furious at his rejection, she drives him into the rain. Joe grabs her and is overcome by passion. The unlikely couple makes love in the muddy street.

Chapter XII—*How Danny's Friends assisted the Pirate to keep a vow, and how as a reward for merit the Pirate's dogs saw a holy vision*

Big Joe steals Pirate's hoard of money. Pirate's friends beat him brutally, for his treasure has become "the symbolic center of the friendship, the point of trust about which the fraternity revolved." Danny counts the recovered money, and discovers that Pirate now has enough to buy the golden candlestick. Pirate gives the money to the priest, who promises to purchase the offering for the following Sunday's mass. The friends prepare to celebrate. Pirate dresses in his best clothes and leaves for the mass. The service is interrupted when the five dogs burst into the church. After the service, Pirate takes them to the forest and repeats the priest's stories of Saint Francis's love for animals, whereupon the dogs have a vision of the saint.

Chapter XIII—How Danny's Friends threw themselves to the aid of a distressed lady

Jose Maria Corcoran sets out to help Teresina Cortez and her family of nine children who are facing starvation because of the failure of the year's bean crop, the only food upon which the large family survives. Danny's friends set out to provide food for the sprawling brood, stealing comestibles until the house overflows with fruits and vegetables and meats. Teresina begins to complain, however, when her children get sick. Embarrassed, she tells the friends that the only proper food for a child is beans. The friends steal four 100-pound sacks of beans, ensuring the family's survival.

Chapter XIV—Of the good life at Danny's House, of a gift pig, of the pain of Tall Bob, and of the thwarted love of the Viejo Ravanno

The boys entertain one another with gossip and stories: Danny recounts how Emilio Murietta gave a stolen pig to Cornelia Ruiz. Pablo tells the story of Tall Bob Smoke, the town dogcatcher who shot off the tip of his nose in a failed suicide attempt. Jesus Maria tells the story of Old Pete Ravanno, who hanged himself accidentally while trying to win the affections of a young girl.

Chapter XV—How Danny brooded and became mad. How the devil in the shape of Torrelli assaulted Danny's House

Danny longs for the freedom of the old days. He disappears from the house and goes on a drunken rampage, stealing and fighting and committing outrages throughout the Flat and the surrounding communities. His friends decide he is crazy. They try to find him, but to no avail. In a moment of drunken depravity Danny sells his house to Mr. Torelli. Danny's friends steal the bill of sale and destroy it. Finally, sad and exhausted, Danny returns to his home.

Chapter XVI—Of the sadness of Danny. How through sacrifice Danny's Friends gave a party. How Danny was translated

Danny is overcome with apathy. His friends decide to throw a party to raise his spirits. Word spreads and everybody in the town plans to attend. That night the party rages and Danny is transformed. Waving a table leg he rushes into the night in search of The Enemy, only to fall to his death at the bottom of a dry watercourse.

Chapter XVII—How Danny's sorrowing Friends defied the conventions. How the Talismanic Bond was burned. How each Friend departed alone

After the friends hold a funeral for Danny, they gather one last time to drink and reflect. Since Danny, their leader, has died, they find it impossible to honor their original commitment. They burn the house and walk away, each one walking alone.

CHARACTERS AND PLACES

Corcoran, Jesus Maria A character in *Tortilla Flat*, Jesus is one of Danny's *paisano* friends. He tries to win the affection of Arabella Gross, a local whore. When he and Pablo and Pilon burn down their rented house, they move in with Danny. He befriends a young Mexican corporal and his sick infant son, and organizes the relief effort for Teresina Cortez and her nine children.

Cortez, Teresina A character in *Tortilla Flat*, Teresina is the mother of nine children. She lives with her poor mother Angelica, who feeds the children beans collected from the chaff that remain after the Monterey bean harvest. When the harvest fails, Teresina's family faces starvation. She is saved by Jesus Maria Corcoran and his friends.

Danny A character in *Tortilla Flat*, Danny is a small, dark, and charming *paisano* with a love for drinking and fighting. Danny returns from the war to find that he is the heir to his grandfather's two houses in Tortilla Flat. He rents one house to his friend Pilon, who accidentally burns it down. Ever forgiving, Danny invites his friends to come and live with him in the second house. He wins the affection of Delores Engracia "Sweets" Ramirez by presenting her with the only vacuum cleaner in all of Tortilla Flat. When his settled, peaceful life begins to make him despondent, Danny runs away and engages in an orgy of drinking and immorality. His friends decide to make him a party to pull him out of his lethargy. During his final great party, Danny is transformed: Wielding a table leg, he rushes into the night to challenge the Enemy and falls to his death at the bottom of a dry riverbed. After his funeral his friends burn down his house and the group separates.

Gross, Arabella A character in *Tortilla Flat*, Arabella is Jesus Maria Corcoran's favorite prostitute. He determines to win her affections by making her a present of a silk brassiere.

Ignacia, Tia A character in *Tortilla Flat*, Tia is a middle-aged widow of long standing and some success. She beats Big Joe Portagee when he ignores her advances.

Morales, Mrs. A character in *Tortilla Flat*, Mrs. Morales is the old widow who lives next to Danny on Tortilla Flat. Danny seduces her when he discovers that she has more than $200 in the bank.

paisano Term referring to the inhabitants of the uphill district of Monterey called Tortilla Flat in the book *Tortilla Flat*. Steinbeck defines a *paisano* as "a mixture of Spanish, Indian, Mexican, and assorted Caucasian bloods." According to Steinbeck, the ancestors of a *paisano* have "lived in California for a hundred or two years," and speak "English with a *paisano* accent and Spanish with a *paisano* accent." When *paisanos* are asked about their race, they indignantly claim pure Spanish blood.

Pilon A character in *Tortilla Flat*, Pilon is one of Danny's *paisano* friends, Pilon is a great logician and a master of justifications. Upon returning from the infantry, he rents his friend Danny's second house, which is destroyed in an accidental fire. Full of contrition, Pilon moves in with Danny. He sets out to steal Pirate's stash of quarters, but is defeated by his friend's trust and his own sense of honor. Pilon and Big Joe Portagee hunt for buried treasure on Saint Andrew's Eve. Pilon sets out to rescue his friend Danny when he is overcome with sadness.

Pirate A character in *Tortilla Flat*, Pirate is a large man whose tremendous black and bushy beard earned him his nickname. He lives with his five dogs, Enrique, Pajarito, Rudolph, Fluff and Señor Alec Thompson. He sells pitchwood and saves his money to buy a golden candlestick for Saint Francis. Pirate is befriended by Pilon, who is intent on discovering where he hides his money. His dogs are visited with a vision when he gives them a sermon on Saint Francis and the animals.

Big Joe Portagee Character in *Tortilla Flat*. One of Danny's *paisano* friends, Big Joe is a large, muscular man who spends most of his time sleeping or in jail. He enlists to fight the Germans during WORLD WAR II, but he spends most of his army career in the brig for insubordination. He assists Pilon on his search for buried treasure. During a rainy evening he has an impassioned affair with the old widow Tia Ignacia. When Big Joe steals the money that Pirate has entrusted them to guard, he is brutally beaten.

Ramirez, Dolores Engracia "Sweets" A character in *Tortilla Flat*, Sweets is a shrill-voiced, hard-faced woman whose sleepy passion excited the attention of those Tortilla Flat residents to whom "the flesh is important." Danny seduces Sweets with the gift of a vacuum cleaner that he purchases in the local pawnshop. The sweeping machine raises her to the peak of the Tortilla Flat social scale and she pushes it proudly through her house, even though it has no motor and there is no electricity.

Ravanno, Petey A character in *Tortilla Flat*, Petey is a Tortilla Flat resident, who hangs himself after being rejected by Gracie Montez, the woman he loves. He is rescued by his father, Old Pete, and is married to Gracie. Old Pete then decides to use the same trick to win the affection of Gracie's younger sister, 'Tonia, but the plan fails and the suicide succeeds.

Ruiz, Cornelia A character in *Tortilla Flat*, Cornelia is renowned for her wild amorous adventures because she goes through husbands in rapid succession. Although "not a very steady woman," she inspires Pilon's admiration because she still has masses sung for her father, now 10 years dead.

Sanchez, Pablo A character in *Tortilla Flat*, Pablo is one of Danny's *paisano* friends. Pablo is sentenced to jail for stealing a goose, but is paroled when the judge determines that the sentence did him no good. Pablo agrees to pay $15 a month to rent a room in Pilon's rented house. When the house burns down Pablo and Pilon move in with Danny.

Simon's Investment, Jewelry, and Loan Company The *Tortilla Flat* pawnshop where Danny purchased the vacuum cleaner that bought him the affection of Dolores Engracia "Sweets" Ramirez.

Smoke, Tall Bob A character in *Tortilla Flat*, Tall Bob is the Monterey dogcatcher. A tall, proud man who is always beset by some disaster which makes the people laugh at him. Filled with self-pity he shoots off his nose in a botched suicide attempt.

Torrelli, Mr. Mr. Torrelli is a character in *Tortilla Flat*. He is the fat Italian owner of Torrelli's, the store where Danny and his friends trade for wine and food. He finds Danny with his wife, Mrs. Torrelli, and takes his revenge by tricking Danny into selling him his house.

THE FILM: *TORTILLA FLAT* (MGM, 1942)

Based on the novel by John Steinbeck

  Screenplay: John Lee Mahin and Benjamin
    Glazer
  Director: Victor Fleming
  Producer: Sam Zimbalist
  Pilon: Spencer Tracy
  Danny: John Garfield
  Dolores: Hedy Lamarr
  The Pirate: Frank Morgan
  Pablo: Akim Tamiroff

Steinbeck was not actively involved in the production of the film version of his famous novel. Louis B. Mayer, the head of MGM, authorized the recreation of an entire *paisano* neighborhood on a three-acre lot for the movie, and put pressure on Warner Bros. Studio for permission to use Garfield for the lead role of Danny. Later Hedy Lamarr insisted the role of Dolores was the best of her career. The actor Frank Morgan was nominated for an Academy Award for best supporting actor for his portrayal of the dull-witted Pirate.

FURTHER READING

Benét, William Rose. "Affectionate Bravos." *Saturday Review,* June 1, 1935, 12.
Warren French. *John Steinbeck's Fiction Revisited.* New York: Twayne, 1994.
Gannett, Lewis. "Books and Things." *New York Herald Tribune,* May 29, 1935, 17.
———. Introduction to *The Portable Steinbeck.* New York: Viking, 1946.
Hansen, Harry. "The First Reader." *New York World Telegram,* May 28, 1935, 23.
Jackson, Joseph Henry. "A Bookman's Notebook." *San Francisco Chronicle,* May 28, 1935, 16.
Lisca, Peter. *John Steinbeck: Nature and Myth.* New York: Crowell, 1978.
Marsh, Fred T. "Life in a California Shantytown." *New York Times Book Review,* June 2, 1935, 5.
Neville, Helen. "Aristocrats without Money." *Nation,* June 19, 1935, 720.
Shillinglaw, Susan. "John Steinbeck." In *American National Biography.* Oxford: Oxford University Press, 1995.
Steinbeck, John. *Tortilla Flat.* New York: Covici and Friede, 1935.
Winter, Ella. "Sketching the Author of *Tortilla Flat.*" *San Francisco Chronicle,* June 2, 1935, Section D, 4.

Travels with Charley in Search of America (1962)

Steinbeck's last full-length book, *Travels with Charley in Search of America,* is the account of the author's 11-week journey around the country in the company of his faithful blue French poodle, Charley Dog. The aging author conceived of the idea after a series of illnesses. The trip, therefore, served a dual purpose: to prove the author's continued physical vigor, and to renew his contact with the common people who had been the inspiration for his most successful works. Steinbeck planned his trip with enthusiasm, ordering a custom-built pickup-truck/camper. The resulting book is a record of the author's impressions of a country with which he has almost lost touch. VIKING PRESS published *Travels with Charley in Search of America* in 1962, only a few weeks before the author was awarded the NOBEL PRIZE IN LITERATURE. The book received enthusiastic reviews and soon made it to the top of best-seller lists across the country.

The book takes the form of a travelogue, but it actually is a study of human nature, both of Steinbeck's own personality and that of his fellow citizens. Steinbeck relates not only his fears about the direction Americans have taken in the 20th century but also a guarded optimism about the future of the country. Later he expanded on this theme in THE WINTER OF OUR DISCONTENT, and AMERICA AND AMERICANS.

After meeting people of various regions, Steinbeck drew quite a few conclusions about his fellow countrymen, calling them "a restless people," and saying that the country was settled by people who "hungered to move." As for the American landscape, the book reminds readers that the United States has become a fuller industrialized nation, with villages giving way to cities and people populating every corner of the land. While Steinbeck does portray the natural beauty of the country, readers often find the writer asking "Why does progress so often look like destruction?"

EARLY CRITICISM

Like many of Steinbeck's previous books, *Travels with Charley: In Search of America* was not positively received by every critic. Some critics ridiculed the book as a poorly written travel guide to the United States. But most reviewers credited the original thoughts shared by the writer about his country. One critic, Edward Weeks of *The Atlantic Monthly* compared the work to the best writing of Henry David Thoreau. Reviewing the book for the *New York Herald Tribune*, LEWIS GANNETT empha-

sized that Steinbeck's new book provides the writer's objective view of the country. Gannett not only senses Steinbeck's wish that the United States should remain rural and clean, but he also notices Steinbeck's vision of the ethnic makeup of this new nation. Not many early critics or reviewers paid enough attention to Steinbeck's belief that Americans are a new breed, made of a mixture of ethnicities. However, *New York Times* reviewer Eric E. Goldman observes that Steinbeck's intentions with *Travels with Charley* are to see "beyond the stubborn regionalism" and to find a common American character for the nation.

CONTEMPORARY PERSPECTIVES

Contemporary critics like John Ditsky and Geralyn Strecker have recently studied *Travels with Charley* and *America and Americans* to present Steinbeck's efforts to explore different facets of America, because both works have people and places of the United States as their subjects. They argue that although each has a distinct vision, Steinbeck's text in both works is American in that he realizes that his reading of America is unique to his own experience, influenced by factors in his life at any given time. According to these critics, *Travels with Charley* constitutes Steinbeck's efforts to read America, an enormous task.

SYNOPSIS

Part One

In an introduction to the journey that he will take, Steinbeck discusses his compulsion or "itch" to travel, which at the age of 58 still plagues him. He writes that once an idea of a trip is conceived, it often develops an individual character, and concludes that "we do not take a trip, a trip takes us."

Feeling that he has lost touch with his own country, Steinbeck realizes he needs to rediscover "this monster land" if he intends to continue writing about America. He determines to travel alone and incognito, rather than allow his fame to become an obstacle. To this end, he commissions the manufacture of a three-quarter-ton pickup truck with a self-contained camping unit on the back. He names his vehicle ROCINANTE after Don Quixote's horse. Concerned about arousing suspicion among those he meets on his journey, he stocks the vehicle with hunting and fishing equipment, allowing himself the pretext of a sportsman's holiday. He decides to take his blue French poodle, CHARLEY, to provide him with companionship and protection during his long drive.

Determined to get under way soon after Labor Day, Steinbeck parks his new truck at his home in SAG HARBOR, NEW YORK, to make preparations for his journey. He notes that everyone who sees Rocinante looks upon it longingly, making him conclude that nearly every American has a hunger to move, a theme that he will return to throughout the book. Meanwhile, Hurricane Donna strikes the East Coast, doing some damage to his house, and endangering his beloved boat, Fayre Eleyne, which he is forced to rescue in the middle of the storm.

Part Two

As his departure date approaches, Steinbeck finds himself hesitant to leave. He confesses that one of his motivations for taking the trip is the poor health that he suffered during the previous year. His journey is to be an act of rebellion against the "kind of second childhood" that overtakes so many older men when they fall ill and must allow others to take care of them on a semipermanent basis.

Finally on September 23 he begins his journey, taking ferries from Sag Harbor to the coast of Connecticut. As he passes through the industrial cities of the north, he laments the waste and pollution of American industries.

Steinbeck continues north through Maine, hoping to begin his travels from "the roof" of America. As he nears Bangor, he is taken with an overwhelming sadness that returns time and again throughout the novel—in effect, he gives every indication of being homesick. The splendor of the aurora borealis late that evening shakes him from his depression. The next day he heads for Deer Island, Maine, a place recommended to him by his friend and literary agent, ELIZABETH OTIS. He finds himself unable to describe the strange island. Hunting season has begun, and fearing Charley might be mistaken for wildlife, he ties a scrap of red cloth around the dog's neck.

Steinbeck drives to the potato country of northern Maine where he meets a family of Canucks, migrant French Canadian farmers who cross the border each fall to harvest the potato crop. At the edge of a migrant camp, he parks his truck, and sends out Charley as his "ambassador" in order to make acquaintance with the workers. He invites his neighbors to his camper for a drink. Driving south the next morning, he notes with sadness that many of the small New England towns are almost abandoned because of Americans' rush to an urban or suburban life.

Following the changing foliage, he descends through New Hampshire and into Vermont. On Sunday, he attends services at a John Knox church in a small town. He comments on modern Americans' preference for sermons without any mention of sin or its consequences, but rather for psychological excuses for bad behavior. He applauds the small-town preacher for his refusal to exculpate sin. The author leaves the service feeling sinful, and exhilarated.

While in New York State, he visits Niagara Falls before attempting to cross the border into Ontario, thus bypassing Pennsylvania and Ohio. He is turned back at the border, because Charley lacks vaccination certification.

In the course of his travels, Steinbeck slowly becomes aware of a new phenomenon in modern American living: mobile homes. The author marvels at the economy and practicality of these rolling residences, which he proclaims a "revolution in living." He associates the advent of mobile homes with the lack of permanence, and the uncertainty he finds throughout the country. After questioning a mobile home owner about the lack of roots implicit in his mobile lifestyle, the author concludes that the restlessness he observes may be a more powerful urge than the need for a durable connection with people or places.

Driving through Ohio, Michigan, and Illinois, he is impressed by the huge increase of population in the Middle West, and by the obvious energy of the people, so different from the laconic lifestyle of New England. He laments the disappearance of regional patterns of speech due to the influence of radio and television, even though he recognizes the change is inevitable. He remarks on the sadness and waste of effort by those who attempt to hold back change and progress. In northern Michigan, he befriends a young man with a wife who Steinbeck believes is an obstacle to the husband's self-realization.

Having arranged to meet his wife, Elaine, in Chicago for a short break in his journey, Steinbeck now hurries westward, abandoning country lanes for a busy interstate highway. He arrives early in the morning at the exclusive Ambassador East, where the management is clearly uncomfortable with his disheveled appearance. To mollify the hotel staff, Steinbeck agrees to spend the morning waiting for the arrival of his wife in a room still untidy from a previous occupant. Taking note of what had been left behind by the former customer, Steinbeck engages in an exercise of imagination. Based on the objects in the room—an empty bottle of whiskey, traces of pale lipstick, a half written note to the man's wife—he invents Lonesome Harry, a businessman whom he imagines engaged in a tryst with an professional woman named Lucille.

Part Three

Steinbeck takes obvious relief in the brief break from his journey, perhaps indicating the extent of his homesickness. For the sake of continuity, however, the author chooses not to write about the events in Chicago, resuming his narrative when he crosses Wisconsin. He is deeply impressed by the beauty of Wisconsin, and comments on the enchantment of the Wisconsin, as well as the Middle American kitsch that makes Swiss Candy possible.

In Minnesota, he becomes lost on a pilgrimage to Sauk Centre, the birthplace of Sinclair Lewis. He notes how the people of Lewis's hometown turned their backs on their native son after his less than flattering portrayal of them in the book *Main Street*. Now Lewis has become a major tourist attraction for Sauk Centre. Steinbeck pauses at a campsite and reflects on his experiences during the trip. He concludes, cynically, that American restaurants have put cleanliness first, at the expense of taste; the emotional life of the nation is so bland it must be spiced up with sex and sadism from paperbacks and newspapers; intellectual fare

has become as flavorless as the food; and strong political opinions are discouraged because of an abundance of caution and disinterest.

Steinbeck crosses the Badlands and leaves the desolation of the Dakotas for the ruggedness of Montana. He falls in love with the state, which he describes as "a great splash of grandeur."

In Yellowstone National Park he discovers that friendly, passive Charley is driven to a mad rage by the park's bears. Because of the dog's fury, Steinbeck is forced to leave the park. He crosses the Great Divide. In Washington State, Charley begins to suffer from an attack of prostatitis, which requires an emergency visit to a Spokane veterinarian. Finally, the two travelers reach the Pacific Ocean. Steinbeck expresses amazement at the population increase in Seattle, and notes "progress looks so much like destruction."

Finally, Steinbeck arrives in the familiar territory of Northern California, his birthplace, and the focus of much of his writing. His homecoming is bittersweet. He visits Cannery Row, and is overwhelmed by the changes from his last visit. He tells his friend, Jonny Garcia, that he feels like a stranger or a ghost.

Realizing the wisdom of Thomas Wolfe's insistence that "you can't go home again," Steinbeck leaves California as quickly as possible, crossing the Mojave Desert into Arizona, and then into New Mexico in a hurried rush towards Texas.

Part Four

Steinbeck arrives in Texas. The size and nature of the state impress the author, and he observes that Texas has "a mystique approaching a religion." In Amarillo, Charley once again becomes ill, and Steinbeck is forced to leave him with a vet for four days. His wife, Elaine, was born in Texas, and the author arranges for his wife to celebrate Thanksgiving in the state. They both stay at the home of a friend, followed up by hunting and fishing on a ranch owned by a Texas millionaire.

Continuing his trip, Steinbeck's attention is drawn to the public outcry over the admission of Negro children to a New Orleans school. He decides he is unfit to judge the controversy, since he grew up in an area where the problem of segregation did not exist. Driving through New Orleans, he decides to visit the school where the infamous "Cheerleaders," a group of intolerant, white racist mothers, shout epithets at young black children. He is sickened by what he sees.

Emotionally exhausted from his experiences in the South, Steinbeck hurries back toward New York, discontinuing his narrative before he reaches his final destination. By the time he reaches Virginia, the trip has lost all interest for him, and he feels as if he has been "stranded far from home."

FURTHER READING

Ditsky, John. *John Steinbeck and the Critics.* Woodbridge, U.K.: Camden House, 2000.

Gannett, Lewis. "From Coast to Coast, He Met No Strangers." *New York Herald Tribune*, July 29, 1962, 3.

Goldman. Eric E. "Steinbeck's America, Twenty Years After." *New York Times Book Review*, July 29, 1962, 5.

Steinbeck, John. *Travels with Charley: In Search of America.* New York: Viking, 1962.

Strecker, Geralyn. "Reading Steinbeck (Re)-Reading America: *Travels with Charley and America and Americans.*" In *After "The Grapes of Wrath": Essays on John Steinbeck in Honor of Tetsumaro Hayashi*, edited by Donald Coers, Robert DeMott, and Paul Ruffin. Athens: Ohio University Press, 1995, 214–227.

Weeks, Edward. "Seeing Our Country Close." *Atlantic Monthly*, August 1962, 138–139.

"Trust Your Luck" (1957)

"Trust Your Luck," first published January 12, 1957, in *The Saturday Review,* was an article written while Steinbeck vacationed in Paris with his two young sons. Sitting on their balcony one evening, the boys make a wish upon the evening star that they might have horses of their very own. Steinbeck teases them that the stars in the sky are French stars, and so they will receive French horses. Catching himself in the act, he realizes that adults have the tendency to defraud the wishes and beliefs of youth.

He remembers one son telling him that he feels like the luckiest boy in the world. Steinbeck almost advises the boy that he should not trust his luck, but realizes that to do so would be a disservice. The author speculates about children's obsession with space travel and promises to buy his boys a telescope to show them that stars are not slaves to national boundaries.

"Unsecret Weapon" (1953)

A story published in two parts in the February 14 and February 21, 1953, editions of *Picture Post.* "Unsecret Weapon" is a two-part story in which Steinbeck proposes a chilling new weapon against tyranny. In the first part, the narrator details his initial pitch of this weapon to President FRANKLIN ROOSEVELT during WORLD WAR II. Frontal assaults on a country, even on a country whose people are horribly oppressed, only serve to stiffen the people's resolve against the aggressor. The weapon the narrator and his friend proposed was designed to break down a system of tyranny from the inside out. Although Roosevelt loved the idea, everyone else, from the secretary of the treasury to the ambassador of Britain, abhorred it as a threat to something many people hold dearer than life. The weapon was never used.

In 1953 Stalin was crushing the Soviet Union, and the narrator offers a view of how the weapon might be used against the USSR. The weapon? Capitalism's greatest: money. For the price of a single destroyer, billions of counterfeit rubles could be manufactured, so close to the original as to be undetectable. They could then be floated into Soviet airspace in balloons and dropped over unsuspecting towns.

The rest of the story goes on to detail a possible scenario of how this would cause the entire Soviet system to break down. Steinbeck details the initial drop over the town of Gemil. The deputy, who has had all initiative and creativity trained out of him, waits desperately for word from Kiev, and then from Moscow, on how to deal with the situation. Although he sends out people to collect all of the money that they can find, he cannot stop people in the streets from furtively gathering it up. Even he is tempted into pocketing some of the money. Eventually, Moscow sends a troubleshooter who gloomily informs them that there is no way to combat this. They cannot even retaliate in kind, because the United States relies much more heavily on checks than on cash. The only recourse is to pretend it never happened and hope the United States thinks it did not work. The story ends with five balloons being spotted over Smolensk.

"The Vegetable War" (1956)

"The Vegetable War" is a short, humorous article about English cooking first published in the July 21, 1956, edition of *Saturday Review*. Steinbeck claims to like the English very much, noting that he first came to know them at home during WORLD WAR II. The English trait that has most puzzled the rest of the world, he says, is their treatment of food. The author proposes two schools of thought to explain this. The first is that it reflects the masochistic tendency of the English. He even suggests that it is a form of sacrifice to the weather gods. His second theory is that it is how the English deal with basic human savagery. They take it out on their food. As an example, Steinbeck considers the Brussels sprout, which is easily cooked. The English method, however, requires time and great effort to produce a "gray mess." He comments on the sexless nature of some Englishmen, suspecting that they must procreate through pollination, resulting in their dislike of vegetables. Finally, he tells of the treacherous British who bemoan the failure of Napoleon to conquer the island, because a French invasion would have improved the cooking.

"The Vigilante" (1936)

Originally published as "The Lonesome Vigilante" in the October 1936, edition of *Esquire*, "The Vigilante" was subsequently included as part of the collection of short stories in THE LONG VALLEY, published by VIKING PRESS in 1938. Steinbeck based the story on a notorious lynching, which took place on November 16, 1933, in San José, California, the hometown of his first wife, CAROL HENNING STEINBECK BROWN. Two men, John Holmes and Thomas Thurmond, incarcerated for the ransom kidnapping and brutal murder of the son of a locally prominent businessman, were dragged by a mob from the San José jail, and hanged in a public park by a crowd of citizens, estimated by eyewitness accounts at from 5,000 to 10,000 people. The passions of the mob had previously been inflamed by statements from the current governor of California, James J. Rolph, who refused to send assistance to the San José constabulary, and instead declared he would not "protect kidnappers who willfully killed a fine boy. . . ."

Steinbeck, distracted as he was during this time period by the terminal illness of his mother, OLIVE HAMILTON STEINBECK, found the story of the lynching to comport with his evolving philosophy of the PHALANX, by which group behavior should be distinguished from individual action. For Steinbeck, an individual human being, an isolated unit, demonstrates far different characteristics when included in a community. He compared the disparate behavior of individual human beings and group human beings to the differences between the interaction of our cell structure, and the overall functioning of those cells contributing to who we are as individuals. According to Steinbeck, in letters and journal entries of the time, "When acting as a group men do not partake of their ordinary natures at all." In other words, when acting as a group we become "cells," contributing to a group organism, and become much altered from our individual identity. In a 1933 letter to CARLTON SHEFFIELD, Steinbeck stated that "[G]roups do not resemble the human atoms which compose them."

Unlike the more positive depictions of "group man" depicted in IN DUBIOUS BATTLE and THE GRAPES OF WRATH, wherein constructive goals impel the characters, Steinbeck unflinchingly confronts the aftermath of a vicious act of mass violence, and the response of one individual participant, Mike. From the start, it becomes clear that Mike is an ordinary human being. Nothing about him distinguishes him from the rest of humanity. He is not a psychopath or a crazed killer. Mike gets caught up in what he believes is an appropriate community response to the purported actions of a "nigger fiend." For Steinbeck, Mike's ideational motivation to join a lynch mob has no interest. Indeed, the actual lynching, though described in graphic terms as the story progresses, is not the core of the story. Not until the third paragraph does the reader understand a lynching has taken place. Rather, in Steinbeck's depiction, Mike's participation, his emotional and psychological response, and his self-satisfaction are typical of human group behavior, whether for good or ill, and it is the individual's connection to the group that carries weight for Steinbeck. Oddly, Mike is not a totally unsympathetic character.

CRITICAL SUMMARY

At the outset of the story, Mike finds himself enervated and detached from the violent events of the evening, despite his active participation, and he even protests mildly when stragglers attempt to mutilate the body of the hanged man by setting fire to his feet. For Mike justice has been done, and the efforts of "sneaky lawyers" to free the hanged man have been circumvented. But, he says, "it don't do no good to try to burn him." Mike retains a sense of skewed humanity and repugnance to unjustified cruelty without confronting his own injustice and cruelty.

As he makes his way home, Mike feels lonely and exhausted, having been separated from the camaraderie and exhilaration of the mob. Moreover, he realizes he had been injured slightly in the rush on the jail cell of the lynched man. Crushed by the weight of the crowd in its eagerness to seize the prisoner, Mike only becomes aware of the pain of strained muscles in his chest in the aftermath of the violence. He has been anesthetized by his actions. He seeks the affirmation of another human being in a bar empty of customers, and discovers that the bartender had witnessed the final moments of the hanging, and had rushed back to open up his saloon in the hope of selling whiskey and beer to thirsty participants.

Mike begins to relate the grotesque details of the night, treating the bartender almost as a father confessor. The bartender eagerly presses for more and more information, which Mike willingly supplies, of how an assemblage of outraged citizens, fueled by an afternoon of drinking, stormed the jail; of how the sheriff, after a token resistance, and fearful the mob might hang the wrong prisoner, gave directions to the correct cell; of how the vengeful crowd broke into the cell, and assaulted the prisoner, beating him into unconsciousness; and how the prisoner was then stripped of his clothes in a final act of degradation, before being dragged to a city park to be killed. Mike speculates that the blow to the prisoner's head during the struggle killed him before the lynching, perhaps giving himself a way to mitigate his participation. Then, in one of the most macabre parts of the story, Mike displays a souvenir from the evening's mayhem—a scrap of "torn blue denim" from the hanged man's pants. The bartender, desperate to feel part of the night's events, avidly encourages Mike to sell the scrap of cloth to hang on the wall behind the bar as a memento of the grisly occasion, because his customers "will like to look at it." Somewhat reluctantly, Mike accepts the exorbitant offer of two silver dollars, and a free beer.

Disappointed by the lack of customers other than Mike, the bartender closes the bar, and offers to walk part of the way home with Mike, since he lives only a couple of blocks away from Mike's home, and is still interested in further detail. Once again feeling lonely, Mike accepts the companionship. During the short walk, the two encounter a policeman walking a beat, and behaving as if nothing untoward had happened during the night, showing no interest in either Mike or the bartender. The bartender tentatively queries Mike about the guilt or innocence of the hanged man, saying, "I've known some pretty nice niggers." Mike protests that he, too, has known "some damn fine niggers" but that the newspapers had made clear this man had been a "fiend." Shortly before they separate, the bartender asks Mike what he felt during the lynching and afterwards, and Mike indicates he feels "cut off and tired, but kind of satisfied, too." The two part company in front of Mike's house, and when he enters his home, Mike's wife accuses of him of having been with another woman because of the look on his face. Mike scoffs and tells her to read the newspapers the next morning, but examining his face in a mirror, he realizes his wife's observation is completely accurate. Only sexual activity can compare to his experiences with the lynch mob, and his lassitude, sense of separation, yet curious contentment resemble a postcoital condition.

For Steinbeck the pleasure of group activity, whether as part of lynch mob as in "The Vigilante," or as part of a labor movement as in his "proletariat" fiction, impels us to join others of our species in collective behavior. We need the affirmation of others. We need to feel part of a crowd or an assembly, and participation in this activity changes us both subtly and profoundly.

EARLY CRITICISM

"The Vigilante" received widespread circulation with the publication of *The Long Valley*. Based as it was on an actual highly publicized event, the story's graphic brutality, yet oddly sensitive treatment of the central character, drew mostly positive attention from leading critics. In a column for the *Los Angeles Times*, Wilbur Needham commented on the strength of Steinbeck's "quietly bitter" and "shocking" presence which "takes command of 'The Vigilante.'" Elinor Davis, writing for the *Saturday Review*, said Steinbeck's stories were "packed with truth," and that "The Vigilante" was particularly notable for its veracity. Stanley Young, a critic for the *New York Times Book Review*, made note of Steinbeck's "directness of impression," and remarked on Steinbeck's ability to render Mike "so sympathetically understandable." In the *New Republic*, T. K. Whipple suggested that the vigilantes from the tale would "take their place in the immemorial spectacle of the ill fated race of men." Lastly, in a mixed review of *The Long Valley*, the critic for the *Times Literary Supplement* (London) described "The Vigilante" as pathological, but still praised Steinbeck's "extraordinary" artistry.

CONTEMPORARY PERSPECTIVES

As a stark portrayal of mob violence, and a fascinating psychological study, "The Vigilante" still draws attention. R. S. Hughes has noted that Steinbeck's "images of light and darkness . . . echo Mike's feelings" throughout the story. Other critics have noted that reality and dreams intermingle in Mike's consciousness. Lastly, John Timmerman stated that "The Vigilante" was a turning point for Steinbeck, in which he discovered the "difference between writing for himself or writing for an audience," and "the difference between philosophical exposition and art."

SYNOPSIS

A lynch mob slowly disperses and Mike, his excitement quickly falling, turns to walk home. He notices that a few men are lighting newspapers in an attempt to burn the dangling Negro's body. "That don't do no good," he says to a man who hurries away in the dark. Mike tries to record the scene in his memory, but he is too emotionally drained from the excitement. Walking through the dark town, a feeling of loneliness falls on him. He enters a bar for a drink and discusses the lynching with the bartender. Mike boasts that he was with the mob when they broke into the jail and dragged their victim out of his cell. He shows the man a torn piece of blue denim—a piece of the pants worn by the executed man. The bartender offers to buy the cloth so that he can hang it above his bar. Mike agrees to sell him half of the fragment, dividing it with a knife. Discovering that they live near one another, the two men decide to walk home together. The bartender asks Mike whether he could tell what kind of man the victim was. He admits that he could not tell, since the prisoner had been too still and quiet and resigned to his fate. He tells the bartender that a lynching makes a person tired, but satisfied at the same time. Mike's wife confronts him after he arrives home with the charge of being with another woman, because of the gratified look on his face. Mike dismisses her charge by explaining he had helped lynch a prisoner from the jail. He then looks at his face in the bathroom mirror, and realizes his expression suggests a sexual encounter.

FURTHER READING

Davis, Elinor. "The Steinbeck Country." *Saturday Review*, September 24, 1938, 11.
Hughes, R. S. "Steinbeck and the Art of Story Writing." In *The Steinbeck Question: New Essays in Criticism*,

edited by Donald Noble. Troy, N.Y.: Whitston Publishing, 1993, 37–50.

———. "Steinbeck, the Short Story Writer." In *Steinbeck's Short Stories in "The Long Valley": Essays in Criticism,* edited by Tetsumaro Hayashi. Steinbeck Monograph Series, No. 15. Muncie, Ind.: Ball State University Press, 1991, 78–89.

"The Long Valley." Times Literary Supplement, February 4, 1939, 75.

Needham, Wilbur. "New Steinbeck Book: Event of Autumn." *Los Angeles Times,* September 18, 1938, Part 3, 6.

Timmerman, John. Introduction to *The Long Valley,* by John Steinbeck. New York: Penguin, 1995, vii–xxx.

Whipple, T. K. "Steinbeck: Through a Glass, though Brightly." *New Republic,* October 12, 1938, 274–275.

Viva Zapata! (1952)

Steinbeck began researching a screenplay based on the life of the Mexican revolutionary leader Emiliano Zapata (1879–1919) while living in Cuernavaca, Mexico, in 1945. At the time he was writing his short novel, THE PEARL. Steinbeck made many trips to MEXICO, as well as STANFORD UNIVERSITY to research the life of the revolutionary. He produced a long manuscript, in reality a narrative history of the Mexican revolution, based loosely on Edgcumb Pinchon's book, *Zapata, the Unconquerable.* Steinbeck's narrative, often written in first person, gives many of the author's impressions and observations about Mexico at the time of the revolution, and lays down the general plot of the film. With the help of screenwriter Jules Buck, this initial work was later pared down to the *Viva Zapata!* screenplay, which was released in 1952 by Twentieth Century–Fox. The movie was a tremendous success, earning more than $3 million in its first month. The *Viva Zapata!* screenplay, as well as Steinbeck's original narrative essay on Emiliano Zapata, were subsequently edited with commentary by Robert E. Morsberger and published under the title *Zapata* by VIKING PRESS in 1975. It seems that

scholars of today have paid little attention to the literary values of this screenplay.

SYNOPSIS

Part One (Zapata: A Narrative, in Dramatic Form, of the Life of Emiliano Zapata)

(I)

Steinbeck presents a short summary of the history of the Spanish conquest of Mexico. The author describes the structure of the Aztec civilization and surmises that conquistador Hernán Cortés's greatest weapons were firearms, smallpox, and the Roman Catholic Church. Great landholdings are awarded to the men who fought in the conquests, while certain areas are reserved for the indigenous communities. A mestizo culture develops, creating a society of classes, with pureblooded Spaniards at the top, and Indians at the bottom. The author dwells on Mexico's long history of foreign occupation and the local effects of the American and French Revolutions.

(II)

The author details the political history of Mexico after it achieves independence from Spain. Under the Indian Benito Juárez, Mexico develops a constitution. Porfirio Díaz, "the Strongman of Mexico," becomes president and then de facto dictator for more than 34 years. He maintains power by tightly controlling the country's wealth and resources, forming an alliance with the powerful rural elite. He enforces his rule with a well-armed and violent police force, often stripping the Indians of their communal lands, which he subsequently distributes to his cronies. The Mexican people grow poorer and education disappears almost completely, except among the very rich. Steinbeck then describes the state of Morelos, south of Mexico City, the birthplace of Emiliano Zapata. He describes the inhabitants of Morelos as gentle and soft-spoken, but filled with energy. One of the largest cash crops in Morelos is sugarcane, and it is the co-optation of Indian lands for the production of sugarcane that leads to the outbreak of the Zapatista revolution. Steinbeck describes the typical Morelos town, as well as the splendor of the great haciendas, and compares the haciendas to medieval baronies.

(III)

For the benefit of the producer and the director, the author lists some of the customs, habits, costumes, and appearances of the people of the state of Morelos. He describes their clothing, hats, and tools, as well as the religious and social structures, the church and the town fair.

(IV)

The author lists some of the customs of small Mexican towns in the early 1900s, declaring that in many cases they have disappeared with the introduction of roads and electricity. He describes in detail the annual fairs held in each village, during which time the people come from all around to barter, celebrate, and attend religious services. The author discusses how various activities of the fair can be utilized in the film, and describes in detail the *corrida,* or bullfight, an activity never portrayed in the film. Emiliano Zapata came from the class of *charros,* or Mexican cowboys, and Steinbeck elaborates in great detail about their peculiarities, including their elegant habits of dress. Finally, the author devotes a lengthy section to a discussion of the *curandera,* or village healer, whom Steinbeck envisions as being an important character in the film, but who is excluded in the final screenplay.

(V)

Steinbeck writes about the force that the Zapata legend still carries in Mexico, as well as his controversial place in Mexican history. He proposes omitting using names of the important figures in the film to avoid the political problems that might arise from offending powerful people who are still living. The remainder of *Zapata* is a lengthy narrative interspersed with cultural observations and suggestions for the direction and production of the film. With the help of Jules Beck, who was hired by the producer specifically for the job, the text was ultimately cut and condensed into the final screenplay, and will therefore not be included here.

Part Two (Viva Zapata! The Screenplay)

A group of peasants from the state of Morelos arrives at the presidential palace to plead before President Díaz for the return of their communal lands. The president listens to their case and assures

them that he will remand their complaint to the courts. He urges them to go back to their village to verify the boundary stones that mark the land. Emiliano Zapata comes forward and asks for the president's authority to cross the fences that have been erected so that they might verify the boundaries. Díaz tells them that he does not have the authority to do such a thing. As the group leaves, the president asks the name of the outspoken man. He carefully circles it on a list, making sure that Zapata understands the implied threat.

Zapata leads a large group of villagers to the fences that have been erected on their lands. He orders that the barriers be cut. The villagers enter, searching for the boundary stones. Suddenly a group of mounted *rurales* (local police) charges toward the group. As the villagers retreat, they are cut down by a machine gun. They attempt to capture Zapata, but he escapes.

A young man, Fernando Aguirre, seeks Zapata out in his hidden encampment. He tells him that Francisco Madero is leading a fight against Díaz and he invites Zapata to join. Zapata sends his man Pablo to Texas to seek out Madero and find out if he is trustworthy.

Zapata sneaks into town to meet Josefa, the daughter of a shopkeeper, whom he wishes to marry. Josefa refuses his proposal, saying that she wants to marry a rich man who can protect her.

Zapata takes a job on the hacienda of Don Nacio. He whips the stable manager for beating a hungry peasant boy whom he has caught stealing the mash which is fed to the horses. Don Nacio breaks up the fight and warns Zapata that he cannot be the conscience of the world.

Pablo returns from Texas with Fernando. They bring a message from Madero instructing Zapata to organize an army. Zapata refuses. The men come upon a group of mounted police dragging an old man behind their horses. Zapata unsuccessfully tries to free the man, who is dragged behind the horses and killed.

Zapata asks Josefa's father, Señor Espejo, for his daughter's hand in marriage. Espejo rejects the proposal, because the suitor has no land and no money. When the angry Zapata leaves the store, he is captured and taken into custody by the *rurales.* A

Marlon Brando (right) as Emiliano Zapata rejecting the reward his brother Eufemio (Anthony Quinn) tries to pin on his suit in the 1952 film *Viva Zapata!* *(Photofest)*

group of peasants surrounds the column of soldiers and frees Zapata.

(Here the film differs from the published screenplay, which has Zapata approaching Don Nacio for help in restoring the village lands. When Nacio fails, Zapata's men ambush a contingent of federal troops leading a mule train.)

Zapata's men ambush a troop train, killing the soldiers and taking the supplies. The rebels then dynamite the citadel of a garrison town. The villagers hold a party to celebrate their victory. One by one, they approach Zapata to congratulate him and offer him gifts. A guerrilla fighter tells of a young boy who has captured a federal machine gun. Zapata offers the boy a reward for his courage.

The boy asks for Zapata's favorite stallion, which the revolutionary reluctantly surrenders. Señor Espejo announces that Madero has made Zapata a general, and he offers him his daughter Josefa's hand.

Zapata is paying a formal visit to his fiancée when word arrives that Díaz has fled the country. Madero requests that Zapata join him in the capitol. Zapata confesses to Josefa that he is ashamed to go because he does not know how to read.

Madero offers Zapata a ranch as a reward for his service, but Zapata refuses, demanding that the new president restore the village lands to the people. Madero assures him that he will do it, but in good time. He orders Zapata to disarm his troops now that the war is won. Zapata warns the president that his men will never relinquish their weapons because they must defend themselves. General Huerta warns Madero that Zapata must be killed.

Madero visits Zapata and convinces his men to turn in their arms. Zapata's brother Eufemio warns them that Huerta is arriving with troops. Madero is bewildered. He assures Zapata that there must be some mistake. Zapata's men ambush Huerta's force.

Madero is held prisoner by Huerta in the presidential palace. Huerta has the president executed. Meanwhile, Zapata reluctantly executes his friend Pablo, who was seen consorting with the enemy.

Pancho Villa sends word that he has defeated Huerta. The exhausted Zapata returns home to rest and be with Josefa.

(Here the published screenplay again departs from the film: In the screenplay Pablo's widow steals into the Zapata house and tries to stab Josefa, whose hand is wounded in the skirmish. The anguished Zapata cries that the killing must stop. Zapata takes pity on the widow and frees her.)

Zapata and Villa meet in the capitol to determine the future of the republic. Villa appoints the unwilling Zapata president.

Zapata sits in the palace judging cases. A contingent from his village arrives to complain that Zapata's brother, Eufemio, has forced them off their land and killed one of them. He grows angry with one of the men's impertinence, and is slowly circling his name on a list, exactly as Díaz once did with him, when he realizes that he is becoming the same kind of man he fought to defeat. He abandons the presidency, and returns to Morelos, where he confronts his brother, who is killed by the jealous husband of his mistress.

A staff of army officers determines that Zapata must be killed.

(Here the published screenplay departs from the film: Fernando convinces an old colonel, Guajardo, to set a trap for Zapata by convincing him that he has switched sides, and wishes to join the rebel army.)

Guajardo sends word that he wishes to join Zapata's rebel army. He offers to bring badly needed troops and stores of ammunition with him. As proof of his loyalty, he kills a corrupt police chief. Zapata decides to meet with the man. Josefa has a premonition that it is a trap and she begs her husband not to go. Zapata ignores his wife's pleading, telling her that he must go, because his forces are desperate for arms and ammunition.

Zapata and a few of his men ride to the ruined hacienda at Chinameca to meet with Guajardo. Outside the building, they greedily examine the piles of weapons and ammunition that they so badly need. Inside the hacienda, Guajardo is holding Zapata's lost white stallion. Zapata asks the colonel where he found the missing horse. Guajardo tells him it was in the possession of a federal officer that he killed, and he offers the horse to Zapata as a sign of friendship. Zapata walks happily to the stallion, which nuzzles him in recognition. Guajardo raises his arm and a barrage of bullets rain down on Zapata, who is knocked to the ground by the force of the lead pouring into him. He is killed instantly. The horse bolts and escapes through the hacienda gate.

Zapata's body lies bleeding in the sun. A federal general warns Guajardo that sometimes a man is more dangerous dead than alive. Fernando understands his point and orders that Zapata's body be dumped in the town plaza so that the people will see that he is indeed dead. The soldiers dump the body, and the village women gather around to compose it and decorate it with flowers. An old man approaches and inspects the body. He announces that it is not Zapata. He claims that Zapata must have escaped into the mountains and that if they ever need him he will come back. The men look up and see Zapata's white stallion running off in the distance.

THE FILM: *VIVA ZAPATA!* (MGM, 1952)

Screenplay: John Steinbeck
Director: Elia Kazan
Producer: Darryl Zanuck
Emiliano Zapata: Marlon Brando
Josefa Zapata: Jean Peters
Eufemio: Anthony Quinn
Fernando: Joseph Wiseman
Don Nacio: Arnold Moss
Pancho Villa: Alan Reed

Soldadera: Margo
Madero: Harold Gordon
Pablo: Lou Gilbert
Señora Espejo: Mildred Dunnock
Huerta: Frank Silvera
Captain: Abner Biberman
Señor Espejo: Florenz Ames
Old General: Richard Garrick
President Díaz: Fay Roope

The film received five ACADEMY AWARD nominations, including for best screenplay (Steinbeck) and for best actor (Marlon Brando), Anthony Quinn won the award for best supporting actor. In a review in the *New York Times* on February 8, 1952, Thomas Pryor wrote that, despite its flaws and lack of historical accuracy, the movie "throbs with a rare vitality, and a masterful picture of a nation in revolutionary torment has been got by director ELIA KAZAN."

The Wayward Bus (1947)

Steinbeck's 16th novel, *The Wayward Bus* is the allegorical tale of a group of unlikely passengers traveling across the California countryside in a battered old bus. When the bus suddenly breaks down, each of the passengers is forced to confront his desires or frustrations. VIKING PRESS published the book in 1947. It was the first novel that Steinbeck dictated to a tape recorder instead of writing by hand.

Steinbeck intended the novel to be a character study similar, in some respects, to the examination of human reaction to adversity he developed in *LIFEBOAT*. In both works, a group of diverse people, isolated by circumstance, is forced to interact and cooperate in order to resolve a dilemma. The characters in *The Wayward Bus* do not face the jeopardy of wartime, as was the case in *Lifeboat,* but they do have to face their strengths and weaknesses, and either succeed or fall by the wayside. In this depiction, Steinbeck intended to portray a universal human journey through life.

EARLY CRITICISM

Early critics of *The Wayward Bus* often disagreed as to whether the novel offered the reader anything

different from the writer's previous works, though most noted that the book was the first full-length novel after THE GRAPES OF WRATH. Harrison Smith, writing for *Saturday Review,* lauds Steinbeck's accomplishment in presenting "the natural man" and "the natural woman" in the novel. In Smith's view the character Juan Chicoy is no longer the kind of underdog Steinbeck usually depicts; instead, Steinbeck's new character is "Everyman" with all the qualities of the *"homo simplicimus"*— love, desires, passion, and sexual urges. *The Wayward Bus* is such a change that Smith views it as totally different from Steinbeck's previous novels. According to Smith, the new novel does not possess "the tenderness of THE PASTURES OF HEAVEN and TORTILLA FLAT" or "the fierce brutality in *Of Mice and Men,*" nor does it present bitter social and political disputes as IN DUBIOUS BATTLE and *The Grapes of Wrath.* Different as it may be, Smith firmly believes that *The Wayward Bus* is still a genuine story by a writer "as distinctively American as Mark Twain."

Other reviews were mixed. Bernard de Voto of the *New York Herald Tribune* praised Steinbeck's "unsentimental detachment," while J. M. Lalley of the *New Yorker* called it a "sermonizing" book, in which the characters "are not definite individuals, like Ma Joad, for example, or Casy the Preacher, but personified generalities." Some negative reviewers evaluated the book from a moralistic perspective. For instance, reviewing *The Wayward Bus* for the *Atlantic* (March 1947), Edward Weeks writes that the intensified examination of sex in the book is "forced" and "tedious." In reviewing the novel, Weeks, who acknowledges that he may sound like a puritan, pays special attention to Steinbeck's portraits of the five noticeable women in this book and expresses disapproval with his work.

CONTEMPORARY PERSPECTIVES

Regrettably contemporary study of *The Wayward Bus* has been slim. Probably the most scholarly study of the novel is Brian Railsback's "*The Wayward Bus:* Misogyny or Sexual Selection?" included in *After The Grapes of Wrath: Essays on John Steinbeck* (1995). Disapproving of Harrison Smith's opinions, Railsback views *The Wayward Bus* as Steinbeck's extended biological perspective into human relations as seen in *In Dubious Battle* and other previous works by the writer. The only difference, as Railsback would argue, is that the novel uses sexual relations to illustrate Darwin's theory of sexual selection. According to Railsback, a significant aspect of *The Wayward Bus* is its "cold measurement" of the characters by their control over human biological instinct.

SYNOPSIS

Chapter 1
Rebel Corners is a rural crossroads where Juan Chicoy owns and operates a restaurant–service station and bus route. Kit "Pimples" Carson assists him. Juan's wife, Alice Chicoy, runs the lunchroom with the help of Norma, a daydreaming 19-year-old who is secretly in love with the movie star, Clark Gable.

Chapter 2
Juan Chicoy and Pimples repair the bus, "Sweetheart," which broke down the previous morning, stranding its passengers at Rebel Corners. Having given up their beds to the stranded passengers, the Chicoys, Pimples, and Norma have spent a restless night sleeping in chairs. While they work, Pimples asks Juan to call him "Kit." Juan agrees, wondering why he has never realized the youth's aversion to his nickname.

Chapter 3
Alice has a capricious temper. She is angry with Juan for surrendering their bed to the stranded passengers. She forces back her anger for fear that Juan will hit her, or worse, that he will leave her. It begins to rain suddenly and heavily. Ernest Horton, a novelty salesman, enters limping and grunting in exaggerated pain. Elliot Pritchard comes out of the bedroom and orders breakfast for his wife. He is taking his family to MEXICO, a vacation that he does not really want to take. Alice refuses to serve breakfast in the bedroom. Ernest continues limping and complaining. He unlaces his shoe to reveal three horribly crushed toes. Delighted by the horror on his unsuspecting audience's face, he laughs gleefully and removes the "Little Wonder Artificial Sore Foot," one of his novelty products. Mr. Pritchard admiringly buys a half dozen.

Chapter 4
Norma is in her bedroom when Mr. Horton returns to remove his suitcase. She asks him to deliver a letter from her to Clark Gable, who she claims is her cousin. The starry-eyed girl recounts a fantastic story about her life among the stars in Hollywood. Mr. Horton is awed by the naked intensity of her lie, and he agrees to take the letter. Alice finds them alone in the bedroom and accuses Mr. Horton of making a pass at the young girl. She advances on Norma with doubled fists, but is stopped by Juan, who leads his hysterical wife to the bedroom and puts her to bed.

Chapter 5
The rain stops and the sky clears. Ernest Norton explains his invention to Mr. Pritchard: a kit to convert a dark suit into a tuxedo. Mr. Pritchard admires the idea and suggests that the two men do business together. Van Brunt, a bitter old farmer, arrives at the restaurant. He warns that with all the rain, the San Ysidro River is rising and threatening to wash out the bridge. Juan calls Breed's Service Station at the bridge crossing and learns that the bridge is all right.

Chapter 6
Alice broods over the incident with Norma. She is surprised by Juan's gentleness with her and thinks that it is a sign that he no longer cares for her. She suspects that Juan is attracted to one of the Pritchard women. She decides to get drunk as soon as Juan leaves with the bus.

Chapter 7
In San Ysidro, Louie prepares to load the passengers and baggage aboard his large Greyhound bus. He sets his sights on a beautiful young woman, whom he attempts to pick up. The woman is Camille Oaks (not her real name), a stripper and prostitute who is returning to Los Angeles. She is accustomed to men like Louie and expertly rebuffs his advances, getting off the bus in Rebel Corners.

Chapter 8
Juan and Pimples unload a shipment of pies from the Greyhound bus. They watch the beautiful Miss Oaks with admiration. Juan suggests that perhaps Pimples would like to accompany him on the run to

San Juan de la Cruz. Mr. Pritchard suspects that he has seen the woman somewhere before. He asks Camille if they have met somewhere. She realizes that he must have seen her perform at a stag party and she replies nervously that she is a dental nurse. Norma becomes suspicious at Alice's long absence from the lunchroom. She goes to her bedroom where she finds Alice rummaging through her personal belongings. Outraged, Norma quits, packs her suitcase, and boards the bus. Pimples puts on his best suit and saddle oxfords for the trip. Alice is nervous about the blonde Miss Oaks, and she watches her husband warily. Juan wonders why he stays with Alice, concluding that it is because she is the only woman outside of Mexico that knows how to cook beans properly, and because she loved him. He loads the passengers and drives toward San Juan de la Cruz. The sky is pregnant with rain.

Chapter 9

Norma and Camille fall into deep conversation. Norma can barely contain her excitement when she learns that Camille is from Los Angeles. She suggests that they rent an apartment together. Camille basks in Norma's admiration, but is non-committal. Mildred Pritchard, the Pritchards' daughter, is attracted to Juan. She feels a deep jealousy as she observes him watching the blonde in the mirror. Mr. Pritchard moves closer to Camille on the pretext of discussing the tuxedo idea with Mr. Horton. The businessman's enthusiasm arouses Mr. Horton's suspicion. He decides to patent his idea as soon as he gets to Los Angeles.

Chapter 10

Mr. Breed, the owner of Breed's General Store, nervously watches the San Ysidro River. He fears that its rising waters may be too much for the simple wooden bridge, which is already straining under the weight of the water.

Chapter 11

Alice Chicoy is relieved to be alone at Rebel Corners. She closes the lunchroom and proceeds to get thoroughly drunk. As she drinks she talks to her reflection in a mirror, examining the disappointments of her life and worrying over her relationship with Juan.

Chapter 12

Mr. Breed and Juan examine the bridge and decide that it is dangerous to cross. Juan is feeling restless. He tells Mr. Breed how his father fought with Pancho Villa and how one day he did not return home, an idea that appeals to him. Juan determines to let the passengers decide whether to proceed or go back to San Ysidro.

Chapter 13

Camille teaches Norma how to make up her face, creating a startling transformation. Van Brunt suggests that they avoid the bridge in favor of the old road to San Juan de la Cruz. Everyone agrees, and the group climbs aboard the bus.

Chapter 14

The old road is slippery with mud. Juan fantasizes about escaping and going to Mexico. The idea gives him pleasure and a sense of freedom. He resolves to turn his fate over to Virgin of Guadalupe: If the bus makes it to San Juan de la Cruz he will continue his life as usual, but if the bus becomes stuck, he will disappear and never go back to Alice. Pimples stares at the newly made-up Norma. He wonders why he has never noticed her before. Norma tells Camille about her fantasy of marrying Clark Gable. Camille is disgusted by Norma's naïveté and decides to dump her as soon as possible. Juan continues to fantasize about Mexico. He wonders what had kept him for so long in Rebel Corners. He speeds up recklessly, causing the bus to slide into a ditch, and then he spins the wheels to ensure that the bus is stuck. High above the stranded bus is a steep cliff painted with the ominous word "Repent." Juan offers to walk out and send a car back for the stranded passengers. Exhausted and feeling guilty about what he has just done, he walks to an abandoned farm and falls asleep in a pile of old hay.

Chapter 15

Bernice Pritchard attacks her husband for traveling by bus. She screams that the money they are wasting would have better been used to build the orchid house that she has coveted for so long. Mrs. Pritchard becomes afraid that she has spoiled her chances of getting her orchid house. Mildred leaves the bus in disgust and follows Juan's footprints. Mrs. Pritchard eavesdrops with excited interest while Camille tells Norma the story of how her friend Loraine got a mink coat out of her boyfriend by provoking him to hit her, and then making him feel sorry for his anger.

Chapter 16

Mildred fantasizes about running away and leaving her controlling parents behind. She follows Juan's muddy tracks to the abandoned farm where she finds him sleeping in the barn. Juan awakens to find her watching him. She tells Juan her dream of escape. She falls into his arms and they make love in the straw.

Chapter 17

Pimples and Mr. Pritchard make a bed for Mrs. Pritchard in a nearby cave. Ernest attacks Mr. Pritchard's hypocrisy. Mr. Pritchard feels the venom of Mr. Horton's words. He returns to the bus and invites Camille to talk with him outside. He proposes that she come and work for him as a receptionist. Camille lays into Mr. Pritchard for being too cowardly to say that he wants to go to bed with her. She tells him that he recognizes her because she performed a striptease at his club and then storms away. Mr. Pritchard walks to the cave where his wife is resting and rapes her. When he leaves her, she stops crying and a look of fierceness comes over her face. She carefully slashes her cheek with her fingernails, rubbing dirt in the resulting wound.

Chapter 18

Mildred and Juan leave the barn. The rain has stopped and the sun is shining beautifully. As they walk hand in hand back toward the bus to dig it out, Juan admits that he planned to abandon the passengers and run away to Mexico. They realize that their brief affair is over, and they say good-bye.

Chapter 19

Van Brunt lies in the bus thinking about the two recent strokes that have left him very afraid. He remembers how his father died of the same condition after lingering for 11 months in a state of paralysis, leaving his family penniless. He thinks of his failed resolve to commit suicide by taking cyanide. Suddenly, he is stricken by another stroke that leaves him paralyzed on the bus seat.

Chapter 20

Norma fights off Pimples's sexual advances. When he calls Camille a tramp, Norma flies into a raging defense of her friend, and chases Pimples off the bus.

Chapter 21

Mildred and Juan return and organize the passengers to dig out the bus. Mr. Pritchard takes care of Van Brunt while he silently punishes himself for attacking his wife. He resolves to build the largest orchid house money can buy for her.

Chapter 22

While Juan drives the bus slowly onward, Mrs. Pritchard fantasizes about the lovely orchid house that her husband will now build her in his guilt. Mr. Pritchard looks at Van Brunt and hates him because he is dying. He feels ashamed for his thoughts. Ernest apologizes for his outburst and the two agree that they might be able to do business together. Norma silently wishes that Camille would agree to live with her. San Juan appears in the distance.

CHARACTERS AND PLACES

Breed's General Store   A small grocery store and gas station in *The Wayward Bus*. It sits next to a wooden bridge that crosses the San Ysidro River between Rebel Corners and San Juan de la Cruz, California, and is run by Mr. and Mrs. Breed, the unofficial custodians of the bridge. An old friend of Juan Chicoy, Mr. Breed suggests that, because of the rising river, the bridge is too dangerous to drive the bus across.

Brunt, Van   A character in *The Wayward Bus*, Van Brunt is a tall, stooped old man who continuously complains to Juan Chicoy on the route to San Juan de la Cruz. Van Brunt has recently suffered from a series of mild strokes that left his hands numb and make him pantingly attracted to young women and even little girls. He is paralyzed by a stroke in the back seat of the bus.

Carson, Kit "Pimples"   A character in *The Wayward Bus*, Pimples Carson is Juan Chicoy's assistant at the Rebel Corners service station. A lank and slender-waisted boy of 17, he eats sweets incessantly and is obsessed by the terrible acne that ravages his face. Pimples asks Juan Chicoy to call him Kit, instead of "Pimples," after the famous explorer Kit Carson who led several expeditions to California and who Pimples claims was a distant relative. On the bus to San Juan de la Cruz he makes a crude sexual advance to Norma, the ex-waitress at Rebel Corners.

Chicoy, Alice   A character in *The Wayward Bus*, Alice is a middle-aged, wide-hipped and sag-chested cook and waitress at the Rebel Corners lunchroom. She is married to Juan Chicoy, whom she loves passionately. Alice lives in fear that her husband will hit, or worse, leave her, for she is convinced that he has left other women. She fights viciously with her waitress, Norma, who discovers her reading her private correspondence. Left alone for the afternoon of the bus trip, Alice closes the restaurant and gets drunk.

Chicoy, Juan   A character in *The Wayward Bus*, Juan Chicoy is the owner and operator of the service station and lunchroom at Rebel Corners, where he lives with his wife, Alice Chicoy. Juan presides over the garage and gas pumps when he is not running the bus service between Rebel Corners and San Juan de la Cruz. When his bus gets stuck in the mud, Juan resolves to abandon his passengers and his wife and run away to Mexico. He walks to an abandoned farmhouse where Mildred Pritchard catches and seduces him. Finally abandoning his plan to run away, he digs out the bus and delivers his passengers safely to their destination.

Horton, Ernest   A character in *The Wayward Bus*, Ernest is a recently discharged veteran and traveling salesman of novelty products who is stranded at Rebel Corners when Juan Chicoy's bus breaks down. He has a sharp face with bright questioning eyes. He had once been married, but on the

Joan Collins and Rick Jason as Alice and Juan Chicoy in the 1957 film *The Wayward Bus* (*Photofest*)

second day he walked out. He describes his idea for a kit that converts black suits into tuxedos to Elliot Pritchard. He attacks Mr. Pritchard for being dishonest and opportunistic.

Loraine A character in *The Wayward Bus*, Loraine is a friend and ex-roommate of Camille Oaks. A hustler and talented manipulator of men. Loraine gets a mink coat out of her boyfriend by provoking him to hit her and then making him feel remorse for his anger.

Louie A character in *The Wayward Bus*, Louie is a stout driver of the southbound Greyhound bus that stops at Rebel Corners. He fails in his attempts to seduce Camille Oaks.

McElroy, "Mac" A character in *The Wayward Bus*, Mac is a farmer in the San Juan Valley. McElroy's prize bull is washed away and drowned when the San Ysidro River floods its banks.

Norma A character in *The Wayward Bus*, Norma is a waitress at the Rebel Corners lunchroom. A plain, lonely young girl with a flat chest and skinny legs, she is madly in love with Clark Gable and dreams of moving to Hollywood and becoming an actress. She quits her job when she discovers Alice Chicoy reading her private letters. On the bus to San Juan de la Cruz she is befriended by Camille Oaks, with whom she dreams of sharing an apartment. She fights off the advances of hot-blooded Pimples Carson.

Oaks, Camille The alias used by the beautiful blonde prostitute and stripper in *The Wayward Bus*. She has a lovely body and widely set blue eyes. Married women always hate her, and men always find her irresistible, a fact that causes her many problems but which she has learned to use to make a living. She dodges the advances of a portly Greyhound driver on the way to Rebel Corners. When Juan Chicoy's bus gets stuck in the mud, she is stranded with Elliot Pritchard, a businessman who recognizes her from a stag performance. When Mr. Pritchard offers her a job, she rejects him saying that he is only trying to seduce her.

Pritchard, Bernice Elliot Pritchard's wife in *The Wayward Bus*. A rather pretty woman with a straight nose and violet-colored, myopic eyes, she is feminine and dainty and completely asexual. She laboriously maintains the illusion of a perfect marriage while manipulating her husband's every action. She and her family are on their way to a vacation in Mexico when their bus gets stuck in the wilderness, and Mr. Pritchard rapes her. She resolves to use the incident to force her husband to build her the orchid house she has always dreamed of.

Pritchard, Elliot The president of a medium-sized corporation in *The Wayward Bus*, Elliot Pritchard dresses and looks like a successful businessman. A man of set opinions, he is comfortable only among men of his own kind. He is thoroughly controlled and manipulated by his wife, Bernice Pritchard. He advises Ernest Norton on his idea for making a kit to turn a dark suit into a tuxedo. He recognizes Camille Oaks, but does not realize that he saw her do a striptease at a stag party. When he offers Camille a job in his business, she rejects him, saying that the job offer is just a plan to seduce her. Pritchard reacts by raping his wife in a cave where they have taken shelter. He is wracked by remorse and vows to build her a large orchid house.

Pritchard, Mildred A character in *The Wayward Bus*, Mildred is a pretty and intellectual girl who seeks to free herself from her parents' smothering embrace. She and her family are on their way to a vacation in Mexico when their bus gets stuck in the wilderness. She follows the bus driver, Juan Chicoy, to an abandoned farm and seduces him.

Rebel Corners A crossroad 42 miles south of San Ysidro, California, on the north-south highway in *The Wayward Bus*. Graced by great white oaks that grew around the garage and restaurant, Rebel Corners was named after the efforts of the Blanken family, who started a blacksmithy there in the last century. The Blankens were proud, violent Kentuckians. When California sided with the Union during the Civil War, they announced the secession of their 160 acres, defending it proudly until the end of the war. The Blankens later lost Rebel Corners to foreclosure. The land changed hands many times until it was converted into a service station and lunchroom run by Juan Chicoy and his wife, as well as the bus station for the line running between Rebel Corners and San Juan de la Cruz.

San Juan de la Cruz   A small town in the great San Juan Valley in *The Wayward Bus.* Juan Chicoy drives the bus route between San Juan de la Cruz and his service station at Rebel Corners.

San Ysidro River   This river in *The Wayward Bus* runs through the San Juan Valley until it discharges in the Pacific Ocean at Black Rock Bay. The river floods, forcing Juan Chicoy to make the detour in his bus route that results in the bus getting stuck.

Sweetheart   Sweetheart is Juan Chicoy's old four-cylinder bus that he drives daily between Rebel Corners and San Juan de la Cruz in *The Wayward Bus.* Sweetheart has been rebuilt and painted with aluminum paint. The inside is upholstered in red oilcloth. The oaken floorboards are scooped and polished by the feet of passengers. Hanging from the top of the windshield are Juan Chicoy's icons: a baby's shoe for protection; a tiny boxing glove for power; a plastic kewpie doll for the pleasures of the flesh. In the center of the dashboard stands a small metal Virgin of Guadalupe.

Virgin of Guadalupe   The patron saint of Mexico and Juan Chicoy's personal saint in *The Wayward Bus.* A small metal statue of the Virgin sits on the dashboard of Mr. Chicoy's bus, Sweetheart.

THE FILM: *THE WAYWARD BUS* (TWENTIETH CENTURY–FOX, 1957)

Based on the novel by John Steinbeck

Screenplay: Ivan Moffat
Director: Victor Vicas
Producer: Charles Brackett
Johnny Chicoy: Rick Jason

Alice Chicoy: Joan Collins
Camille: Jayne Mansfield
Ernest Horton: Dan Dailey
Norma: Betty Lou Keim
Mildred Pritchard: Dolores Michaels
Mr. Pritchard: Larry Keating
Morse: Robert Bray
Mrs. Pritchard: Kathryn Givney

Twentieth Century–Fox, perhaps with hope of repeating its previous year's success with Marilyn Monroe on a bus (*Bus Stop*), released this movie in 1957 with Jayne Mansfield as the blonde bombshell on a bus stranded in the middle of nowhere. The cast was unremarkable, the acting overdone, and the special effects laughable. The movie garnered neither popular nor critical success.

FURTHER READING

Lalley, J. M. "Books." *New Yorker,* February 22, 1947, 87–90.

Railsback, Brian. "*The Wayward Bus:* Misogyny or Sexual Selection?" In *After The Grapes of Wrath: Essays on John Steinbeck,* edited by Donald V. Coers, Paul D. Ruffin, and Robert J. DeMott. Athens: Ohio University Press, 1995, 125–135.

Steinbeck, John. *The Wayward Bus.* New York: Viking, 1947.

Smith, Harrison. "John Steinbeck Does It Again." *Saturday Review,* February 15, 1947, 14–15.

de Voto, Bernard. "Books." *New York Herald Tribune Books,* February 16, 1947, 1.

Weeks, Edward. "California Bus Ride." *Atlantic,* March 1947, 126, 128.

"The White Quail" (1935)

Steinbeck's short story "The White Quail" first appeared in print in *North American Review* magazine in 1935. It was subsequently reprinted in the collection of short stories, THE LONG VALLEY, published by VIKING PRESS in 1938. Throughout Steinbeck's works, his characters identify with the land and view it as a living entity. From Joseph Wayne to Tom Joad to Ethan Hawley, the land

and nature are central to their understanding of themselves, and to their patterns of behavior. In "The White Quail," Mary Teller's identification with the land, as symbolized by her garden and the creatures within, cannot be separated from her own consciousness and her own sense of worth and identity.

Mary's garden is not the rugged landscape of other Steinbeck settings. It is totally contrived and artificial, a bulwark against the intrusion of a much wilder and more natural countryside at the edge of her property, and a metaphor for her withdrawal from real life into an idealized fantasy. It also presents a contrast between the artificiality of a civilized life, and its attendant solipsism; and the attraction of a less contrived, more natural existence. Steinbeck explores as well the ramifications of modern relationships, in which man and woman have no communication, and no shared attraction. Indeed, Harry Teller and Mary share only space and a mutual misperception of the other. Nothing in the story indicates the two ever share a bed.

CRITICAL SUMMARY

From her childhood, Mary has dreamed of a perfect garden. She has made elaborate plans for a particular piece of property on the outskirts of town since adolescence, and only accepts Harry's marriage proposal because the future "garden seemed to like him." Harry is drawn to Mary with promises of future kisses, and because "She is very pretty." From the beginning, he does not recognize the strength of her obsession, and she refuses to acknowledge his sexual hunger for her. She sends him away after accepting his proposal, and spends her evening as a new fiancée penning her future married name in a copybook, writing "Mary Teller" far more often than "Mrs. Harry E. Teller," already establishing her separation from her future husband.

Before the marriage takes place, Harry purchases the lot Mary had identified as the perfect location and a house is built. The two marry, move into the new home, and Mary begins the construction of her faultless garden. She excludes Harry from every aspect of the planning, the planting, and the choice of plants. At one point she politely offers

him some input, and is relieved when he demurs, saying he is happy she has such a nice pastime. Afterward, she expresses the hope that nothing will ever be changed in her utopian horticultural design. The couple's only shared activities are ridding the garden of pests, with Harry doing the "actual killing" while Mary excitedly directs the hunt; and entertaining Harry's clients. Each has a separate bedroom, and Mary routinely keeps the door to her room locked. Harry turns the doorknob almost every night, making as little noise as possible, and Mary ignores the surreptitious hint. Instead, she turns off the light, and admires the view of the garden through the window in the moonlight.

Eventually, the communication between Harry and Mary breaks down entirely. Mary distances herself from her husband so completely that she begins to imagine an alternative persona. There is the Mary of the House, sitting quietly in an armchair in the marital companionship of Harry, and the Mary of the Garden, spiritual and noncorporeal, observing the Mary of the House through the dormer window. Harry initially has very little conception of his wife's peculiarities. Aside from the lack of sexual congress, he is pleased with her feminine skills and with her attractive appearance. Increasingly he grows frustrated by her obsession with the garden, and her coldness to his need for warmth and companionship. Mary even refuses Harry's request for a dog, because of the potential damage a puppy might do to her carefully laid out garden plot.

Matters come to a head when the inexorable forces of nature intervene. Almost concurrently, a white quail and a gray cat enter Mary's sanctuary. Mary immediately identifies her own being with the white quail—a symbol of purity and of inviolability—though Harry calls the bird a freak of nature. The gray cat stalks the birds, and in hysteria, Mary demands that Harry poison the cat to protect the white quail. He refuses and instead suggests he will use an air gun to stun the cat and scare it permanently away from the garden. Before dawn the next day, Harry takes up a position in the garden with the gun. The gray cat never appears; instead the flock of quail emerge from the brush and approach the garden pond. Harry raises his weapon and shoots a white quail, killing it with a BB shot below its right eye. He carefully hides the bird's carcass in the wild undergrowth behind the house, and then tells Mary he has dealt with the threat from the gray cat. At the close, Harry must come to terms with the nature of his actions. He has killed his wife, symbolically.

Steinbeck's symbolism and metaphor are not very subtle in this story. Even the names of the central characters suggest Steinbeck's intent. Mary, whose name comes from the Virgin Mary, and Harry, whose name suggests a hirsute primitive, establish an irresolvable conflict. Purity versus primordial passion, both tempered by civilizing influences, set up a tension from the beginning. Mary's purity is compromised by her willingness to allow kisses from her husband when he pleases her. Harry bows to convention in both the pursuit of his wife, and in his expression of remorse when he kills the white quail. Harry stalks his wife the way the gray cat stalks the white quail, the essence of Mary's spirit, when he turns the doorknob to her room every night. The garden represents their marriage and Mary's rejection of the pain of life. She recalls forbidden treats sent to her by her father in his travels, and the announcement of his death, and determines never again to expose herself to the ordinary troubles of life, including conjugal relations, and childbirth. Her garden keeps her isolated from her husband and from life. Harry remarks on Mary's strength and untouchability, but both are based on her ability to detach herself from reality.

As a character in the larger collection of short stories in *The Long Valley*, Mary Teller is often compared and contrasted with Elisa Allen in "THE CHRYSANTHEMUMS." Both women have an obsession with their gardens, and both live estranged from their husbands. However, Elisa Allen lives in the present, and she is not delusional. Mary lives in an almost platonic realm, wherein she creates an idealized world, and refuses to accept any deviation from her construct. She is "unnatural" in the face of nature, whether it is the ebb and flow of life and death, or the natural progression of human relationships. Mary's efforts to control her environment absolutely, whether in her marriage or in her garden, lead inevitably to disappointment.

EARLY CRITICISM

Perhaps because of Steinbeck's unusual treatment of a woman as a protagonist, reactions to "The White Quail" were mixed. William Soskin from the *New York Herald Tribune* called Steinbeck's characterization of Mary, "synthetic and psychologically phony," and suggested that Steinbeck should confine himself to "mothers, ranch wives, eccentrics and clods." Harry Hansen, writing for the *New York World Telegram*, praised *The Long Valley* overall, but said "The White Quail" was "artificial and not impressive." Clifton Fadiman, the critic for the *New Yorker*, noted that the story was "beautifully written," but that Steinbeck was "trying a mite too hard to be sensitive and Open to Beauty." The only unqualified praise came from Stanley Young writing for the *New York Times Book Review*. Mr. Young marveled at the story's "delicacy and symbolism and design" and further remarked on the "subtlety and grace unlike anything Steinbeck has yet written."

CONTEMPORARY PERSPECTIVES

"The White Quail" remains a subject of academic discussion. Marilyn Mitchell notes Mary's "aggressive manipulation in feminine frailty" as a comment in a larger essay on the strength of Steinbeck's women. Stanley Renner suggests that the story "anatomizes the sexual revulsion and fear that have been traditionally associated with idealized woman. . . ," and that the relationship between Mary and Harry in "The White Quail," present a "particularly bad bargain for men." Robert Hughes concludes the story might be partially autobiographical because of the disintegration of Steinbeck's marriage to CAROL HENNING STEINBECK BROWN during the time the story was written.

SYNOPSIS

(I)

Mary Teller sits contentedly by the fireplace in her perfect living room admiring the perfect garden outside. The garden, lying at the edge of a wild, overgrown hillside, is painstakingly designed, with large oaks, a shady, immaculate lawn, and a shallow garden pool. She remembers how she imagined every detail of her house and her garden in her mind before setting out to find an appropriate man to build her dream for her. Such a man was Harry E. Teller, her husband.

(II)

Mary remembers how she and Harry purchased the lot, built the house, and were married. Harry admires her for her determination and efficiency in creating the beautiful garden, but he tells her that he is a little afraid of her, too. To him, she's untouchable, and inscrutable, and he is afraid of disturbing her just as he is afraid of disturbing her plants.

(III)

Mary frets that no birds come down from the wild hillside to drink in the shallow pool, and is relieved when a family of quail begin visiting the pool in the evenings. She pictures her garden as an island of peace separating her from the "rough and tangled and unkempt" world. Harry senses that he sits on the outside of her peaceful garden, and outside of her mind as well.

(IV)

One night Mary stands outside in her garden gazing through the large dormer window into the living room where Harry is reading the paper. She pictures herself inside and discovers that she can divide herself in two, one Mary who remains protected in her personal garden, and the other Mary that lives with Harry E. Teller.

(V)

Mary adopts the habit of spending her evenings sitting quietly by herself on a bench in the garden to watch the birds gather next to the shallow pool. One evening a beautiful solitary white quail comes to the pool to drink. Mary identifies herself in the lovely, remote bird.

(VI)

Mary starts with horror when she sees a gray cat sneak out of the brush to attack the quail. She screams and the quail escapes up the hillside. Harry rushes outside and finds his wife shuddering and crying hysterically. She explains to him about the cat, and asks him to poison it to protect her birds. Afraid that he might accidentally poison a dog, Harry promises to wait for the cat's return with his air gun. Mary tells him how she identifies with the white quail, as her alter ego. Early the next morning, Harry sits in the garden with his air gun waiting for the cat to reappear. As the garden grows light, the white quail arrives at the edge of the garden pool. He shoots the quail and buries it on the hillside. Afterward, he feels guilty for what he has done. Then he becomes overwhelmed by his loneliness.

FURTHER READING

Hughes, Robert. "Searching for Subjects: Steinbeck's Uncollected Stories." In *Rediscovering Steinbeck: Revisionist Views of His Art, Politics, and Intellect,* edited by Cliff Lewis and Carroll Britch. Lewiston, N.Y.: The Edwin Mellen Press, 1989, 104–124.

Mitchell, Marilyn L. "Steinbeck's Strong Women: Feminine Identity in the Short Stories." In *Modern Critical Views: John Steinbeck,* edited by Harold Bloom. New York: Chelsea House, 1987, 91–101.

Renner, Stanley. "Sexual Idealism and Violence in 'The White Quail.'" *Steinbeck Quarterly,* XVII: 1–2 (Winter/Spring 1984): 76–87.

The Winter of Our Discontent (1961)

The Winter of Our Discontent, the last of Steinbeck's novels, was first published in June 1966 by VIKING PRESS. Although Steinbeck, in preparing this novel, had read many books and plays, the major influence was an earlier short story of his entitled "How Mr. Hogan Robbed a Bank," published in the *Atlantic Monthly* in March, 1956.

The brief, epigraphical statement with which Steinbeck prefaces the novel suggests its connections to both the content and style of his earlier work: "Readers seeking to identify the fictional people and places here described would do better to inspect their own communities and search their own hearts, for this book is about a large part of America today." Suggesting that his theme will again cover, or at least address, the subject of America, and that his focus on the misbehavior of characters will allow readers to draw conclusions and cast aspersions on the failings of human behavior which they will not want to connect to themselves, Steinbeck perhaps thought of the receptions of his great successes 20 and 30 years earlier. His interest in human morality, and in particular American conduct, also look forward to his last two published works, both of nonfiction, TRAVELS WITH CHARLEY and AMERICA AND AMERICANS. *The Winter of Our Discontent* is the only one of Steinbeck's novels to be set in an eastern seacoast town; several critics mark a seeming connection to the California coastal locations of CANNERY ROW, but the vividness of the earlier settings is, if not dimmed, at least overshadowed by the vigorously etched portrait of the central character, Ethan Allen Hawley.

The Winter of Our Discontent is the only novel Steinbeck wrote in the first person. The decision to shift point of view after chapter 2, to return to an objective narrator at the beginning of part 2 and to shift perspectives again after one chapter moved Steinbeck away from the openly farcical tone and cartoonish characterization that marks the opening of the book, but it does not sufficiently resolve the questions created by juxtaposing Ethan's initial outrage at the moral relativism of his contemporaries, with his eventual plotting and subsequent despair. In some respects, Ethan is a reworking of *Cannery Row's* Doc; his decision at the very end to return and pass on the talisman to Ellen seems to revise Doc's own despairing demise, but Steinbeck's mixed characterization of Ellen, who is alternately sprightly and vicious and yet irrationally beloved by her father, seems an insufficient cause for him to return to live out his life. The relationship of Ethan and Danny Taylor pulls some of the threads of the relationship between Lennie and George from OF MICE AND MEN; Ethan's wistful remembrance of his friendship seems at first as if it might compel him to find a way to save the landpoor drunk, but Ethan's light starts to dim when his initial outrage that Mr. Baker had tried to swindle Danny out of his patrimony with a bottle of expensive liquor turns to lust when he realizes he can do the same, but with a slightly different kind of bribe.

Perhaps more interesting than Steinbeck's seeming allusions to his own earlier work are the references to the work of other writers. Critics make no note of Steinbeck's allusions to American writers in *The Winter of Our Discontent*, perhaps because there is such a wealth of more obvious, more pointed references to the medieval and Renaissance texts that so preoccupied Steinbeck's mind late in his career. Yet, given the northeastern location of the story, it is harder to dismiss the echoes of Nathaniel Hawthorne than it would be if the work were set in Steinbeck's usual locus, the "long valley" of California. Ethan's sense of his family's decline from a once-patrician past recalls the resentful nostalgia of Hepzibah Pyncheon of Hawthorne's *The House of the Seven* Gables, and his shame at being reduced to clerking in a grocery store mirrors Hebzibah's sense of humiliation that she must open a cent-shop and sell candy to little schoolboys in order to keep her place in the grand old house. Ethan's desire to escape his despair by fleeing from his home and family mirrors the shortlived exuberance of Clifford Pyncheon during his temporary escape from his destiny as he and Hepzibah ride the train to nowhere. Most significant are Ethan's parallels to Jaffrey Pyncheon, the conniving current head of the Pyncheon family, who schemes to cheat Clifford out of his patrimony as Ethan schemes to cheat Danny. Like Jaffrey, Ethan also imagines the images of his patrician ancestors watching him from their places of rest, judging him, advising him, and similar to Jaffrey, he senses his ancestors guiding him to restore the family's greatness. In the end, Steinbeck's allusions to Hawthorne's ancestral sensibilities are a mixed success, and his appropriation of some of Hawthorne's characterizations and thematic interests are far less successful than those of Henry James or Willa Cather.

Steinbeck's references to medieval and Renaissance literatures also have mixed success, but they were likely of more importance to Steinbeck himself. Ethan's despair at the discovery of the depths of his own son's treacherous amorality mirrors the epic tragedy and betrayals of the MORTE D'ARTHUR that had preoccupied Steinbeck for so many years, much to the dismay of his editor and publisher.

Ethan's sense of disaffection at the falling off of past ethical standards that is so obviously referenced in the title, taken from Shakespeare's *Richard III*, connects not only to the play that is the source for the title, but to another of Shakespeare's historical tragedies. Certainly Ethan's displacement of the objective narrator to tell his own tale echoes the behavior of Richard III in his many unwelcome asides to the audience in the play. Likewise, Ethan's machinations to reposition himself at the forefront of New Baytown society, regardless of the cost to others, echoes Richard's movements to claim the throne. His deliberate betrayal of Marullo and his plan to hogtie Baker into compliance with his scheme echo the vengeful machinations of those other Shakespearean villains, Edmund (*King Lear*) and Iago (*Othello*). But perhaps the most interesting Shakespearean allusions are to *Macbeth*. Ethan's frustrated wishes that he were more than he is echo those of the Scottish lord, as his response to Mary's mildly expressed disappointment in Ethan's reserve parallels Macbeth's reaction to the more direct and pointed criticisms of his lady. Like Macbeth, Ethan is tantalized by the predictions of a fortune teller, the ubiquitous Margie Young-Hunt, and her promise to Mary that Ethan will be her fortune plays a large role in Ethan's decision to act. Ethan is further tantalized by the wishes and hopes of his daughter Ellen, who cruelly wonders when they will be rich, and whose sleepwalking caresses of the family talisman serve as an epiphany for her father. Together, the three women approximate an appropriately disjointed reworking of the Weird Sisters of the Scottish play in their effect on Ethan. An even more obvious reworking of Shakespeare exists in Ethan's reconfiguring of his relationship to Danny Taylor, whose patrimonial meadow Ethan must usurp in order to establish himself as the financial leader of New Baytown. Ethan's fond nostalgia for their boyhood days does not prevent him from following through with his plan. At the same time, Ethan knows he will be "visited" by Danny's ghost, much as Macbeth is haunted by Macduff, and his sense that the tidal waves washing over him will overwhelm him parallels not only the end of *Richard III*, but the end of *Macbeth*, as well. All of these allusions are perhaps part of what led Stein-

beck to write in letters that he was working on something important. Ultimately, as most critics agree, the results don't meet the grandness of the resources.

However, as time has progressed to the 21st century, it is interesting to notice how Steinbeck's concerns over individual morals and their social consequence have foretold what we witness today of ethics in corporate business, politics, and government operations. It may be reasonable to believe that as long as ethical issues remain important, *The Winter of Our Discontent* will continue to be relevant.

EARLY CRITICISM

Like much of Steinbeck's later work, *The Winter of Our Discontent* received mostly polite but fairly lukewarm reviews. Many early reviews of the book tended to allude to the writer's work of the 1930s and 1940s as a substitute for more direct criticism of the recent novel. Notices were relatively brief and straightforward, but only a few reviewers really cared to call Steinbeck's new book serious writing. A few early analyses focused on the presence of mythic elements and Steinbeck's uses of naturalism. But other early critics were troubled by Steinbeck's seeming inability to decide if the work was a moral teaching or a satire of modern man, and they found the combination of mythical elements too confusing.

Virgilia Peterson, in her review of *The Winter of Our Discontent* in the *New York Herald Tribune*, called it a novel worth scrutiny simply because of the author's previous work, although like many other critics, she found it ultimately inferior to his other books. Peterson stated that Steinbeck is a writer with "two literary faces," one "gleeful," as shown in Tortilla Flat and *Cannery Row,* and the other "outraged" as shown in *The Grapes of Wrath* and In Dubious Battle. Peterson further suggested that Steinbeck shows an angry and moralistic face in *The Winter of Our Discontent.* Although she credited Steinbeck for exposing the "incontrovertible" fact that "American honesty is losing reputation," Peterson pointed out that the author failed to present his characters as realistically as he did in previous works. For example, Peterson found the author's portrayal of Ethan Hawley, "a man of innocence and principle," to be naïve and unacceptable. Similarly, a book review in *Time* complained that the novel contains little passion and that the writer's "moral anathema" was nothing but "late-middle-aged petulance."

Critics who viewed the story in the book as fable rather than reality tended to appreciate the messages conveyed by Steinbeck. Peter Harcourt was one of the few early critics who valued Steinbeck's fables in *The Winter of Our Discontent*. Writing for the English *Time and Tide*, Harcourt contends that Steinbeck is more concerned with the social consequences of a corrupted individual, whose moral corrosion "spills over and begins to spoil the lives of people around him." From this perspective Harcourt views the novel as expressing Steinbeck's continued faith that our society needs to retain moral goodness so "the light of life can continue burning." Writing from a similar standpoint, Eric Keown of the English *Punch* calls the book "a study of an innocent whose character is corrupted by the discovery that graft is easy." Harold Gardiner, writing in *America*, regards the novel as a story that concerns the moral decay of a good man.

In addition to its teaching on morality, other critics noted that *The Winter of Our Discontent* may offer readers some sociological perspective to reflect on the rapid changes in mid-20th-century American life. A year after the novel was published, the *Yale Review* carried an article called "The Return of Moral Passion," by J. N. Hartt, who argues that *The Winter of Our Discontent* conveys Steinbeck's very serious and passionate concern about the decaying morals due to the trend of urbanization. In Hartt's view, the novel juxtaposes and contrasts "the cause of American small-town virtue" with "the juggernaut of urbanization." Perceived from this standpoint, Hartt believes, the novel tells us that what we call progress "is often a move toward the moral jungle."

CONTEMPORARY PERSPECTIVES

Contemporary studies of *The Winter of Our Content* have focused a great deal on the ethics the novel explores. Critics like Warren French, Peter Lisca, Michael Meyer, and Stephen George have argued that typical of Steinbeck's later work, *The Winter of Our Discontent* indicates Steinbeck's shift in emphasis from broad social issues to individual moral concerns. As George has recently pointed out, *The Winter of Our Discontent* "indeed speaks with a clear moral voice, a voice concerned not only with our moral development as individuals, but with the ability of those same individuals to provide a light by which others may see the way." According to George, *The Winter of Our Discontent* deserves far more attention than it has been given to.

More recently, the Internet has made available various forums for lay readers to respond to Steinbeck's work; a surprising number of them pay attention to *The Winter of Our Discontent*. Perhaps less surprising, they are receptive to the critique of corrupted morality and appreciative of Ethan's aspirations and his despair. Steinbeck's decision to avoid an apocalyptic ending is commended by several of these "popular" critics.

SYNOPSIS
Part 1

(I)

On Good Friday, Ethan Allen Hawley, the poor but proud member of one of New Baytown's oldest families, opens the grocery store that was once his before he lost it due to his own mismanagement. Joey Morphy, the popular teller at First National Bank, stops to order a sandwich, and jokingly explains to Ethan his theory for robbing banks without getting caught, saying he would do it just before a long weekend. Mr. Baker, the bank president and a longtime friend of the Hawleys, reminds Ethan that the Hawley family was once a great family in the town. Ethan discusses the origin of the decline of his family fortune with another store clerk, suggesting it was gradual, and unstoppable until it was too late. Mr. Marullo, the Italian owner of the store, reminds Ethan that he lost the store because he was too nice, and without any business sense. Ethan receives a visit from Mr. Bigger, a drummer for a wholesale house, who suggests to Ethan that he place his orders through his rival firm, offering to pay him a 5 percent kickback. Ethan rejects the proposal. Ethan discusses the offer with Joey, who advises him to take the money, reminding him that he has a family to think about.

(II)

Back home, Ethan's teenage children, Ellen and Allen, inform him that they are going to write essays for the national "I Love America" contest. Allen asks his father where he can find examples of old patriotic speeches. His wife, Mary, tells him excitedly that her friend Margie Young-Hunt read his tarot cards and predicted that Ethan is going to become rich. His wife tells him that money would allow her to hold up her head and stop the townspeople from sneering at him because he is a grocery clerk.

(III)

Late that night Ethan walks down to the Old Harbor to his secret cave in the ruins of the family pier to reflect on the day's events. He begins to understand the nature of business and of money, and he realizes that he needs money to regain the Hawleys' social position. Returning home, he meets his childhood friend, Danny Taylor, the town drunk. Like Ethan, Danny was once a member of the town's elite. Ethan tells Danny to sell the family's property, the Taylor Meadow, and get treatment for his drinking. Danny refuses to sell the only thing he has left.

(IV)

The next morning Ethan reviews in his mind Joey's instructions for robbing a bank. He asks Mr. Baker if he can visit him to get some investment advice. Marullo comes into the store painfully flexing his arthritic hands. Ethan suggests that he take a vacation to Sicily. Marullo admits that he hasn't been back since he left 47 years earlier.

(V)

Ethan shows his son the dusty books of patriotic speeches in the attic. Margie comes over for dinner and agrees to reads Ethan's fortune. She is shocked when she sees a vision of a rattlesnake changing its skin.

(VI)

Lying in bed, Ethan realizes that in his smugness about being a "Good Man" he has lost sight of the corruption and dishonesty that are all around him. He has come to a conclusion without realizing it: he will rob the First National Bank and rebuild the Hawley fortune.

(VII)

The next morning Marullo comes to the house with an Easter gift for the children, and tells Ethan that he knows about the rejection of Mr. Bigger's proffer of a "kickback." That afternoon the Hawleys visit the Bakers. Mr. Baker confides that New Baytown is on the verge of growth and that he and a few of his friends intend to take advantage of it. Ethan realizes that Mr. Baker plans to take over the town council during the next elections.

(VIII)

Ethan visits Danny Taylor. He warns his friend that Mr. Baker will do anything to get the Taylor Meadow. He offers to give Danny money to get treatment. Danny asks for $1,000, which Ethan promises to deliver to him on Wednesday. Ethan feels sick because he knows that his friend will spend the money on alcohol. That night he follows his sleepwalking daughter and watches as she removes his talisman, a small translucent stone with a strange interwoven shape carved into its surface, from the living room cabinet. He watches his sleeping daughter caress the stone, kissing it and holding to her breast.

(IX)

The pieces fall into place. Joey tells Ethan of his suspicion that Marullo immigrated illegally and is unable to return to Italy because he is unable to get a passport. He also explains to Ethan how the timed lock on the bank's safe opens every day at 9:00. Ethan notices that Joey puts a piece of paper in the lock of the bank's back door to keep it from shutting. The robbery now begins to take shape. That evening he walks to the waterfront and leaves the money in Danny's shack. At home, Ellen attempts to tell her father that Allen is plagiarizing his essay, but he does not listen to her.

(X)

The next morning Ethan finds an envelope shoved under the door of the store. Inside is Danny's will, which leaves Ethan the Taylor Meadow in the event of his death. It is attached to a note that reads simply: "Dear Eth: This is what you want."

Part 2

(XI)

It is the month of June. Ethan calls the Immigration and Naturalization Service and anonymously reports Mr. Marullo. At home, he reproaches Allen for his immorality and materialism.

(XII)

Margie Young-Hunt is desperate to find a husband. She tells Ethan that she can see that his fortune is coming true and that she wants to ride along. A man from the Justice Department arrives asking questions about Marullo. Mr. Baker comes to the store and asks him if he has seen Danny Taylor. He tells Ethan that the governor has called him to Albany and that there is going to be an investigation of corruption in the town government.

(XIII)

Ethan is silently amazed at how one thing has led to another: the bank, the Taylor Meadow, and now Marullo. Marullo is agitated when he comes to the store. The old Italian gives him some money and lends him his car for the upcoming Fourth of July holiday. The next day, Ethan tells Mr. Baker that Marullo is in trouble and that he thinks that there is a chance he might be able to buy back the store. The banker agrees to prepare the necessary papers.

(XIV)

Ethan resolves to take back his security and his dignity and then resume his habit of honesty, just as he killed men in the war but did not become a killer. He wakes up early and takes the talisman out of the cabinet, puts it in his pocket, and walks to work. Mr. Baker brings him the promised conveyances for the store, and advises him to bargain hard. That evening it is announced on the radio that officials of New Baytown have been subpoenaed to appear before a grand jury on charges of corruption. In the morning, Ethan wakes up and prepares nervously to enact his carefully planned bank robbery.

(XV)

Ethan is poised to commit the crime when a man from the Justice Department suddenly arrives, forc-

ing him to call everything off. The man tells him that Marullo is going to be deported for illegal entry, and that Marullo has decided to give the store to Ethan as a tribute to the only truly honest man that he has ever met. Ethan feels sick from the secret knowledge that he has betrayed his benefactor.

(XVI)

Joey tells Ethan that he woke up in the morning with the suspicion that the bank was going to be stuck up, and that he took extra precautions. Ethan realizes how close he came to getting caught. He closes the store and sits in the dark. Running his fingers over the design in the talisman, he wonders what price he will pay for his actions.

(XVII)

Ethan and his wife plan to leave town for the Fourth of July holiday. Ellen tells her father that the talisman is gone. He takes it out of his pocket and gives it to his daughter. His wife asked him why he took it. Ethan explains he took it for luck.

(XVIII)

Ethan and Mary check into a small hotel. He tells Mary that he now owns the store. She cries with joy when she discovers that he is no longer a clerk. Margie calls the hotel to tell them that Allen has won honorable mention in the "I Love America" essay contest. The proud parents start for home to greet their son.

(XIX)

The Hawleys have a party to celebrate their son's success. The next morning Mr. Baker suggests that Ethan run for town manager. The drummer, Mr. Bigger, comes into the store. Ethan tells him that he will give him the store's account for a 6 percent discount. Stonewall Jackson Smith tells Ethan that Danny's body was found in the ruins of the old Taylor house in the Taylor Meadow where he swallowed a bottle of sleeping pills.

(XX)

Ethan shows Mr. Baker Danny's will. He sees fear in the banker's eyes for the first time. He tells Mr. Baker that he can have the meadow for 51 percent of the partnership that he is forming to revitalize the town. He tells Mr. Baker that he cannot be town manager because it would be a conflict of interest.

(XXI)

Ethan goes walking in the night. Margie intercepts him, and the two go together to her house. She tells him she knows what he has done to Danny and Mr. Marullo. Back at home, Ethan learns that his son plagiarized his winning essay from the speeches of Clay and Lincoln. When he confronts his unrepentant son, Allen tells him that everyone is dishonest, and accuses his father of being less than honorable. Ethan takes a package of razor blades from the bathroom and leaves the house. His daughter intercepts him at the door, and hugs him desperately, asking him to take her with him.

(XXII)

Ethan walks to his hiding place at the old Hawley pier. He reaches into his pocket to get the razor blades to slash his wrists, and discovers the talisman. He decides not to commit suicide, but to return home and give the talisman to his daughter, so that her future will not be blighted by his actions.

CHARACTERS AND PLACES

Baker, Mr. A character in *The Winter of Our Discontent*. The president of First National Bank in New Baytown, he agrees to help Ethan Allen Hawley remake his fortune. He plots to have the New Baytown town council removed so that he and his associates can take over. He is furious to learn that Ethan outmaneuvered him and gained control of the title to the Taylor Meadow, where Baker planned to build an airport.

Belle-Adair A great whaling ship, one of the last built and finest of all whaling bottoms, owned by the Hawley family in *The Winter of Our Discontent*. It was burned to the waterline in a fire that Ethan Allen Hawley suspects was started by the Baker family in order to collect the insurance money.

Bigger, Mr. Minor character in *The Winter of Our Discontent*. A drummer for a grocery wholesaler who offers Ethan a kickback for placing his grocery orders with his company.

Hawley, Ethan Allen A character in *The Winter of Our Discontent*, Ethan Allen Hawley is a man of education and iron integrity whose family was once powerful and respected in their small New England town. He loses the remnants of the family fortune and ends up working as a clerk in a grocery store that he once owned. He and his wife, Mary, an Irishwoman from Boston, have two children, Allen and Mary Ellen. He decides to set aside his strict morality to rehabilitate the family fortune. He gains control of the valuable Taylor Meadow by providing cash for Danny Taylor's fatal drinking spree. He decides to commit the perfect bank robbery but must abort the plan at the last minute. When Ethan learns that he cannot reverse the process of his own corruption he decides to commit suicide, but changes his mind at the last minute for the sake of his young daughter.

Marullo, Mr. A character in *The Winter of Our Discontent*, Mr. Marullo is the stodgy Italian owner of Marullo's grocery store in New Baytown. A large man with wet, sly eyes, he is plagued by chronic, painful arthritis. When he is deported for living in the country illegally, he leaves his grocery store to Ethan Allen Hawley, the only truly honest man that he has ever met. Unbeknownst to him, it was Mr. Hawley who turned him in.

Morphy, Joseph (Joey) A character in *The Winter of Our Discontent*, Joey is the popular teller at New Baytown's First National Bank. His friends often call him "the Morph." He has the inside information on everything that happens in New Baytown. Joey gives Ethan Allen Hawley the idea of robbing the bank by explaining his theory of the perfect bank robbery. He suspects that Mr. Marullo is an illegal immigrant.

New Baytown A fictional, handsome town that was once famous for its whaling industry, the center of *The Winter of Our Discontent*. The story is set around 1960s New Baytown, which Steinbeck tells the reader had flourished during the whaling days of the mid-19th century. John Steinbeck modeled New Baytown after SAG HARBOR, NEW YORK, where he lived during the writing of the novel.

Smith, Stonewall Jackson A character in *The Winter of Our Discontent*, Smith is the New Baytown day constable. He is forced to testify before a grand jury about the corrupt practices that many of the New Baytown town officials are engaged in. He asks Ethan Allen Hawley to identify Danny Taylor's body.

Taylor, Danny A character in *The Winter of Our Discontent*, Danny is New Baytown's town drunk and Ethan Allen Hawley's childhood best friend. Danny comes from one of the town's best families. When he was expelled from the Naval Academy, the shame killed his parents and most of him. In the end, Danny kills himself with whiskey and sleeping pills, leaving the family estate, the Taylor Meadow, to his friend and betrayer, Ethan.

Young-Hunt, Margie A character in *The Winter of Our Discontent*, Margie is an attractive, clever woman nearing middle age. Her two marriages failed because her husbands were weak. The granddaughter of a Russian witch, she reads Ethan Allen Hawley's tarot cards and discovers that he is going to become rich. Reading his cards a second time she has a vision of a rattlesnake shedding its skin. She sets out to seduce Ethan Allen Hawley, only to discover that she has set in motion a chain of events that she cannot control.

FURTHER READING

French, Warren. *John Steinbeck's Fiction Revisited*. New York: Twayne, 1994.

Gardiner, Howard. "The Old Pro and Three Newcomers." *America*, July 22, 1961, 554.

George, Stephen. "The Philosophical Mind of John Steinbeck: Virtue Ethics and His Later Fiction." In *Beyond Boundaries: Rereading John Steinbeck*, edited by Susan Shillinglaw and Kevin Hearle. Tuscaloosa: The University of Alabama Press, 2002, 266–276.

Harcourt, Peter. "Steinbeck's Fables." *Time and Tide*, June 6, 1961, 1031–1032.

Hartt, J. N. "The Return of Moral Passion." *Yale Review* (Winter 1962): 305–306.

Keown, Eric. "New Novels." *Punch*, July 5, 1961, 31–32.

Lisca, Peter. *The Wide World of John Steinbeck*. New Brunswick, N.J.: Rutgers University Press, 1958.

Meyer, Michael. "Citizen Cain: Ethan Hawley's Double Identity in *The Winter of Our Discontent*." In *After The Grapes of Wrath: Essays on John Steinbeck*, edited by Donald V. Coers, Paul D. Ruffin, and Robert J. DeMott. Athens: Ohio University Press, 1995, 197–213.

Peterson, Virgilia. "John Steinbeck's Modern Morality Tale." *New York Herald Tribune Weekly Book Review*, June 25, 1961, 29.

Steinbeck, John. *The Winter of Our Discontent*. New York: Viking, 1961.

The Wizard of Maine

Musical comedy begun in the mid-1940s by John Steinbeck and his close friend, the Broadway composer Frank Loesser. The two men worked off and on producing the story idea about a snake oil salesman who travels through the country performing good deeds. Steinbeck assigned his neighbor George Frazier to write the stage adaptation of the story. After making a serious attempt to complete both the book and the stage versions of the story, *The Wizard of Maine* was finally abandoned.

"Women and Children in the USSR" (1948)

A photo-essay published in the February 1948 edition of the *Ladies' Home Journal*. Not long after WORLD WAR II, Steinbeck traveled to the USSR with photographer ROBERT CAPA to investigate the day-to-day life of Russian women and children for the Ladies Home Journal. They spent about two months traveling between Leningrad, Moscow, Kiev, Stalingrad, Tiflis, and Batum. It was the first report in an American magazine on day-to-day life in the Soviet Union.

Capa and Steinbeck were generally encouraged to see and talk to as many people as they liked. They were, however, detained briefly by Moscow police for taking pictures of children playing amongst the rubble. Steinbeck dryly observes that the camera must be a terrifying weapon. In the essay, Steinbeck contrasted the life of women in the USSR with that of American women. He wrote with admiration about the women who took over working in the fields and rebuilding the wartorn cities, to fill in for the 10 million Russian men who died in the war.

He told of women who lived in the German-destroyed cities in little more than caves built from the rubble, or in the cellars of bombed-out buildings, as they worked to rebuild housing and schools. Children were afforded the best of everything: the warmest clothes, the last of the milk, and even circus entertainment in nearly every city. Steinbeck noticed a haunted look about the children from the destroyed areas, though, as if they had seen too much already. The country folk were hospitable, and curious about American women. They were surprised when Steinbeck reported that American women were quite like them, not pampered.

Although the word in America was that religious freedom was suppressed in the USSR, Steinbeck found the churches filled with men, women, and children of all ages. Religious icons, he said, were more commonplace than were Bibles in the Midwest. He summarized by agreeing with a little boy who told his mother, in wonder, that Americans were just like them.

PART III

Related People, Places, and Topics

Academy Awards Organized in May 1927, the Academy of Motion Picture Arts and Sciences is a professional honorary organization that gives annual awards known as Oscars. The Oscar statuette was designed by MGM's chief art director, Cedric Gibbons. It depicts a knight holding a crusader's sword and standing on a reel of film with five spokes—each representing the original parts of the academy: actors, writers, directors, producers, and technicians.

A number of Steinbeck's screenplays, as well as many other film adaptations of his novels, were nominated for Academy Awards during his long and productive career in HOLLYWOOD, CALIFORNIA. Films included: *LIFEBOAT* (1944), nominated for best original story and best director; *A MEDAL FOR BENNY* (1945), nominated for best original story and best supporting actor; *VIVA ZAPATA!* (1952), nominated for five awards, including best story and screenplay, best actor, art and set direction, and musical score, and received the award for best supporting actor; *EAST OF EDEN* (1955), nominated for best director, best screenplay, best actor, and received the award for best supporting actress; *TORTILLA FLAT* (1942), nominated for best supporting actor. Steinbeck himself never received an Oscar for his work as a screenwriter.

Ainsworth, Elizabeth (Beth) Steinbeck (1894–1992) Steinbeck's elder sister Beth was the second of four children. She graduated from Mills College and became one of the first women in the nation to earn a graduate business degree. She went on to become a successful businesswoman and mother. Steinbeck often sought his sister's help while researching the family history for his novel, *EAST OF EDEN*. Elizabeth Steinbeck lived in PACIFIC GROVE, CALIFORNIA, and remained close to her brother, corresponding and visiting frequently until his death in 1968.

Albee, George (1905–1964) One of Steinbeck's oldest friends, Albee met Steinbeck in the 1930s in EAGLE ROCK, CALIFORNIA, where the two young writers lived and worked to build their respective careers. A regular member of the now famous circle of artists and writers that Steinbeck surrounded himself with during the 1930s, Albee became an intimate correspondent with Steinbeck and one of his great supporters during the difficult early years, often serving as a sounding board for the author's ideas and frustrations as he struggled with such early novels as *TO A GOD UNKNOWN*. Albee even lent Steinbeck money on one occasion to allow him to continue writing during the GREAT DEPRESSION. Albee's surviving correspondence with the young Steinbeck provides many insights into the creative process that led to the author's early novels. Among other topics, Steinbeck wrote of the constant revisions required for his works in progress; of the unimportance of setting and background material if the human story has merit; and of the care he took with idiomatic accuracy for his characters' speech patterns. The MCINTOSH & OTIS LITERARY AGENCY in NEW YORK represented both writers. During his mostly lackluster career, Albee wrote a number of novels, including *Not in a Day*. As Steinbeck's career blossomed, Albee's stagnated. He began to resent his friend's success, forcing Steinbeck to confront him about his jealousy. Their relationship remained strained for many years until the two men resumed their friendship in the 1950s.

Allen, Fred (1894–1956) Legendary comedian, radio personality, and host of *The Fred Allen Show,* he became a close friend of John and Gwyndolyn Steinbeck during the 1940s. Allen's popular and innovative radio show featured comedic sketches on current events, and skits involving a recurring cast of characters. At one point, Steinbeck collaborated with FRANK LOESSER on a musical play called *THE WIZARD OF MAINE,* which was to be a vehicle for Allen's introduction to the Broadway stage. Although the play never materialized, Allen and Steinbeck remained intimate. Allen's autobiography, *Much Ado About Me,* contains an introduction relating Steinbeck's advice to him on writing. Steinbeck suggested that the beginning writer should adopt a stream-of-consciousness approach by writing down as much detail of the subject as possible without worrying about chronology, or a particular form. Eventually, the form and organization would be shaped by the accumulation of detail.

American Academy of Arts and Letters Steinbeck was elected as a member of the academy, which was founded in 1904 to honor distinguished contributors to American letters. The author received the appointment on November 23, 1948, along with WILLIAM FAULKNER, Mark Van Doren, and Leon Kroll. Although Steinbeck placed little stock in awards, he was proud of this achievement and pleased to be recognized as an equal among the "serious" American authors. In 1976, the American Academy merged with the National Institute of Arts and Letters.

Army Air Corps On the recommendation of President FRANKLIN ROOSEVELT, Steinbeck was assigned as "special civilian consultant" to the Army Air Corps during WORLD WAR II. His assignment was to write a movie script about a bomber crew with the purpose of glorifying the air corps' role in the war effort and thereby encouraging Congress to increase its appropriations to the force.

His effort resulted in the book *BOMBS AWAY!* Determined not to benefit financially for fulfilling what he saw as his duty, the author donated all wages and royalties that he earned as an air corps consultant to the Air Force Aid Society.

Arroyo del Ajo Spanish for "garlic gulch," this was the name of a small house built in 1936 by Steinbeck and his wife, Carol, on an isolated plot of land in the countryside outside of LOS GATOS, CALIFORNIA. The Steinbecks lived in the Arroyo del Ajo house until the author decided that the area had become too developed, at which time he and Carol bought a more remote piece of property called the BIDDLE RANCH.

Arvin Sanitary Camp Founded under the auspices of the Federal Farm Security Administration to provide relief for the migrant DUST BOWL refugees flowing into California during the 1930s, Arvin Sanitary Camp provided the model for the Weedpatch Camp in Steinbeck's novel *THE GRAPES OF WRATH.* The camp's administrator, TOM COLLINS, became Steinbeck's friend and collaborated with him often as he worked on the famous novel.

Farm Security Administration camp for migrants in Farmersville, California, 1939 *(Library of Congress, Prints and Photographs Division, FSA/OWI Collection, photographed by Dorothea Lange)*

B

Bailey, Margery (1891–1963) Steinbeck's professor of English at STANFORD UNIVERSITY and one of the principal forces behind the Stanford English Club that Steinbeck was intensely involved with while a student in the 1920s. A Yale Ph.D. famous for her strong character and an independent-mindedness that earned her the nickname "the Dragon Lady" from Stanford undergraduates, Bailey identified Steinbeck's talent early and gave the young writer important support and encouragement. Steinbeck frequently brought his work to Bailey for her criticism and suggestions. A charismatic woman, she was surrounded by a retinue of writers, including Elizabeth Anderson, who greatly influenced Steinbeck during his early years as a writer. Bailey introduced the author to his lifelong friend WEBSTER "TOBY" STREET. She later became a good friend of Steinbeck and continued to visit him at his various California residences during the early years of his success. During her long career, Bailey ran one of the nation's first creative writing programs at Stanford, where she inspired many young writers.

Ballou, Robert O. (1892–1977) A New York publisher and one-time literary editor for the *Chicago Daily News* during the late 1920s, Ballou accepted Steinbeck's manuscript for THE PASTURES OF HEAVEN while he was editor for the American office of the British publishing firm Cape and Smith. Within weeks of agreeing to publish the novel, Cape and Smith declared bankruptcy. Ballou switched to the firm Brewer, Warren & Putnam, taking *The Pastures of Heaven* with him, and stuck by his promise

to publish the novel. The book, however, sold few copies and his new firm also entered rocky financial territory. Ballou decided to cast off and start his own publishing company. Taking a great risk demonstrative of the writer's loyalty to those who supported him, Steinbeck agreed to stay with Ballou to publish TO A GOD UNKNOWN. The author continued to stand by Ballou when the publisher nearly went bankrupt in the GREAT DEPRESSION. Ballou, however, was disappointed with the book's sales and backed out of his option on Steinbeck's next novel, IN DUBIOUS BATTLE, agreeing to hand over his rights to PASCAL COVICI of the New York firm Covici-Friede. Covici would become Steinbeck's editor for the remainder of his career, even after Covici transferred to VIKING PRESS when his publishing house also went bankrupt. To a large extent, Ballou's dedication to publishing Steinbeck's early work was responsible for the artist's success.

Benchley, Nathaniel (1915–) Son of the Hollywood star Robert Benchley, Nathaniel became Steinbeck's close friend in the mid-1940s when he and his wife rented the other half of a New York duplex owned by Steinbeck and his wife Gwen. Benchley was a journalist at *Newsweek* and later a freelance writer known for his biographies and children's books. Steinbeck and the younger Benchley became close friends and spent a lot of time together carousing in New York while their wives Gwen and Margaret were both pregnant with their first children. The Benchleys witnessed the rapid deterioration of Steinbeck's second marriage and stood by their friend during the emotionally rocky divorce that followed. Benchley coauthored a short play called *The Circus of Doctor Lao* with Gwen Steinbeck, which had a short, unsuccessful run in Chicago, and he later went on to write a novel called *Side Street*. In later years, Benchley frequently spent time with John and Elaine Steinbeck, as both couples had houses in the SAG HARBOR area of Long Island. The two men remained close friends for the remainder of the author's life.

Berry, Anthony (Tony) (unknown)   A sardine fisherman and the captain of the WESTERN FLYER, a 76-foot purse-seiner that Steinbeck and Ricketts chartered for their scientific expedition to the GULF OF CALIFORNIA, which resulted in the book SEA OF CORTEZ: A LEISURELY JOURNAL OF TRAVEL AND RESEARCH.

Beskow, Bo (1906–1989)   Swedish painter whom Steinbeck met while making a European tour of the Nordic countries and Russia with his wife Carol, soon after his first commercial success with the novel OF MICE AND MEN. Steinbeck and the painter remained close friends and faithful correspondents, particularly during the personally devastating period after the author's break-up with his second wife, GWENDOLYN CONGER. The two men visited each other frequently. Beskow painted three portraits of Steinbeck during his career.

Beswick, Katherine (Kate) (unknown)   Steinbeck's intimate friend from the Stanford English Club. After graduating, she moved to NEW YORK to pursue a career as a writer but remained devoted to the young Steinbeck. The two writers maintained a long-running platonic relationship by mail during the difficult years before Steinbeck's success. Beswick was a constant influence in the young writer's life, lavishing continuous encouragement on him. Beswick often critiqued and retyped Steinbeck's disorderly manuscripts before sending them on to his agent, TED MILLER, who would then hand-deliver them to New York publishing houses. On at least one occasion she sent Steinbeck money so that he could quit his job and dedicate himself to finishing a novel. Despite their close relationship, Steinbeck and Beswick never met again face to face after their brief time together at Stanford.

Biddle Ranch   Small ranch near LOS GATOS, CALIFORNIA, where John and Carol Steinbeck lived from the end of the 1930s until their divorce in 1943. During their time at the Biddle Ranch, they played host to an ever-growing circle of friends, including such Hollywood legends as CHARLES CHAPLIN and DOUGLAS FAIRBANKS, JR.

bindlestiffs   Wandering laborers who drifted from ranch to ranch carrying all their belongings in small bundles slung from their shoulders. Steinbeck became interested in bindlestiffs while he was working on ranches in the Salinas Valley during his periodic leaves of absence from STANFORD UNIVERSITY. The plight of the bindlestiff is the principal theme of many of his novels, including OF MICE AND MEN and THE GRAPES OF WRATH.

Blaine, Mahlon (1894–1969)   An artist from NEW YORK whom Steinbeck met during his journey from San Francisco to New York on the freighter *KATRINA*. Blaine helped Steinbeck through his difficult first visit to New York and then again when the young writer needed help finding a publisher for his novel CUP OF GOLD. Blaine presented Steinbeck to Guy Holt, an employee at Robert M. McBride & Company, who agreed to publish the novel on the condition that Blaine illustrate the volume. Blaine's fame as an illustrator, Holt hoped, would guarantee sales for *Cup of Gold*. Steinbeck, however, was unhappy with the cover, which included a picture of a dashing swashbuckler that he felt lent the impression that the book was a juvenile pirate fantasy instead of a serious work of literature. Blaine moved west to work in HOLLYWOOD and joined up with the Steinbecks in PACIFIC GROVE, where he worked for a time in a business venture to sell a new plastic modeling material with Carol Steinbeck and some friends.

Brigham family   A wealthy California family for whom Steinbeck worked as a young man. Steinbeck was hired by the widowed Alice Brigham to work as the caretaker of the family's large estate on the south shore of Lake Tahoe. Steinbeck was introduced to her by his friend CARLTON "DOOK"

SHEFFIELD's mother-in-law, Mrs. Price, the owner of a nearby guesthouse where the young author had worked during previous summers. Steinbeck remained on the Brigham estate for two years and spent the long winters there in almost total isolation. During this time Steinbeck made ample use of the Brighams' large library to read and do research for some of his early short stories. It was here during the winter of 1927–28 that Steinbeck completed his first novel, CUP OF GOLD.

Brown, Carol Henning Steinbeck (1906–1983) John Steinbeck's first wife. The author met Carol Henning in 1928 while he worked as an assistant to his friend LLOYD SHEBLEY in the Tallac Hatchery in Tahoe City, California. Carol and her sister Idell were on vacation when they decided to drop in on their friend Shebley. Steinbeck immediately fell for the young woman, and the two spent the remainder of Carol's short vacation together. The young woman returned to SAN FRANCISCO, where she worked in the advertising department of the *San Francisco Chronicle*. At the end of September, Steinbeck left his job and moved to San Francisco to be near Carol. He quickly tired of life in the city, however, and moved back to the family cottage in PACIFIC GROVE, near MONTEREY, where he would write during the week and visit with Carol on the weekends. Their relationship blossomed, but Steinbeck was reluctant to marry before he had made a success of his work. The two became engaged after CUP OF GOLD was accepted for publication, and were later married in a private ceremony in 1930 before settling into the Steinbeck cottage in Pacific Grove with a $50 stipend from John's father as their only financial support.

An attractive woman with a strong air of personal independence, a riotous sense of humor, and a biting sarcasm, Carol seemed to be the perfect match for the sometimes shy and often brooding Steinbeck. Together they formed a tight, interdependent relationship during the early 1930s as the young author struggled to make his way in the literary world. Carol worked in the Monterey Chamber of Commerce, a publicity company, and in EDWARD RICKETTS's laboratory as the two struggled to make ends meet during the worst years of

John and Carol Steinbeck, 1935   *(Center for Steinbeck Studies)*

the GREAT DEPRESSION. She had literary aspirations and wrote poetry, some of which was published in the *Monterey Beacon* under the pseudonym, Amnesia Glasscock. Steinbeck's biographers commonly accept the important role Carol played in Steinbeck's early fiction. She encouraged her husband to press ahead, and provided cogent criticisms of the manuscripts, which she would then correct and type. Carol's interest in organized labor and other social issues inspired many of Steinbeck's early novels, including IN DUBIOUS BATTLE and THE GRAPES OF WRATH.

Having sacrificed her own career to support her husband's writing, Carol became increasingly defensive and resentful as Steinbeck achieved success. She reacted to the pressure by drinking heavily, and the gregarious behavior that her husband first enjoyed eventually became an embarrassment to him. Their marriage became strained and finally fell apart when Carol learned that Steinbeck was in love with another woman. The infidelity resulted in an extended and acrimonious separation, and the marriage finally ended in divorce on March 18, 1943. Eleven days later Steinbeck married GWYNDOLYN CONGER, who had been his lover for some time. Carol, too, eventually remarried to a man named William Brown.

Burrows, Abe (1910–1985)   Abe Burrows was a famous comedian, theater director, and playwright, whose credits include *Guys and Dolls, Can-Can,* and *How to Succeed in Business without Really Trying.* He became a close friend and associate of Steinbeck during the 1940s through their mutual friend FRANK LOESSER. Steinbeck often turned to the playwright for advice and criticism of his theatrical work, including the play BURNING BRIGHT. Burrows once cast the Steinbecks' sheepdog, Willie, in one of his plays.

C

Campbell, Joseph (1904–1977)   Campbell was a prolific author and thinker whose volumes on comparative mythology have become classics. He was introduced to John and CAROL HENNING STEINBECK BROWN by Carol's sister Idell. Campbell became the Steinbecks' neighbor in Monterey, California, during the 1930s when he moved into the house next door to EDWARD RICKETTS. For some time he was a fixture of Steinbeck's contingent of artists and dilettantes, taking part in the intense discussions held in Ed Ricketts's lab, as well as the uproarious parties of the CANNERY ROW scene. Campbell's interest in the psychology of Sigmund Freud and the symbolism of Carl Jung had a profound effect on Steinbeck's novels TO A GOD UNKNOWN and IN DUBIOUS BATTLE, both of which experimented with the usage of archetype and symbol. Campbell later became a professor at Sarah Lawrence College and the author of *The Hero with a Thousand Faces* and *The Masks of God*, among other works. Steinbeck's relationship with the intellectual became strained due to Campbell's increasingly obvious, albeit platonic, interest in Steinbeck's wife Carol.

Cannery Row   An area of MONTEREY, CALIFORNIA, consisting of sardine canneries, honkytonks, whorehouses, and flophouses, which Steinbeck used as the backdrop for two of his novels, CANNERY ROW, and SWEET THURSDAY. Monterey's economic livelihood from the mid 19th century until the mid 20th century largely derived from the fishing industry, especially salmon and sardine fishing, creatures in abundance in the coastal waters of California. The first cannery was built next to Fisherman's Wharf in Monterey Harbor, but the overwhelming stench of processed fish, and the problems of waste disposal dictated the relocation of the canneries to a rocky, coastal road leading from Monterey to PACIFIC GROVE and China Point, called Ocean View Avenue. The inhabitants and employees of the area knew it as Cannery Row. Steinbeck was intimately acquainted with the people and habits of the region during his long friendship with the marine biologist, EDWARD RICKETTS, who lived and worked on Ocean View Avenue.

The fish canning and processing industry eventually died out in Monterey, because the supply of sardines, once believed inexhaustible, disappeared through overharvesting, especially during WORLD WAR II when canned goods became necessary for the war effort. Cannery Row turned into a sad collection of abandoned, derelict buildings. However, the curious began to arrive in the 1950s and 1960s, driven by an interest sparked by Steinbeck's vivid descriptions in his fiction. Recognizing the potential of the area as a tourist attraction, Monterey redeveloped Ocean View Avenue to include hotels, boutiques, and fine restaurants, and officially renamed it Cannery Row in 1958. Today, it receives more visitors than any other section of Monterey.

Hovden Cannery, 886 Cannery Row, Monterey, California, 1921 *(Library of Congress, Prints and Photographs Division, photographed by Julie Packard)*

Capa, Robert (1913–1954)   Capa was one of the most intriguing of Steinbeck's associates and collaborators. Capa had an illustrious career as a photojournalist. Born Andre Friedmann, Capa invented wholesale the persona of a glamorous bon vivant and made a name for himself in journalism with his stirring photos of the Spanish civil war. Having found his genre, Capa went on to photograph every major international conflict between the 1920s and the 1960s. Steinbeck first met the photographer during his stint in the European war theater during WORLD WAR II as a correspondent for the *New York Herald Tribune.* The two men later traveled together to the Soviet Union on a journey that Steinbeck documented in *A RUSSIAN JOURNAL.* The two men became extremely close and Steinbeck was devastated when, in 1954, Capa was killed when he stepped on a land mine in French Indochina (Vietnam). In the introduction to Steinbeck's collection of war correspondence, ONCE THERE WAS A WAR, Steinbeck writes admiringly of his friend.

Carmel, California   Beautiful region of valleys and farms in central California near MONTEREY. John and Carol Steinbeck moved to Carmel soon after they were married in 1930. They rented a small home in EAGLE ROCK, close to the home of Steinbeck's friend CARLTON SHEFFIELD. When the landlord evicted them from the Eagle Rock house, the young couple moved briefly to a small house on the edge of the Angeles National Forest. They were soon forced to move north, however, when a number of strange incidents led Carol to believe that the house was haunted. It was during his time in Carmel that Steinbeck wrote much of his unpublished novel DISSONANT SYMPHONY, as well as his novels TO A GOD UNKNOWN and IN DUBIOUS BATTLE. John and Carol left and then returned to the Carmel area a number of times, always attracted by the large colony of artists and literary people, such as ELLA WINTER, Lincoln Steffens, and FRANCIS WHITAKER. The Carmel Valley Road is mentioned in *TRAVELS WITH CHARLEY,* and the Carmel Valley was the setting for the famous frog-hunting scene in *Cannery Row*.

Central Avenue   Central Avenue is a residential street and site of Steinbeck's birth in Salinas, California. John Steinbeck was born at 132 Central Avenue, in a two-story Victorian house where he lived for 17 years before leaving to study at Stanford University in Palo Alto, California. During the 1930s Steinbeck returned to the family house for close to a year to care for his dying mother and ailing father. During this time he wrote many of his most famous short stories, as well as parts of *The Red Pony* and *Tortilla Flat*. For the remainder of Steinbeck's career, Central Avenue would evoke memories of the solidity and conventionality of middle-class bourgeois society. The street figures prominently as the home of Adam Trask in Steinbeck's novel *East of Eden*.

Cervantes, Miguel de (1547–1616)   Miguel de Cervantes is one of the most celebrated Spanish novelists, playwrights, and poets, whose classic book *Don Quixote* is among the literary works that had the greatest influence on Steinbeck and his fiction. While Steinbeck's early novels are concerned with the behavior of groups of men moving and acting together, his later novels are much more oriented toward the integrity and nobility of the individual, an idea that Steinbeck saw in the works of Cervantes and Sir Thomas Malory. In the mid-1940s Steinbeck spent much time writing and rewriting a novel called *The Wizard of Maine*, based on the adventures of Don Quixote; although he never finished the novel, some of the earlier work was included in the novel *The Wayward Bus*. A few years later, the author prepared to write a book called *Don Keehan*, a modern western based on the *Don Quixote* story. Although the project never went ahead, Steinbeck did not give up the idea. When he made his 1961 journey across the United States chronicled in *Travels with Charley*, he traveled in a truck named Rocinante, after Don Quixote's horse; and at one point he proposed writing a play called "A Colloquy of Bugs," based loosely on Cervantes's novel *Colloquy of Dogs*.

Chaplin, Charles (1889–1977)   Chaplin was the legendary actor and director who became internationally famous for his portrayal of "the Tramp." He became friends with John Steinbeck during the 1930s after paying an unexpected visit to Steinbeck's home in Carmel, California, to meet the man who had written *In Dubious Battle,* which Chaplin admired. The two men remained friends throughout their careers and often crossed paths, first in Hollywood and later in London, England, after Chaplin's reentry permit was revoked during the stormy years of the Joseph McCarthy hearings in the 1950s.

Charley (Charles le Chien)   Charley was Steinbeck's 10-year-old blue French poodle that accompanied him during his travels for the book *Travels with Charley in Search of America*. Born in Bercy on the outskirts of Paris, and trained in France, he responded quickly only to commands in French.

Colletto, Tiny (unknown)   Tiny was a seaman on *Western Flyer*, a 76-foot ship that Steinbeck and Edward Ricketts chartered for their scientific expedition to the Gulf of California that resulted in the book, *Sea of Cortez: A Leisurely Journal of Travel and Research*.

Collins, Tom (Thomas) (unknown)   The administrator of the Arvin Sanitary Camp for migrant laborers, near Bakersfield, California, Collins worked under the auspices of the Federal Farm Security Administration to provide relief for the migrant Dust Bowl refugees flowing into California during the 1930s. Arvin Sanitary Camp provided the model for the Weedpatch Camp in Steinbeck's novel *The Grapes of Wrath*.

In an article in the *Journal of Modern Literature* (April 1976), published posthumously, Steinbeck describes Collins during their first meeting as a short, unkempt man, surrounded by desperate migrant workers in a dripping tent. Despite the miserable conditions, the workers focused their attention on an exhausted Collins, looking to him for solutions, because they viewed him as their only hope.

Collins trained for the priesthood before studying psychology and then worked in the Resettlement Administration, an administration relief program during the FRANKLIN ROOSEVELT administration. He made the camps successful by granting large amounts of autonomous authority to the people living in them, encouraging them to form committees and solve their own problems, establishing a sort of simple democracy that restored the inhabitants' pride. Later, in 1937, Collins and Steinbeck traveled together to research the roots of the westward migration for Steinbeck's novel *The Grapes of Wrath*. Steinbeck later claimed that he and Collins followed the entire trail of westward migration along Route 66 from Oklahoma to California, although evidence indicated that the two men probably traveled only as far east as the Nevada

Tom Collins, manager of the Arvin Sanitary Camp, and adviser to Steinbeck on the conditions of migrant workers during the writing of *The Grapes of Wrath* (Library of Congress, Prints and Photographs Division, FSA/OWI Collection, photographed by Dorothea Lange)

border. On Steinbeck's suggestion, Collins spent a few years working to turn his extensive notes on life in Arvin Sanitary Camp into a novel about the dust bowl immigrants. One of his versions was accepted for publication before being abandoned by the publisher.

Commonwealth Club of California   Founded in SAN FRANCISCO, CALIFORNIA, in 1903, the Commonwealth Club of California is a nonprofit, nonpartisan education organization that focuses on public affairs. Steinbeck was awarded the 1935 Commonwealth Club of California Gold Medal for Best Book by a Californian for his book TORTILLA FLAT. Steinbeck was awarded the 1936 Commonwealth Club of California Fiction Gold Medal for IN DUBIOUS BATTLE. The Commonwealth Club is the nation's oldest and largest public affairs forum, bringing together its 14,000 members for more than 400 annual events on topics ranging across politics, culture, society, and the economy.

communism   Communism (or Marxism) is a leftist political ideology that argues that the state ought to control the means of production for the good of the many. In an ideal application of communism, the state itself would wither away and the masses would live in a utopia of equality. Because of Steinbeck's critical views on the many undesired consequences of capitalism, early critics often labeled his writing as "red" or "radical," terms that allude to communism, or they accused him of harboring communist sympathies. These charges were propagated in the 1930s with the publication of the novels IN DUBIOUS BATTLE and THE GRAPES OF WRATH, as well as the series of inflammatory articles "THE HARVEST GYPSIES," all of which contain poignant criticism of the power and abusive habits of the large landowners in California's agricultural regions as well as overt approval of attempts to organize agricultural laborers. Although Steinbeck was highly critical of the anticommunist witch hunt that took a high toll among his friends and colleagues during the era of Joseph McCarthy's chairmanship of the Senate Committee on Government Operations, in fact he became increasingly critical of communism after traveling to the Soviet Union and witnessing the constraints imposed on individual rights by Stalin's totalitarian regime.

COMMUNISM AND *THE GRAPES OF WRATH*

Because the material in Steinbeck's masterpiece *The Grapes of Wrath* was so true to the real situation during the GREAT DEPRESSION, it caused a tremendous stir. Some argued that Steinbeck's portrayal of the Joad family proved the inability of the government to provide for the poor. Others saw Steinbeck as a communist seeking to use his literary talent to foment a revolution.

Indeed, *The Grapes of Wrath* struck the nation in a realistic but painful way. The revelation of the hard social reality hit right at the center of the problem. Steinbeck's depiction of society echoes the concern for the poor espoused by the communist movement in the 1930s. Yet, being sympathetic with the poor does not make a writer communist. Many writers in the early 20th century, such as WILLIAM FAULKNER, Sherwood Anderson, and even Robert Cantwell, offered devastating social and cultural criticisms of industrialism without romanticizing the communist utopia. As Steinbeck biographer Jackson Benson has noted, Steinbeck feared being labeled as a social-political writer because he felt the messages in the novel transcended the transient politics of his time. As Steinbeck writes in the novel, the reason that the Joads have to leave their homeland is not just social injustice; rather, the uncertainty of life itself forces the move.

During his lifetime Steinbeck was often disappointed by critics who insisted that an artist should join the major trend of social development and enlighten the common people. Steinbeck's writing does not reflect such a view of literature, for Steinbeck never directed his writing to a particular political or social group.

Further Reading

Benson, Jackson J. *John Steinbeck, Writer.* New York: Penguin, 1990.

Conger, Gwyndolyn (ca. 1916–1975) Steinbeck's second wife, a young, pretty woman who, shortly before they met, had moved to Los Angeles to work

Wedding photograph of John Steinbeck and Gwyndolyn Conger, 1943 *(Center for Steinbeck Studies)*

as a singer in radio and band music. Their mutual friend MAX WAGNER introduced Gwyn to the famous author in 1939. The couple hit it off immediately, even though at 38 years old, Steinbeck was perhaps 14 years her senior. Gwyndolyn's exact birth date is not known. Their relationship developed slowly during Steinbeck's intermittent trips to LOS ANGELES from his home in CARMEL, CALIFORNIA. Those trips became more and more frequent, however, as the author sought to escape the tension of his decaying marriage to CAROL HENNING STEINBECK BROWN. As soon as the Steinbecks separated in 1941, Gwyn and John made plans to move to NEW YORK and live together until the divorce was final, when they planned to be married. The couple moved into a farm owned by Steinbeck's friend BURGESS MEREDITH and Steinbeck immediately went to work with the FOREIGN INFORMATION SERVICE. In March 1943 Steinbeck was notified that the final papers for his divorce from Carol would be filed, clearing the way for him and Gwyn to get married. On March 18, 1943, Steinbeck obtained the final divorce papers and married Gwyn 11 days later in a private ceremony in New Orleans.

An active, strong-willed woman, Gwyn soon discovered that Steinbeck had more than just her to worry about. To have more time to write and report on the war, Steinbeck preferred that his wife stay at home to take care of domestic issues. Gywn obliged her husband, but tensions grew as the author's responsibilities kept him frequently away on business.

The situation worsened when, soon after they were married, Steinbeck agreed to travel to Europe as a WAR CORRESPONDENT for the *New York Herald Tribune*, leaving his young wife alone for almost six months. From the beginning of his trip to England as a correspondent, Gwyn had opposed it, but Steinbeck was steadfast with his plan. When he refused to listen, she accused him of choosing the war over her. To stop him, she claimed to be pregnant. So when Steinbeck left for England, he was filled with worry for his newly married wife. But to punish him, Gwyn would not write to him for weeks. However, the worst was that Gwyn was never pregnant as she had told her husband. This experience made Steinbeck learn that domestic matters could have a huge impact on his career and life. On August 2, 1944, Gwyn gave birth to THOMAS STEINBECK, the first of two sons she would have with the author. Their second son, JOHN STEINBECK IV, was born on June 12, 1946. Tension worsened between Gwyn and Steinbeck until, in 1948, she left her husband and filed for divorce. During her marriage to Steinbeck, Gwyn helped her husband research for his screenplay *VIVA ZAPATA!* coordinated the music for the film adaptation of *THE PEARL*, and cowrote a play script, "The Circus of Doctor Lao," with the writer NATHANIEL BENCHLEY.

Covici, Pascal (Pat) (1888–1964)   Covici was Steinbeck's lifelong editor and close friend. Covici discovered Steinbeck's short stories in 1934. He quickly recognized the young author's talent and agreed to publish the novel *IN DUBIOUS BATTLE*, which had recently been rejected by Steinbeck's publisher ROBERT BALLOU due to the poor sales posted by the author's earlier books (*THE PASTURES OF HEAVEN* and *TO A GOD UNKNOWN*). Covici published *In Dubious Battle* and *OF MICE AND MEN* in quick succession. He also acquired the rights to rerelease Steinbeck's earlier novels. Ironically, in 1937 on the eve of the completion of Steinbeck's greatest work, *THE GRAPES OF WRATH*, Covici-Friede went bankrupt. Covici was hired by VIKING PRESS's chief, HAROLD GUINZBURG, who agreed to honor Covici's commitment to Steinbeck. Viking would remain Steinbeck's publisher and Covici would remain his editor for the rest of the author's career. The relationship between Covici and Steinbeck grew increasingly intimate over the years, and the publisher was a frequent visitor to the Steinbeck household. During the breakup of Steinbeck's marriage to GWYNDOLYN CONGER, Covici provided the distraught author with emotional support. He also played an active role in the creation of Steinbeck's novels, pushing the author to write and then reading, proofing, and offering suggestions on the resulting manuscripts. Covici suggested that Steinbeck keep a journal during the writing of *EAST OF EDEN*, the result of which would be published after Steinbeck's death as *Journal of a Novel*. To acknowledge his friend's efforts, Steinbeck presented Covici with a hand-carved wooden box containing the final manuscript of the novel. Covici died on October 14, 1964, and Steinbeck gave the eulogy at his funeral, saying that "For thirty years Pat was my collaborator and my conscience. He demanded of me more than I had and thereby caused me to be more than I should have been without him."

D

Dekker, Mary Steinbeck (1905–1965) Mary Steinbeck Dekker was John Steinbeck's younger sister. The two enjoyed a close relationship throughout their lives. Mary followed her brother to STANFORD UNIVERSITY in the early 1920s and remained there after he dropped out in 1926 before she graduated, married, and moved to SAN FRANCISCO. In 1923 she and John enrolled together in a summer program at the HOPKINS MARINE STATION in MONTEREY, CALIFORNIA. They lived together in the family's cottage in nearby PACIFIC GROVE. She married Bill Dekker, the son of a wealthy San Francisco family. Mary and her husband helped the young writer on a number of occasions as he struggled with art and romance in San Francisco. Her relationship with her brother became strained during the late 1930s because her politically conservative views conflicted with his own more radical stance. When her husband died during WORLD WAR II, however, the two grew close again and Mary became good friends with John's third wife, ELAINE ANDERSON SCOTT STEINBECK. Steinbeck dedicated his last, uncompleted book, THE ACTS OF KING ARTHUR AND HIS NOBLE KNIGHTS to Mary.

de Kruif, Dr. Paul (1884–1974) De Kruif was the author of many book about the struggle to improve human living conditions, including *The Microbe Hunters, The Fight for Life* and *The Hunger Fighters.* He became a close friend of John Steinbeck during the 1930s. Steinbeck later worked with the documentary filmmaker PARE LORENTZ on a screen version of THE FIGHT FOR LIFE, which tells the story of the country's efforts to reduce the rate of infant mortality.

Dos Passos, John (1896–1970) One of the principal writers of the "Lost Generation," a term coined by Gertrude Stein for the artists, intellectuals, and writers who fled to PARIS during the 1920s seeking a bohemian lifestyle and rejecting American materialism. Aside from Dos Passos, the best known of the group were F. Scott Fitzgerald, and ERNEST HEMINGWAY, but included, as well, were Sherwood Anderson, Hart Crane, and Alice B. Toklas. Dos Passos's experimental novels *Manhattan Transfer* and *The 42nd Parallel* had an important influence on Steinbeck during his early years as a writer. Perhaps the most radical of the critically acclaimed authors of the 1920s, Dos Passos investigated new forms for literature in which the story or plot no longer was central to the reader's experience, but rather the manner of telling, the style, and format affected a reader's perception. Steinbeck did not directly imitate contemporary authors, because he was motivated strongly toward independence in establishing his own style, but he did attempt to use, in the manner of Dos Passos, diaries, newspapers, and other written documents as sources for his literary creations. After several false starts, Steinbeck's second published novel, THE PASTURES OF HEAVEN, reflected the experimentation with literary style that emerged from the 1920s.

du Bois, William Pène (1916–1993) Illustrator for Steinbeck's novel *THE SHORT REIGN OF PIPPIN IV: A FABRICATION*. William Pène Sherman du Bois, an American author and illustrator of children's books, is especially known for his comic coterie of peculiar characters. Winner of the Newbery Medal for his best-known book, *The Twenty-One Balloons,* du Bois also illustrated many other works for authors such as Jules Verne, Sir Arthur Conan Doyle, and Roald Dahl. Born into a family of artists, du Bois studied art in France, then published books for children from the mid-1930s. He served in WORLD WAR II as a correspondent for *Yank* and other magazines, and became the first art director for *The Paris Review* in 1953.

dust bowl During the GREAT DEPRESSION of the 1930s, the term *dust bowl* referred to a region of the Great Plains that extended throughout Texas, Arkansas, and Oklahoma, where, due to drought and poor farming practices, the soil of large areas of farmland was carried away by strong winds, resulting in a disaster of catastrophic proportions for the largely poor sharecropper farmers that populated the area. The dust bowl conditions spurred the westward migration of hundreds of thousands of families that Steinbeck documented in his book *THE GRAPES OF WRATH.*

E

Eagle Rock, California   A suburb of LOS ANGE-LES, CALIFORNIA, where John and CAROL STEIN-BECK moved soon after their marriage in 1930, to be close to Steinbeck's friend CARLTON SHEFFIELD, who used to be his roommate at Stanford. There they occupied a small house until they were evicted by the landlord. The Steinbecks relocated to another house in nearby Glendale, and then again to an area just north of Eagle Rock called Tujunga.

El Gabilan   The Salinas High School yearbook of which Steinbeck was associate editor during his senior year in 1919. The young writer contributed a number of short pieces to the yearbook, including a Class Will and a short essay titled "How, When and Where of High School."

Enea, Sparky   A seaman on *WESTERN FLYER*, a 76-foot purse-seiner that Steinbeck and EDWARD RICKETTS chartered for their scientific expedition to the GULF OF CALIFORNIA that resulted in the book, *SEA OF CORTEZ: A LEISURELY JOURNAL OF TRAVEL AND RESEARCH.*

Fairbanks, Douglas, Jr. (1909–2000) Fairbanks was a famous Hollywood actor and independent television producer. He became friends with John Steinbeck through their mutual friend CHARLES CHAPLIN. While working as a war correspondent in WORLD WAR II, John Steinbeck spent some time in the Mediterranean aboard the destroyer *Knight*, which was under Fairbanks's command. Indeed, the author wrote in his war dispatches for the *New York Herald Tribune* about his experiences while in Fairbanks's unit, including the famous account of how the crew of the *Knight* managed to capture an island held by a superior German force. The two men remained friends for the rest of their lives and Fairbanks later helped Steinbeck gain access to important private libraries in England in order to research his book on SIR THOMAS MALORY and the legend of King Arthur.

Farm Security Administration Established by the FRANKLIN D. ROOSEVELT administration in an attempt to deal with the growing agricultural crisis caused by the DUST BOWL in the 1930s. The Farm Security Administration (FSA) established a number of experimental camps in California for the rapidly increasing number of migratory workers that moved there in search of employment only to find the conditions of slow starvation. One such camp was the ARVIN SANITARY CAMP, made famous by John Steinbeck as the Weedpatch camp in his novel THE GRAPES OF WRATH. Steinbeck worked with the FSA on a number of occasions while researching articles and books.

farms/farmworkers Having grown up in the Central Valley of California—one of the nation's most intensely agricultural regions—Steinbeck felt a strong emotional attachment to farms and farmworkers. During his childhood he often spent time at his grandfather SAMUEL HAMILTON's ranch on the hills outside of KING CITY, CALIFORNIA, where he learned such skills as horseback riding and planting. Later, the aspiring author often took extended leaves from STANFORD UNIVERSITY to spend time working on the ranches in and around California's Central Valley. Steinbeck's experiences among

Family of a migrant agricultural worker, Nipomo, California, 1936 *(Library of Congress, Prints and Photographs Division, FSA/OWI Collection, photographed by Dorothea Lange)*

Pea pickers near Calipatria, California, 1939 *(Library of Congress, Prints and Photographs Division, FSA/OWI Collection, photographed by Dorothea Lange)*

farmworkers inspired many of his novels, such as OF MICE AND MEN and THE RED PONY and added to the brutal veracity and realism of his novels.

Faulkner, William (1897–1962)   William Faulkner was an American novelist and short story writer whose credits include *As I Lay Dying, The Sound and the Fury,* and *Light in August.* Faulkner was elected, together with Steinbeck, Mark Van Doren, and Leon Kroll, to the AMERICAN ACADEMY OF ARTS AND LETTERS in 1949. Later that year Faulkner received the NOBEL PRIZE IN LITERATURE. Steinbeck and Faulkner met on a number of occasions during the 1950s and worked together on the writer's committee of the

Dwight D. Eisenhower administration's People to People program to counteract Soviet anti-American propaganda, on which Faulkner served as chairman. According to the biographer Jackson Benson, Steinbeck sometimes referred to the writer as part of "the neurosis belt of the South" for his fascination with sickness, decay, and abnormality.

Fayre Eleyne   Steinbeck's boat, which he named after his wife, ELAINE ANDERSON STEINBECK. In his book *TRAVELS WITH CHARLEY IN SEARCH OF AMERICA* Steinbeck recounts how he rescued the *Fayre Eleyne* during Hurricane Donna when the boat was in danger of crashing against its mooring.

Fenton, Frank (1906–1970)   A friend from Steinbeck's college years, Fenton edited the STANFORD SPECTATOR, where he published some of Steinbeck's first short stories, including "FINGERS OF CLOUD" and "ADVENTURES IN ARCADEMY." He later became the president of San Francisco State University.

Figaro Littéraire   During the summer of 1954, Steinbeck, his wife, Elaine, and his children lived in PARIS, where he wrote a series of weekly short articles and opinion pieces for the popular French magazine. In his articles he proposed to offer the Parisians the Steinbeck vision of Paris. Steinbeck wrote the *Figaro* articles in English and had them translated to French for publication. The author later reused much of the material for articles in American and British periodicals such as *Holiday,* *Saturday Review,* and *Punch.*

Fisher, John   An interior decorator from New York, his wife, Shirley Fisher, worked for Steinbeck's literary agents MCINTOSH & OTIS LITERARY AGENCY. The couple became close friends with Steinbeck and his third wife, Elaine, and often visited the Steinbecks in their vacation home near the Fishers' home in SAG HARBOR, NEW YORK.

Fonda, Henry (1905–1982)   Fonda was a well-known Hollywood actor. He starred as Tom Joad in ELIA KAZAN's film adaptation of THE GRAPES OF WRATH. Steinbeck was impressed with the actor's portrayal of the important character, and the two men became close friends. Henry Fonda would later marry Susan Blanchard, the stepdaughter of Steinbeck's good friend and associate OSCAR HAMMERSTEIN. Steinbeck wrote a profile of Henry Fonda in the November 1966 edition of *Harper's Bazaar* in which he praises Fonda's talent and dedication. The actor later read a selection of Steinbeck's favorite poems at the writer's funeral at St. James Episcopal Church in NEW YORK.

Foreign Information Service   Part of the Office of Strategic Services (OSS), an agency created by the FRANKLIN D. ROOSEVELT administration to support U.S. efforts in WORLD WAR II, the FIS was headed by Robert E. Sherwood and assigned the job of combating Nazi propaganda. Steinbeck was invited to participate in the FIS and spent much of the early war working as a consultant in the agency's Washington, D.C., headquarters. Although he was never a formal employee of the FIS, he wrote his novel THE MOON IS DOWN on assignment for the agency. The novel, however, was rejected out of concern that it would be bad for the public moral. Steinbeck continued to work informally for the FIS, writing text for radio broadcasts throughout the duration of the war and on into the 1950s.

G

Gabilan Mountains A low mountain range lying east of the Salinas Valley. In *THE RED PONY*, Jody names his new pony Gabilan after the pleasant range.

Galbraith, John Kenneth (1908–) Galbraith is an economist, author of *The Affluent Society*, and a former speechwriter for JOHN F. KENNEDY. Galbraith met John Steinbeck while on vacation. The two men shared a mutual passion for politics and would later work together on ADLAI STEVENSON's presidential campaign. Steinbeck and Galbraith remained friends and correspondents for the rest of Steinbeck's life, and his work influenced many of Steinbeck's later efforts, including *TRAVELS WITH CHARLEY*, *AMERICA AND AMERICANS*, and *THE WINTER OF OUR DISCONTENT*, all of which reflect the idea of postwar American decadence.

Gannett, Lewis (1891–1966) Literary critic at the *New York Herald Tribune*, Lewis Gannett became a longtime friend of John Steinbeck. Gannett's wife illustrated the first edition of Steinbeck's novel *TORTILLA FLAT*.

Gemmell, Margaret (1904–1988) Steinbeck's first serious girlfriend while he was attending STANFORD UNIVERSITY. The relationship ended when Steinbeck decided to abandon his studies and travel to NEW YORK to become a writer. Steinbeck returned to California less than a year later intent on resuming the romance with Gemmell, only to find that the young woman was no longer interested in him.

Gipson, Sam M., Jr. (unknown) Marine major from Texas who was assigned by the Military Office of Information to be Steinbeck's guide during the six weeks that he traveled through Vietnam as a reporter for the New York newspaper *Newsday*. The two men corresponded for some time after their brief meeting.

government As a young man, Steinbeck maintained a somewhat wary attitude toward government, due in part to the role of sheriffs and other law enforcement officials in the California strike-breaking activities of the 1930s. Local and state governments almost always backed the farmers and growers in their resistance to higher wages and decent living conditions for the farm laborer. Moreover strike leaders and organizers were routinely arrested for violating California's criminal syndicalism law, and thrown into prison for lengthy terms. Although Steinbeck had very little sympathy for the Marxist ideology of many of these organizers, he was appalled by the destitution and living conditions of migrant workers, and recognized the need for organization to force change. He hoped the publication of a series of articles he wrote for the *San Francisco News*, and for the *Nation* about the starvation and deprivation he witnessed in the camps would lead an enlightened citizenry to pressure democratic institutions for reform. In this sense, Steinbeck, while considered a radical during those conservative times, had great faith in the foundations and institutions of the United States

When Pearl Harbor was attacked, Steinbeck immediately donated his services to his country and wrote a series of nonfiction essays in support of the war effort, in addition to THE MOON IS DOWN for the OFFICE OF WAR INFORMATION. He also consulted informally with President FRANKLIN D. ROOSEVELT. After being rejected by his local draft board because of supposed communist ties from his associations with labor organizers, Steinbeck lobbied to become a war correspondent, and participated in the successful Allied efforts to liberate Italy, though he was officially a noncombatant. From WORLD WAR II on, Steinbeck demonstrated a great respect for the institution of government and often felt himself duty-bound to use his talent and his celebrity in its service. Steinbeck went on to serve the cause of government in many different capacities both formal and informal, including a 1961 trip to Eastern Europe as a cultural representative of the United States government. In 1964 Steinbeck was awarded the Medal of Freedom for his long history of service to the United States government.

Great Depression   The period between the stock market crash of October 29, 1929, and WORLD WAR II, when the United States and most of the rest of the Western world experienced the most severe economic decline of the 20th century. The causes for the crash, and subsequent economic catastrophe remain a subject of controversy. Certainly, hyperinflated stock values and blundering attempts by the newly formed Federal Reserve to control excessive investment speculation contributed to the initial "crash" when American common stocks lost an estimated 10 percent of their value. As the economic crisis deepened, businessmen, financiers, and politicians all expected the moderate recession to be self-limiting. That is, in previous economic cycles and downturns, the capitalist "law" of supply and demand had reasserted itself, and both increasing unemployment and plunging productivity hit a plateau, and then reversed. Unfortunately the predictions of self-correction did not hold true. At the height of the Great Depression in 1932, production had fallen to

a level 40 percent below what it had reached before 1929, and more than 25 percent of the American workforce was unemployed. Banks and businesses failed. Farmers fell into bankruptcy. The environmental calamity of the DUST BOWL caused by poor agricultural practices and years of sustained drought further contributed to the economic misery, as farmers in the Midwest and Plains states could no longer grow crops in the severely depleted soil.

The Great Depression was at its worst during the years that Steinbeck made his first serious attempts to become a writer. It forms the background for five of his novels, IN DUBIOUS BATTLE, OF MICE AND MEN, THE GRAPES OF WRATH, CANNERY ROW, and SWEET THURSDAY, of which In Dubious Battle and the Grapes of Wrath were most deeply influenced by the economic turmoil of the times. Strikes, and other forms of labor unrest became common during the 1930s. In California conflicts between workers and employers often involved the agricultural conglomerates, which controlled California farming. Because Steinbeck had spent many of his summers working on farms and ranches around Salinas during his college career, he was already familiar with the problems of migrant farm laborers. In 1933, with the encouragement of his first wife, CAROL HENNING STEINBECK BROWN, Steinbeck attended several meetings of strike organizers, and from those meetings, he derived the idea for In Dubious Battle. The idea for The Grapes of Wrath originated during his first journalistic assignment in 1936 when he was tasked with covering the burgeoning migration of dust bowl refugees to California for the San Francisco News. The series of articles was published under the title "The HARVEST GYPSIES" in September 1936.

In his essay "ABOUT ED RICKETTS," the author writes about the personal impact of the Great Depression on him and his wife. He claims, perhaps without being fully candid, that the lack of money and employment was not terribly difficult. No one they knew had any money, and whatever food they needed could be gotten through fishing in Monterey Bay, barter, and "a minimum of theft." What Steinbeck fails to mention is the monthly stipend provided by his parents while he labored at his writing, and the family cottage in PACIFIC GROVE in which he and Carol lived rent free. Moreover, Carol took numerous odd jobs to support the household. The economic crisis ended for Steinbeck well before it ended for the nation at large, however, when the 1935 publication of *TORTILLA FLAT* and the 1937 publication of *Of Mice and Men* made the author a rich man.

Greenwood Lane Near LOS GATOS, CALIFORNIA, John and CAROL HENNING STEINBECK BROWN built a house on this road to escape the growing attention of reporters and curiosity seekers that arose following the success of *TORTILLA FLAT* and *IN DUBIOUS BATTLE*. This was the first of a string of refuges that Steinbeck would build in California and later in NEW YORK to meet his intense need for privacy while he was working.

Gregory, Sue (1885–unknown) A Spanish teacher at Monterey High School and a poet, she introduced Steinbeck to the *paisano* inhabitants of MONTEREY and spent many hours telling the young writer about the speech and customs of the small and vibrant community. Gregory's influence led Steinbeck to investigate a fascinating group of local residents whose colorful lives were later transformed into his first commercially successful novel, *TORTILLA FLAT*. Steinbeck was accused by at least one critic of stealing his material from Gregory, a criticism that fell away as he demonstrated his talent and inventiveness in other novels, such as *CANNERY ROW* and its successor, *SWEET THURSDAY*.

Grossteinbeck, John Adolph (1852–1913) Steinbeck's paternal grandfather. Born in Dusseldorf, Germany, John Adolph traveled to Jerusalem with his brother, sister and brother-in-law to convert the Jews of Palestine to Christianity. While on this quixotic journey, John Adolf met and married Almira Dickson, the American niece of another missionary in the region. During the mission, John's brother was stabbed and killed and his sister raped in a raid by Bedouin tribesmen. Discouraged in his missionary work, John moved to the town of his wife's family in Massachusetts, where he set up a workshop and practiced woodworking and cabinet

making. Growing restless, he packed up his new family and moved to Florida, where he was conscripted into the Confederate Army during the Civil War. He deserted and sneaked back to the North, whereupon he sent for his family. Almira was granted passage and soon joined her husband in New England. After the war, John Adolf migrated again, this time to California, which had recently been granted statehood. He spent his savings to purchase 10 acres of farmland in the Salinas Valley and began his new life as a dairy farmer. Although he died before John Steinbeck got a chance to know him, he remained a vivid figure in the author's imagination as a person willing to take risks in order to achieve his goals.

Guggenheim, Alicia Patterson (1906–1963) Daughter of the founder of the *New York Daily News*, she became the editor of the Long Island, New York, tabloid *Newsday*, which was purchased for her by her third husband, HARRY F. GUGGENHEIM. Alicia Guggenheim became friends with John Steinbeck in 1956 and urged him to write occasional articles for *Newsday*. After her death in 1963, Steinbeck agreed to write a series of articles that he presented in the form of letters to the dead woman. These so-called "LETTERS TO ALICIA" comprise some of Steinbeck's least known and most controversial work, including as they do attacks on the decline of morality in America as well as the author's dispatches from an extended tour in Southeast Asia during which he took pains to defend the LYNDON B. JOHNSON administration's policies in the VIETNAM WAR.

Guggenheim, Harry F. (1890–1971) Harry was the publisher and editor of the Long Island, New York, tabloid *Newsday* after the death of his wife, ALICIA PATTERSON GUGGENHEIM. He encouraged Steinbeck to write the series of articles that became known as the "LETTERS TO ALICIA."

Guinzburg, Harold (1899–1961) The president of VIKING PRESS, he hired the editor, PASCAL COVICI, who had a long-term commitment with Steinbeck from a previous publishing contract, and thus brought the author into the company. Soon thereafter the firm published THE GRAPES OF WRATH, which went on to break Viking sales records. Guinzburg was supportive of Steinbeck's many endeavors and invested personally in some of the author's more unlikely projects, such as the documentary film THE FORGOTTEN VILLAGE. He became a close friend of Steinbeck, and hosted the author's marriage ceremony to ELAINE ANDERSON STEINBECK in his family home. Guinzburg took a more involved role in criticizing and encouraging Steinbeck's work as the two men became friends. For instance, Guinzburg took on the role of early critical commentary for the rough drafts of EAST OF EDEN, when Steinbeck determined Covici was too close to the project.

H

Hamilton, Joe (1878–unknown) Steinbeck's uncle on his mother's side. Joe was a successful businessman and pioneer in the field of advertising. When his young nephew John was having troubles finding work in New York City, Uncle Joe offered to get him a job as an advertising copywriter. Steinbeck turned him down, however—he wanted only to be a writer. Uncle Joe patiently pulled some strings and helped Steinbeck to land a job as a cub reporter for the *New York American*, one of the William Randolph Hearst papers, from which he was fired a few months later. Ironically, many years later Steinbeck served as a WORLD WAR II combat journalist for the Hearst syndicate.

Hamilton, Samuel (ca. 1833–ca. 1903) Steinbeck's maternal grandfather, he migrated to the United States from Ballykelly, Ireland. Samuel married Elizabeth Fagen in 1849 in New York City and then moved to SALINAS, CALIFORNIA to establish himself as one of the town's founding fathers. Samuel later moved his family to a large ranch near KING CITY, CALIFORNIA, where he and Elizabeth raised a family of nine children and eked out a living digging wells and running a small blacksmithy. Although Samuel died while Steinbeck was still an infant, he remained a flamboyant figure in the author's memory, and was later given a place of honor in the novel EAST OF EDEN. Late in his career Steinbeck returned to Ballykelly in search of his roots only to discover that the Hamilton family had died out, and that the town's inhabitants had forgotten his grandfather.

Hammerstein, Oscar (1895–1960) One half of the famous Broadway duo of RODGERS & HAMMERSTEIN, he was an associate of ELAINE ANDERSON STEINBECK from her days working on the New York production of the hit musical *Oklahoma!* Hammerstein became John Steinbeck's friend and agreed to help him prepare the stage version of his PLAY-NOVELETTE, BURNING BRIGHT, for which Rodgers & Hammerstein subsequently purchased the production rights. The play, however, was almost universally panned by the critics and enjoyed only a brief run before being abandoned. Later Oscar Hammerstein expressed interest in composing a musical version of Steinbeck's CANNERY ROW and SWEET THURSDAY. The play, renamed *Pipe Dream*, was also a failure. Hammerstein remained a close friend of the Steinbecks until his death in 1960.

Hemingway, Ernest (1899–1961) Hemingway was a quickly rising literary star when the young Steinbeck was struggling to publish his first novels in the late 1920s and early 1930s. His books such as *In Our Time*, a collection of short stories, and *The Sun Also Rises*, based on his experiences in World War I, were well known and admired among writers. Hemingway's plain, powerful style had a strong impact on the young Steinbeck, who would later place Hemingway's short stories among his favorite works of American literature. Together with his admiration for Hemingway, Steinbeck also harbored a sense of professional envy, and he spent much of his career refuting the accusation that he copied his style from the famous author. The two men met a number of times but never established a friendship.

Highway 66   Running from Chicago, Illinois, to LOS ANGELES, CALIFORNIA, Highway 66 is the main route used by the evicted sharecroppers who migrated westward toward California looking for work. Construction on the road began in 1926, and the planners intended the road to link rural and urban communities in a major national thorough-fare for the first time, making it far easier for small farmers to ship their products to market via large trucks. John Steinbeck dubbed U.S. Highway 66 the "Mother Road," and it was along this highway that more than 210,000 victims of the DUST BOWL made their way to points west. Steinbeck's descrip-tion of the highway led to its immortalization in the imagination of Americans. A song recorded by Nat King Cole in 1946 brought the phrase "Get your kicks on Route 66" into common speech, and a popular television series in the 1960s, *Route* 66, also contributed to the road's legendary quality. In October 1984 the last portion of Route 66 was replaced by Interstate 40 near Flagstaff, Arizona.

Hollywood, California   The principal seat of the United States's film industry, the pioneers of American motion pictures found Hollywood to be well suited to their needs for abundant sunshine, mild temperatures, varied nearby scenery for loca-tion shots, and inexpensive labor. Hungry for well-known writers to brighten up their hackneyed and unimaginative movie scripts, Hollywood studios constantly courted Steinbeck, who had become a hot property after the phenomenal success of both the book and play versions of OF MICE AND MEN. Although tempted by the startlingly large salaries that he was offered in exchange for his collabora-tion as a screenwriter, Steinbeck was reluctant to work for a studio, because he feared compromising his artistic integrity. Indeed, collaborators very sel-dom had artistic control over the pictures they worked on in Hollywood. Although he claimed to harbor a dislike for the Hollywood "swimming pool set," the star-struck Steinbeck was often beguiled by its glamour, and spent more and more time in the company of the industry's best and brightest.

Moreover, though he never worked as a screen-writer for a particular studio, Steinbeck became the American novelist whose work was most often, and most successfully, translated to film.

hooptedoodle   A word introduced by Steinbeck in the prologue to SWEET THURSDAY. It is also the title of the third chapter, "Hooptedoodle 1," and the 38th chapter, "Hooptedoodle 2." Steinbeck indicated the word warned his reader of extraneous and not necessarily pertinent information in the novel, which allowed the author to engage in a flight of fancy.

Hooverville   Slang term given to the temporary camps set up by migratory workers. They are usu-ally found on the outskirts of towns and near sources of water and firewood. "Hoovervilles" derived their name from Herbert Hoover, who was president at the outset of the GREAT DEPRESSION, and who was blamed by many of the unemployed and homeless for their desperate circumstances. These shantytowns sprang up spontaneously along the edges of many urban areas, as the economy grew worse, and the ranks of the unemployed increased, especially among blue-collar workers.

Migrants' winter quarters, Farmersville, Tulare County, California, 1939 *(Library of Congress, Prints and Photographs Division, FSA/OWI Collection, photographed by Dorothea Lange)*

Hopkins Marine Station A marine institute located near MONTEREY, CALIFORNIA. Steinbeck studied there with his sister MARY STEINBECK DEKKER in the summer of 1923. His studies at Hopkins are thought to have provoked of his interest in biology and nature that would later become important themes in his writings, and especially in the book SEA OF CORTEZ, which Steinbeck wrote with his close friend EDWARD RICKETTS.

Horton, Chase (1897–1985) The owner of the Washington Square Bookshop near Steinbeck's New York residence, he became the author's close friend and adviser, often reading and offering advice on the author's manuscripts. Chase encouraged Steinbeck to undertake a modern retelling of SIR THOMAS MALORY's legends of King Arthur, and then dedicated himself to helping him with his research. The project occupied much of Steinbeck's creative energies during the last decade of his life, but he was never able to complete the proj-

ect to his satisfaction. Chase Horton later convinced the author's widow, ELAINE ANDERSON STEINBECK, to allow the publication of the unfinished manuscript, which became Steinbeck's last book, THE ACTS OF KING ARTHUR AND HIS NOBLE KNIGHTS.

House Un-American Activities Committee (HUAC) The House Un-American Activities Committee was a Congressional Committee devoted to stamping out communism in America. HUAC's campaign ultimately deteriorated into an anticommunist witch hunt. Steinbeck would speak out against HUAC when his friend ARTHUR MILLER was faced with charges of contempt of Congress for refusing to testify before the committee. Steinbeck's action was a tremendous personal and professional risk in an environment characterized by irrational fear. He wrote a scathing critique of what he called "one of the strangest and most frightening dilemmas that a people and a government has ever faced."

J

Jackson, Joseph Henry (1894–1955) Book critic from the *San Francisco Chronicle,* he and his wife, Charlotte, became close friends of John and CAROL HENNING STEINBECK BROWN, often inviting them to parties at their Berkeley, California, home. Steinbeck and Jackson met after Jackson's positive reviews of Steinbeck's early works in the mid-1930s, prior to the national recognition of Steinbeck's talent. The two couples later traveled together to MEXICO after Steinbeck's success with the novel *TORTILLA FLAT.*

Johnson, Lyndon B. (1908–1973) Lyndon Johnson was the 36th president of the United States. Architect of the Great Society program, which was his domestic agenda for his presidency, he is often remembered for his role in escalating the fighting in Vietnam. ELAINE ANDERSON STEINBECK met Lyndon Johnson's wife, Lady Bird, at the University of Texas, and she and John later became frequent visitors to the White House during the Johnson administration. Steinbeck helped Johnson write his acceptance speech for the 1964 Democratic Convention. The author became a loyal supporter of the president, backing him when his popularity diminished and even standing behind his wildly unpopular policies in the VIETNAM WAR. Johnson awarded Steinbeck the Medal of Freedom and appointed him to the Council of the National Endowment for the Arts.

Johnson, Nunnally (1897–1977) Nunnally Johnson was the Hollywood screenwriter who prepared the script for DARRYL ZANUCK's adaptation of Steinbeck's *THE GRAPES OF WRATH.* Steinbeck and Johnson became good friends while working together on the script. Johnson eventually wrote the screenplay for the film adaptation of *THE MOON IS DOWN.* Indicating his confidence in the man, the author gave Johnson explicit permission to make several important alterations to the story to make it more fitting for the screen. The two men remained close friends for the rest of Steinbeck's life.

John Steinbeck Library Originally the SALINAS, CALIFORNIA, Public Library, it was renamed after the town's most famous native son in March 1969, a year after the author's death. Among the library's archives are original Steinbeck manuscripts, rare editions of the author's works, and a collection of his correspondence. Although most of these materials have been moved to the NATIONAL STEINBECK CENTER, which is also located in Salinas, the John Steinbeck Library still holds many critical works on Steinbeck studies, including books, journals, degree theses, and dissertations.

Katrina Steinbeck left California in 1925 aboard the *Katrina*, a small freighter traveling from SAN FRANCISCO, CALIFORNIA, to NEW YORK via the Panama Canal. On this voyage Steinbeck became fascinated with the small Central American nation of PANAMA, an experience that would play an important part in his first novel, CUP OF GOLD. Among his traveling companions on the *Katrina* was the illustrator MAHLON BLAINE, who would later help Steinbeck sell his early novels, as well as illustrating the cover of *Cup Of Gold.*

Kaufman, George S. (1899–1961) American playwright and stage director who directed the smash stage adaptation of Steinbeck's novella OF MICE AND MEN. Kaufman and Steinbeck worked together on the script for the stage version, but then had a falling out when Steinbeck refused to remain in NEW YORK for the rehearsal of the play. Kaufman became even angrier when the author failed to attend the play's opening night. Despite the author's strange behavior, however, Kaufman's production of *Of Mice and Men* opened at New York's Music Box Theatre on November 23, 1937 to rave reviews, winning the New York Drama Critics Circle Award for best play.

Kazan, Elia (1909–2003) Kazan was a well-known Broadway director who later became a successful Hollywood director and producer. Kazan worked with John Steinbeck on the movie VIVA ZAPATA!, providing the author with an outline for

John Steinbeck (right) with director Elia Kazan, at the premiere of *East of Eden,* 1955 *(Photofest)*

the story and then working with him to edit the final version of the screenplay. He became Steinbeck's intimate friend and a source of emotional support during the breakup of the writer's second marriage. Kazan and his family later moved into a house just a few blocks from Steinbeck's NEW YORK residence. After their success with *Zapata*, Kazan directed the film adaptation of Steinbeck's novel *EAST OF EDEN*, based on the last section of the book, that earned him an ACADEMY AWARD nomination for best director. Steinbeck later defended Kazan's controversial decision to testify before the HOUSE UN-AMERICAN ACTIVITIES COMMITTEE.

Kennedy, John F. (1917–1963)   John F. Kennedy was the 35th president of the United States. On November 22, 1963, when he was hardly past his first thousand days in office, Kennedy was killed by an assassin's bullets as his motorcade wound through Dallas, Texas. Although Steinbeck was a strong supporter of Kennedy's rival for the Democratic presidential nomination, ADLAI STEVENSON, he came to respect the young president after his election in 1960. Steinbeck attended Kennedy's 1961 inauguration with his wife, ELAINE ANDERSON STEINBECK. After hearing President Kennedy's inauguration speech, Steinbeck was so moved that he wrote a letter to the president. It would start a close relationship between the writer and the president for the next few years before JFK's assassination. The president appointed Steinbeck to travel to the Soviet Union and the other Eastern Bloc countries as a cultural representative of the United States Information Agency. Kennedy later selected Steinbeck to receive the Medal of Freedom in 1964, but the president was assassinated before the award was presented.

King City, California   A small town in central California, some 60 miles south of Steinbeck's boyhood home of SALINAS. Steinbeck's grandfather

SAMUEL HAMILTON homesteaded the area, founding a large ranch in the dry hills 10 miles outside the town. There Steinbeck spent many summers of his youth with his uncle Tom Hamilton, learning to do chores and ranch work. Steinbeck's uncle Will Hamilton owned the town's garage and Ford dealership. King City and the Hamilton ranch held an important place in Steinbeck's imagination and were later used by the author as the setting for many of the author's stories and novels, most notably *THE RED PONY* and *EAST OF EDEN*.

King Haakon Liberty Cross   The King Haakon Liberty Cross was established in May 1945 and awarded for outstanding and decisive contributions to the Norwegian cause during WORLD WAR II. Steinbeck was awarded the King Haakon Liberty Cross in 1946 by the king of Norway for his book *THE MOON IS DOWN*, which had served to inspire the citizens of Norway during the Nazi occupation. The award had previously only been given to Norwegian heroes of the resistance.

Kline, Herbert (1909–1999)   Kline was a Hollywood director who proposed the original story idea for the semidocumentary *THE FORGOTTEN VILLAGE* to Steinbeck. Steinbeck was interested in making a documentary film and he quickly accepted the idea. Together with Steinbeck, Kline invested his own money in the project, and the two men spent considerable time on site in MEXICO preparing and filming the movie, which was released in December 1941, only days before the bombing of Pearl Harbor and the entry of the United States into WORLD WAR II. Although it was not distributed widely, *The Forgotten Village* earned Kline critical acclaim.

L

labor unions   After witnessing the terrible abuses committed against the migrant OKIE farmworkers in California in the 1930s, Steinbeck became a vocal proponent of organized labor. Indeed in his series of articles "THE HARVEST GYPSIES," the author decried the policies that were leading to the development of a "peon class" and urged the government to establish a migratory labor board that would regulate wages and normalize relations between employer and laborer. His proposals to organize farmworkers were viewed as radical and even as incipient COMMUNISM by the California growers' associations, and Steinbeck quickly became persona non grata in the region where he was born and raised. Steinbeck's short story "THE RAID" is a tense study of the psychology of the radical organizers who were attempting to stir interest in labor unions and Communist Party organizations during the 1930s, and his classic novel IN DUBIOUS BATTLE tells the story of a small group of men attempting to organize the migrant fruit pickers in the apple orchards of California's Central Valley.

La Paz, Mexico   La Paz is the largest town on the Baja Peninsula, the crew of the WESTERN FLYER landed here for supplies. It was also here that Steinbeck first heard the legend of a young boy who discovered a great pearl, a legend that would later become his novella THE PEARL.

literary criticism   As an author, Steinbeck had little use for literary criticism of any sort. Throughout his career he was constantly at odds with the American critical establishment, which it seemed he could never please after his early success with the novel THE GRAPES OF WRATH. Because many of Steinbeck's early works dealt with the "common man" and the plight of the marginalized poor, even his more comedic books, reviewers believed later he had abandoned his early commitment to social justice. Despite the author's claims to be uninterested in what the critics had to say about his work, the truth is he expressed frustration with what he saw as their inability to perceive what he was trying to say in his novels. Steinbeck was often driven to distraction and even depression that his novels were not taken seriously, and he spent much of his career in a futile attempt to prove his critics wrong. Although Steinbeck professed a policy of never answering his critics, no matter how unfavorable or inaccurate their reviews, on several occasions he was unable to contain his displeasure. Steinbeck's critics never rested; indeed, they launched a new round of attacks on the author when he was awarded the 1962 NOBEL PRIZE FOR LITERATURE. So vicious were the condemnations of his work that he felt the necessity to make reference to them in his acceptance speech, stating that "literature was not promulgated by a pale and emasculated critical priesthood singing their litanies in empty churches—nor is it a game for the cloistered elect, the tinhorn mendicants of low calorie despair."

Loesser, Frank (1910–1969)   Composer and songwriter who wrote many Broadway musicals including the smash hit *Guys and Dolls*. Loesser's wife,

Lynn, was a singer and close friend of GWYNDOLYN CONGER, Steinbeck's second wife. Steinbeck and Frank Loesser quickly became good friends during the time Steinbeck first became acquainted with Gwyndolyn Conger, and, after Steinbeck's subsequent marriage to Gwyn, the two couples spent considerable time together during the 1940s. Frank Loesser often advised John Steinbeck on his projects, and the two men collaborated on a number of musicals that never materialized, included one titled THE WIZARD OF MAINE, which they wrote as a vehicle to introduce their mutual friend FRED ALLEN to Broadway. The two men also entertained the idea of making a musical version of CANNERY ROW, a project that never got off the drawing board. Steinbeck often sought out Loesser's support when his marriage to Gywn was falling apart, and the two men maintained an active friendship and correspondence for the rest of their lives.

Loesser, Lynn (1916–1986)   A singer, and the wife of the Broadway composer FRANK LOESSER, she shared a voice coach with John Steinbeck's second wife, GWYNDOLYN CONGER. The two women became close friends and were even pregnant with their first children at the same time, thus deepening their kinship. Lynn Loesser played an important role in introducing the Steinbecks to the theater society of NEW YORK.

London, England   Steinbeck arrived in London for the first time aboard a troop transport ship in 1943, when he traveled to Europe as a war correspondent for the *New York Herald Tribune*. He immediately fell in love with the city and wrote with admiration of its inhabitants' ability to doggedly go about their lives in the middle of the nightly German bombing attacks. The author returned to London on many occasions in the company of his third wife, ELAINE ANDERSON STEINBECK. During his later career, he wrote a number of articles for the London papers the *Evening Standard* and the *Sunday Times,* as well as the weekly literary review *Punch.* Steinbeck became friends with his English agent, GRAHAM WATSON, and thereafter returned frequently to the city that he described as one of his favorite places in Europe.

Lorentz, Pare (1905–1992)   A film critic turned documentary filmmaker, Lorentz made the DUST BOWL documentary *The Plow That Broke the Plains,* as well as the acclaimed film *The River.* Lorentz's work had an important influence on Steinbeck's THE GRAPES OF WRATH, which touched on many similar themes of agricultural poverty and the devastation caused by the climatological changes in the plains states. Lorentz used a documentary approach of alternating chapters that describe the phenomenon of the westward migration from the devastated plains states to the West Coast, as desperate tenant farmers lost their land and livelihood. He invited Steinbeck to write the narrative portions of the film THE FIGHT FOR LIFE, which was based on DR. PAUL DE KRUIF's book about the struggle to lower the country's infant mortality rate. His collaboration with Lorentz inspired Steinbeck to make the semidocumentary film THE FORGOTTEN VILLAGE. Lorentz's frustrating work habits caused Steinbeck to decline further opportunities to work with the filmmaker on other projects, including his documentary film *The Land.* Lorentz maintained his friendship with Steinbeck throughout his colorful career, often paying visits to Steinbeck's homes in California and then New York.

Los Angeles, California   As a young man, Steinbeck stayed in Los Angeles on a number of occasions with his good friends CARLTON SHEFFIELD, who had taken a job teaching English at Occidental College, and the aspiring novelist GEORGE ALBEE. Steinbeck lived near Los Angeles in EAGLE ROCK and Glendale with his wife, CAROL HENNING STEINBECK BROWN, briefly during the early 1930s, but financial problems soon forced him to return to the family cottage in PACIFIC GROVE, CALIFORNIA, near Monterey. As Steinbeck's fame mushroomed after the publication of his novel OF MICE AND MEN, he became friends with a number of celebrities, including CHARLES CHAPLIN and HENRY FONDA. The previously shy author began to spend ever greater amounts of time rubbing elbows with his new friends and making the rounds of the HOLLYWOOD scene. This proved particularly true as his marriage to Carol began to fall apart, causing Steinbeck to escape to the refuge of Los Angeles hotel room and, later, the apartment of his new lover GWYNDOLYN CONGER.

Los Gatos, California   A wooded, hilly area 50 miles north of MONTEREY, CALIFORNIA, where Steinbeck lived between 1936 and 1941. In 1936, after Steinbeck's success with the novel and play OF MICE AND MEN, the author and his wife, CAROL HENNING STEINBECK BROWN, built a house in an isolated plot in the countryside outside Los Gatos. Steinbeck named his small piece of property ARROYO DEL AJO, Spanish for "garlic gulch." There they developed a close group of local friends and spent many evenings hosting visitors such as EWARD RICKETTS, WEBSTER "TOBY" STREET, and CARLTON "DOOK" SHEFFIELD. Steinbeck lived in the Arroyo del Ajo house until he decided that the area was overrun with development, whereupon he and Carol bought a more remote piece of property called the BIDDLE RANCH. Steinbeck lived at the ranch until his separation from Carol, when he moved to NEW YORK to be with GWYNDOLYN CONGER, the woman who would become his second wife.

Lovejoy,   Ritchie (1914–1994)   and   **Natalya** (1908–1968)   Longtime friends of John and CAROL HENNING STEINBECK BROWN from their days in PACIFIC GROVE, CALIFORNIA, the two couples were frequently in one another's company during the 1930s. A writer and illustrator, Ritchie Lovejoy shared a professional as well as a personal interest in Steinbeck's work. Natalya (Tal) Lovejoy and Carol Steinbeck formed a company to market a new plastic modeling compound. The company failed, but it formed yet another link in the couple's growing friendship. Together with EDWARD RICKETTS and CARLTON "DOOK" SHEFFIELD, the Lovejoys formed the core of Steinbeck's contingent of friends and artists in the MONTEREY and CARMEL area during the GREAT DEPRESSION of the 1930s. Steinbeck later gave the money from his 1939 PULITZER PRIZE to Ritchie Lovejoy so that the would-be author could quit his job and concentrate on finishing a novel that he had worked on for some time. John and Ritchie's relationship came under strain as Steinbeck's fame grew, and the two men parted ways after Ritchie Lovejoy accepted an assignment for *Life* magazine that Steinbeck had rejected.

Malory, Sir Thomas (ca. 1405–1471) Sir Thomas Malory is the most famous author of the Arthurian legends. Little is known of his personal life. As a young man, Steinbeck was heavily influenced by Malory's MORTE D'ARTHUR, the first English recounting of the legend of King Arthur. The structure of Malory's famous tale lies at the foundation of many of Steinbeck's works, including the classic novel TORTILLA FLAT, wherein Danny's house was similar to the Round Table of Arthurian legend and Danny's friends were not unlike the knights. Indeed Steinbeck's interest in Malory was so great that the author spent much of his later career working on a project to "bring to present-day usage" Malory's tales of King Arthur and the Knights of the Round Table, an effort that was published posthumously in 1976 as THE ACTS OF KING ARTHUR AND HIS NOBLE KNIGHTS. The author undertook extensive research on Malory, even traveling on multiple occasions to Italy and England. For the most part Steinbeck based his work on the Winchester Manuscript, a newly discovered manuscript of the Malory legends, and depended frequently on the assistance of the famed Malory scholar, Professor EUGENE VINAVER.

Martin, Mollie Hamilton (unknown) The older sister of Steinbeck's mother, OLIVE HAMILTON STEINBECK. In the introduction to his novel THE ACTS OF KING ARTHUR AND HIS NOBLE KNIGHTS, Steinbeck expresses his gratitude to his Aunt Mollie for introducing him to SIR THOMAS MALORY's depiction of the Arthurian legend in MORTE D'ARTHUR, a story that influenced the author heavily throughout his career.

McIntosh, Mavis (1902–1986) One of the two founding partners of the MCINTOSH & OTIS LITERARY AGENCY, Mavis McIntosh took on John Steinbeck as a client in 1931 shortly after the publication of his first novel, CUP OF GOLD, and served as his agent for the remainder of his career—nearly 40 years. Along with her partner, ELIZABETH OTIS. McIntosh became a close friend of the author, diligently supporting him during his many periods of emotional distress, and always encouraging him on to the next project. She often offered suggestions to Steinbeck regarding the nature of his work. For instance, Steinbeck originally intended to write a nonfiction narrative of his encounters with Communist labor organizers during the California farmworker strikes of the 1930s. McIntosh advised the author to convert his experiences into a novel, from which came his first major success, IN DUBIOUS BATTLE. She enjoyed a particularly close relationship with Steinbeck during the early years of his career, when the author was constantly under intense economic pressure. McIntosh maintained a vigorous correspondence with the artist throughout his life.

McIntosh & Otis Literary Agency New York literary agency founded by MAVIS MCINTOSH and ELIZABETH OTIS that represented Steinbeck for nearly 40 years, from 1931 until his death in 1968. The agency continues to represent Steinbeck's estate. McIntosh & Otis accepted Steinbeck as a client based on a recommendation from Steinbeck's friend John Breck and immediately began working on finding a publisher for his novel TO A GOD UNKNOWN, as well as some of his short stories. Although it was difficult to sell the fiction of unknown writers during those economically distressed times, McIntosh & Otis stood by Steinbeck and encouraged him to keep writing and submitting manuscripts. The agency finally found a publisher for THE PASTURES OF HEAVEN, which became the author's second published book. Steinbeck's other novels followed one after another in quick succession. Over the years Steinbeck became close friends with both Mavis McIntosh and Elizabeth Otis, and the two women worked diligently to support him in his many periods of emotional distress and to encourage him always on to the next project.

Meredith, Burgess (1907–1997) Burgess was an actor and close friend of John Steinbeck. The two men met when Meredith played the role of George in Stanley Kaufman's adaptation of Steinbeck's novel OF MICE AND MEN. The two men liked one another immediately and maintained a fairly close friendship for the remainder of the author's life. Steinbeck invited Meredith to his ranch in LOS GATOS, CALIFORNIA, to meet EDWARD RICKETTS and the rest of the writer's contingent of friends. A few years later Meredith narrated Steinbeck's semidocumentary film THE FORGOTTEN VILLAGE. During Steinbeck's acrimonious separation from his first wife, CAROL HENNING STEINBECK BROWN, Meredith lent the author his New York farmhouse as a refuge for him and his new love GWYNDOLYN CONGER. The two men were in London during WORLD WAR II, where Steinbeck was working as a correspondent for the New York Herald Tribune and Meredith made films for the army. Steinbeck and Meredith remained friends for the rest of their lives and at one time discussed producing a Broadway play about the legendary Joan of Arc, an idea that never materialized.

Mexico Steinbeck felt an intense fascination with Mexico and traveled there on a number of occasions during his career. He first planned to cross the border with his best friend CHARLTON "DOOK" SHEFFIELD, when the two young men where studying together at STANFORD UNIVERSITY in the 1920s. The plan never materialized, however, and Steinbeck's wish remained unfulfilled until the success of the novel OF MICE AND MEN made him a rich man, at which time he and his wife, CAROL HENNING STEINBECK BROWN, traveled to Mexico City for a few months to escape the deluge of public interest that the success of the novel had inspired. The couple rented a house in the capital city and traveled extensively in the mountainous central region. Later Steinbeck returned to Mexico with his friend EDWARD RICKETTS to undertake a six-week scientific study of the marine life in the Gulf of California. The resulting work, SEA OF CORTEZ, is a fascinating look at a relatively unexplored region of Mexico. Steinbeck continued to make periodic visits to Mexico as he worked on a number of projects, including the production of his quasi-documentary film about life in a Mexican village, THE FORGOTTEN VILLAGE, and the film adaptation of his novel, THE PEARL, both of which used Mexican actors and film crews. After WORLD WAR II, Steinbeck returned yet again to Mexico to research the life of Emiliano Zapata for the film about the Mexican revolutionary leader, VIVA ZAPATA!

Milestone, Lewis (1895–1980) Milestone was the Hollywood director of All Quiet on the Western Front, a World War I story about the tragedy of war. He directed the 1939 film adaptation of Steinbeck's novel OF MICE AND MEN. The two men were introduced by their mutual friend, the documentary filmmaker PARE LORENTZ, and were soon working together closely with the screenwriter Eugene Solow to draft the film's screenplay. Milestone quickly became one of Steinbeck's growing group of Hollywood celebrity friends, often visiting the Steinbecks at their home in the hills outside of LOS GATOS, CALIFORNIA. The director eventually produced and directed the film adaptation of Steinbeck's classic novelette THE RED PONY, which was released in 1949 after production delays due to the war. The two men remained friends for the remainder of Steinbeck's life.

Miller, Arthur (1915–2005)   Playwright Arthur Miller's best-known works include *The Crucible* and *Death of a Salesman.* Steinbeck met him in the early 1940s when Miller was still relatively unknown. Over the years Steinbeck developed a great respect for the younger man's work. Both writers were published by VIKING PRESS and had frequent contact during the latter half of Steinbeck's career. In the 1950s, when Arthur Miller refused to testify during the infamous RED purges of the HOUSE UN-AMERICAN ACTIVITIES COMMITTEE (HUAC) and was faced with charges of contempt of Congress, Steinbeck took a tremendous personal and professional risk to defend his friend. He wrote a scathing critique of what he called "one of the strangest and most frightening dilemmas that a people and a government has ever faced." The two men would remain friends for the rest of Steinbeck's life, although their relationship would later become strained due to Steinbeck's increasingly supportive relationship with the Johnson administration and his defense of the VIETNAM WAR.

In a 2002 essay by Miller on Steinbeck's centennial, however, Miller wrote that he thought of Steinbeck as a friend even though their lives ran parallel and never really crossed. Miller had read Steinbeck's writing in college. As for his opinion of Steinbeck as a writer, Miller said, "I can't think of another American writer, with the possible exception of Mark Twin, who so deeply penetrated the political life of the country."

Further Reading

Benson, Jackson J. *John Steinbeck, Writer.* New York: Penguin, 1990.

Miller, Arthur. "Tribute to Steinbeck." In *John Steinbeck: A Centennial Tribute,* edited by Stephen George. Westport, Conn., and London: Praeger, 2002.

Miller, Ted (unknown)   Steinbeck's college buddy, and a fellow member of the Stanford English Club. After finishing a law degree, Miller moved to New York to pursue a career as a lawyer. He soon met Steinbeck again, when the aspiring author moved to New York to work for the *Herald Tribune.* Steinbeck was soon fired from his job, and quickly became destitute. He turned to Miller, who helped him obtain a berth upon a San Francisco–bound freighter. Some time later, Miller agreed to work informally as Steinbeck's literary agent, dutifully carrying copies of the young author's manuscript for his first novel, CUP OF GOLD, to potential publishers. Miller managed to place the novel eight months later with Robert M. McBride & Company, but he was unable to find a firm interested in publishing *To an Unknown God,* Steinbeck's first draft of the novel that would later be published by ROBERT O. BALLOU under the slightly altered title *TO A GOD UNKNOWN.*

Mirrielees, Edith Ronald (1878–1962)   Steinbeck's professor of creative writing at STANFORD UNIVERSITY, she probably had greater impact on his development as a writer than any other single person, according to Steinbeck's biographer, Jackson J. Benson. It was Mirrielees who discouraged Steinbeck's early tendency toward ornate and turgid writing, and who also emphasized the importance of constant revision. Mirrielees was a published writer of short stories who earned her Ph.D. at Stanford and went on to be a pioneer in the field of creative writing, an academic course of study that hardly existed as a formal discipline when she began her career. Mirrielees would later become a fixture of the famous Bread Loaf School of English, a summer graduate program of Middlebury College in Vermont, which offers courses taught by renowned English professors. During her career, she edited two anthologies of short fiction that are now considered classics in the field of creative writing, *The Story Writer,* and *Story Writing.* Late in his career, Steinbeck wrote a preface for a paperback edition of Edith Mirrielees's textbook *Story Writing.*

Model T Ford   Henry Ford's famous automobile was a fixture of Steinbeck's youth and early adulthood. The author owned a beat-up Model T during the years that he worked in the Lake Tahoe region, a car that he later eulogized in the article "A Model T Named 'It' " that he published in the *Ford Times* magazine in 1953. Steinbeck's books *IN DUBIOUS BATTLE* and *EAST OF EDEN* both contain detailed descriptions of the odd procedures for starting the automobile, an operation that was celebrated yet again by the director ELIA KAZAN in his film adaptation of the novel *East of Eden.*

Monterey, California   A coastal town in central California, Monterey was an important location in Steinbeck's childhood and early adulthood. The Monterey coast was one of the author's favorite places, and it became the setting for some of his most famous novels, including TORTILLA FLAT, CANNERY ROW, and SWEET THURSDAY. In *Tortilla Flat,* Steinbeck offers a picture of the town that he loved so much: "Monterey sits on the slope of a hill, with a blue bay below it and with a forest of tall dark pine trees at its back." Like many members of the SALINAS middle class, the Steinbeck family maintained a weekend home in PACIFIC GROVE, a small community on the outskirts of Monterey. Thus young John spent his summers slouching over the tide pools and sneaking around the canneries of the famous port town. Later, after dropping out of STANFORD UNIVERSITY, Steinbeck spent much of his time living in the family cottage and exploring the area that, during the GREAT DEPRESSION, had become famous for the sardine canneries that provided an inexpensive staple for the poor. Monterey gained an even greater hold on the author when he became friends with a local personality, EDWARD RICKETTS. Steinbeck and his new wife, CAROL HENNING STEINBECK BROWN, remained in the Monterey area until 1936, during which time Steinbeck wrote *Tortilla Flat,* a tribute to the town's *paisano* inhabitants, and gathered the images and experiences that would later populate his novels *Cannery Row* and *Sweet Thursday.* Many years later, while on the journey that would become the book TRAVELS WITH CHARLEY, Steinbeck returned to Monterey to find it had changed dramatically.

Morgan, Henry (1635–1688)   Henry Morgan was a famous 17th-century Welsh buccaneer who served as the inspiration for Steinbeck's unpublished short story "A LADY IN INFRA-RED" that would later become his first published novel, CUP OF GOLD.

Morte d'Arthur   Written by SIR THOMAS MALORY, it is the first account in English prose of the legend of King Arthur. *Morte d'Arthur* was the book that had the greatest influence on John Steinbeck as both a person and a writer. This influence, although apparent throughout the author's body of work, is evidenced most starkly in the novel TORTILLA FLAT, where he overtly compares Danny and his friends to the Knights of the Round Table. Steinbeck eventually spent much of his later years researching and writing a modern-language version of *Morte d'Arthur,* and although he never finished the project to his satisfaction, the unfinished manuscript was eventually published after his death as THE ACTS OF KING ARTHUR AND HIS NOBLE KNIGHTS. In the introduction to his book, Steinbeck describes his fascination with Malory's work and attributes to it many of the elements that inspire his own writing: "I think my sense of right and wrong, my feeling of noblesse oblige, and any thought I may have against the oppressor and for the oppressed, came from this secret book."

N

National Steinbeck Center Located in the historic center of SALINAS, CALIFORNIA, the NATIONAL STEINBECK CENTER is a nonprofit organization dedicated to the life and work of Salinas's favorite native son. Founded in 1998, the center includes a permanent exhibit of the author's life and works, as well as an extensive archive of Steinbeck materials for academic research.

New York, New York Steinbeck first traveled to New York in 1925 as a young man aspiring to write in the capital city of the Jazz Age. The city horrified him, he later remembered: "there was something monstrous about it—all tall buildings looming in the sky and the lights shining through the falling snow." He briefly obtained a job as a reporter for the New York *American* before being fired for his lackluster work. After less than a year, Steinbeck returned to his native California. He moved back to the New York in 1941 with his soon-to-be second wife, GWYNDOLYN CONGER. From that point on, when not traveling abroad, Steinbeck would spend most of the rest of his life living in or around New York City. The author slowly came to love his new home. Over the years he built up a large group of friends and acquaintances there who doted on him and supported him in his artistic endeavors, much as he had done previously in the CARMEL region of California. Later, the writer and his third wife, ELAINE ANDERSON STEINBECK, purchased a house in SAG HARBOR on nearby Long Island where they spent their summers, returning to the city for the winter months. Late in his career Steinbeck wrote glowingly of his adopted city: "New York is the world with every vice and blemish and beauty. . . . What more could you ask for?"

New York American Steinbeck obtained a job with the *American,* one of the many newspapers owned by William Randolph Hearst, in the late 1920s, a job secured for him by his influential uncle JOE HAMILTON. Unhappy with Steinbeck's work as a street reporter, the *American*'s editor soon reassigned the young writer to cover the federal courts. Steinbeck, however, continued to show little interest in reporting and was soon fired.

Nobel Prize in literature The Nobel Prize in literature, with the other Nobel Prizes, was established in the will of Alfred Nobel, a Swedish industrialist. John Steinbeck was first nominated for the Nobel Prize in literature in 1945, though he did not win. He also received consideration for the award on various occasions during the late 1940s and early 1950s before his reputation as a writer began to fade under the barrage of negative critical opinions of his work. Thus it came as an immense surprise to the Steinbecks when, one morning during the tense period of the Cuban missile crisis in October 1962, they turned on their television set at SAG HARBOR for the news and heard the words: "John Steinbeck has been awarded the Nobel Prize for literature." Even for a writer so often ill-treated by the critical establishment, the reaction to the

Nobel Committee's selection was astonishingly negative, even brutal. And although the author bore the attack with dignity, in truth he was terribly hurt by it. Indeed, Steinbeck even felt the necessity to make reference to it in his acceptance speech, stating that "literature was not promulgated by a pale and emasculated critical priesthood singing their litanies in empty churches—nor is it a game for the cloistered elect, the tinhorn mendicants of low calorie despair."

However, when John and ELAINE ANDERSON STEINBECK traveled to Stockholm, he received a very different sort of reception—for even as his reputation was tarnished in America, in Europe he was viewed as one of the foremost American writers. The Swedish Academy stated that Steinbeck had been awarded the prize "for his realistic as well as imaginative writings, distinguished by a sympathetic humour and a keen social perception." Although the European ardor went a long way toward ameliorating the damage done by the fierce critical attacks at home, Steinbeck would live the rest of his days under the cloud of a powerful insecurity about his writing. Indeed, after winning the Nobel Prize, the author would never again produce a work of fiction, preferring instead to stay in the relatively uncontroversial waters of journalism and opinion.

Office of War Information A WORLD WAR II agency devoted to PROPAGANDA and organized by the FRANKLIN D. ROOSEVELT administration to prepare the country for the coming war. Steinbeck had spoken to the president on a number of occasions to warn him of the need to organize a strategy to counteract the Nazi Party's propaganda efforts in the United States and abroad. Steinbeck, feeling that it was his duty to participate in the government's new effort, volunteered to work in the newly formed OWI He was assigned to the office of the Foreign Information Service, where he was put to work writing scripts for radio broadcasts. At this time, Steinbeck also worked on his novelette THE MOON IS DOWN, the story of a small town whose citizens silently but steadfastly resist enemy occupation. The story was turned down by Steinbeck's superiors at the OWI out of fear that it would be bad for the country's moral. Steinbeck continued his collaborations with the OWI and the FIS throughout the duration of the war, writing for a number of films, including the cinematic classic LIFEBOAT, as well as both the film and book versions of the air force propaganda film BOMBS AWAY: THE STORY OF A BOMBER TEAM.

O'Hara, John (1905–1970) O'Hara was a stage writer hired by Herman Shumlin to turn Steinbeck's novel IN DUBIOUS BATTLE into a Broadway play. The young writer became a lifelong friend of Steinbeck and was the first person to encourage Steinbeck to write a novel in the form of a play, the result of which was the author's most successful theatrical adaptation, OF MICE AND MEN. Steinbeck described this new form as the PLAY-NOVELETTE, a style that he continued to experiment with during the remainder of his career.

O. Henry's Full House (Twentieth Century–Fox, 1952) This movie is an anthology film that compiles five of O. Henry's greatest short stories into one film. The stories are *The Ransom of Red Chief*, *The Gift of the Magi*, *The Cop and the Anthem*, *The Last Leaf*, and *The Clarion Call*. Many famous actors such as Marilyn Monroe were part of this film. Steinbeck served as the film's narrator.

Okie Pejorative name originally denoting an Oklahoman, used to describe any migrant worker.

Otis, Elizabeth (unknown–1981) One of the two founding partners of MCINTOSH & OTIS LITERARY AGENCY, established in 1928, she and her partner, MAVIS MCINTOSH, took on John Steinbeck as a client in 1931 shortly after the publication of his first novel, CUP OF GOLD. Otis developed a lifelong friendship with the author and participated heavily in the editing, revision, and direction of almost all of his writing. She enjoyed a particularly close relationship with

Oklahoma dust bowl refugees, San Fernando, California, 1935 *(Library of Congress, Prints and Photographs Division, FSA/OWI Collection, photographed by Dorothea Lange)*

Steinbeck during the later years of his career, after Steinbeck had achieved a stunning literary success with the publication of OF MICE AND MEN. She also maintained a vigorous correspondence with the artist throughout his life and was often a visitor at the Steinbeck house in SAG HARBOR, NEW YORK.

Pacific Biological Laboratories   Edward Ricketts's biological supply company in the Cannery
Row district of Monterey, California. The small,
disorderly laboratory was located in an old house
that Ricketts had bought and transformed specifically for that purpose. Steinbeck described the laboratory in his essay "About Ed Ricketts."
According to Steinbeck, the low building contained four rooms in addition to a basement storage
area, and was redolent with the odor of living and
dead animals. Though seemingly disorganized,
each room had a specific purpose from breeding
and housing laboratory animals to preserving and
mounting specimens. Pacific Biological Laboratories became a meeting place for a large group of
friends that surrounded Steinbeck and Ricketts
during the heyday of their friendship in the 1930s.
In 1939 Steinbeck purchased half of Pacific Biolog-
icals to save the business from bankruptcy. The
author would remain Ed Ricketts's silent partner
until Ricketts died in an automobile accident in
1948.

Pacific Grove, California   Pacific Grove is a
small community on the outskirts of Monterey,
California. Steinbeck's parents had a vacation
cottage there on 11th Street where the young, penniless writer often found refuge. Steinbeck wrote
his novel To a God Unknown in the Pacific
Grove cottage in 1929 and then returned there
again with Carol Henning Steinbeck Brown
soon after they were married in 1930. The young

couple would fall back on the rent-free cottage a
number of times during their financially strapped
1930s. It was while living in Pacific Grove that
Steinbeck made the acquaintance of Edward
Ricketts, his lifelong best friend. Throughout his
life, the author would return to the Pacific Grove
cottage whenever he was troubled or in need of

Pacific Grove cottage, 1935   *(Center for Steinbeck Studies)*

307

rest. In *Sweet Thursday*, Steinbeck tells the story of a Great Roque War in Pacific Grove and describes it as the home of the Pacific Grove Butterfly Festival.

Palo Alto, California   Home of Stanford University, where Steinbeck studied periodically between 1919 and 1925. The young writer lived in a dormitory on the Stanford campus before moving into a small shed behind the Palo Alto home of his friend John Breck.

Panama   Steinbeck passed through the Central American country while crossing the Panama Canal aboard the ship *Katrina* on the way to New York City. Panama became the setting for a short story, *A Lady in Infra-Red*, as well as his quasi-historical novel *Cup of Gold: A Life of Sir Henry Morgan, Buccaneer, with Occasional Reference to History*.

Paris, France   Steinbeck first traveled to Paris with his second wife, Gwyndolyn Conger, in 1946. He immediately fell in love with the City of Light and returned on numerous occasions during the course of his career, often renting a house or villa in order to accommodate his entire family. During the summer of 1954, Steinbeck, his third wife, Elaine Anderson Steinbeck, and his children lived in Paris while he wrote a series of weekly short articles and opinion pieces for the popular French magazine *Figaro Littéraire*. In his articles he proposed to offer the Parisians the Steinbeck view of Paris. While living in Paris, Steinbeck conceived the story that became one of his most unusual creations, *The Short Reign of Pippin IV: A Fabrication*.

Pastures of Heaven   The Pastures of Heaven is a long, fertile valley in central California that was protected against the fog and wind by the hills that surrounded it. A lovely place, it is the setting of the stories in Steinbeck's *The Pastures of Heaven*.

PEN   The International Association of Poets, Playwrights, Editors, Essayists and Novelists. Founded in 1924 by Mrs. C. A. Scott, and John Galsworthy, the noted British author, PEN is the only international organization of writers, and is dedicated to the promotion of contemporary literature, and worldwide freedom of expression. Steinbeck became involved with PEN and was keynote speaker at the association's 1956 congress in Tokyo. Shocked to learn that the group never met in the United States because many important writers could not get the required entry visas due to their affiliations with leftist organizations, Steinbeck wrote an editorial for the *Saturday Review* decrying American immigration policy. It was entitled "A Game of Hospitality."

phalanx   An ancient Greek military tactic consisting of a large group of soldiers standing shoulder to shoulder and moving as a unit. Steinbeck used the word *phalanx* to describe his theory of group behavior illustrated in his novel *The Grapes of Wrath* and explicitly described in his book *Sea of Cortez*. The phalanx theory suggests that a group of men acting together takes on the properties of an individual and that the strength of such a group exceeds the sum of its parts.

play-novelette   A genre that Steinbeck used in *Of Mice and Men*, *The Moon Is Down*, *The Pearl*, and *Burning Bright*. Steinbeck defined the form as "a play that is easy to read or a short novel that can be played simply by lifting out the dialogue." He believed, though he was not completely certain, that the format was unique and original to his writing. The author praised the play-novelette because it obliged the writer to be disciplined and to write clearly and concisely. The play-novelette was a genre particularly suited to Steinbeck's talent for recording speech patterns and dialects because of its heavy emphasis on dialog instead of narrative description. It was Steinbeck's use of the play-novelette form that made so many of Steinbeck's works particularly adaptable for theater and film.

politics and Steinbeck's fiction   Although works such as *In Dubious Battle*, "The Harvest Gypsies," and *The Grapes of Wrath* indicate that Steinbeck had his own notions of right and wrong, as well as strong opinions about what the government should have done to help migrant laborers, the author demonstrated very little interest in politics during the first half of his career. In general terms, Steinbeck liked to define himself as a "New Deal Democrat" and he made no secret of his admiration for President FRANKLIN D. ROOSEVELT, a man whom he had the opportunity to meet with on a number of occasions as his literary fame increased. The author's overt participation in politics did not surface, however, until he discovered ADLAI STEVENSON in the 1950s. Expressing a profound admiration for the presidential candidate from Chicago, Steinbeck immediately agreed to write a foreword for a book of Stevenson's political speeches. He also became active in the Stevenson campaign, aiding the candidate with his speeches and organizing the support of other celebrities. Steinbeck later became a close friend and avid defender of President LYNDON B. JOHNSON, although his support of the man seems to have been motivated more by personal loyalty than shared political ideals.

Because of his connections to politicians, many people considered Steinbeck's writing itself to be political. The publication of *The Grapes of Wrath* in 1939 immediately gained Steinbeck the reputation of being an advocate of COMMUNISM. Like many social novels of the first half of the 20th century, *The Grapes of Wrath* and his earlier novel *In Dubious Battle* were conveniently labeled as protest works with political messages. As a result of the political cleansing from the 1930s to the 1950s and the ideological influence of the cold war years, Steinbeck's works were often examined within some ideological framework forged by politicians and their followers among the intelligentsia. The rhetoric in Steinbeck criticism often links the author to such terms as "leftist," "political," and "ideological," which insinuate an impression that Steinbeck was not a true artist or a writer of the first caliber.

In this ideological climate, *The Grapes of Wrath* had little chance of being accepted and evaluated purely as a piece of fiction. From the very beginning it was debated on its merits as a document rather than as a novel. Within two months after the publication of *The Grapes of Wrath*, there appeared a volume called *Grapes of Gladness: California's Refreshing and Inspiring Answer to John Steinbeck's "Grapes of Wrath."* It questioned the "facts" in the novel. Another book, *The Truth About John Steinbeck and the Migrants* accuses the novel of advancing the idea of class war and promoting hatred of class against class. Critic R. W. B. Lewis argues that instead of arriving at an artistic conclusion *The Grapes of Wrath* is committed to politics. According to Lewis, Steinbeck's rebellious sympathy for the wretched and the luckless leaves readers with the merely political.

In general, because of Steinbeck's alleged connection to "social protest," "revolution" and "communism," a number of influential social critics have faulted his works with "lack of artistic invention" and "close attachment to politics and reality." Steinbeck's works are therefore seen as aesthetically flawed by critics who maintain that art should be for art's sake. In *The Modern American Political Novel 1900–1960* (1966), Joseph Blotner notes that *The Grapes of Wrath* is a proletarian novel, and that *In Dubious Battle* is "essentially a strike novel," because the former is about the experience of those impoverished people during the Great Depression, and the latter "deals with Communist manipulation of a strike for Communist purposes . . . and the emphasis is upon one particular tactic—the subversion of the strike for partisan aims—and upon the economic and social plight of migrant workers."

Critics who focus on the political struggles in Steinbeck's novels often miss the true values of Steinbeck's artistic talent at a much deeper layer. This is exactly why a critic such as Edmund Wilson fails to see Steinbeck's craftsmanship. Wilson believes that most of Steinbeck's writings are burdened with "mawkish verbiage" that displays "a certain color of style which for some reason does not possess what is called magic." Joseph Warren Beach in Steinbeck and His Critics, quotes from *The Grapes of Wrath* to find fault with Steinbeck's style:

> For man, unlike any other thing organic or inorganic in the universe, grows beyond his work, walks up the stairs of his concepts, emerges ahead of his accomplishments. Having stepped forward, he may slip back, but only half a step, never the full step back. This you may say and

know it and know it. And this you can know—fear the time when Manself will not suffer and die for a concept, for this one quality is the foundation of Manself, and this one quality is man, distinctive in the universe.

To Beach, Steinbeck's observations about man are more didactic than artistic, so Beach refuses to consider them as literary art.

However, as an author who was widely loved, often by ordinary readers, Steinbeck had his own view of art, which is very different from that held by many of his critics. In Steinbeck's mind, the novelist must understand the world he creates and must serve as "the watch-dog of society . . . to satirize its silliness, to attack its injustices, to stigmatize its faults." To accomplish his task as a writer, Steinbeck consciously employed what may be called fictional, as opposed to empirical or "truthful," forms. Seen in this perspective, Steinbeck's preference for myths and fable is an attempt not to escape from reality but to create a world that exists within the work of fiction. In the 1930s he did research in the field to improve his control of material, and several of his books, which are now usually called the social novels, show that he was not often a realist in method and never wholly realistic in mode. For instance, under Steinbeck's artistic "manipulation," the main character, Doc, in *In Dubious Battle* refuses to exercise partisanship, nor does he show any revolutionary tendency. Instead Steinbeck presents an overview of the complex condition out of which the strike evolved.

As for his artistic intention, Steinbeck states in SEA OF CORTEZ that he is not a writer particularly concerned with specific causes or with social criticism per se, but one striving instead for an all-encompassing vision of life itself. For instance, when Jim, the Communist agitator in *In Dubious Battle*, tries to convince Doc of "the right cause" of the strikers, Doc answers: "You can only build a violent thing with violence." Responding to Jim's next Marxist slogan that "All great things have violent beginnings," Doc answers, "There aren't any beginnings. . . . Nor any ends. It seems to me that man has engaged in a blind and fearful struggle out of a past he can't remember, into a future he can't fore-

see nor understand." What Steinbeck means through Doc is that, compared with the long history of humanity, the current cause of asking for a little increase in salary makes no sense at all, if one has to shed blood or even die for that "cause." To further explain his point, Steinbeck continues, "the other side of the struggle is also made of men." As he writes, "Mankind must be the same. . . . We fight ourselves and we can only win by killing every man." To portray an alternative view of how human beings should live with one another, Steinbeck ends *The Grapes of Wrath* with Rose of Sharon feeding a dying man with her own breast. Therefore, it is reasonable to say that neither in *The Grapes of Wrath* nor in *In Dubious Battle* does the author have a fundamental advocacy of any political ideology.

Further Reading

Beach, Joseph Warren. *American Fiction 1920–1940.* New York: Russell & Russell, 1941.

Blotner, Joseph. *The Modern American Political Novel 1900–1960.* Austin: University of Texas Press, 1966.

Lewis, R. W. B. "John Steinbeck: The Fitful Daemon." In *The Young Rebel in American Literature,* edited by Carl Bode. London: Heinemann, 1959, 131–134.

Miron, George Thomas. *The Truth About John Steinbeck and the Migrants.* Los Angeles: Haynes Corporation, 1939.

Steinbeck, John. *The Grapes of Wrath.* New York: Penguin Books, 1992.

———. *In Dubious Battle.* New York: Penguin Books, 1992.

———. *A Russian Journal.* New York: Penguin Books, 1999.

Wilson, Edmund. *The Boys in the Back Room: Notes on California Novelists.* San Francisco: Colt Press, 1941.

Presidential Medal of Freedom   The Presidential Medal of Freedom, the nation's highest civilian award, recognizes exceptional meritorious service. The medal was established by President Harry S. Truman in 1945 to recognize notable service in the war. In 1963, President JOHN F. KENNEDY reintroduced it as an honor for distinguished civilian service in peacetime. He selected Steinbeck to receive the award, but did not live to carry out the honor. Steinbeck received the award from LYNDON B. JOHNSON on September 14, 1964.

propaganda   During WORLD WAR II and the cold war that followed, Steinbeck worked regularly as a propaganda agent for the American government. The author's interest in the subject first revealed itself when, upon returning from a trip to MEXICO before the war, Steinbeck expressed his concern about the effectiveness of the Nazis' propaganda machine in Germany. When President Roosevelt formed the OFFICE OF WAR INFORMATION, Steinbeck quickly agreed to write scripts for government radio broadcasts. A number of Steinbeck's artistic creations were products of his work with the government's war propaganda effort, including *THE MOON IS DOWN*, *LIFEBOAT*, and *BOMBS AWAY*. Further study of Steinbeck's work as propaganda may be found in Donald V. Coers, *John Steinbeck as Propagandist:* The Moon Is Down *Goes to War.*

See also COMMUNISM.

Pulitzer Prize   One of the highest American awards for excellence in letters, Steinbeck won the Pulitzer Prize for fiction in 1939 for his novel *THE GRAPES OF WRATH*. Other 1939 Pulitzer Prize recipients included the playwright William Saroyan and the poet Carl Sandburg. Earlier that year Steinbeck won the National Book Award for the same work. Remembering the many people who had supported him during his early years as a struggling writer, Steinbeck presented the $1,000 Pulitzer Prize money to his friend RITCHIE LOVEJOY, a young author attempting to complete and publish his first novel. The Pulitzer Prize compounded Steinbeck's frustration about his growing celebrity by making him the object of unending press attention. Soon after receiving the prize, Steinbeck moved temporarily to Mexico City to escape the commotion caused by his sudden notoriety.

Pym, Peter   Pen name used by Steinbeck to conceal his identity as author of the pulp mystery-thriller *MURDER AT FULL MOON*.

R

Red Pejorative name originally denoting membership in the Communist Party, it is applied to anybody perceived to be a troublemaker or labor agitator in THE GRAPES OF WRATH and IN DUBIOUS BATTLE.

religion Although he came from a Presbyterian family and was raised with a solid education in the Bible and religious themes, John Steinbeck himself was not a particularly religious man. Indeed, many of his novels and short stories lightly poke fun at what the author believed to be the hypocrisy and general silliness of religious people. Steinbeck was a man who valued tolerance highly, and too often he had observed that intolerance was frequently a characteristic of those who wore religion like a mantle. On the other hand, Steinbeck's strong sense of morality had a definite Judeo-Christian character. However, his view on God and religion was perhaps best summed up in a letter that Steinbeck wrote to his doctor a few years before his death. In that letter, Steinbeck explained that he did not have hope for heaven or fear of hell in the afterlife, because he did not believe, based upon his experience, that either existed.

Steinbeck's use of God figures may be found in writings throughout his career. For instance, it is significant to note, in TO A GOD UNKNOWN (1933), the author's description of Joseph Wayne's wedding in the church. The church wedding between Elizabeth McGreggor and Joseph Wayne is simply a prelude to their real marriage, when they pass through a mountain cut above the Nuestra Senora Valley. The challenge to the church wedding is seen in what Joseph says to Elizabeth:

> Listen, Elizabeth, do not be afraid. I tell you I have thought without words . . . Yesterday we were married and it was no marriage. This is our marriage—through the pass—entering the passage like sperm and egg that have become a single unit of pregnancy. This is a symbol of the undistorted real. I have a moment in my heart, different in shape, in texture, in duration, from any other moment.

Notable here is that for Joseph it is the un-Christlike sexual and erotic imagery of penetration and resultant pregnancy that is most important.

Another incident in *To a God Unknown* that indicates the author's attitude toward religion is when Joseph learns that his younger brother Benjy has been killed by Juanito. Normally, this would be a sad moment for anyone, but for Joseph it makes little difference. He is neither sad nor glad that Benjy is dead. As Steinbeck conveys it through Joseph, "All things are one, and all a part of me." His attitude is central to the novel, because Joseph is a hero who represents the interaction between the contents of the unconscious and of consciousness. As Robert DeMott has pointed out, it is not God who reconciles life and death, but Joseph Wayne. He is both literally and symbolically the central source in the Wayne family, the man of imagination who can create symbols and fictions that explain the many unknowns. *To a God Unknown* brings forth another aspect of Steinbeck's attitude toward his religion, the idea of the cosmos as an organic whole. All of nature in the novel is interconnected—plants, animals, rocks, dust, and water; the moon and sun; the cycles of weather and the cycles of life.

Much has been written about Steinbeck's use of biblical parallels in THE GRAPES OF WRATH, but the most obvious allusion to the Bible in Steinbeck's works may be found in his later novel, EAST OF EDEN. The book's title comes from Genesis 4:1–16. In the novel the Bible story is carefully discussed by Adam, Lee, and Samuel as they search for names for Adam's twin sons, whose names and stories later unfold as a parallel to the Cain-Abel story.

The major theme of *East of Eden* is not simply a moral dilemma over good and evil or the mixture of both; rather, Steinbeck examines the repetitive punishment for errors in human choices. Nonetheless, many early critics judged *East of Eden* a literary disaster, blaming Steinbeck for not understanding the biblical story and the American experience. They assumed the story of Adam to be the story of the fall of Man. But *East of Eden* is something quite different: a story of the rise of Man. To Steinbeck, Eden may be built anywhere. Steinbeck's rewriting of the biblical story makes Man immortal and God-like with power and soul ebbing and flowing; the writer has dignified human existence and glorified human experience, be it laudable or lamentable. In dignity Lee chooses to serve the Trasks, and Samuel Hamilton opts to have his land yield modestly. Yet both find harmony, comfort, and satisfaction in their choices of life.

Other noteworthy allusions to the Bible appear in *The Grapes of Wrath* and in many of Steinbeck's short stories, such as those in *The Long Valley*. Recently Steinbeck scholars like John Ditsky, Michael J. Meyer, Stephen George, and Barbara Heavilin all have examined the biblical implications in Steinbeck's major works. At the same time, scholars in Asia are noticing the Buddhist and Taoist elements in Steinbeck's works. Thus one can say that Steinbeck's literary texts have widespread and profound religious resonance.

Further Reading

DeMott, Robert. Introduction to *To a God Unknown,* by John Steinbeck New York: Penguin Books, 1995, vii–xxxvii.

Steinbeck, John. *To a God Unknown.* New York: Penguin Books, 1995.

reporter, Steinbeck as In 1926, Steinbeck worked as a cub reporter for William Randolph Hearst's paper, the NEW YORK AMERICAN, a job secured for him by his influential uncle JOE HAMILTON. Unhappy with the young writer's results, the *American's* editor soon reassigned him to cover the federal courts. Steinbeck showed little interest in reporting, however, and was soon fired. Although he would work as a correspondent and syndicated columnist throughout his career, the writer never again attempted to write as a straightforward reporter; rather, his work is distinguished by the typically "Steinbeck" style that mixed objective reporting with his characteristic humor and wry observation. The best known examples of Steinbeck's later reporting are his WORLD WAR II dispatches for the *New York Herald Tribune* (collected and republished by Viking Press in the volume ONCE THERE WAS A WAR) and his reports from the 1956 Republican and Democratic National Conventions for the *Louisville* (Kentucky) *Courier-Journal.*

Ricketts, Edward F. (1897–1948) Ricketts was Steinbeck's best friend and close colleague during much of the writer's career. Dark-haired, small, and full of energy, Ricketts was a marine zoologist who studied at the University of Chicago before moving to PACIFIC GROVE, CALIFORNIA to open a biological supply company called PACIFIC BIOLOGICAL LABORATORIES. He later moved the laboratory to CANNERY ROW in Monterey, where he met Steinbeck in a dentist's waiting room in the fall of 1930. Steinbeck once said that listening to Ricketts talk was like "hearing himself think aloud, only more clearly." The two men found an immediate affinity for one another and Ricketts remained Steinbeck's best friend and mentor for 18 years until Ricketts was killed in 1948 when his

Ed Ricketts, 1937 *(Mr. Pat Hathaway Photo Collection, Monterey)*

car collided with the Del Monte Express train at a Monterey crossing.

Ricketts inspired characters in many of Steinbeck's novels, including IN DUBIOUS BATTLE, THE GRAPES OF WRATH, THE MOON IS DOWN, CANNERY ROW, BURNING BRIGHT, and SWEET THURSDAY, as well as the short story "THE SNAKE." He also brought out Steinbeck's innate interest in science, and the author would spend hours each day gazing into microscopes and discussing specimens with Ricketts during the 1930s. Indeed, Steinbeck and Ricketts's mutual love of nature led to their expedition to the Gulf of California, a voyage that was documented in Steinbeck's book SEA OF CORTEZ: A LEISURELY JOURNAL OF TRAVEL AND RESEARCH.

Rocinante   Rocinante is the name of Don Quixote's horse. Steinbeck gave this name to his three-quarter-ton pickup truck-camper unit that

he drove across the United States to write TRAVELS WITH CHARLEY IN SEARCH OF AMERICA.

See also CERVANTES, MIGUEL DE.

Rodgers, Esther Steinbeck (1892–1986)   The eldest of Steinbeck's three sisters, she married a farmer and moved to Watsonville, California. Steinbeck was often frustrated with her and her husband's small-town conservatism and would argue with them about politics. He consulted with Esther for her knowledge of the family history while writing the novel EAST OF EDEN.

Rodgers & Hammerstein   The famous Broadway duo of Richard Rodgers (1902–79) and OSCAR HAMMERSTEIN created such hits as *Oklahoma!* and produced the stage adaptations of two Steinbeck works, BURNING BRIGHT and *Pipe Dreams* (based on SWEET THURSDAY). Both were unsuccessful in critical and popular terms.

Roosevelt,   Franklin   Delano (1882–1945)   Throughout much of his career Steinbeck considered himself a "New Deal Democrat" in the spirit of the legendary American president Franklin D. Roosevelt whom he admired greatly. During the 1930s the author collaborated with the documentary filmmaker PARE LORENTZ on THE FIGHT FOR LIFE, a film about the struggle against infant mortality commissioned by the Roosevelt administration as a vehicle to stir public support for a national health bill. As Steinbeck's celebrity grew, he began to offer advice to the president. On one such occasion he warned Roosevelt of the country's need to counteract the extremely effective Nazi propaganda machine that he had witnessed firsthand on a trip to Mexico. On another occasion the author arranged a meeting with the president to propose undermining the German war effort by flooding Germany with counterfeit currency. Although the plan was never acted upon, Roosevelt added Steinbeck to his pool of available talent and later called upon the writer to join the FOREIGN INFORMATION SERVICE under William J. Donovan. Steinbeck's involvement in the FIS led to his penning the novel THE MOON IS DOWN, as well as the story idea for the movie *LIFEBOAT*. On another occasion Roosevelt charged Steinbeck to cooperate with the Army Air Force in writing a book about the importance of long-range strategic bombers that resulted in *BOMBS AWAY*. In 1942, the president's wife, Eleanor, intervened on Steinbeck's behalf to free his film *THE FORGOTTEN VILLAGE* from the New York State Board of Censors, which had voted to prevent its opening.

S

Sag Harbor, New York   Sag Harbor is close (a little over 100 miles) to NEW YORK CITY and yet isolated from the stresses of urban life. The small resort village served as John and ELAINE ANDERSON STEINBECK's refuge during the 1950s and 1960s after the couple purchased a two-acre peninsula on the edge of a small inland bay. The setting, no doubt, brought back to the author the familiar sights and sounds of the ocean that played such an important role in his youth and early adulthood. Steinbeck fixed up the small cottage and built an isolated writing room where he spent most mornings working. The cottage at Sag Harbor became a sort of refuge for the aging artist, and he and his wife spent the remainder of their summers there until his death in 1968. An important whaling port in the 19th century, Sag Harbor is thought to have been the inspiration for the hamlet of New Baytown, the setting of Steinbeck's last novel, THE WINTER OF OUR DISCONTENT.

Salinas, California   The governmental seat of Monterey County, California, Salinas sits just east of Monterey Bay at the mouth of a wide, long, and fertile valley in central California. Steinbeck's birthplace as well as the location of the Steinbeck family home, it is the setting for many of the author's novels and short stories, including EAST OF EDEN. Salinas is a largely agricultural town famous for its year-round crops, particularly lettuce. Steinbeck spent much of his adolescence working on the ranches and farms around the Salinas area before

migrating to nearby PACIFIC GROVE. Salinas is currently home to the NATIONAL STEINBECK CENTER, a nonprofit organization that houses a permanent exhibit of the author's life and works, as well as an extensive archive of Steinbeck materials for academic research. The city of Salinas also has a public library, the John Steinbeck Library, named after its native son. Salinas was a multiethnic community even in the early days. Today it remains a multicultural city with residents from many different ethnic groups, and its Spanish heritage is reflected in the names of its streets, lakes, shopping centers, recreation areas and school districts.

Steinbeck's reflections of his hometown are often meditative and serious, as in "A PRIMER ON THE '30S" and "Conversation at Sag Harbor." In his "Always Something to Do in Salinas," the author reflects mixed emotions about his hometown. He remembers the days of roaming the countryside on his pony during his childhood, but he also chides the community's conservativeness. The following excerpt from "Always Something to Do in Salinas" expresses a typical view:

> Salinas was never a pretty town. It took a darkness from the swamps. The high gray fog hung over it and the ceaseless wind blew up the valley, cold and with a kind of desolate monotony. The mountains on both sides of the valley were beautiful, but Salinas was not and we knew it. Perhaps that is why a kind of violent assertiveness and energy like the compensation for sin grew up in the town. . . .

Main Street, Salinas, California, 1929 *(Mr. Pat Hathaway Photo Collection, Monterey)*

It is a kind of metropolis now and there must be nearly fourteen thousand people living where once a blacksmith shop stood in the swamp. The whole face of the valley has changed. But the high, thin, gray fog still hangs overhead and every afternoon the harsh relentless wind blows up the valley from King City. And the town justifies the slogan given it when it was very young . . . Salinas is!

Further Reading

Steinbeck, John. "Always Something to Do in Salinas." In *America and Americans and Selected Nonfiction,* edited by Susan Shillinglaw and Jackson J. Benson. New York: Viking, 2002, 4–12.

Salinas High School   John Steinbeck attended Salinas High School, graduating in 1919. While a student, he worked in the yearbook committee and served as class president during his senior year.

San Francisco, California   Situated on a peninsula between the Pacific Ocean and San Francisco Bay, this important port city had a continual influence in John Steinbeck's life during his adolescence and early adulthood. The author and his mother would often travel to the city to see cultural events that were not available in their small town of SALINAS, CALIFORNIA. Later, when Steinbeck was a student at nearby STANFORD UNIVERSITY, San Francisco provided the young man with another sort of entertainment, namely women. After dropping out of Stanford in 1925, Steinbeck returned to San Francisco on various occasions to live and work in the city's intellectual Bohemian culture.

Scott, Waverly (1936–)   Waverly is John Steinbeck's stepdaughter from his third marriage, to ELAINE ANDERSON STEINBECK. She lived with her mother and Steinbeck after their 1950 marriage and often traveled with them on their trips abroad.

scriptwriter Unlike many popular novelists at the time, including his contemporaries ERNEST HEMINGWAY and WILLIAM FAULKNER, Steinbeck had a remarkably successful career as a Hollywood scriptwriter. Refusing to work as a paid screenwriter for any of the major Hollywood studios, Steinbeck preferred to work on his own projects and thus maintain control of the final product. Films in which Steinbeck wrote or coauthored the script include: THE FORGOTTEN VILLAGE, LIFEBOAT (story), A MEDAL FOR BENNY (story, with JACK WAGNER), THE PEARL (with Emilio Fernandez and Jack Wagner), THE RED PONY, and VIVA ZAPATA! Many of Steinbeck's novels were also successfully adapted to the screen by other writers, including OF MICE AND MEN, THE GRAPES OF WRATH, THE MOON IS DOWN, and EAST OF EDEN. Steinbeck never received an ACADEMY AWARD for his scriptwriting, although he was nominated on a number of occasions.

Shebley, Lloyd (1906–1981) An employee of the Department of Fish and Game in Tallac, near Tahoe City, he became Steinbeck's friend during the years that the author worked as caretaker for the BRIGHAM FAMILY on Lake Tahoe. It was while working as Shebley's assistant at a Tahoe City hatchery that Steinbeck met his future wife, CAROL HENNING STEINBECK BROWN. A handsome man, Shebley later abandoned his work to try his luck at a career in Hollywood. He did not have much success, however, and was later forced to find work as a commercial fisherman.

Sheffield, Carlton (Dook) (1901–1989) Steinbeck's lifelong friend and correspondent. The two young men met as undergraduate students at STANFORD UNIVERSITY, where they shared a room. Sheffield planned to be a writer and, together with Steinbeck, joined the Stanford English Club. Later, during the summer break between classes, Sheffield and Steinbeck worked together for a surveyor team and then the SPRECKELS SUGAR Company. Steinbeck stayed with Dook and his wife, Ruth, on various occasions during the difficult early years, and often sought his friend's opinion on his work.

Sheffield became an English professor at Occidental College and the two men remained in almost constant contact for the remainder of their lives. In 1983, Sheffield wrote a memoir about Steinbeck entitled *John Steinbeck: The Good Companion.*

The Smoker's Companion The Smoker's Companion was a small magazine that paid Steinbeck his first royalties, $7, when it published his short story "THE GIFTS OF IBAN." Steinbeck wrote the story while he was working as a caretaker of the BRIGHAM FAMILY estate near Lake Tahoe. The story was published under the pseudonym JOHN STERN.

social justice Many of Steinbeck's most important works, including IN DUBIOUS BATTLE, "THE HARVEST GYPSIES" and THE GRAPES OF WRATH show that the author had clearly conceived notions of the dignity and justice that should be afforded all human beings. His work took on an increasingly angry tone when he was confronted by conditions that were clearly unjust, even tragic, particularly in the case of the treatment of migrant laborers in California during the 1930s. Steinbeck brought to the attention of the public the sufferings of men and women whom he knew to be hardworking and moral; he became a vocal proponent of government intervention to end injustice. Indeed in the series of articles "The Harvest Gypsies," the author decried the policies that were leading to the development of a "peon class" and urged the government to establish a migratory labor board that would regulate wages and normalize relations between employer and laborer. This sort of activism made Steinbeck a folk hero to many Americans.

Sphincter Steinbeck's nickname for the small tack shed behind John Breck's house on Palo Alto Avenue, where he lived for a time after his final attempt to earn a degree at STANFORD UNIVERSITY.

Spreckels Sugar One of the largest employers in the Salinas Valley during Steinbeck's childhood, Spreckels Sugar employed Steinbeck's father as plant accountant. John Steinbeck worked there periodically as a caretaker, crew boss, and sugar chemist during the summers and dropout periods while he attended STANFORD UNIVERSITY in the 1920s. The writer's experiences on the Spreckels sugar-beet ranches afforded him many of the contacts with the wandering laborers that would inform his early novels and short stories.

Stanford Spectator At STANFORD UNIVERSITY the *Stanford Spectator* was the student magazine that published Steinbeck's first works, including two short stories, "FINGERS OF CLOUD" and "ADVENTURES IN ARCADEMY" in 1924.

Stanford University Stanford University was called the Leland Stanford Junior University when Steinbeck entered as a freshman in the fall of 1919. Steinbeck was just 17 years old then; he attended the university periodically for six years before finally abandoning his studies without ever earning a degree. Determined to be a writer and unwilling to spend time on what he viewed to be a futile waste of effort, Steinbeck never adjusted well to academic life. Due to his poor performance, he was often on academic probation and had to beg for readmittance on several occasions. Although he did not do well by conventional standards, Steinbeck used his time at Stanford to concentrate intensely on his goal of becoming a writer. He made extensive use of the university's library, and took a number of creative writing and other classes that interested him. Steinbeck also met many people who would play important roles in his development as a writer, including the Stanford professors MARGERY BAILEY and EDITH MIRRIELEES. The young writer also found in the Stanford English Club a forum for developing his talent and meeting other people interested in writing. Stanford's greatest contributions to the author may have been the friendships he developed there, with CARLTON "DOOK" SHEFFIELD, CARL WILHELMSON, and John Breck, relationships that he would maintain for the rest of his life. Sheffield was Steinbeck's roommate. The two corresponded for the rest of their lives. Sheffied later wrote of their friendship at Stanford in *John Steinbeck: The Good Companion,* recalling vivid experiences of Steinbeck's days during those years. In addition, some of

Steinbeck's early writing samples are revealed in this memoir.

Steinbeck finally left Stanford in the spring of 1925. His younger sister, MARY STEINBECK, graduated from the university. Stanford now has significant holdings of Steinbeck materials, including manuscripts, notes, correspondence, photographs, and ephemera in the Special Collection Department of the university's Green Library.

Steinbeck, Elaine Anderson (1915–2003) Steinbeck's third wife, she met the writer in 1949 while still married to the Hollywood actor Zachary Scott, the father of her only child, WAVERLY SCOTT. Steinbeck fell immediately in love with the sophisticated woman from Texas, and the two corresponded in secret for almost a year, seeing each other as much as possible until Elaine finally announced to her husband that she wanted a divorce. The couple moved to separate apartments in New York, and Steinbeck busied himself introducing her to his circle of friends and acquaintances. Having spent time stage-directing RODGERS & HAMMERSTEIN's Broadway production *Oklahoma!,* Elaine was able to introduce the author to the ways of the New York stage, which inspired Steinbeck to dedicate much of his energy to stage writing during the coming years. On December 28, 1950, John and Elaine were married at the New York home of Steinbeck's friend and longtime publisher HAROLD GUINZBURG. Over the next 17 years John became increasingly dependent on his wife, often requiring her to entertain his children and keep away unwanted guests while he applied himself to his work. The Steinbecks developed the custom of spending the winter in their NEW YORK CITY brownstone and then retiring to the nearby seaside town of SAG HARBOR for the pleasant summer months. They also shared a mutual passion for traveling and spent much time abroad, either touring or simply renting a house in England or France, where they could entertain their families and friends. Steinbeck often wrote articles to finance their travels, and Elaine learned the art of photography in order to illustrate the author's work. Elaine took great care of her husband during the final year of his life as his health rapidly deteriorated. After his death on December 20, 1968, Elaine Steinbeck acted as executrix of the vast liter-

John and Elaine Anderson Steinbeck *(Photofest)*

ary estate left behind by her husband. Among other projects, she oversaw the compilation of a volume of his correspondence and directed the publication of the unfinished manuscript THE ACTS OF KING ARTHUR AND HIS NOBEL KNIGHTS.

Steinbeck, John Ernst (1863–1935)   John Ernst Steinbeck was John Steinbeck's father. As a young man, John Ernst learned to mill flour on his family's farm. Later he became a manager at the Sperry Flour Mill in SALINAS. He was an active and respected member of the community. When he lost his job at the flour mill in 1910, he became an introspective, quiet man, forcing his wife, OLIVE HAMILTON STEINBECK, to assume most of the control of the large family of three girls and one boy. Hoping to restore his luck, he opened a feed store in Salinas that was soon driven out of business because of the automobile's arrival in the valley. Throughout the Steinbecks' long string of economic misfortune, the community rallied around the family. A friend eventually arranged a job for John as an accountant at the SPRECKELS SUGAR plant, the same place where John Ernst would later find employment for his errant son, John. John Ernst was eventually appointed Monterey County Treasurer, a job that suited his bourgeois sensibilities and that he held until he was forced by illness to retire in the mid 1930s.

Steinbeck, John, IV (1946–1991)   The second of Steinbeck's two sons by his wife GWYNDOLYN CONGER, John Junior was called "Catbird" by his father because he liked to sit on the floorboard of the family car, which John Steinbeck, Sr., called the "catbird seat." After his parents' divorce in 1948, custody of him and his brother, THOMAS STEINBECK, was awarded to their mother. During their childhood, the boys spent summers with their father, often joining him and their stepmother, Elaine, on vacations in foreign cities. Both Thom and John, Jr., experienced a difficult relationship with their sometimes generous, often preoccupied father. Their mother, Gwyn, who took every opportunity to turn the two boys against her ex-husband, made the troublesome situation much worse, according to John, Jr.'s autobiography. Nevertheless, they grew closer to their father as they matured, and in the end developed a close relationship with him.

In 1965, John, Jr., was drafted into the army and served as a war correspondent in Vietnam, where his father joined him for a brief time in 1967. Shortly before his discharge from the service in 1967, John, Jr., drew the attention of the press when 20 pounds of marijuana was discovered in his apartment in the District of Columbia under rather suspicious circumstances. At the time, he had been preparing an article for *The Washingtonian* titled *The Importance of Being Stoned in Vietnam*, which exposed the high rate of drug usage by soldiers in Vietnam. He was later acquitted of all charges.

In 1968, John, Jr., returned to Vietnam as a journalist accompanied by the photojournalist Sean Flynn, son of the actor Errol Flynn. Sean Flynn subsequently disappeared in Cambodia and was presumed killed. During this time, John, Jr., converted to Buddhism. He later wrote of his experiences in a 1969 memoir titled *In Touch*. In 1971, John, Jr., won an Emmy award for his work on the CBS documentary, *The World of Charlie Company*, narrated by Walter Cronkite.

While studying Tibetan Buddhism in Boulder, Colorado, in 1975, he met his future wife, Nancy Harper. They were married in 1982, and John, Jr., adopted his wife's two children, Megan and Michael. In 1984, John, Jr., was diagnosed with a genetic disorder, hemochromatosis, which causes excessive buildup of iron in the body. Because the condition is made worse by drug and alcohol abuse, John, Jr., sought successful treatment for a lifelong addiction to drugs and alcohol. After a diagnosis of a ruptured disc, John, Jr., underwent corrective surgery in 1991, and died during the operation. His autobiography, *The Other Side of Eden*, was completed by his wife, and published by Prometheus Books in 2001.

Steinbeck, Olive Hamilton (1867–1934)   Olive was John Steinbeck's mother, one of nine children, the youngest daughter, born to SAMUEL and ELIZABETH HAMILTON. She grew up on the Hamilton Ranch in KING CITY, CALIFORNIA, and attended high school in nearby SALINAS, where she studied to be a teacher. At 17 Olive received her teaching certificate and began working in a small school in Monterey County until she met JOHN ERNST STEINBECK, the manager of a Salinas flour mill, at a church social in King City. The couple soon married and relocated to Salinas, where they eventually had four children, three girls and one world-famous author. Olive Steinbeck was a religious woman with a strict sense of right and wrong, who tended to make the important family decisions while her meek husband stood quietly by. She was a very active figure in the community, often chairing local committees and charities. Olive Steinbeck may well be the source of John Steinbeck's puritanical sense of morality, as well as his interest in the poor and less fortunate. She died on February 19, 1934, after a long, lingering illness and stroke.

Steinbeck, Thomas (1944–)   The first of Steinbeck's two sons by his second wife, GWYNDOLYN CONGER, Thomas (Thom) Steinbeck was born on August 2, 1944. After his parent's divorce in 1948, custody of him and his brother, JOHN STEINBECK IV, was awarded to their mother. During his childhood the boys spent summers with their father, often joining him and their stepmother Elaine on vacations in foreign cities. Both Thom and his brother had a difficult relationship with their sometimes generous, often preoccupied father. And things were made much worse by their mother, Gwyn, who, never having remarried, took every opportunity to play the wronged wife and turn the two boys against her ex-husband. Still, they grew closer to their father as they matured and in the end developed a close relationship with him. Maybe influenced by his father, Thom has written numerous original screenplays and documentaries, as well as adaptations of his father's work. In 2003 Thom Steinbeck published the story collection *Down to a Soundless Sea* (Ballantine Books).

As the late writer's heirs, Thom Steinbeck and Blake Smyle, daughter of John Steinbeck IV and granddaughter of the writer, sued the estate of ELAINE ANDERSON STEINBECK and MCINTOSH & OTIS, Steinbeck's New York literary agency, in 2004. In the lawsuit Thom Steinbeck and Smyle allege that Elaine Steinbeck and the agents "engaged in a 30-year hidden conspiracy to deprive John Steinbeck's blood heirs of their rights in the intellectual properties of John Steinbeck" (*New York Times*, August 3, 2004).

Stern, John John Stern is the pseudonym that Steinbeck used when he published his first short story "THE GIFTS OF IBAN" in *THE SMOKER'S COMPANION*.

Stevenson, Adlai Ewing (1900–1965) American politician and diplomat who helped found the United Nations and later served as ambassador to the UN from 1961 to 1965. Steinbeck was impressed after reading a number of Stevenson's speeches and immediately wrote the politician a letter expressing his admiration. Steinbeck then agreed to write a foreword for a collection of Stevenson's speeches that was published as part of the man's presidential campaign effort. Both Stein-

beck and his wife, ELAINE ANDERSON STEINBECK, became active supporters of the Stevenson candidacy, often working to recruit other celebrities to appear at Stevenson rallies. The author also collaborated directly with the candidate on a number of occasions during the 1952 and 1956 campaigns, although he is not believed to have written any of Stevenson's speeches directly. For the rest of his life Steinbeck would refer to himself as a "Stevenson Democrat." The author finally met the candidate at the 1956 Democratic Convention in Chicago, and the two men immediately became good friends. Stevenson and Steinbeck often corresponded and spent time together during the following years.

Street, Webster (Toby) (1899–unknown) Toby Street was a World War I veteran who became Steinbeck's lifelong friend when the two aspiring writers met in the Stanford English Club at STANFORD UNIVERSITY. After Steinbeck abandoned his studies to concentrate on his work, he and Street lived together for some time in Street's small SAN FRANCISCO apartment, a time that the author fondly remembered as his "tour of duty as an intellectual Bohemian." Street was working on a play called "THE GREEN LADY," which he later abandoned when he was unable to reconcile its multiple elements. He gave Steinbeck the play's manuscript and offered to let the young writer use the material for a novel. Fascinated with the complex story, Steinbeck spent more than two years trying to rewrite it as a novel. After considerable rewriting and changes, "The Green Lady" eventually became Steinbeck's third novel, TO A GOD UNKNOWN. Street gave up his plans of being a writer, married, and returned to Stanford to earn a law degree. Over the years the two men remained close friends and Street often served as Steinbeck's adviser, and at times his legal counsel, even performing the duties of attorney during the author's first divorce from CAROL HENNING STEINBECK BROWN.

T

Tortilla Flat The uphill district above the town of MONTEREY, CALIFORNIA, in the novel, *TORTILLA FLAT*, where the majority of *paisanos* resided. SUE GREGORY, the teacher and poet who provided many of the basic outlines for stories in the book, had extensive contact with many of the *paisanos* and Mexican Americans who lived in a wooded area on the edges of Monterey, and it is to this geographic area Steinbeck refers. However, it appears he appropriated the place-name "Tortilla Flat" from a hilly site near CARMEL, CALIFORNIA.

Travis, Tex (unknown) Tex was the engineer on the *WESTERN FLYER*, a 76-foot ship that Steinbeck and EDWARD RICKETTS chartered for their scientific expedition to the Gulf of California that resulted in the book *SEA OF CORTEZ: A LEISURELY JOURNAL OF TRAVEL AND RESEARCH.*

V

Vietnam War The Vietnam War was the longest and most unpopular armed conflict ever fought by Americans. Officially, it began in 1959 when President Dwight Eisenhower assigned military advisers to the Republic of South Vietnam's government to assist the South Vietnamese in their struggle against the Communist North Vietnamese led by Ho Chi Minh. However, United States involvement actually began shortly after WORLD WAR II, when President Harry Truman sent troops to assist the French who had reinstated their colonial administration of Vietnam at the conclusion of the war, and who encountered increasing popular resistance from the Vietnamese. In 1956 the defeated French abandoned their efforts to regain the colony, and the United Nations partitioned Vietnam into two separate sections, Communist North Vietnam, and anticommunist South Vietnam. With the passage of the Gulf of Tonkin Resolution in 1965, which authorized massive American troop deployment in Vietnam, the United States became the lead military force in the defense of South Vietnam against the North. From 1959 until January 1973, when the Paris Peace Accords brought United States participation to a conclusion, more than 58,000 American lives were lost, and close to 2.5 million Vietnamese lost their lives as well.

Steinbeck was one of the few American writers to support the Johnson administration's policy in Southeast Asia and particularly in Vietnam. President LYNDON B. JOHNSON attempted on a number of occasions to send Steinbeck to Asia to report on local conditions and the progress of the war. Wishing to avoid an overtly political involvement, however, Steinbeck sidestepped the president's requests. In November 1966, Steinbeck agreed to travel to Asia as a special correspondent for the Long Island, New York, tabloid *Newsday*, with which he had a contractual obligation for the "LETTERS TO ALICIA" series. During the next few months, he traveled with his wife, Elaine, to Vietnam, Laos, Thailand, Indonesia, and Japan, stopping first in California to visit his older son, THOMAS STEINBECK, who was taking basic training before being sent himself to Vietnam. Steinbeck's younger son, JOHN STEINBECK, IV was already serving with the army in Vietnam. After a briefing in Hawaii, Steinbeck arrived in Saigon in December, where he was assigned Marine MAJOR SAM GIPSON, JR., to be his guide. For six weeks the author made field trips during which he participated in numerous military operations, at times traveling across enemy lines and even witnessing combat. His dispatches for *Newsday* received harsh public criticism for their defense of the government's increasingly unpopular policies.

There were a few reasons for which Steinbeck was considered a pro-war writer. First, he was a friend of Lyndon Johnson. He had personal invitations from the president and frequented the White House and Camp David on many occasions. At the beginning of the Johnson administration, he was awarded the Medal of Freedom and had been encouraged by the president to visit Vietnam and to report his views privately and directly to Johnson, and on the occasion of Steinbeck's son's departure for Vietnam in May 1966, the president invited both father and son to the White House. Second, Steinbeck did use his *Newsday* columns to express his concerns over the anti-war protests back home. His "Letters to Alicia" in *Newsday* were taken as enthusiastic support for the war itself, although he avoided discussing the war in any general terms, concentrating on the daily life of soldiers instead. Third, Steinbeck was reluctant to join other writers and university scholars in lending his name to lists in opposition to the war, although he shared some of their views. Before his visit to Vietnam, the Russian poet Genya Yevtushenko in a poem published in *The New York Times* chided Steinbeck, who had visited Moscow in 1963, to speak out in opposition to this American war. Steinbeck's reply asserted his principles regarding the war in Vietnam:

> In your poem, you asked me to speak out against the war in Vietnam. You know well how I detest all war, but for this one I have particular hatred. I am against this Chinese-inspired war. I don't know a single American who is for it. But, . . . you asked me to denounce half a war, our half. I appeal to you to join me in denouncing the whole war.

Yet Steinbeck did recognize flaws in the government's approach to the war and Johnson's handling of it. As biographer Jackson J. Benson puts it, "He came to see the war as a kind of quicksand of deceit and confusion [believing that] we would be here for at least a generation and [that] there would be no victory." In a letter to Jack Valenti, Steinbeck wrote, "There is no way of justifying sending troops to another man's country. And there is no way to do anything but praise the man who defends his own land. . . . The government we are supporting [South Vietnam] is about as smelly as you can get." Later Steinbeck met with General Westmoreland and learned more about the ongoing war. Benson wrote, "He soon realized that Westmoreland and the others were lying to the president about the war, and he determined to tell the president himself what was really going on, then write about it."

Viking Press   Steinbeck's publisher from 1937 until the present. Steinbeck began his relationship with Viking when his previous publisher Covici-Freide went bankrupt. One of the co-owners of the defunct firm, PASCAL COVICI, was hired as an editor by the head of Viking Press, HAROLD GUINZBURG, who agreed to honor Covici's commitment to Steinbeck. Viking, which is now part of Penguin Putnam, continues to publish Steinbeck's work under copyright, as well as posthumous releases and collections.

Vinaver, Eugène   (1899–unknown)   An illustrious SIR THOMAS MALORY scholar at the University of Manchester in England, Vinaver assisted John Steinbeck on a number of occasions with the author's research for his book *THE ACTS OF KING ARTHUR AND HIS NOBLE KNIGHTS*. On one occasion the two men combed through the private libraries of various wealthy English families for new material. Together they discovered a previously unknown Malory manuscript that shed important light on the discipline. Steinbeck and Vinaver remained occasional correspondents for the remainder of the author's life.

Wagner, Jack (1897–1965)   The brother of Max Wagner, and a close friend of Steinbeck from his boyhood in Salinas, California. As a Hollywood screenwriter, he collaborated with Steinbeck on the screenplay for *The Pearl,* and on the story and screenplay for the 1945 film, *A Medal for Benny,* which was later nominated for Academy Awards for best original story and best supporting actor.

Wagner, Max (1903–1975)   Steinbeck's close friend from his boyhood in Salinas, the two men grew up as neighbors and remained friends throughout their lives. During the late 1930s they often spent time together in Hollywood where Max was working with his brother Jack Wagner. In 1939 he introduced Steinbeck to a beautiful singer named Gwyndolyn Conger, the woman who eventually became Steinbeck's second wife. Max helped the author hide his affair with Gwyn until Steinbeck finally separated from his first wife, Carol Henning Steinbeck Brown, in 1943.

war correspondent   Always ready to do his duty for his country, Steinbeck was too old for service at the beginning of World War II. Eager to see some action, the author was granted permission in 1943 to travel to the European war theater as a correspondent for the *New York Herald Tribune.* Only recently married to his second wife, Gwyndolyn Conger, Steinbeck remained in Europe from June to October, traveling first to England, then Africa, and finally Italy and the Mediterranean. Instead of using the objective style of reporting that was already being done by such celebrated war correspondents as Ernie Pyle and Clark Lee, the author chose a style very similar to the storytelling that had made him famous, recounting interesting anecdotes and personal accounts that were both intimate and alive with detail. His columns were immensely popular and were soon syndicated and reproduced throughout the United States and the world. Steinbeck's war correspondence was later collected and published in 1958 as *Once There Was a War.*

Steinbeck would once again fill the role of war correspondent when, during the Vietnam War in 1966, he agreed to travel to Asia as a special correspondent for the Long Island, New York, tabloid *Newsday.* During the next few months he traveled with his wife, Elaine Anderson Steinbeck, to Vietnam, Laos, Thailand, Indonesia, and Japan, stopping first in California to visit his son Thomas Steinbeck, who was in basic training before being sent to Vietnam. For six weeks the author made field trips during which he participated in numerous military operations, at times traveling across enemy lines and even witnessing combat. His dispatches for *Newsday,* which constituted a continuation of his "Letters to Alicia" series, lacked the warmth and humanity of his work in World War II and they received harsh public criticism for their defense of the government's increasingly unpopular policies.

Watson, Graham (1913–2002)   Steinbeck's literary agent in the United Kingdom, Graham Watson was employed by Curtis Brown. He became close friends with the author and his third wife, ELAINE ANDERSON STEINBECK, and often served as the Steinbecks' host and tour guide during their frequent visits to England in the 1950s and 1960s.

Western Flyer The boat owned by ANTHONY BERRY, which Steinbeck chartered for his expedition to the Gulf of California in 1940. The boat was fairly new, measured 76 feet, and had a 165-horsepower diesel engine. A 50-foot-long hold below was used to store the specimens collected on the trip. The boat had bunks to sleep 12, though only seven people made the journey. The expedition is described in Steinbeck's book SEA OF CORTEZ: A LEISURELY JOURNAL OF TRAVEL AND RESEARCH.

Whitaker, Francis (1907–1999) A blacksmith and iron sculptor from Philadelphia, Whitaker met John Steinbeck in CARMEL, CALIFORNIA, in the early 1930s. Whitaker and his wife were deeply involved political radicals and Whitaker himself was the leader of the John Reed Club, a socialist organization. They both worked diligently to convert the young writer and his wife, CAROL HENNING STEINBECK BROWN, to socialism. The Whitakers became regular members of Steinbeck's circle of artists and friends in the Carmel/Monterey area. During the next couple of years, Whitaker introduced Steinbeck to a number of radical labor organizers who were probably important models for his book IN DUBIOUS BATTLE.

Wilhelmson, Carl (1889–1968) A Finnish veteran of World War I, he met Steinbeck at the Stanford English Club. Steinbeck found Wilhelmson's nonconformist attitude appealing, but more important, he admired Wilhelmson's talent and persistence as a writer. Wilhelmson spent some time with the young author at the BRIGHAM FAMILY estate in Tahoe. Wilhelmson published one novel, *Midsummernight*, in 1930, and a children's book, *Speed of the Reindeer*, in 1954. He also wrote an unpublished book with the working title "Blind Bargain." Unlike Steinbeck, he never achieved success as an author, though he became a decent businessman. The two men remained friends for the duration of their lives.

Williams, Annie Laurie (1894–1977) Steinbeck's film and theater agent from the MCINTOSH & OTIS LITERARY AGENCY, Williams negotiated the rights for many of the author's most important works, including THE GRAPES OF WRATH. She used her background in theater to help Steinbeck write the original play script for GEORGE S. KAUFMAN's Broadway production of OF MICE AND MEN, by instructing him on the mechanics of stage direction, including where to insert exits and entrances. The astounding success of the play made Steinbeck a national sensation and object of endless interest from the big HOLLYWOOD picture studios. In what was perhaps the biggest coup of her career, Williams sold the film rights to Steinbeck's novel THE MOON IS DOWN for $300,000, the largest sum that had ever been paid for movie rights at that time.

Winter, Ella (1898–1980) Winter was a radical leader in the 1930s and the wife of the journalist and political philosopher Lincoln Steffens. The couple were neighbors of John and CAROL HENNING STEINBECK BROWN in CARMEL, CALIFORNIA, during the 1930s. She introduced Steinbeck to a group of farm laborers and organizers who would serve as models for his book THE GRAPES OF WRATH.

World War II The United States entered World War II after the Japanese attacked the American Pacific fleet at Pearl Harbor, Hawaii, without warning on December 7, 1941. Prior to this date, most of Europe and Asia had been overrun by the Axis countries, Nazi Germany, Fascist Italy, and Imperial Japan. The war was triggered by Germany's invasion of Poland in September 1939. The United States had resisted entering the war until Japan's assault. After a series of setbacks, by 1943 the Allied Forces of Great Britain, the United States, and Free France had succeeded in regaining some of the territory conquered by the Axis.

In 1943, Steinbeck was granted permission by the U.S. War Department to travel to the European front as a correspondent for the *New York Herald Tribune*. Only recently married to his second wife, GWYNDOLYN CONGER, Steinbeck remained in

Europe from June to October, traveling first to England, then North Africa, and finally Italy. Rather than emulating the objective reporting of celebrated journalists such as Ernie Pyle and Clark Lee, the author chose a style very similar to the storytelling that had made him famous. He recounted interesting anecdotes and personal accounts that were both intimate and alive with detail. His columns proved to be immensely popular and were soon syndicated and reproduced throughout the United States and the world. In one of his most memorable dispatches, the author describes in intimate detail the combat that he experienced during the invasion of the Italian coastal city of Salerno. Writing in the third person, he tells of a young girl eviscerated by a shell, and of a young soldier crying over a fallen comrade. He writes graphically, too, of his own physical discomfort—of skin worn raw from a filthy woolen uniform, and of swollen feet from ill-fitting combat boots. While on his tour of duty he met the photojournalist ROBERT CAPA, who would later join Steinbeck for a tour of the Soviet Union that resulted in his book A RUSSIAN JOURNAL. Steinbeck's time in Europe was a powerful experience for the middle-aged author and he returned to his home in New York physically exhausted and with eardrums burst by an exploding shell. The author's war correspondence was later collected and published in 1958 as ONCE THERE WAS A WAR.

Z

Zanuck, Darryl F. (1902–1979)   Zanuck was a producer and director for Twentieth Century–Fox. Zanuck met John Steinbeck when he purchased the film rights for the novel *THE GRAPES OF WRATH*. Initially, Steinbeck did not think that Zanuck was the right person to produce the work, but, Steinbeck was pleased with the resulting film, which he felt to be an effective vehicle for conveying the plight of the migrant workers in California. The two men worked together again in the 1950s on the film *VIVA ZAPATA!*, whose original screenplay was written by Steinbeck at Zanuck's urging.

PART IV

Appendices

CHRONOLOGY

1902

February 27: John Ernst Steinbeck III is born in Salinas, California. He is the third of four children and the only son of John Ernst and Olive Hamilton Steinbeck.

1905

January 9: Steinbeck's younger sister, Mary Blanch Steinbeck, is born in Salinas.

1906

April 18: Steinbeck lives through the great earthquake, which literarily shakes Salinas apart.

1908

Fall: Steinbeck enters the first grade at what is known as the Salinas "Baby School."

1910

Fall: At eight years old, Steinbeck begins grammar school in the third grade at the West End School near his home.

1911

Early February: The Sperry Flour Mill is shutting down, leaving John Ernst senior out of work; he has been the manager since the middle of the 1890s when the family settled in Salinas.

1912

January: John Ernst senior buys out Blackie's Feed Store in Salinas and starts his own business.

John is given his own chestnut-colored Shetland pony, Jill; like Jody in *The Red Pony,* he is expected to care for her.

Fall: Steinbeck is allowed to skip the fifth grade and enter the sixth grade at the West End School, making him a year younger than most of his classmates through high school.

1914

July 28: World War I begins.

1915

Fall: Steinbeck enters Salinas Union High School as a freshman.

1919

February: A general strike, organized by a procommunist, paralyzes Seattle.

June 16: Steinbeck graduates from Salinas Union High School.

September: Organized by the Industrial Workers of the World (IWW), a total of 343,000 steelworkers walk off their jobs. In the same month, the Boston police strike.

October 1: Steinbeck registers as a freshman at Stanford University, listing English as his major field of study. He rooms with George Mors.

October–December: Steinbeck meets Carlton "Dook" Sheffield while taking his French class, and they become close friends.

1920

Sinclair Lewis publishes *Main Street*; F. Scott Fitzgerald publishes *This Side of Paradise*.

April 5: After two months' leave of absence due to a serious flu, Steinbeck returns to Stanford and registers for the spring term, signing up for courses in American history, elementary economics, and English literature.

Early May: An attack of acute appendicitis puts Steinbeck in the hospital for surgery and makes him unable to complete the remainder of the spring term at Stanford.

June–September: With the help of his father, Steinbeck and George Mors (his roommate at Stanford) work for a surveying crew and find the working conditions unbearable. After they quit the job, John's father finds another job for them with the maintenance crew at the Spreckels factory near Salinas.

October 1: Steinbeck registers for the autumn quarter at Stanford where he rooms again with George Mors.

Late November: With a number of incompletes to make up, Steinbeck is on probation at Stanford. He is more interested in reading and writing than attending classes. One Sunday morning, his roommate, George Mors, wakes up to find John gone and a note saying, "Gone to China. See you again sometime. Please free the chipmunk." Steinbeck goes to the San Francisco area and stays for a time with friends. He is unsuccessful in trying to get to China or finding other employment. He finally winds up as a straw boss supervising pickup crews at a Spreckels ranch near Chualar, about 10 miles south of Salinas.

December 31: Steinbeck is "officially" requested to withdraw from Stanford University.

1921

January: Steinbeck works with a dredging crew and at the same time works on his writing.

1922

February 2: James Joyce's *Ulysses* is published by Shakespeare & Company.

June: Steinbeck returns to Spreckels as a bench chemist. Encouraged by his parents, John decides to return to Stanford.

November 11: Steinbeck applies for readmission to Stanford, submitting some letters of reference.

1923

January 2: Steinbeck registers for the winter quarter at Stanford as an English/journalism major.

February 26: John Ernst Steinbeck, Sr., is appointed Monterey County Treasurer by the county board of supervisors.

April–May: Steinbeck continues his participation in the English Club at Stanford.

June 19: Steinbeck registers for the summer quarter, which is held at the Hopkins Marine Station, located near the Steinbeck summer cottage in Pacific Grove. Steinbeck takes a class in zoology, which reveals his interest in nature and natural processes that would later manifest itself in his writing.

September: Steinbeck returns to Salinas, living with his parents and working as a bench chemist at Spreckels. At this point, John begins a practice, which he carries on throughout his life, of using letter-writing as a way of warming up for his fiction.

1924

January: Steinbeck takes a class in short-story writing with Edith Ronald Mirrielees, whose influence on his development as a writer is significant.

February: Steinbeck publishes his short story "Fingers of Cloud" in *The Stanford Spectator*, a campus literary magazine.

June: Steinbeck's second short story, "Adventures in Arcademy," is published in *The Stanford Spectator*.

1925

April 10: Fitzgerald's *The Great Gatsby* is published by Scribners.

June 17: Steinbeck packs up his belongings and leaves Stanford for the last time.

November: John sets out for New York City on a freighter, the *Katrina*, which sails from Wilmington in southern California.

December: Steinbeck arrives in New York. His brother-in-law, Gene Ainsworth, helps John to get a job as a laborer on the construction of Madison Square Garden. He works at this job for about five or six weeks but quits after a worker falls from a scaffold, landing near him. At the same time Steinbeck is writing short stories but has difficulties finding publishers.

1926

March: John's uncle, Joe Hamilton, helps him get a job as a reporter for the *New York American.*

May: Steinbeck does not do well in his job as a reporter and is fired. Then John spends the next month trying his hand as a freelance writer, but after a number of failures to get his stories published, he decides to return to California.

Mid-June: Steinbeck returns to California and continues to write, supporting himself with a variety of jobs.

September–January: Steinbeck is hired by Mrs. Alice Brigham, the wealthy widow of a prominent San Francisco surgeon, as a caretaker of her summer home on the south shore of Lake Tahoe. Here Steinbeck spends most of his time writing.

October: Ernest Hemingway publishes *The Sun Also Rises.*

1927

March: Steinbeck's short story, "The Gifts of Iban," is published in the *Smoker's Companion* under the pseudonym of John Stern.

April: With the help of his new acquaintance, Lloyd Shebley, who works for the California Fish and Game Department, Steinbeck gets a part-time job at the Tallac Hatchery.

May: On a vacation, Steinbeck goes home to Salinas and takes several trips to Palo Alto and San Francisco. He becomes interested in a play Toby Street is working on called "The Green Lady." This work would later become the basis for Steinbeck's novel, *To a God Unknown.*

Mid-June: Steinbeck returns to the Tahoe area and works for the Brigham family for the remainder of the summer, during which he writes his novel, *Cup of Gold.*

1928

January: Steinbeck completes the *Cup of Gold* manuscript. Katherine Beswick, a Stanford friend, agrees to type the manuscript without charge. Ted Miller in New York agrees to be his informal agent to see if he can get the manuscript published.

February: Steinbeck starts planning a new novel, "The Green Lady," after the Toby Street play, which would later be titled *To a God Unknown* (1933).

May: Steinbeck starts the first draft of his new novel, quits his work with the Brighams, and takes a vacation before starting his new job at the Tahoe City hatchery.

June: Steinbeck meets Carol Henning in Tahoe City.

August: Lloyd Shebley leaves the hatchery to seek a film career in Hollywood, and Steinbeck is left alone.

September: After Steinbeck and a coworker wreck the hatchery superintendent's new truck, he is laid off and returns to the family cottage in Pacific Grove; he then works as warehouseman in San Francisco until he quits the job in late December.

1929

January: Steinbeck receives word from Ted Miller in New York that after seven rejections the "Cup of Gold" manuscript has been accepted for publication by Robert M. McBride. At the same time Steinbeck is working hard on the manuscript of "The Green Lady."

July: After abandoning the first version of "The Green Lady," Steinbeck is working on a second version of the same story.

August: Cup of Gold is published by McBride. Even though the book receives little critical attention, it sells fairly well. Steinbeck, however, is not happy with the garish dust jacket designed by his artist friend Mahlon Blaine.

September 27: Hemingway's *A Farewell to Arms* is published by Scribner's Sons.

October 29: The New York Stock Exchange crashes, marking the beginning of the Great Depression.

November: John and Carol announce their intention to marry, and the following month they travel south to Los Angeles and stay with Carlton Sheffield and his wife.

December: Steinbeck reads Hemingway's work for the first time and realizes that Hemingway's prose style is very close to what he has been working toward.

1930

January 14: John Steinbeck and Carol Henning get married in Glendale, California, with Carlton Sheffield as a witness, and they settle in Eagle Rock in the hills east of Los Angeles.

March: Steinbeck changes the title of the recently completed "Green Lady" to "To an Unknown God," which came from a Vedic hymn.

July: Steinbeck finishes the manuscript for "Dissonant Symphony," an experimental novel, and sends it to Scribner's for possible publication. Later, Scribner's turns it down.

August: John and Carol move out of their home in Eagle Rock, and after several moves within the area of Glendale and Eagle Rock, they move back to the family cottage in Pacific Grove by the end of August.

October: Steinbeck meets Ed Ricketts for the first time, one of the most important meetings in his life. During this time of the year, Steinbeck hears from an old Stanford friend, Elizabeth Smith, about a new literary agency in New York, McIntosh & Otis, which he would contact later.

December: Steinbeck sends his murder mystery manuscript, "Murder at Full Moon," to Ted Miller to see if he can find a publisher.

1931

January: Steinbeck becomes a frequent visitor to the Pacific Biological Laboratories located on Cannery Row in Monterey, California.

April: Steinbeck urges Ted Miller to try a new literary agency, McIntosh and Otis, to place his manuscripts.

August 18: After receiving the rejection for his manuscript, "To an Unknown God," Steinbeck plans to rewrite the novel and sends his manuscript for "Dissonant Symphony" to Ted Miller to pass along to McIntosh & Otis, which marks his permanent association with Mavis McIntosh and Elizabeth Otis, his literary agents.

December: Carol finishes typing the "Pastures" manuscript, and it is sent to Ted Miller in New York to pass along to McIntosh & Otis.

1932

February 27: On his 30th birthday, Steinbeck receives a telegram from McIntosh & Otis, telling him that "The Pastures of Heaven" has been accepted for publication by the publisher, Jonathan Cape and Harrison Smith.

March: Carol Steinbeck gets a job working for Ed Ricketts that pays her $50 a month.

May: Cape and Smith go bankrupt, and "Pastures" is picked up by Brewer, Warren & Putnam. Steinbeck sends a manuscript, "St. Katy the Virgin," to his agents, but they are unable to place it.

June: Carol and Joseph Campbell have a brief romantic encounter, which is terminated by mutual consent when Campbell leaves with Ed Ricketts on a specimen-collecting trip to Alaska.

July: With the promise of money from "Pastures of Heaven" and because Carol no longer works for Ed Ricketts, the Steinbecks move back to southern

California, settling in the Montrose area just north of Eagle Rock.

October: *The Pastures of Heaven* is published.

November 8: Franklin D. Roosevelt is elected president.

1933
January: John and Carol are experiencing financial problems. Steinbeck asks McIntosh and Otis to withdraw his manuscript "Dissonant Symphony." Eventually Steinbeck destroys this manuscript.

January 3: Steinbeck writes to publisher Robert O. Ballou that he will have the manuscript "To a God Unknown" to him by the end of February and explains that the word "unknown" in the title means "unexplored."

February 11: Steinbeck sends the manuscript "To a God Unknown" to McIntosh and Otis.

Mid-March: Steinbeck moves into the family home in Salinas to take care of his mother, who suffers serious illness. For the summer, Carol works at part-time jobs in Monterey while John does his writing, using the dining room table outside his mother's room.

May: The Agricultural Adjustment Act lifts agricultural prices to "parity" with industrial prices.

June 30: Steinbeck has finished his story, "The Red Pony," while taking care of his mother.

August 9: Steinbeck writes to Carl Wilhelmson, telling him that he has been working on several stories and complaining that it is difficult to write when his parents are in bad health. Some of these stories will later be incorporated into *The Red Pony* and others used in *Tortilla Flat* (1935).

September: *To a God Unknown* is published by Robert O. Ballou.

November: Steinbeck's short story, "The Red Pony," later retitled "The Gift," appears in the *North American Review.*

December: "The Great Mountains" appears the *North American Review.* "The Gift" and "The Great Mountains" were the first two parts of *The Red Pony* (1937) and are later included in *The Long Valley* (1938).

1934
February 19: Steinbeck's mother, Olive Hamilton Steinbeck, dies in Salinas as the result of a second stroke.

February 25: Steinbeck has just finished a short story, "The Chrysanthemums," while taking care of his father.

Early March: Steinbeck finishes the manuscript of "Tortilla Flat" and sends it to McIntosh & Otis.

March: John and Carol accompany Ed Ricketts on a specimen-collecting trip to Laguna Beach for a week.

April: Another short story, "The Murder," by Steinbeck is published in the *North American Review.* "The Murder" wins the O. Henry Prize.

May: John and Carol divide their time between Pacific Grove and the family home in Salinas. Steinbeck begins research on labor unions and migrant workers by going on various expeditions, collecting firsthand information on migrant workers, communists, and labor organizations for a novel.

During this time, Steinbeck is working on more short stories, which later appear in *The Long Valley* (1938). "The Harness" (originally entitled "The Fool"), "Flight" (originally "Manhunt"), "The White Quail," and "Johnny Bear" (originally "The Sisters") have been written this summer.

August: Steinbeck begins writing his novel about a farm worker; strike novel, later to be titled *In Dubious Battle* (1936).

October: Another short story by Steinbeck, "The Raid," appears in the *North American Review.*

November–December: Ben Abramson, a well-known Chicago bookseller, introduces Steinbeck's writings to publisher and editor Pascal Covici, who would be his friend and editor till his death.

1935

February 4: Steinbeck has completed the manuscript for *In Dubious Battle.* He signs a contract with Covici-Friede to publish *Tortilla Flat.*

March: Elizabeth Otis takes over from Mavis McIntosh to handle Steinbeck's career for the agency. A short story, "The White Quail," is published in the *North American Review.*

May 23: After a long illness, Steinbeck's father, John Ernst Steinbeck, dies at his daughter Esther's house in Watsonville.

May 28: Tortilla Flat is published and is an instant best seller.

June 22: Steinbeck's short story, "The Snake," appears for the first time in *The Monterey Beacon* (newspaper).

August: Steinbeck signs a contract with Covici-Friede for "In Dubious Battle," after it had been rejected by an editor who was sitting in for Pascal Covici while he was away on a promotional trip. Covici is furious that the substitute rejected Steinbeck's manuscript.

Also in this month, Covici travels to San Francisco on a business trip and meets Steinbeck for the first time.

September: John and Carol travel to Mexico and on to New York to escape publicity.

October: While in Mexico, John and Carol receive a telegram from McIntosh & Otis, telling them that Paramount Pictures had purchased the motion picture rights to *Tortilla Flat* for $4,000.

1936

Early January: The Steinbecks return home via New York to sign the Paramount contract and then on to Pacific Grove.

January 15: In Dubious Battle is published by Covici-Friede in a limited as well as a regular trade edition. It has moderately good sales.

Mid-April: Steinbeck is working on "Something That Happened," which would eventually become *Of Mice and Men.*

May 11: John and Carol purchase two acres of land near Los Gatos in Santa Clara County, California, to gain some privacy.

May 27: Steinbeck reports that his setter pup has destroyed nearly half of his manuscript of "Of Mice and Men."

May–June: Steinbeck meets John O'Hara, who has been hired to write a play based on *In Dubious Battle.*

June 11: Steinbeck receives the California Literature Gold Medal (Commonwealth Club of California) for *Tortilla Flat.*

August: Steinbeck works on a series of articles on migrant workers for the *San Francisco News.* On one of his fact-finding trips for these articles, Steinbeck is introduced to Tom Collins, who manages a federal government labor camp. By mid August, Steinbeck completes the second writing of "Of Mice and Men" and finishes the newspaper articles. Also in this month, his short story, "The Leader of the People," is published in *Argosy* (London).

An essay entitled "The Way It Seems to John Steinbeck" appears in the Fall issue of the periodical *Occident.*

September 12: A condensed version of his newspaper article entitled "Dubious Battle in California" appears in *The Nation.*

October: Another short story, "The Lonesome Vigilante," is published in *Esquire.*

October 5–12: Steinbeck's series of newspaper articles on migrant workers is published in the *San Francisco News* under the alternate titles "The Harvest Gypsies" or "California's Harvest Gypsies."

November 3: Franklin D. Roosevelt is reelected president.

November 9: Another short story, "Breakfast," appears in this issue of the *Pacific Weekly.*

November 25: The lab on Cannery Row in Monterey burns down. Ed Ricketts is unable to save much except some clothing. All of his records, personal possessions, documents, and books are lost.

November–December: Steinbeck begins work on a long novel, which he entitled "L'Affaire Lettuceberg." Some of the writing later contributed to the draft of "The Grapes of Wrath."

December: St. Katy the Virgin is privately printed in a limited edition by Covici-Friede as a Christmas gift for friends.

1937

February 6: The novel *Of Mice and Men* is published by Covici-Friede and is chosen by the Book-of-the-Month Club. The book hits the best-seller lists almost immediately.

February 28: John and Carol plan a trip to Europe.

March 23: The Steinbecks sail for the East Coast via the Panama Canal aboard the SS *Sagebrush.*

April 15: The Steinbecks arrive in Philadelphia. Then the couple travel by train to New York, where he attends a dinner honoring Thomas Mann. The event makes Steinbeck miserable because he does not like publicity.

During their stay in New York, John and Carol fight and further realize that their marriage is disintegrating.

Late May–early June: The Steinbecks leave for Europe aboard the SS *Drottningholm* in late May. Early the following month they arrive in Göteborg, Sweden. They spend the first part of the month in Copenhagen and then travel on to Stockholm, where they develop a friendship with the Swedish painter, Bo Beskow, whom Steinbeck had met briefly in the Covici-Friede office in the winter of 1936. Beskow paints his first of three portraits of Steinbeck.

June 5: The Commonwealth Club of California awards a second gold medal to Steinbeck for *In Dubious Battle.*

July: The Steinbecks travel from Sweden to Helsinki, Finland, and then on to Leningrad and Moscow in the Soviet Union.

August: The Steinbecks return to New York on a small freighter.

August 23: John and Carol confer with the well-known playwright-director George S. Kaufman on the play version of *Of Mice and Men.* At Kaufman's farm in Pennsylvania, Steinbeck works intensively for a week and completes the final script.

John and Carol purchase a red Chevrolet in New York and start for California via Chicago, where they visit Uncle Joe Hamilton and bookseller Ben Abramson. Then they continue their journey following Route 66 through Oklahoma to California.

Steinbeck's short story, "The Promise," is published in *Harper's Magazine.*

September: Another Steinbeck short story, "The Ears of Johnny Bear," appears in *Esquire.*

October: Steinbeck's best-known short story, "The Chrysanthemums," first appears in *Harper's Magazine.*

Mid-October: Steinbeck sets off for another trip to the migrant camps to gather information and returns to Los Gatos early the following month.

November 23: The play version of *Of Mice and Men* begins its run on Broadway at the Music Box Theater in New York City. It is a success and runs for 207 performances.

A book version of the play *Of Mice and Men* is published by Viking Press.

1938

January 12: The play version of *Tortilla Flat,* adapted by playwright Jack Kirkland, opens in New York. The play lasts only four performances.

February: Steinbeck starts work on the manuscript for "L'Affaire Lettuceberg."

Mid-February: Steinbeck goes to Visalia for about 10 days with Tom Collins to assist with the problems of migrant workers.

Steinbeck meets the well-known film critic and maker of documentary films, Pare Lorentz. Lorentz and Steinbeck are both involved in works related to the migrant labor problems of the time.

March 7: Steinbeck goes on a trip to visit migrant labor camps with *Life* photographer, Horace Bristol.

April: "Their Blood Is Strong," a nonfiction account of the migrant labor problem in California, is published by the Simon J. Lubin Society (San Francisco).

April 15: "Starvation Under the Orange Trees," an article on migrant labor, appears in the *Monterey Trader.*

May: Steinbeck receives the New York Drama Critics Award for the play of *Of Mice and Men.*

Steinbeck completes the first draft of his novel, "L'Affaire Lettuceberg." Unhappy with this manuscript, Steinbeck decides to burn it and starts work on a new version of his long novel.

June: A short story, "The Harness," is published in *The Atlantic Monthly.*

Late July: Publisher Pascal Covici declares bankruptcy and is hired as a senior editor at Viking Press.

September: A second short-story collection, entitled *The Long Valley,* incorporating the fourth part of *The Red Pony,* is published.

Carol invents a new title for Steinbeck's long novel: "The Grapes of Wrath."

Late October: Steinbeck completes "The Grapes of Wrath" manuscript, and Carol finishes typing it.

1939

January: Elizabeth Otis visits with the Steinbecks in Los Gatos to negotiate some changes in "The Grapes of Wrath" manuscript. She persuades John Steinbeck to make some changes, but he will not change much of the language or the controversial ending of the novel.

Mid-January: Steinbeck is elected to the National Institute of Arts and Letters, an honor that he accepts gratefully.

Mid-April: *The Grapes of Wrath* is published and becomes an immediate best seller.

About this time, *Between Pacific Tides* by Ed Ricketts and Jack Calvin is published by the Stanford University Press.

April 25: Steinbeck travels to Chicago to help Pare Lorentz with a documentary film, *The Fight for Life,* and stays about a month.

May: After leaving Chicago, Steinbeck makes a hurried trip to New York and Washington, D.C., and returns secretly to Los Gatos.

June: Steinbeck spends most of the month in Los Angeles working with Lorentz on *The Fight for Life.* Also in this month, a boyhood friend, Max Wagner, introduces John to band singer Gwyndolyn Conger.

August: The marriage between John and Carol continues to disintegrate; after a fight Carol returns home to Los Gatos, and John returns to the ranch.

September 1: Hitler's troops invade Poland, provoking Great Britain and France to declare war, marking the beginning of World War II.

September: Carol and John take a getaway trip. They travel to the Pacific Northwest to see the sights and to visit with friends. Then they move on to Chicago to see Uncle Joe Hamilton and check with Pare Lorentz, who is still working on *The Fight for Life.*

October–November: John spends time between Los Gatos and Pacific Grove reading, studying, and helping Ed Ricketts. They also make a number of field trips together.

December 15: Steinbeck is in Los Angeles to view the screenings of *The Grapes of Wrath* and *Of Mice and Men.*

December 22: The motion picture of *Of Mice and Men* opens in Hollywood.

Late December: Carol becomes pregnant just after Christmas. John persuades her to get an abortion, from which an infection develops, and she has to have a hysterectomy.

1940

January 24: The motion picture of *The Grapes of Wrath* has its world premiere at the Rivoli Theatre in New York City and receives overwhelming endorsements from critics.

February 16: The motion picture version of *Of Mice and Men* opens at the Roxy Theatre in New York City.

March 11–April 20: John, Carol, Ricketts, and four crew members embark on the *Western Flyer* to the Gulf of California to collect specimens and take notes for an extensive book on the marine life of the area.

May: Steinbeck receives two awards for *The Grapes of Wrath,* one from the American Booksellers Association, and the other from the editors of the journal *Social Work Today.*

May 6: *The Grapes of Wrath* receives the Pulitzer Prize for fiction.

May 23: Steinbeck is back in Mexico working on a film script for a documentary about life in a traditional Mexican village, which he titles *The Forgotten Village.*

June 22: Steinbeck travels to Washington, D.C., to present his views about Nazi propaganda to President Roosevelt.

July: Steinbeck begins writing "The God in the Pipes," a new play-novel that introduces some of the characters who will appear in 1945 in *Cannery Row.*

September 12: John returns to Washington, D.C., and meets with President Roosevelt, urging him to institute a plan he devised would ruin the German economy and prevent the spread of Nazism. Roosevelt is sympathetic but ignores the plan.

Mid-October: Steinbeck returns to Mexico to work on the filming of *The Forgotten Village.*

November: Steinbeck leaves Mexico and arrives in Hollywood to meet Gwyn; his affair with Gwyn accompanies his deteriorating relationship with Carol.

November 5: Franklin D. Roosevelt wins the campaign for a third term.

1941

Mid-January: Steinbeck writes a preface for Tom Collins's semiautobiographical novel, *They Die to Live,* and the copy for a word-picture story, to be published in *Life.*

Steinbeck begins work on his part of the "Sea of Cortez" manuscript.

February: Because Carol is having a difficult time getting over the flu, which has bothered her since the past December, John talks her into taking a vacation in Hawaii.

February 7: Carol sails for a vacation in Hawaii. During this time Gwyn comes to Monterey for visits, and John travels to Los Angeles occasionally.

March: Mavis McIntosh visits Steinbeck in Monterey, and he shows her around and introduces her to his friends.

April 2: Carol returns home, and John tells her all about his affair with Gwyn. John sends for Gwyn and she comes to Monterey. A terrible confrontation results.

Late April: Carol and John separate permanently, and he moves into the Eardley Street house in Pacific Grove, which they had purchased in January.

May: The book version of *The Forgotten Village* is published by Viking Press.

July 4: Steinbeck has completed his work on the first draft of "Sea of Cortez" and is working on another manuscript called "God in the Pipes."

August: The short story, "How Edith McGillcuddy Met R. L. Stevenson," is first published in *Harper's Magazine.*

September: Steinbeck starts on the film script for *The Red Pony.*

Steinbeck decides to move to the East Coast. He asks Gwyn to go with him, and she agrees.

October 7–8: Steinbeck flies to Washington, D.C., to attend a conference dealing with a propaganda agency, the Foreign Information Service (FIS).

John and Gwyn move into a house on a farm owned by actor Burgess Meredith near Suffern, New York. John begins writing material for the FIS.

November 16: Steinbeck and Gwyn move into a two-bedroom apartment in a residential hotel, The Bedford, on East 40th Street in Manhattan.

The film version of *The Forgotten Village* runs into legal difficulties with the New York State Board of Censors as allegedly being obscene. After a public hearing, the ban is lifted, and the documentary is shown.

Late November: Steinbeck begins work on "The New Order," the original title of the 1942 novel *The Moon Is Down.*

December 5: Sea of Cortez (coauthored by Steinbeck and Edward F. Ricketts) is published by Viking Press.

December 7: Japan attacks Pearl Harbor.

Mid-December: Steinbeck submits the manuscript for "The Moon Is Down" to Viking Press.

Late December: John and Gwyn spend Christmas and New Year's Day in Roark Bradford's French Quarter home in New Orleans.

1942
January 7: John and Gwyn return to New York. During this winter, Steinbeck is busy working on a play script for "The Moon Is Down."

March 6: The novel *The Moon Is Down* is published by Viking Press. It sells well and becomes a Book-of-the-Month Club selection.

Carol files papers for a divorce on grounds of mental cruelty.

April 7: The play version of *The Moon Is Down* opens on Broadway. Also around this time, Steinbeck is offered a permanent job with the Office of War Information (OWI), but has to go through a security check.

Mid-May: Steinbeck is offered another temporary assignment to write two books for the air force.

May 23: The Moon Is Down closes on Broadway. The film version of *Tortilla Flat* opens in New York.

Late May–June: Steinbeck travels with photographer John Swope and air force trainees on a 20,000-mile trip gathering information from first-hand experience for his book.

November 27: Bombs Away: The Story of a Bomber Team is published by Viking Press. The royalties from the sale of this book are donated to the Air Force Aid Society Trust Fund.

December: Steinbeck begins work on a script for an air force training film.

Mid-December: Jack Wagner, Max's brother, approaches Steinbeck with an idea for a film. Over the next few weekends Steinbeck and Wagner produce a script for the film *A Medal for Benny,* released in 1945.

1943
January: Steinbeck is working on a script for the Alfred Hitchcock motion picture *Lifeboat.*

Mid-January: Steinbeck finishes the screenplay for *Lifeboat.* John and Gwyn move to an apartment in New York City.

March: The film *The Moon Is Down* is released. Steinbeck applies for a job as a war correspondent and is hired by the *New York Herald Tribune.*

March 18: Final notice of Carol and John's divorce is issued.

March 29: John and Gwyn travel to New Orleans and are married in the home of a friend, Lyle Saxon.

April 5: Steinbeck receives word from the War Department that he has been accredited as a correspondent for the European theater.

May: Steinbeck spends the month preparing for his new job. Gwyn objects to his going, but Steinbeck is determined to go.

June 3: Steinbeck leaves for England aboard a troopship.

June 8: Steinbeck arrives in London.

July–October: Steinbeck reports on the war from various points in Britain, North Africa, and Italy.

October 15: Steinbeck returns to the United States and arrives home in poor shape physically and emotionally.

November: Steinbeck begins work on the "Cannery Row" manuscript.

December: The Steinbeck Pocket Book, with an introduction by Pascal Covici, is published by the Blakston Co. and distributed by Pocket Books.

Mid-December: Steinbeck starts writing a novella with a Mexican setting called "The Good Little Neighbor."

1944

Mid-January: While traveling in Mexico with Gwyn, Steinbeck plans for a future novel, *The Pearl* (1947). Also in this month, Gwyn announces that she is pregnant.

Steinbeck sees the movie *Lifeboat* for the first time and is very unhappy with Hitchcock for changing some of the things he had written. He asks Twentieth Century–Fox to remove his name from the screen credits.

Spring: Steinbeck meets Ernest Hemingway at a party in New York at Tim Costello's on Third Avenue. The meeting ends with a disaster, when Hemingway breaks a walking stick that was a gift to writer John O'Hara from Steinbeck.

June–July: Steinbeck continues to work on "Cannery Row" in an office provided by Viking Press. He completes the work in six weeks.

August 2: Gwyn gives birth to a boy, whom they name Thomas Myles Steinbeck.

September: Steinbeck envisions a new novel that takes place in the Salinas Valley. He persuades Gwyn to move back to California to be near the source for the novel.

Early October: The Steinbecks move back to California, John driving, and Gwyn and the baby arriving by plane.

Late November: Steinbeck begins work on "The Pearl."

Early December: Although the official publication of *Cannery Row* was not scheduled until January of 1945, the booksellers are already selling the book by the thousands.

1945

January 2: Cannery Row is officially published by Viking Press.

February 9: John and Gwyn arrive in Mexico City to assist in the casting, locations, and music for the film, *The Pearl.*

April 12: President Roosevelt dies, and Harry S. Truman becomes president.

May: The motion picture *A Medal for Benny* is released and receives a mixed critical reaction.

August: John works with Max Wagner and Emilio (Indio) Fernández on the script for *The Pearl.*

November: After a brief visit to his home in New York, John returns to Mexico and stays there for three weeks to work on the filming of *The Pearl.*

December: "The Pearl of the World" is published in the *Woman's Home Companion.*

Mid-December: Steinbeck returns to New York from Mexico.

1946

January–May: Steinbeck is working on "The Wayward Bus" manuscript.

June 12: Steinbeck's second son, John Steinbeck IV, is born.

July: Steinbeck returns to Mexico briefly for some postproduction work on *The Pearl.*

October 18: John and Gwyn sail for Sweden aboard the SS *Drottningholm,* leaving the two boys at home with a nursemaid.

November 15: Steinbeck receives the King Haakon Liberty Cross (Norway) for *The Moon Is Down.*

Winter: Swedish artist Bo Beskow paints a second portrait of Steinbeck. After a brief trip to Paris, the Steinbecks return to New York.

1947

January: Steinbeck is writing a play entitled "The Last Joan" based on an idea given to him by Burgess Meredith.

John and Gwyn have been experiencing marital difficulties since his return from Europe and the war.

Early February: Viking Press publishes *The Wayward Bus.* The book is selected by the Book-of-the-Month Club.

March: Steinbeck discusses with noted photographer Robert Capa the idea of taking a trip to Russia to write articles for the *New York Herald Tribune,* which would finance the trip.

April: Steinbeck gives up on the play, "The Last Joan," and destroys it. Instead, he spends much time preparing for his trip to Russia.

May 14: Steinbeck's travel plans are interrupted when he suffers injuries from a fall from the second-story balcony at his brownstone when the railing gives way. He is hospitalized due to knee injuries.

June: John and Gwyn travel to Paris.

July 18: Gwyn returns to New York.

July 21: Steinbeck and Capa set out for Russia.

Late July–September: Steinbeck and Capa tour the Soviet Union, Steinbeck taking notes and Capa taking photographs.

Late September: Steinbeck returns to New York.

November: Steinbeck's short novel, *The Pearl,* is published by Viking Press, with illustrations by José Clemente Orozco.

December: The First Watch, a pamphlet printed by the Ward Richie Press in Los Angeles, is published and distributed to friends by Steinbeck as a Christmas gift. The content of this pamphlet was a letter from Steinbeck to a "Mr. G" dated January 5, 1938.

1948

Early January: Steinbeck flies to California to do research for his next novel about the Salinas Valley. While in California, he visits old friends and works with Ed Ricketts.

February 17: The film *The Pearl* is released and shown at the Sutton Theatre in New York.

Mid-March: Steinbeck returns to New York.

April: A Russian Journal is published by Viking Press.

Steinbeck enters the hospital to have varicose veins removed from his legs. After leaving the hospital, he separates from Gwyn and the boys and takes a room at New York's Bedford Hotel.

May 7: Ed Ricketts's car is hit by a train in Monterey, and he is seriously injured.

May 11: Ricketts dies from his injuries before Steinbeck can reach his bedside.

Mid-May: After Ed's funeral, Steinbeck and a close friend, George Robinson, go to the lab on Cannery Row and go over Ed's things. Steinbeck burns his letters to Ed.

June–July: Gwyn confronts John with a demand for a divorce when he returns to New York. After this confrontation, Gwyn takes the boys with her to Los Angeles, and John spends most of his summer in Mexico working on the "Zapata" film.

August: Steinbeck travels between Mexico, Los Angeles, and New York.

Early September: Steinbeck moves back into the family cottage on 11th Street in Pacific Grove. With him is a former navy steward, James Neale, a domestic servant with the Steinbecks in New York.

October: Gwyn is granted a divorce in a Reno courtroom.

Early November: Steinbeck meets Elia Kazan in Los Angeles, and the two fly to Mexico City for the filming of *Viva Zapata!*

Mid-November: Steinbeck returns to Pacific Grove.

November 23: Steinbeck is elected to membership in the American Academy of Arts and Letters.

December 25: A short story, "Miracle of Tepayac," is published in *Collier's.*

1949

January: The film *The Red Pony* is released after a delay of seven years. Steinbeck sees the film for the first time in Los Angeles.

Late March: While working on the script for "Zapata," Steinbeck is also writing short stories and taking notes for the big novel that in 1952 will be published as *East of Eden.*

April–May: Steinbeck finishes the first draft of the "Zapata" script.

Steinbeck invites one of his Hollywood friends, actress Ann Sothern, to visit him in Pacific Grove on the Memorial Day weekend. Sothern brings with her a friend, Elaine Scott, the wife of actor Zachary Scott. Elaine and John fall in love at this time.

Summer: John and Elaine agree to get married if Elaine can obtain a divorce from her husband.

August: Steinbeck is working on an experimental play/novelette manuscript entitled "Everything," later titled "In the Forest of the Night," and finally *Burning Bright,* published in 1950. Steinbeck borrowed the last two titles from William Blake's poem "Tyger."

September: A short story, "His Father," appears in *The Reader's Digest.*

November 1: Elaine calls John to tell him that she and her husband have agreed to a divorce.

Late November: Steinbeck returns to New York.

December: Elaine and her daughter, Waverly, travel to New York to join Steinbeck.

1950

January: Steinbeck starts writing the play "Burning Bright." His enthusiasm for plays becomes stronger with his exposure to Elaine's circle of Broadway friends.

February: Steinbeck is polishing "Burning Bright" and in the meantime, making notes for his next project, a drama script for *Cannery Row.*

March–April: John and Elaine fly to Texas to meet her family, returning to New York in early April.

Early August: Steinbeck sets aside the dramatization of *Cannery Row;* instead, he works on his profile of Ed Ricketts and submits the draft to Viking.

October 18: The play of *Burning Bright* opens in New York at the Broadhurst Theater and draws heavy criticism. The play runs only a few performances before it closes.

November 11: Steinbeck lashes out at his critics in an article titled "Critics, Critics, Burning Bright," which appears in the *Saturday Review.*

December 21: Elaine's divorce from Zachary Scott becomes final.

December 27: John and Elaine are married in a quiet ceremony at the home of his publisher, Harold Guinzburg.

1951

January: John and Elaine begin their New Year with a honeymoon in Bermuda. Then the couple spends much time in Hollywood to work on "Zapata," and visit with family and friends in Northern California.

Late January: John and Elaine return to New York.

Early February: Steinbeck begins work on his big novel, "The Salinas Valley."

At this time, Steinbeck develops a distinctive writing pattern by keeping a journal in the form of letters to his editor, Pat Covici.

Late April: Steinbeck has finished about one-fourth of the projected manuscript.

June: While reading Genesis 4:1–16 in the Bible, Steinbeck decides that a better title for his big novel would be "East of Eden."

Mid-July: Steinbeck has written more than 135,000 words for the "East of Eden" manuscript. He makes a lined box for the manuscript as a present for Pat Covici with the Hebrew word *timshel* on the lid. (According to Steinbeck's research, *timshel* means "thou mayest" rather than "thou should.")

September: The Log from the Sea of Cortez, a portion of *Sea of Cortez* (1941) with an original essay, "About Ed Ricketts," is published by Viking.

Early November: Steinbeck completes the first draft of "East of Eden."

1952

January: Steinbeck starts revising "East of Eden." This works takes him a few months.

February 7: The movie of *Viva Zapata!* is released and shown at the Rivoli Theatre in New York and is an immediate commercial success.

Late March: John and Elaine depart New York on a freighter bound for Genoa, Italy, and then Greece. The ship changes its destination, stopping first at Casablanca in North Africa, then goes on to Algiers. The couple then take a boat to Marseilles, France. From there they rent a car and drive down the east coast of Spain.

Mid-May: While in Paris, Steinbeck starts writing travel articles for *Collier's.*

June–July: John and Elaine travel on to various cities in Italy. While in Italy in June, Steinbeck is criticized by Italian communists for his political views.

July: John and Elaine return to Paris and then travel to England, and then move on to Ireland to visit the home of Steinbeck's Hamilton ancestors.

August 31: The Steinbecks fly back to New York from Paris.

Steinbeck's articles, "Duel Without Pistols" and "The Soul and Guts of France," are published in *Collier's.*

September: East of Eden is published by Viking Press, and it soon becomes a best seller.

September–October: Steinbeck and Elaine are working for the Democratic presidential candidate, Adlai E. Stevenson.

November 4: Dwight D. Eisenhower is elected president.

1953

January: Steinbeck's articles for *Collier's,* "The Secret Weapon We Were Afraid to Use" and "I Go Back to Ireland," are published.

John and Elaine go to the Virgin Islands for a winter vacation.

March–May: Steinbeck sets aside his plan to write a musical play based on *Cannery Row.*

June–July: In New York, Steinbeck works on a novel that he titles "Bear Flag," which will turn out, when published in 1954, to be *Sweet Thursday.*

September: The first edition of a combined work, *The Short Novels of John Steinbeck,* with an introduction by Joseph Henry Jackson, is published by Viking Press.

Mid-September: The first draft of the "Sweet Thursday" manuscript is completed.

Mid-October: Steinbeck enters Lenox Hill Hospital with a mysterious illness after he returns from Long Island where he rented a house for a month. It turns out to be depression. Later in the year John consults with psychologist Gertrudis Brenner to get himself out of the depression.

1954

January: While on vacation at Caneel Bay on St. John, Steinbeck meets the John Kenneth Galbraiths, with whom he becomes good friends.

Early February: John and Elaine plan for an extensive trip to Europe.

Mid-March: The Steinbecks sail for Europe.

March 26: John and Elaine arrive in Lisbon, Portugal, then they rent a car for most of the trip in Europe. They tour Spain and then head to Paris.

May 27: During their tour in Europe, Steinbeck receives word that Robert Capa has been killed in Vietnam by a land mine.

June 10: Viking Press publishes *Sweet Thursday.*

During his stay in Paris, Steinbeck contributes a short article every week to *Figaro Littéraire,* a weekly newspaper magazine.

Early July: John and Elaine go to Munich, Germany, at the request of Radio Free Europe. While in Munich, Steinbeck records a personal statement of his position on the situation in Eastern Europe, which is broadcast over Radio Free Europe.

October–November: After a two-week trip to London, the Steinbecks return to Paris, close up their rental house, and then move on to Florence, Rome, Athens, and then Naples on a leisurely journey.

Late December: John and Elaine return to New York aboard the *Andrea Doria,* arriving just before Christmas.

1955

January: Steinbeck meets William Faulkner for the first time.

March 9: The film *East of Eden,* starring James Dean, is released with Steinbeck attending the opening at the Astor Theatre in New York. The film receives mixed reviews.

March 10: The article "How to Tell Good Guys from Bad Guys" is published in *The Reporter.*

April: A short story, "The Affair at 7, Rue de M——," is published in *Harper's Bazaar.*

April–May: Steinbeck begins his long association with the *Saturday Review* to which he will contribute editorials and articles.

June: John and Elaine move into the Sag Harbor house (on Long Island, New York) that they purchased the previous winter.

September: Pipe Dream, a musical comedy version of *Sweet Thursday* that Steinbeck has been working on with Richard Rodgers and Oscar Hammerstein goes into production.

October 24: Pipe Dream opens in New Haven.

November 30: Pipe Dream opens on Broadway at the Sam S. Shubert Theatre in New York.

1956

Early February: John and Elaine return to Sag Harbor after their winter vacation in Trinidad, and John resumes work on an experimental novel entitled "Pi Root."

March: A short story, "How Mr. Hogan Robbed a Bank," is published in *The Atlantic.*

Mid-March: Steinbeck is writing a satire, "The Short Reign of Pippin IV."

April: Steinbeck agrees to cover this year's political conventions for the *Louisville* (Kentucky) *Courier-Journal.*

May: Steinbeck is introduced to Alicia Patterson Guggenheim and her husband, Harry Guggenheim, at the Ethridge estate in Louisville while Steinbeck is there for the Kentucky Derby. This meeting will lead Steinbeck to write for *Newsday,* a Long Island newspaper, years later.

July 14: Waverly Scott, Elaine's daughter, is married to Frank Skinner.

August 4: Steinbeck's article, "The Mail I've Seen," is published in *The Saturday Review.* In this article Steinbeck discourages teachers from assigning their students to ask authors to comment on their work, because it would take too much of an author's time to respond.

August 10: John and Elaine attend the Democratic Convention in Chicago to report for the *Louisville Courier-Journal.* Steinbeck confers with the candidate, Adlai Stevenson.

Late August: John and Elaine attend the Republican Convention in San Francisco. After the conventions, Steinbeck sends speech material to the Stevenson campaign.

September: During the election campaign, Steinbeck writes speech materials and broadcasts for Radio Free Europe and the United States Information Service.

October: Steinbeck begins work with the Eisenhower administration's People to People Program.

As a member of a writer's committee, Steinbeck helps in drafting proposals about world conditions.

November: After finishing the "Pippin" manuscript, Steinbeck decides to work on putting Malory's *Morte d'Arthur* into simple prose in modern English, yet without changing anything of the original stories.

November 6: Dwight D. Eisenhower is reelected president.

1957

January: John and Elaine plan and prepare for a research trip to Europe on the Malory project. The trip will be financed by articles to the *Louisville Courier-Journal.*

March 25–early April: John and Elaine, together with John's sister Mary Dekker, sail to Naples, Italy, aboard the *Saturnia.* During their visits in Florence and Rome, John gathers material on Malory while Elaine takes pictures for a projected *Holiday* article on Florentine craftsmanship.

Viking Press publishes *The Short Reign of Pippin IV: A Fabrication,* and it becomes a Book-of-the-Month Club selection.

April 20: Steinbeck's article, "A Game of Hospitality," appears in *The Saturday Review.* He criticizes U.S. immigration officials who will not allow foreign writers into the country because their work is considered leftist.

Late April: In Florence Steinbeck meets Robert Wallsten, who was an actor and later turned to writing, for the first time.

June: The Steinbecks leave Italy and arrive in Paris, then go to London for a week and then on to Denmark and Sweden.

In Stockholm John and Elaine visit with Dag Hammarskjöld and the artist Bo Beskow, who paints Steinbeck's third portrait.

The Steinbecks then go to London to visit and become acquainted with Malory county. At Manchester, John meets Eugène Vinaver, who is professor of French language and literature at the University of Manchester and the world's leading authority on Malory. Steinbeck and Vinaver become friends immediately and Vinaver agrees to help Steinbeck with his Malory project.

July: The Steinbecks tour Malory country, taking notes and photographs.

July 25: John and Elaine sail on the *Queen Elizabeth* for home.

September: Steinbeck flies to Tokyo to attend a meeting of PEN (International Association of Poets, Playwrights, Editors, Essayists and Novelists) where he give a brief speech and catches influenza, which delays his return to the United States.

Late September: John returns to Sag Harbor and resumes his work on Malory.

Mid-November: The Steinbecks move to a house on 72nd Street where John continues his work on Malory and *Morte d'Arthur.*

1958

Spring: Steinbeck continues his study and research on Malory and plans another trip to England. Steinbeck spends most of the season in Bruton, Somerset, England, working on *Morte d'Arthur.*

Early June: John and Elaine fly to England and spend a month searching for physical traces of Malory.

Early July: The Steinbecks return from England to Sag Harbor.

August 23: Steinbeck publishes "The Easiest Way to Die" in *The Saturday Review.*

Late September: Steinbeck sends the completed Malory project to Elizabeth Otis and Chase Horton for their suggestions but receives dull responses.

Viking Press publishes *Once There Was a War,* a collection of Steinbeck's World War II dispatches in Europe and North Africa.

October: Steinbeck decides to set aside his Malory project and starts work on what he calls a modern western, titled "Don Keehan."

November–December: Steinbeck works on "Don Keehan" but becomes dissatisfied with the first draft. He tries to rewrite it several times but finally gives up the entire work itself. Then he decides to take another research trip to England to resume his Malory project.

1959

Late February: John and Elaine set out for England. During this journey they meet another important writer and his wife, Erskine and Virginia Caldwell.

Summer: During their stay in England, the Steinbecks entertain such guests as Elia Kazan, Adlai Stevenson, John's sister Mary Dekker, and the Robert Wallstens.

Mid-October: The Steinbecks return from Somerset, England, to their home in New York, and John realizes that he is coming down with a kidney infection.

December 3: Steinbeck suffers a stroke and is hospitalized for two weeks.

1960

January 11: John and Elaine go to Caneel Bay for two weeks to recover.

Late February: Steinbeck completes several essays for *The Saturday Review.*

March: Once again, Steinbeck lays aside the Malory project and begins work on his last novel, "The Winter of Our Discontent," published in 1961.

June: Steinbeck has a special vehicle constructed for his upcoming travel plans. He names the truck "Rocinante" in honor of Don Quixote's horse.

Mid-July: Steinbeck completes the manuscript of "The Winter of Our Discontent."

September 23–October: Steinbeck starts a journey with his pet poodle, Charley. Beginning in the Northeast and going to the Midwest, he collects material that will become *Travels with Charley.*

November 8: John F. Kennedy is elected president.

1961

Early January: From the Midwest Steinbeck travels to the western states and then on to the West Coast,

where he meets Elaine in Seattle. Then the Steinbecks travel down the coast before Elaine flies on to Texas where John joins her later. After brief stays in New Orleans and Alabama, Steinbeck heads back home to New York.

January 20: The Steinbecks attend the inauguration of John F. Kennedy.

Early February: The Steinbecks start their annual vacation in the Caribbean and Barbados.

Steinbeck begins work on the manuscript for "Travels with Charley."

March: Steinbeck leaves for San Diego to act as a historian for the Mohole expedition, which is exploring the Earth's composition by drilling a 12,000-foot hole off the coast of Mexico.

April: Steinbeck has to leave the Mohole project and return home. He is hospitalized for surgery to repair a torn hernia.

The Winter of Our Discontent is published by Viking Press. This novel immediately becomes a Book-of-the-Month Club selection.

September 1: Steinbeck completes the manuscript for "Travels with Charley."

Early October: The Steinbecks travel to Paris, where Elaine receives a muscle injury in an automobile accident.

November 25: Just before Thanksgiving, John and Elaine take a train to Milan, Italy. While in Milan, Steinbeck suffers a major heart attack.

December: The Steinbecks travel to Rome where they spend Christmas.

December 24: On Christmas Eve, John and Elaine have an audience with Pope John XXIII.

1962

January–March: Steinbeck continues his world tour even though he is still recovering from his heart attack. He spends a lot of time reading and reflecting.

April: When John's health is restored, the Steinbecks travel extensively in Italy and Greece and among the Greek islands.

May 28: Steinbeck writes to Elizabeth Otis from his hotel in Mykonos, Greece, telling her that the trip is over and that he and his family are returning to the United States.

June: Viking Press publishes *Travels with Charley,* and the book receives positive reviews and is a Book-of-the-Month Club selection.

October 25: On this morning at their Sag Harbor home, the Steinbecks turn on their TV for the news and learn that Steinbeck has been awarded the Nobel Prize in literature.

Steinbeck sends a cable to Anders Oesterling of Svenska Akademien Stockholm to express his gratitude and commitment to go to Stockholm.

October 30: In a letter to the artist Bo Beskow, Steinbeck reports that he has received overwhelming attention from the media, meeting 75 reporters and cameramen at one time in New York.

November: John is busy answering congratulatory messages, which arrive 400 to 500 a day. He feels obliged to write individual thanks. Among his responses are to Carlton A. Sheffield, John O'Hara, Eugène Vinaver, Princess Grace of Monaco, Adlai Stevenson, Elizabeth Otis, and an old friend named Natalya Lovejoy, whom he asks for help to find Carol's address and her present name.

December 8: John and Elaine fly to Stockholm, Sweden, for the ceremony.

December 10: John Steinbeck receives the Nobel Prize for Literature.

Mid-December: A few days after the ceremony, John and Elaine fly to London.

1963

Spring: Steinbeck meets with President John F. Kennedy several times during the year, and he is selected to receive the Medal of Freedom.

Steinbeck is invited by Leslie Brady, cultural attaché to the American Embassy in Moscow, later deputy commissioner of the U.S. Information Agency, to visit the Soviet Union under the auspices of the Cultural Exchange Program.

May 13: Steinbeck writes to Leslie Brady suggesting that Edward Albee, a young playwright, should be invited to go along to Russia with John.

Late June: One morning, John awakes to find that one of his eyes cannot see: a detached retina. Surgery is performed at Southampton Hospital on June 24.

September: The Steinbecks and Edward Albee attend a series of briefings at the State Department in Washington, D.C., in preparation for their trip to the Soviet Union.

October 11: The Steinbecks arrive in Helsinki, Finland, to begin the trip of cultural exchanges.

They meet Albee in the Soviet Union and meet with Soviet authors and officials.

November 15: The Steinbecks fly to Warsaw, Poland.

November 22: In Warsaw John and Elaine learn of President Kennedy's assassination. They decide to continue the job that Kennedy had given them to do. They travel to Vienna to rest and attend a funeral service held there for the president, then move on to Budapest, Hungary.

From Budapest, they travel to Prague, Czechoslovakia, and from Prague to West Berlin.

Early December: The Steinbecks return to the United States.

December 17: John and Elaine go to Washington, D.C., for the three days of debriefing by the State Department and are invited to a private dinner at the White House on their last evening in the capital.

1964

February: Steinbeck meets with Jacqueline Kennedy concerning her request that Steinbeck write a biography of President Kennedy. For various reasons this project was never undertaken.

April: John and Elaine travel to Rome for Easter and return in mid-month for a trial in New York Family Court regarding Gwyn's request for an increase in alimony and child support. But the judge gives Gwyn only a slight raise, which makes her very angry.

Early June: John and Elaine move back to Sag Harbor, where John resumes work on the Malory project.

August: Thomas H. Guinzburg, who has taken over after his father's death as head of Viking Press, approaches Steinbeck with a collection of photographs, requesting that Steinbeck add text that would capture the spirit of America and Americans.

September 14: Steinbeck receives the Presidential Medal of Freedom at the White House.

October 14: Pascal Covici, Steinbeck's longtime friend and editor, dies.

Following Covici's funeral, John and Elaine fly to California for a family reunion in Watsonville.

December: The Steinbecks spend Christmastime with John Huston at his home in Ireland.

1965

January: The Steinbecks go to London from Ireland and then on to Paris.

January 23: Mary Steinbeck Dekker, John's younger sister, dies of cancer in Carmel, California.

Mid-April: Steinbeck has been working on his essays on America.

Late April: John and Elaine are invited to the White House to spend a weekend with the Johnsons.

Late Summer: John receives a job offer from Harry E. Guggenheim, the publisher of *Newsday* on Long Island, to write a column on topics of his choosing. This column is written in the form of letters called "Letters to Alicia" and runs in *Newsday* from November 1965 through May of 1967, averaging about four articles a month.

Early December: John and Elaine fly to London, arriving around the first of December to search private libraries for Malory materials.

While at Alnwick Castle near the Scottish border, Steinbeck and Eugène Viniver discover a manuscript relating to the Arthur legend, which they believe is unknown.

Late December: John and Elaine go to Ireland to spend another Christmas with John Huston. After Christmas they tour Ireland.

1966

January: The John Steinbeck Society of America is founded at Kent State University by Tetsumaro Hayashi and Preston Beyer.

April: President Johnson appoints Steinbeck to the Council of the National Endowment for the Arts.

Steinbeck's son, John IV, finishes his basic training in the U.S. Army and requests assignment to Vietnam.

May: It is around this time that Steinbeck abandons his "Arthur" project.

June–August: Steinbeck has a battle of words with the Russian poet Yevgeny Yevtushenko over his views on the Vietnam conflict.

September: Steinbeck's article "Let's Go After the Neglected Treasures Beneath the Seats" appears in this month's issue of *Popular Science.*

October: John and Elaine are accredited as correspondents for *Newsday* and leave for Vietnam. They stop in California to see Thom, who is in basic training at Fort Ord, and other family members. From there they fly to Hawaii, to Guam, and then on to Vietnam.

October 12: Viking Press publishes *America and Americans.*

November–December: John and Elaine are busy covering the war as correspondents.

1967

January: Steinbeck continues to report on combat missions in Vietnam until the third week of this month.

Late January: John and Elaine leave Vietnam and fly to Bangkok, Thailand, and from there to Laos, which was then a neutral country.

From Laos they return to Bangkok briefly to meet with the king and queen of Thailand. Then they travel by train down the Malay Peninsula to the island of Penang, where they rest and work on the articles for *Newsday*.

April: The Steinbecks visit Singapore and Jakarta, and from there go to Hong Kong. While in Hong Kong, Steinbeck injures his back when helping a man pull a heavy hand truck of beer up a set of steps.

Later they travel to Tokyo for a visit with son John IV.

Late April: John and Elaine return to New York at the end of the third weekend of April.

Mid-May: John and Elaine are invited to stay for a weekend at the White House.

John is having much physical discomfort from bursitis in his right shoulder and arm and cannot write. On Memorial Day, the Steinbecks are in Sag Harbor when John's back gives out again.

October 23: Steinbeck undergoes a five-hour operation to repair a ruptured spinal disk. The operation is successful.

Mid-November: Steinbeck is learning to walk again and begins swimming and pool therapy.

December: John and Elaine fly to Grenada in the Virgin Islands where John can recuperate.

1968

January: For most of the month, John and Elaine stay in Grenada.

Late January: The Steinbecks return to Sag Harbor in the last week of January.

February: The Steinbeck Quarterly begins publication under the editorship of Tetsumaro Hayashi at Kent State University.

May: On Memorial Day weekend, while eating in a restaurant in Sag Harbor, John suffers a small stroke and is hospitalized for a week.

Early July: John suffers an episode of heart failure and is again hospitalized.

July 11: Steinbeck is transferred to New York Hospital, and his condition worsens. The doctors con-

sider bypass surgery but decide against it because of Steinbeck's severe condition.

August 21: John returns to Sag Harbor.

Early November: John's condition becomes so severe that he has to move to the New York apartment where treatment is more readily available.

December: Tetsumaro Hayashi, Robert DeMott, and others start the *Steinbeck Newsletter*, which later became *The Steinbeck Quarterly* under the editorship of Tetsumaro Hayashi at Ball State University.

December 20: John Steinbeck dies at 5:30 P.M. in New York City.

December 23: Steinbeck's funeral service is held at St. James Episcopal Church on Madison Avenue in New York City.

December 24: Elaine and Thom bring John's ashes back to California. John's older sisters arrange a small family service on Point Lobos, and his ashes are buried in the family plot in the Garden of Memories Cemetery in Salinas, California.

1969

December: A collection of letters entitled *The Journal of a Novel* is published by Viking Press. This is a daily account of the writing of *East of Eden* published in 1952.

1970

A new edition of *The Portable Steinbeck*, revised by Pascal Covici, Jr., is published by Viking Press.

1971

The Portable Steinbeck is republished, with an introduction by Pascal Covici, Jr.

1973

John Steinbeck and Edward F. Ricketts: The Shaping of a Novelist by Richard Astro is published by the University of Minnesota Press.

1974

May 4: "Steinbeck and the Sea" conference takes place at the Marine Science Center Auditorium, Newport, Oregon.

1975

Steinbeck: A Life in Letters, edited by Elaine Steinbeck and Robert Wallsten, is published by Viking Press.

The film script of *Viva Zapata!,* edited by Robert E. Morsberger, is published in paperback by Viking Press.

"New York: The Burdens and the Glories . . . and Just Yesterday, Men Who Loved It So" by Steinbeck is printed in the *New York Times* (May 5, 1973).

December 30: Gwyndolyn Conger Steinbeck (second wife) dies in Boulder, Colorado. She was 59 years old.

1976

The Acts of Kings Arthur and His Noble Knights (Steinbeck's Malory project), edited by Chase Horton, is published by Farrar, Straus and Giroux, New York.

Steinbeck's Foreword to Thomas A. Collins's *From Bringing in the Sheaves of Windsor Drake* is reprinted in the Journal of Modern Literature 5.2 (April 1976).

1978

Letters to Elizabeth: A Selection of Letters from John Steinbeck to Elizabeth Otis, edited by Florian J. Shasky and Susan F. Riggs, is published by The Book Club of California.

The John Steinbeck Society of Japan *Newsletter* begins publication.

1979

The Intricate Music: A Biography of John Steinbeck by Thomas Kiernan, the first extensive biography of John Steinbeck, is published by Little, Brown and Company.

Steinbeck and Covici: The Story of a Friendship, by Thomas Fensch, is published by P. S. Eriksson.

1980

Steinbeck and Hemingway: Dissertation Abstracts and Research Opportunities, edited by Tetsumaro Hayashi, is published by Scarecrow.

1981

Steinbeck's Unhappy Valley by Joseph Fontenrose is published.

1983

February 8: Carol Janella Henning Steinbeck Brown (first wife) dies in Carmel, California. She was 76 years old.

1984

The most extensive John Steinbeck biography, *The True Adventures of John Steinbeck,* by Jackson J. Benson, is published by Viking Press.

Steinbeck's Reading: A Catalogue of Books Owned and Borrowed, by Robert DeMott, is published by Garland.

1985

John Steinbeck's Re-Vision of America, by Louis Owens, is published by the University of Georgia Press.

1986

John Steinbeck's Fiction: The Aesthetics of the Road Taken, by John H. Timmerman, is published by the University of Oklahoma Press.

1987

Fall: The Steinbeck Newsletter, under the editorship of Susan Shillinglaw of the Steinbeck Research Center at San José State University, begins publication.

1988

Conversations with John Steinbeck, edited by Thomas Fensch, is published by the University Press of Mississippi.

1989

John Steinbeck's Working Days: The Journal of The Grapes of Wrath, *1938–1941,* edited by Robert DeMott, is published by Viking Press.

Critical Essays on Steinbeck's "The Grapes of Wrath," edited by John Ditsky, is published by G.K. Hall.

1990

The Dramatic Landscape of John Steinbeck's Short Stories, by John Timmerman, is published by the University of Oklahoma Press.

1991

February 7: John Steinbeck IV dies. He was 44 years old.

November: Zapata, an original biographical narrative of the life of Emiliano Zapata, together with Steinbeck's long introduction, is published by The Yolla Bolly Press of Covelo, California.

John Steinbeck as Propagandist: "The Moon Is Down" Goes to War, by Donald V. Coers, is published by the University of Alabama Press.

1992

Steinbeck's short story "Breakfast" is published in pamphlet form by Anchor Acorn Press of Petaluma, California, with wood engravings by Colleen Dwire Weaver in a limited edition.

1993

October: A new motion picture version of *Of Mice and Men* is released, starring John Malkovich as Lennie Small and Gary Sinise as George Milton.

The Steinbeck Question: New Essays in Criticism, edited by Donald Noble, is published by Whitston.

1994

John Steinbeck's Fiction Revisited, by Warren French, is published by Twayne.

John Steinbeck: Novels and Stories, 1932–1937: The Pastures of Heaven / To a God Unknown / Tortilla Flat / In Dubious Battle / Of Mice and Men, edited by Robert DeMott and Elaine A. Steinbeck, is published by Library of America.

1995

Another extensive authorized biography, by Jay Parini, entitled *John Steinbeck: A Biography,* is published by H. Holt.

1996

Steinbeck's Typewriter: Essays on His Art is published by Whitston Publishing.

John Steinbeck's Nonfiction Revisited, by Warren French, is published by Twayne.

John Steinbeck: The War Years, 1939–1945, by Roy Simmonds, is published by Bucknell University Press.

1997

Steinbeck and the Environment: Interdisciplinary Approaches, edited by Susan F. Beegel, Susan Shillinglaw, and Wesley N. Tiffney, Jr., is published by the University of Alabama Press. The Fourth International Steinbeck Congress (March 19–23) is held at San José State University, Salinas, and Monterey, California.

1998

A $12 million museum—the National Steinbeck Center—is constructed and opened at the head of Main Street in Steinbeck's hometown, Salinas, California.

The Hayashi Steinbeck Bibliography, 1982–1996, edited by Michael Meyer, is published by Scarecrow.

2000

John Steinbeck and the Critics, by John Ditsky, is published by Camden House.

The Critical Response to John Steinbeck's The Grapes of Wrath, edited by Barbara A. Heavilin, is published by Greenwood Press.

John Steinbeck: from Salinas to Stockholm, a catalog by William McPheron, is published by Stanford University Libraries.

2001

While many academic institutions, public libraries, and Steinbeck-related organizations are getting ready to celebrate the Steinbeck centennial (February 27, 2002), a coalition of 26 nonprofit cultural organizations nationwide, led by the Center for Steinbeck Studies at San José State University in California, and the Mercantile Library of New York, has received a $260,000 grant from the National Endowment for the Humanities to commemorate the centennial.

Starting with its Winter 2001 issue, the *Steinbeck Newsletter,* a publication at San José State University, changes its name to *Steinbeck Studies.*

2002

January: The Steinbeck Centennial Collection: The Grapes of Wrath, Of Mice and Men, East of Eden, The Pearl, Cannery Row, Travels With Charley, in Search of America (Boxed Set), is published by Penguin.

Beyond Boundaries: Rereading John Steinbeck, edited by Susan Shillinglaw and Kevin Hearle, is published by the University of Alabama Press.

John Steinbeck: America and Americans and Selected Nonfiction, edited by Susan Shillinglaw and Jackson J. Benson, is published by Viking.

John Steinbeck: A Centennial Tribute, edited by Stephen K. George, is published by Praeger Publishers.

2003

April 27: Elaine Anderson Steinbeck (third wife) dies in New York City. She was 88 years old.

2004

Spring: The first issue of *The Steinbeck Review* is published by the Scarecrow Press. Its editors-in-chief are Stephen K. George and Barbara A. Heavilin.

2005

March: The Moral Philosophy of John Steinbeck, edited by Stephen K. George, is published by the Scarecrow Press.

John Steinbeck: A Documentary Volume, edited by Luchen Li, is published by Thomson Gale.

SELECTED STEINBECK
AWARDS AND HONORS

1934
O. Henry Award ("The Murder")

1935
Commonwealth Club of California Gold Medal for Best Novel by a Californian (*Tortilla Flat*)

1936
Commonwealth Club of California Gold Medal for Best Novel by a Californian (*In Dubious Battle*)

1938
New York Drama Critics' Circle Award (*Of Mice and Men*)

O. Henry Award ("The Promise")

1939
Member of National Institute of Arts and Letters

American Booksellers' Award

1940
Pulitzer Prize in fiction (*The Grapes of Wrath*)

1944
Academy Award nominee for Best Story (*Lifeboat*)

1945
Academy Award nominee for Best Story (with Jack Wagner, *A Medal for Benny*)

1946
King Haakon Liberty Cross (*The Moon Is Down*)

1948
Member of American Academy of Arts and Letters

1952
Academy Award nominee for Best Original Screenplay (*Viva Zapata!*)

1962
Nobel Prize in literature

1963
Honorary Consultant in American Literature to the Library of Congress

1964
United States Medal of Freedom

Press Medal of Freedom

1966
Member of the National Arts Council

STEINBECK IN FILM, TELEVISION, AND THEATER

Feature Films

Twenty-nine Academy Award nominations and four Academy Awards were given for films adapted from John Steinbeck stories.

Of Mice and Men (1939)

Producer: Lewis Milestone

Director: Lewis Milestone

Notable Cast Members: Burgess Meredith as *George Milton*; Betty Field as *Mae Jackson*; Lon Chaney Jr as *Lennie Small*; Charles Bickford as *Slim*; Roman Bohnen as *Candy*; Bob Steele as *Curley Jackson*

Original Music: Aaron Copland

Screenplay: Eugene Solow

The Grapes of Wrath (1940)

Producer: Darryl F. Zanuck

Director: John Ford

Notable Cast Members: Henry Fonda as *Tom Joad*; Jane Darwell as *Ma Joad*; John Carradine as *Casy*; Charley Grapewin as *Grandpa*; Dorris Bowdon as *Rosasharn*; Russell Simpson as *Pa Joad*

Screenplay: Nunnally Johnson

Musical Score: Gregg Toland

The Forgotten Village (1941)

Producers: Alexander Hammid (as Alexander Hackenschmid); Herbert Kline

Director: Herbert Kline

Notable Cast Member: Burgess Meredith as *Narrator*

Documentary Story and Screenplay: John Steinbeck

Music: Hanns Eisler

Tortilla Flat (1942)

Producer: Sam Zimbalist

Director: Victor Fleming

Notable Cast Members: Spencer Tracy as *Pilon*; Hedy Lamarr as *Dolores "Sweets" Ramirez*; John Garfield as *Danny*; Frank Morgan as *Pirate*; Akim Tamiroff as *Pablo*; Sheldon Leonard as *Tito Ralph*

Screenplay: Lee Mahin and Benjamin Glazer

The Moon Is Down (1943)

Producer: Nunnally Johnson

Director: Irving Pichel

Notable Cast Members: Cedric Hardwicke as *Col. Lanser*; Henry Travers as *Mayor Orden*; Lee J. Cobb as *Dr. Albert Winter*; Dorris Bowdon as *Molly Morden*; Margaret Wycherly as *Mme. Orden*; Peter van Eyck as *Lt. Tonder*

Screenplay: Nunnally Johnson

20th Century–Fox

Lifeboat (1944)

Producer: Kenneth McGowan

Director: Alfred Hitchcock

Notable Cast Members: Tallulah Bankhead as *Constance "Connie" Porter*; William Bendix as *Gus Smith*; Walter Slezak as *Willy*; Mary Anderson as *Alice MacKenzie*; John Hodiak as *John Kovac*; Henry Hull as *Charles D. "Ritt" Rittenhouse*

Screenplay: Jo Swerling
20th Century–Fox

A Medal for Benny (1945)

Producer: Paul Jones
Director: Irving Pichel
Notable Cast Members: Dorothy Lamour as *Lolita Sierra*; Arturo de Córdova as *Joe Morales*; J. Carrol Naish as *Charley Martin*; Mikhail Rasumny as *Raphael Catalina*; Fernando Alvarado as *Chito Sierra*; Frank McHugh as *Edgar Lovekin*; Rosita Moreno as *Toodles Castro*; Grant Mitchell as *Mayor of Pantera*; Douglass Dumbrille as *General*
Screenplay: Frank Butler
Story: John Steinbeck and Jack Wagner
Paramount

The Pearl (1947)

Producer: Óscar Dancigers
Director: Emilio Fernández
Notable Cast Members: Pedro Armendáriz as *Quino*; María Elena Marqués as *Juana*
Also Known As: *La Perla*
Screenplay: John Steinbeck, Emilio Fernández, and Jack Wagner
RKO

The Red Pony (1949)

Producers: Charles K. Feldman (executive producer); Lewis Milestone
Director: Lewis Milestone
Notable Cast Members: Myrna Loy as *Alice Tiflin*; Robert Mitchum as *Billy Buck*; Louis Calhern as *Grandfather*; Shepperd Strudwick as *Mr. Fred Tiflin*; Peter Miles as *Tom "Mr. Big Britches" Tiflin*
Screenplay: John Steinbeck
Original Music: Aaron Copland
Republic

Viva Zapata! (1952)

Producer: Darryl F. Zanuck
Director: Elia Kazan
Notable Cast Members: Marlon Brando as *Emiliano Zapata*; Jean Peters as *Josefa Zapata*; Anthony Quinn as *Eufemio*; Joseph Wiseman

as *Fernando*; Arnold Moss as *Don Nacio*; Alan Reed as *Pancho Villa*
Screenplay: John Steinbeck
20th Century–Fox

O. Henry's Full House (1952)

Narrator: John Steinbeck
Based on Five Stories: "The Cop and the Anthem," "The Clarion Call," "The Last Leaf," "The Gift of the Magi," "The Ransom of Red Chief."
20th Century–Fox

East of Eden (1955)

Producer: Elia Kazan
Director: Elia Kazan
Notable Cast Members: Julie Harris as *Abra*; James Dean as *Cal Trask*; Raymond Massey as *Adam Trask*; Burl Ives as *Sam the Sheriff*; Richard Davalos as *Aron Trask*; Jo Van Fleet as *Kate*
Also Known As: *John Steinbeck's East of Eden*
Screenplay: Paul Osborn Warner

The Wayward Bus (1957)

Producer: Charles Brackett
Director: Victor Vicas
Notable Cast Members: Joan Collins as *Alice Chicoy*; Jayne Mansfield as *Camille Oaks*; Dan Dailey as *Ernest Horton*; Rick Jason as *Johnny Chicoy*
Screenplay: Ivan Moffat
20th Century–Fox

Flight (1961)

Producer: Barnaby Conrad
Director: Louis Bispo
Screenplay: Barnaby Conrad
Music Written and Played: Laurindo Almeida

Cannery Row (1982)

Producer: Michael Phillips
Director: David S. Ward
Notable Cast Members: Nick Nolte as *Doc*; Debra Winger as *Suzy*; Audra Lindley as *Fauna*; Frank McRae as *Hazel*; M. Emmet Walsh as *Mack*; Tom Mahoney as *Hughie*
Also Known As: *John Steinbeck's Cannery Row*

Of Mice and Men (1992)

> Producers: Alan Bloomquist (executive producer); Russell Smith; Gary Sinise
> Director: Gary Sinise
> Notable Cast Members: John Malkovich as *Lennie Small*; Gary Sinise as *George Milton*; Ray Walston as *Candy*; Casey Siemaszko as *Curley*; Sherilyn Fenn as *Curley's Wife*; John Terry as *Slim, Team Leader*

TV Movies

There have been numerous adaptations of Steinbeck's works for television. The list below is not comprehensive.

Molly Morgan (1950)

> Barbara Bel Geddes as *Molly Morgan*

O. Henry's Full House (1952)

> Producer: Andre Hakim
> Directors: Henry Hathaway (segment "The Clarion Call"); Howard Hawks (segment "The Ransom of Red Chief"); Henry King (segment "The Gift of the Magi"); Henry Koster (segment "The Cop and the Anthem"); Jean Negulesco (segment "The Last Leaf")
> Notable Cast Members: Fred Allen as *Sam* (*The Ransom of Red Chief*); Anne Baxter as *Joanna* (*The Last Leaf*); Jeanne Crain as *Della* (*The Gift of the Magi*); Farley Granger as *Jim* (*The Gift of the Magi*); Charles Laughton as *Soapy* (*The Cop and the Anthem*); Oscar Levant as *Bill* (*The Ransom of Red Chief*); Marilyn Monroe as *Streetwalker* (*The Cop and the Anthem*); Jean Peters as *Susan* (*The Last Leaf*)
> Narrator: John Steinbeck

America and Americans (1956)

> Notable Cast Member: Henry Fonda as *Narrator*

Travels with Charley (1968)

> Notable Cast Member: Henry Fonda as *Narrator*

The Harness (1969)

> Producer: William Sackheim
> Director: Boris Sagal
> Notable Cast Members: Lorne Greene as *Peter Randall*; Julie Sommars as *Jennifer Shagaras*;

Murray Hamilton as *Roy Kern*; Lee Montgomery as *Tor Shagaras*

Of Mice and Men (1970)

> Notable Cast Members: George Segal as *George*; Nicol Williamson as *Lennie*

The Red Pony (1973)

> Producers: Frederick Brogger; James Franciscus
> Director: Robert Totten
> Notable Cast Members: Henry Fonda as *Carl Tiflin*; Maureen O'Hara as *Ruth Tiflin*

East of Eden (1981)

> Producers: Mace Neufeld (executive producer); Barney Rosenzweig
> Director: Harvey Hart
> Notable Cast Members: Timothy Bottoms as *Adam Trask*; Jane Seymour as *Cathy/Kate Ames*; Bruce Boxleitner as *Charles Trask*; Soon-Tek Oh as *Lee*; Karen Allen as *Abra*

Of Mice and Men (1981)

> Producers: Robert Blake; Gino Grimaldi; Robert Hargrove
> Director: Reza Badiyi
> Notable Cast Members: Robert Blake as *George Milton*; Randy Quaid as *Lenny Small*; Lew Ayres as *Candy*; Mitch Ryan as *Slim*; Ted Neeley as *Curley*; Cassie Yates as *Mae*

The Winter of Our Discontent (1983)

> Producers: Gary Adelson and Malcolm Stuart (executive producers); R. W. Goodwin
> Director: Waris Hussein
> Notable Cast Members: Donald Sutherland as *Ethan Hawley*; Teri Garr as *Mary Hawley*; Tuesday Weld as *Margie Young-Hunt*
> Also Known As: John Steinbeck's Winter of Our Discontent

The Grapes of Wrath (1991)

> Producers: Michael Bronson; John Williams
> Directors: Kirk Browning; Frank Galati
> Notable Cast Members: Jeff Perry as *Noah Joad*; Gary Sinise as *Tom Joad*; Lois Smith as *Ma Joad*

Theater

The following is a noncomprehensive list of openings of theater adaptations and musical adaptations of Steinbeck's work:

Of Mice and Men
(The Green Street Theatre, San Francisco, May 21, 1937)

Of Mice and Men
(Music Box Theatre, New York City, Nov. 23, 1937)

Tortilla Flat
(Henry Miller Theatre, New York City, Jan. 12, 1938)

The Moon Is Down
(Martin Beck Theatre, New York City, April 7, 1942)

Burning Bright (musical)
(Broadhurst Theatre, New York City, Oct. 19, 1950)

Pipe Dream (musical)
(Shubert Theatre, New York City, Nov. 30, 1955)

Here's Where I Belong (musical based on *East of Eden*)
(Billy Rose Theatre, New York City, March 3, 1968)

Of Mice and Men (opera)
(Seattle, Washington, Jan. 22, 1970)

The Pearl
(Chimera Theatre, St. Paul, Minnesota, Nov. 1, 1974)

The Long Valley
(Theatre de Lys, New York City, Jan. 6, 1975)

The Grapes of Wrath
(National Premiere Stage Tour premiere, San Diego State University, Jan. 1978)

The Grapes of Wrath
(Netherbow Theatre, Edinburgh, Scotland, Aug. 10, 1987)

The Grapes of Wrath
(Steppenwolf Theatre, Chicago, Sept. 1988)

East of Eden
(The Western Stage, Salinas, California, August 7, 1992)

Burning Bright (opera)
(Yale University, New Haven, Connecticut, Nov. 5, 1993)

Steinbeck Country (musidrama)
(Steinbeck Center Foundation, Salinas, California, 1994)

East of Eden (musical)
(Takarazuka Revue Company, Flower Troupe, Takarazuka Grand Theater, Japan, June 30, 1995)

Cannery Row
(The Western Stage, Salinas, California, July 28, 1995)

CHRONOLOGICAL BIBLIOGRAPHY OF STEINBECK'S WORKS

This bibliography contains citations to all published writings during Steinbeck's lifetime. The bibliography does contain some reprints. This is especially helpful when the original title of the article was changed in the reprint. Under each year, books published in that year start the list, then contributions to publications that are dated only by the year, and then dated materials by month and/or month and day.

1919

"The How, When and Where of the High School." *El Gabilan* (Salinas High School Yearbook). 1919: 19.

"Class Will." *El Gabilan.* 1919: 36.

"Student Body." *El Gabilan.* 1919: 43.

"Woodwork." *El Gabilan.* 1919: 50.

1924

"Adventures in Arcademy: A Journey into the Ridiculous," *The Stanford Spectator* 2, 9 (June 1924): 291.

"Fingers of Cloud: A Satire on College Protervity," *The Stanford Spectator* 2, 9 (February 1924): 161–164.

1926

"Atropos," *The Stanford Lit* I, 4 (March 1926): 95.

"The Game of Authors," *The Stanford Lit* I, 4 (March 1926): 94–95.

1927

"The Gifts of Iban." *The Smokers Companion* I, 1 (March 1927): 18–19, 70–72.

1929

Cup of Gold. New York: Robert M. McBride, 1929.

1932

The Pastures of Heaven. New York: Brewer, Warren & Putnam, 1932.

1933

To A God Unknown. New York: Robert O. Ballou, 1933.

"The Great Mountains," *The North American Review* 236, 6 (December 1933): 493–500.

"The Red Pony," *The North American Review* 236, 5 (November 1933): 422–438.

1934

Foreword. In *Morgan Sails the Caribbean,* by Berton Braley. New York: Macmillan, Co. 1934, vii–x.

"The Murder," *The North American Review* 237, 4 (April 1934): 306–312.

"The Murder," *Lovat's Dickson's Magazine* 3, 4 (October 1934): 442–456 [Text from *The North American Review,* April 1934.]

"The Raid," *The North American Review* 238, 4 (October 1934): 300–305.

1935

Tortilla Flat. New York: Covici-Friede, 1935.

"Four Shades of Navy Blue," *Monterey Beacon* 1 (January 26, 1935): 12.

"The Genius," *Monterey Beacon* 1 (January 26, 1935): 12.

"Ivanhoe," *Monterey Beacon* 1 (January 26, 1935): 12.

"The Snake," *Monterey Beacon* I, 44 (June 22, 1935): 10–11, 14–15.

"The White Quail," *The North American Review* 239, 3 (March 1935): 205–211.

1936

In Dubious Battle. New York: Covici-Friede, 1936.

"A Depiction of Mexico by an Author with No Pattern to Vindicate," *San Francisco Chronicle* May 31, 1936, D4.

"The Leader of the People." *Argosy* 20 (August 1936), 99–106.

"Dubious Battle in California." *Nation* September 12, 1936, 302–304.

"The Harvest Gypsies," *San Francisco News*, October 5–12, 1936.

"The Lonesome Vigilante." *Esquire*, October 1936, 35, 186A–186B.

"The Way It Seems to John Steinbeck." *The Occident* 29 (1936): 5.

"Breakfast." *Pacific Weekly*, November 9, 1936, 300.

1937

Of Mice and Men. New York: Covici-Friede, 1937.

Of Mice and Men [Play]. New York: Covici-Friede, 1937.

The Red Pony. New York: Covici-Friede, 1937.

"The Promise." *Harper's Magazine*, August 1937, 244–252.

"The Ears of Johnny Bear." *Esquire*, September 1937, 35, 195–200.

"The Chrysanthemums." *Harper's Magazine*, October 1937, 514–519.

"Prophet with Honor in His Country." *The Coast* (December 1937): 14–15.

1938

The Long Valley. New York: Viking Press, 1938.

"Their Blood is Strong." San Francisco: Simon J. Lubin Society, 1938.

"Steinbeck's Letter." *Writers Take Sides: Letters about the War in Spain from 418 American Authors.* New York: League of American Writers, 1938: 56–57.

"The novel might benefit by the discipline and terseness of the drama . . ." *Stage* 15 (Jan. 1938): 50–51.

"A Snake of One's Own." *Esquire*, February 1938, 31, 178–180.

"The Murder." *Redbook Magazine*, May 1938, 38–39, 78–80. Text from *The North American Review*, April 1934.

"The Harness." *Atlantic Monthly*, June 1938, 741–749.

"Starvation Under the Orange Trees." *Monterey Trader* April 15, 1938.

"A Letter to the Inmates of the Connecticut State Prison." *Monthly Record* (Connecticut State Prison) (June 1938): 3.

"The Stars Point to Shafter." *Progressive Weekly* December 24, 1938, 2.

1939

The Grapes of Wrath. New York: Viking Press, 1939.

"No Riders." *Saturday Review*, April 1, 1939, 13, 14, 16. Text from *The Grapes of Wrath*.

"Their Blood is Strong." *Progressive Weekly*, April 29, 1939, 3.

"The Squatter's Camp." *Progressive Weekly*, May 6, 1939, 2.

1940

"Of Beef and Men." In *Famous Recipes by Famous People*. San Francisco: Lane Publishing Co., 1940, 11. Text from *"Tortilla Flat" Famous Recipes by Famous People, Hotel Del Monte*, 1936.

1941

The Forgotten Village. (Film Script) New York: Viking, 1941.

Sea of Cortez: A Leisurely Journal of Travel and Research. With Edward F. Ricketts. New York: Viking, 1941.

"Johnny Bear." *Argosy*, January 1941, 97–111. Text from *Esquire*, September 1937.

"Murder." *Argosy*, March 1941, 31–40. Text from *The North American Review*, April 1934.

"Of Mice and Men." *Argosy*, April 1941, 151–157.

"How Edith McGillcuddy Met R. L. Stevenson." *Harper's Magazine*, August 1941, 253–358.

"Steinbeck Lashes Out at Bungled Goodwill Drive in Latin Sates: A Reply to American Censorship." *Carmel Cymbal* September 4, 1941, 1941: 3.

1942

Bombs Away. Photographs by John Swope. New York: Viking Press, 1942.

The Moon Is Down. New York: Viking Press, 1942.

The Moon Is Down (Play). New York: Viking Press, 1942.

"The Moon Is Down." *Reader's Digest*, June 1942, 116–152. Condensed text from *The Moon Is Down*.

"The Moon Is Down." *Argosy*, September 1942, 91–124. Text from *The Moon Is Down*, chapters 1–4.

"The Moon Is Down." *Argosy*, October 1942, 89–124. Text from *The Moon Is Down*, chapters 5–8.

" 'Our Best'—Our Fliers." *New York Times Magazine*, November 22, 1942, 16–17, 29. Text from *Bombs Away*.

1943

"Free Ride to Monterey." *Argosy*, March 1943, 69–76. Text from "How Edith McGillcuddy Met R. L. Stevenson," *Harper's Magazine*, 1941.

"War Dispatches." *New York Herald Tribune* (86 articles between June 21, 1943, and December 15, 1943). These dispatches were reprinted in several newspapers including *Daily Express* (June–October 1943),

Cincinnati Enquirer (October–December 1943), *New York Herald Tribune* (November–December 1943). A single dispatch entitled "Steinbeck Says Blitz Stories All Hang on Some Small Detail" appeared in the *Amarillo Sunday* (July 11, 1943).

"Johnny Bear." *Avon Modern Short Story Monthly*, 1943, 12–24. Text from *The Long Valley.*

"The Bomber—Our Best Weapon." *Science Digest*, July 1943, 62–66. Condensed chapter from *Bombs Away.*

"The Long Valley." *Avon Modern Short Story Monthly*, 1943, 12–62. Text from *The Long Valley.*

"John Steinbeck Writes Appeal for Third War Loan Drive." *Monterey Peninsula Herald*, September 17, 1943.

"The Moon Is Down." *Strand Magazine*, September 1943, 57–71, 86–89, 91, 93–96. Condensed text from *The Moon Is Down.*

"Aerial Engineer." *Scholastic*, December 6, 1943, 17–18.

1944

"Nothing So Monstrous." *Avon Modern Short Story Monthly*, 1944, 53–69. Text from *The Pastures of Heaven.*

"Over There." *Ladies Home Journal*, February 1944, 20–21, 137, 139–142, 144–158.

"Troopship." *Reader's Digest*, March 1944, 67–70. Condensed from *The New York Herald Tribune.*

" 'Shark' Wicks." *The Avon Annual*, 1944, 12–25. Text from *The Pastures of Heaven.*

1945

Cannery Row. New York: Viking Press, 1945.

"Cannery Row." *Coronet*, June 1945, 145–161. Condensed from *Cannery Row.*

"The Harness." *Argosy*, June 1945, 15–25.

"Cannery Row." *Omnibook Magazine*, June 1945, 3–40. Condensed from *Cannery Row.*

"Work of W. F. Cody." *Saturday Review of Literature*, July 7, 1945, 18–19.

"Cannery Row." *Argosy*, September 1945, 17–34. Condensed from *Cannery Row.*

"The Hanging at San Quentin." *Avon Modern Short Story Monthly*, 1945, 11–22. Text from *The Pastures of Heaven.*

"The Pearl of the World." *Woman's Home Companion*, December 1945, 17–18, 85–86, 90, 92, 96–100, 104–105, 109–113, 120. Published later as *The Pearl.*

1946

"This Is the Monterey We Love," *Monterey Peninsula Herald* July 3, 1946, Sec. 3, 1.

"Molly Morgan." *Avon Short Story Monthly*, 1946, 150–162. Text from *The Pastures of Heaven.*

"The Origin of Tularecito." *The Avon Annual*, 1946, 11–20. Text from *The Pastures of Heaven.*

1947

The Pearl. New York: Viking Press, 1947.

The Wayward Bus. New York: Viking Press, 1947.

Vanderbilt Clinic. Photographs by Victor Keppler. New York: Presbyterian Hospital, 1947.

The First Watch. Los Angeles: Ward Ritchie Press, 1947.

"The Time the Wolves Ate the Vice-Principal." 47 *The Magazine of the Year*, March 1947, 26–27.

"The GI's War in a Book Far from Brass." *New York Herald Tribune Weekly Book Review*, May 18, 1947, 1. Review of *Yank! The GI Story of the War.*

"The Wayward Bus." *Omnibook Magazine*, August 1947, 3–40. Condensed from *The Wayward Bus.*

1948

A Russian Journal. Photographs by Robert Capa. New York: Viking, 1948.

Foreword. In *Between Pacific Tides* by Edward Ricketts and Jack Calvin. Revised edition. Stanford, Calif.: Stanford University Press, 1948.

"Russian Journal." *New York Herald Tribune*, (18 articles between January 14, 1948 and January 31, 1948).

"Women and Children in the U.S.S.R." *Ladies Home Journal*, February 1948, 45–49.

"The Pearl." *Omnibook*, March 1948, 105–122. Condensed from *The Pearl.*

"Journey into Russia: People of the Soviet." *Illustrated*, May 1, 1948, 3–22.

"Miracle of Tepayac." *Collier's*, December 25, 1948, 22–23.

1949

"The Miracle." *Argosy*, April 1949, 97–101. Text from "Miracle of Tepeyac," *Collier's*, 1948.

"His Father." *Reader's Digest*, September 1949, 19–21.

1950

Foreword. In *Burning Bright.* New York: Viking, 1950, 9–13.

"My Ideal Woman." *Flair*, July 1950, 30–33.

"Foreward to Burning Bright." *New York Times*, October 15, 1950, sec. 2 (Theater).

"How Edith McGilcuddy Skipped Sunday-school." *Chamber's Journal*, November 1950, 641–646.

"Critics, Critics, Burning Bright." *Saturday Review*, November 11, 1950, 20–21.

"The 'Inside.' on the Inside." *The Iron Gate of Jack and Charlie's "21."* Edited by Francis T. Hunter. New York: Kriendler Memorial Foundation, 1950, 27.

1951

The Log from The Sea of Cortez. New York: Viking, 1951.

"Some Random and Randy Thoughts on Books." *The Author Looks at Format,* edited by Ray Freiman. New York: American Institute of Graphic Arts, Inc. (1951): 27–34.

"About Ed Ricketts." Preface to *The Log from* The Sea of Cortez. New York: Viking, 1951, vii–lxvii.

"Do You Like Yourself?" *New York Herald Tribune,* January 21, 1951, Sec. 7, 2.

"The Naked Book." *Vogue,* November 15, 1951, 119, 161.

"The Farmer's Hotel." Letter to the editor, *New York Times Book Review,* December 2, 1951, 40.

1952

East of Eden. New York: Viking Press, 1952.

Foreword. In *Speeches of Adlai Stevenson.* New York: Random House, 1952, 5–8.

"Who Said the Old Lady Was Dying?" (Article on London Theatre) *Evening Standard,* (England) August 1, 1952.

"Your Audiences Are Wonderful." *Sunday Times,* August 10, 1952, 5.

"Duel Without Pistols." *Collier's,* August 23, 1952, 13–15.

"The Soul and Guts of France." *Collier's,* August 30, 1952, 26–30.

"For Stevenson: Rivals Contrasted," Letter to the editor, *New York Times,* October 26, 1952, Sec. 4, 9.

"We Don't Want to Be America's Colony." *Reader's Digest,* November 1952, 18–23. Condensed text from "The Soul and Guts of France," *Collier's,* August 30, 1952.

1953

Introduction. In *The World of Li'l Abner* by Al Capp. New York: Farrar, Straus, and Young, 1953.

"The Stevenson Letter." *New Republic,* January 5, 1953, 13–14.

"The Secret Weapon We Were Afraid to Use." *Collier's,* January 10, 1953, 9–13.

"Ballantine Ale." *Life,* January 26, 1953, 92–93.

"I Go Back to Ireland." *Collier's* January 31, 1953, 48–50.

"Autobiography: Making of a New Yorker." *New York Times Magazine,* February 1, 1953, 26–27; 66–67.

"Unsecret Weapon [Part I]." *Picture Post,* February 14, 1953, 31.

"Unsecret Weapon [Part II]." *Picture Post,* February 21, 1953, 31.

"The King Snake and the Rattlers: A Parable for Americans." *Brief,* April 1953, 23–27.

"A Model T Named 'It'." *Ford Times,* July 1953, 34–39.

"Positano." *Harper's Bazaar,* May 1953, 158, 185, 187–190, 194. Reprinted as Positano. Salerno, Italy: Ente Provinciale Per Il Turismo, 1954.

"A Model T Named 'It.'" *Ford Times,* July 1953, 34–39.

"My Short Novels." *Wings,* October 1953, 4–8.

"Voices of Authors: Johnny Bear." *Life,* October 12, 1953.

1954

Sweet Thursday. New York: Viking Press, 1954.

"Circus." *Ringling Bros. and Barnum & Bailey Circus Program* (1954): 6–7.

"Trade Winds: When, Two Summers Ago . . ." *Saturday Review,* February 27, 1954, 8.

"In Awe of Words." *The Exonian* March 3, 1954, 4.

"One American in Paris." *Le Figaro Littéraire* (17 articles appearing between June 12–September 18, 1954).

"Death with a Camera." *Picture Post* (London) June 12, 1954.

"Jalopies I Cursed and Loved." *Holiday,* July 1954, 44–45; 89–90.

"Fishing in Paris." *Punch,* August 25, 1954, 248–49.

"Robert Capa: An Appreciation." *Photography,* September 1954, 48.

"The Miracle of Joan." *John O'London's Weekly,* September 19, 1954, 907. Text from *Le Figaro.*

"Good Guy—Bad Guy." *Punch,* September 22, 1954, 375–78.

"Of Fish and Fishermen." *Sports Illustrated,* October 4, 1954, 45. Text from *Le Figaro.*

"And Some Cars of Yesterday." *Reader's Digest* (British Edition), November 1954, 53–57. Text from "Jalopies I Cursed and Loved." *Holiday,* July 1954.

"Steinbeck's Voices of America." *Scholastic,* November 3, 1954, 15.

"Reality and Illusion." *Punch,* November 17, 1954, 616–17. Text from *Le Figaro.*

"How to Fish in French." *Reader's Digest,* December 1954, 129–131.

1955

"An Appreciation." *Elia Kazan's Production of John Steinbeck's "East of Eden."* Warner Brothers, 1955.

Souvenir booklet for the world premiere presentation of the film at the Astor Theater in New York City.

"A Plea for Tourists." *Punch*, January 26, 1955, 148–49. Text from *Le Figaro*.

"The Affair at 7, Rue de M—" *Harper's Bazaar*, April 1955, 112, 202, 213. Text from *Le Figaro*.

"The Death of a Racket." *Saturday Review*, April 2, 1955, 26.

"Cooks of Wrath." *Everybody's*, April 9, 1955. Text from *Le Figaro*.

"Capital Roundup: Paris" *Saturday Review*, April 16, 1955, 41. Text from *Le Figaro*.

"A Plea to Teachers." *Saturday Review*, April 30, 1955, 24.

"The Summer Before." *Punch*, May 25, 1955, 647–51.

"Some Thoughts on Juvenile Delinquency." *Saturday Review*, May 28, 1955, 22.

"Always Something to Do in Salinas." *Holiday*, June 1955, 58–59, 152–153, 156.

"Report on America." *Punch*, June 22, 1955, 754–55.

"Bricklaying Piece." *Punch*, July 27, 1955, 92.

"A Letter on Criticism." *Colorado Quarterly* 4, 2 (Autumn 1955): 218–219.

"How to Recognize a Candidate." *Punch*, August 10, 1955, 146–48.

"Critics—From a Writer's Viewpoint." *Saturday Review*, August 27, 1955, 20, 28.

"Dear Teachers, Sweet Teachers I Beg You . . . Call Them Off!" *NEA Journal* 44, 6 (September 1955): 359.

"Random Thoughts on Random Dogs." *Saturday Review*, October 8, 1955, 11.

". . . like captured fireflies." *CTA Journal* (November 1955): 7.

"We're Holding Our Own." *Lilliput* (November 1955): 18–19.

"Writer's Mail." *Punch*, November 2, 1955, 512–13.

"Trade Winds: In a Radio Broadcast Beamed to Listeners in Foreign Countries, John Steinbeck Had This to Say about New York City." *Saturday Review*, November 26, 1955, 8–9.

"Dreams Piped from Cannery Row." *New York Times*, Sec. 2, November 27, 1955, 1, 3.

"What Is the Real Paris?" *Holiday*, December 1955, 94. Text from *Le Figaro*.

"More About Aristocracy: Why Not a World Peerage?" *Saturday Review*, December 10, 1955, 11.

1956

Pipe Dream. New York: Viking Press, 1956.

Foreword. In *Much Ado About Me* by Fred Allen. Boston: Little Brown, 1956.

"The Yank in Europe." *Holiday*, January 1956, 25. Text from *Le Figaro*.

"The Joan in All of Us." *Saturday Review*, January 14, 1956, 43. Text from *Le Figaro*.

"Miracle Island of Paris." *Holiday*, February 1956, 43. Text from *Le Figaro*.

"How Mr. Hogan Robbed a Bank." *Atlantic*, March 1956, 58–61.

"Madison Avenue and the Election." *Saturday Review*, March 31, 1956, 11.

"Needles-Derby Day Choice for President?" *Louisville* (Kentucky) *Courier-Journal*, May 6, 1956, 8.

"Green Paradise." *Argosy*, May 1956, 41–47.

"The Vegetable War." *Saturday Review*, July 21, 1956, 34–35.

"Discovering the People of Paris." *Holiday*, August 1956, 36. Text from *Le Figaro*.

"The Mail I've Seen." *Saturday Review*, August 4, 1956, 16, 34.

Reporting on 1956 Democratic and Republican Conventions in the *Louisville* (Kentucky) *Courier-Journal* (August 12–August 25, 1956). These reports were also published in the *Oakland* (California) *Tribune* and the *Chicago Daily News*.

"The Cab Driver Doesn't Give a Hoot." *Daily Mail* (London), August 14, 1956.

"The Hostess with the Mostest in the Hall." *Daily Mail* (London), August 14, 1956.

1957

The Short Reign of Pippin IV. New York: Viking Press, 1957.

"A Postscript from Steinbeck." *Steinbeck and His Critics: A Record of Twenty-five Years*, edited by Ernest W. Tedlock and C. V. Wicker. Albuquerque: University of New Mexico Press, 1957, 307–308.

"Trust Your Luck." *Saturday Review*, January 12, 1957, 42–44. Text from *Le Figaro*.

"My War with the Ospreys." *Holiday*, March 1957, 72–73; 163–165.

"John Steinbeck States His Views on Cannery Row," *Monterey Peninsula Herald*, March 8, 1957, 1.

"Letters to the Courier-Journal," *Louisville* (Kentucky) *Courier-Journal*, April 17–July 17, 1957. Series of 23 travel articles.

"A Game of Hospitality." *Saturday Review*, April 20, 1957, 24.

"The Trial of Arthur Miller." *Esquire*, June 1957, 86.

"Red Novelist's [Sholokoff's] Visit Produces Uneasy Talk," *Louisville* (Kentucky) *Courier-Journal,* July 17, 1957.

"Television and Radio," *New York Herald Tribune,* August 23, 1957, Sec. 2, 1.

"Open Season on Guests." *Playboy,* September 1957, 21.

"Steinbeck and the Flu," *Newsday,* September 9, 1957, 37.

" 'D' for Dangerous." *McCall's,* October 1957, 57, 82.

"Dichos: The Way of Wisdom." *Saturday Review,* November 9, 1957, 13.

1958

Once There Was a War. New York: Viking Press, 1958.

"Short Story of Mankind." *Playboy,* April 1958.

"Salinas . . . And Its Valley." *Spreckles Sugar News,* June 1958.

"Dedication." *Journal of the American Medical Association* 167, 11 (July 12, 1958): 1388–1389.

"The Easiest Way to Die." *Saturday Review,* August 23, 1958, 12, 37.

"Healthy Anger." *Books and Bookman,* October 1958, 24.

"The Spivacks Beat the Odds." *Reader's Digest,* October 1958, 153–154. Condensed from "Dedication," *Journal of the American Medical Association* (July 12, 1958).

"The Golden Handcuff." *San Francisco Examiner,* November 23, 1958.

1959

The Winter of Our Discontent. New York: Viking Press, 1959.

"If You See Me on the Hoe with a Puma." *Daily Mail* (London), September 30, 1959.

"Writer Catches Lions By Tale," *Monterey Peninsula Herald,* October 3, 1959.

"Adlai Stevenson and John Steinbeck Discuss the Past and the Present," *Newsday,* December 2, 1959, 34–35.

1960

"A Teddy Bear Called Miz Hicks," *News Chronicle,* January 18, 1960.

"Have We Gone Soft?" *New Republic,* February 15, 1960, 11–15.

"Steinbeck Replies," *Newsday,* March 1, 1960, 27.

"Our 'Rigged' Mortality." *Coronet,* March 1960, 144.

"A Primer on the Thirties." *Esquire,* June 1960, 85–93.

"Atque Vale." *Saturday Review,* July 23, 1960, 13.

1961

"Conversation at Sag Harbor." *Holiday,* March 1961, 60–61, 129–31, 133.

"Black Man's Ironic Burden." *Negro History Bulletin* 24 (April 1961): 146.

"High Drama of Bold Thrust Through Ocean Floor." *Life,* April 14, 1961, 110, 118, 120, 122.

"Camping Is for the Birds." *Popular Science,* May 1961, 26.

"In Quest of America" (Part I). *Holiday,* July 1961, 27–33, 79–85.

"The Critic Defined" (Letter to the Editor) *Newsweek,* July 10, 1961, 2.

"Sorry—If I Had Any Advice to Give I'd Take It Myself." *Writer's Digest,* September 1961.

"In Quest of America" (Part II). *Holiday,* December 1961, 60–65, 116–18, 120–21, 124, 126–28, 130–31, 134–36.

1962

Travels with Charley in Search of America. New York: Viking Press, 1962.

Speech Accepting the Nobel Prize for Literature. New York: Viking Press, 1962.

Preface. In *Story Writing* by Edith Ronald Mirrielees. New York: Viking, 1962, vii–viii.

"In Quest of America" (Part III). *Holiday,* February 1962, 58–63, 122.

Letter of tribute to Oscar Hammerstein II. Program for the Oscar Hammerstein II Memorial Festival, 46th Street Theatre, New York City, April 8, 1962.

"California: The Exploding State." *Sunday Times Colour Section* (London), December 16, 1962, 2.

"According to Steinbeck." *Time,* December 21, 1962. Text from Nobel Prize speech.

1963

"On Learning Writing." *Writer's Yearbook* 34 (1963): 10.

"To the Swedish Academy." *Story* 36 (March–April 1963): 6–8. Acceptance speech for Nobel Prize.

"Reflections on a Lunar Eclipse." *New York Sunday Herald Tribune,* October 6, 1963, Book Week 3.

Quote about Berlin Wall. *Time,* December 20, 1963, 28.

1964

"A Letter from John Steinbeck." San Francisco and Los Angeles: Roxburghe and Zamorano Clubs, 1964.

"A Letter from Steinbeck." *The Thinking Dog's Man,* edited by Ted Patrick. New York: Random House, 1964, 3–10.

In Memoriam V. *Pascal Covici, 1888–1964.* New York: Meriden Gravure Company, 1964, 19–20.

"John Every." *John Emery.* Zachery Scott. Privately printed, 1964. 200 copies. A Tribute.

"The Pure West." *Montana, the Big Sky Country: Official Publication of the Montana Territorial Centennial Commission* 1, 1 (1964): 6–9, 30, 35. Text from *Travels with Charley.*

"A President, . . . Not a Candidate." Democratic Convention Program Book Committee (1964).

"Open Seasons on Guests." *VIP: The Playboy Club Magazine* February 1964, 20–21.

Letter to Samuel Tankel, Publisher. *Short Story International* 1, 6 (April 1964).

"The Language of Courtesy." *New World Review* 32 (December 1964): 26.

1965

"Steinbeck's Letter to the Author." *Modern Fiction Studies* (Spring 1965): 75–78.

"Then My Arm Glassed Up." *Sports Illustrated,* December 20, 1965, 94–96, 99–102.

"Letters to Alicia," *Newsday* (November 20, 1965–May 28, 1966).

1966

America and Americans. New York: Viking Press, 1966.

"How Steinbeck's Religious Career Ended." *Salinas Californian,* February 26, 1966, 16.

"The Waiter Is Liable to Lose Face," *Newsday,* February 28, 1966, 35.

"The Short-Short Story of Mankind." *Broadside,* June 1966, 14.

"America and the Americans." *Saturday Evening Post,* July 2, 1966, 33–38, 40–41, 44, 46–47.

"An Open Letter to the Poet Yevtushenko," *Newsday,* July 11, 1966, 3.

"Let's Go After the Neglected Treasures Beneath the Seas." *Popular Science,* September 1966, 84–87.

"My Dear Friend Genya." *Reader's Digest,* September 1966, 128. Condensed from "An Open Letter to the Poet Yevtushenko," *Newsday,* July 11, 1966.

"Popping Off." *Cavalcade,* September 1966, 28.

"Henry Fonda." *Harper's Bazaar,* November 1966, 215.

"The March Hare Mother." *Library Journal,* December 1966.

"John Steinbeck's America." *Newsday,* November 12–19, 1966. Seven essays from *America and Americans.*

"Letters to Alicia," *Newsday,* December 3, 1966–May 20, 1967.

1967

Foreword. In *Hard Hitting Songs for Hard-Hit People.* Compiled by Alan Lomax. New York: Oak Publications, 1967, 8–9.

"A Warning to the Viet Cong—Keep New Year's Truce or Else," *Los Angeles Times,* January 1, 1967, C2.

"Challenge to Soviets," *Newsday,* January 5, 1967, 5, 75.

"Steinbeck in Vietnam: 'Pravda Called Me an Accomplice in a Murder, But Do They Know the Facts?' " *Daily Sketch,* January 6, 1967, 6.

"Hungarians Criticise Steinbeck," *Newsday,* January 23, 1967.

"Soviet Youth Answers the Great Steinbeck." Pamphlet. (Gravenhurst, Ontario, Canada: Northern Book House, 1967).

"John Steinbeck vs. Erle Stanley Gardner" ("Camping Is for the Birds"). *Popular Science,* May 1967, 160, 204–205.

Quotation Weekly Messenger (of the Presbyterian Hospital in the City of New York) (May 29, 1967).

"John Steinbeck to a Russian Friend." *Reader's Digest* (British edition), August 1967, 41.

"A Day, a Mood, a Faith." *Good Housekeeping,* December 1967, 82–83.

1968

"Minority Rights and Majority Power." In *Politics of Literature,* edited by Henry Holland, Jr. Englewood Cliffs, N.J.: Prentice Hall 1968, 146–148.

1969

Journal of a Novel. New York: Viking Press, 1969.

1975

A Life in Letters. New York: Viking Press, 1975.
Viva Zapata! New York: Viking/Compass 1975.

1976

Acts of King Arthur and His Noble Nights. New York: Farrar, Straus & Giroux 1976.

1988

The Harvest Gypsies. Berkeley, Calif.: Heyday Books 1988. Reprint of "Their Blood Is Strong" (1938).

1989

Working Days. New York: Viking Press, 1989.

ALPHABETICAL BIBLIOGRAPHY
OF STEINBECK'S WORKS

This bibliography is an alphabetical listing of all of the works contained in the Chronological Bibliography.

A

"About Ed Ricketts." Preface to *The Log from the Sea of Cortez*. New York: Viking, 1951, vii–lxvii.

"According to Steinbeck." *Time*, December 21, 1962. Text from Nobel Prize Speech.

Acts of King Arthur and His Noble Knights. New York: Farrar, Straus & Giroux 1976.

"Adlai Stevenson and John Steinbeck Discuss the Past and the Present." *Newsday*, December 2, 1959, 34–35.

"Adventures in Arcademy: A Journey into the Ridiculous" *Stanford Spectator*, June 1924, 291.

"Aerial Engineer." *Scholastic*, December 6, 1943, 17–18.

"The Affair at 7, Rue de M—" *Harper's Bazaar*, April 1955, 112, 202, 213. Text from *Le Figaro*.

"Always Something to Do in Salinas." *Holiday*, June 1955, 58–59, 152–153, 156.

America and Americans. New York: Viking Press, 1966.

"America and the Americans." *Saturday Evening Post*, July 2, 1966, 33–38, 40–41, 44, 46–47.

"And Some Cars of Yesterday." *Reader's Digest* (British edition), November 1954, 53–57. Text from "Jalopies I Cursed and Loved." *Holiday*, July 1954.

"An Appreciation." *Elia Kazan's Production of John Steinbeck's "East of Eden."* Warner Brothers, 1955. Souvenir booklet for the world premiere presentation of the film at the Astor Theater in New York City.

"Atque Vale." *Saturday Review*, July 23, 1960, 13.

"Atropos." *Stanford Lit*, March 1926, 95.

"Autobiography: Making of a New Yorker." *New York Times Magazine*, February 1, 1953, 26–27; 66–67.

B

"Ballantine Ale." *Life*, January 26, 1953, 92–93.

"Baubles." *Monterey Beacon*, January 5, 1935, 7.

"Black Man's Ironic Burden." *Negro History Bulletin*, April 1961, 146.

"The Bomber—Our Best Weapon." *Science Digest*, July 1943, 62–66. Condensed chapter from *Bombs Away*.

Bombs Away. Photographs by John Swope. New York: Viking Press, 1942.

"Breakfast." *Pacific Weekly*, November 9, 1936, 300.

"Bricklaying Piece." *Punch*, July 27, 1955, 92.

C

"The Cab Driver Doesn't Give a Hoot," *Daily Mail*, (London) August 14, 1956.

"California: The Exploding State." *Sunday Times Colour Section* (London), December 16, 1962, 2.

"Camping Is for the Birds." *Popular Science*, May 1961, 26.

Cannery Row. New York: Viking Press, 1945.

"Cannery Row." *Argosy*, September 1945, 17–34. Condensed from *Cannery Row*.

"Cannery Row." *Coronet*, June 1945, 145–161. Condensed from *Cannery Row*.

"Cannery Row." *Omnibook Magazine*, June 1945, 3–40. Condensed from *Cannery Row*.

"Capital Roundup: Paris." *Saturday Review*, April 16, 1955, 41. Text from *Le Figaro*.

"Challenge to Soviets," *Newsday*, January 5, 1967, 5, 75.

"The Chrysanthemums." *Harper's Magazine*, October 1937, 514–519.

"Circus." *Ringling Bros. and Barnum & Bailey Circus Program*, 1954, 6–7.

"Class Will." *El Gabilan*, 1919, 36.

"Conversation at Sag Harbor." *Holiday,* March 1961, 60–61; 129–131, 133.

"Cooks of Wrath." *Everybody's,* April 9, 1955. Text from *Le Figaro.*

"The Critic Defined" (Letter to the Editor). *Newsweek,* July 10, 1961, 2.

"Critics, Critics, Burning Bright." *Saturday Review,* November 11, 1950, 20–21.

"Critics—From a Writer's Viewpoint." *Saturday Review,* August 27, 1955, 20, 28.

Cup of Gold. New York: Robert M. McBride, 1929.

D

"A Day, a Mood, a Faith." *Good Housekeeping,* December 1967, 82–83.

"Dear Teachers, Sweet Teachers I Beg You . . . Call Them Off!" *NEA Journal,* September 1955, 359.

"The Death of a Racket." *Saturday Review,* April 2, 1955, 26.

"Death with a Camera." *Picture Post* (London), June 12, 1954.

"Dedication." *Journal of the American Medical Association,* 167, 11 (July 12, 1958), 1388–1389.

"A Depiction of Mexico by an Author with No Pattern to Vindicate," *San Francisco Chronicle,* May 31, 1936, D4.

"'D' for Dangerous." *McCall's,* October 1957, 57, 82.

"Dichos: The Way of Wisdom." *Saturday Review,* November 9, 1957, 13.

"Discovering the People of Paris." *Holiday,* August 1956, 36. Text from *Le Figaro.*

"Do You Like Yourself?" *New York Herald Tribune,* January 21, 1951, Sec. 7, 2.

"Dreams Piped from Cannery Row," *New York Times,* November 27, 1955, Sec. 2, 1, 3.

"Dubious Battle in California." *Nation,* September 12, 1936, 302–304.

"Duel Without Pistols." *Collier's,* August 23, 1952, 13–15.

E

"The Ears of Johnny Bear." *Esquire,* September 1937, 35, 195–200.

"The Easiest Way to Die." *Saturday Review,* August 23, 1958, 12, 37.

East of Eden. New York: Viking Press, 1952.

F

"The Farmer's Hotel" (Letter to the editor), *New York Times Book Review,* December 2, 1951, 40.

"Fingers of Cloud: A Satire on College Protervity." *Stanford Spectator,* February 1924, 161–164.

The First Watch. Los Angeles: Ward Ritchie Press, 1947.

"Fishing in Paris." *Punch,* August 25, 1954, 248–249.

Foreword. In *Between Pacific Tides* by Edward Ricketts and Jack Calvin. Revised edition. Stanford, Calif.: Stanford University Press, 1948.

Foreword. In *Burning Bright.* New York: Viking, 1950, 9–13.

Foreword. In *Hard Hitting Songs for Hard-Hit People.* Compiled by Alan Lomax. New York: Oak Publications, 1967, 8–9.

Foreword. In *Morgan Sails the Caribbean* by Berton Braley. New York: Macmillan, 1934, vii–x.

Foreword. In *Much Ado About Me* by Fred Allen. Boston: Little Brown, 1956, np.

Foreword. In *Speeches of Adlai Stevenson.* New York: Random House, 1952, 5–8.

"Foreword to Burning Bright," *New York Times,* October 15, 1950, sec. 2, Theatre.

The Forgotten Village. (Film Script) New York: Viking, 1941.

"For Stevenson: Rivals Contrasted" (Letter to the editor), *New York Times,* October 26, 1952, Sec. 4, 9.

"Four Shades of Navy Blue." *Monterey Beacon* January 26, 1935, 12.

"Free Ride to Monterey." *Argosy,* March 1943, 69–76. Text from "How Edith McGillcuddy Met R. L. Steveson," *Harper's Magazine,* August 1941.

G

"The Game of Authors." *Stanford Lit* I, 4 (March 1926), 94–95.

"A Game of Hospitality." *Saturday Review,* April 20, 1957, 24.

"The Genius," *Monterey Beacon* January 26, 1935, 12.

"The Gifts of Iban." *Smokers Companion,* March 1927, 18–19, 70–72.

"The GI's War in a Book Far from Brass." *New York Herald Tribune Weekly Book Review,* May 18, 1947, 1. Review of *Yank! The GI Story of the War.*

"The Golden Handcuff," *San Francisco Examiner,* November 23, 1958.

"Good Guy—Bad Guy." *Punch,* September 22, 1954, 375–378.

The Grapes of Wrath. New York: Viking Press, 1939.

"The Great Mountains." *North American Review* 236, 6 (December 1933): 493–500.

"Green Paradise." *Argosy,* May 1956, 41–47.

H

"The Hanging at San Quentin." *Avon Modern Short Story Monthly*, no. 25 (1945), 11–22. Text from *The Pastures of Heaven*.

"The Harness." *Atlantic Monthly*, June 1938, 741–749.

"The Harness." *Argosy*, June 1945, 15–25.

"The Harvest Gypsies," *San Francisco News*, October 5–12, 1936.

The Harvest Gypsies. Berkeley, Calif.: Heyday Books, 1988. Reprint of "Their Blood Is Strong" (1938).

"Have We Gone Soft?" *New Republic*, February 15, 1960, 11–15.

"Healthy Anger." *Books and Bookman*, October 1958, 24.

"Henry Fonda." *Harper's Bazaar*, November 1966, 215.

"High Drama of Bold Thrust Through Ocean Floor." *Life*, April 14, 1961, 110, 118, 120, 122.

"His Father." *Reader's Digest*, September 1949, 19–21.

"The Hostess with the Mostest in the Hall," *Daily Mail* (London), August 14, 1956.

"How Edith McGillcuddy Met R. L. Stevenson." *Harper's Magazine*, August 1941, 253–358.

"How Edith McGilcuddy Skipped Sunday-school." *Chamber's Journal*, November 1950, 641–646.

"How Mr. Hogan Robbed a Bank." *Atlantic*, March 1956, 58–61.

"How Steinbeck's Religious Career Ended," *Salinas Californian*, February 26, 1966, 16.

"How to Fish in French." *Reader's Digest*, December 1954, 129–131.

"How to Recognize a Candidate." *Punch*, August 10, 1955, 146–148.

"The How, When and Where of the High School." *El Gabilan* (Salinas High School Yearbook), 1919, 19.

"Hungarians Criticise Steinbeck," *Newsday*, January 23, 1967.

I

"If You See Me on the Hoe with a Puma," *Daily Mail* (London), September 30, 1959, 6.

"I Go Back to Ireland." *Collier's*, January 31, 1953, 48–50.

"In Awe of Words." *Exonian*, March 3, 1954, 4.

In Dubious Battle. New York: Covici-Friede, 1936.

In Memoriam Pascal Covici, 1888–1964. New York: Meriden Gravure Company, 1964, 19–20.

"In Quest of America" (Part I), *Holiday*, July 1961, 27–33, 79–85.

"In Quest of America" (Part II), *Holiday*, December 1961, 60–65, 116–18, 120–21, 124, 126–28, 130–31, 134–36.

"In Quest of America" (Part III), *Holiday*, February 1962, 58–63, 122.

"The 'Inside' on the Inside." *The Iron Gate of Jack and Charlie's "21."* Edited by Francis T. Hunter. New York: Jack Kriendler Memorial Foundation, 1950, 27.

Introduction to *The World of Li'l Abner*, by Al Capp. New York: Farrar, Straus, and Young, 1953, np.

"Ivanhoe," *Monterey Beacon*, January 26, 1935, 12.

J

"Jalopies I Cursed and Loved." *Holiday*, July 1954, 44–45, 89–90.

"The Joan in All of Us." *Saturday Review*, January 14, 1956, 43. Text from *Le Figaro*.

"John Every." John Emery. Zachary Scott. Privately printed, 1964

"Johnny Bear." *Argosy*, January 1941, 97–111. Text from *Esquire*, September 1937.

"Johnny Bear." *Avon Modern Short Story Monthly*, no. 7 (1943), 12–24. Text from *The Long Valley*.

"John Steinbeck's America." *Newsday*, November 12–19, 1966. Seven essays from *America and Americans*.

"John Steinbeck States His Views on Cannery Row." *Monterey Peninsula Herald*, March 8, 1957, 1.

"John Steinbeck to a Russian Friend." *Reader's Digest* (British edition), August 1967, 41.

"John Steinbeck vs. Erle Stanley Gardner" ("Camping Is for the Birds"). *Popular Science*, May 1967, 160, 204–205.

"John Steinbeck Writes Appeal for Third War Loan Drive," *Monterey Peninsula Herald*, September 17, 1943.

Journal of a Novel. New York: Viking Press, 1969.

"Journey into Russia: People of the Soviet." *Illustrated*, May 1, 1948, 3–22.

K

"The King Snake and the Rattlers: A Parable for Americans." *Brief* 1, 4 (April 1953): 23–27.

L

"The Language of Courtesy." *New World Review* 32 (December 1964): 26.

"The Leader of the People." *Argosy*, August 1936, 99–106.

"Let's Go After the Neglected Treasures Beneath the Seas." *Popular Science*, September 1966, 84–87.

"A Letter from John Steinbeck." San Francisco and Los Angeles: Roxburghe and Zamorano Clubs, 1944.

"A Letter from Steinbeck." *The Thinking Dog's Man*, edited by Ted Patrick. New York: Random House, 1964, 3–10.

"Letter of tribute to Oscar Hammerstein II." Program for the Oscar Hammerstein II Memorial Festival, 46th Street Theatre, New York City (April 8, 1962).

"A Letter on Criticism." *Colorado Quarterly* 4, 2 (Autumn 1955, 218–219.

"Letters to Alicia," *Newsday*, December 3, 1966–May 20, 1967.

"Letters to Alicia," *Newsday*, November 20, 1965–May 28, 1966.

"Letters to the Courier-Journal," *Louisville* (Kentucky) *Courier-Journal*, April 17–July 17, 1957. Series of 23 travel articles.

"Letter to Samuel Tankel, Publisher." *Short Story International* 1, 6 (April 1964).

"A Letter to the Inmates of the Connecticut State Prison." *Monthly Record* (Connecticut State Prison), June 1938, 3.

"A Letter Written in Reply to a Request for a Statement about His Ancestry." Stamford, Conn.: Overbrook Press, 1940.

A Life in Letters. New York: Viking Pres, 1975.

". . . like captured fireflies." *CTA Journal* (November 1955): 7.

The Log from the Sea of Cortez. New York: Viking, 1951.

"The Lonesome Vigilante." *Esquire*, October 1936, 35, 186A–186B.

The Long Valley. New York: Viking Press, 1938.

"The Long Valley." *Avon Modern Short Story Monthly*, no. 9 (1943): 12–62. Text from *The Long Valley*.

M

"Madison Avenue and the Election." *Saturday Review*, March 31, 1956, 11.

"The Mail I've Seen." *Saturday Review*, August 4, 1956, 16, 34.

"Mammy," *Monterey Beacon*, January 5, 1935, 7.

"The March Hare Mother." *Library Journal* (December 1966).

"Minority Rights and Majority Power." In *Politics of Literature*, edited by Henry Holland, Jr. Englewood Cliffs, N.J.: Prentice Hall, 1968, 146–148.

"The Miracle." *Argosy*, April 1949, 97–101. Text from "Miracle of Tepeyac," *Collier's*, 1948.

"Miracle Island of Paris." *Holiday*, February 1956, 43. Text from *Le Figaro*.

"The Miracle of Joan." *John O'London's Weekly*, September 19, 1954, 907. Text from *Le Figaro*.

"Miracle of Tepayac." *Collier's*, December 25, 1948, 22–23.

"A Model T Named 'It'." *Ford Times*, July 1953, 34–39.

"Molly Morgan." *Avon Short Story Monthly*, no. 31 (1946): 150–162. Text from *The Pastures of Heaven*.

"Monterey: Steinbeck's View of a Simpler Time." *Monterey Peninsula Herald*, July 1946.

The Moon Is Down (Play). New York: Viking Press, 1942.

The Moon Is Down. New York: Viking Press, 1942.

"The Moon Is Down." *Reader's Digest*, June 1942, 116–152. Condensed text from *The Moon Is Down*.

"The Moon Is Down." *Argosy*, September 1942, 91–124. Text from *The Moon Is Down*, chapters 1–4.

"The Moon Is Down." *Argosy*, October 1942, 89–124. Text from *The Moon Is Down*, chapters 5–8.

"The Moon Is Down." *Strand Magazine*, September 1943, 57–71, 86–89, 91, 93–96.

"More About Aristocracy: Why Not a World Peerage?" *Saturday Review*, December 10, 1955, 11.

"The Murder." *North American Review*, April 1934, 306–312.

"The Murder." *Lovat's Dickson's Magazine*, October 1934, 442–456. Text from *North American Review*, April 1934.

"The Murder." *Redbook Magazine*, May 1938, 38–39, 78–80. Text from *North American Review*, April 1934.

"Murder." *Argosy*, March 1941, 31–40. Text from *North American Review*, April 1934.

"My Dear Friend Genya." *Reader's Digest*, September 1966, 128. Condensed from "An Open Letter to the Poet Yevtushenko," *Newsday*, July 11, 1966.

"My Ideal Woman." *Flair*, July 1950, 30–33.

"My Short Novels." *Wings* 26 (October 1953): 4–8.

"My War with the Ospreys." *Holiday*, March 1957, 72–73, 163–165.

N

"The Naked Book." *Vogue*, November 15, 1951, 119, 161.

"Needles-Derby Day Choice for President?" *Louisville* (Kentucky) *Courier-Journal*, May 6, 1956, 8.

"No Riders." *Saturday Review,* April 1, 1939, 13, 14, 16. Text from *The Grapes of Wrath.*

"Nothing So Monstrous." *Avon Modern Short Story Monthly,* 1944, 53–69. Text from *The Pastures of Heaven.*

"The novel might benefit by the discipline and terseness of the drama . . ." *Stage,* January 1938, 50–51.

O

"Of Beef and Men." In *Famous Recipes by Famous People.* San Francisco: Lane, 1940: 11. Text from *"Tortilla Flat" Famous Recipes by Famous People.* Del Monte, Calif.: Hotel Del Monte, 1936.

"Of Fish and Fishermen." *Sports Illustrated,* October 4, 1954, 45. Text from *Le Figaro.*

Of Mice and Men (Play). New York: Covici-Friede, 1937.

Of Mice and Men. New York: Covici-Friede, 1937.

"Of Mice and Men." *Argosy,* April 1941, 151–157.

Once There Was a War. New York: Viking Press, 1958.

"One American in Paris." *Le Figaro Littéraire* (17 articles appearing June 12–September 18, 1954).

"On Learning Writing." *Writer's Yearbook* (1963): 10

"An Open Letter to the Poet Yevtushenko," *Newsday,* July 11, 1966, 3.

"Open Season on Guests." *Playboy,* September 1957, 21.

"Open Seasons on Guests." *VIP: The Playboy Club Magazine,* February 1964, 20–21.

"The Origin of Tularecito." *Avon Annual,* 1946, 11–20. Text from *The Pastures of Heaven.*

"'Our Best'—Our Fliers." *New York Times Magazine,* November 22, 1942, 16–17, 29. Text from *Bombs Away.*

"Our 'Rigged' Mortality." *Coronet,* March 1960, 144.

"Over There." *Ladies Home Journal,* February 1944, 20–21, 137, 139–142, 144–158.

P

The Pastures of Heaven. New York: Brewer, Warren & Putnam, 1932.

The Pearl. New York: Viking Press, 1947.

"The Pearl." *Omnibook,* March 1948, 105–122. Condensed from *The Pearl.*

"The Pearl of the World." *Woman's Home Companion,* December 1945, 17–18, 85–86, 90, 92, 96–100, 104–105, 109–113, 120. Published later as *The Pearl.*

Pipe Dream. New York: Viking Press, 1956.

"A Plea for Tourists." *Punch,* January 26, 1955, 148–49. Text from *Le Figaro.*

"A Plea to Teachers." *Saturday Review,* April 30, 1955, 24.

"Popping Off." *Cavalcade,* September 1966, 28.

"Positano." *Harper's Bazaar,* May 1953, 158, 185, 187–190, 194. Reprinted as *Positano.* Salerno, Italy: Ente Provinciale Per Il Turismo, 1954.

"A Postscript from Steinbeck." In *Steinbeck and His Critics: A Record of Twenty-five Years,* edited by Ernest W. Tedlock and C. V. Wicker. Albuquerque: University of New Mexico Press, 1957, 307–308.

Preface. In *Story Writing* by Edith Ronald Mirrielees. New York: Viking, 1962, vii–viii.

"A President, . . . Not a Candidate." Democratic Convention Program Book Committee, 1964.

"A Primer on the Thirties." *Esquire,* June 1960, 85–93.

"The Promise." *Harper's Magazine,* August 1937, 244–252.

"Prophet with Honor in His Country." *Coast,* December 1937, 14–15.

"The Pure West." In *Montana, the Big Sky Country: Official Publication of the Montana Territorial Centennial Commission* 1, 1 (1964): 6–9, 30, 35. Text from *Travels with Charley.*

Q

Quotation Weekly Messenger (Presbyterian Hospital, City of New York), May 29, 1967.

Quote about Berlin Wall. *Time,* December 20, 1963, 28.

R

"The Raid." *North American Review,* October 1934, 300–305.

"Random Thoughts on Random Dogs." *Saturday Review,* October 8, 1955, 11.

"Reality and Illusion." *Punch,* November 17, 1954, 616–617. Text from *Le Figaro.*

"Red Novelist's [Sholokoff's] Visit Produces Uneasy Talk." *Louisville* (Kentucky) *Courier-Journal,* July 17, 1957.

"The Red Pony." *North American Review,* November 1933, 422–438.

The Red Pony. New York: Covici-Friede, 1937.

"Reflections on a Lunar Eclipse." *New York Sunday Herald Tribune,* October 6, 1963, Book Week, 3.

Reporting on 1956 Democratic and Republican Conventions. *Louisville* (Kentucky) *Courier-Journal,* August 12–August 25, 1956. These reports were also published in the *Oakland* (California) *Tribune* and the *Chicago Daily News.*

"Report on America." *Punch,* June 22, 1955, 754–755.

"Robert Capa: An Appreciation." *Photography*, September 1954, 48.

"Russian Journal." *New York Herald Tribune*. Eighteen articles between January 14 and January 31, 1948.

A Russian Journal. Photographs by Robert Capa. New York: Viking, 1948.

S

"Salinas . . . And Its Valley." *Spreckles Sugar News*, June 1958.

Sea of Cortez: A Leisurely Journal of Travel and Research. With Edward F. Ricketts. New York: Viking, 1941.

"The Secret Weapon We Were Afraid to Use." *Collier's*, January 10, 1953, 9–13.

"'Shark' Wicks." *Avon Annual*, 1944, 12–25. Text from *The Pastures of Heaven*.

The Short Reign of Pippin IV. New York: Viking Press, 1957.

"The Short-Short Story of Mankind." *Broadside*, June 1966, 14.

"Short Story of Mankind." *Playboy*, April 1958.

"The Snake." *Monterey Beacon*, June 22, 1935, 10–11, 14–15.

"A Snake of One's Own." *Esquire*, February 1938, 31, 178–180.

"Some Random and Randy Thoughts on Books." *The Author Looks at Format*, edited by Ray Fliman. N.P.: American Institute of Graphic Arts, 1951 31–34.

"Some Thoughts on Juvenile Delinquency." *Saturday Review*, May 28, 1955, 22.

"Song of the Disgusted Modern," *Monterey Beacon*, January 5, 1935, 7.

"Sorry—If I Had Any Advice to Give I'd Take It Myself." *Writer's Digest*, September 1961.

"The Soul and Guts of France." *Collier's*, August 30, 1952, 26–30.

"Soviet Youth Answers the Great Steinbeck" (Pamphlet). Gravenhurst, Ontario, Canada: Northern Book House, 1967.

Speech Accepting the Nobel Prize for Literature. New York: Viking Press, 1962.

"The Spivacks Beat the Odds." *Reader's Digest*, October 1958, 153–154. Condensed from "Dedication." *Journal of the American Medical Association*, July 12, 1958.

"The Squatter's Camp." *Progressive Weekly*, May 6, 1939, 2.

"The Stars Point to Shafter." *Progressive Weekly*, December 24, 1938, 2.

"Starvation Under the Orange Trees." *Monterey Trader*, April 15, 1938.

"Steinbeck and the Flu," *Newsday*, September 9, 1957, 37.

"Steinbeck in Vietnam: 'Pravda Called Me an Accomplice in a Murder, But Do They Know the Facts?'" *Daily Sketch*, January 6, 1967, 6.

"Steinbeck Lashes Out at Bungled Goodwill Drive in Latin States: A Reply to American Censorship." *Carmel Cymbal*, September 4, 1941, 3.

"Steinbeck Replies." *Newsday*, March 1, 1960, 27.

"Steinbeck's Letter." In *Writers Take Sides: Letters about the war in Spain from 418 American Authors*. New York: League of American Writers, 1938, 56–57.

"Steinbeck's Letter to the Author." *Modern Fiction Studies*, Spring 1965, 75–78.

"Steinbeck's Voices of America." *Scholastic*, November 3, 1954, 15.

"The Stevenson Letter." *New Republic*, January 5, 1953, 13–14.

"Student Body." *El Gabilan*, 1919, 43.

"The Summer Before." *Punch*, May 25, 1955, 647–51.

Sweet Thursday. New York: Viking Press, 1954.

T

"A Teddy Bear Called Miz Hicks." *News Chronicle*, January 18, 1960.

"Television and Radio." *New York Herald Tribune*, August 23, 1957, Sec. 2: 1.

"Their Blood Is Strong." San Francisco: Simon J. Lubin Society, 1938.

"Their Blood Is Strong." *Progressive Weekly*, April 29, 1939, 3.

"Then My Arm Glassed Up." *Sports Illustrated*, December 20, 1965, 94–96, 99–102.

"This Is the Monterey We Love." *Monterey Peninsula Herald*, July 3 1946, Sec. 3, 1.

"The Time the Wolves Ate the Vice-Principal." *47 The Magazine of the Year*, vol. 1, no. 1 (March 1947): 26–27.

To a God Unknown. New York: Robert O. Ballou, 1933.

"To Carmel." *Monterey Beacon*, January 5, 1935, 7.

Tortilla Flat. New York: Covici-Friede, 1935.

"Tortilla Flat" Famous Recipes by Famous People, Hotel Del Monte. Compiled by Herbert Cerwin. Del Monte, Calif.: Hotel Del Monte, 1936, 18.

"To the Swedish Academy." *Story*, vol. 36 (March–April 1963): 6–8. Acceptance speech for Nobel Prize.

"Trade Winds: In a Radio Broadcast Beamed to Listeners in Foreign Countries, John Steinbeck had this to say about New York City." *Saturday Review,* November 26, 1955, 8–9.

"Trade Winds: When, Two Summers Ago . . ." *Saturday Review,* February 27, 1954, 8.

Travels with Charley in Search of America. New York: Viking Press, 1962.

"The Trial of Arthur Miller." *Esquire,* June 1957, 86.

"Troopship." *Reader's Digest,* March 1944, 67–70.

"Trust Your Luck." *Saturday Review,* January 12, 1957, 42–44. Text from *Le Figaro.*

U

"Unsecret Weapon (Part I)." *Picture Post,* February 14, 1953, 31.

"Unsecret Weapon (Part II)." *Picture Post,* February 21, 1953, 31.

V

Vanderbilt Clinic. Photographs by Victor Keppler. New York: Presbyterian Hospital, 1947.

"The Vegetable War." *Saturday Review,* July 21, 1956, 34–35.

"The Visitor." *Monterey Beacon* January 5, 1935, 7.

Viva Zapata! New York: Viking Press, 1975.

"Voices of Authors: Johnny Bear." *Life,* October 12, 1953.

W

"The Waiter Is Liable to Lose Face," *Newsday,* February 28, 1966, 35.

"War Dispatches," *New York Herald Tribune* (86 articles between June 21 and December 15, 1943). These dispatches were reprinted in several newspapers, including *Daily Express* (June–October 1943), *Cincinnati Enquirer* (October–December 1943), *New York Herald Tribune* (November–December 1943). A single dispatch entitled "Steinbeck Says Blitz Stories All Hang on Some Small Detail" appeared in the *Amarillo Sunday* (July 11, 1943).

"A Warning to the Viet Cong—Keep New Year's Truce or Else," *Los Angeles Times,* January 1, 1967, C2.

"The Way It Seems to John Steinbeck." *Occident,* 29 (1936): 5.

The Wayward Bus. New York: Viking Press, 1947.

"The Wayward Bus." *Omnibook Magazine,* August 1947, 3–40. Condensed from *The Wayward Bus.*

"We Don't Want to Be America's Colony." *Reader's Digest,* November 1952, 18–23. Condensed text from "The Soul and Guts of France," *Collier's,* August 30, 1952.

"We're Holding Our Own." *Lilliput,* November 1955, 18–19.

"What Is the Real Paris?" *Holiday,* December 1955, 94. Text from *Le Figaro.*

"The White Quail," *North American Review,* March 1935, 205–211.

"Who Said the Old Lady Was Dying?" *Evening Standard,* London, August 1, 1952.

The Winter of Our Discontent. New York: Viking Press, 1959.

"Women and Children in the U.S.S.R." *Ladies Home Journal,* February 1948, 45–49.

"Woodwork." *El Gabilan,* 1919, 50.

Working Days. New York: Viking Press, 1989.

"Work of W. F. Cody." *Saturday Review of Literature,* July 7, 1945, 18–19.

"Writer Catches Lions by Tale." *Monterey Peninsula Herald,* October 3, 1959.

"Writer's Mail." *Punch,* November 2, 1955, 512–513.

Y

"The Yank in Europe." *Holiday,* January 1956, 25. Text from *Le Figaro.*

"Your Audiences Are Wonderful." *Sunday Times* (London), August 10, 1952.

CATEGORIZED BIBLIOGRAPHY OF STEINBECK'S WORKS

Books

Cup of Gold. New York: McBride, 1929; London & Toronto: Heinemann, 1937.

The Pastures of Heaven. New York: Brewer, Warren & Putnam, 1932; London: Allan, 1933.

To a God Unknown. New York: Ballou, 1933; London & Toronto: Heinemann, 1935.

Tortilla Flat. New York: Covici-Friede, 1935; London: Heinemann, 1935.

In Dubious Battle. New York: Covici-Friede, 1936; London & Toronto: Heinemann, 1936.

Of Mice and Men. New York: Covici-Friede, 1937; London & Toronto: Heinemann, 1937.

Of Mice and Men: A Play in Three Acts. New York: Covici-Friede, 1937.

The Red Pony. New York: Covici-Friede, 1937; enlarged edition, New York: Viking, 1945.

Their Blood Is Strong. San Francisco: Simon J. Lubin Society, 1938.

The Long Valley. New York: Viking, 1938; London & Toronto: Heinemann, 1939.

The Grapes of Wrath. New York: Viking, 1939; London & Toronto: Heinemann, 1939.

The Forgotten Village. New York: Viking, 1941.

Sea of Cortez: A Leisurely Journal of Travel and Research, coauthored by Steinbeck and Edward F. Ricketts (New York: Viking, 1941); republished in part as *The Log from the Sea of Cortez* (New York: Viking, 1951; London, Melbourne & Toronto: Heinemann, 1958, with "About Ed Ricketts," by Steinbeck).

The Moon Is Down. New York: Viking, 1942; London & Toronto: Heinemann, 1942.

The Moon Is Down: A Play in Two Parts. New York: Dramatists Play Service, 1942; London: English Theatre Guild, 1943.

Bombs Away: The Story of a Bomber Team. New York: Viking, 1942.

Cannery Row. New York: Viking, 1945; London & Toronto: Heinemann, 1945.

The Wayward Bus. New York: Viking, 1947; London & Toronto: Heinemann, 1947.

The Pearl. New York: Viking, 1947; Melbourne, London & Toronto: Heinemann, 1948.

A Russian Journal. New York: Viking, 1948; London, Melbourne & Toronto: Heinemann, 1949.

Burning Bright. New York: Viking, 1950; Melbourne, London & Toronto: Heinemann, 1951.

Viva Zapata! (Rome: Edizioni Filmcritica, 1952); new edition, ed. Robert Morsberger (New York: Viking, 1975).

East of Eden. New York: Viking, 1952; Melbourne, London & Toronto: Heinemann, 1952.

Sweet Thursday. New York: Viking, 1954; Melbourne, London & Toronto: Heinemann, 1954.

The Short Reign of Pippin IV: A Fabrication. New York: Viking, 1957; Melbourne, London & Toronto: Heinemann, 1957.

Once There Was a War. New York: Viking, 1958; London, Melbourne & Toronto: Heinemann, 1959.

The Winter of Our Discontent. New York: Viking, 1961; London, Melbourne & Toronto: Heinemann, 1961.

Travels with Charley in Search of America. New York: Viking, 1962; London, Melbourne & Toronto: Heinemann, 1962.

Speech Accepting the Nobel Prize for Literature. New York: Viking, 1962.

America and Americans. New York: Viking, 1966; London: Heinemann, 1966.

The Acts of King Arthur and His Noble Knights, ed. Chase Horton. New York: Farrar, Straus & Giroux, 1976.

Working Days: The Journals of the Grapes of Wrath, 1938–1941, ed. Robert DeMott. New York: Viking, 1989.

Plays
Of Mice and Men, New York, Music Box Theatre, November 23, 1937.
The Moon Is Down, New York, Martin Beck Theatre, April 7, 1942.
Burning Bright, New York, Broadhurst Theatre, October 18, 1950.

Screenplays
The Forgotten Village, Arthur Mayer-Joseph Burstyn, 1941.
Lifeboat, screen story by Steinbeck, Twentieth Century–Fox, 1944.
A Medal for Benny, screen story by Steinbeck and Jack Wagner, Paramount, 1945.
The Pearl, by Steinbeck, Emilio Fernandez, and Jack Wagner, RKO, 1948.
The Red Pony, Republic, 1949.
Viva Zapata!, Twentieth Century–Fox 1952.

Periodical Publications (Fiction)
"Fingers of Cloud: A Satire on College Protervity," *Stanford Spectator* 2 (February 1924): 149, 161–165.
"Adventures in Arcademy: A Journey into the Ridiculous," *Stanford Spectator* 2 (June 1924): 279, 291.
"How Edith McGillcuddy Met R. L. Stevenson," *Harper's* 183 (August 1941): 253–358.
"Miracle of Tepayac," *Collier's* 122 (December 25, 1948): 22–23.
"His Father," *Reader's Digest* 55 (September 1949): 19–21.
"Sons of Cyrus Trask," *Collier's* 130 (July 12, 1952): 14–15.
"How Mr. Hogan Robbed a Bank," *Atlantic* 197 (March 1956): 58–61.

Periodical Publications (Nonfiction)
"Dubious Battle in California," *Nation* 143 (September 13, 1936): 302–304.
"The Stars Point To Shafter," *Progressive Weekly* (December 24, 1938).
"The Secret Weapon We Were Afraid to Use," *Collier's* 131 (January 10, 1953): 9–13.
"Jalopies I Cursed and Love," *Holiday* 16 (July 1954): 44–45; 89–90.
"Fishing in Paris," *Punch* 227 (August 25, 1954): 248–249.

"How to Fish in French," *Reader's Digest* 66 (January 1955): 59–61.
"Some Thoughts on Juvenile Delinquency," *Saturday Review* 38 (May 28, 1955): 22.
"Always Something to Do in Salinas," *Holiday* 17 (June 1955): 58 ff.
"Conversations at Sag Harbor," *Holiday* 29 (March 1961): 60–61, 129–131, 133.

Letters
Journal of a Novel: The East of Eden Letters. New York: Viking, 1969: London: Heinemann, 1970.
Steinbeck: A Life in Letters, ed. Elaine Steinbeck and Robert Wallsten. New York: Viking, 1975.
Letters to Elizabeth: A Selection of Letters from John Steinbeck to Elizabeth Otis, ed. Florian J. Shasky and Susan F. Riggs. San Francisco: Book Club of California, 1978.
Steinbeck and Covici: The Story of a Friendship, ed. Thomas Fensch. Middlebury, Vt.: Paul S. Eriksson, 1979.
Working Days: The Journal of "The Grapes of Wrath," ed. Robert DeMott. New York: Viking, 1988.

Collections
Selected Essays of John Steinbeck, ed. Hidekazu Hirose and Kiyoshi Nakayama. Tokyo: Shinozake Shorin Press, 1981.
Uncollected Stories of John Steinbeck, ed. Kiyoshi Nakayama. Tokyo: Nan'un Do, 1986.

Other
Galati, Frank, adaptor. *"The Grapes of Wrath."* London: Warner Chappell Plays, 1991.

Biographies
Benson, Jackson. *The True Adventures of John Steinbeck, Writer.* New York: Viking, 1984.
Enea, Sparky. *With Steinbeck in the Sea of Cortez.* Los Osos, Calif.: Sand River Press, 1991.
Kiernan, Thomas. *The Intricate Music: A Biography of John Steinbeck.* Boston: Little Brown, 1979.
Lynch, Audry. *Steinbeck Remembered: Interviews with Friends and Acquaintances of John Steinbeck.* Santa Barbara, Calif.: Fithian Press, 2000.
Parini, Jay. *John Steinbeck: A Biography.* New York: Henry Holt, 1995.
Steinbeck, John, IV, and Nancy Steinbeck. *The Other Side of Eden: Life with John Steinbeck.* Essex, U.K.: Prometheus Books, 2001.

BIBLIOGRAPHY OF SECONDARY SOURCES

Astro, Richard, and Tetsumaro Hayashi, eds. *Steinbeck: The Man and His Work*. Corvallis: Oregon State University Press, 1971.

Astro, Richard. *John Steinbeck and Edward F. Ricketts: The Shaping of a Novelist*. Minneapolis: University of Minnesota Press, 1973.

Astro, Richard, and Joel W. Hedgpeth, eds. *Steinbeck and the Sea*. Corvallis: Oregon State University Press, 1975.

Astro, Richard. *Edward F. Ricketts*. Boise, Idaho: Boise State University Press, 1976.

Beach, Warren Joseph. "John Steinbeck: Art and Propaganda." *In American Fiction 1920–1940*. New York: Russell & Russell, 1960.

Beck, Warren. "On John Steinbeck." *Talks With Authors*, ed. Charles F. Madden. Carbondale: Southern Illinois University Press, 1968.

Beegel, Susan F., Susan Shillinglaw, and Wesley N. Tiffney, Jr., eds. *Steinbeck and the Environment: Interdisciplinary Approaches*. Tuscaloosa: University of Alabama Press, 1997.

Benson, Jackson J. *Looking for Steinbeck's Ghost*. Norman: University of Oklahoma Press, 1988.

———. *The True Adventures of John Steinbeck, Writer*. New York: Viking, 1984.

———, ed. *The Short Novels of John Steinbeck: Critical Essays with a Checklist to Steinbeck Criticism*. Durham, N.C.: Duke University Press, 1990.

———. *Steinbeck's "Cannery Row": A Reconsideration*. Muncie, Ind.: Steinbeck Research Institute, Ball State University, 1991.

Blake, Nelson Manfred. "The Lost Paradise." In *Novelists' America: Fiction as History, 1910– 1940*. Syracuse, N.Y.: Syracuse University Press, 1969.

Bloom, Harold, ed. *John Steinbeck*. New York: Chelsea House, 1987.

Bluefarb, Sam. "The Joads: Flight into the Social Soul." In *The Escape Motif in the American Novel: Mark Twain to Richard Wright*. Ohio State University Press, 1972.

Burrows, Michael. *John Steinbeck and His Films*. St. Austell, U.K.: Primestyle, 1971.

Burress, Lee. "*The Grapes of Wrath*: Preserving Its Place in the Curriculum." In *Censored Books: Critical Viewpoints*. Metuchen, N.J.: Scarecrow Press, 1993.

Coers, Donald V. *John Steinbeck as Propagandist: The Moon Is Down Goes to War*. Tuscaloosa: University of Alabama Press, 1991.

Coers, Donald V., Paul D. Ruffin, and Robert J. DeMott, eds. *After The Grapes of Wrath: Essays on John Steinbeck in Honor of Tetsumaro Hayashi*. Athens: Ohio University Press, 1995.

Cook, Sylvia Jenkins. "Steinbeck, the People, and the Party." *American Fiction: 1914–1945*. Harold Bloom, ed. New York: Chelsea House Publishers, 1987.

———. "Steinbeck's Poor in Prosperity and Adversity." *The Steinbeck Question: New Essays in Criticism*, ed. Donald R. Noble, Troy, N.Y.: Whitson Publishing Co., 1993.

Covici, Pascal, ed. *The Portable Steinbeck*. New York: Viking, 1971.

Crouch, Steve. *Steinbeck Country*. Palo Alto, Calif.: American West, 1973.

Davis, Robert Con, ed. *Twentieth Century Interpretations of "The Grapes of Wrath."* Englewood Cliffs, N.J.: Prentice-Hall, 1982.

Davis, Robert Murray, ed. *Steinbeck: A Collection of Critical Essays*. Englewood Cliffs, N.J.: Prentice-Hall, 1972.

DeMott, Robert. *Steinbeck's Reading: A Catalogue of Books Owned and Borrowed*. New York: Garland Publishing, 1984.

———. *Steinbeck's Typewriter: Essays on His Art.* Troy, N.Y.: Whitson Publishing, 1996.

———, ed. *Working Days: The Journals of* The Grapes of Wrath. New York: Viking, 1989.

Ditsky, John. *Essays on "East of Eden."* Muncie, Ind.: Steinbeck Research Institute, Ball State University, 1977.

———. *John Steinbeck: Life, Work, and Criticism.* Fredericton, N.B.: York Press, 1985.

———. *John Steinbeck and the Critics.* Woodbridge, U.K.: Camden House, 2000.

———, ed. *Critical Essays on Steinbeck's "The Grapes of Wrath."* Boston: G. K. Hall, 1989.

Donohue, Agnes McNeill, ed. *A Casebook on* The Grapes of Wrath. New York: Thomas Y. Crowell Co., 1968.

Enea, Sparky. *With Steinbeck in the Sea of Cortez.* Los Osos, Calif.: Sand River Press, 1991.

Etheridge, Charles Larimo. "Dos Passos, Steinbeck, Faulkner, and the Narrative of the Thirties." *Dissertation Abstracts International.* Ann Arbor, Mich.: 1990 March, 50:9, 2895A.

Evans, Thomas G. "Impersonal Dilemmas: The Collision of Modernist and Popular Traditions in Two Political Novels, *The Grapes of Wrath* and *Ragtime.*" *South Atlantic Review* 52 (January 1987): 1, 71–85.

Fensch, Thomas. *Conversations with John Steinbeck.* Jackson: University Press of Mississippi, 1988.

———. *Steinbeck and Covici: The Story of a Friendship.* Middlebury, Vt.: Paul S. Eriksson, 1979.

Fontenrose, Joseph. *John Steinbeck: An Introduction and Interpretation.* New York: Holt, Rinehart and Winston, 1963.

———. *Steinbeck's Unhappy Valley.* Berkeley, Calif.: Joseph Fontenrose, 1981.

French, Warren. *Filmguide to "The Grapes of Wrath."* Bloomington: Indiana University Press, 1973.

———. *John Steinbeck.* New York: Grossett & Dunlap, 1961.

———. *John Steinbeck,* rev. ed. Boston: Twayne, 1975.

———. "John Steinbeck." In *The Politics of Twentieth-Century Novelists,* ed. George A. Panichas. New York: Hawthorn Books, Inc., 1971.

———. *John Steinbeck's Fiction Revisited.* New York: Twayne, 1994.

———. *John Steinbeck's Nonfiction Revisited.* New York: Twayne, 1996.

———. *The Social Novel at the End of An Era.* Carbondale: Southern Illinois University Press, 1966.

———, ed. *A Companion to "The Grapes of Wrath."* New York: Viking, 1963.

Frohock, W. M. "John Steinbeck: The Utility of Wrath." In *The Novel of Violence in America, 1920–1950.* Dallas, Tex.: Southern Methodist University Press, 1950.

Gale, Robert L. *Barron's Simplified Approach to Steinbeck: "Grapes of Wrath."* Woodbury, N.Y.: Barron's, 1967.

Gannett, Lewis. *John Steinbeck: Personal and Bibliographical Notes.* New York: Viking, 1939.

———, ed. *The Portable Steinbeck.* New York: Viking, 1946.

Geismar, Maxwell. "John Steinbeck: Of Wrath or Joy." In *Writers in Crisis: The American Novel, 1925–1940.* New York: E. P. Dutton, 1971.

Garcia, Reloy. *Steinbeck and D. H. Lawrence: Fictive Voices and the Ethical Imperative.* Muncie, Ind.: Steinbeck Research Institute, Ball State University, 1972.

Gladstein, Mimi Reisel. "*America and Americans:* The Arthurian Consummation." In *After* The Grapes of Wrath: *Essays on John Steinbeck in Honor of Tetsumaro Hayashi.* Athens: Ohio University Press, 1995.

———. *The Indestructible Woman in Faulkner, Hemingway, and Steinbeck.* Ann Arbor, Mich.: UMI Research Press, 1986.

George, Stephen, ed. *John Steinbeck: A Centennial Tribute.* Westport, Conn.: Praeger Publishers, 2002.

———. *The Moral Philosophy of John Steinbeck.* Lanham, Md.: Scarecrow Press, 2005.

Gray, James. *John Steinbeck.* Minneapolis: University of Minnesota Press, 1971.

Hadella, Charlotte Cook. *Of Mice and Men: A Kinship of Powerlessness.* New York: Twayne, 1995.

Hayashi, Tetsumaro. *John Steinbeck and the Vietnam War (Part I).* Muncie, Ind.: Steinbeck Research Institute, Ball State University, 1986.

———. *A New Steinbeck Bibliography, 1971–1981.* Metuchen, N.J.: Scarecrow, 1983.

———. *A New Steinbeck Bibliography, 1929–1971.* Metuchen, N.J.: Scarecrow, 1973.

———. *Steinbeck's World War II Fiction, "The Moon Is Down": Three Explications.* Muncie, Ind.: Steinbeck Research Institute, Ball State University, 1986.

———. *A Student's Guide to Steinbeck's Literature: Primary and Secondary Sources.* Muncie, Ind.: Steinbeck Research Institute, Ball State University, 1986.

———, ed. *A Handbook for Steinbeck Collectors, Librarians, and Scholars.* Muncie, Ind.: Steinbeck Research Institute, Ball State University, 1981.

———, ed. *John Steinbeck: A Guide to the Doctoral Dissertations.* Muncie, Ind.: Steinbeck Research Institute, Ball State University, 1971.

———, ed. *John Steinbeck: The Years of Greatness, 1936–1939*. Tuscaloosa: University of Alabama Press, 1993.

———, ed. *John Steinbeck on Writing*. Muncie, Ind.: Steinbeck Research Institute, Ball State University, 1988.

———, ed. *A New Study Guide to Steinbeck's Major Works, with Critical Explications*. Metuchen, N.J.: Scarecrow, 1993.

———, ed. *Steinbeck and the Arthurian Theme*. Muncie, Ind.: Steinbeck Research Institute, Ball State University, 1975.

———, ed. *Steinbeck Criticism: A Review of Book-Length Studies (1939–1973)*. Muncie, Ind.: Steinbeck Research Institute, Ball State University, 1974.

———, ed. *Steinbeck's Literary Dimension: A Guide to Comparative Studies*. Metuchen, N.J.: Scarecrow, 1973.

———, ed. *Steinbeck's Literary Dimension: A Guide to Comparative Studies, Series II*. Metuchen, N.J.: Scarecrow, 1991.

———, ed. *Steinbeck's Short Stories in "The Long Valley" Essays in Criticism*. Muncie, Ind.: Steinbeck Research Institute, Ball State University, 1991.

———, ed. *Steinbeck's Travel Literature: Essays in Criticism*. Muncie, Ind.: Steinbeck Research Institute, Ball State University, 1980.

———, ed. *Steinbeck's "The Grapes of Wrath": Essays in Criticism*. Muncie, Ind.: Steinbeck Research Institute, Ball State University, 1990.

———, ed. *Steinbeck's Women: Essays in Criticism*. Muncie, Ind.: Steinbeck Research Institute, Ball State University, 1979.

———, ed. *A Study Guidebook to Steinbeck: A Handbook to His Major Works*. Metuchen, N.J.: Scarecrow, 1974.

———, ed. *A Study Guidebook to Steinbeck (Part II)*. Metuchen, N.J.: Scarecrow, 1979.

———, ed. *A Study Guide to Steinbeck's "The Long Valley."* Ann Arbor, Mich.: Pierian, 1976.

——— and Beverly K. Simpson, eds. and comps. *John Steinbeck: Dissertation Abstracts and Research Opportunities*. Metuchen, N.J.: Scarecrow, 1994.

Hayashi, Tetsumaro, and Kenneth D. Swan, eds. *Steinbeck's Prophetic Vision of America*. Upland, Ind.: Taylor University Press, 1976.

——— and Thomas J. Moore, eds. *Steinbeck's Posthumous Work: Essay in Criticism*. Muncie, Ind.: Steinbeck Research Institute, Ball State University, 1989.

Hayashi, Tetsumaro, Yasuo Hashiguchi, and Richard F. Peterson, eds. *John Steinbeck: East and West*. Muncie, Ind.: Steinbeck Research Institute, Ball State University, 1978.

Hedgpeth, Joel W., ed. *The Outer Shores*, Part One. Eureka, Calif.: Mad River Press, 1978.

Hedgpeth, ed. *The Outer Shores*, Part Two. Eureka, Calif.: Mad River Press, 1979.

Hughes, R. S. *Beyond The Red Pony: A Reader's Companion to Steinbeck's Complete Short Stories*. Metuchen, N.J.: Scarecrow, 1987.

———. *John Steinbeck: A Study of the Short Fiction*. Boston: Twayne, 1989.

Ingram, Forrest L. "John Steinbeck: *The Pastures of Heaven*." In *Representative Short Story Cycles of the Twentieth Century: Studies in a Literary Genre*. Paris: Mouton & Co., 1971.

Jain, Sunita. *John Steinbeck's Concept of Man*. New Delhi: New Statesman Publishing Co., 1979.

Jones, Lawrence William. *John Steinbeck as Fabulist*, ed. Marston LaFrance. Muncie, Ind.: Steinbeck Research Institute, Ball State University, 1973.

Kennedy, John S. "John Steinbeck: Life Affirmed and Dissolved." In *Fifty Years of the American Novel: A Christian Appraisal*, ed. Harold C. Gardiner. New York: Scribner's, 1952.

Levant, Howard. *The Novels of John Steinbeck: A Critical Study*. Columbia: University of Missouri Press, 1974.

Lewis, Cliff, and Carroll Britch, eds. *Rediscovering Steinbeck: Revisionist Views of His Art, Politics and Intellect. Studies in American Literature* 3. Lewiston, N.Y.: Edwin Mellen Press, 1989.

Li, Luchen. *John Steinbeck: A Documentary Volume*. Farmington Hills, Mich.: Thomson Gale, 2005.

Lisca, Peter. *John Steinbeck: Nature and Myth*. New York: Thomas Y. Crowell Co., 1978.

———. *The Wide World of John Steinbeck*. New Brunswick, N.J.: Rutgers University Press, 1958.

———, ed. *John Steinbeck: "The Grapes of Wrath": Text and Criticism*. New York: Viking, 1972.

Lisca, Peter, and Kevin Hearle, eds. *"The Grapes of Wrath" Text and Criticism*. New York: Penguin, 1997.

Magny, Claude-Edmonde. "Steinbeck, or the Limits of the Impersonal Novel." In *The Age of the American Novel: The Film Aesthetic of Fiction Between the Two Wars*, trans. Eleanor Hochman. New York: Frederick Ungar, 1972.

Marks, Lester J. *Thematic Design in the Novels of John Steinbeck*. The Hague, Netherlands: Mouton & Co. N.V., 1969.

Marsden, John L. "'California Dreamin': The Significance of 'A Coupla Acres' in Steinbeck's *Of Mice and Men*." *Western American Literature* 29, 4 (February 1995): 291–297.

Martin, Stoddard. *California Writers: Jack London, John Steinbeck, the Tough Guys*. New York: St. Martin's Press, 1983.

McCarthy, Paul. *John Steinbeck*. New York: Ungar, 1980.

McElrath, Joseph R., Jr., Jesse S. Crisler, and Susan Shillinglaw, eds. *John Steinbeck: The Contemporary Reviews*. New York: Cambridge University Press, 1996.

Meyer, Michael, ed. *The Hayashi Steinbeck Bibliography, 1982–1996*. Lanham, Md.: Scarecrow, 1998.

Millichap, Joseph R. *Steinbeck and Film*. New York: Frederick Ungar, 1983.

Minter, David. "The Search for Shared Purpose: Struggle on the Left." In *A Cultural History of the American Novel*. Cambridge University Press, 1994.

Miron, George Thomas. *The Truth About John Steinbeck and the Migrants*. Los Angeles: Haynes Corporation, 1939.

Moore, Harry Thornton. *The Novels of John Steinbeck: A First Study*. Chicago: Normandie House, 1939.

Noble, Donald R., ed. *The Steinbeck Question: New Essays in Criticism*. Troy, N.Y.: Whitston Publishing, 1993.

O'Connor, Richard. *John Steinbeck*. New York: McGraw-Hill, 1970.

Owens, Louis. *"The Grapes of Wrath": Trouble in the Promised Land*. Boston: Twayne, 1989.

———. *John Steinbeck's Re-Vision of America*. Athens: University of Georgia Press, 1985.

Pratt, John Clark. *John Steinbeck*. Grand Rapids, Mich.: Eerdmanns, 1970.

Railsback, Brian E. *Parallel Expeditions: Charles Darwin and the Art of John Steinbeck*. Moscow: University of Idaho Press, 1995.

Schmitz, Anne-Marie. *In Search of Steinbeck*. Los Altos, Calif.: Hermes, 1978.

Shasky, Florian J., and Susan F. Riggs, eds. *Letters to Elizabeth: A Selection of Letters From John Steinbeck to Elizabeth Otis*. San Francisco: Book Club of California, 1978.

Shindo, Charles J. "The Perfectibility of Man: John Steinbeck and *The Grapes of Wrath*." In *Dust Bowl Migrants in the American Imagination*. Lawrence: University Press of Kansas, 1997.

Simmonds, Roy S. *John Steinbeck: The War Years, 1939–1945*. Lewisburg, Pa.: Bucknell University Press, 1996.

———. *Steinbeck's Literary Achievement*. Muncie, Ind.: Steinbeck Research Institute, Ball State University, 1976.

Smith, Joel A., ed. *Steinbeck: On Stage & Film*. Louisville, Ky.: Actors Theatre of Louisville, 1996.

Steinbeck, Elaine, and Robert Wallsten, eds. *Steinbeck: A Life in Letters*. New York: Viking, 1975.

Stoneback, H. R. "Rough People . . . Are the Best Singers: Woody Guthrie, John Steinbeck, and Folksong." In *The Steinbeck Question: New Essays in Criticism*, ed. Donald R. Noble. Troy, N.Y.: Whitson Publishing, 1993.

St. Pierre, Brian. *John Steinbeck: The California Years*. The Literary West Series. San Francisco: Chronicle Books, 1983.

Stuckey, W. J. *The Pulitzer Prize Novels: A Critical Backward Look*. Norman: University of Oklahoma Press, 1966.

Tedlock, E. W., Jr., and C. V. Wicker, eds. *Steinbeck and His Critics: A Record of Twenty-five Years*. Albuquerque: University of New Mexico Press, 1957.

Timmerman, John H. *The Dramatic Landscape of John Steinbeck's Short Stories*. Norman: University of Oklahoma Press, 1990.

———. *John Steinbeck's Fiction: The Aesthetics of the Road Taken*. Norman: University of Oklahoma Press, 1986.

Valjean, Nelson. *John Steinbeck: The Errant Knight*. San Francisco: Chronicle, 1975.

Watt, F. W. *John Steinbeck*. New York: Grove, 1962.

Visser, Nicholas. "Audience and Closure in *The Grapes of Wrath*." *Studies in American Fiction* 22, 11 (Spring 1994): 19–36.

Wagenknecht, Edward. "Two Kinds of Novelist: Steinbeck and Marquand." New York: Henry Holt, 1952, 438–448.

Walcutt, Charles Child. "Later Trends in Forms: Steinbeck, Hemingway, Dos Passos." *American Literary Naturalism, a Divided Stream*. Minneapolis: University of Minnesota Press, 1956.

Watt, F. W. *John Steinbeck*. New York: Grove Press, 1962.

Weber, Tom. *Cannery Row: A Time to Remember*. Monterey, Calif.: Orenda/Unity, 1983.

Whitebrook, Peter. *Staging Steinbeck: Dramatising The Grapes of Wrath*. London: Cassell Publishers Ltd., 1988.

Wollenberg, Charles. "Introduction to *The Harvest Gypsies*." Berkeley, Calif.: Heyday Books, 1988.

Wyatt, David, ed. *New Essays on "The Grapes of Wrath."* New York: Cambridge University Press, 1990.

Yano, Shigeharu, Tetsumaro Hayashi, Richard F. Peterson, and Yasuo Hashiguchi. *John Steinbeck: From Salinas to the World.* Tokyo: Gaku Shobo Press, 1986.

Special Journals
Steinbeck Newsletter. Kent, Ohio: John Steinbeck Bibliographical Society, 1968–ca. 1969.
Steinbeck Quarterly. Ball State University, Indiana, 1969–1993.
Steinbeck Newsletter. Steinbeck Research Center, San José State University, 1987–2001.
Steinbeck Studies. Steinbeck Research Center, San José State University, 2001–.

Steinbeck Review. Lanham, Md.: Scarecrow Press, 2004–.

Papers
Most of John Steinbeck's papers are at the Steinbeck Research Center, San José State University, the National Steinbeck Center, Salinas, California; the Special Collection Department of Stanford University. Other major collections of Steinbeck material are at the Beyer Collection of Princeton University; the Harry Ransom Humanities Research Center of the University of Texas at Austin, the University of Virginia Library; Ball State University; and the John Steinbeck Library, Salinas, California.

INDEX